D0024968

Attitudes and Attitude Change

FRONTIERS OF SOCIAL PSYCHOLOGY

Series Editors:
Arie W. Kruglanski, *University of Maryland at College Park*
Joseph P. Forgas, *University of New South Wales*

Frontiers of Social Psychology is a new series of domain-specific handbooks. The purpose of each volume is to provide readers with a cutting-edge overview of the most recent theoretical, methodological, and practical developments in a substantive area of social psychology, in greater depth than is possible in general social psychology handbooks. The Editors and contributors are all internationally renowned scholars, whose work is at the cutting-edge of research.

Scholarly, yet accessible, the volumes in the *Frontiers* series are an essential resource for senior undergraduates, postgraduates, researchers, and practitioners, and are suitable as texts in advanced courses in specific sub-areas of social psychology.

Published titles
Negotiation Theory and Research, Thompson
Close Relationships, Noller & Feeney
Evolution and Social Psychology, Schaller, Simpson, & Kenrick
Social Psychology and the Unconscious, Bargh
Affect in Social Thinking and Behavior, Forgas
The Science of Social Influence, Pratkanis
Social Communication, Fiedler
The Self, Sedikides & Spencer
Personality and Social Behavior, Rhodewalt
Attitudes and Attitude Change, Crano & Prislin

Forthcoming titles
Social Cognition, Strack & Förster
Exploration in Political Psychology, Krosnick & Chiang
Social Psychology of Consumer Behavior, Wänke
Social Motivation, Dunning
Intergroup Conflicts and their Resolution, Bar-Tal

For continually updated information about published and forthcoming titles in the *Frontiers of Social Psychology* series, please visit: **www.psypress.com/frontiers**

Attitudes and Attitude Change

Edited by
William D. Crano and Radmila Prislin

Psychology Press
Taylor & Francis Group

New York   London

Psychology Press
Taylor & Francis Group
270 Madison Avenue
New York, NY 10016

Psychology Press
Taylor & Francis Group
27 Church Road
Hove, East Sussex BN3 2FA

© 2008 by Taylor & Francis Group, LLC

Printed in the United States of America on acid-free paper
10 9 8 7 6 5 4 3 2

International Standard Book Number-13: 978-1-84169-481-8 (0)

Except as permitted under U.S. Copyright Law, no part of this book may be reprinted, reproduced, transmitted, or utilized in any form by any electronic, mechanical, or other means, now known or hereafter invented, including photocopying, microfilming, and recording, or in any information storage or retrieval system, without written permission from the publishers.

Trademark Notice: Product or corporate names may be trademarks or registered trademarks, and are used only for identification and explanation without intent to infringe.

Visit the Taylor & Francis Web site at
http://www.taylorandfrancis.com

and the Psychology Press Web site at
http://www.psypress.com

This book is dedicated with love to Suellen and Igor

Contents

PART VII ATTITUDES: THE SOCIAL CONTEXT

About the Editors

William Crano is the Oskamp Professor of Psychology at Claremont Graduate University. Before Claremont, he was Professor of Psychology at Michigan State University, Texas A&M, and the University of Arizona. His work is concerned with minority influence, and the application of persuasive principles to prevention of drug abuse and HIV/AIDS in young adolescents.

Radmila Prislin is Professor of Psychology at San Diego State University. Her research interests are in the areas of social influence and social change, group dynamics in the aftermath of social change, attitudes and persuasion, and the evaluation of public health programs.

Contributors

Icek Ajzen, PhD
Department of Psychology
University of Massachusetts—Amherst

Dolores Albarracín, PhD
Department of Psychology (and Marketing)
University of Florida

Christopher J. Armitage, PhD
Centre for Research in Social Attitudes
Department of Psychology
University of Sheffield

John N. Bassili, PhD
Department of Life Sciences
University of Toronto at Scarborough

Gerd Bohner, PhD
Faculty of Psychology and Sport Science
Department of Psychology
University of Bielefeld

Mark Conner, PhD
Institute of Psychological Sciences
University of Leeds

Nicole Gilbert Cote
Department of Psychology
University of Massachusetts—Amherst

Thierry Devos, PhD
Department of Psychology
San Diego State University

Hans-Peter Erb, PhD
Faculty for Humanities and Social Sciences
Helmut Schmidt University, Hamburg

Nicholas C. Fernandez
Department of Psychology
University of Arizona

Joseph P. Forgas, PhD
School of Psychology
University of New South Wales

Antonis Gardikiotis, PhD
School of Psychology
Aristotle University of Thessaloniki

Geoffrey Haddock, PhD
School of Psychology
Cardiff University

Miles Hewstone, PhD
Professor of Social Psychology
University of Oxford

Michael A. Hogg, PhD
School of Behavioral & Organizational Sciences
Claremont Graduate University

Blair T. Johnson, PhD
Department of Psychology
University of Connecticut

Richard V. Kendrick, PhD
Department of Psychology
University of Tennessee

Tina Langer, PhD
Department of Psychology
University of Trier

Hong Li
Department of Psychology
University of Florida

Gregory R. Maio, PhD
School of Psychology
Cardiff University

Pearl Y. Martin, PhD
Work & Organisational Psychology
Group
Aston Business School
Aston University

Robin Martin, PhD
Work & Organisational Psychology
Group
Aston Business School
Aston University

Kenji Noguchi, PhD
Department of Psychology
University of Florida

Michael A. Olson, PhD
Department of Psychology
University of Tennessee

Tania Rendón
Department of Psychology
California State University, San
Marcos

P. Wesley Schultz, PhD
Department of Psychology
California State University, San
Marcos

Norbert Schwarz, PhD
Institute for Social Research
University of Michigan

Frank Siebler, PhD
Department of Psychology
University of Tromsø, Norway

Joanne R. Smith, PhD
School of Psychology
University of Exeter

Jeff Stone, PhD
Department of Psychology
University of Arizona

Jennifer J. Tabanico, PhD
Department of Psychology
California State University, San
Marcos

Zachary L. Tormala, PhD
Graduate School of Business
Stanford University

Eva Walther, PhD
Department of Psychology
University of Trier

Wei Wang
Department of Psychology
University of Florida

Susan E. Watt, PhD
School of Psychology
University of New England

I

Introduction

1

Attitudes and Attitude Change
The Fourth Peak

RADMILA PRISLIN
San Diego State University

WILLIAM D. CRANO
Claremont Graduate University

The field [social psychology] has been a mosaic of heterogeneous pieces from the start, but attitudes have always been one of the central elements of the design. (McGuire, 1985)

*I*t is reasonable to begin a text on attitudes with Allport's (1935, p. 798) famous dictum that attitudes are "the most distinctive and indispensable concept in American social psychology." The gist of Allport's observation undoubtedly was true at the time of its publication, and is largely true even today, more than seven decades later, but McGuire's measured appraisal also is true, and reflects social psychology's less than unremitting romance with attitudes over the past half-century. An attitude

represents an evaluative integration of cognitions and affects experienced in relation to an object. Attitudes are the evaluative judgments that integrate and summarize these cognitive/affective reactions. These evaluative abstractions vary in strength, which in turn has implications for persistence, resistance, and attitude-behavior consistency. (Crano & Prislin, 2006, p. 347)

Our best chroniclers have noted the ebb and flow of the field's fascination with attitudes (Jones, 1988), and McGuire (1985, p. 235) even identified "Three peakings of attitude research," which describe periods of the field's most insistent focus on this construct. The first peaking, in the1920s and 1930s, reflected social psychology's concern with the fundamental nature of attitudes and their measurement. The second peaking, which occurred in the 1950s and 1960s, was focused on factors that affected attitude change. The third peaking, from the1980s and (McGuire predicted) into the 1990s, was focused on attitude systems, a "structuralist surge" that focused on the "content, structure, and functioning of attitude complexes" (p. 236).

To McGuire's three peaks we suggest a fourth peaking, the Modern Era, which reflects trends in the field that have occurred since his seminal publication, and whose description constitutes the core of the present volume. This fourth peaking has been stimulated largely by three important movements: the development of dual process models, which absorbed the energies of a considerable fraction of the field for a number of years; the revitalization of the field that followed Moscovici's (1980, 1985) seminal work on the persuasive power of minorities (Crano, 2000); and a new focus on the *implicit* measurement of attitudes, and the follow-on possibility that attitudes implicated by these measures are in some ways qualitatively different from attitudes tapped via traditional self-reports. The parallels between the earlier peak usage periods and theorizing and research in the fourth peaking are intriguing. Certainly, continuity between prior theory and research and today's contributions is obvious, but just as certainly, we not only have consolidated prior knowledge, but also have added to it in significant and qualitatively different ways. Perhaps Ecclesiastes was wrong—maybe there is something new under the sun.

ATTITUDES: NATURE AND MEASUREMENT

The Basics

The first of the organizing themes of the book is concerned with the fundamental nature of attitudes and their measurement. This section corresponds to the first peak period in McGuire's framework, when attitude theorists were concerned with the basic elaboration and identification of the attitude construct. This process was materially facilitated by an evolving sophistication in measurement. The pioneering work of Thurstone and his contemporaries (Guttman, 1944; Likert, 1932; Thurstone & Chave, 1929) and later researchers (Osgood, Suci, & Tannenbaum, 1957) laid the essential foundation, which allowed those who followed to study attitudes in a rigorous and scientifically defensible manner. Arguably, the measurement approach developed by Thurstone set the stage for almost all that has followed in the field of attitudes and, by extension, social psychology. Thurstone's insistence on the fundamental evaluative nature of attitudes, which can be inferred clearly from his measurement model, and which was reinforced later by the work of Osgood and his colleagues (1957), has shaped theory and measurement in the field up to the present day. Although definitions of attitude have evolved over time, a central core of all of them follows from the assumption that attitudes are fundamentally concerned with evaluation (Albarracín, Johnson, Zanna, & Kumkale, 2005; Zanna & Rempel, 1988).

In the opening substantive chapter of this volume, Albarracín, Wang, Li, and Noguchi discuss the basic structure of attitudes. By its very nature, this chapter anticipates almost all that follows in this text. It provides a general overview of many of the central issues considered, and provides a framework within which the various constructs under consideration may be integrated.

In much previous theorizing, in addition to being seen primarily as evaluative structures, attitudes were conceptualized as representational. That is, attitudes were "things" that in some way resided in memory. When asked about an attitude, the memory trace that held the requisite information was polled, and the attitude was produced. Of course, it has long been recognized that social and contextual features might influence an attitude's expression, but the trace was accepted as an established feature of the reporter's memory. More recent constructionist views conceptualize attitudes as judgments that are formed on the spot, and whose expression is dependent on the social context in which they are assessed, the internal state of the attitude reporter, and so on. Albarracín and her colleagues, as well as Schwarz, consider these contrasting views of attitudes, as representational vs. constructed, and discuss the implications of these conceptualizations for our understanding of attitude development, attitude structure, and attitude change.

Measurement Then and Now

The classic scaling approaches of Thurstone, Guttman, Likert, and Osgood, the latter two still widely used today, require respondents to report their evaluations and beliefs overtly. Recently, these manifest response methods were extended by measures that purport to assess attitudes implicitly (e.g., Greenwald & Banaji, 1995). These newer approaches seek to provide information about respondents' attitudes and beliefs unfettered by their concerns to paint a flattering self-portrait. The data generated with these measures are viewed as being largely outside the conscious control of the respondent, and thus may supply a more accurate picture of the individual's true attitudes. The search for evaluations unadulterated by mundane extraneous factors, social psychology's Holy Grail, has been a consistent theme in the field at least since Asch's (1951) time. However, establishing the validity of the novel implicit approaches is daunting. Echoing Campbell's (1969, p. 16) plaint, we are faced with "a very unsatisfactory predicament: We have only other invalid measures against which to validate our tests: we have no 'criterion' to check them against." In validations of implicit measures, we sometimes find researchers comparing responses obtained through these approaches with those collected via more standard manifest (or overt) response formats. We can guess that Campbell would not see this approach as entirely satisfactory, inasmuch as a positive, null, or even negative relation between implicit and manifest measures could be taken as supportive of the validity of the implicit (or explicit) measure, depending on the attitude of the researcher. More promising by far are studies in which a behavioral outcome is used as a criterion, and the implicit (or manifest) measure the predictor.

Schwarz provides a useful consideration of the implicit approaches, along with a discussion of the more traditional manifest response methods. The logic of the chapter is evident from the start. It begins with a consideration of direct attitude measurement, including a consideration of the cognitive processes involved in answering direct (or manifest) attitude questions. It then moves on to a consideration of the implicit approaches, most of which are dependent on response latency measurement. As Schwarz suggests, many of the context dependencies found to affect manifest attitude measures affect implicit measurements as well. The final section of this chapter is devoted to a consideration of the representational vs. constructed nature of attitudes, an issue raised earlier by Albarracín and her colleagues.

Implicit Attitudes: A Closer Look

Devos continues the conversation with a chapter focused on the theoretical underpinnings of implicit attitudes. Among other issues considered in this chapter are the relationship between implicit and explicit attitudes, and the association of implicit attitudes with behavior. Devos's chapter supplies an insightful correction to much of the earlier work in this area which, perhaps unavoidably, focused on the measurement of implicit attitudes (a reliability issue) at the expense of considerations of validity.

ATTITUDES: FORMATION AND ORIGINS

Attitude Formation

Allied with the consideration of implicit (measures of) attitudes and cognitions are the processes of evaluative conditioning. Chapters by Walther and Langer and Olson and Kendrick both weigh in on this topic. The historic link of evaluative conditioning to earlier attitude research is very strong. It was not too long ago that social psychology was behavioristic in its orientation. The seminal work of Hovland and his colleagues (e.g., Hovland, Janis, & Kelley, 1953), after all, was framed largely in terms of Hovland's translation and extension of Clark Hull's learning theory model to issues of communication and persuasion. With Festinger's (1957) classic theory of cognitive dissonance, all of that changed, and we moved to a more intense consideration of the cognitive features of attitudes and the attitude-behavior link. It would be a mistake, however, to throw out the baby with the bathwater. There is no doubt that evaluative conditioning plays a role in our attitudes and actions. Walther and Langer detail the manner in which this phenomenon operates and distinguish evaluative conditioning from more traditional forms of S-R conditioning. The utility of the evaluative conditioning model, among others, is that this form of influence can occur without conscious awareness of the contingency between conditioned and unconditioned stimuli, and appear highly resistant to extinction. Earlier research had suggested that evaluative conditioning was a force to be reckoned with only when dealing with attitude formation: In other words, evaluative conditioning could facilitate the development of attitudes, but not their change. Walther and Langer challenge the validity of this comforting thought.

Origins

Olson and Kendrick continue with a consideration of the origins of attitudes, and bring our story back to the beginning chapters, which were concerned with the fundamental nature of attitudes. They show how attitudes may form either through implicit, or unconscious processes, or through more explicit, conscious, overtly thoughtful means. Neither is favored, both appear to operate, and these authors describe the conditions that facilitate the occurrence of one or the other. In developing their position, Olson and Kendrick frame their early discussion in terms of the tripartite model of attitude structure, in which cognition, affect, and behavior independently contribute to the content of the attitude. This model has been a part of the literature for many years (Katz, 1960), but its relevance to current considerations of attitude development is reestablished here. In addition to the tripartite model, Olson and Kendrick discuss the possible roles of evolution and genetics in attitude formation, the topic of rising interest and controversy in social psychology (Forgas, Haselton, & von Hippel, 2007).

Affect: A Corrective to the Common Cold Cognition Approach

Forgas's discussion of the role of affect in attitudinal phenomena touches on another topic of enduring interest to the field—that of the interplay between the emotional and the rational aspects of human nature. Long neglected in attitude research, affects or temporary feelings are increasingly considered in theorizing about attitude structure, content, and change. Defying simplistic views of affects as saboteurs of thoughts, recent research demonstrates that affective influences go beyond thought suppression to include thought selection and channeling into complex processing strategies that underlie attitude formation, maintenance, and change.

ATTITUDES: CHANGE AND RESISTANCE

Information Processing Approaches to Persuasion

In McGuire's (1985) classification, the second peaking of the attitude construct occurred in the 1950s and 1960s. He identified this period as the decades of attitude change. Some earlier efforts had been devoted to attitude change, but it was during this period that persuasion came into full flower in social psychology. Persuasion remains a staple of attitude research, with dual-process models, the elaboration likelihood model (Petty & Cacioppo, 1986) and the heuristic-systematic model (Chaiken, 1987), reigning supreme. Their generative power is evident in an impressive library of research that accounts for a host of persuasive phenomena. As detailed in Bohner, Erb, and Siebler's chapter, these models differentiate two qualitatively different types of processing: one relatively effortful that parses information in a persuasive message, and another relatively effortless that focuses on superficial, extraneous (e.g., source attractiveness) information. Both models postulate motivation and ability as conditions sine qua non for effortful processing. The main difference between the two models is their conceptualization of the effortless processing. Both models have evolved since their inception in the 1980s, increasing in complexity to provide a comprehensive framework for the study of persuasion.

The basic tenet of dual-process models has been challenged by an approach that postulates persuasion as a single process of drawing conclusions from available information (Kruglanski & Thompson, 1999). The unimodel functionally equates message-related and extraneous information, postulating that both are processed as evidence for persuasive conclusions depending on their subjective relevance. Introduction of the unimodel to persuasion research created quite a stir (*Psychological Inquiry*, 1999), suggesting that Bohner et al.'s claim about the model representing an evolution rather than a revolutionary break from dual process models is not uniformly shared. Clearly, discussion about the nature of information processing in persuasion continues (e.g., Kruglanski et al., 2006), with new accounts including the connectionist approach (Van Overwalle & Siebler, 2005), contributing to the discourse.

Attitude Functions in Persuasion

Extending attitude theory to the motivational domain, the functionalist approach to persuasion posits that any information processing in a persuasive context is motivated. Motives that guide information processing in persuasive contexts are encapsulated in the functions that targeted attitudes serve. Initial formalizations of this idea—a trio of motives proposed by Smith, Bruner, and White (1956) and Katz, McClintock, and Sarnoff's (1957) quartet of functions—were short-lived. Their near-tautological reasoning, difficulties in identifying attitude functions a priori, and an overall unwelcoming theoretical (cognitive) zeitgeist conspired to cause their early demise.

Improvements in a priori means for identifying and manipulating functions of attitudes have breathed new life into this approach. Watt, Maio, Haddock, and Johnson review these newer developments, along with evidence showing that persuasive information tailored to match a functional need is more effective in changing attitudes than persuasive information unrelated to such a need. Watt and her colleagues take theorizing about attitude functions beyond enumeration of motives (functions). They argue that those functions that have been consistently identified are best understood within a hierarchical framework. Modeling attitude functions as a hierarchical structure requires further conceptual clarifications of specific functions to stipulate how some functions may be nested within others. Initial steps toward this goal by Maio and Olson (2000) suggest that hierarchical approach may constructively inform research on the role of psychological needs in persuasion.

Resistance to Persuasion

A recent revival of a long-dormant interest in resistance to persuasion (McGuire, 1964) combines earlier motivational with more contemporary process-oriented approaches to examine resistance as the outcome of a persuasive attempt (Wood & Quinn, 2003). Implied in much of this research is the idea that successful resistance to persuasion leaves targeted attitudes intact. Tormala challenges this assumption, postulating instead that resistance has important consequences for targeted attitudes. Highlighting the role of meta-cognitive factors, Tormala and his colleagues document how perceptions of resistance and the context in which resistance occurs combine to affect postresistance attitude strength. The innovative predictions of the resistance appraisal framework lend themselves to applications in many domains, including health interventions. Together with other approaches to attitude resistance (Knowles & Linn, 2004), the resistance appraisal approach provides a valuable alternative view of persuasive phenomena.

ATTITUDES: BEYOND EVALUATION

Attitude Strength

Not all attitudes are created equal. This holds true even for attitudes that seem identical in terms of responses to attitudinal inquiries. This fact became painfully obvious after the first generation of research on the predictive validity of attitudes revealed that seemingly identical attitudes could result in hugely variable behaviors (Wicker, 1969). This sobering observation sent attitude researchers back to the drawing board to rethink the very nature of their construct. Correcting their initial and, in retrospect, naïve assumption that attitudes always guide behavior, attitude researchers acknowledged that some (but not all) attitudes do so, just as some (but not all) attitudes are resistant to change, and are persistent over time. This recognition gave rise to the construct of attitude strength, which encapsulates the idea of variability in attitude impact and durability (Krosnick & Petty, 1995; Scott, 1959).

The search for properties that make an attitude strong has been fruitful (Petty & Krosnick, 1995), naturally leading to questions about the dimensionality of more than a dozen strength indicators that have been discussed in the literature. Bassili's chapter on attitude strength documents how thorny the issue of strength dimensionality is. Beyond a repeated finding that strength cannot be reduced to a single latent dimension, there is little agreement in the literature about the structure of attitude strength. Bassili reasons that the structure emerges from the processes underlying attitudinal responses. His distinction between meta-attitudinal indicators that are based on one's impressions about one's own attitudes, and operative indicators of strength that originate from the judgmental processes responsible for attitude responses, has paved the way for more theory-based approaches to dimensionality of strength. Recent attempts have focused on the antecedents and consequences of various strength features (Visser, Bizzer, & Krosnick, 2006). The logic guiding these attempts is that to the extent that strength-related features reflect the same latent dimension, they should originate from the same antecedents and generate the same consequences, but they should not cause each other. Research based on this reasoning requires comparing the commonalities and divergencies of the causes and consequences of various pairs or sets of strength features. Given that more than a dozen identified strength features could be paired and organized in numerous sets, this is quite a formidable task. Obviously, the Gordian knot of the dimensionality of attitude structure awaits its Alexander.

Attitudinal Ambivalence

Conner and Armitage's chapter on attitudinal ambivalence nicely illustrates how reasoning about this feature of attitude strength evolved from the conceptualization of an attitude as a concurrent set of positive and negative evaluations. Moreover, the conceptualization of an attitude as a situated construal (rather than a representation stored in memory) accounts for the evidence that features of the environment, typically the attitude object itself, give rise to ambivalence. Intuitively, ambivalence should weaken attitudes. The evidence supporting this intuition, however, is equivocal. On the one hand, higher levels of ambivalence appear to make attitudes more susceptible to persuasion and less likely to guide behavior. On the other hand, higher levels of ambivalence do not necessarily lower the impact of attitudes on information processing or their temporal stability.

Some of this complexity may stem from two different operational definitions of the ambivalence construct: felt or self-reported ambivalence, and potential ambivalence derived from attitude judgment processes or its outcomes. In Bassili's categorization, the former would represent a meta-attitudinal index and the latter would represent an operative index of strength. Importantly, some attitudinal effects appear due to felt ambivalence, others to potential ambivalence, and still others to both. Conner and Armitage point out that the apparent independence of the two operationalizations of ambivalence may suggest different origins—a possibility that warrants investigation. Future research also should clarify how ambivalence involving two components of an attitude—affective-cognitive inconsistency in the parlance of consistency theories (Rosenberg, 1956, 1968)—relates to ambivalence within a single component. This research may reconcile some contradictions in the findings about strengthlike aspects of ambivalence.

ATTITUDES: MUTUAL IMPACTS OF BELIEFS AND BEHAVIORS

Attitudes as Predictors of Behavior

The continuing popularity of the construct of attitudes stems from the assumption that attitudes predict behavior. This assumption has survived numerous challenges (Wicker, 1969), which have inspired theorizing about conditions under which the assumption is tenable and the processes responsible for linking attitudes and action. Aiding in the understanding of the link is Ajzen and Cotes's distinction between global attitudes and attitudes toward behavior. Both are related to behavior according to the principle of compatibility, which asserts that a strong attitude–behavior relationship will ensue when the measures of both constructs correspond in terms of action, target, content, and time elements.

Processes linking attitudes to behavior have been formalized in several models. The MODE (motivation and opportunity as determinants of behavior) model (Fazio, 1990) assumes that attitudes guide behavior either through spontaneous (automatic) or deliberate (reasoned) processes. The former depends on the strength of the attitude-evaluation association (accessibility); the latter is activated by strong motivation and the opportunity to engage in conscious deliberation. The most prominent of the deliberative process models is the theory of planned behavior (Ajzen, 1985), in which overt actions are thought to originate from behavioral intentions, which are derived from attitudes toward behavior, subjective norms or perceived social pressure regarding behavior, and perceived behavioral control or perceived capability of behavior. The latter component also may influence behavior directly, bypassing intentions. As Ajzen and Cote explain, the core assumption of the theory of planned behavior is the reasoned nature of human action. Behavioral intentions are formed and translated into behavior through the process of logical, though not necessarily unbiased, reasoning. The impressive volume of research that the theory has inspired in various behavioral domains speaks eloquently about its impact on field. Such a large volume allows for quantitative syntheses that examine each of the paths postulated by the theory. Emerging from these meta-analyses is reasonably strong support for the theory. Equally important, these analyses have uncovered questions to be addressed in future research (Sheeran, 2002). These developments suggest that the generative power of the theory of planned action matches its explanatory power.

Behavior as a Predictor of Attitudes: The Cognitive Dissonance Approach

The attitude–behavior relationship is a two-way street, with influence flowing in both directions. Of the several accounts of the effects of behavior on attitudes, none has had more impact than cognitive dissonance theory. Since its inception (Festinger, 1957), the theory has provided insights into people's capacity to justify their counterattitudinal behavior, difficult decisions, and ill-invested efforts. In the engaging overture to their chapter, Stone and Fernandez illustrate how this justification process operates in the contemporary political arena.

The original formulation of dissonance as a negative motivational state created by the presence of two inconsistent cognitions has inspired many revisions, including those that situate the motivational source of dissonance in the aversive consequences of any behavior, consistent and inconsistent alike. The self-consistency and self-affirmation versions agree that the (positive) self plays an important role in dissonance but disagree about the nature of that role. Reconciling divergent views, the self-standards model holds that inconsistent results might be attributed to dissimilar standards that people set for themselves, and the consequences of variations in self-esteem for discrepancies between these standards and actions. Because of varying self-standards, discrepancies between standards and actions could cause differences in dissonance.

Discrepancies from standards involve actions that contradict standards, and also failures to act in accordance with one's self-standards. The latter is an example of hypocrisy that presumably challenges a sense of self-integrity that people are motivated to uphold. Recent studies have documented that this hypocrisy may motivate behavioral changes toward the advocated standard. Extending dissonance research to the cross-cultural domain, recent studies suggest that dissonance may be universal in that it involves anxiety about the self, but also culture-specific in that it is differently configured in terms of the culture-specific views of the self. Yet, dissonance does not appear to be a solely intraindividual phenomenon. Recent research on groups as sources of dissonance and a means of its reduction (Norton, Benoit, Cooper, & Hogg, 2003) takes dissonance research back to the group setting where it began (Festinger, Riecken, & Schachter, 1956).

ATTITUDES: THE SOCIAL CONTEXT

Social Identity and Attitudes

Although early research conceptualized attitudes as social commitments, much contemporary research examines attitudes in socially impoverished contexts. Making a strong case for socially situated study of attitudes, Smith and Hogg describe how social identity theory can inform the study of attitudinal phenomena. In this approach, attitudes are inextricably blended with group membership, in that they originate from group prototypes in an expression of one's identification with the group. This group-based approach to attitudes has important implications for understanding persuasion. Because the phenomenological validity of persuasive information is derived from in-group norms, persuasive communication from in-group sources, including those in numerical minority, should be more carefully scrutinized and ultimately more influential than persuasive communication from out-group sources. Also, attitudes and behaviors should be aligned to the extent that they are normatively consistent with important reference groups. This implies that individual attitudes of group members are manifested in collective action when both are derived from and contribute to salient social identities. These hypotheses are amply supported in empirical research reviewed in Smith and Hogg's chapter.

The motivational aspect of the social identity approach to attitudes accounts not only for its explanatory but also its generative power. Recent theorizing about the reduction of self-related uncertainty as a primary motive driving group dynamics opens new avenues for the study of attitudinal phenomena (Hogg, in press). The motivational approach championed in this framework represents an important counterpoint to the dominant information-processing orientation. Together, they hold promise to contribute to much needed cumulative understanding of attitudes (Prislin & Wood, 2005).

Persuasion from Majority and Minority Groups

Attitude change induced by groups that differ in size, normativeness, and power over others is a special case in persuasion. In their review of research on this group-induced attitude change, Martin, Hewstone, Martin, and Gardikiotis follow four chronological phases. The initial, functionalist, approach placed the power to influence solely in the hands of the majority, because of its presumed means of control over others (minority). This asymmetrical, dependency-based model of influence was overthrown with Moscovici's seminal demonstrations of the power of minorities to influence. His conceptualization of influence as originating from conflict between source and target balanced the scale, in that both minorities and majorities could create conflict and therefore exert influence. Moscovici's position, clearly in the minority when it was introduced, single handedly changed the field to become an example par excellence of the power of minority to influence.

Once adopted, the symmetrical approach to influence flourished in comparisons involving variations in minority and majority influence. This third phase of research produced numerous models of social influence that focus on either conflict resolution or the role of social identification. Incorporated in some of these models is consideration of intraindividual processes that are activated in response to minority or majority advocacy—a theme that dominates current research on social influence. A hallmark of the prevailing information-processing approach is the examination of cognitive responses, either in their own right or as mediators of attitude change. Importantly, these processes are examined in a socially impoverished context. Martin and his collaborators recognize theoretical and methodological advantages of this approach, but they justifiably call for a broader approach that would account for a more complex social context and causal processes underlying majority and minority influence.

Normative Beliefs and Influence

Though typically not included in volumes on attitudes and persuasion, research on normative influence is important for the understanding of these phenomena as it underscores their social foundation. In their review of normative influence, Schultz, Tabanico, and Rendón emphasize how descriptive norms or perceptions of what others do, and injunctive norms or perceptions of what others approve of (or should do), can powerfully regulate behavior not only in controlled laboratory settings but also in various applied domains. Numerous accounts of normative influence clearly call for future integrative theorizing that should clarify the processes through which different types of norms influence behavior.

We hope this brief introduction has served to motivate readers to delve deeply into the many interesting and useful chapters contained here. There is much we know about attitudes—how they are formed, their structures, the ways they may be measured, and the implications of their change. The work presented on the following pages represents the richness of a mature field that is still in the process of dynamic growth, for although we know much, there is much still to know.

REFERENCES

Ajzen, I. (1985). From intentions to actions: A theory of planned behavior. In J. Kuhl & J. Beckman (Eds.), *Action-control: From cognition to behavior* (pp. 11–39). Heidelberg, Germany: Springer.

Albarracín, D., Johnson, B. T., & Zanna, M. P. (Eds.). (2005). *Handbook of attitudes*. Hillsdale, NJ: Erlbaum.

Allport, G. W. (1935). Attitudes. In C. Murchison (Ed.), *A handbook of social psychology* (pp. 798–844). Worcester, MA: Clark University Press.

Asch, S. E. (1951). Effects of group pressure on the modification and distortion of judgments. In H. Guetzkow (Ed.), *Groups, leadership, and men* (pp. 177–190). Pittsburgh, PA: Carnegie.

Campbell, D. T. (1969). Definitional versus multiple operationism. *et al.*, *2*, 14–17.

Chaiken, S. (1987). The heuristic model of persuasion. In M. P. Zanna, J. M. Olson, & C. P. Herman (Eds.), *Social influence: The Ontario Symposium* (Vol. 5, pp. 3–39). Hillsdale, NJ: Erlbaum.

Crano, W. D. (2000). Milestones in the psychological analysis of social influence. *Group Dynamics: Theory, Research, and Practice*, *4*, 68–80.

Crano, W. D., & Prislin, R. (2006). Attitudes and persuasion. *Annual Review of Psychology*, *57*, 345–374.

Fazio, R. H. (1990). Multiple processes by which attitudes guide behavior: The MODE model as an integrative framework. In M. P. Zanna (Ed.), *Advances in experimental social psychology* (Vol. 23, pp. 75–109). San Diego, CA: Academic Press.

Festinger, L. (1957). *A theory of cognitive dissonance*. Evanston, IL: Row, Peterson.

Festinger, L., Riecken, H., & Schachter, S. (1956). *When prophecy fails*. Minneapolis, MN: University of Minnesota Press.

Forgas, J. P., Haselton, M. G., & Hippel, W. v. (Eds.). (2007). *Evolution and the social mind: Evolutionary psychology and social cognition*. New York: Psychology Press.

Greenwald, A. G., & Banaji, M. R. (1995). Implicit social cognition: attitudes, self-esteem, and stereotypes. *Psychological Review*, *102*, 4–27.

Guttman, L. A. (1944). A basis for scaling qualitative data. *American Sociological Review*, *9*, 139–150.

Hogg, M. (in press). Uncertainty-identity theory. In M. P. Zanna (Ed.), *Advances in experimental social psychology* (Vol. 39). San Diego, CA: Academic Press.

Hovland, C. I., Janis, I. L., & Kelley, H. H. (1955). *Communication and persuasion*. New Haven, CT: Yale University Press.

Jones, E. E. (1988). Major developments in five decades of social psychology. In D. T. Gilbert, S. T. Fiske, & G. Lindzey (Eds.), *The handbook of social psychology* (4th ed., Vol. 1, pp. 3–57). Boston, MA: McGraw-Hill.

Katz, D. (1960). The functional approach to the study of attitudes. *Public Opinion Quarterly*, *24*, 163–204.

Katz, D., McClintock, C., & Sarnoff, I. (1957). The measurement of ego defense as related to attitude change. *Journal of Personality*, *25*, 465–474.

Knowles, E. S., & Linn, J. A. (Eds.). (2004). *Resistance and persuasion*. Mahwah, NJ: Erlbaum.

Krosnick, J. A., & Petty, R. E. (1995). Attitude strength: An overview. In R. E. Petty & J. A. Krosnick (Eds.), *Attitude strength: Antecedents and consequences* (pp. 1–24). Mahwah, NJ: Erlbaum.

Kruglanski, A. W., Dechesne, M., Erb, H. P., Pierro, A., Mannetti, L., & Chun, W. Y. (2006). Modes, systems and the sirens of specificity: The issues in gist. *Psychological Inquiry*. *17*, 256–264.

Kruglanski, A. W., & Thompson, E. P. (1999). Persuasion by a single route: A view from the unimodel. *Psychological Inquiry*, *10*, 83–109.

Likert, R. (1932). A new technique for the measurement of attitudes. *Archives of Psychology*, *140*, 5–53.

Maio, G. R., & Olson, J. M. (2000). Emergent themes and potential approaches to attitude function: The function-structure model of attitudes. In G. R. Maio & J. M.

Olson (Eds.), *Why we evaluate: Functions of attitudes* (pp. 417–442). Mahwah, NJ: Erlbaum.

McGuire, W. J. (1964). Inducing resistance to persuasion: Some contemporary approaches. In L. Berkowitz (Ed.), *Advances in experimental social psychology* (Vol. 1, pp. 191–229). New York: Academic Press.

McGuire, W. J. (1985). Attitudes and attitude change. In G. Lindzey & E. Aronson (Eds.), *The handbook of social psychology* (3rd ed., Vol. 2, pp. 233–346). New York: Random House.

Moscovici, S. (1980). Toward a theory of conversion behavior. In L. Berkowitz (Ed.), *Advances in experimental social psychology* (Vol. 13, pp. 209–239). New York: Academic Press.

Moscovici, S. (1985). Social influence and conformity. In G. Lindsey & E. Aronson (Eds.), *The handbook of social psychology* (3rd ed., Vol. 2, pp. 347–412). New York: Random House.

Norton, M. I., Benoit, M., Cooper, J., & Hogg, M. A. (2003). Vicarious dissonance: Attitude change from the inconsistency of others. *Journal of Personality and Social Psychology, 85*, 47–62.

Osgood, C. E., Suci, G. J., & Tannenbaum, P. H. (1957). *The measurement of meaning.* Urbana, IL: University of Illinois Press.

Petty, R. E., & Cacioppo, J. T. (1986). The elaboration likelihood model of persuasion. In L. Berkowitz (Ed.), *Advances in Experimental Social Psychology* (Vol. 19, pp. 123–205). San Diego, CA: Academic Press.

Petty, R. E., & Krosnick, J. A. (1995). *Attitude strength: Antecedents and consequences.* Mahwah, NJ: Erlbaum.

Prislin, R., & Wood, W. (2005). Social influence in attitudes and attitude change. In D. Albarracin, B. T. Johnson, & M. P. Zanna (Eds.), *The handbook of attitudes* (pp. 671–706). Hillsdale, NJ: Erlbaum.

Rosenberg, M. J. (1956). Cognitive structure and attitudinal affect. *Journal of Abnormal and Social Psychology, 53*, 367–372.

Rosenberg, M. J. (1968). Hedonism, inauthenticity, and other goads toward expansion of a consistency theory. In R. P. Abelson et al. (Eds.), *Theories of cognitive consistency: A sourcebook* (pp. 73–111). Chicago, IL: Rand McNally.

Scott, W. A. (1959). Cognitive consistency, response reinforcement, and attitude change. *Sociometry, 22*, 219–229.

Sheeran, P. (2002). Intention-behavior relations: A conceptual and empirical review. In W. Stroebe & M. Hewstone (Eds.), *European review of social psychology* (Vol. 12, pp. 1–36). Chichester, UK: Wiley.

Smith, M. B., Bruner, J., & White, R. (1956). *Opinions and personality.* New York: Wiley.

Thurstone, L. L., & Chave, E. J. (1929). *The measurement of attitude.* Chicago, IL: Chicago University Press.

Van Overwalle, F., & Siebler, F. (2005). A connectionist model of attitude formation and change. *Personality and Social Psychology Review, 9*, 231–274.

Visser, P. S., Bizzer, G. Y., & Krosnick, J. A. (2006). Exploring the latent structure of strength-related attitude attributes. In M. P. Zanna (Ed.), *Advances in experimental social psychology* (Vol. 38, pp. 1–67). San Diego, CA: Academic.

Wicker, A. W. (1969). Attitudes versus actions: The relationship of verbal and overt behavioral responses to attitude objects. *Journal of Social Issues, 25*, 41–78.

Wood, W., & Quinn, J. M. (2003). Forewarned and forearmed? Two meta-analytic syntheses of forewarnings of influence appeals. *Psychological Bulletin, 129*, 119–138.

Zanna, M. P., & Rempel, J. K. (1988). Attitudes: A new look at an old concept. In D. Bar-Tal & A. Kruglanski (Eds.), *The social psychology of knowledge* (pp. 315–334). Cambridge, UK: Cambridge University Press.

II

Attitudes
Nature and Measurement

2

Structure of Attitudes
Judgments, Memory, and Implications for Change

DOLORES ALBARRACÍN, WEI WANG,
HONG LI, & KENJI NOGUCHI
University of Florida

*A*ttitudes are important because they shape people's perceptions of the social and physical world and influence overt behaviors. For example, attitudes influence friendship and animosity toward others, giving and receiving help, and hiring of ethnic minority job candidates. More dramatically, attitudes are at the heart of many violent attacks, including master-minded crimes against humanity (e.g., the Holocaust and the terrorist attacks in New York City on September 11, 2001), but also, attitudes promote major philanthropic enterprises such as a current campaign to end poverty in the world.

When defined as evaluations, attitudes refer to associations between an attitude object and an evaluative category such as *good* vs. *bad* (Albarracin, Johnson, Zanna, & Kumkale, 2005; Zanna & Rempel, 1988). The attitude object can be a concrete target, a behavior, an abstract entity, a person, or an event (Fishbein & Ajzen, 1974). For example, individuals form evaluations of social groups (e.g., prejudice), their own behaviors (attitude toward the behavior; Fishbein & Ajzen, 1975), themselves (self-esteem; Brown, 1998), and other people (person impressions: Wyer & Srull, 1989).

Attitudes have memory and judgment components (Albarracin, Johnson et al., 2005). The memory component involves representations of the attitude in permanent memory; the judgment component involves on-line evaluative thoughts generated about an object at a particular time and place. In this chapter, the structure of attitudes in memory is reviewed, with particular attention to implicit and explicit attitudes. In reviewing memory-structures, we first talk about the internal structure of attitudes and the relation between implicit and explicit attitudes. This section is followed by an account of how judgments are structured by means of reasoned, associative, and configural processes, and a discussion of models depicting the relation between memory structures and judgments.

ATTITUDE REPRESENTATION IN MEMORY

Explicit and Implicit Representations

Learning occurs when one clearly recalls having learned a particular task (explicit memory), but also when skills are acquired in subtle, difficult to recollect ways (implicit memory; Richardson-Klavehn & Bjork 1988; Roediger 1990). Using this explicit/implicit memory distinction, automatic or implicit attitudes have been contrasted with deliberate, explicit attitudes. Whereas explicit attitudes are measured with self-reported evaluations ("President Bush is *good* vs. *bad*"), implicit attitudes are measured with methods that assess the time to link the good vs. bad category with a particular object (e.g., President Bush; Fazio, Jackson, Dunton, & Williams, 1995; Greenwald, McGhee, & Schwartz, 1998; Wittenbrink, Judd, & Park, 1997). For a detailed discussion of implicit attitude measures, see Schwarz (this volume).

The implicit-measurement methods have yielded an impressive amount of evidence about attitudes, as well as generating considerable speculation about the nature of the constructs captured with these measures (see Devos, this volume). In the upcoming sections, we describe various structural aspects of attitudes and the relations between implicit and explicit attitudes.

Internal Structure of Explicit and Implicit Attitudes

Bipolarity A common measure of explicit attitudes is the semantic differential, a 7-point scale with a negative adjective on the left end (-3) and a positive adjective on the right end (+3). The underlying premise of this technique is that ratings of an object as *positive* have extremely high negative correlations with ratings of an object as *negative*. Some evidence suggests that this is in fact the case. For example, according to Watson and Tellegen (1985, 1999), ratings of pleasantness and unpleasantness are bipolar, leading people who report experiencing high pleasure also to report experiencing low displeasure in relation to the same object. More direct evidence comes from work conducted by Judd and Kulik (1980). Their observation that attitudes promote retention and retrieval of both consistent and inconsistent information led them to conclude that the structure of attitudes in memory is bipolar. Specifically, in their work, bipolar questions were more readily answered than unipolar ones, and information processed with bipolar questions was more easily and accurately recalled.

Ambivalence Social psychologists have long identified attitudes entailing simultaneous positive and negative evaluations of an object (Fabrigar, MacDonald, & Wegener, 2005; also see Conner & Armitage, this volume). Ambivalence can occur because of conflict between the implications either among the various beliefs associated with an object or between the beliefs and the affect associated with an object (Ajzen, 2001). Thus, one limitation of bipolar measurement procedures is that it may mask simultaneous negativity and positivity with respect to an object.

Implications of Negative and Positive Evaluations   Even in the absence of ambivalence, the negative and positive dimensions of attitudes have an interesting asymmetry. Specifically, compared with positive information, negative information tends to have a greater impact on attitudes and decisions (Cacioppo, Gardner, & Berntson, 1997; Fiske & Taylor, 1991; Klein, 1996; Matthews & Dietz-Uhler, 1998). People also tend to have better memory for negative vs. positive stimulus words (Ohira, Winton, & Oyama, 1998), and the negative (vs. positive) aspects of an ambivalent attitude can have stronger effects on behavior (Cacioppo & Berntson, 1994; Cacioppo et al., 1997; N. E. Miller, 1944). Also, supporting the notion of greater sensitivity to negative than positive information, an advertising study (Yoon, 2003) revealed that respondents exposed to fictitious brands were slow to perceive the negativity of the information but were more likely to be influenced by it. In contrast, respondents exposed to real brands were quicker to perceive the negativity of the information but were less likely to be influenced by it.

Other lines of research, however, suggest that negative information has greater impact only under certain conditions. For example, messages that are framed negatively or contain negative information are more persuasive than their positive counterparts if the information is difficult to process or recipients are accuracy motivated (Ahluwalia, 2002; Block & Keller, 1995; Homer & Batra, 1994; Meyers-Levy & Maheswaren, 2004; Shiv et al., 2004). However, negative information is not always more powerful in determining attitudes. It is less effective when people have to imagine a story about a potential negative outcome (having a problem during a vacation), presumably because they construct these stories under the most favorable possible light (Adaval & Wyer, 1998). Consistent with this interpretation, the effects of negative (vs. positive) information decrease when people are motivated to process information in an even-handed fashion, but increase when people are motivated to see themselves in a positive light (Ahluwalia, 2002).

Scale   Researchers have developed a variety of scales to assess people's explicit attitudes (Fishbein & Ajzen, 1975; Krosnick, Judd & Wittenbrink 2005; Tesser, Whitaker, Martin, & Ward, 1998). Interestingly, of more than 100 studies of social psychological and political attitudes, 37 used 2-point scales, seven used 3-point scales, 10 used 4-point scales, 27 used 5-point scales, six used 6-point scale, and 21 used 7-point scales (Robinson, Shaver, & Wrightsman, 1999). Despite this diversity, dichotomous-response options appear to have advantages when it comes to understanding the scale (Krosnick et al., 2005) and may appropriately reflect the nature of the representation of evaluations in memory.

It seems unlikely that people have -3 to +3 scales stored in memory. With the exception of specific external requests to use a complex scale, or the need to compare similar objects, most judgments probably entail *good* vs. *bad* options rather than finer distinctions. Moreover, implicit evaluative associations likely link an object with representations or manifestations of visceral affect. Hence, implicit attitudes may be insensitive to variations in the evaluative intensity of the material (Wang, 2005).

Structural Relations between Implicit and Explicit Attitudes

There are at least three possible models of the relation between implicit and explicit attitudes. The following sections address (1) a model in which the explicit and the implicit attitudes are separate (Greenwald & Banaji, 1995); (2) a model in which these two attitudes reflect different levels of processing—and censure—but are not structurally separate (Fazio, 1989); and (3) a model in which the two attitudes are separate but interact (Gawronski & Bodenhausen, 2006; Petty & Briñol, 2006).

Dissociated Systems   Greenwald and Banaji (1995) defined implicit attitudes as introspectively unidentified (or inaccurately identified) traces of past experience that mediate favorable or unfavorable feeling, thought, or action toward an object. These researchers proposed that implicit attitudes reflect unconscious evaluations of an attitude object, whereas explicit attitudes reflect conscious evaluations of an attitude object (Banaji, Lemm, & Carpenter, 2001). Unlike explicit attitudes, implicit measures reflect attitudes of which the person may not be aware, and are not subject to conscious editing on the basis of social or personal concerns. Thus, awareness and disapproval of either negative or positive associations can trigger a dissociation in which the implicit and explicit attitudes can have contradictory implications, or at least low correlations.

This dissociative model is undoubtedly parsimonious and has received support in studies of attitudes toward gender (Greenwald & Farnham, 2000), race, (Banaji, Greenwald, & Rosier, 1997; Greenwald et al., 1998), ethnicity (Greenwald et al., 1998), and age (Mellott & Greenwald, 2000). These findings may be contrasted with lack of dissociation obtained in studies of attitudes toward political candidates (Nosek, Banaji, & Greenwald, 2002) and some consumer products (Brunel, Collins, Greenwald, & Tietje, 1999; Maison, Greenwald, & Bruin, 2001). Presumably, prejudice, but not consumer attitudes, produces dissociations due to attempts at disguising spontaneous yet socially sanctioned negative associations about minority groups.

A meta-analysis of this research (Hofmann, Gawronski, Gschwendner, Le, & Schmitt, 2005) revealed a mean $r = .24$ between IAT measures and self-reported attitudes. This overall low correlation is higher when individuals are likely to rely on their "gut feeling" in a particular domain (as decided by Hofmann et al.'s coders). Correspondingly, the correlation is lower when social desirability is high for a given domain than when it is not. A similar analysis of IAT data collected via the Internet also suggests that self-presentation has a small attenuating effect on the same correlation ($d = .04$), as does believing that one's explicit attitudes are disapproved by one's social group ($d = .24$). In any case, there is no perfect relation between self-presentational concerns and dissociation, as exemplified with a .33

correlation for racial attitudes and a .37 correlation for attitudes about the seasons (i.e., winter and summer).

Separate Interacting Systems   It also is possible to conceive of separate yet interacting explicit and implicit attitudes. For example, Gawronski and Bodenhausen (2006) stated that implicit and explicit attitudes are the result of two different underlying mental processes: associative and propositional processes. Associative evaluations can be activated regardless of whether or not a person considers these evaluations accurate. In contrast, explicit attitudes are evaluative judgments about an attitude object that are rooted in the processes of propositional reasoning.

Importantly, Gawronski and Bodenhausen pointed out that explicit and implicit attitudes have reciprocal influences on each other. People often use automatic-affective reactions (implicit attitudes) towards an object as a basis for evaluative judgments (explicit attitudes) about the object. This influence, however, should occur if and only if the automatic affective reaction is considered valid (i.e., consistent with other propositions). There also are potential influences of evaluative judgments on implicit associations. Presumably, if new propositions make connections between object and an evaluative category, these connections should be represented as implicit attitudes.

Continuum   Fazio and Olson (2003) have questioned the hypothesis that implicit and explicit attitudes are two different attitudes. They argued that research participants are likely unaware that their attitudes are being assessed by means of some implicit measure. However, successful concealment of the research question does not imply that participants are unaware that they possess these attitudes. That is, people may be aware of the evaluative material in implicit measures, but they may lack the opportunity and motivation to correct for their reactions to it. The more sensitive the issue, the greater the likelihood that people will be motivated to exert an influence on overt responses to an explicit measure. In this situation, the implicit measure captures relatively raw material in memory, whereas the direct measure captures reactions altered by the opportunity and motivation to conform to a normative standard (social desirability).

Hypothesizing specific roles for motivation and opportunity leads to the prediction that when an issue is sensitive, motivation and opportunity influence what measure predicts behavior. Clearly, when motivation and opportunity are high, explicit measures should be more predictive because the more desirable associations have been deliberatively selected. Further, Fazio and Olson (2003) also predicted that implicit measures should be more predictive when motivation and opportunity are low. That is, if one cannot engage in careful correction, disguise, or selection of the implicit associations, the explicit measures should be direct translations of the implicit ones.

Distributed Networks   A model by Bassili and Brown (2005; also see Bassili, this volume) suggests that attitudes emerge from microconceptual networks that are activated by particular context configurations. In this model, microconcepts are molecular elements of knowledge that may yield evaluations in combination with other microconcepts in the network. For example, for a person who played competitive tennis as an adolescent, tennis is represented as a collection of microconcepts having to do with the joys of winning, the disappointments of losing, traveling to tournaments, competition, discipline, pressures, fairness, and hanging out with other competitors. These prior experiences together comprise the microconcepts by which the woman evaluates the sport of tennis.

With the framework above, it is relatively easy to explain the structure of explicit and implicit attitudes. According to the model, explicit and implicit attitudes share the same base of microconcepts, but differ in potentiation, which is akin to level of activation. Potentiation depends on recent and current information about the attitude object and cognitive activity in working memory. Implicit attitudes are activations under the potentiation level, which therefore preclude the involvement of deliberate processes. In contrast, explicit attitudes are activated by deliberative process facilitated by working memory.

ATTITUDINAL JUDGMENTS

Processes Underlying Judgments and Corresponding Structures

Online judgments are formed when one considers evaluative aspects of an object either explicitly or spontaneously. Explicitly, one may open a clothing catalog with the intent of evaluating the designs. Alternatively, one may browse the catalog with the intent of selecting pictures for a child's school project and incidentally conclude that some of the designs are attractive. In the following section, we consider whether the processes are associative, reasoned, or configural.

Associative Processes Staats and Staats (1957) showed that pairing nonsense syllables with positive or negative words altered the affective response to the nonsense syllables. That is, the evaluation of the words apparently transferred to initially neutral stimuli by what is referred to as *evaluative conditioning*. In this phenomenon, the positivity of a stimulus transfers to another regardless of the order of presentation. The valenced stimulus can precede, follow, or appear at the same time as the neutral stimulus, suggesting that mere associative processes are at stake.[1] These same processes can explain how one particular association can influence other associations as they come into working memory (see Walther & Langer, this volume).

Reasoned Processes Attitude judgments also can emerge from the application of formal reasoning. For example, expectancy value models have been prominently applied to describe how attitudes are derived from beliefs through the process of formal reasoning. When purchasing a car, people often form their attitudes about a particular car by determining the car's attributes and the desirability of each attribute. In this case, the judgment is determined by the evaluations of attributes or outcomes associated with the car, the strength of the car-attribute associations, and the rule used to combine these cognitions. In Fishbein and Ajzen's (1975) formulation, A_B is the attitude toward the behavior, b_i is the strength of the belief that the behavior will lead to outcome i, e_i is the evaluation of outcome i, and the sum is over all salient outcomes (Fishbein & Ajzen, 1975; also see Ajzen & Gilbert Cote, this volume).

$$A_B = \Sigma b_i e_i \qquad [1]$$

Similarly, a conceptualization proposed by McGuire (1960, 1981) and extended by Wyer and Goldberg (1970; see also Wyer, 1974, 2003) addressed how prior beliefs can influence new beliefs and attitudes. McGuire (1960) stated that two cognitions, A (antecedent) and C (conclusion), can relate to each other by means of a syllogism of the form "A; if A, then C; C." This structure implies that the probability of C (e.g., "an event is good") is a function of the beliefs in the premise or antecedent, and beliefs that "if A is true *and* if $\sim A$ (Not A) is true, C is true." Further, Wyer (1970; Wyer & Goldberg, 1970) argued that C might be true for reasons other than those included in these premises. That is, beliefs in these alternate reasons should also influence the probability of the conclusion ("not A; if not A, then C"). Hence, the belief that C is true, $P(C)$, should be a function of the beliefs in these two mutually exclusive sets of premises, or:

$$P(C) = P(A)P(C/A) + P(\sim A)P(C/\sim A), \qquad [2]$$

where $P(A)$ and $P(\sim A)$ [= $1\text{-}P(A)$] are beliefs that A is and is not true, respectively, and $P(C/A)$ and $P(C/\sim A)$ are conditional beliefs that C is true if A is and is not true, respectively.

A limitation of the conditional inference model described above is the use of a single premise. Although other criteria are considered, these criteria are lumped together in the value of $P(C/\sim A)$, or the belief that the conclusion is true for reasons other than A. In contrast, other formulations consider multiple factors. Slovic and Lichtenstein (1971), for example, postulated that people who predict an unknown event from a set of cues are likely to combine these cues in an additive fashion. Therefore, regression procedures can be used to predict beliefs on the basis of several different pieces of information. In this case, the regression weights assigned to each piece provide an indication of its relative importance (Wiggins, Hoffman, & Taber, 1969). Nevertheless, the assumptions that underlie these linear approaches often are incorrect (Anderson, 1974, 1981; Fishbein & Ajzen, 1975; Tversky, 1969; Wiggins & Hoffman, 1968). Birnbaum and Stegner (1979), for example, found that participants' estimates of a car's value was an *average* of its blue book value and the opinion of another person, with the weight of each piece of information depending on the credibility of its source. Hence, nonlinear models are necessary to understand the influence of beliefs on attitudes.

Configural or Structural Processes   In many instances, neither summative nor averaging models may be applicable (Anderson, 1959; Fishbein & Ajzen, 1975). Kahneman and Tversky (1982) provide strong evidence that people's estimates of the conjunction of two features (e.g., the likelihood that a woman is a feminist bank teller) are not predictable from their estimates of each feature (i.e., being a feminist or being a bank teller) considered in isolation. In these instances, people appear to process the information configurally rather than construing the implications of each piece of information separately (Wyer & Carlston, 1979). One possible configural or structural arrangement relates to *good form,* in the spirit of Gestalt psychology. For example, information that is easier to process often is associated with positive affective reactions. Hence, harmoniously organized information is likely to produce more positive attitudes than disorganized information. Consistent with this hypothesis, Simmons and Nelson (2006) found that people were less confident in predicting the winning of their favorite team over the underdog when the game information was presented in poor, difficult-to-read (vs. easy-to-read) font, which reduced fluency and positive affect (Werth & Strack, 2003).

Another configural process relates to the organization of information in a *familiar form.* As research on mere exposure shows, neutral information gains in favorability with its mere presentation (Zajonc, 1968; see Bornstein, 1989, for a review). For example, Law, Schimmack, and Braun (2003) presented brief video sketches containing one of two brands of food products to a group of participants. One week later, despite their lack of recall or recognition of the presentation, participants liked the previously presented brands better than the unpresented ones.

A third type of configural process is *syntactic parsing, or the arrangement of stimuli using propositional structures* (e.g., a subject-action pair). Judgments emerge from temporally organized information stored in working memory. As stimuli flow through working memory in a particular sequence, the order of stimuli can determine judgments. For example, linguistic propositions may emerge when the order of relatively random material in working memory is syntactically compatible with a given proposition (Chomsky, 1959). Noguchi, Albarracín, and Fischler (2006) investigated the formation of intentions based on implicit propositions formed from random environmental inputs. They reasoned that people could form intentions on the basis of the mere succession of certain words presented in a given behavioral context. In this study, participants who previously played a prisoner's dilemma game (the behavioral context) engaged in a word-detection task. The word-detection task, introduced as a filler while awaiting the scores of the game, required participants to press a key when words began with certain letters (e.g., *A* or *N*). In a series of trials, two sets of words comprised the experimental manipulation. The manipulated words were synonyms of either "act" or "nice." In one condition, participants were exposed to the "act" words (e.g., "play"), followed by "nice" words (e.g., "fair"). In the other condition, participants were exposed to the same words in the opposite order ("nice"—"act").

After the word-detection manipulation, participants played another prisoner's dilemma game. The prediction was that the implicit proposition "act"—"nice" might motivate participants to cooperate because the order suggests a command. In contrast, the implicit proposition "nice"—"act" could be perceived as a compliment. As a result, "nice"—"act" may suggest that participants had already been nice in the prior game. In turn, this assessment may reduce the perceived need to be nice on a future game. Supporting these expectations, the "act"—"nice" sequence increased cooperativeness from the first to the second game. Correspondingly, the "nice"—"act" sequence decreased cooperativeness from the first to the second game. Importantly, these findings were produced with the combination of words; they were not the result of a recency effect in the "be"—"nice" sequence.

Meta-cognitive Processes   Human metacognitive capacity allows individuals first to form attitude judgments, then form judgments about those judgments (Jost, Kruglanski, & Nelson, 1998). These types of processes form multilayered judgments in which each judgment is the object of another judgment. For example, analyses of metacognitive principles have been applied to attitude confidence, defined as a subjective sense of certainty or validity regarding one's attitudes (see Tormala, this volume). In this case, the object of the attitude is the attitude itself, and the metacognitive judgment of attitude confidence entails a judgment about one's attitude. Attitude confidence is higher when one has been repeatedly exposed to the source of the attitude (e.g., an advertisement; Berger & Mitchell, 1989), when one experiences positive affect (Werth & Strack, 2003), and when beliefs and attitudes are univalent rather than complex (Jonas, Diel, & Bröemer, 1997; Prislin, Wood, & Pool, 1998). Attitude confidence has several notable consequences, including using the particular attitude as a basis for later behaviors (Albarracin, Glasman, & Wallace, 2004; Berger, 1992; Fazio, Zanna & Cooper, 1978), and increasing the attitude's resistance to change (Babad, Ariav, Rosen, & Salomon, 1987; Krosnick & Abelson, 1992; Swann et al., 1988).

In addition to studying attitude confidence, researchers have examined confidence in the beliefs or evaluations that underlie a particular attitude toward an object. According to Petty, Briñol, and Tormala (2002), people's confidence in the validity of their thoughts about an object, and the valence of these thoughts influence attitudes. That is, when positive thoughts dominate responses to a communication, increasing confidence in those thoughts makes attitudes toward the message topic more favorable. In contrast, when negative thoughts dominate responses, increasing confidence makes attitudes toward the message topic less favorable.

Another meta-cognitive aspect examined in past research is the perceived strength of the persuasive attack. In a series of studies, Tormala and his collaborators (see Tormala, this volume) demonstrated that participants were more certain about their attitudes after resisting an ostensibly strong message than after resisting an ostensibly weak message or after resisting arguments of undetermined normative strength. The authors concluded that people interpret their personal success in protecting their attitudes from a strong attack as evidence of the correctness of their attitude (thus increasing attitude certainty).

Conventional strength, however, is not the only judgment people make of their attitudes. How intuitive a judgment is, for example, can influence attitude confidence (Simmons & Nelson, 2006). Moreover, judgments based on what is subjectively defined as "intuitive" can last longer than judgments based on what is subjectively defined as "reasoned." Presumably, these intuitions are not questioned, or cognitive resources are recruited to bolster them. Both of these processes can explain the durability of intuitions.

MODELS OF THE RELATION BETWEEN MEMORY REPRESENTATIONS AND JUDGMENTS

Up to now, we considered the structure of attitudes in memory and also the structure of judgments as formed on line without clarifying how memory and online aspects relate to each other. In the following sections, we discuss models that emphasize memory-based influences on judgments, models that assume exclusively on-line influences, and models that consider both memory-based and online influences.

REPRESENTATIONAL MODELS OF ATTITUDES

Memory as the Primary Basis for Judgments

Fazio (1986, 1990, 1995; Fazio & Towles-Schwen, 1999) has stated that attitudes are represented in memory as summary evaluations associated with the attitude object. Although the object-evaluation associations are supposedly integrated into broader representational networks, the model concentrates on the strength of the association between an evaluation and an attitude object. Attitudes are thought to fall on a continuum defined on one end by representations of attitude objects that are not associated with a summary evaluation (i.e., *nonattitudes*, see Converse, 1964, 1974), and on the other end, by representations of attitude objects that are strongly associated with a summary evaluation.

According to this model, attitude accessibility is determined by the strength of the association between an attitude object and its evaluation. When the object-evaluation link is strong, the attitude is highly accessible and exposure to the attitude object will activate the prior evaluation. This automatic process is important because activated evaluations can guide thought and behavior in the presence of the attitude object (Fazio, Powell, & Herr, 1983; also see Ajzen, this volume). For example, highly accessible attitudes exert strong influences on behavior (Fazio, 1990) and can bias perceptions of attitude objects (Fazio, Ledbetter, & Towles-Schwen, 2000). To this extent, information about an object is likely to have a different impact depending on whether or not people possess a prior accessible attitude. Fazio's model, however, does not describe how specific representations are incorporated with other information at the time of making an evaluative judgment.

Models of Rigid Implicit Attitudes

Another example of emphasis on memory-based processes is the assumption that implicit attitudes do not change. Although this assumption later changed, implicit attitudes were initially believed to be difficult to change because they are formed gradually though experiences and learning (see Devos, this volume; Gregg, 2000; Smith & DeCoster, 1999). For example, counterattitudinal information that reliably changes explicit attitudes does not affect implicit attitudes (Gawronski & Strack, 2003; Gregg, Seibt, & Banaji, 2006); McDell, Banaji, & Cooper, 2004). In the area of racial attitudes, white participants directly instructed not to show a bias while performing an Implicit Association Test persisted in showing it (Kim, 2003). Other research suggests that changes that are apparent in explicit attitudes are not observed in implicit ones. In particular, a rise in explicit self-esteem from older to newer generations of East Asian immigrants to the United States is not accompanied by a rise in implicit self-esteem (Hetts, Sakuma, & Pelham, 1999), nor are there cross-generational differences in implicit attitudes toward age (young vs. old) and academic disciplines (math vs. arts) (Nosek, Banaji, & Greenwald, 2002). These findings all support the possibility that implicit attitudes can be stable).

MODELS EMPHASIZING ONLINE INFORMATION

In contrast to traditional representational models of attitudes, constructionist models emphasize that judgments derive from whatever information happens to be accessible at the time. The weak form of Schwarz and Bohner's (2001) model implies that memory-based evaluative information about an attitude object plays a role in current judgments, but this role is not necessarily more important than that of external inputs. The strong form of this argument implies that evaluative judgments are exclusively guided by information present in the external context (Schwarz & Bohner, 2001). For example, individuals may use momentarily experienced affective reactions (e.g., Schwarz & Clore, 1983) or physiological arousal (e.g., Valins, 1966; Wells & Petty, 1980) to determine their evaluations of objects. They may do this without ever bothering to retrieve a previously stored prior attitude about these objects. In this strong version, even when a prior judgment serves as a basis for a subsequent judgment, the judgment is still constructed anew—it is just constructed using old information from memory.

Online use of information as a basis for judgments can be effectively modeled with an inclusion/exclusion model (see Schwarz, this volume). For example, Stapel and Schwarz (1998) drew participants' attention either to Colin Powell's decision (he was a highly popular military leader at the time) to join the Republican Party or his decision to reject an offer to run as a presidential candidate for the Republican Party. Subsequent evaluations of the party were more favorable when participants had thought of Powell joining rather than rejecting a party offer. Presumably, including Powell into the evaluation led to assimilating the party to the highly popular leader. In contrast, distancing Powell from the party led to contrasting the party from him.

MODELS INTEGRATING MEMORY REPRESENTATIONS AND ONLINE INFORMATION

Social Judgment Theory

According to social judgment theory (Eiser, 1973; Eiser & Mower White, 1974; Sherif & Hovland, 1961; for an excellent review, see Eagly & Chaiken, 1993), attitude change is the result of a perceptual process. When the position of the communication appears close to recipients' attitudes, people become closer to the position advocated in the communication by "assimilating" their own attitude to the advocacy. In contrast, when the communication is subjectively distant from their attitudes, there is a "contrast" effect, or perception that one's attitude is more discrepant from the communication than it actually is. In these situations, people resist change, occasionally even changing in opposition to the communication.

Several other predictions of social judgment theory concern the conditions leading to contrast versus assimilation. A chief assumption is that attitude change is a function of the range of positions a person accepts and rejects. When the message position falls within this latitude of acceptance, people assimilate this position to their attitudes. When the position falls within the latitude of rejection, people contrast their attitudes with that position. Furthermore, topics that are highly involving shrink the latitudes of acceptance and expand the latitudes of rejection. The assumption that heightened involvement increases resistance to change has not received consistent support (for reviews, see Eagly & Chaiken, 1993; Johnson, Maio, & Smith-McLallen, 2005).

Information Integration Theory

Anderson (1974) was one of the first researchers to statistically model the effects of prior attitudes and new information. According to his (1959, 1974) *information-integration theory*, if a person receives n items of information, the response (R) to the set of items $(s, i...n)$ is given by:

$$R = w_0s_0 + w_1s_1 + w_2s_2 + ... + w_ns_n, \tag{1}$$

where w_i are the weights and s_i are the scale values of each item. Based on the assumption that information is normally combined by averaging rather than adding, the sum of the weights is typically set to 1. Supporting the averaging model, Birnbaum and Stegner (1979) found that estimates of a car's value were an average of information from the Blue Book and the opinion of another person, each weighted by the credibility of each source of information. However, Fishbein and Ajzen (1975) argued that an additive model is more plausible. The main source of controversy between the additive and averaging models is their ability to account for the set size effect. Whereas additive models naturally account for increases in extremity as new elements of the same value are incorporated (set-size effect), the averaging model needs to assume an initial moderate attitude to account for the set-size effect (Anderson, 1981).

The Activation and Comparison Model

Albarracin, Glasman, and Wallace (2004) also attempted to conceptualize the role of memory representations and online information in producing evaluative judgments. They proposed an activation and comparison model in which attitude change depends on three processes: (1) activating the prior attitude (retrieving it from memory); (2) activating information related to the prior attitude (which can come from memory or an external source); and (3) comparing the prior attitude with the related information. People presumably can activate their prior attitudes as well as information relevant to those attitudes.

Consider the case in which both prior attitudes and new information from a persuasive message (e.g., a political ad) are activated. If one recognizes the message information as being the basis for the prior attitude (redundancy), one may simply select the prior attitude that summarized the information. However, if the retrieved information is new, one may attempt to integrate this information. Integrating this information may entail assigning equal weights by default. Then, both the prior attitude and the new information will be combined through simple average (Anderson, 1974). Alternatively, comparison may ensue (Muthukrishnan, Pham, & Mungalé, 1999, 2001; Pham & Muthukrishnan, 2002). Then, both perceptual comparison as well as comparative validation may determine how the information will be integrated. Perceptually, the new information may appear more invalid when juxtaposed to prior confident attitudes than it would appear alone (Sherif & Sherif, 1964; a perceptual effect). In addition, people may reason that if the new information appears valid even when it is discrepant with one's prior attitudes, this attitude may be more valid when juxtaposed to the attitude than alone (an inferential or comparative validation process). That is, the weights of the prior attitude and the new information may become interdependent.

These observations suggest that there are lower-level, perceptual types of comparative processes as well as inferential forms of comparative validation. Either form of comparison can involve a number of elements. One may simply wish to compare one's prior attitude with a current attitude to determine if the attitude has changed. Or one may compare the direction or validity of the prior information with the direction or validity of the current information. Importantly, these comparisons may be performed very quickly or may require more time. When they require time, the ability to activate the prior attitude quickly increases the chance of comparative processes that modify the weights of the information. Thus, although in many conditions quick recall of the prior attitudes increases stability (Fazio, 1989), by facilitating comparison high prior-attitude activation can also produce *change*.

Models of Malleable Implicit Attitudes

Several recent studies have suggested that implicit attitudes are more flexible than previously thought (Blair & Banaji, 1996; Blair, Ma, & Lenton, 2000). For example, Dasgupta and Greenwald (2001) found that white participants exposed to favorable exemplars of black Americans and unfavorable exemplars of white Americans showed weaker implicit prowhite preferences than did control participants. In addition, levels of automatic racial prejudice decrease with casual social encounters with members of the target group (Lowery, Hardin, & Sinclair, 2001), suggesting that implicit attitudes are fairly malleable.

The above findings of malleability of implicit attitudes greatly interested social psychologists, producing a sizable literature (see Devos, this volume). Reviews of this research by Bassili and Brown (2005), Blair (2002), and Dasgupta and Green-wald (2001), and have identified various conditions in which online information affects implicit attitudes. These conditions include self- and social motives to appear fair (Kinder & Sanders, 1996; Schuman, Steeh, Bobo, & Krysan, 1997; Sinclair & Kunda, 1999); cognitive strategies such as invoking an image that counters an implicit attitude (Blair & Banaji, 1996); attention to an attitude object (e.g., a social category; Macrae, Bodenhausen, Milne, Thorn, & Castelli, 1997; Mitchell, Nosek, & Banaji, 2001); context reminders of the attitude object (Macrae, Boden-hausen, & Milne, 1995; Wittenbrink, Judd, & Park, 2001); and the fit of an external object with the attitude object (Livingston & Brewer, 2002; Macrae, Mitchell, & Pendry, 2002).

The Potentiated Recruitment Framework

As previously mentioned, models inspired by connectionism (Smith, Fazio, & Cejka, 1996) offer an alternative means to account for the influences of both enduring attitudes and the evaluative implications of momentarily accessible information. By explicating the sources of variability in the potentiation of attitudes (e.g., context, goals), this framework integrates prior attitude representations with online information.

FINAL COMMENTS

"Attitude structure" encompasses rich and diverse themes including how attitude-relevant memories are structured, how judgments are constructed, and whether and how the memory and judgment components interact to produce new judgments. For a while, the study of attitude structure involved simply the literature on explicit attitudes, but the last decade has allowed for new and exciting developments in the area of implicit attitudes. We hope that the next decade will bring further integration of our understanding of explicit and implicit attitudes, and that social psychology will continue to be at the forefront of this important theorizing.

AUTHORS' NOTE

Dolores Albarracín, Wei Wang, Hong Li, and Kenji Noguchi, Department of Psychology, University of Florida: The research was supported by grant K02-MH075616 from the National Institute of Mental Health and facilitated by a grant from the National Institutes of Health (R01-NR08325). We thank Casey McCulloch for comments on an earlier version of this chapter. Correspondence about this paper should be sent to Dolores Albarracín, Psychology Department, University of Florida, Gainesville, FL 32608. Electronic e-mail can be sent to dalbarra@ufl.edu.

NOTE

1. By contrast, classical conditioning requires that the valenced (conditioned) stimulus be followed by the unconditioned stimulus, thus ensuring that the conditioned stimulus will signal the unconditioned one.

REFERENCES

Adaval, R., & Wyer, R. S. (1998). The role of narratives in consumer information processing. *Journal of Consumer Psychology, 7*, 207–245.

Ahluwalia, R. (2002). How prevalent is the negativity effect in consumer environments? *Journal of Consumer Research, 29*, 270–279.

Ajzen, I. (2001). Nature and operation of attitudes. *Annual Review of Psychology, 52*, 27–58.

Albarracín, D., Johnson, B. T., Zanna, M. P., & Kumkale, G. T. (2005). Attitudes: Introduction and scope. In D. Albarracín, B. T. Johnson, & M. P. Zanna (Eds.), *Handbook of attitudes* (pp.3–20). Hillsdale, NJ: Erlbaum.

Albarracín, D., Glasman, L. R., & Wallace, H. M.. (2004). Survival and change of attitudes and other social judgments: A model of activation and comparison. In M. P. Zanna (Ed.), *Advances in experimental social psychology* (Vol. 36, pp. 252–315). San Diego, CA: Academic Press.

Anderson, N. H. (1959). A test model of opinion change. *Journal of Abnormal and Social Psychology, 59*, 371–381.

Anderson, N. H. (1974). Cognitive algebra: Integration theory to applied social attribution. In L. Berkowitz (Ed.), *Advances in experimental social psychology* (Vol. 7, pp. 1–101). San Diego, CA: Academic Press.

Anderson, N. H. (1981). Integration theory applied to cognitive responses and attitudes. In R. E. Petty, T. M. Ostrom, & T. C. Brock (Eds.), *Cognitive responses in persuasion* (pp. 361–397). Hillsdale, NJ: Erlbaum.

Babad, E. Y., Ariav, A., Rosen, I., & Salomon, G. (1987). Perseverance of bias as a function of debriefing conditions and subjects' confidence. *Social Behaviour, 2*, 185–193.

Banaji, M. R., Greenwald, A. G., & Rosier, M. (1997, October). Implicit esteem: When collectives shape individuals. Paper presented at the Preconference on Self, Toronto, Ontario, Canada.

Banaji, M. R., Lemm, K. M., & Carpenter, S. J. (2001). The social unconscious. In A. Tesser & N. Schwarz (Eds.), *Blackwell handbook of social psychology: Intraindividual processes* (pp. 134–158). Oxford, UK: Blackwell.

Bassili, J. N., & Brown, R. D. (2005). Implicit and explicit attitudes: Research, challenges, and theory. In D. Albarracín, B. T. Johnson, & M. P. Zanna (Eds.), *Handbook of attitudes and attitude change* (pp.543–574). Mahwah, NJ: Erlbaum.

Berger, I. E. (1992). The nature of attitude accessibility and attitude confidence: a triangulated experiment. *Journal of Consumer Psychology, 1*, 103–123.

Berger, I. E., & Mitchell, A.A. (1989). The effect of advertising repetition on attitude accessibility, attitude confidence/certainty and the attitude-behavior relationship. *Journal of Consumer Research, 16*, 269–279.

Birnbaum, M. H., & Stegner, S. E. (1979). Source credibility in social judgment: Bias, expertise, and the judge's point of view. *Journal of Personality and Social Psychology, 37*, 48–74.

Blair, I. V. (2002). The malleability of automatic stereotypes and prejudice. *Personality and Social Psychology Review, 6*, 242–261.

Blair, I. V., & Banaji, M. R. (1996). Automatic and controlled processes in stereotype priming. *Journal of Personality and Social Psychology, 70,* 1142–1163.

Blair, I. V., Ma, J. E., & Lenton, A. P. (2000). Imagining stereotypes away: The moderation of automatic stereotypes through mental imagery. Unpublished manuscript.

Block, L. G., & Keller, P. A. (1995). When to accentuate the negative: The effects of perceived efficacy and message framing on intentions to perform a health-related behavior. *Journal of Marketing Research, 32,* 192–204.

Bornstein, M. H. (1989). Sensitive periods in development: Structural characteristics and causal interpretations. *Psychological Bulletin, 105,* 179–197

Brown, J. D. (1998). *The self.* New York: McGraw-Hill.

Brunel, F. F., Collins, C. M., Greenwald, A. G., & Tietje, B. C. (1999, October). Making the private public, accessing the inaccessible: Marketing applications of the Implicit Association Test. Paper presented at the Annual Meeting of the Association for Consumer Research, Columbus, OH.

Cacioppo, J. T., & Berntson, G. G. (1994). Relationship between attitudes and evaluative space: A critical review, with emphasis on the separability of positive and negative substrates. *Psychological Bulletin, 115,* 401–423.

Cacioppo, J. T., Gardner, W. L., & Berntson, G. G. (1997). Beyond bipolar conceptualizations and measures: The case of attitudes and evaluative space. *Personality and Social Psychology Review, 1,* 3–25.

Chomsky, N. (1959). On certain formal properties of grammars. *Information and Control, 2,* 137–167.

Converse, P. E. (1964). A network of data archives for the behavioral sciences. *Public Opinion Quarterly, 28,* 273–286.

Converse, P. E. (1974). Comment: The status of non attitudes. *American Political Science Review, 68,* 650–660.

Dasgupta, N., & Greenwald, A. G. (2001). On the malleability of automatic attitudes: Combating automatic prejudice and preference with images of admired group members. *Journal of Personality and Social Psychology, 81,* 800–814.

Devos, T., & Banaji, M. R. (2005). American = White? *Journal of Personality and Social Psychology, 88,* 447–466.

Eagly, A. H., & Chaiken, S. (1993). *The psychology of attitudes.* Fort Worth, TX: Harcourt Brace.

Eiser, J. R. (1973). Judgment of attitude statements as a function of judges' attitudes and the judgmental dimension. *British Journal of Social and Clinical Psychology, 17,* 1–10.

Eiser, J. R., & Mower White, C. J. (1974). Evaluative consistency and social judgment. *Journal of Personality and Social Psychology, 30,* 349–359.

Fabrigar, L. R., MacDonald, T. K., & Wegener, D. T. (2005). The structures of attitudes. In D. Albarracin, B. T. Johnson, & M. P. Zanna (Eds.), *The handbook of attitudes* (pp. 79–124). Mahwah, NJ: Erlbaum.

Fazio, R. H. (1986). On the automatic activation of attitudes. *Journal of Personality and Social Psychology, 50,* 229–238.

Fazio, R. H. (1989). On the power and functionality of attitudes: The role of attitude accessibility. In S. J. Breckler & A. G. Greenwald (Eds.), *Attitude Structure and Function* (pp. 153–179). Hillsdale, NJ: Erlbaum.

Fazio, R. H. (1990). Multiple processes by which attitudes guide behavior: The MODE model as an integrative framework. In M. P. Zanna (Ed.), *Advances in experimental social psychology* (Vol. 23, pp. 75–109). San Diego, CA: Academic Press.

Fazio, R. H. (1995). Attitudes as object-evaluation associations: Determinants, consequences, and correlates of attitude accessibility. In R. E. Petty & J. A. Krosnick (Eds.), *Attitude strength: Antecedents and consequences* (pp. 247–282). Mahwah, NJ: Erlbaum.

Fazio, R. H., Jackson, J. R., Dunton, B. C., & Williams, C. J. (1995). Variability in automatic activation as an unobtrusive measure of racial attitudes: A bona fide pipeline? *Journal of Personality and Social Psychology, 69,* 1013–1027.

Fazio, R. H., Ledbetter, J. E., & Towles-Schwen, T. (2000). On the costs of accessible attitudes: Detecting that the attitude object has changed. *Journal of Personality and Social Psychology, 78,* 197–210.

Fazio, R. H., & Olson, M. A. (2003). Implicit measures in social cognition research: Their meaning and use. *Annual Review of Psychology, 54,* 297–327.

Fazio, R. H., Powell, M. C., & Herr, P. M. (1983). Toward a process model of the attitude-behavior relation: Accessing one's attitude upon mere observation of the attitude object. *Journal of Personality and Social Psychology, 44,* 723–735.

Fazio, R. H., & Towles-Schwen, T. (1999). The MODE model of attitude-behavior processes. In S. Chaiken & Y. Trope (Eds.), *Dual process theories in social psychology* (pp. 97–116). New York: Guilford.

Fazio, R. H., Zanna, M. P., & Cooper, J. (1978). Direct experience and attitude-behavior consistency: An information processing analysis. *Personality and Social Psychology Bulletin, 4,* 48–51.

Fishbein, M., & Ajzen, I. (1974). Attitude toward objects as predictors of single and multiple behavioral criteria. *Psychological Review, 81,* 59–74.

Fishbein, M., & Aizen, I. (1975). *Belief, attitudes, intention, and behavior: an introduction to theory and research.* Reading, MA: Addison-Wesley.

Fiske, S. T., & Taylor, S. E. (1991). *Social cognition* (2nd ed.). New York: McGraw-Hill.

Gawronski, B., & Bodenhausen, G. V. (2006). Associative and propositional processes in evaluation: An integrative review of implicit and explicit attitude change. *Psychological Bulletin, 132*(5), 692–731.

Gawronski, B., & Strack, F. (2003). On the propositional nature of cognitive consistency: Dissonance changes explicit, but not implicit attitudes. *Journal of Experimental Social Psychology, 40,* 535–542.

Greenwald, A. G., & Banaji, M. R. 1995. Implicit social cognition: attitudes, self-esteem, and stereotypes. *Psychological Review, 102,* 4–27.

Greenwald, A. G., & Farnham, S. D. (2000). Using the Implicit Association Test to measure self-esteem and self-concept. *Journal of Personality and Social Psychology, 79,* 1022–1038.

Greenwald, A. G., McGhee, D. E., & Schwartz, J. K. L. (1998). Measuring individual differences in implicit cognition: The Implicit Association Test. *Journal of Personality and Social Psychology, 74,* 1464–1480.

Gregg, A. P. (2000). The hare and the tortoise: The origins and dynamics of explicit and implicit attitudes. Unpublished doctoral dissertation, Yale University, New Haven, CT.

Gregg, A. P., Seibt, B., & Banaji, M. R. (2006). Easier done than undone: Asymmetry in the malleability of implicit preferences. *Journal of Personality and Social Psychology, 90,* 1–20.

Hetts, J. J., Sakuma, M., & Pelham, B. W. (1999). Two roads to positive regard: Implicit and explicit self-evaluation and culture. *Journal of Experimental Social Psychology, 35,* 512–559.

Hofmann, W., Gawronski, B., Gschwendner, T., Le, H., & Schmitt, M. (2005). A meta-analysis on the correlation between the implicit association test and explicit self-report measures. *Personality and Social Psychology Bulletin, 31,* 1369–1385.

Homer, P. M., & Batra, R. (1994). Attitudinal effects of character-based versus competence-based negative political communications. *Journal of Consumer Psychology, 3,* 163–185.

Johnson, B. T., Maio, G. R., & Smith-Mclallen, A. (2005). Communication and attitude change: Causes, processes, and effects. In D. Albarracín, B. T. Johnson, & M. P. Zanna (Eds.), *Handbook of attitudes and attitude change*. Hillsdale, NJ: Erlbaum.

Jonas, K., Diehl, M., & Bröemer, P. (1997). Effects of attitudinal ambivalence on information processing and attitude-intention consistency. *Journal of Experimental Social Psychology, 33,* 190–210.

Jost, J. T., Kruglanski, A. W., & Nelson, T. O. (1998). Social metacognition: An expansionist review. *Personality and Social Psychology Review, 2,* 137–154.

Judd, C. M., & Kulik, J. A. (1980). Schematic effects of social attitudes on information processing and recall. *Journal of Personality and Social Psychology, 38,* 569–578.

Kahneman, D., & Tversky, A. (1982). The psychology of preferences. *Scientific American, 246,* 160–173.

Kim, D. Y. (2003). Voluntary controllability of the Implicit Association Test (IAT). *Social Psychology Quarterly, 66,* 83–96.

Kinder, D. R., & Sanders, L. M. (1996). *Divided by color.* Chicago: University of Chicago Press.

Klein, J. G. (1996). Negativity in impressions of presidential candidates revisited: the 1992 election. *Personality and Social Psychology Bulletin, 22,* 288–295.

Krosnick, J. A., & Abelson, R. P. (1992). The case for measuring attitude strength in surveys. In J. Tanur (Ed.), *Questions about survey questions* (pp. 177–203). New York: Russell Sage.

Krosnick, J. A., Judd, C. M., & Wittenbrink, B. (2005). The measurement of attitudes. In: D. Albarracín, B. T Johnson, & M. P. Zanna (Eds.), *The handbook of attitudes* (pp. 21–76). Mahwah, NJ: Erlbaum.

Law, S., Schimmack, U., & Braun, K. A. (2003). Cameo appearances of branded products in TV shows: How effective are they? Manuscript in preparation.

Livingston, R. W., & Brewer, M. B. (2002). What are we really priming? Cue-based versus category-based processing of facial stimuli. *Journal of Personality and Social Psychology, 82,* 5–18.

Lowery, B. S., Hardin, C. D., & Sinclair, S. (2001). Social influence effects on automatic social prejudice. *Journal of Personality and Social Psychology, 81,* 842–855.

Macrae, C. N., Bodenhausen, G. V., & Milne, A. B. (1995). The dissection of selection in person perception: Inhibitory processes in social stereotyping. *Journal of Personality and Social Psychology, 69,* 397–407.

Macrae, C. N., Bodenhausen, G. V., Milne, A. B., Thorn, T. M. J., & Castelli, L. (1997). On the activation of social stereotypes: The moderating role of processing objectives. *Journal of Experimental Social Psychology, 33,* 471–489.

Macrae, C. N., Mitchell, J. P., & Pendry, L. F. (2002). What's in a forename? Cue familiarity and stereotypical thinking. *Journal of Experimental Social Psychology, 38,* 186–193.

Maison, D., Greenwald, A. G., & Bruin, R. (2001). The Implicit Association Test as a measure of implicit consumer attitudes. *Polish Psychological Bulletin, 32.* Retrieved from http://insight.blackhorse.pl/10012/10012010002a.html.

Matthews, D., & Dietz-Uhler, B. (1998). The black-sheep effect: how positive and negative advertisements affect voter's perceptions of the sponsor of the advertisement. *Journal of Applied Social Psychology, 28,* 1903–1915.

McDell, J. J., Banaji, M. R., & Cooper, J. (2004). Freedom to choose does not matter to implicit attitudes. Unpublished manuscript, Harvard University.

McGuire, W. J. (1960). A syllogistic analysis of cognitive relationships. In M. J. Rosenberg & C. I. Hovland (Eds.), *Attitude organization and change* (pp. 140–162). New Haven, CT: Yale University Press.

McGuire, W. J. (1981). The probabilogical model of cognitive structure and attitude change. In R. E. Petty, T. M. Ostrom, & T. C. Brock (Eds.), *Cognitive responses in persuasion* (pp. 291–307). Hillsdale, NJ: Erlbaum.

Mellott, D. S., & Greenwald, A. G. (2000). But I don't feel old! Implicit self-esteem, age identity, and ageism in the elderly. Unpublished manuscript, University of Washington, Seattle.

Meyers-Levy, J., & Maheswaran, D. (2004). Exploring message framing outcomes when systematic, heuristic, or both types of processing occur. *Journal of Consumer Psychology, 14,* 159–167.

Miller, N. E. (1944). Experimental studies of conflict. In J. McV. Hunt (Ed.), *Personality and the behavior disorders* (Vol. 1, pp. 431–465). New York: Ronald Press.

Mitchell, J. P., Nosek, B. A., & Banaji, M. R. (2001). Contextual variations in implicit evaluation. Manuscript submitted for publication.

Muthukrishnan, A.V., Pham, M.T., & Mungalé, A. (1999). Comparison opportunity and judgment revision. *Organizational Behavior and Human Decision Processes, 80,* 228–251.

Muthukrishnan, A. V., Pham, M. T., & Mungalé, A. (2001). Does greater amount of information always bolster attitudinal resistance? *Marketing Letters, 12,* 131–144.

Noguchi, K., Albarracín, D., & Fischler, I. (2006). Implicit pragmatics: The effect of incidental word order on cooperative behavior. Unpublished manuscript, University of Florida, Gainesville.

Nosek, B. A. & Banaji, M. R. (2001). The go/no-go association task. *Social Cognition, 19,* 625–666.

Nosek, B. A., Banaji, M. R., & Greenwald, A. G. (2002). Harvesting implicit group attitudes and beliefs from a demonstration web site. *Group Dynamics: Theory, Research, and Practice, 6,* 101–115.

Ohira, H., Winton, W. M., & Oyama, M. (1998). Effects of stimulus valence on recognition memory and endogenous eyeblinks: Further evidence for positive-negative asymmetry. *Personality and Social Psychology Bulletin, 24,* 986–993.

Petty, R. E., & Briñol, P. (2006). A metacognitive approach to "implicit" and "explicit" evaluations: Comment on Gawronski and Bodenhausen. *Psychological Bulletin, 132,* 740–744.

Petty, R. E., Briñol, P., & Tormala, Z. L. (2002). Thought confidence as a determinant of persuasion: The self-validation hypothesis. *Journal of Personality and Social Psychology, 82,* 722–741.

Pham, M. T., & Muthukrishnan, A.V. (2002). Search and alignment in judgment revision: Implications for brand positioning. *Journal of Marketing Research, 39,* 18–30.

Prislin, R., Wood, W., & Pool, G. J. (1998). Structural consistency and the deduction of novel from existing attitudes. *Journal of Experimental Social Psychology, 34,* 66–89.

Richardson-Klavehn, A., & Bjork, R. A. (1988). Measures of memory. *Annual Review of Psychology, 39,* 475–543.

Robinson, J. P., Shaver, P. R., & Wrightsman, L. S. (1999). *Measures of political attitudes.* San Diego, CA: Academic Press.

Roediger, H. L. (1990). Implicit memory: retention without remembering. *American Psychologist, 45,*1043–1056.

Schuman, H., Steeh, S., Bobo, L., & Krysan, M. (1997). *Racial attitudes in America: Trends and interpretations* (Rev. ed.). Cambridge, MA: Harvard University Press.

Schwarz, N., & Bohner, G. (2001). The construction of attitudes. In A. Tesser & N. Schwarz (Eds.), *Blackwell handbook of social psychology: Intraindividual processes* (pp. 436–457). Malden, MA: Blackwell.

Schwarz, N., & Clore, G. L. (1983). Mood, misattribution, and judgments of well-being: Informative and directive function of affective states. *Personality and Social Psychology Bulletin, 45*, 513–523.

Sherif, M., & Hovland, C. I. (1961). Placement of items on controversial issues. In M. Sherif & C. Hovland (Eds.), *Social judgment* (pp. 99–126). New Haven, CT: Yale University Press.

Sherif, M., & Sherif, C. (1964) Acceptable and unacceptable behavior defined by group norms. In M. Sherif & C. Sherif (Eds.), *Reference groups: Exploration into conformity and deviation of adolescents*. New York: Harper & Row.

Shiv, B., Britton, J. E., & Payne, J. W. (2004). Does elaboration increase or decrease the effectiveness of negatively versus positively framed messages? *Journal of Consumer Research, 31*, 199–208.

Simmons, J. P., & Nelson, L. D. (2006). Intuitive confidence: Choosing between intuitive and nonintuitive alternatives. *Journal of Experimental Psychology, General, 135*, 409–428.

Sinclair, L., & Kunda, Z. (1999). Reactions to a Black professional: Motivated inhibition and activation of conflicting stereotypes. *Journal of Personality and Social Psychology, 77*, 885–904.

Slovic, P., & Lichtenstein, S. (1971). Comparison of Bayesian and regression approaches to the study of information processing in judgment. *Organizational Behavior and Human Performance, 6*, 649–744.

Smith, E. R., & DeCoster, J. (1999). Associative and rule-based processing: A connectionist interpretation of dual-process models. In S. Chaiken & Y. Trope (Eds.), *Dual-process theories in social psychology* (pp. 323–336). New York: Guilford.

Smith, E. R., Fazio, R. H., & Cejka, M. A. (1996). Accessible attitudes influence categorization of multiply categorizable objects. *Journal of Personality and Social Psychology, 71*, 888–898.

Staats, C. K., & Staats, A. W. (1957). Meaning established by classical conditioning. *Journal of Experimental Psychology, 54*, 74–80.

Stapel, D. A., & Schwarz, N. (1998). Similarities and differences between the impact of traits and experiences: What matters is whether the target stimulus is ambiguous or mixed. *Journal of Experimental Psychology, 34*, 227–245.

Swann, W. B., Jr., Pelham, B. W., & Chidester, T. (1988). Change through paradox: Using self-verification to alter beliefs. *Journal of Personality and Social Psychology, 54*, 268–273.

Tesser, A., Whitaker, D., Martin, L., & Ward, D. (1998). Attitude heritability, attitude change and physiological responsivity. *Personality and Individual Differences, 24*, 89–96.

Tversky, A. (1969). Intransitivity of preference. *Psychology Review, 76*, 31–48.

Valins, S. (1966) Cognitive effects of false heart-rate feedback. *Journal of Personality and Social Psychology, 4*, 400–408.

Wang, W. (2005). The implicit and explicit cognitive bias towards different positive & negative events among Chinese university students. Unpublished thesis, Beijing Normal University.

Watson, D., & Tellegen, A. (1985). Toward a consensual structure of mood. *Psychological Bulletin, 98*, 219–235.

Watson, D., & Tellegen, A. (1999). Issues in the dimensional structure of affect—Effects of descriptors, measurement error, and response formats: Comment on Russell and Carroll. *Psychological Bulletin, 125*, 601–610.

Wells, G. L., & Petty, R. E. (1980). The effects of overt head movements on persuasion: Compatibility and incompatibility of responses. *Basic and Applied Social Psychology, 1*, 219–230.

Werth, L., & Strack, F. (2003). An inferential approach to the knew-it-all-along phenomenon. *Memory, 11,* 411–419.

Wiggins, N., & Hoffman, P. J. (1968). Three models of clinical judgment. *Journal of Abnormal Psychology, 73,* 70–77.

Wiggins, N., Hoffman, P. J., & Taber, T. (1969). Types of judges and cue utilization in judgments of intelligence. *Journal of Personality and Social Psychology, 12,* 52–59.

Wittenbrink, B., Judd, C. M., & Park, B. (1997). Evidence for racial prejudice at the implicit level and its relationships with questionnaire measures. *Journal of Personality and Social Psychology, 72,* 262–274.

Wittenbrink, B., Judd, C. M., & Park, B. (2001). Spontaneous prejudice in context: Variability in automatically activated attitudes. *Journal of Personality & Social Psychology, 81,* 815–827.

Wyer, R. S. (1970). Information redundancy, inconsistency, and novelty and their role in impression formation. *Journal of Experimental Social Psychology, 6,* 111–127.

Wyer, R. S. (1974). *Cognitive organization and change: An Information-processing approach.* Hillsdale, NJ: Erlbaum.

Wyer, R. S. (2003). *Social comprehension and judgment: The role of situation models, narratives, and implicit theories.* Mahwah, NJ: Erlbaum.

Wyer, R. S., & Carlston, D. E. (1979). *Social cognition, inference, and attribution.* Hillsdale, NJ: Erlbaum.

Wyer, R. S., & Goldberg, L. (1970). A probabilistic analysis of the relationships among beliefs and attitudes. *Psychological Review, 77,* 100–120.

Wyer, R. S., & Srull, T. K. (1989). *Memory and cognition in its social context.* Hillsdale, NJ: Erlbaum.

Yoon, D. (2003). The effect of Web-based negative information on brand attitude. *Dissertation Abstracts International Section A: Humanities and Social Sciences, 64*(5-A), 1448.

Zajonc, R. B. (1968). Attitudinal effect of mere exposure. *Journal of Personality and Social Psychology, 9,* 1–27.

Zanna, M. P., & Rempel, J. K. (1988). Attitudes: A new look at an old concept. In D. Bar-Tal & A. Kruglanski (Eds.), *The social psychology of knowledge* (pp. 315–334). Cambridge, UK: Cambridge University Press.

3

Attitude Measurement

NORBERT SCHWARZ

Institute for Social Research, University of Michigan

*A*s currently used in psychology, the term *attitude* refers to a hypothetical construct, namely a predisposition to evaluate some object in a favorable or unfavorable manner (Eagly & Chaiken, 1993; Prislin & Crano, this volume). This predisposition cannot be directly observed and needs to be inferred from individuals' responses to the attitude object. These responses can run from overt behavior (such as approaching or avoiding the object) and explicit verbal statements (e.g., answers to an attitude question) to covert responses, which may be outside of the person's awareness (such as minute facial expressions or the speed with which a letter string can be recognized as a meaningful word). In principle, any one of these responses can be used to infer a person's attitude; however, each response may be influenced by variables other than the person's evaluative predisposition toward the attitude object, raising complex theoretical issues. Moreover, the same person's responses to different attitude measures may suggest different underlying attitudes; for example, a person's verbal statements may not converge with the person's overt behavior or spontaneous facial expressions.

This chapter provides an introduction to the most commonly used measurement procedures; it is organized as follows. The first section addresses direct attitude questions. It reviews the cognitive and communicative processes involved in answering attitude questions and discusses common question and response scale formats. As will become apparent, respondents' answers to attitude questions are highly context dependent and researchers have developed a number of alternative procedures, often in the hope that they would provide a less context dependent assessment of attitudes. The second section reviews some of these recent "implicit" attitude measures, most of which are based on variants of response time measurement (see also Devos, this volume).

A growing body of research indicates that these implicit measures are just as context dependent as explicit attitude reports. Alternatively, researchers can rely on psychophysiological measures or on behavioral observation, reviewed in the third section. The chapter concludes with a discussion of the theoretical implications of the observed context dependency of attitude measurement by juxtaposing the traditional emphasis on evaluative predispositions with the alternative view that attitudes are context sensitive evaluations, constructed on the spot.

DIRECT QUESTIONS: EXPLICIT SELF-REPORTS OF ATTITUDES

Most researchers rely on respondents' answers to direct attitude questions, like, "Do you approve or disapprove of how President Bush is handling his job?" Direct questions are the most feasible procedure for assessing the attitudes of the population at large, as is done in representative sample surveys. In laboratory research, direct questions can be supplemented with more indirect procedures, like psychophysiological or response time measurement. The use of direct questions is based on the premise that people have introspective access to their attitudes and are aware of what they like and dislike (for a discussion see Strack & Schwarz, 2007), whereas most other attitude measures do not require this assumption.

As attitude researchers have known for many decades, self-reports of attitudes are highly context dependent and minor changes in question wording, question format, and question order can profoundly affect the obtained results (for early reviews see Cantril, 1944; Payne, 1951). Since the early 1980s, psychologists and survey methodologists investigated the underlying cognitive and communicative processes and this section summarizes what has been learned. Sudman, Bradburn, and Schwarz (1996) and Tourangeau, Rips, and Rasinski (2000) provide more comprehensive reviews of this work, including self-reports of attitudes as well as behaviors (see also Schwarz & Oyserman, 2001).

Respondents' Tasks

Answering an attitude question involves several tasks. As a first step, respondents need to understand the question to determine which information they are to provide. Next, they need to retrieve relevant information from memory to form an attitude judgment. In most cases, they cannot report this judgment in their own words, but need to format their answer to fit the response alternatives provided by the researcher. Moreover, they may want to edit their judgment before they report it, due to reasons of social desirability and self-presentation. Accordingly, comprehension, retrieval, judgment, formatting, and editing are the key components of the response process (see Strack & Martin, 1987; Sudman et al., 1996, chapter 3, for more detailed discussions). Performance at each of these steps is strongly influenced by contextual features.

Question Comprehension

The key issue at the comprehension stage is whether the respondent's understanding of the question matches what the researcher had in mind: Is the attitude object that the respondent reports on the one that the researcher intended? Does the respondent's understanding tap the intended facet of the issue and the intended evaluative dimension? Not surprisingly, researchers are urged to write clear and simple questions and to avoid unfamiliar or ambiguous terms. Bradburn, Sudman, and Wansink (2004) provide excellent advice in this regard. Even familiar terms, however, are open to interpretation and respondents draw on the context of the question to infer which meaning the researcher has in mind. Hence, the term *drugs* acquires a different meaning in the context of a health insurance survey than in the context of a crime survey. This use of contextual information is licensed by the tacit norms that underlie the conduct of conversation in daily life (Grice, 1975), where listeners are expected to take the content of preceding utterances into account when they interpret the next one. Research participants bring these conversational norms to the research situation and assume that all contributions of the researcher are relevant to the ongoing "conversation" (for reviews see Clark & Schober, 1992; Schwarz, 1994, 1996). These contributions include the study introduction and the content of preceding questions, as well as the specific wording of the question and many apparently "formal" features of the questionnaire.

Suppose, for example, that respondents are asked to report how successful they have been in life, along an 11-point rating scale, ranging from "not so successful" to "extremely successful." To provide a rating, they need to determine what "not so successful" means: Does it refer to the absence of outstanding achievements or to the presence of failure? To infer the intended meaning they may draw on formal characteristics of the rating scale. When the numeric values of the scale run from 0 = "not so successful" to 10 = "extremely successful," respondents interpret "not so successful" as pertaining to the absence of noteworthy achievements; but when the scale runs from -5 = "not so successful" to +5 = "extremely successful," they interpret "not so successful" as pertaining to the presence of failure. Because people are more likely to lack great achievements than to experience great failures, these differences in interpretation result in dramatic shifts in the obtained ratings. Specifically, 34% of a German sample endorsed a value between 0 and 5 on the 0 to 10 scale, whereas only 13% endorsed a formally equivalent value between -5 and 0 on the -5 to +5 scale (Schwarz, Knäuper, Hippler, Noelle-Neumann, & Clark, 1991). In general, a minus-to-plus rating scale format conveys that the researcher has a bipolar dimension in mind, where one endpoint refers to the opposite of the other. In contrast, a format that presents only positive numbers conveys that the researcher has a unipolar dimension in mind, where the numbers pertain to different degrees of the presence of the same attribute. Schwarz (1994, 1996) has reviewed what respondents infer from different elements of a questionnaire and the procedures used in laboratory experiments, and highlights how their inferences are consistent with normal conversational conduct in everyday life.

To safeguard against unintended question interpretations, researchers developed cognitive interviewing techniques to assess respondents' interpretation of questions at the pretest stage. Willis (2004) and the contributions in Schwarz and Sudman (1996) review these methods and provide advice on their use. Given the context dependency of question interpretations, these techniques should not be applied to isolated questions; instead, the question needs to be presented in the context in which it will be used in the actual study. When properly employed, cognitive interviewing at the questionnaire development stage, and sensitive revisions, can ensure that respondents understand the final question as intended.

Information Retrieval and Judgment

Once respondents determine what the question refers to, they need to recall relevant information from memory. In some cases, they may have direct access to a previously formed judgment that they can offer as an answer. In most cases, however, they will not find an appropriate answer readily stored in memory and will need to develop a judgment on the spot. To do so, they need to form a mental representation of the attitude object, and of a standard against which the object is evaluated. The resulting judgment depends on which information happens to come to mind at that point in time and on how this information is used.

As a large body of social cognition research demonstrates, people rarely retrieve all information that may bear on an attitude object; rather, they truncate the search process as soon as enough information has come to mind to form a judgment with sufficient subjective certainty (for reviews see Bodenhausen & Wyer, 1987; Wyer & Srull, 1989). Hence, the judgment is disproportionately influenced by the first few pieces of information that come to mind. Whereas some information may always come to mind when the person thinks of a particular object (and is therefore called chronically accessible), other information may be only temporarily accessible, for example, because it has been brought to mind by preceding questions. Changes in what is temporarily accessible are at the heart of many context effects in attitude measurement, including question order and response order effects, as discussed below. In contrast, chronically accessible information contributes some stability to attitude judgments.

Question Order Effects   How accessible information influences the judgment depends on how it is used (Schwarz & Bless, 1992, 2007). Information that is included in the temporary representation formed of the target results in assimilation effects; that is, the inclusion of positive (negative) information results in a more positive (negative) judgment. The size of assimilation effects increases with the amount and extremity of temporarily accessible information and decreases with the amount and extremity of chronically accessible information included in the representation of the target (Bless, Schwarz, & Wänke, 2003). For example, Schwarz, Strack, and Mai (1991) asked respondents to report their marital satisfaction and their general life-satisfaction in different question orders. When the general life-satisfaction question was asked first, it correlated with marital satisfaction $r = .32$. Reversing the question order, however, increased this correlation to $r = .67$. This reflects that the marital satisfaction question brought marriage related information to mind, and respondents included the information in the representation formed of their lives in general.

This increase in correlation was attenuated ($r = .43$) when questions about three different life-domains (job, leisure time, and marriage) preceded the general question, thus bringing a more diverse range of information to mind. Parallel influences were observed in the mean reports. Happily married respondents reported higher, and unhappily married respondents reported lower, general life-satisfaction when their attention was drawn to their marriage by the preceding question. However, the same piece of accessible information that may elicit an assimilation effect may also result in a contrast effect; that is, in a more negative (positive) judgment, the more positive (negative) information is brought to mind. This is the case when the information is excluded from, rather than included in, the cognitive representation formed of the target (Schwarz & Bless, 1992, 2007). As a first possibility, suppose that a given piece of information with positive (negative) implications is excluded from the representation of the target category. If so, the representation will contain less positive (negative) information, resulting in less positive (negative) judgments. This possibility is referred to as a subtraction based contrast effect. The size of subtraction based contrast effects increases with the amount and extremity of the temporarily accessible information that is excluded from the representation of the target, and decreases with the amount and extremity of the information that remains in the representation of the target.

For example, the above study (Schwarz et al., 1991) included a condition in which the marital satisfaction and life-satisfaction questions were introduced with a joint lead-in that read, "We now have two questions about your life. The first pertains to your marriage and the second to your life in general." This lead-in was designed to evoke the conversational maxim of quantity (Grice, 1975), which enjoins speakers to avoid redundancy when answering related questions. Accordingly, respondents who had just reported on their marriage should now disregard this aspect of their lives when answering the general life-satisfaction question. Confirming this prediction, happily married respondents now reported lower general life-satisfaction, whereas unhappily married respondents reported higher life-satisfaction, indicating that they excluded the positive (negative) marital information from the representation formed of their lives in general. These diverging effects reduced the correlation to r = .18, from r = .67 when the same questions were asked in the same order without a joint lead-in. Finally, a control condition in which the general life-satisfaction question was reworded to, "Aside from your marriage, which you already told us about, how satisfied are you with your life in general?" resulted in a similarly low correlation of r = .20. Such subtraction based contrast effects are limited to the specific target (here, one's life in general), reflecting that merely "subtracting" a piece of information (here, one's marriage) does only affect this specific representation.

As a second possibility, respondents may not only exclude accessible information from the representation formed of the target, but may also use this information in constructing a standard of comparison or scale anchor. If the implications of the temporarily accessible information are more extreme than the implications of the chronically accessible information used in constructing a standard, they result in a more extreme standard, eliciting contrast effects for that reason. The size of comparison based contrast effects increases with the extremity and amount of temporarily accessible information used in constructing the standard, and decreases with the amount and extremity of chronically accessible information used in making this construction. In contrast to subtraction based comparison effects, which are limited to a specific target, comparison based contrast effects generalize to all targets to which the standard is applicable.

As an example, consider the impact of political scandals on assessments of the trustworthiness of politicians. Not surprisingly, thinking about a politician who was involved in a scandal, say Richard Nixon, decreases trust in politicians in general. This reflects that the exemplar is included in the representation formed of the target "politicians in general." If the trustworthiness question pertains to a specific politician, however, say Bill Clinton, the primed exemplar cannot be included in the representation formed of the target—after all, Bill Clinton is not Richard Nixon. In this case, Richard Nixon may serve as a standard of comparison, relative to which Bill Clinton seems more trustworthy than would otherwise be the case. An experiment with German exemplars confirmed these predictions (Schwarz & Bless, 1992b): Thinking about a politician who was involved in a scandal decreased the trustworthiness of politicians in general, but increased the trustworthiness of all specific exemplars assessed.

If a given piece of information is used in constructing a representation of the attitude object (resulting in assimilation effects), or of a standard of comparison (resulting in contrast effects), depends on a host of different variables, which are beyond the scope of this chapter. Schwarz and Bless (2007) and Sudman et al. (1996) review these variables and present a theoretical model that predicts the direction, size, and generalization of question order effects in attitude measurement.

Response Order Effects   Respondents' judgments are also influenced by the order in which response alternatives are presented within a question. To understand the underlying processes, suppose you are asked to provide a few good reasons why "divorce should be easier to obtain." You can easily do so, but you could just as easily provide some reasons why "divorce should be more difficult to obtain." When such alternatives are juxtaposed within a question (as in "Should divorce be easier to obtain or more difficult to obtain?"), the outcome depends on which alternative is considered first. When respondents first consider "easier" and generate some supportive thoughts, they are likely to truncate the search process and endorse this response option; but had they considered "more difficult," the same process would have resulted in an endorsement of that option. Again, respondents' judgments are based on the temporary representation formed of the attitude object ("divorce"), which is a function of the thoughts brought to mind by the response option considered first.

Which option respondents consider first depends on the order and mode in which the response alternatives are presented (Krosnick & Alwin, 1987). When presented in writing, respondents read down the list of response alternatives and elaborate on their implications in the order in which they are presented. In this mode, an alternative that elicits supporting thoughts is more likely to be endorsed when presented early rather than late on the list, giving rise to primacy effects. In contrast, when the alternatives are read to respondents, their opportunity to think about the early ones is limited by the need to listen to the later ones. In this case, they are more likely to work backwards, thinking first about the last alternative read to them, which is still "in their ears." When the last alternative heard elicits supporting thoughts, it is likely to be endorsed, giving rise to recency effects. As a result, a given alternative is more likely to be endorsed when presented early rather than late in a visual format (primacy effect), but when presented late rather than early in an auditory format (recency effect). Sudman et al. (1996) review these processes in more detail.

Response order effects are most likely to be obtained when respondents can generate supporting thoughts for several of the response alternatives presented to them, as in the above divorce example. When one alternative is attractive and the other unattractive, the order in which they are presented is unlikely to make a difference (Sudman et al., 1996). Finally, response order effects are more pronounced for older and less educated respondents (see Knäuper, 1999, for a meta-analysis), whose limited cognitive resources further enhance the focus on a single response alternative. This age-sensitivity of response order effects can invite misleading conclusions about cohort differences in the reported attitude, suggesting, for example, that older respondents are more liberal than younger respondents under one order condition, but more conservative under the other (see Schwarz & Knäuper, 2000).

Response Formatting

Once respondents have formed a judgment, they can only report it in their own words when an open response format is used. Because open answers require cumbersome and expensive coding prior to statistical analysis, open response formats are rarely used in practice. Instead, respondents are usually asked to provide an answer in a closed response format, either by rating the attitude object along a scale or by selecting one of several substantive response alternatives presented to them.

Categorical Response Alternatives   When the question offers several distinct opinions and asks the respondent to select the one that is closest to his or her own position, it is important to ensure that the set of response alternatives offered covers the whole range of plausible positions. Any opinion omitted from the list is unlikely to be reported, even when respondents are offered a general "other" response option, which they rarely use. For example, Schuman and Presser (1981) asked respondents what they consider "the most important thing for children to prepare them for life." When the answer, "To think for themselves" was offered as part of a list, 61.5% of a representative sample endorsed it—yet only 4.6% volunteered an answer that could be assigned to this category when an open response format was used (Schuman & Presser, 1981). Such discrepancies reflect that the response alternatives clarify what the researcher is interested in and remind respondents of aspects they might otherwise not consider. Similarly, few respondents report not having an opinion on an issue when this option is not explicitly provided—yet, they may be happy to report so when "Don't know" is offered as an alternative. Throughout, respondents work within the constraints imposed by the question (see Krosnick & Fabrigar, in press, for a review). In addition, respondents' judgments are influenced by the order in which response alternatives are presented, as already seen.

Rating Scales   Rating scales are the most commonly used response format in attitude measurement. Typically, a numerical scale with verbally labeled endpoints (e.g., -3 = strongly disagree; +3 = strongly agree) is presented and respondents are asked to check the number that best represents their opinion. As noted, the numeric values may themselves influence the interpretation of the verbal endpoints. Alternatively, each point of the rating scale may be labeled, a format that is more commonly used in telephone interviews than in self-administered questionnaires or laboratory experiments. In general, the retest reliability of fully labeled scales is somewhat higher than that of partially labeled scales. Moreover, retest reliability decreases as the number of scale points increases beyond seven, reflecting the difficulty of making many fine-grained distinctions. Krosnick and Fabrigar (in press) provide a comprehensive review of the relevant literature.

Respondents' use of rating scales is highly context dependent. As numerous studies demonstrated, respondents use the most extreme stimuli to anchor the endpoints of a rating scale. As a result, a given stimulus will be rated as less extreme if presented in the context of a more extreme one, than if presented in the context of a less extreme one. In addition, if the number of stimuli to be rated is large, respondents attempt to use all categories of the rating scale about equally often to be maximally informative. Accordingly, the specific ratings given also depend on the frequency distribution of the presented stimuli. These processes have been conceptualized in a number of related models of rating scale use, of which Parducci's (1965) range-frequency model is the most comprehensive. As a result, ratings of the same object cannot be directly compared when they were collected in different contexts, rendering comparisons over time or between studies difficult.

Other Scale Format   In representative sample surveys, as well as most psychological experiments, respondents' attitudes toward an object are typically assessed by asking only one or two questions, despite the usual textbook admonition to use multi-item scales. In fact, the classic textbook examples of multi-item attitude scales, like the Thurstone or Guttman scales, are rarely used in practice. All of these scales require extensive topic-specific item development and pretesting to arrive at a set of items that forms an internally consistent scale. Himmelfarb (1993) provides an excellent review of these and other classic scale formats.

In contrast, Osgood and colleagues' (1957) semantic differential scale is a ready-to-use scale that can be applied to any topic without new development work, making it considerably more popular. Respondents are asked to rate the attitude object (e.g., "abortion") on a set of 7-point bipolar adjective scales. The adjectives used as endpoint labels reflect three general factors, namely evaluation (e.g., good-bad; pleasant-unpleasant), potency (e.g., strong-weak; small-large), and activity (e.g., active-passive; fast-slow). Of these factors, evaluation is considered the primary indicator of respondents' attitude toward objects, as reflected in the objects' (relatively global) connotative meanings.

Response Editing

Finally, respondents may hesitate to report their attitude when they are concerned that their answer may present them in a negative light. If so, they may want to edit their privately formed judgment before they communicate it, essentially providing a more "acceptable" answer. As may be expected, editing on the basis of social desirability is particularly likely when the question is highly threatening (Bradburn et al., 2004; De Maio, 1984). Moreover, it is more pronounced in face-to-face interviews than in self-administered questionnaires, which provide a higher degree of confidentiality (e.g., Krysan et al., 1994; T. W. Smith, 1979).

To reduce socially desirable responding, researchers developed a number of different techniques. Some techniques attempt to ensure the confidentiality of respondents' answers. Relevant procedures range from simple assurances of anonymity and confidentiality to complex randomized response techniques (Bradburn et al., 2004; Himmelfarb, 1993). In the latter case, respondents are presented with two different questions, an innocuous one and a socially sensitive one, and a draw a card that determines which one they are to answer. Given properly worded response alternatives, the interviewer remains unaware of the question to which the answer pertains, thus ensuring the highest possible level of confidentiality. Other techniques create conditions that present a disincentive for socially desirable responding. For example, Sigall and Page's (1972) "bogus pipeline" technique involves convincing participants that the researcher can discern their true attitude independent of what they say, thus making lying an embarrassment. Empirically, these various techniques have been found to increase the frequency of socially undesirable answers (Himmelfarb, 1993).

Although socially desirable responding is undoubtedly a threat to the validity of attitude reports, many of the more robust findings commonly attributed to its influence may reflect the impact of several distinct processes. For example, white respondents have frequently been found to mute negative sentiments about African Americans when the interviewer is black rather than white (e.g., Hatchett & Schuman, 1976). From a social desirability perspective, these context dependent answers presumably do not reflect respondents' "true" attitude. However, the friendly conversation with a middle-class African-American interviewer may itself serve as input into the attitude judgment, resulting in a (temporary) "real" attitude change, much as incidental exposure to pictures or names of liked African Americans has been found to affect attitudes toward the group in laboratory experiments (e.g., Bodenhausen, Schwarz, Bless, & Wänke, 1995). Hence, the impact of social desirability per se often is difficult to isolate. Moreover, social desirability certainly affects everyday behavior, including interracial interactions, indicating that it is not a mere artifact observed in measurement contexts—nor is it obvious that we should disregard social desirability influences when our goal is to predict such everyday behavior.

Summary   As this selective review indicates, asking people to report on their attitudes will almost always result in an answer—but it often remains unclear what exactly the answer means. Attitude reports are highly context sensitive and minor variations in question wording, format, or sequence can profoundly affect the obtained results. The underlying processes are systematic and increasingly well understood. Sudman and colleagues (1996) and Tourangeau and colleagues (2000) provide comprehensive reviews of what has been learned about the cognitive processes involved in answering questions about one's attitudes and behaviors.

The observed context dependency of respondents' answers is particularly problematic in survey research. Researchers conduct surveys to generalize from the answers provided by a representative sample to the attitudes of a population that was never exposed to the context in which the sample answered the questions. Hence, any contextual influence on the answers of the sample may lead to erroneous inferences about the population. The problem is less profound in experimental research. In most experiments, we are primarily interested in differences between experimental conditions. As long as the attitude questions (including their format and ordering) are constant across conditions, observed differences between conditions are meaningful, although slightly different questions may have resulted in different answers.

Implicit Measures of Attitudes

Given the context dependency of respondents' answers to direct attitude questions, researchers developed a number of techniques that replace explicit self-reports of attitudes with more indirect measures. The use of indirect measures is based on the theoretical assumption that attitudes exert a systematic influence on people's performance on a variety of tasks and that the size of this influence can serve as an index of the underlying attitude. Accordingly, indirect measures do not require the assumption that people are aware of their attitudes (in contrast to direct questions, which can only be answered on the basis of awareness and introspective insight). To infer a person's attitude from his or her performance on another task, we need clear bridging rules that specify the theoretical and empirical relationship between the attitude and the task. Not surprisingly, these bridging rules have varied widely over the history of attitude research. From the early use of projective tests (e.g., Proshensky, 1943) to the current use of response latency measures (reviewed below), the history of indirect measures mirrors historical shifts in the conceptualization of attitudes and their underlying processes (see Vargas, Sekaquaptewa, & von Hippel, 2007, for an informative review). The respective theoretical assumptions gave rise to numerous controversies, which are beyond the scope of this chapter (see the contributions in Wittenbrink & Schwarz, 2007, for controversies surrounding current reaction time measures).

In addition to requiring no introspective insight into one's attitudes, indirect attitude measures promise to solve the problem of response editing in ways that go beyond what can be achieved in the context of explicit self-reports. First, respondents are presumably unaware of the relationship between their response to indirect measures and their attitudes. Hence, they have few incentives and opportunities for deliberate self-presentation—and wouldn't know how to present themselves in a favorable light even if they wanted to. Second, some researchers have been concerned that deception and self-presentation may not only be directed toward others, but also toward the self (e.g., Paulhus, 1984). From this perspective, people may sometimes hold attitudes of which they are not aware, and hence can't report on, or which they don't even want to admit to themselves. Indirect measures may capture such attitudes because they do not require that respondents are aware of them; nor does their opaque nature confront the person with the implications of his or her response.

In addition, many researchers also hope that (some) indirect measures may reduce the context dependency observed in explicit attitude reports (for a review see Ferguson & Bargh, 2007). According to one influential conceptualization (Fazio, 1995), attitudes are stored object-evaluation links that are automatically activated upon exposure to the attitude object. From this perspective, context effects reflect noise that results from the deliberate consideration of contextual information, and this noise may be avoided by limiting the degree of deliberate processing (see Ferguson & Bargh, 2007). Hence, fast-paced response latency procedures, which provide little opportunity for deliberation, may limit context effects and may provide a "bona fide pipeline" (Fazio, Jackson, Dunton, & Williams, 1995) to people's true attitudes.

Next, I turn to these measures and some technologically less demanding paper-and-pencil alternatives. Because these measures do not require awareness of the attitude and entail no explicit attitude report, they are commonly referred to as "implicit" attitude measures (see Devos, this volume, for a more detailed theoretical discussion).

Response Time Measures

The currently most widely used implicit attitude measures rely on response time measurement. Some of these measures take advantage of the observation that preceding exposure to a stimulus facilitates subsequent responses to related stimuli; others draw on the observation that a stimulus is responded to more slowly when it contains multiple features that give rise to competing responses. Bassili (2001) and the contributions in Wittenbrink and Schwarz (2007) provide detailed reviews of these measures and their underlying logic (see Bassili, this volume).

Sequential Priming Procedures   As a large body of research in cognitive psychology indicates (for a review see Neely, 1991), exposure to a concept (e.g., "doctor") facilitates the subsequent recognition of related concepts (e.g., "nurse"). A common explanation for this phenomenon holds that exposure to the initial concept (the prime) activates semantically related concepts in memory, thus reducing the time needed for their identification.

Concept priming procedures take advantage of this facilitation effect to assess a person's associations with an attitude object. They present target words with evaluative meaning (e.g., lazy, smart) and ask participants to identify the word as fast as possible. Speed of identification can be assessed by having participants pronounce the word or by having them decide whether a letter string is a word or a nonword. Of interest is whether a preceding prime that represents the attitude object (e.g., black, white) affects the speed with which different target words can be identified. For example, Wittenbrink, Judd, and Park (1997) exposed participants to African American or white primes and assessed how quickly they could identify subsequently presented trait terms of positive or negative valence that were or were not part of the cultural stereotype about the group. The observed facilitation patterns provide information that bears on three questions: First, does exposure to the group prime activate associated stereotypical traits, independent of their valence? If so, stereotypical traits will be recognized faster than stereotype unrelated traits. Second, is the automatic activation evaluatively biased? For example, are negative stereotypic traits identified more quickly than positive ones, indicating that the negative traits are more accessible? Third, does exposure to the group prime activate general evaluative associations (e.g., good, bad), independent of their stereotypicality?

Evaluative priming procedures (e.g., Fazio, Sanbonmatsu, Powell, & Kardes, 1986) focus on the speed with which the evaluative meaning of a word can be identified. Of interest is whether exposure to the attitude object affects the speed of the evaluative response to the target words. In a typical experiment, participants are exposed to a prime (e.g., a black or white face) and decide whether a subsequent target word (e.g., pleasant, awful) is positive (press the "good" key) or negative (press the "bad" key). If the attitude prime is strongly associated with a positive evaluation, it speeds up the identification of positive words as "good" and slows down the identification of negative words as "bad." Devos (this volume), Fazio (1995), and Wittenbrink (2007) review representative findings. Unfortunately, the observed facilitation patterns depend to some extent on the general accessibility of the target words and some experiments produced reversals of the usually obtained patterns when the target words have a very high frequency in everyday language use (Chan, Ybarra, & Schwarz, 2006).

In sum, evaluative priming procedures assess whether an attitude object triggers an automatic evaluation, whereas concept priming procedures assess descriptive associations that may have evaluative content. Wittenbrink (2007) reviews these procedures, provides advice on their implementation, and summarizes representative findings.

Response Competition Procedures   A second class of response time procedures is based on interference effects that may occur when different features of attitude objects imply different responses. The best known of these procedures is the Implicit Associations Test (IAT; Greenwald, McGhee, & Schwartz, 1998). It presents two discrimination tasks that are combined in specific ways across a sequence of five steps. To assess attitudes toward African Americans and European Americans, for example, the first discrimination task may present names that are typical for the respective group and participants are asked to categorize each name as "white" vs. "black." They do so by pressing a response key assigned to "white" with their left hand or a response key assigned to "black" with their right hand. Next, a second discrimination task presents words with pleasant (e.g., love) or unpleasant (e.g., poison) connotations, which participants classify as positive vs. negative by pressing the left vs. right response key. At the third step, these two tasks are superimposed and participants press the left key when either a white name or a pleasant word is shown, but the right key when either a black name or an unpleasant word is shown. As in the facilitation paradigms, this task is easier when evaluatively associated categories share the same response key; for example, when white participants press the left key to categorize white names and pleasant words. Going beyond this assessment of response facilitation, the IAT involves two more steps. At the fourth step, the assignment of keys to white and black names is reversed, so that participants who first used the left key for white names now use the left key for black names. Finally, the two discrimination tasks are again super-imposed, resulting in an assignment of "black" and "pleasant" to the left response key and "white" and "unpleasant" to the right response key.

Of key interest is the speed with which participants can perform the two superimposed discrimination tasks at step 3 and step 5. Do participants respond faster when a given response key pertains either to the pairing of white names + pleasant words or black names + unpleasant words (step 3) than when this pairing is reversed and a given response key pertains either to white names + unpleas-ant words or black names + pleasant words (step five)? In the present example, a faster response at step 3 than at step 5 is thought to indicate that white names and positive evaluations and black names and negative evaluations are more strongly associated than the reverse pairings.

Lane, Banaji, Nosek, and Greenwald (2007) review the underlying logic, report representative findings, and provide hands-on advice for the implementation and scoring of the IAT. Related response competition tasks include the Go/No-go Association Task (GNAT; Nosek & Banaji, 2001) and the Extrinsic Affective Simon Task (EAST; De Houwer, 2003).

Low Tech Alternatives

Whereas response time procedures require a high degree of instrumentation and technical sophistication, other implicit measures of attitudes are decidedly low tech. Some of these measures take advantage of the observation that attitudes and expectations influence individuals' information processing in systematic ways. For example, people are more likely to spontaneously explain events that discon-firm rather than confirm their expectations (e.g., Hastie, 1984), suggesting that the amount of explanatory activity can serve as an indirect measure of a person's expectations. The Stereotypic Explanatory Bias (SEB) measure developed by Sekaquaptewa and colleagues (2003) builds on this observation and uses the num-ber of explanations generated in response to stereotype-consistent vs. stereotype-inconsistent behaviors as an implicit measure of stereotyping. Similarly, people describe expected or stereotype-consistent behaviors in more abstract terms than unexpected or stereotype-inconsistent behaviors, a phenomenon known as the Linguistic Intergroup Bias (LIB; e.g., Maass, Salvi, Accuri, & Semin, 1989). The size of this bias can again be used as an indirect measure to gauge the underly-ing expectations. Vargas and colleagues (2007) review such measures and provide advice on their use.

Context Effects on Implicit Measures

The initial hope that responses to implicit measures that limit deliberation may be less context dependent than responses to explicit attitude questions has not been supported (for reviews see Blair, 2002; Ferguson & Bargh, 2007). Instead, these measures are subject to pronounced context effects that usually parallel the patterns observed on explicit attitude measures. For example, Dasgupta and Greenwald (2001) observed that exposure to pictures of liked African Americans and disliked European Americans resulted in shifts on a subsequent IAT that parallel the effects of exposure to liked or disliked exemplars on explicit measures of attitudes (e.g., Bodenhausen et al., 1995). Similarly, Wittenbrink, Judd, and Park (2001) found that the same black face primes elicited more negative automatic responses when the faces were presented on the background of an urban street scene rather than a church scene. Other findings parallel the observed influence of interviewer race and ethnicity in the survey research literature (e.g., Hatchet & Schuman, 1976; Weeks & Moore, 1981). For example, Lowery, Hardin, and Sinclair's (2001) obtained more positive automatic evaluations of African Americans when the experimenter was black rather than white. Note that the low transparency of Lowery et al.'s implicit attitude measure makes it unlikely that these responses were based on a deliberate self-presentation strategy. Instead, the accumulating findings suggest that experimenters and interviewers may serve as highly accessible positive exemplars when respondents evaluate the group in general, paralleling the influence of incidental exposure to liked exemplars in other research (e.g., Bodenhausen et al.,1995; Dasgupta & Greenwald, 2001).

To account for the context dependency of implicit measures, Ferguson and Bargh (2007) suggest that automatic attitudes are responses to object-centered contexts rather than to the attitude object in isolation. I return to this issue in the final section of this chapter.

PSYCHOPHYSIOLOGY AND BEHAVIORAL OBSERVATION

Because of their involuntary and hard to control nature, physiological correlates of evaluative responses have long been of interest to attitude researchers who doubted respondents' explicit self-reports.

Psychophysiological Measures

Early uses of physiological measures drew on the observation that strong affective reactions to an attitude object are associated with increased activation of the sympathetic nervous system (e.g., Rankin & Campbell, 1955). Increased sympathetic activation results in increased sweat glands activity, which can be measured by assessing the resistance of the skin to low level electric currents, a procedure known as electrodermal measurement. However, electrodermal responses do not reflect the direction (favorable or unfavorable) of the evaluative response, which limits their usefulness.

More promising are attempts to assess changes in individuals' facial expression in response to an attitude object. Overt facial expressions (like smiling or frowning) may often be observed in response to attitude objects that elicit strong reactions. But these expressions may be intentionally concealed and many evaluative reactions may be too subtle to evoke overt expressive behaviors. Even subtle evaluative reactions are associated, however, with low-level activation of facial muscles that can be detected by electromyography (EMG). These muscle reactions reflect the direction (favorable vs. unfavorable) as well as the intensity of the evaluative response (see Cacioppo, Bush, & Tassinary, 1992, for an example). However, the obtained measures can be distorted by facial movements that are unrelated to the evaluative reaction.

Another approach involves the measurement of brain activity through electro-encephalography (EEG), the assessment of small electric signals recorded from the scalp. This procedure, however, does not lend itself to a direct assessment of positive or negative responses. Instead, it capitalizes on the observation that unexpected stimuli evoke brain wave activity that differs from the activity evoked by expected stimuli. Hence, one may detect if a target object is evaluated positively or negatively by embedding its presentation in a long series of other objects with a known evaluation. The brain activity evoked by the target object will then indicate if its evaluation is consistent or inconsistent with the evaluation of the context objects (see Cacioppo, Crites, Berntson, & Coles, 1993, for an example).

Ito and Cacioppo (2007) review these and other measures, including recent developments in the brain imaging techniques, which provide a promising avenue for future work in this area. Throughout, the implementation of psychophysiological measures requires sophisticated technology and high expertise, and their analysis poses complex issues of data reduction. For these reasons, they are best used in collaboration with a skilled colleague.

Behavioral Observation

In principle, a person's attitude toward some object may be inferred from his or her behavior toward it. However, people's behaviors are influenced by many variables other than their attitudes. Hence, the attitude–behavior relationship is typically weak, unless other variables are taken into account (see Ajzen & Cote, this volume). As a result, the mere observation of a behavior is a poor indicator of the person's attitude per se and behavioral observation is rarely used as a measurement strategy.

THEORETICAL IMPLICATIONS: CONTEXT DEPENDENCY AND THE NATURE OF ATTITUDES

As this review of different attitude measurement techniques indicates, attitude reports are highly context dependent. This observation holds for traditional "explicit" measures (direct questions) as well as for the more recent "implicit" measures (response time procedures). While the findings are undisputed, their theoretical implications are controversial: Do context effects indicate that attitudes are "constructed" on the spot, based on whatever information is accessible at the time of judgment? Or do they merely reflect some "noise" that does not call the existence of enduring attitudes into question?

Taking the latter position, Eagly and Chaiken (2005, p. 747) suggested that "context effects should be and are pervasive...because attitudinal judgments are not pure expressions of attitude but outputs that reflect both attitude and the information in the contemporaneous setting." While the contemporaneous setting gives rise to variability in attitude expression, the "inner state or latent construct that constitutes the attitude can be relatively stable. Therefore, judgments often vary around an average value that is defined by the tendency that constitutes the attitude" (Eagly & Chaiken, 2005, p. 747). In contrast, attitude construction models question the assumption that people "have" enduring attitudes and instead focus on the cognitive and affective processes underlying evaluative judgment (e.g., Lord & Lepper, 1999; Schwarz, 2007; Schwarz & Bohner, 2001; Smith & Conrey, 2007). These models identify the processes that give rise to variation in attitude judgments and specify the conditions under which attitude judgments are stable across time and contexts, as well as the conditions under which attitude judgments predict behavior (see Schwarz, 2007; Schwarz & Bohner, 2001).

More important, both approaches differ in their metatheoretical perspectives (see Schwarz, 2007, for a more detailed discussion). Construal models start with the premise that evaluative judgment stands in the service of action, which requires high context sensitivity. Because action is always located in a specific context, any adaptive system of evaluation should be informed by past experience, but highly sensitive to the specifics of the present. It should overweight recent experience at the expense of more distant experience, and experience from similar situations at the expense of experience from dissimilar situations. In addition, it should take current goals and concerns into account to ensure that the assessment is relevant to what we attempt to do now, in this context. Only such context-sensitive evaluation can guide behavior in adaptive ways by alerting us to problems and opportunities when they exist; by interrupting ongoing processes when needed (but not otherwise); and by rendering information highly accessible that is relevant now, in this situation.

A large body of diverse findings indicates that human cognition meets these requirements (for reviews see Barsalou, 2005; Schwarz, 2002; Smith & Semin, 2004)—and it is presumably no coincidence that the above list of desirable context sensitivities reads like a list of the conditions that give rise to context effects in attitude judgments.

In contrast to this situated construal approach, traditional attitude theories treat attitudes as personal dispositions, that is, "a psychological tendency that is expressed by evaluating a particular entity with some degree of favor or disfavor" (Eagly & Chaiken, 1993, p. 1). In the eyes of critics, this conceptualization derives its considerable intuitive appeal from its compatibility with humans' pervasive tendency to explain others' behavior in terms of their dispositions—a tendency otherwise known as the "fundamental attribution error" (Ross, 1977). From a dispositional perspective, context effects are undesirable because they cloud the underlying disposition and undermine the observer's ability to predict an actor's behavior on the basis of his or her attitude. Yet from the actor's own perspective, context sensitive evaluation is an asset, not a liability.

To date, attitude research has predominantly taken the observer's perspective, deploring the context "dependency" of attitude reports, which presumably obscures the actor's "true" attitude. Once we adopt the actor's perspective, deplorable context "dependency" turns into laudable context "sensitivity." If so, there may be more to be learned from exploring the dynamics of context sensitive evaluation than from ever more sophisticated attempts to discover a person's "true" enduring attitude—attempts that have so far mostly resulted in a reiteration of the same basic lesson: evaluations are context sensitive. Such a shift in theoretical orientation would require a methodological approach to attitude measurement that focuses on evaluation-in-context (Ferguson & Bargh, 2007; Schwarz, 2007), raising new challenges for future research.

REFERENCES

Barsalou, L. W. (2005). Situated conceptualization. In H. Cohen & C. Lefebvre (Eds.), *Handbook of categorization in cognitive science* (pp. 619–650). Amsterdam: Elsevier.

Bassili, J. (2001). Cognitive indices of social information processing. In. A. Tesser & N. Schwarz (Eds.), *Blackwell handbook of social psychology: Intraindividual processes* (pp. 68–87). Oxford, UK: Blackwell.

Blair, I. V. (2002). The malleability of automatic stereotypes and prejudice. *Personality and Social Psychology Review, 6*, 242–261.

Bless, H., Schwarz, N., & Wänke, M. (2003). The size of context effects in social judgment. In J. P. Forgas, K. D. Williams, & W. von Hippel (Eds.), *Social judgments: Implicit and explicit processes* (pp. 180–197). Cambridge, UK: Cambridge University Press.

Bodenhausen, G. V., Schwarz, N., Bless, H., & Wänke, M. (1995). Effects of atypical exemplars on racial beliefs: Enlightened racism or generalized appraisals? *Journal of Experimental Social Psychology, 31*, 48–63.

Bodenhausen, G. V., & Wyer, R. S. (1987). Social cognition and social reality: Information acquisition and use in the laboratory and the real world. In H. J. Hippler, N. Schwarz, & S. Sudman (Eds.), *Social information processing and survey methodology* (pp. 6–41). New York: Springer Verlag.

Bradburn, N., Sudman, S., & Wansink, B. (2004). *Asking questions* (2nd ed.). San Francisco: Jossey-Bass.

Cacioppo, J. T., Bush, L. K., & Tassinary, L. G. (1992). Microexpressive facial reactions as a function of affective stimuli. *Personality and Social Psychology Bulletin, 18*, 515–526.

Cacioppo, J. T., Crites, S. L., Berntson, G. G., & Coles, M. G. H. (1993). If attitudes affect how stimuli are processed, should they not affect event-related brain potential? *Psychological Science, 4*, 108–112.

Cantril, H. (1944) *Gauging public opinion.* Princeton, NJ: Princeton University Press.

Chan, E., Ybarra, O., & Schwarz, N. (2006). Reversing the affective congruency effect: The role of target word frequency of occurrence. *Journal of Experimental Social Psychology, 42*, 365–372.

Clark, H. H., & Schober, M. F. (1992). Asking questions and influencing answers. In J. M. Tanur (Ed.), *Questions about questions* (pp. 15–48). New York: Russell Sage Foundation.

Dasgupta, N., & Greenwald, A. G. (2001). On the malleability of automatic attitudes: Combating automatic prejudice with images of liked and disliked individuals. *Journal of Personality and Social Psychology, 81*, 800–814.

De Houwer, J. (2003). The extrinsic affective Simon task. *Experimental Psychology, 50*, 77–85.

DeMaio, T. J. (1984). Social desirability and survey measurement: A review. In C. F. Turner & E. Martin (Eds.), *Surveying subjective phenomena* (Vol. 2, pp. 257–281). New York: Russell Sage Foundation.

Eagly, A. H., & Chaiken, S. (1993). *The psychology of attitudes*. Fort Worth, TX: Harcourt, Brace, Jovanovich.

Eagly, A. H., & Chaiken, S. (2005). Attitude research in the 21st century: The current state of knowledge. In D. Albarracin, B. T. Johnson, & M. P. Zanna (Eds.), *The handbook of attitudes* (pp. 743–768). Mahwah, NJ: Erlbaum.

Fazio, R. (1995). Attitudes as object-evaluation associations: Determinants, consequences, and correlates of attitude accessibility. In R. Petty & J. A. Krosnick (Eds.), *Attitude strength: Antecedents and consequences* (pp. 247–282). Mahwah, NJ: Erlbaum.

Fazio, R. H., Jackson, J. R., Dunton, B. C., & Williams, C. J. (1995). Variability in automatic activation as an unobtrusive measure of racial attitudes. A bona fide pipeline? *Journal of Personality and Social Psychology, 69*, 1013–1027.

Fazio, R. H., Sanbonmatsu, D. M., Powell, M. C., & Kardes, F. R. (1986). On the automatic activation of attitudes. *Journal of Personality and Social Psychology, 50*, 229–238.

Ferguson, M. J., & Bargh, J. A. (2007). Beyond the attitude object: Automatic attitudes spring from object-centered-contexts. In B. Wittenbrink & N. Schwarz (Eds.), *Implicit measures of attitudes: Progress and controversies* (pp. 216–246). New York: Guilford.

Greenwald, A. G., McGhee, D. E., & Schwarz, J. L. K. (1998). Measuring individual differences in implicit cognition: The Implicit Association Test. *Journal of Personality and Social Psychology, 74*, 1464–1480.

Grice, H. P. (1975). Logic and conversation. In P. Cole, & J.L. Morgan (Eds.), *Syntax and semantics: Vol.3. Speech acts* (pp. 41–58). New York: Academic Press.

Hastie, R. (1984). Causes and effects of causal attribution. *Journal of Personality and Social Psychology, 46*, 44–56.

Hatchett, S., & Schuman, H. (1976). White respondents and race-of-interviewer effects. *Public Opinion Quarterly, 39*, 523–528.

Himmelfarb, S. (1993). The measurement of attitudes. In A. H. Eagly & S. Chaiken, *The psychology of attitudes* (pp. 23–43). Fort Worth, TX: Harcourt, Brace, Jovanovich.

Ito, T. A., & Cacioppo, J. T. (2007). Attitudes as a mental and neural state of readiness: Using physiological measures to study implicit attitudes. In B. Wittenbrink & N. Schwarz (Eds.), *Implicit measures of attitudes: Progress and controversies* (pp. 125–158). New York: Guilford.

Knäuper, B. (1999). The impact of age and education on response order effects in attitude measurement. *Public Opinion Quarterly, 63*, 347–370.

Krosnick, J. A., & Alwin, D. F. (1987). An evaluation of a cognitive theory of response order effects in survey measurement. *Public Opinion Quarterly, 51*, 201–19.

Krosnick, J. A., & Fabrigar, L. R. (in press). *Handbook of questionnaire design*. New York: Oxford University Press.

Krysan, M., Schuman, H., Scott, L. J., & Beatty, P. (1994). Response rates and response content in mail versus face-to-face surveys. *Public Opinion Quarterly, 58*, 381–399.

Lane, K. A., Banaji, M. R., Nosek, B. A., & Greenwald, A. G. (2007). Understanding and using the Implicit Association Test: IV. What we know (so far) about the method. In B. Wittenbrink & N. Schwarz (Eds.), *Implicit measures of attitudes: Progress and controversies* (pp. 59–102). New York: Guilford.

Lord, C. G., & Lepper, M. R. (1999). Attitude representation theory. *Advances in Experimental Social Psychology, 31*, 265–343.

Lowery, B. S., Hardin, C. D., & Sinclair, S. (2001). Social influence on automatic racial prejudice. *Journal of Personality and Social Psychology, 81*, 842–855.

Maass, A., Salvi, D., Arcuri, L., & Semin, G. (1989). Language use in intergroup contexts: The linguistic intergroup bias. *Journal of Personality and Social Psychology, 57,* 981–993.

Neely, J. H. (1991). Semantic priming effects in visual word recognition: A selective review of current findings and theories. In D. Besner & G. W. Humphreys (Eds.), *Basic processes in reading: Visual word recognition.* Hillsdale, NJ: Erlbaum.

Nosek, B. A., & Banaji, M. R. (2001). The go/no-go association task. *Social Cognition, 19,* 625–666.

Osgood, C. E., Suci, G. J., & Tannenbaum, P. H. (1957). *The measurement of meaning.* Urbana, IL: University of Illinois Press.

Parducci, A. (1965). Category judgments: A range-frequency model. *Psychological Review,* 72, 407–418.

Paulhus, D. L. (1984). Two-component models of socially desirable responding. *Journal of Personality and Social Psychology, 46,* 598–609.

Payne, S. L. (1951). *The art of asking questions.* Princeton, NJ: Princeton University Press.

Proshensky, H. M. (1943). A projective method for the study of attitudes. *Journal of Abnormal and Social Psychology, 38,* 393–395.

Rankin, R. E., & Campbell, D. T. (1955). Galvanic skin response to Negro and white experimenters. *Journal of Abnormal and Social Psychology, 51,* 30–33.

Ross, L. (1977). The intuitive psychologist and his shortcomings: Distortions in the attribution process. *Advances in Experimental Social Psychology, 10,* 173–220.

Schuman, H., & Presser, S. (1981). *Questions and answers in attitude surveys.* New York: Academic Press.

Schwarz, N. (1994). Judgment in a social context: Biases, shortcomings, and the logic of conversation. *Advances in Experimental Social Psychology, 26,* 123–162.

Schwarz, N. (1996). *Cognition and communication: Judgmental biases, research methods and the logic of conversation.* Hillsdale, NJ: Erlbaum.

Schwarz, N. (2002). Situated cognition and the wisdom of feelings: Cognitive tuning. In L. Feldman Barrett & P. Salovey (Eds.), *The wisdom in feelings* (pp.144–166). New York: Guilford.

Schwarz, N. (2007). Attitude construction: Evaluation in context. *Social Cognition, 25,* 638–656.

Schwarz, N., & Bless, H. (1992a). Constructing reality and its alternatives: Assimilation and contrast effects in social judgment. In L. L. Martin & A. Tesser (Eds.), *The construction of social judgment* (pp. 217–245). Hillsdale, NJ: Erlbaum.

Schwarz, N., & Bless, H. (1992b). Scandals and the public's trust in politicians: Assimilation and contrast effects. *Personality and Social Psychology Bulletin, 18,* 574–579.

Schwarz, N., & Bless, H. (2007). Mental construal processes: The inclusion/exclusion model. In D. A. Stapel & J. Suls (Eds.), *Assimilation and contrast in social psychology* (pp. 119–141). New York: Psychology Press.

Schwarz, N. & Bohner, G. (2001). The construction of attitudes. In A. Tesser & N. Schwarz (Eds.), *Blackwell handbook of social psychology: Intraindividual processes* (pp. 436–457). Malden, MA: Blackwell.

Schwarz, N., & Knäuper, B. (2000). Cognition, aging, and self-reports. In D. Park & N. Schwarz (Eds.), *Cognitive aging. A primer* (pp. 233–252). New York: Psychology Press.

Schwarz, N., Knäuper, B., Hippler, H. J., Noelle-Neumann, E., & Clark, F. (1991). Rating scales: Numeric values may change the meaning of scale labels. *Public Opinion Quarterly, 55,* 570–582.

Schwarz, N., & Oyserman, D. (2001). Asking questions about behavior: Cognition, communication and questionnaire construction. *American Journal of Evaluation, 22,* 127–160.

Schwarz, N., Strack, F., & Mai, H.P. (1991). Assimilation and contrast effects in part-whole question sequences: A conversational logic analysis. *Public Opinion Quarterly, 55,* 3–23.

Schwarz, N., & Sudman, S. (Eds.) (1996). *Answering questions: Methodology for determining cognitive and communicative processes in survey research.* San Francisco: Jossey-Bass.

Sekaquaptewa, D., Espinoza, P., Thompson, M., Vargas, P., & von Hippel, W. (2003). Stereotypic explanatory bias: Implicit stereotyping as a predictor of discrimination. *Journal of Experimental Social Psychology, 39,* 75–82.

Sigall, H., & Page, R. (1972). Reducing attenuation in the expression of interpersonal affect via the bogus pipeline. *Sociometry, 35,* 629–642.

Smith, E. R., & Conrey, F. R. (2007). Mental representations are states not things: Implications for implicit and explicit measurement. In B. Wittenbrink & N. Schwarz (Eds.), *Implicit measures of attitudes: Progress and controversies* (pp. 247–264). New York: Guilford.

Smith, E. R., & Semin, G. R. (2004). Socially situated cognition: Cognition in its social context. *Advances in Experimental Social Psychology, 36,* 53–117.

Smith, T. W. (1979). Happiness. *Social Psychology Quarterly, 42,* 18–30.

Strack, F., & Martin, L. (1987). Thinking, judging, and communicating: A process account of context effects in attitude surveys. In H. J. Hippler, N. Schwarz, & S. Sudman (Eds.), *Social information processing and survey methodology* (pp. 123–148). New York: Springer Verlag.

Strack, F., & Schwarz, N. (2007). Asking questions: Measurement in the social sciences. In M. Ash & T. Sturm (Eds.), *Psychology's territories: Historical and contemporary perspectives from different disciplines* (pp. 225–250). Mahwah, NJ: Erlbaum.

Sudman, S., Bradburn, N. M., & Schwarz, N. (1996). *Thinking about answers: The application of cognitive processes to survey methodology.* San Francisco, CA: Jossey-Bass.

Tourangeau, R., Rips, L. J., & Rasinski, K. (2000). *The psychology of survey response.* Cambridge, UK: Cambridge University Press.

Vargas, P. T., Sekaquaptewa, D., & von Hippel, W. (2007). Armed only with paper and pencil: "Low-tech" measures of implicit attitudes. In B. Wittenbrink & N. Schwarz (Eds.), *Implicit measures of attitudes: Progress and controversies* (pp. 103–124). New York: Guilford.

Weeks, M. F., & Moore, R. P. (1981). Ethnicity-of-interviewer effects on ethnic respondents. *Public Opinion Quarterly, 45,* 245–249.

Willis, G. B. (2004). *Cognitive interviewing. A tool for improving questionnaire design.* Thousand Oaks, CA: Sage.

Wittenbrink. B. (2007). Measuring attitudes through priming. In B. Wittenbrink & N. Schwarz (Eds.), *Implicit measures of attitudes: Progress and controversies* (pp. 17–58). New York: Guilford.

Wittenbrink, B., Judd, C. M., & Park, B. (1997). Evidence for racial prejudice at the implicit level and its relationships with questionnaire measures. *Journal of Personality and Social Psychology, 72,* 262–274.

Wittenbrink, B., Judd, C. M., & Park, B. (2001). Spontaneous prejudice in context: Variability in automatically activated attitudes. *Journal of Personality and Social Psychology, 81,* 815–827.

Wittenbrink, B., & Schwarz, N. (Eds.). (2007). *Implicit measures of attitudes: Procedures and controversies.* New York: Guilford.

Wyer, R. S., & Srull, T. K. (1989). *Memory and cognition in its social context.* Hillsdale, NJ: Erlbaum.

4

Implicit Attitudes 101
Theoretical and Empirical Insights

THIERRY DEVOS
San Diego State University

O ver the past two decades, a substantial body of research has established that attitudes operate at two distinct levels. More precisely, evaluations based on controlled or deliberate processes have been distinguished from evaluations operating outside of conscious awareness or control (Fazio & Olson, 2003; Greenwald & Banaji, 1995; Petty, Fazio, & Briñol, in press; Wittenbrink & Schwarz, 2007). Research on implicit attitudes examines evaluations or feelings that are not available to introspection or that cannot be consciously controlled. To grasp the enthusiasm for this topic, it suffices to skim the premier research outlets in the field. Our journals are replete with theoretical and methodological contributions shedding light on the vicissitudes and ramifications of implicit attitudes. At the same time, some have met these recent developments with skepticism, and have triggered stimulating debates inherent to paradigmatic shifts in scientific disciplines (Arkes & Tetlock, 2004; Blanton & Jaccard, 2006; Karpinski & Hilton, 2001).

Without allegiance to a specific theoretical model or technique, the goal of the present chapter is to describe and discuss major advances in this field. Theoretical and empirical contributions are deliberately emphasized, rather than methodological issues that have been duly recognized in the literature (Fazio & Olson, 2003; Nosek, Greenwald, & Banaji, 2006). Arguably, research on implicit social cognition should be evaluated less by the sophistication or pitfalls of its techniques than by the insights that it generates. The present chapter selectively addresses four important questions. First, different sources of implicit attitudes are discussed. Second, the complex interconnections between implicit and explicit attitudes are examined. Third, evidence for the flexibility of attitudes operating outside of conscious awareness or control is reviewed. Finally, revisiting a classic issue in the attitude literature, the extent to which implicit attitudes account for behavioral responses is considered.

CONCEPTUALIZATION AND MEASUREMENT OF IMPLICIT ATTITUDES

Before addressing these substantive areas of research, a few preliminary clarifications are needed. Implicit attitudes often are conceptualized as reactions that reflect processes operating without awareness, control, intention, or attentional resources (Bargh, 1994). Indirect assessments of attitudes rarely meet all of these criteria. In addition, each defining feature encompasses multiple facets. For example, when the term *implicit* is used to imply lack of awareness or unconsciousness, it can refer to a lack of conscious awareness of the origin of an attitude (source awareness), the attitude itself (content awareness), or the influence of the attitude on other psychological processes (impact awareness) (Gawronski, Hofmann, & Wilbur, 2006). The concept of *control* also can designate distinct processes (Payne, 2005). For instance, it may refer to attempts at providing an accurate depiction of the environment, or to self-regulatory processes aimed at inhibiting an unwanted response. Although these distinctions are important, the term *implicit* is used in this chapter to include both processes that occur without conscious awareness and those that occur without conscious control.

Research on implicit social cognition has been greatly facilitated by the introduction of new techniques (Fazio & Olson, 2003). The development of indirect measures has been motivated by the need to circumvent the limitations of self-reports (Schwarz, this volume). Two reasons are commonly provided to justify the use of implicit measures. First, attitudes are not necessarily available to introspection. Therefore, self-reports do not always provide an accurate assessment of people's evaluations and feelings. Second, social desirability, impression management, or demand characteristics can affect self-report of attitudes. From this perspective, implicit measures allow investigators to capture attitudes that individuals are unwilling to report.

In a pioneer contribution published more than two decades ago, Fazio, Sanbonmatsu, Powell, and Kardes (1986) adapted a sequential priming technique to measure the extent to which an object automatically activates an associated evaluation from memory. On each trial, the prime presented is the name of the attitude object and it is followed by a positive or negative adjective. Participants are asked to indicate, as quickly as possible, the evaluative connotation (positive or negative) of the target word. The latencies of these judgments constitute the dependent measure. The technique is based on the assumption that if the attitude object automatically activates a negative evaluation, response to negative target adjectives should be facilitated. Such facilitation effects provide evidence for automatic evaluations and have been obtained in many experiments relying on similar procedures (for a review, see Fazio, 2001).

Another widely used technique to study implicit attitudes is the Implicit Association Test (IAT; Greenwald, McGhee, & Schwartz, 1998). The IAT is based on the assumption that the strength of associations between two pairs of concepts can be revealed by the ease with which participants discriminate (or pair) stimuli representing these concepts under different conditions. The technique does not require introspective access and minimizes the role of conscious control or intention. Devos and Banaji (2005) used the IAT to measure implicit attitudes of American respondents toward the concept *American* (relative to *foreign*). Participants were asked to categorize, as quickly as possible, pictures of American or foreign symbols (e.g., flags, landmarks, maps) and pleasant or unpleasant words (e.g., gift, rainbow, death, disaster). In one block of trials, American symbols were paired with pleasant words, and foreign symbols were combined with unpleasant words. In another block of trials, American symbols were combined with unpleasant words, and foreign symbols were paired with pleasant words. Participants performed the categorization task more quickly when American symbols and pleasant words shared the same response key, suggesting that the concept *American* elicited a more positive attitude than the concept *foreign*. The IAT has been used to assess implicit associations in a variety of domains and disciplines (for a review, see Nosek et al., 2006).

A dominant feature of the IAT is that it captures the relative associations between two pairs of concepts. Alternative techniques have been developed to provide more absolute assessments of associations (De Houwer, 2003b; Nosek & Banaji, 2001). Relying on response latencies is not the only means to infer implicit attitudes. Research on automatic evaluations and affective responses has also taken advantage of such techniques as functional magnetic resonance imaging (Cunningham, Johnson, Gatenby, Gore, & Banaji, 2003), facial electromyography (Vanman, Saltz, Nathan, & Warren, 2004), or startle eye blink response (Amodio, Harmon-Jones, & Devine, 2003). Although some of these techniques yield convergent findings and are reliably intercorrelated (Cunningham, Preacher, & Banaji, 2001), important differences among them should not been overlooked (Olson & Fazio, 2003). For example, some indirect measures of prejudice assess the automatic activation of an evaluative response when encountering a member of a target group, whereas other measures capture the extent to which prejudice is automatically applied in judgment (Brauer, Wasel, & Niedenthal, 2000). Structural analyses of available techniques help elucidate their similarities and differences (De Houwer, 2003a). For example, responses on the IAT might be determined by the valence of one particular feature of the stimulus, whereas responses on a sequential priming task might be driven by the global attitude toward the stimulus.

Finally, several scholars have stressed that indirect measures of attitudes should not be conceptualized as *process-pure* assessments of automatic attitudes (Conrey, Sherman, Gawronski, Hugenberg, & Groom, 2005; Payne, Jacoby, & Lambert, 2005). Instead, they should be viewed as tapping a mix of automatic and controlled processes. For instance, a process dissociation framework can be used to decompose performances on sequential priming tasks into controlled and automatic estimates (Payne et al., 2005): The controlled estimate reflects the ability to respond in accordance with task instructions, whereas the automatic estimate taps an unintentional accessibility bias (e.g., "Blacks are more likely than whites to carry guns") used to resolve ambiguities when control fails. Extending this approach, the Quad model was developed to disentangle the contribution of four distinct processes on several tasks (Conrey et al., 2005; Sherman, 2006). The processes are conceptualized as the automatic activation of an association, the ability to determine the correct response, the success at overcoming automatically activated associations, and a guessing bias operating when sources of responses are unavailable. These refinements promise to move the field beyond a simplistic distinction between implicit and explicit attitudes that is often confounded with measurement techniques.

FOUNDATIONS OF IMPLICIT ATTITUDES

Where do implicit attitudes stem from? Although this is an important question, it has received surprisingly little attention. Many scholars have relied on broad and largely untested assumptions. An array of factors shape attitudes (Olson & Kendrick, this volume; Rudman, 2004). In many cases, these factors are inextricably linked. To clarify what we know regarding the sources of implicit attitudes, we distinguish and discuss the role of three important factors. Although these factors may contribute to both implicit and explicit attitudes, they are often assumed to play a more potent role when it comes to responses operating outside of conscious awareness or control.

Experiences and Socialization

A prominent view of the origins of implicit attitudes holds that they stem from repeated experiences and develop through socialization processes (Devine, 1989). According to Greenwald and Banaji (1995), implicit attitudes reflect introspectively unidentified (or inaccurately identified) traces of past experiences. Consistent with this hypothesis, Rudman and Goodwin (2004) found that early attachment to maternal caregivers was associated with implicit gender attitudes. More precisely, individuals raised primarily by their mothers showed a stronger implicit preference for women over men. Focusing on the roots of implicit self-esteem, DeHart, Pelham, and Tennen (2006) examined the extent to which implicit self-esteem among young adults correlated with parenting styles assessed based on reports provided by these young adults or their mothers. Controlling for explicit self-esteem, a more nurturing parenting style was related to higher implicit self-esteem and a more overprotective parenting style was associated with lower implicit self-esteem.

Implicit attitudes may also be shaped by fairly recent experiences. For instance, participation in diversity training has been shown to reduce prejudice toward African Americans (Rudman, Ashmore, & Gary, 2001). Although this form of intervention seemed to improve both explicit and implicit attitudes, change at the more deliberate level was driven by an increased awareness of bias and motivation to overcome it, whereas change observed at the automatic level appeared to be mediated by emotion-based variables (e.g., fear of blacks, liking for the African American instructor). Exploring the role of experiences in the development of racial attitudes among undergraduate students, Towles-Schwen and Fazio (2001) found that more positive automatically activated attitudes toward blacks were associated with recent (high school) positive interactions with blacks, whereas self-reported concerns about appearing prejudiced were linked to experiences at all school levels and with perceptions of parents' racial attitudes. Although measures of experiences included in this study were retrospective self-reports and the data were correlational, these findings suggest that early experiences may not be as critical in shaping automatic affective responses as it often is assumed. Implicit attitudes may continually be updated based on recent or ongoing experiences. Moreover, implicit attitudes are not necessarily based on first-hand experiences with attitude objects. They also develop via exposure to socializing agents starting in childhood (Devine, 1989). For example, Sinclair, Dunn, and Lowery (2005) found a reliable correspondence between parental self-reported racial attitudes and children's implicit prejudice; in particular among children who were highly identified with their parents. These findings provide preliminary evidences for common assumptions regarding the roots of implicit attitudes. Longitudinal and experimental studies still are needed to elucidate the causal mechanisms accounting for the interconnections between socialization processes and implicit attitudes.

The role of experiences and socialization is consistent with basic principles of classical conditioning (Walther & Langer, this volume). Recent studies provide strong support for the idea that implicit attitudes develop through the repeated pairings of potential attitude objects with positively and negatively valenced stimuli (Olson & Fazio, 2001, 2002). According to this view, an automatic preference for a consumer product may result from its frequent pairing with attractive individuals and racial prejudice may develop through repeated exposure to minority-group members portrayed negatively (e.g., criminals, drug addicts, gang members, etc.).

Self-Related Attitude Objects

The extent to which attitude objects are linked to the self has a potent influence on automatic or unconscious evaluations. Several compelling lines of research show that the mere ownership of an object or its association to the self is sufficient to enhance its attractiveness. Nuttin (1985) found that when individuals were asked to choose a preferred letter from each of several pairs consisting of one letter from their names and one not, they preferred letters that were included in their names. This *name letter effect* has been replicated in many different countries and cultures (Nuttin, 1987) and it seems to reflect an automatic or unconscious preference for the self. Pelham, Mirenberg, and Jones (2002) have shown that implicit positive self-evaluations were reflected in what people choose to do for a living and where they choose to live. Across a dozen studies, they found that people were more likely to choose careers and to live in cities or states whose names share letters with their own first or last names. In the same vein, participants were attracted to people whose arbitrary experimental code numbers resembled their own birth dates, whose surnames shared letters with their own surnames, and whose jersey number had been paired subliminally with their own names (Jones, Pelham, Mirenberg, & Carvallo, 2004). As a whole, these findings suggest that personal choices and interpersonal attraction may be indicative of *implicit egotism*.

Objects attached to the self are immediately endowed with increased value. This proposition is consistent with the well-documented impact of group membership on implicit attitudes: In-groups automatically elicit more positive feelings than out-groups (for a review, see Devos & Banaji, 2003). Given that group membership in natural groups or social categories is often confounded with such factors as familiarity, the most compelling evidence for the implication of the self on intergroup biases comes from research that disentangles group membership from its possible confounds. Thus, it has been shown that a minimal social categorization is sufficient to automatically or unconsciously activate positive attitudes toward self-related groups and negative or neutral attitudes toward non-self-related groups (Ashburn-Nardo, Voils, & Monteith, 2001; Otten & Moskowitz, 2000; Otten & Wentura, 1999). Recently, Greenwald, Pickrell, and Farnham (2002) discovered that briefly studying the name of four members of a hypothetical group was sufficient to produce identification with and attraction to that group. This phenomenon, labeled *implicit partisanship*, emerged even when the relations between the two groups that were compared (studied vs. nonstudied) were cooperative and when the groups consisted of nonhuman objects (bogus car brands). Implicit partisanship was significantly reduced when the studied group was identified with a rival university (Pinter & Greenwald, 2004). In sum, these findings revealed introspectively unidentified or uncontrollable effects of the self on evaluations.

The role of the self in implicit attitudes also emerges from tests of the unified theory proposed to account for patterns of interrelations among self-esteem, self-concept, and attitude (Greenwald, Banaji, Rudman, et al., 2002). This framework draws its inspiration from theories of affective-cognitive consistency that dominated social psychology in the 1960s (Abelson et al., 1968). A core principle of the unified theory is that attitudes toward self and concepts closely associated with self (i.e., components of self-concept) tend to be of similar valence. This balance–congruity principle can be tested by examining the extent to which one of these constructs (implicit self-esteem, implicit self-concept, or implicit attitude) can be predicted as a function of the other two. Each construct should be a multiplicative function of the other two. In line with the balance–congruity principle, Devos, Diaz, Viera, and Dunn (2007) showed that the more college women identified with motherhood (relative to college education), the stronger the correlation between self-esteem and liking for motherhood (relative to college education). Support for similar hypotheses was found in studies on gender, race, and age identities (Greenwald et al., 2002; Rudman & Goodwin, 2004). Interestingly, the balance–congruity principle always received stronger support when tested with implicit than explicit measuring tools, suggesting that introspective limits and self-presentational concerns may partially obscure the operation of consistency processes.

Cultural Evaluations

In many circumstances, implicit attitudes reflect cultural evaluations. In other words, automatic or nonconscious evaluations are influenced by sociocultural realities. To some extent, the role of experiences and socialization is consistent with the idea that implicit attitudes are shaped by the cultural milieu in which individuals are immersed. In some cases, experiences and cultural evaluations operate in opposite directions, thus highlighting the fact that implicit attitudes are social constructions. For example, Swanson, Rudman, and Greenwald (2001) found that smokers' attitudes toward smoking were relatively positive at the explicit level, but their implicit attitudes were as negative as those observed among nonsmokers. This suggests that bolstering socially denounced behaviors (e.g., smoking) is more likely at a deliberate level than outside of conscious awareness or control. The influence of the cultural milieu is also nicely illustrated by a study showing that Japanese and Korean Americans who were more strongly immersed in their culture of origin exhibited a more pronounced automatic preference for their own ethnic group (Greenwald et al., 1998).

Several lines of research reveal that in-group favoritism is constrained by sociocultural evaluations of social groups. For example, Nosek, Banaji, and Greenwald (2002) reported data showing that, on an explicit measure, white respondents reported a preference for whites over blacks, and black respondents reported an even stronger preference for blacks over whites. This strong explicit liking reported by black respondents stood in sharp contrast to performances on the implicit measure. Unlike white respondents, who continued to show a strong preference for their own group, black respondents displayed no such preference on the implicit measure. Two studies conducted by Livingston (2002) documented that the more blacks perceived negativity in the mainstream culture toward their group, the more they exhibited in-group favoritism at the explicit level, but the less they displayed in-group favoritism at the implicit level. In sum, individuals who belong to high-status or privileged groups often exhibit a stronger implicit in-group favoritism than members of low-status or disadvantaged groups (Jost, Pelham, & Carvallo, 2002; Lane, Mitchell, & Banaji, 2005; Rudman, Feinberg, & Fairchild, 2002).

The picture emerging from this literature is that disadvantaged group members exert effort to report positive attitudes on explicit measures, but the lower social standing of their group is internalized sufficiently to eliminate in-group favoritism at the implicit level. On the other hand, advantaged group members' in-group preferences reflect the combined effect of in-group liking and the sociocultural advantage assigned to their group. Such results are consistent with the notion of *system-justification* (Jost & Banaji, 1994), or the idea that members of dominant and subordinate groups share thoughts, feelings, and behaviors that reinforce or justify the status quo, even when such justifications reflect poorly on one's self or social group. Ideological bolstering is most likely to occur outside conscious awareness, and this prevents perceivers and even targets of prejudice from questioning the legitimacy of social arrangements (Jost, Banaji, & Nosek, 2004).

The idea that implicit attitudes are reflections of cultural evaluations has sometimes been interpreted as a challenge to the validity of indirect measures. For example, Karpinski and Hilton (2001) criticized the IAT on the ground that the technique does not measure attitudes per se, but captures culturally shared knowledge that is not necessarily accepted by the individual (environmental associations). According to these authors, the lack of correspondence between self-reported attitudes toward apples vs. candies and implicit preferences for apples vs. candies assessed by an IAT casts doubts on the validity of the IAT as a measure of individual differences. To them, the technique merely reveals how these objects are valued in society rather than a personal orientation toward these objects. In a similar vein, Arkes and Tetlock (2004) contend that reaction time measures of racial attitudes reflect shared cultural stereotypes rather than prejudice, defined as antipathy directed toward a group. In both cases, the assumption is that only responses that are accepted or endorsed by individuals can be defined as attitudes (or prejudices). As explained at the onset of this chapter, however, an important aim of indirect measures is precisely to assess responses that may be disavowed by individuals.

Olson and Fazio (2004) offered a more nuanced version of this criticism. They argued that *extrapersonal* associations that do not contribute to the evaluation of the attitude object, but are nonetheless available in memory, contaminate performances on the IAT. These associations may include cultural evaluations (e.g., the majority's negative depictions of minority groups). The premise here is that attitudes are inherently personal associations and that an individual's attitude can differ from what he or she knows to be the cultural norm. Explicitly, people can easily distinguish between their personal attitude and evaluations displayed by others ("I don't like this movie, but most people enjoyed it"). At the implicit level, the distinction between personal (attitude) and extrapersonal (evaluative knowledge) evaluations is tenuous. Moreover, evidence reviewed in the last section of this chapter suggests that indirect measures (IAT included) capture meaningful individual differences in automatic evaluations.

To conclude, implicit evaluations reflect traces of experiences within a given social or cultural context. Unless one assumes a complete separation between the self and the cultural milieu, these automatic evaluations are an integral feature of the individual embedded in that environment (Banaji, 2001; Banaji, Nosek, & Greenwald, 2004).

RELATIONSHIP BETWEEN IMPLICIT AND EXPLICIT ATTITUDES

To what extent do measures of implicit and explicit attitudes converge? Some theoretical frameworks assume that implicit and explicit measures are taping distinct constructs (Devine, 1989; Greenwald & Banaji, 1995). The notions of *dual attitudes* (Wilson, Lindsey, & Schooler, 2000) and *implicit ambivalence* (Petty, Tormala, Briñol, & Jarvis, 2006) capture the idea that people may hold discrepant implicit and explicit attitudes toward the same object. Other theoretical perspectives assume a single attitude construct and posit that implicit and explicit measures differ only in the extent to which intentional or conscious processes can alter the attitudinal response (Fazio, 2001). In both cases, the correspondence between evaluations based on deliberative processes and evaluations produced when conscious control is relatively unavailable is a question of interest.

Variability in the Correspondence between Implicit and Explicit Attitudes

Dovidio, Kawakami, and Beach (2001) found a modest correlation between implicit and explicit measures of prejudice ($r = .24$). A meta-analysis based on 126 studies, covering a wide range of attitude objects, revealed a mean correlation of $r = .24$ between the IAT and self-reported attitudes (Hofmann, Gawronski, Gschwendner, Le, & Schmitt, 2005). Bosson, Swann, and Pennebaker (2000) examined systematically the correlations between various measures of implicit and explicit self-esteem. The observed correlations were relatively small (all $rs < .27$), and only some implicit measures correlated significantly with explicit measures. Modest associations between implicit and explicit measures are not surprising if one assumes that they are tapping distinct constructs. More intriguing is the extreme variability of correlations reported in the literature. This variability cannot be explained entirely by differences in the measures used. In some cases, variations in the magnitude of these associations remained despite similarities between the measures. For example, a wide range of correlations between the Modern Racism Scale (McConahay, 1986) and implicit measures of racial attitudes has been obtained (e.g., Dovidio, Kawakami, Johnson, Johnson, & Howard, 1997; Rudman, Ashmore, & Gary, 2001; Wittenbrink, Judd, & Park, 1997).

In some studies, weak correlations between implicit and explicit attitudes can be attributed to methodological pitfalls or to characteristics of the measures. For instance, failing to evaluate measurement error or a lack of conceptual correspondence between implicit and explicit assessments may lead to misleading conclusions regarding the dissociation between implicit and explicit attitudes. Researchers tackling these methodological shortcomings have typically documented robust interconnections between these two levels. For example, structural equation modeling studies that corrected for measurement error often support the contention that implicit and explicit evaluations are distinct, but related constructs (Cunningham, Johnson, et al., 2001; Cunningham, Nezlek, & Banaji, 2004). The meta-analysis conducted by Hofmann et al. (2005) also underscores the importance of methodological variables: Correlations between the IAT and self-reports systematically increased as a function of the conceptual correspondence between the measures and the spontaneity of self-reports. This being said, methodological features only partially account for the extreme heterogeneity of implicit–explicit associations. The fact that the magnitude of the implicit–explicit relationship varies across studies, domains, and individuals suggests that it might be moderated by additional factors (Nosek, 2005). Researchers have mostly focused their attention on the role of self-presentation and attitude strength as potential moderators.

Self-Presentation

Self-presentation refers to attempts to alter a response for personal or social purposes. In the present domain, it typically applies to circumstances where individuals are unwilling to report or express their affective response toward an object. People may not be willing to report the evaluation that comes to mind because they either do not want other people to know about it or they do not consciously accept or deliberately endorse this evaluation. That is, individuals may be tempted to deceive others by not reporting how they feel toward an object or they may reject their spontaneous affective reaction toward an object because it does not fit their principles or values. By definition, implicit measures are less vulnerable than explicit measures to deliberate control. Thus, self-presentation may shape explicit, but not implicit responses. This implies that as self-presentational concerns increase, the correlation between implicit and explicit attitudes should decrease.

In a systematic examination of the relationship between implicit and explicit evaluations of 57 pairs of objects using multilevel modeling techniques, Nosek (2005) tested hypotheses about several moderators of the implicit-explicit bond, including self-presentation. As predicted, greater overlap between implicit and explicit attitudes emerged when individuals were less concerned about expressing negativity (e.g., preferences for Coke vs. Pepsi) than when they were internally or externally motivated to conceal their negativity (e.g., preferences for thin people vs. fat people). The impact of self-presentation might just be one specific case in an array of motivations that lead individuals to tailor overtly expressed attitudes (Hofmann, Gschwendner, & Schmitt, 2005). Usually, consistency between implicit and explicit attitudes is reduced to the extent that such adjustment processes are executed.

Several studies on the motivation to control prejudiced reactions also indicate that motivational aspects can be more effectively incorporated in deliberative responses (Dunton & Fazio, 1997; Plant & Devine, 1998). Fazio et al. (1995) found greater consistencies between the Modern Racism Scale (McConahay, 1986) and an unobtrusive measure of racial attitudes among individuals with weak motivations to control prejudiced reactions. However, individuals who displayed a high internal and low external motivation to respond without prejudice exhibited lower levels of implicit prejudice than others (Devine, Plant, Amodio, Harmon-Jones, & Vance, 2002). This pattern suggests that when this motivation is internalized, it may facilitate successful regulation or inhibition of automatic evaluative responses (Amodio et al., 2003; Maddux, Barden, Brewer, & Petty, 2005).

Attitude Strength

Other potential moderators can be integrated under the umbrella of *attitude strength*. In contrast to weak attitudes, strong attitudes are stable, resistant to persuasion, guide information processing, and predict behavior (Bassili, this volume). Attitude strength can be assessed using numerous indicators, including importance, knowledge, familiarity, frequency of thought, extremity, and ambivalence regarding the attitude object. Important for the present discussion is a common assumption that the more individuals express their attitudes or think about an attitude object, the more automatized their attitudes become. From this perspective, attitude strength should increase the correspondence between explicit and implicit attitudes. Over time, deliberate or conscious thinking should shape automatic responses, resulting in greater overlap between implicit and explicit evaluations. One also could posit a reciprocal dynamic by which the more individuals practice their attitude, the more it is likely to become highly accessible and automatically activated upon mere presentation of the attitude object. Several investigators have provided evidence for the role of various aspects of attitude strength as a moderator of the relationship between implicit and explicit measures of attitudes. For example, Karpinski, Steinman, and Hilton (2005) found that self-reported interest in and perceived importance of politics and an upcoming presidential election moderated the relationship between explicit and implicit attitudes toward George W. Bush and Al Gore. As predicted, these indicators of attitude strength increased the overlap between assessments reflecting deliberate processes and associations operating outside of conscious control. These authors obtained convergent findings using consumer products as attitude objects and showed that giving participants the opportunity to elaborate on their attitudes resulted in a stronger implicit–explicit correlation.

Additional Moderators

Across a large set of attitude objects and aggregating multiple indicators of attitude strength, Nosek (2005) also found evidence for the moderating role of attitude strength. He also hypothesized about other moderators that have received less scrutiny, suggesting that the dimensionality or structure of the evaluative responses may account for the magnitude of the implicit–explicit relation. Some attitude objects may be evaluated along a single dimension, whereas other attitude objects might be evaluated more independently. Evaluations elicited by the two sides of dichotomies such as gun control vs. gun rights or Democrats vs. Republicans, are often mirror images of one another: to a large extent, being in favor of gun control means being opposed to gun rights. However, liking Julia Roberts does not necessarily imply antipathy for Meg Ryan. From an information processing perspective, an attitudinal response should be easier to make when the objects trigger responses that fit a unidimensional structure. In contrast, multidimensional evaluations are more complex, less stable, and more difficult to retrieve (Connor & Armitage, this volume). In line with this principle, Nosek (2005) observed greater consistency between implicit and explicit attitudes for pairs of objects that can be evaluated along a single dimension than for objects that are assessed independently.

The extent to which people perceive a discrepancy between their own evaluation and what they assume is the norm can also moderate implicit–explicit relationships. Indeed, highly distinctive evaluations are more likely to be seen as defining features of the self-concept and as such are more likely to be linked to efficient and precise self-observation. Following this line of thought, the correlation between implicit and explicit attitudes intensified as distinctiveness increased (Nosek, 2005). Hofmann et al. (2005) examined the extent to which people's awareness of their implicit attitude moderated the implicit–explicit consistency. They suggested that awareness of the implicit attitude affected how strongly the conscious representation of the attitude reflected the implicit attitude. Evidence for the role of awareness is not conclusive, but further work may elucidate the circumstances under which it might have an effect.

The work reviewed in this section provides insights into when implicit and explicit evaluative processes will converge or diverge. The consistency between implicit and explicit attitudes appears to be systematically influenced by multiple moderators. Future research should investigate how these variables may jointly, or interactively, influence the implicit–explicit correspondence. For example, the effect of self-presentational concerns may depend on people's awareness of their implicit attitudes. As awareness of implicitly held attitudes increases, the motivation to tailor self-reported attitudes may become more evident. The moderating factors are often conceptualized as dispositional, but they could also be viewed as situational factors. From this perspective, it is important to identify features of social contexts that may activate these dynamics. An important challenge for future research is also to test more systematically the processes through which the moderators operate. In some cases, it is likely that the moderating factors shape explicit responses. In other cases, they might affect implicit attitudes, and some variables may simultaneously influence both.

FLEXIBILITY OF IMPLICIT ATTITUDES

Contrary to the assumption that implicit attitudes reflect highly stable mental representations, a growing literature indicates that implicit attitudes are malleable or flexible (for reviews, see Blair, 2002; Gawronski & Bodenhausen, 2006). Performances on tasks developed to assess implicit attitudes are responsive to a wide range of cognitive, motivational, and contextual factors. Under some circumstances, these factors are capable of eliciting radically different patterns of evaluations. To account for the malleability of implicit associations, several theorists have relied on a constructivist view of mental representations (Gawronski & Bodenhausen, 2006; Mitchell, Nosek, & Banaji, 2003). According to this approach (Schwarz, this volume; Schwarz & Bohner, 2001; Wilson & Hodges, 1992), attitudes are not merely retrieved from memory but rather are constructed on the spot. They should be conceptualized as momentarily constructed representations integrating contextual information and selective subsets of associative knowledge. In other words, mental representations are not inert entities stored in memory and retrieved from memory when needed. Rather, they are dynamically constructed or re-created based on available information and contextually activated knowledge (Smith, 1996).

Accessibility Effects

Studies showing that exposure to different kinds of information prior to completing an implicit measure influences performance on the measure are consistent with this framework. It could be argued that the initial exposure phase influences how individuals construe the attitude object. Supporting this reasoning are the results of studies showing that being exposed to admired black individuals and disliked white individuals reduced implicit prejudice toward blacks (Dasgupta & Greenwald, 2001). Similarly, after having watched a video clip of an African-American group at an outdoor barbecue, weaker implicit prejudice was exhibited than after having been exposed to a gang-related situation involving African Americans (Wittenbrink, Judd, & Park, 2001). Similar findings have been obtained by having participants interact with a black experimenter (Lowery, Hardin, & Sinclair, 2001) or with a black partner assigned situational power (Richeson & Ambady, 2003). In all these cases, it is likely that contextually activated knowledge is incorporated in the mental representation produced in reaction to the experimental manipulation.

A constructivist approach also can easily integrate the idea that most targets (object, person, or group) are represented in a multifaceted manner and that the presence of particular cues is sufficient to influence which subset of associative knowledge is activated. Thus, the *same* target can be automatically evaluated differently as a function of the specific context in which it is encountered. Mitchell et al. (2003) have shown that automatic evaluations elicited by famous individuals varied as a function of whether they were categorized based on their race or based on their occupation. They compared the relative evaluations of targets that differed both in terms of race and occupation (white politicians vs. black athletes). When the IAT required categorization based on race, the White politicians were evaluated more favorably than the black athletes. When categorizations were based on occupation, a bias favoring black athletes relative to white politicians was obtained. Subtly varying the race and gender composition of the context in which a particular social group is evaluated also affected implicit attitudes. More precisely, white women expressed a more negative attitude toward black women when race (rather than gender) was the distinctive categorization criterion. On the other hand, highlighting gender (rather than race) elicited a more negative attitude toward white men. In a similar vein, cueing specific social roles moderated automatic racial bias (Barden, Maddux, Petty, & Brewer, 2004). In sum, implicit attitudes are shaped by the frame through which a given situation is filtered. Individuals may hold multiple sets of associations about a target, and access these associations at different times based on contextual circumstances.

Impact of Stimuli Sets

The flexibility of implicit associations also emerges from studies showing that different mental representations might be temporarily activated by different sets of stimuli. Several researchers have examined whether exemplars determine performances on the IAT (Nosek et al., 2006). For example, Govan and Williams (2004) showed that changing the affective valence of stimuli could eradicate or reverse well-documented IAT effects. They found that the preference for flowers over insects was reversed when the stimuli were pleasant insects (e.g., ladybird, butterfly) and unpleasant flowers (e.g., nettles, poison ivy). Further, evidence for a prowhite bias was eradicated when admired blacks celebrities (movie stars, athletes) were contrasted to infamous white individuals (mass murderers, etc.). Bluemke and Friese (2006) also reported compelling evidence for the influence of stimuli on IAT effects. Using a between-subject design, they systematically manipulated the relation of target stimuli (East, Neutral, or West German stimuli) to the evaluative dimension, and the relation of the evaluative stimuli (positive, neutral, or negative traits) to the target dimension. Data from a sample of West German Internet users indicated that the strength and direction of these cross-category associations influenced the direction and magnitude of automatic intergroup attitudes. The effects obtained ranged from a very strong in-group bias to a strong out-group bias. According to these authors, the conceptual overlap between the stimuli influences the ease of the sorting process. In sum, there is growing evidence that effects obtained on the IAT are not solely a function of the concepts or labels contrasted.

In this section, we demonstrated why implicit attitudes should not be conceptualized as stable mental representations. Rather, they are dynamically constructed within the parameters of a given social context. This being said, the specific mechanisms underlying contextual influences on indirect measures of attitudes are not fully understood (Gawronski & Bodenhausen, 2006). There is no doubt that multiple mental processes are likely to come into play. For example, Gawronski and Bodenhausen (2005) have shown that performance on tasks based on response compatibility processes is influenced not only by the direct activation of associative knowledge, but also by subjective feelings of ease or difficulty in retrieving relevant information from memory. Most studies reported in this section document assimilation effects, but contrast effects have also been obtained (Gawronski, Deutsch, & Seidel, 2005). Other researchers have offered explanations for contextual variations that are not strictly cognitive, arguing that social motives shape performances on implicit measures. For example, the need to adjust one's perspective and communications to match the experimenter's presumed attitudes (social tuning) may account for the impact of the experimenter's ethnicity on implicit racial attitudes (Lowery et al., 2001). Threat to one's self-image also is likely to moderate implicit biases (Frantz, Cuddy, Burnett, Ray, & Hart, 2004). Finally, priming a multicultural (rather than color-blind) perspective has been shown to reduce implicit prejudice (Richeson & Nussbaum, 2004).

Establishing the malleability of implicit attitudes was an important step because it challenged a common assumption about evaluations or feelings operating outside of conscious control. Work on this topic is now starting to provide more solid and integrative theoretical accounts of these effects (Gawronski & Bodenhausen, 2006). This shift in perspective also raises important questions about the relative stability of implicit and explicit attitudes. In a series of experiments, Gregg, Seibt, and Banaji (2006) demonstrated that implicit and explicit preferences for imagined social groups could easily be induced. However, newly formed implicit preferences (in contrast to explicit ones) could not easily be reversed by various counterinductions (e.g., asking participants to imagine that the associations were diametrically opposite to those learned initially). These findings are consistent with the idea that implicit evaluations are less malleable than self-reported ones.

IMPLICIT ATTITUDES AND BEHAVIORS

A central aim of measuring attitudes is to predict behavior. It is well established that explicitly held attitudes do not always strongly account for behavioral responses (Ajzen & Gilbert Cote, this volume). The distinction between implicit and explicit attitudes may prove useful in better grasping the complex interplay between attitudinal and behavioral responses (for a meta-analysis, see Greenwald, Poehlman, Uhlmann, & Banaji, in press).

Implicit Attitudes Predict Behavioral Responses

Consistent with a functional perspective, evaluations operating outside of conscious awareness or control result in behavioral tendencies. For example, Chen and Bargh (1999) demonstrated that automatic evaluations elicited by various attitude objects translated directly in behavioral predispositions toward these stimuli. A negative evaluation prompted an immediate avoidance tendency (pulling a lever away), whereas a positive evaluation produced an immediate approach tendency (pulling a lever toward). In other words, the automatic categorization of stimuli as either good or bad has direct behavioral consequences. A person does not need to be aware of the operation of attitudes for attitudes to orient the person toward the environment.

Several studies indicate that some behaviors are better predicted by implicit rather than explicit attitudes. For instance, Fazio, Jackson, Dunton, and Williams (1995) found that the more participants displayed automatic prejudice toward African Americans, the less friendly were their verbal and nonverbal behaviors toward an African-American experimenter. Automatic racial attitudes accounted for the extent to which participants smiled, made eye contact, and expressed interest in the debriefing delivered by the experimenter. Self-reported racial attitudes did not correlate with these behavioral reactions. In the same vein, McConnell and Leibold (2001) found that as participants' performances on an IAT reflected more negative attitudes toward blacks than Whites, their interactions were less positive with a black (vs. a white) experimenter. This was evident in assessments offered by the experimenters themselves and by trained judges. In addition, implicit prejudice predicted shorter speaking time, less smiling, fewer social comments, more speech errors or hesitations when interacting with a black (vs. a white) experimenter. Explicit attitudes did not predict these behavioral responses. Similarly, Bessenoff and Sherman (2000) found that automatic negative attitudes toward fat people predicted how far participants chose to sit from an overweight woman with whom they expected to interact. Self-reported attitudinal measures were not reliably correlated with this behavioral response. Overall, these studies demonstrate that at least under some circumstances, implicit evaluations predict behavioral responses, whereas overtly expressed evaluations do not.

Spontaneous, Uncontrollable, or Nonconscious Behaviors

It would be wrong to conclude that indirect measures of attitudes systematically outperform self-reported attitudes in predicting behavior. There is a growing consensus in the field that explicit and implicit measures of attitudes are both systematically related to behavior, albeit different types of behaviors. As the previously described studies suggested, implicitly assessed attitudes predict behavior that evades strategic control. Examining the correspondence between attitudes toward people with AIDS and avoidance behaviors, Neumann, Hülsenbeck, and Seibt

(2004) found that performance on an IAT correlated with automatic approach and avoidance predispositions as assessed by the speed with which a computer mouse was pulled toward (approach) or pushed away from (avoidance) the body, whereas explicit attitudes were correlated with behavioral intentions measured through a questionnaire. Dovidio, Kawakami, Johnson, et al. (1997) found that implicit attitudes were related to such nonverbal responses to an African-American interaction partner as blinking and eye contact, whereas explicit attitudes specifically predicted participants' ratings of their partners. These findings are consistent with dual-process theories positing that consciously endorsed attitudes influence controlled actions, whereas automatic attitudes determine spontaneous actions (Devine, 1989; Fazio, 2001; Wilson et al., 2000). Despite efforts to behave in a nonprejudiced manner, automatic prejudice transpired from nonverbal behaviors.

There is variability in the extent to which people are aware and vigilant to such nonverbal reactions as smiling, spatial distance, or eye contact. Recently, Dasgupta and Rivera (2006) examined several potential moderators of the extent to which implicit attitudes translate into actions in the domain of antigay attitudes. The authors focused on the impact of traditional belief systems about gender and sexuality and behavioral control (awareness of and ability to control subtle nonverbal behaviors during interpersonal interactions). They found that among participants who endorsed traditional beliefs about gender and sexuality, implicit antigay attitudes were related to subtle discriminatory reactions toward a gay confederate. However, for traditional participants who were high in behavioral control, implicit prejudice translated into friendlier reactions toward a gay confederate, suggesting that these participants overcorrected their behavior to avoid potential bias.

The fact that prejudices leak out in ways that cannot be consciously controlled or identified by individuals holding these negative attitudes may partially account for the fact that *perpetrators* and *targets* of prejudicial reactions often develop very different perspectives on intergroup interactions. Dovidio, Kawakami, and Gaertner (2002) showed that white and black individuals based their impressions about the quality of interracial interactions on different types of information. Impressions of white individuals stemmed from overt verbal cues communicated during the interaction and related to their explicit racial attitudes. In contrast, black individuals based their impression to a much larger extent on subtle nonverbal cues communicated by white individuals and related to these individuals' level of implicit prejudice toward blacks.

Motivation and Opportunity for Control

The picture emerging from these studies is that implicit attitudes better predict relatively spontaneous, uncontrollable, or unconscious behaviors, whereas explicit attitudes are a more potent predictor of deliberate behavioral responses. However, several studies reveal that implicitly held evaluations shape behaviors that presumably involve deliberative processes (Greenwald et al., in press). For example, implicit racial attitudes assessed using facial electromyography accounted for the selection of an applicant for a prestigious teaching fellowship (Vanman et al., 2004). In a similar vein, the more African-American participants displayed an implicit preference for whites over blacks, the less favorably they evaluated a potential black partner compared to a white partner (Ashburn-Nardo, Knowles, & Monteith, 2003), suggesting once again that members of ethnic minorities can display responses that are detrimental to the interest of their group. The fact that implicit attitudes play a role in the initiation of deliberate or controllable behaviors is consistent with a substantial body of work emphasizing the ubiquity of automaticity in everyday life (Bargh & Chartrand, 1999).

According to Fazio's (2001) MODE model, people's motivation and opportunity to respond carefully determine whether automatic or controlled processes drive attitudes and behaviors; that is, the consistency of attitudes and behaviors depends on processing capacities and motivation: If they are high, behaviors will reflect deliberative processes. When processing capacities are limited or motivation is lacking, behaviors are more likely to stem from automatic evaluations. Based on this theoretical framework, several studies examined whether the motivation to control prejudiced reactions moderated the relation between implicit racial attitudes and behavioral responses. This motivation may reflect a concern about appearing prejudiced or a desire to avoid disputes. These two motivational orientations are sources of distinct moderating effects (Dunton & Fazio, 1997). For individuals who indicated that they were not motivated to avoid interracial disputes, automatic prejudice accounted for less positive ratings of a black student. In contrast, for individuals who reported a strong desire to avoid interracial disputes, automatic prejudice translated into more positive evaluations of the target, suggesting that these participants overcorrected for their potential bias. In a similar vein, Towles-Schwen and Fazio (2003) examined participants' anticipated comfort and willingness to interact with a black partner. They found that participants who held more negative automatic attitudes toward blacks felt more uncomfortable about the idea of interacting with a black person, particularly if they anticipated the interaction to be fairly unscripted. Participants who were motivated to avoid interracial conflicts admitted this discomfort in particular if they were not concerned about appearing biased, whereas participants who were concerned about appearing prejudiced reported less anticipated discomfort, probably in an attempt to correct for their prejudices. In sum, participants' anticipated reactions and behavioral intentions stemmed from the conjoint influences of motivations to control prejudiced reactions and characteristics of the situation.

Discrepancies between Implicit and Explicit Attitudes

As suggested earlier, there is great variability in the extent to which implicit and explicit attitudes overlap. In a meta-analysis on the predictive validity of the IAT, Greenwald et al. (in press) tested the hypothesis that a lack of correspondence between implicit and explicit responses may reduce the extent to which these measures predict criterion variables. For instance, the predictive power of self-report measures might be reduced because the implicit response pulls in an opposite direction. In addition, conscious attempts to override the automatic response may reduce the predictive validity of the implicit measure. In line with this proposition, Greenwald et al. (in press) found that when the IAT and self-reports were strongly correlated they both predicted criterion measures more effectively than when there was a low correspondence between implicit and explicit assessments. At the same time, internal conflicts between automatic and controlled attitudes potentially have important motivational and behavioral consequences. For example, discrepancies between implicit and explicit self-esteem are particularly potent in determining behavior when people become aware of their ambivalent self-views (Jordan, Spencer, & Zanna, 2005; Jordan, Spencer, Zanna, Hoshino-Browne, & Correll, 2003). According to this perspective, self-esteem might often operate at an automatic or unconscious level, but at times implicit views may seep into consciousness. When this occurs, discrepancies between implicit and explicit self-evaluations motivate people to reduce this ambivalence, and they have powerful effects on self-image maintenance. Thus, situations bringing to mind a discrepancy between explicit and implicit attitudes are likely to trigger motivated behavioral reactions.

Despite the fact that indirect measures of attitudes have been introduced only recently, the skepticism about their ability to predict behaviors seems unwarranted. There is a compelling body of work showing that implicit attitudes influence people's judgments, decisions, and behaviors in subtle but systematic ways. Research on implicit attitudes has enriched our understanding of the complex interplay between automatic evaluations and behavioral responses. More precisely, circumstances under which implicit attitudes account for behavioral responses are well understood. Even when attitudes are automatically activated, the extent to which people are aware of their potential influence, are motivated to control their impact, and are able to exert control on their behavioral response determine whether automatic attitudes shape behavior.

To conclude this section, it is important to emphasize that the interconnections between implicit attitudes and behaviors should not be studied exclusively with the assumption that attitudes guide behaviors. It also is possible that the behaviors people engage in shape their attitudes. Consider, for example, an interesting study by Jellison, McConnell, and Gabriel (2004) showing that implicit and explicit measures of sexual orientation attitudes were related to distinct behaviors among gay men. Implicit attitudes were more strongly related to activities reflecting an involvement or immersion in the gay culture, whereas explicit attitudes correlated more strongly with self-presentational behaviors (not passing as straight or disclosure to others). As the authors acknowledge, the correlational nature of the data does not provide evidence for specific causal pathways.

CONCLUSION

The initial enthusiasm for the concept of implicit attitude was driven largely by the prospect of circumventing the limitations of self-report measures. However, the existing body of research on implicit attitudes suggests that the virtues of indirect measures do not stem solely from their capacity to access attitudes that do not fully enter consciousness, or to bypass social desirability, impression management, or demand characteristics. More importantly, research on implicit attitudes has lead to many theoretical and empirical insights. Attitudes, evaluations, and preferences are shaped by a myriad of psychosocial processes marked by a lack of conscious awareness, control, intention, or self-reflection. Recent advances in the study of implicit attitudes provide concepts, theories, paradigms, and methods that allow researchers to understand these processes. Capitalizing on pioneer demonstrations of automatic or unconscious evaluations and on the development of an arsenal of techniques, scientists are now in a position to tackle questions that have important theoretical and practical implications. Refinements in the conceptualization of implicit attitudes have been proposed. Various factors that play a role in the development of implicit attitudes have been identified. The emphasis on dissociations between implicit and explicit attitudes has given way to a more thorough understanding of the circumstances under which implicit and explicit attitudes converge or diverge. The idea that implicit attitudes are fixed or rigid entities has been shown to be untenable and firmer theoretical accounts of contextual influences on implicit attitudes are starting to emerge. Finally, much has been learned about the interconnections between implicit attitudes and behavior. Theoretical and empirical contributions discussed in this chapter have also profoundly changed the concept of attitude itself.

REFERENCES

Abelson, R. P., Aronson, E., McGuire, W. J., Newcomb, T. M., Rosenberg, M. J., & Tannenbaum, P. (Eds.). (1968). *Theories of cognitive consistency: A sourcebook*. Chicago: Rand-McNally.

Amodio, D. M., Harmon-Jones, E., & Devine, P. G. (2003). Individual differences in the activation and control of affective race bias as assessed by startle eyeblink response and self-report. *Journal of Personality and Social Psychology, 84*, 738–753.

Arkes, H. R., & Tetlock, P. E. (2004). Attributions of implicit prejudice, or "Would Jesse Jackson 'fail' the Implicit Association Test?" *Psychological Inquiry, 15*, 257–278.

Ashburn-Nardo, L., Knowles, M. L., & Monteith, M. J. (2003). Black Americans' implicit racial associations and their implications for intergroup judgment. *Social Cognition, 21*, 61–87.

Ashburn-Nardo, L., Voils, C. I., & Monteith, M. J. (2001). Implicit associations as the seeds of intergroup bias: How easily do they take root? *Journal of Personality and Social Psychology, 81*, 789–799.

Banaji, M. R. (2001). Implicit attitudes can be measured. In H. L. Roediger, III, J. S. Nairne, I. Neath, & A. Surprenant (Eds.), *The nature of remembering: Essays in honor of Robert G. Crowder* (pp. 117–150). Washington, D.C.: American Psychological Association.

Banaji, M. R., Nosek, B. A., & Greenwald, A. G. (2004). No place for nostalgia in science: A response to Arkes and Tetlock. *Psychological Inquiry, 15*, 279–310.

Barden, J., Maddux, W. W., Petty, R. E., & Brewer, M. B. (2004). Contextual moderation of racial bias: The impact of social roles on controlled and automatically activated attitudes. *Journal of Personality and Social Psychology, 87*, 5–22.

Bargh, J. A. (1994). The four horsemen of automaticity: Awareness, intention, efficiency, and control in social cognition. In R. S. Wyer, Jr. & T. K. Srull (Eds.), *Handbook of social cognition* (Vol. 1, pp. 1–40). Hillsdale, NJ: Erlbaum.

Bargh, J. A., & Chartrand, T. L. (1999). The unbearable automaticity of being. *American Psychologist, 54*, 462–479.

Bessenoff, G. R., & Sherman, J. W. (2000). Automatic and controlled components of prejudice toward fat people: Evaluation versus stereotype. *Social Cognition, 18*, 329–353.

Blair, I. V. (2002). The malleability of automatic stereotypes and prejudice. *Personality and Social Psychology Review, 6*, 242–261.

Blanton, H., & Jaccard, J. (2006). Arbitrary metrics in psychology. *American Psychologist, 61*, 27–41.

Bluemke, M., & Friese, M. (2006). Do features of stimuli IAT effects? *Journal of Experimental Social Psychology, 42*, 163–176.

Bosson, J. K., Swann, W. B., & Pennebaker, J. W. (2000). Stalking the perfect measure of implicit self-esteem: The blind men and the elephant revisited. *Journal of Personality and Social Psychology, 79*, 631–643.

Brauer, M., Wasel, W., & Niedenthal, P. (2000). Implicit and explicit components of prejudice. *Review of General Psychology, 4*, 79–101.

Chen, M., & Bargh, J. A. (1999). Consequences of automatic evaluation: Immediate behavioral predispositions to approach or avoid the stimulus. *Personality and Social Psychology Bulletin, 25*, 215–224.

Conrey, F. R., Sherman, J. W., Gawronski, B., Hugenberg, K., & Groom, C. J. (2005). Separating multiple processes in implicit social cognition: The Quad model of implicit task performance. *Journal of Personality and Social Psychology, 89*, 469–487.

Cunningham, W. A., Johnson, M. K., Gatenby, J. C., Gore, J. C., & Banaji, M. R. (2003). Neural components of social evaluation. *Journal of Personality and Social Psychology, 85*, 639–649.

Cunningham, W. A., Nezlek, J. B., & Banaji, M. R. (2004). Implicit and explicit ethnocentrism: Revisiting the ideologies of prejudice. *Personality and Social Psychology Bulletin, 30*, 1332–1346.

Cunningham, W. A., Preacher, K. J., & Banaji, M. R. (2001). Implicit attitude measures: Consistency, stability, and convergent validity. *Psychological Science, 12*, 163–170.

Dasgupta, N., & Greenwald, A. G. (2001). On the malleability of automatic attitudes: Combating automatic prejudice with images of admired and disliked individuals. *Journal of Personality and Social Psychology, 81*, 800–814.

Dasgupta, N., & Rivera, L. M. (2006). From automatic antigay prejudice to behavior: The moderating role of conscious beliefs about gender and behavioral control. *Journal of Personality and Social Psychology, 91*, 268–280.

De Houwer, J. (2003a). A structural analysis of indirect measures of attitudes. In J. Musch & K. C. Klauer (Eds.), *The psychology of evaluation: Affective processes in cognition and emotion* (pp. 219–244). Mahwah, NJ: Erlbaum.

De Houwer, J. (2003b). The extrinsic affective Simon task. *Experimental Psychology, 50*, 77–85.

DeHart, T., Pelham, B. W., & Tennen, H. (2006). What lies beneath: Parenting style and implicit self-esteem. *Journal of Experimental Social Psychology, 42*, 1–17.

Devine, P. G. (1989). Stereotypes and prejudice: Their automatic and controlled components. *Journal of Personality and Social Psychology, 56*, 5–18.

Devine, P. G., Plant, E. A., Amodio, D. M., Harmon-Jones, E., & Vance, S. L. (2002). The regulation of explicit and implicit race bias: The role of motivations to respond without prejudice. *Journal of Personality and Social Psychology, 82*, 835–848.

Devos, T., & Banaji, M. R. (2003). Implicit self and identity. In M. R. Leary & J. P. Tangney (Eds.), *Handbook of self and identity* (pp. 153–175). New York: Guilford.

Devos, T., & Banaji, M. R. (2005). American = White? *Journal of Personality and Social Psychology, 88*, 447–466.

Devos, T., Diaz, P., Viera, E., & Dunn, R. (2007). College education and motherhood as components of self-concept: Discrepancies between implicit and explicit assessments. *Self and Identity, 6*, 256–277.

Dovidio, J. F., Kawakami, K., & Beach, K. R. (2001). Implicit and explicit attitudes: Examination of the relationship between measures of intergroup bias. In R. Brown & S. L. Gaertner (Eds.), *Blackwell handbook of social psychology: Intergroup processes* (pp. 175–197). Oxford, UK: Blackwell.

Dovidio, J. F., Kawakami, K., & Gaertner, S. L. (2002). Implicit and explicit prejudice and interracial interaction. *Journal of Personality and Social Psychology, 82*, 62–68.

Dovidio, J. F., Kawakami, K., Johnson, C., Johnson, B., & Howard, A. (1997). On the nature of prejudice: Automatic and controlled processes. *Journal of Experimental Social Psychology, 33*, 510–540.

Dunton, B. C., & Fazio, R. H. (1997). An individual difference measure of motivation to control prejudiced reactions. *Personality and Social Psychology Bulletin, 23*, 316–326.

Fazio, R. H. (2001). On the automatic activation of associated evaluations: An overview. *Cognition & Emotion, 15*, 115–141.

Fazio, R. H., Jackson, J. R., Dunton, B. C., & Williams, C. J. (1995). Variability in automatic activation as an unobtrusive measure of racial attitudes: A bona fide pipeline? *Journal of Personality and Social Psychology, 69*, 1013–1027.

Fazio, R. H., & Olson, M. A. (2003). Implicit measures in social cognition research: Their meaning and uses. *Annual Review of Psychology, 54*, 297–327.

Fazio, R. H., Sanbonmatsu, D. M., Powell, M. C., & Kardes, F. R. (1986). On the automatic activation of attitudes. *Journal of Personality and Social Psychology, 50*, 229–238.

Frantz, C. M., Cuddy, A. J. C., Burnett, M., Ray, H., & Hart, A. (2004). A threat in the computer: The race Implicit Association Test as a stereotype threat experience. *Personality and Social Psychology Bulletin, 30*, 1611–1624.

Gawronski, B., & Bodenhausen, G. V. (2005). Accessibility effects on implicit social cognition: The role of knowledge activation and retrieval experiences. *Journal of Personality and Social Psychology, 89*, 672–685.

Gawronski, B., & Bodenhausen, G. V. (2006). Associative and propositional processes in evaluation: An integrative review of implicit and explicit attitude change. *Psychological Bulletin, 132*, 692–731.

Gawronski, B., Deutsch, R., & Seidel, O. (2005). Contextual influences on implicit evaluation: A test of additive versus contrastive effects of evaluative context stimuli in affective priming. *Personality and Social Psychology Bulletin, 31*, 1226–1236.

Gawronski, B., Hofmann, W., & Wilbur, C. J. (2006). Are "implicit" attitudes unconscious? *Consciousness and Cognition, 15*, 485–499.

Govan, C. L., & Williams, K. D. (2004). Changing the affective valence of the stimulus items influences the IAT by re-defining the category labels. *Journal of Experimental Social Psychology, 40*, 357–365.

Greenwald, A. G., & Banaji, M. R. (1995). Implicit social cognition: Attitudes, self-esteem, and stereotypes. *Psychological Review, 102*, 4–27.

Greenwald, A. G., Banaji, M. R., Rudman, L. A., Farnham, S. D., Nosek, B. A., & Mellot, D. S. (2002). A unified theory of implicit attitudes, stereotypes, self-esteem, and self-concept. *Psychological Review, 109*, 3–25.

Greenwald, A. G., McGhee, D. E., & Schwartz, J. L. K. (1998). Measuring individual differences in implicit cognition: The implicit association test. *Journal of Personality and Social Psychology, 74*, 1464–1480.

Greenwald, A. G., Pickrell, J. E., & Farnham, S. D. (2002). Implicit partisanship: Taking sides for no reason. *Journal of Personality and Social Psychology, 83*, 367–379.

Greenwald, A. G., Poehlman, T. A., Uhlmann, E., & Banaji, M. R. (in press). Understanding and using the Implicit Association Test: III. Meta-analysis of predictive validity. *Journal of Personality and Social Psychology.*

Gregg, A. P., Seibt, B., & Banaji, M. R. (2006). Easier done than undone: Asymmetry in the malleability of implicit preferences. *Journal of Personality and Social Psychology, 90*, 1–20.

Hofmann, W., Gawronski, B., Gschwendner, T., Le, H., & Schmitt, M. (2005). A meta-analysis on the correlation between the Implicit Association Test and explicit self-report measures. *Personality and Social Psychology Bulletin, 31*, 1369–1385.

Hofmann, W., Gschwendner, T., & Schmitt, M. (2005). On implicit-explicit consistency: The moderating role of individual differences in awareness and adjustment. *European Journal of Personality, 19*, 25–49.

Jellison, W. A., McConnell, A. R., & Gabriel, S. (2004). Implicit and explicit measures of sexual orientation attitudes: Ingroup preferences and related behaviors and beliefs among gay and straight men. *Personality and Social Psychology Bulletin, 30*, 629–642.

Jones, J. T., Pelham, B. W., Carvallo, M., & Mirenberg, M. C. (2004). How do I love thee? Let me count the Js: Implicit egotism and interpersonal attraction. *Journal of Personality and Social Psychology, 87*, 665–683.

Jordan, C. H., Spencer, S. J., & Zanna, M. P. (2005). Types of high self-esteem and prejudice: How implicit self-esteem relates to ethnic discrimination among high explicit self-esteem individuals. *Personality and Social Psychology Bulletin, 31*, 693–702.

Jordan, C. H., Spencer, S. J., Zanna, M. P., Hoshino-Browne, E., & Correll, J. (2003). Secure and defensive high self-esteem. *Journal of Personality and Social Psychology, 85*, 969–978.

Jost, J. T., & Banaji, M. R. (1994). The role of stereotyping in system-justification and the production of false consciousness. *British Journal of Social Psychology, 33*, 1–27.

Jost, J. T., Banaji, M. R., & Nosek, B. A. (2004). A decade of system justification theory: Accumulated evidence of conscious and unconscious bolstering of the status quo. *Political Psychology, 25*, 881–920.

Jost, J. T., Pelham, B. W., & Carvallo, M. R. (2002). Non-conscious forms of system justification: Implicit and behavioral preferences for higher status groups. *Journal of Experimental Social Psychology, 38*, 586–602.

Karpinski, A., & Hilton, J. L. (2001). Attitudes and the implicit association test. *Journal of Personality and Social Psychology, 81*, 774–788.

Karpinski, A., Steinman, R. B., & Hilton, J. L. (2005). Attitude importance as a moderator of the relationship between implicit and explicit attitude measures. *Personality and Social Psychology Bulletin, 31*, 949–962.

Lane, K. A., Mitchell, J. P., & Banaji, M. R. (2005). Me and my group: Cultural status can disrupt cognitive consistency. *Social Cognition, 23*, 353–386.

Livingston, R. W. (2002). The role of perceived negativity in the moderation of African Americans' implicit and explicit racial attitudes. *Journal of Experimental Social Psychology, 38*, 405–413.

Lowery, B. S., Hardin, C. D., & Sinclair, S. (2001). Social influence effects on automatic racial prejudice. *Journal of Personality and Social Psychology, 81*, 842–855.

Maddux, W. W., Barden, J., Brewer, M. B., & Petty, R. E. (2005). Saying no to negativity: The effects of context and motivation to control prejudice on automatic evaluative responses. *Journal of Experimental Social Psychology, 41*, 19–35.

McConahay, J. B. (1986). Modern racism, ambivalence, and the modern racism scale. In J. F. Dovidio & S. L. Gaertner (Eds.), *Prejudice, discrimination, and racism* (pp. 91–125). San Diego, CA: Academic Press.

McConnell, A. R., & Leibold, J. M. (2001). Relations among the implicit association test, discriminatory behavior, and explicit measures of racial attitudes. *Journal of Experimental Social Psychology, 37*, 435–442.

Mitchell, J. P., Nosek, B. A., & Banaji, M. R. (2003). Contextual variations in implicit evaluation. *Journal of Experimental Psychology: General, 132,* 455–469.

Neumann, R., Hulsenbeck, K., & Seibt, B. (2004). Attitudes toward people with AIDS and avoidance behavior: Automatic and reflective bases of behavior. *Journal of Experimental Social Psychology, 40,* 543–550.

Nosek, B. A. (2005). Moderators of the relationship between implicit and explicit evaluation. *Journal of Experimental Psychology: General, 134,* 565–584.

Nosek, B. A., & Banaji, M. R. (2001). Measuring implicit social cognition: The go/no-go association task. *Social Cognition, 19,* 625–666.

Nosek, B. A., Banaji, M. R., & Greenwald, A. G. (2002). Harvesting implicit group attitudes and beliefs from a demonstration website. *Group Dynamics, 6,* 101–115.

Nosek, B. A., Greenwald, A. G., & Banaji, M. R. (2006). The Implicit Association Test at age 7: A methodological and conceptual review. In J. A. Bargh (Ed.), *Social psychology and the unconscious: The automaticity of higher mental processes* (pp. 265–292). New York: Psychology Press.

Nuttin, J. M. (1985). Narcissism beyond Gestalt and awareness: The name letter effect. *European Journal of Social Psychology, 15,* 353–361.

Nuttin, J. M. (1987). Affective consequences of mere ownership: The name letter effect in twelve European languages. *European Journal of Social Psychology, 17,* 381–402.

Olson, M. A., & Fazio, R. H. (2001). Implicit attitude formation through classical conditioning. *Psychological Science, 12,* 413–417.

Olson, M. A., & Fazio, R. H. (2002). Implicit acquisition and manifestation of classically conditioned attitudes. *Social Cognition, 20,* 89–104.

Olson, M. A., & Fazio, R. H. (2003). Relations between implicit measures of prejudice: What are we measuring? *Psychological Science, 14,* 636–639.

Olson, M. A., & Fazio, R. H. (2004). Reducing the influence of extrapersonal associations on the Implicit Association Test: Personalizing the IAT. *Journal of Personality and Social Psychology, 86,* 653–667.

Otten, S., & Moskowitz, G. B. (2000). Evidence for implicit evaluative in-group bias: Affect-biased spontaneous trait inference in a minimal group paradigm. *Journal of Experimental Social Psychology, 36,* 77–89.

Otten, S., & Wentura, D. (1999). About the impact of automaticity in the Minimal Group Paradigm: Evidence from affective priming tasks. *European Journal of Social Psychology, 29,* 1049–1071.

Payne, B. K. (2005). Conceptualizing control in social cognition: How executive functioning modulates the expression of automatic stereotyping. *Journal of Personality and Social Psychology, 89,* 488–503.

Payne, B. K., Jacoby, L. L., & Lambert, A. J. (2005). Attitudes as accessibility bias: Dissociating automatic and controlled processes. In R. R. Hassin, J. S. Uleman, & J. A. Bargh (Eds.), *The new unconscious.* (pp. 393–420). New York: Oxford University Press.

Pelham, B. W., Mirenberg, M. C., & Jones, J. K. (2002). Why Susie sells seashells by the seashore: Implicit egotism and major life decisions. *Journal of Personality and Social Psychology, 82,* 469–487.

Petty, R. E., Fazio, R. H., & Briñol, P. (Eds.). (in press). *Attitudes: Insights from the new wave of implicit measures.* Mahwah, NJ: Erlbaum.

Petty, R. E., Tormala, Z. L., Briñol, P., & Jarvis, W. B. G. (2006). Implicit ambivalence from attitude change: An exploration of the PAST model. *Journal of Personality and Social Psychology, 90,* 21–41.

Pinter, B., & Greenwald, A. G. (2004). Exploring implicit partisanship: Enigmatic (but genuine) group identification and attraction. *Group Processes & Intergroup Relations, 7,* 283–296.

Plant, E. A., & Devine, P. G. (1998). Internal and external motivation to respond without prejudice. *Journal of Personality and Social Psychology, 75,* 811–832.

Richeson, J. A., & Ambady, N. (2003). Effects of situational power on automatic racial prejudice. *Journal of Experimental Social Psychology, 39,* 177–183.

Richeson, J. A., & Nussbaum, R. J. (2004). The impact of multiculturalism versus color-blindness on racial bias. *Journal of Experimental Social Psychology, 40,* 417–423.

Rudman, L. A. (2004). Sources of implicit attitudes. *Current Directions in Psychological Science, 13,* 79–82.

Rudman, L. A., Ashmore, R. D., & Gary, M. L. (2001). "Unlearning" automatic biases: The malleability of implicit prejudice and stereotypes. *Journal of Personality & Social Psychology, 81,* 856–868.

Rudman, L. A., Feinberg, J., & Fairchild, K. (2002). Minority members' implicit attitudes: Automatic in-group bias as a function of group status. *Social Cognition, 20,* 294–320.

Rudman, L. A., & Goodwin, S. A. (2004). Gender differences in automatic in-group bias: Why do women like women more than men like men? *Journal of Personality and Social Psychology, 87,* 494–509.

Schwarz, N., & Bohner, G. (2001). The construction of attitudes. In A. Tesser & N. Schwarz (Eds.), *Blackwell handbook of social psychology: Intraindividual processes* (pp. 436–457). Oxford, UK: Blackwell.

Sherman, J. S. (2006). On building a better process model: It's not only how many, but which ones and by which means. *Psychological Inquiry, 17,* 173–184.

Sinclair, S., Dunn, E., & Lowery, B. S. (2005). The relationship between parental racial attitudes and children's implicit prejudice. *Journal of Experimental Social Psychology, 41,* 283–289.

Smith, E. R. (1996). What do connectionism and social psychology offer each other? *Journal of Personality and Social Psychology, 70,* 893–912.

Swanson, J. E., Rudman, L. A., & Greenwald, A. G. (2001). Using the Implicit Association Test to investigate attitude-behaviour consistency for stigmatised behaviour. *Cognition & Emotion, 15,* 207–230.

Towles-Schwen, T., & Fazio, R. H. (2001). On the origins of racial attitudes: Correlates of childhood experiences. *Personality and Social Psychology Bulletin, 27,* 162–175.

Towles-Schwen, T., & Fazio, R. H. (2003). Choosing social situations: The relation between automatically activated racial attitudes and anticipated comfort interacting with African Americans. *Personality and Social Psychology Bulletin, 29,* 170–182.

Vanman, E. J., Saltz, J. L., Nathan, L. R., & Warren, J. A. (2004). Racial discrimination by low-prejudiced Whites facial movements as implicit measures of attitudes related to behavior. *Psychological Science, 15,* 711–714.

Wilson, T. D., & Hodges, S. D. (1992). Attitudes as temporary constructions. In L. L. Martin & A. Tesser (Eds.), *The construction of social judgments* (pp. 37–65). Hillsdale, NJ: Erlbaum.

Wilson, T. D., Lindsey, S., & Schooler, T. Y. (2000). A model of dual attitudes. *Psychological Review, 107,* 101–126.

Wittenbrink, B., Judd, C. M., & Park, B. (1997). Evidence for racial prejudice at the implicit level and its relationship with questionnaire measures. *Journal of Personality and Social Psychology, 72,* 262–274.

Wittenbrink, B., Judd, C. M., & Park, B. (2001). Spontaneous prejudice in context: Variability in automatically activated attitudes. *Journal of Personality and Social Psychology, 81,* 815–827.

Wittenbrink, B., & Schwarz, N. (Eds.). (2007). *Implicit measures of attitudes: Procedures and controversies.* New York: Guilford.

III

Attitudes
Origin and Formation

5

Attitude Formation and Change through Association
An Evaluative Conditioning Account

EVA WALTHER and TINA LANGER
University of Trier

*H*ardly any topic in social psychology has attracted more attention than attitude research. Because attitudes are seen as providing guidance in a complex world, social behavior without attitudes is difficult to imagine. Beyond the question of how attitudes guide behavior (e.g., Ajzen, 1991; Fazio, 1990), two major topics have been of primary interest in attitude research: attitude formation and attitude change.

Traditionally, the question of attitude formation has been addressed by accounts that emphasize the significance of affective processes (Eagly & Chaiken, 1993). The most prominent example is research on evaluative conditioning (for reviews, see De Houwer, Thomas, & Baeyens, 2001; Walther, Nagengast, & Trasselli, 2005). In a prototypical evaluative conditioning (EC) study, a subjectively neutral picture of a human face (conditioned stimulus; CS) is repeatedly presented with a subjectively liked or disliked human face (unconditioned stimulus; US). The common result is a substantial shift in the valence of the formerly neutral CS, such that it acquires the evaluative quality of the US. This evaluative conditioning effect is usually explained by the formation of an association between the cognitive representation of the CS and the US (De Houwer et al., 2001; Walther, 2002).

Although there is ample evidence that attitudes can be formed by the mere association of affective cues (De Houwer et al., 2001; Walther et al., 2005), theorists in the Fishbein and Ajzen (1975) tradition argue that attitude formation is confined to cognitive processes. More specifically, these accounts focus on cognitive structures (i.e., beliefs) to explain the development of attitudes (Ajzen & Fishbein, 1980; Fishbein & Middlestadt, 1995). This view can be illustrated by

Fishbein and Middlestadt's proposition that "findings indicating that variables other than beliefs and their evaluative aspects contribute to attitude formation and change can best be viewed as methodological artifacts resulting from the use of inappropriate predictors and/or criteria" (p. 184).

This position recently has been challenged by numerous experimental studies providing supportive evidence for the affect based attitude account (e.g., De Houwer, Baeyens, Vansteenwegen, & Eelen, 2000; Dijksterhuis, 2004; Hammerl & Grabitz, 2000; Olson & Fazio, 2001, 2002; Walther, 2002; Walther & Grigoriadis, 2004). Thus, it has been shown that attitudes can be influenced by the mere contiguity of a neutral stimulus (e.g., person or object) with affective stimuli (e.g., (dis)liked persons, music, or (un)pleasant objects). For instance, Olson and Fazio (2001) found evidence that the mere co-occurrence of a fictitious character (i.e., a Pokemon) with negative words or pictures leads to a negative reaction toward this fictitious character. Further evidence for affect-based EC effects was provided by Hammerl and Grabitz (2000) who showed that EC emerges in the haptic domain. In their studies, neutral tactile textures (CS) acquired evaluative meaning after frequent pairing with pleasant and unpleasant tactile textures (US). EC effects have also been found in the gustatory domain. In these studies, the CS usually is a flavor mixed in plain water and the US is the same flavor mixed with pleasant (sugar) or unpleasant (soap) flavors (Baeyens, Crombez, & Hendrickx, 1995; Zellner, Rozin, Aron, & Kulish, 1983). Additionally, there is evidence for EC even when CS and US are of different modalities. The combination of CS and US can be visual-auditory (e.g., geometric shapes and music; Bierley, McSweeney, & Vannieuwkerk, 1985) or visual-olfactory (e.g., photographs of faces and odors; Todrank, Byrnes, Wrzesniewski, & Rozin, 1995). Van Reekum, van den Berg, and Frijda (1999) paired abstract paintings (CS) with liked or disliked sounds (US). Their result confirmed the previous findings that the affective evaluation of the previously neutral paintings shifted in the direction of the affective auditory stimuli.

Interestingly, in many studies, conditioning effects have been particularly pronounced when cognitive processes were hindered by a distractive, secondary task applied during conditioning (Bakker-De Pree, Defares, & Zwaan, 1970; Walther, 2002), or by subliminally presented stimuli (De Houwer, Baeyens, & Eelen, 1994; De Houwer, Hendrickx, & Baeyens, 1997; Dijksterhuis, 2004; Krosnick, Betz, Jussim, & Lynn, 1992; Niedenthal, 1990). Consistent with this observation, evaluative conditioning seems to be most effective in participants who are unaware of the co-occurrence (i.e., the contingency) between the CS and the US (Baeyens, Eelen, & van den Bergh, 1990; De Houwer et al., 2001; Fulcher & Hammerl, 2001; Hammerl & Grabitz, 2000). In other words, affective attitudes were most influenced under conditions of limited cognitive resources. Thus, people form affective attitudes neither knowing why they suddenly like a certain attitudinal object, nor being consciously aware that their attitude was influenced.

A closer look at the putative disagreement between the affectively and the cognitively based lines of research suggests that they might refer to different phases in the processes of attitude formation and change. While proponents of the cognitively based approach regard cognitively based beliefs as the core concept in explaining *attitude change* (Ajzen & Fishbein, 1980; Petty & Cacioppo, 1984; Petty, Cacioppo, & Goldman, 1981), proponents of the affectively based approach point to the primary stage of *attitude formation* (Olson & Fazio, 2002; Walther, 2002, Walther & Trasselli, 2003). Thus, it may be that simple affective mechanisms determine the origin of attitudes, whereas more deliberate, cognitively based processes are necessary to change already existing attitudes. After all, attitude change typically has been addressed by theories that emphasize the significance of cognitive processes (Eagly & Chaiken, 1993). For instance, research in the tradition of cognitive response models (Greenwald, 1968) argues that the effectiveness of a persuasive message in changing attitudes depends on the particular thoughts that a recipient generates in response to the message.

However, as useful the distinction between attitude formation and attitude change may be in reconciling cognitive and affective attitude accounts, it has recently been undermined by the finding that evaluative conditioning mechanisms may also contribute to attitude change (Walther, Gawronski, Blank, & Langer, 2007). Specifically, is has been demonstrated that attitudes toward a given CS can be changed indirectly by merely changing the valence of the US associated with the CS. Most importantly, because this effect is driven by the mere association between CS and US, such attitude changes emerge even when the CS is never encountered with the new evaluative information. This indirect mechanism goes beyond previous research on persuasion in which attitude change is typically the result of a *direct* link between evaluative information (e.g., a persuasive message) and an attitudinal object (e.g., a consumer product).

ATTITUDE FORMATION AND CHANGE THROUGH ASSOCIATION: A CLOSER LOOK AT EC

EC and CC (Classical Conditioning):[1] Similarities and Differences

There are three essential characteristics of EC that render this paradigm particularly interesting for social psychological research on attitude formation. First, as already mentioned, people in an EC experiment usually do not know why they started to like a particular individual. Thus, in contrast to classical conditioning (CC), EC effects seem to be independent of contingency awareness. However, in some studies, only participants aware of the contingencies exhibit EC effects (Allen & Janiszewski, 1989; Fulcher & Cocks, 1997; Ghuman & Bar, 2006; Shimp, Stuart, & Engle, 1991). This contradictory finding may be the result of the fact that (1) there is no standardized EC paradigm and EC studies differ on nearly all parameters that are involved in EC, and (2) there is no agreement on how awareness should be assessed (Baeyens, Hermans, & Eelen, 1993; Dawson & Reardon, 1973; Field, 2000, 2001; Field & Moore, 2005; Hammerl, 2000; Lovibond & Shanks, 2002). This latter issue is especially troubling because the way contingency awareness is measured strongly determines whether an individual is categorized as aware or unaware (Pleyers, Corneille, Luminet, & Yzerbyt, 2007; Walther & Nagengast, 2006).

The debate of whether likes and dislikes can actually be formed without contingency awareness is important because the relationship between awareness and conditioning speaks to the processes underlying evaluative learning and to the question of whether or not EC should be considered as a type of learning different from CC. This is because a growing body of evidence suggests that conscious awareness of the contingencies between CS and US is a necessary precondition for CC to occur (Brewer, 1974; Dawson, 1973; Dawson & Schell, 1987). In other words, the contemporary conception of CC as signal learning takes higher cognitive processes (e.g., rule learning) into account, making CC an associative mechanism that allows the organism to make predictions about significant events in the environment (Rescorla & Wagner, 1972). A prototypical CC procedure involves a tone as a CS followed contingently by a shock as a US. Thus, what the organism learns within the CC paradigm is an if–then relationship between CS and US; that is, the organism acquires an expectancy that the shock will follow if the tone occurs.

Is EC fundamentally different from CC, or just a much simpler version of the same basic principle? If EC could be identified as a variety of signal, which means cognitive learning, this would also imply that attitude formation is confined to cognitive processes as suggested by the Fishbein and Ajzen (1975) model. In contrast, showing that EC is independent of awareness and therefore much less cognitively based than CC would cast doubt on the general notion that all attitudes are cognitively based.

Second, as a logical consequence of the formation of expectancies, the contingency (i.e., statistical correlation) between CS and US is a crucial determinant of CC. One factor that limits the application of CC in social psychology is that a strict contingency between CS and US hardly ever occurs in the real world, where individuals usually encounter each other in different group compositions and settings. Because EC is not restricted to strong CS-US contingency, it increases the range of contexts in which evaluative learning can be applied.

Third, after successful EC, single CS presentations do not alter the valence of the stimulus; that is, EC is resistant to extinction (Baeyens, Crombez, van den Bergh, & Eelen, 1988). In other words, EC is stable over time, which means that the affective meaning of an individual, once acquired, is not impaired if the person is presented in different settings after conditioning. This is because EC is not based on an expectancy that the US is going to occur if the CS is presented. In view of its resistance to extinction, EC is more plausibly explained as a transfer of valence such that the CS acquires some affective attributes of the US (De Houwer et al., 2001; Hammerl & Grabitz, 1996).

Besides these differences, there also are similarities between EC and CC, which suggest to some researchers that both paradigms are based on the same learning mechanisms. These similarities are evident in the word use and the constituents of the paradigms. In both paradigms, a former neutral CS gains meaning through its co-occurrence with an already meaningful stimulus, the US. Both paradigms are sensitive to sensory preconditioning, which means that the affective value of the CS is transferred to objects or events that are preassociated with the stimulus due to prior learning (Barnet, Grahame, & Miller, 1991; Hammerl & Grabitz, 1996;

Rizley & Rescorla, 1972; Walther, 2002). Furthermore, as will be discussed later, there is evidence in both paradigms for the US-revaluation effect (Baeyens, Eelen, van den Bergh, & Crombez, 1992; Delamater & Lolordo, 1991; Hosoba, Iwanaga, & Seiwa, 2001; Walther et al., 2007) and second-order conditioning (Barnet et al., 1991; Rizley & Rescorla, 1972; Walther, 2002), which indicates that the CS itself attains the power of a US through conditioning. In other words, the CS is first made affectively meaningful through CC before it is used as a US in a subsequent phase of the experiment.

Whereas CC traditionally has been confined to aversive USs, recent evidence extends it to appetitive conditioning in the area of animal learning (Jennings & Kirkpatrick, 2006). Taken together, there is mixed evidence for the assumption that EC is a learning mechanism different from CC. On the one hand, some features clearly separate EC from CC. Most importantly, EC is not dependent on contingency awareness and is resistant to extinction. On the other hand, phenomena like sensory preconditioning, the US-revaluation effect, and second-order conditioning that appear in EC, as well as in CC, cast doubt on the assumption that EC is indeed a learning mechanism distinct from CC.

APPLICATIONS OF EC

EC in Social Psychology

Besides its implications for attitude formation and change, EC provides a simple account for many phenomena in social psychology. For instance, EC is involved in the famous "*kill-the-messenger effect*" whereby transmitters are inevitably associated with the valence of the message they have conveyed (Manis, Cornell, Moore, & Jeffrey, 1974). Whereas in persuasion, a neutral message (CS) usually is revaluated because of its co-occurrence with an evaluated communicator (US), the opposite mechanism occurs in the kill-the-messenger effect: The messenger (CS) is revaluated because of his or her association with bad news (US).

Similar association-based effects were obtained in a series of intriguing studies by Skowronski, Carlston, Mae, and Crawford (1998), who demonstrated that communicators involuntarily become associated with their verbal description of others. Although descriptions of other people are (psycho) logically independent of the communicator, simple associative processes nevertheless link these two events together and produce such boomeranglike phenomena.

The idea that conditioning also may contribute to *stigmatization* was evident in recent studies by Hebl and Mannix (2003), who examined how the company of a stigmatized (i.e., obese) person affected the evaluation of associated individuals. The results indicated that job applicants were judged more negatively when they were accompanied by an obese (vs. average weight) female. The mere co-occurrence of the applicant with an overweight woman was sufficient to cause the applicant to be judged more negatively than a control person on several job-relevant scales. Characteristically for EC processes, this stigmatization was independent of high-level (controlled) cognitive factors, such as knowledge about the relationship of the applicant to his companion, an existing explicit antifat attitude, or other compensating information. However, the applicant was never judged independently of the context in which the obese person was present. Thus, it could be the case that the obese individual serves as a negative anchor for the subsequent judgment. If an EC effect occurred, the negative evaluation of the applicant also should emerge when she is presented alone.

If transfer of stigmatization is similar to EC, it should be enduring and hard to change. Evidence for the particular stability of conditioned affective attitudes has come from studies by Sherman and Kim (2002). These authors demonstrated that the affective preferences for objects (i.e., Chinese ideographs) persevered even after the cognition that gave rise to the affect ceased to be valid. That is, the affective meaning associated with the Chinese ideographs persisted even though this meaning was invalidated—a phenomenon the authors called *"affective perseverance."* These findings suggest that evaluatively conditioned attitudes are relatively resistant to cognitive change strategies such as discounting.

Evaluative conditioning documented in the many domains of social psychology appears restricted to situations in which there is direct contact between a neutral and a valued event. However, in many social situations, attitudes are formed without such a contact, as it is the case when the evaluatively conditioned attitude spreads to other stimuli that are preassociated with the CS (spreading attitude affect). The liability of a family for the crime of a family member or the devaluation of an individual due to the bad reputation of her in-group are the most blatant examples of the spreading attitude effect (Ito, Chiao, Devine, Lorig, & Cacioppo, 2006; Walther, 2002). The spreading attitude effect refers to the phenomenon that a favorably or unfavorably evaluated stimulus may influence not only the evaluation of an event that co-occurs with the stimulus, but also other stimuli that are merely associated with it. Using the picture–picture paradigm, Walther (2002) first presented participants with pairs of evaluatively neutral male faces. In the subsequent evaluative conditioning phase, one of the neutral pictures (the CS) was paired with a negatively evaluated face (the US). The author found that the EC procedure not only affected the evaluation of the CS, but also "spread" to the face that was only preassociated with the CS: Both previously neutral faces were evaluated more negatively, although only one of them (the CS) was in direct contact with the aversive event.

Transferred to real life settings, the spreading attitude effect implies that a person's bad behavior not only affects his or her own evaluation but also the judgment that is passed on people associated with the person, including family members, friends, colleagues, or in-group members (Ito et al., 2006). The mechanism that underlies this amazing effect is presumably as follows: The contiguous presentation of the two neutral stimuli during co-occurrences develops an association in memory between the two. In the conditioning phase, one of the formerly neutral stimuli serves as CS and acquires valence through its co-occurrence with an aversively or favorably evaluated stimulus. The acquired affective tone of the CS, however, influences other (pre)associated stimuli that are connected with this stimulus in memory.

This finding from the spreading attitude paradigm opens up a wide range of possible applications in several areas of basic and applied social psychology. The implications of the spreading attitude effect for attitude formation in social psychology are clear: Attitudes are not always based on a direct positive or aversive experience. Many prejudiced people have never encountered the targets of their antipathy. Instead, attitudes are often based on prior experiences with similar attitudinal targets, on second-hand information, or on mere preassociations. It is important to note, however, that evaluative learning does not affect each and every (similar) target, but only those highly specific individuals actually associated with the CS through prior experience. Demonstrating the spreading attitude phenomenon is of theoretical relevance to the EC literature because preconditioning effects indicate that associative mechanisms are at work in this paradigm.

Although the concept of EC may provide a parsimonious explanation for many social phenomena including attitude formation, the ultimate impact of this account in social psychology would presumably depend on the degree to which the comparatively simple valence-driven mechanisms of evaluative conditioning are compatible with or integrated into other kinds of socially relevant information, such as category information (e.g., in-groups/out-groups) or sentiments (e.g., relations). As a matter of fact, many social situations consist not only of the valence of individuals, but also of a variety of other information that determines the social life of an individual. In addition to basic likeability impressions, the relation to other individuals, for example, may strongly determine social judgments. A theoretical approach that aims at covering social attitude formation must take into account both the multiple facets of the social network and the valence of the individual. A theoretical account that meets this criterion is balance theory.

EC and Balance Theory

Consistent with EC theory, Heider (1958) suggested that many attitudes are not derived from direct experience with attitude objects. Rather, most interpersonal attitudes are inferred from the valence of, and relationships among, individuals who need not interact directly. Taking only valence information into account, the predictions of balance theory are congruent with those of EC: an individual (CS) associated with a liked or disliked person (US) will be judged similar to this evaluated person. This process of unit formation indicates that the attitude toward an individual is based on the evaluation of the persons associated with her. Although balance theory belongs to the standard canon of psychological theories, the mechanisms that underlie unit formation have never been investigated intensively.

Not only can EC theory explain the when and how of unit formation, it also may elucidate the associative mechanism underlying affective attitude formation. Note that in addition to the evaluation of a person, balance theory postulates that the relationship between individuals, the so-called sentiment relation, may be of critical importance in social situations. Liking someone who is liked by a friend might be easy, but liking someone who is liked by a nasty colleague might be a different thing. In such cases, balance theory predicts that people strive for a balanced sentiment triad in which people like individuals who are liked by friends and dislike individuals who are disliked by friends. Also, triads are balanced when (1) people dislike individuals who are liked by those whom they personally dislike, and

(2) people like individuals who are disliked by those whom they personally dislike. Interestingly, unit formation (EC) and balanced sentiment triads may have contradictory implications for particular conditions. Let us assume observing a disliked individual (A) meets another person (B) whom he or she does not like. Unit formation should lead to a negative attitude toward B because of his or her association with A. Sentiment formation, however, should lead to a positive attitude because the resultant triad would be balanced ("my enemy's enemy is my friend").

These contradictory implications of EC-like unit development and balance-postulated sentiment development in the formation of interpersonal attitudes were investigated in a series of studies by Gawronski, Walther, and Blank (2005). The authors examined under which conditions the conglomerate of (a priori) attitudes and observed sentiment relations results in a balanced sentiment triad, and under which conditions interpersonal attitude formation is dominated by EC. Based on empirical evidence obtained in the EC paradigm, it was hypothesized that unit formation can be considered as the result of the mere spatio-temporal co-occurrence between two stimuli. Hence, evaluations implied by unit formation may reflect simple associative processes (Olson & Fazio, 2001, 2002; Walther, 2002). Balanced sentiment triads, in contrast, may require higher order cognitive processes, such as inferring a positive evaluation of someone who is disliked by a disliked person. Gawronski et al. (2005) found that balanced sentiment triads emerge only when perceivers already have a positive or negative attitude toward a given individual at the time they learn about his or her sentiment relation to another target but not in the case of a neutral target. A possible explanation for this finding is that an a priori attitude is needed to create tensions toward balance when perceivers learn about the sentiment relation between two individuals. A further explanation for this finding is that the existence of an a priori attitude at the time when perceivers learn about the sentiment relation between two individuals is a necessary precondition for the application of the balanced sentiment schema. If, however, perceivers have neutral attitudes toward two individuals at the time they learn about their sentiment relation, the sentiment relation itself obviously has no clear-cut balanced sentiment implication.

EC and Self

Besides the valence of and the relation among individuals, another important source of interpersonal attitudes is self-evaluation (Greenwald & Banaji, 1995). There is considerable evidence that (normally positive) self-evaluations may influence the evaluation of objects, individuals, and events. The mere ownership effect (Feys, 1991, 1995), for instance, holds that people have a preference for objects belonging to the self. Giving people an object (e.g., a pen) leads to a more favorable attitude toward this object compared to a not-owned object (Beggan, 1992).

Preference for aspects associated with the self also is supported by the name letter effect, which suggests that people like letters that are part of their own names better than other letters (Nuttin, 1985; see also Koole, Dijksterhuis, & van Knippenberg, 2001). Pelham, Mirenberg, and Jones (2002) showed that the name letter preference might even affect major life decisions. The authors found a contingency between people's initials and decisions such as whom to marry, where to live, and what career to choose.

Although there are several demonstrations that the evaluation of the self plays a crucial role in evaluating other objects and events, the mechanisms that lead to these attitude formation processes are not entirely clear. We argue that most of these effects can be explained with simple EC. In terms of EC, self-evaluation can be conceptualized as a US and other individuals or objects as CSs. According to evaluative learning theory (De Houwer et al., 2001), the mere spatiotemporal CS-US co-occurrence is a sufficient condition for the transfer of valence from the US to the CS (Martin & Levey, 1978). Given that self-evaluation is predominantly positive, associating an object or event with the self may therefore lead to a favorable attitude toward this object or event.

The same principle could be involved in people's evaluations of other individuals, thus reversing the Stapel and Koomen notion that "people use others to evaluate themselves" (2000, p. 1068). Drawing on an EC account (De Houwer et al., 2001; Walther, 2002), we assume that the valence of the self serves as a source (a US) of interpersonal attitudes. In contrast to self-anchoring (Cadinu & Rothbart, 1996) or self-projection (Krueger, 2000) approaches, which conceptualize the self as a cognitive heuristic based on self-other similarity, we suggest that a simple affective mechanism, the transfer of valence from the self to others, may be involved in interpersonal (dis)liking. Since social projection extends only to in-group members (Clement & Krueger, 2002), EC is less restricted and predicts perceived self-other similarities even in out-group members. Naturally, in most cases, categorizations as an in-group go along with stronger associations between self and others, and therefore, with increased perceived similarity. However, whether the "boundaries of social categories are a veritable firewall against the spread of projection," as Clement and Krueger (2002, p.219) suggested, or whether there are only quantitative differences in the transfer of valences to in- and out-group members, must be addressed in future research.

The idea that self-evaluation may serve as a (unconscious) source of interpersonal attitudes was examined in a series of studies by Walther and Trasselli (2003). The authors hypothesized that if the idea of the self-as-US is correct, the mere association of the positively or negatively evaluated self with another otherwise unrelated and neutral target should lead to self-other evaluative similarity. The results indicated that a target associated with the self was indeed evaluated more similarly to the self than a control person who did not co-occur with the self during a learning phase. However, Walther and Trasselli (2003) also found this effect could be counteracted by higher cognitive processes. Taken together, the studies discussed in this section supported the notion that self-evaluation can serve as a source of interpersonal evaluative attitudes under certain conditions. To reconcile Krueger's (2000) notion of self-projection and the EC account, it could be argued that EC is a basic mechanism that is less restricted but often overridden by higher cognitive processes (e.g., categorization, anchoring). Specifically, the self is associated with another individual through the EC procedure, which leads to a perceived similarity between self and other. This simple affective associative mechanism entails a transfer of valence from the self to the other and thus can be sufficient to cause interpersonal evaluative attitudes. However, cognitive processes like categorization of the other into in- or out-group, as suggested by Krueger (2000), also come into play when judging other people and can possibly override or counteract the effects of the associative EC mechanism.

The idea that self-evaluation serves not only as a source (US) but also as an object (CS) of attitude formation was recently demonstrated by Dijksterhuis (2004). In a series of intriguing studies, Dijksterhuis (2004) presented participants with evaluatively positive words preceded by the word *I*. Relative to a control condition, this procedure enhanced (implicit) self-evaluation even if both words were presented subliminally, a technique that effectively ruled out demand effects. It is important to note, however, that these studies addressed the change of already existing attitudes rather than the formation of them. Based on the self-esteem literature (Greenwald & Banaji, 1995), it could be assumed that the concept of self is occupied with preexisting (positive) cognitive and affective meaning. Given the aforementioned persistence and stability of affective attitudes (Sherman & Kim, 2002) one might argue that there is a fundamental difference between creating an attitude in a neutral stimulus and the mere change of an already existing meaning. This difference is reflected in attitude change theories that typically emphasize the significance of cognitive processes (Eagly & Chaiken, 1993), whereas attitude formation is typically addressed by conditioning models (De Houwer et al., 2001).

Conceptualizing the self as a source of interpersonal attitudes can also provide alternative explanations for several phenomena in social psychology. A prominent example to which our account could contribute is in-group favoritism in the minimal-group paradigm (Tajfel, Billig, Bundy, & Flament, 1971). While recent studies have shown that in-groups are automatically associated with positive affect, the underlying mechanisms remain unclear (Otten & Wentura, 1999, 2001). Evidence in support of the EC account of in-group biases comes from Perdue, Dovidio, and Gurtman (1990), who found that the use of words referring to in-group or out-group status, such as *us* or *them*, may unconsciously serve as a source of evaluation. In one of their studies, nonsense syllables unobtrusively paired with "in-group" designating pronouns (e.g., *we*) were rated as more pleasant than syllables paired with "out-group" designators (e.g., *they*). We propose that this automatic positive evaluation of the in-group may be due to simple EC mechanisms in which the individual serves as a positive US and the associated group as CS. As speculative as this idea may seem, the implications can be put to a simple empirical test: given that depressive individuals, by definition, possess a negative self-image, the minimal group effect should at least be reduced if a depressive group is tested for its reaction to the in-group.

EC in Advertising

Companies have spent enormous amounts of time and energy introducing new brands and products. However, there are many reasons that new product launches fail. Expert magazines estimate that between 35% and 45% of product introductions are considered failures (Boulding, Morgan, & Staelin, 1997). What makes the launching of brands and products such a risky and difficult business? Beyond market and customer identification, placement and sales management, the most important determinant of the fate of the goods is advertising. It is the ultimate goal of advertising to induce favorable attitudes toward products, goods, and brands. The idea is that a high evaluation of products and brands is related with sales success in the long run. Whereas hardly anybody would question this goal, it is widely debated which psychological method is most effective in reaching it.

Although the "conditioning of attitudes toward products and brands has become generally accepted and has developed into a unique research stream within consumer behavior" (Till & Priluck, 2000, p. 57), hardly any work reflects contemporary theoretical advances in this area. For instance, several researchers in this field do not distinguish between signal learning and evaluative learning. That is, most researchers try to apply signal learning to the advertising context. This is surprising because there are several factors that limit the application of signal learning in consumer psychology and highlight the advantage of EC. The first is that a strict contingency between the CS and US hardly ever occurs in real world consumer settings, where individuals usually encounter products in compositions and settings very different from those used in the ads. The second restriction is that signal learning is highly sensitive to extinction. In contrast, one of the most frequently cited properties of evaluative learning is the stability of conditioned effects (Baeyens et al., 1988; Grossman & Till, 1998). The affective meaning of a brand or product, once acquired, is not impaired if the product is presented in different settings after conditioning. The third restriction is that signal learning is mostly applied to aversive events. This is at odds with almost all advertising contexts that promote the acquisition of positive rather than negative product attitudes. The fourth distinction of EC in consumer research is the fact that evaluative learning is not dependent on deliberate attention, but turns out to be even stronger when participants are distracted (see Walther, 2002). Since most ads pass by without receiving much attention, using an attitude formation technique that actually profits from inattention may be of critical importance.

In light of the theoretical limitations of signal learning approaches, it is clear that second-order conditioning may be relevant for advertising and consumer research. For example, the concept of brand extension can only work if the positive attitude toward the brand is extended to other products associated with the brand. Whereas there is a vast amount of research pertaining to this topic (Barone, Miniard, & Romeo, 2000; Flaherty & Pappas, 2000; Lane, 2000; Till & Priluck, 2000), the underlying mechanisms of the how-and-when of brand extensions remain unclear. Thus, a theoretical account is needed to explain whether or not brand-extension may be profitable. We believe that EC provides such an account.

EC also can be fruitfully applied to contexts in which consumers acknowledge a product's claim but do not personally like the product because it elicits uncomfortable affective reactions. Examples of the dissociations between affective and cognitive reactions toward brands and products are not rare. For instance, most people in Western Europe know that organic food is healthier than conventional food products. Despite this belief, however, many people avoid organic products because they appear to be old-fashioned and uncool. An advertising campaign in which organic food is presented with affective cues of youthfulness in a modern lifestyle context may be a remedy against the outmoded image of organic food. A similar strategy was applied by American Airlines to counter fear of flying after September 11, 2001. Although most people were well aware that the risk of losing one's life flying this airline was extremely low, they nevertheless exhibited strong fear. American Airlines tried to fight this negative affective reaction toward their product by airing commercials in which very pleasant feelings of security (e.g., meeting friends, coming home) were transmitted. The idea behind this counter-conditioning strategy was that the repeated presentation of the product with a highly positive life-scene (i.e., an appetitive US) would alter the former negative reaction (Bouton, 2000, 2002). That is, an existing affective reaction should be changed into the opposite valence by presenting the CS with a new US. Although counterconditioning is a widespread practice in advertising, empirical evidence that this strategy is indeed effective in changing human attitudes is surprisingly rare (Baeyens, Eelen, van den Bergh, & Crombez, 1989). In contrast, counterconditioning has been well documented with animals (Amundson, Escobar, & Miller, 2003; Brooks, Hale, Nelson, & Bouton, 1995). Richardson, Riccio, and Smoller (1987), for instance, examined the counterconditioning of an aversively motivated response in male rats, using presentation of a highly palatable sugar solution. They found the counterconditioning procedure was effective in modifying the aversive response. Thus, further empirical research is necessary to test whether the same basic principles that are successful in animal training also apply to human attitude change processes.

It is common in advertising campaigns to present the product along with stimuli other than the US. For instance, in many cases such mood inducing procedures as music are presented along with the product. This technique is based on the belief that the number of positive cues is proportional to the extremity of positive evaluations of the product. Consistent with this view, negative cues are almost always avoided in advertising. For example, the idea that sad mood has negative influences on product evaluation is part of the unquestioned wisdom in consumer research and practice. Coca Cola does not air commercials on news channels because the company is afraid that the sad feeling induced by bad news may affect the evaluation of their (fun) product. This avoidance of bad feelings in the context of advertising is founded on the mood congruency hypothesis (Bower, 1981). However, Walther and Grigoriadis (2004) found no evidence for mood congruency in their EC paradigm. Instead, they obtained strong support for the idea that negative mood enhances the acquisition of positive valence by guiding attention to the (pleasant) environment, rather than to inner processes. This counterintuitive result is at odds with most advertising practice in which the induction of positive attitudes is mostly aspired by the induction of positive mood.

Forbidden Fantasies and Phobias: EC in Clinical Psychology

The interplay between affect and cognition is not only a topic relevant to attitude researchers in social psychology but also is one of the most debated issues in clinical research (Lazarus, 1984; Zajonc, 1980). This is because findings on affective learning challenged the conviction of cognitive therapy that emotional reactions (e.g., fear, disgust, anger) can only be changed through a process of cognitive redefinition (Goldfried, Linehan, & Smith, 1978; Lazarus, 1974; Matthews & Litwack, 1995). In a demonstration of affective learning, Eifert, Craill, Carey, and O'Connor (1988) showed that fear reactions toward animals can be substantially reduced by presenting pleasant stimuli (music) along with the phobic objects. Thus, counterconditioning was an effective means of changing even pathological affective reactions. Additional support for counterconditioning comes from recent studies showing its effectiveness in the treatment of posttraumatic stress disorder (Paunovic, 2003), spider phobia (de Jong, Vorage, van den Hout, 2000), and obsessive–compulsive behavior (Kearney, 1993).

The idea that evaluative conditioning is involved in the genesis of these diseases came from the observation that some patients do not benefit from exposure therapies that are based on extinction of the conditioned stimulus (Rachman, 1985). That is, although people may learn to control their physiological fear reaction during exposure therapy, they nevertheless experience strong aversive emotional reaction when facing the phobic stimulus. For instance, a claustrophobic patient may have learned to avoid panic reactions while riding the elevator but may still have strong negative affective reactions toward elevators. Within the EC framework, this could be explained by the observation that conditioned attitudes are resistant to extinction. The apparent persistence of conditioned reactions seemingly contradicts the findings obtained in research following the Pavlovian tradition. This research, however, relies mostly on autonomic physiological responses (e.g., skin conductance response, SCR) as indices of learning. In contrast, EC studies generally make use of evaluative ratings as dependent variables. Thus, it could be speculated that physiological reactions are indeed subject to extinction while subjective evaluative responses are not. This idea was recently put to test by Vansteenwegen, Francken, Vervliet, De Clercq, and Eelen (2006). In these studies, participants underwent a conditioning procedure in which human pictures served as CSs and shocks as USs. In a departure from previous studies, however, the authors assessed not only physiological reactions such as skin conductance response (SCR) but also evaluation measures (affective priming) before and after extinction. Interestingly, they found a decrease in physiological reactions due to extinction but a stable reaction when affective attitudes were tested. Thus, the often mentioned discrepancy in sensitivity to extinction between EC and other forms of conditioning may at least be partly attributed to the different dependent measures used in both paradigms.

WHAT IS LEARNED? ADDRESSING THE MECHANISMS UNDERLYING EC WITH THE US-REVALUATION PARADIGM

Although EC has been investigated for almost 30 years now, the processes underlying evaluative learning are still not sufficiently well understood (De Houwer et al., 2001). Specifically, it is not clear whether EC represents an instance of stimulus-response (S-R) or an instance of stimulus-stimulus (S-S) learning. There seem to be two possible effects of the repeated co-occurrence of CS and US during conditioning. The first, which is in line with Pavlov's (1927) original notion of associative learning, assumes the development of a connection between the CS and the US at the response level. According to this account, the CS acquires its own response that mimics the conditioned response (CR) elicited by the US (S-R learning). The second possibility assumes that EC leads to a mental connection between the cognitive representations of the CS and the US. Thus, exposure to the CS after conditioning will activate the representation of the US, which in turn activates its corresponding response (S-S learning).

The US-revaluation paradigm provides a straightforward test of these two possibilities. US-revaluation indicates that postconditional changes in the valence of a US lead to corresponding changes in the valence of preassociated conditioned stimuli (CS). For instance, Walther et al. (2007) postconditionally presented positive USs with negative statements (e.g., "often makes jokes at the expense of other colleagues") and negative USs with positive phrases (e.g., "is always there for colleagues when they need help"). Subsequently, participants had to judge the likeability of the USs as well as the CSs. The revaluation procedure not only led to a reversal in the valence of the US, but also to a change of the affective quality of the CS in the direction of the revaluated US. Most important, this effect occurred even though the CS had never been paired with the revaluating behavioral information. In other words, changing the attitude toward a given object (US) led to corresponding changes in attitudes toward other stimuli that were merely associated with that object (CS). The implications of these results for EC theory are clear: Whereas S-R learning implies that responses to the CS should be unaffected by US revaluation, S-S learning implies that responses to the CS should reflect the new valence of revaluated US. The present data strongly supports the idea of S-S, rather than S-R, learning in the EC paradigm.

Another theoretically important issue in the EC literature is the question of whether the CS is associated merely with the valence of the US, or whether the CS is associated with a nominal stimulus consisting of additional features other than valence. If individuals are merely storing the valence of the US, the correct US should not be distinguishable from a stimulus of the same valence in a postconditional awareness test (Baeyens et al., 1993; Baeyens, Eelen, Crombez, & van den Bergh, 1992; Field, 2000; Fulcher & Hammerl, 2001). However, if the nominal stimulus is encoded, participants in a postconditional awareness test should be able to distinguish the US presented in the study from a distractor stimulus of the same valence that was not presented in the study. Consistent with previous work (Walther & Nagengast, 2006), the studies conducted by Walther et al. (2007) supported the notion that nominal stimuli are indeed connected with the CS. If CSs were not connected to a particular US, revaluation of the US left CS evaluations unaffected.

Beyond its theoretical significance for EC research, the US-revaluation effect has important implications for attitude change in social and applied settings. If the spreading attitude effect (Walther, 2002) already implies a lack of control over attitude formation processes in the social world, this is even more true for US-revaluation. An association with positively evaluated individuals, such as highly respected experts or admired celebrities, should have a positive impact on one's own image only as long as a positive evaluation of the associated other persists. If the associated individual loses his or her prestige, this slip may also affect one's own reputation. Thus, basking in the reflective glory of highly respected individuals (Cialdini & De Nicholas, 1989) may be a risky strategy when the positive evaluation of these individuals is fragile.

Similar consequences pertain to advertising. To create positive evaluations of products, a common strategy among advertisers is to present brands and products (e.g., AOL, Nike) along with well-known individuals, a strategy called celebrity endorsement. Many examples—including those of Boris Becker who cheated on his wife, or Kobe Bryant who was charged with sexually assaulting a hotel worker—suggest that this advertising strategy can be quite risky. Within the logic of the US-revaluation effect, the loss of the celebrity's positive public image due to socially undesirable behavior can have negative consequences for associated brands and products.

Finally and most important, the US-revaluation effect has important implications for the debate of whether attitudes can be formed and changed by merely affective cues. The US-revaluation effect suggests that not only attitude formation, but also attitude change, can be explained by the association of an attitudinal object with simple affective stimuli. In contrast to other models of attitude change that assume a high degree of cognitive activity, attitude change through revaluation is subtle, simple, and does not demand cognitive elaboration.

US-revaluation has also implications for contemporary models of persuasion, such as the Elaboration Likelihood Model (ELM, Petty & Cacioppo, 1986), the Heuristic-Systematic Model (HSM, Chaiken, Liberman, & Eagly, 1989), and the Unimodel (UM, Kruglanski & Thompson, 1999). Notwithstanding some fundamental differences, all of these models focus primarily on attitude changes resulting from direct links between evaluative information and an attitude object. The US-revaluation effect expands on these theories by indicating that peripheral cues, such as source attractiveness, may influence attitudes even when the original message is not available anymore. If an originally likeable source acquires a negative valence, this change in source valence can affect attitudes toward the object without any additional contact to the original message. This perspective suggests that contemporary models of persuasion can be expanded by considering the effects of the associative representation of evaluative information in memory (Gawronski & Bodenhausen, 2006). Future studies combining the general findings of evaluative conditioning and persuasion research may provide an important step in this direction.

DIRECTIONS FOR FUTURE RESEARCH: PROCESSES, PREFERENCES AND INFERENCES

Given the empirical differences between EC and CC with respect to awareness, extinction, and dependency on contingency, it appears that two different learning principles may be at work in these paradigms. With respect to recent developments in the attitude domain, one might conclude that EC represents an example of implicit learning, and CC an example of explicit learning (see Devos, this volume). Consistent with the contemporary distinction between associative vs. propositional models (Gawronski & Bodenhausen, 2006), the empirical differences between EC and CC suggest the application of dual-process models (see also Kruglanski & Dechesne, 2006). This perspective is supported by the finding that EC decreases under awareness but CC apparently benefits from conscious awareness. Further support for this view comes from Olson and Fazio (2001) who successfully used an implicit learning paradigm to induce conditioned attitudes (see Olson, this volume). However, in both domains there are findings that contradict the dual-process perspective. For instance, Schienle, Schäfer, Walter, Stark, and Vaitl (2005) found that disgust was conditioned in phobic individuals only when people were aware of the contingencies. There also is evidence that CC conditioning occurs without awareness under certain conditions (Öhman, Esteves, & Soares, 1995; Öhman & Soares, 1998; Schell, Dawson, & Marinkovic, 1991). However, the question remains as to what actually constitutes the differences between EC and CC on an empirical level. Schienle et al. (2005) called their study an EC experiment; however, the fact that they (1) presented strong aversive USs; (2) for a very long time interval (8.5 sec); and (3) assessed physiological measurements raises the question whether or not this study would be more appropriately categorized as an instance of CC.

Is the distinction of implicit and explicit attitudes helpful here? On the one hand, this distinction refers to the acquisition of attitudes. Indeed in most experimental settings of EC the learning context is more implicit than in CC studies. That is, in EC studies participants are not instructed that they should acquire an attitude, they are shown fewer and more briefly presented USs and CSs, and the affective intensity is much lower than in the typical CC study. In EC, mild aversive and appetitive USs, such as pictures of human faces are used, whereas CC studies apply shock, or strong aversive pictures, such as the IAPS (Tracy, McFall, & Steinmetz, 2005), to their participants. However, the question remains whether these differences constitute a qualitative or simply a quantitative difference in the processes underlying these paradigms. On the other hand, the terms *explicit* and *implicit* refer to measurements used to assess attitudes. EC effects have been found in a wide array of implicit and explicit attitude measurements. In most cases a strong correlation has been obtained between direct and indirect assessments of attitudes in this domain (Olson & Fazio, 2001; Walther et al., 2007). However, with the exception of the research of Vansteenwegen et al. (2006), no other study assessed classical conditioned responses by means of implicit measures.

In the present chapter, we have summarized empirical evidence that attitudes can be formed and changed through EC mechanisms. This challenges cognitive attitude accounts, which assume that beliefs are the core concepts in the attitudinal process. Moreover, we argued that EC is involved in many social, clinical, and applied phenomena that are usually explained by other cognitive or motivational mechanisms. However, it also should be noted that mechanisms underlying EC are not yet well understood. For instance, it is not clear whether EC and CC refer to similar or different processes. One conclusion, shared by many EC researchers, is that EC is a form of implicit learning and CC a form of explicit learning (Olson & Fazio, 2001, 2006).

However, all these conclusions may be premature with respect to one point: it is often overlooked that despite the differences in the paradigms, the basic parameters are similar in both accounts. Thus, in both kinds of learning, evaluative responses are elicited by environmental stimuli that can be expressed in terms of (dis-)liking. In a more integral perspective, therefore, it could be assumed that EC and CC refer to the same mechanism, whereby EC is the more basic effect, instigated by the mere co-occurrence of affective cues, and not dependent on awareness. However, with increasing numbers of trials, US intensity, and presentation intervals, cognitive aspects become more and more involved in the process that may result in awareness of the contingencies. A first step to establish this one-model perspective (vs. a dual-process orientation) would be to settle on a binding learning paradigm in which the relevant parameters are varied. However, despite these questions and remaining issues, we believe in the theoretical potential of EC to explain socially relevant phenomena. In summarizing the major advantages of the EC paradigm, one must mention its simplicity on the one hand and its scope on the other. Moreover, EC highlights the affective nature of attitude formation processes (Zajonc, 1980). Applying the EC logic to social psychology is fruitful because the affective and cognitive domains complement each other superbly. Taking EC into account contributes to our understanding of attitude formation driven by basic learning mechanisms that often receive little attention in social psychology and that are not covered by other current theories. Conversely, applying EC to the social area speaks to the boundary conditions of so called primitive learning principles and therefore stimulates theory formation in this area.

NOTE

1. The terms *classical conditioning* (CC), *Pavlovian conditioning* (PC), and *signal learning* will be used interchangeably throughout the chapter.

REFERENCES

Ajzen, I. (1991). The theory of planned behavior. *Organizational Behavior and Human Decision Processes, 50,* 179–211.

Ajzen, I., & Fishbein, M. (1980). *Understanding attitudes and predicting social behavior.* Englewood Cliffs, NJ: Prentice Hall.

Allen, C. T., & Janiszewski, C. A. (1989). Assessing the role of contingency awareness in attitudinal conditioning with implications for advertising research. *Journal of Marketing and Research, 26,* 30–43.

Amundson, J. C., Escobar, M., & Miller, R. (2003). Proactive interference between cues trained with a common outcome in first-order Pavlovian conditioning. *Journal of Experimental Psychology: Animal Behavior Processes, 29,* 311–322.

Baeyens, F., Crombez, G., & Hendrickx, H. (1995). Parameters of human evaluative flavor-flavor conditioning. *Learning and Motivation, 26,* 141–160.

Baeyens, F., Crombez, G., van den Bergh, O., & Eelen, P. (1988). Once in contact always in contact: Evaluative conditioning is resistant to extinction. *Advances in Behaviour Research and Therapy, 10,* 179–199.

Baeyens, F., Eelen, P., Crombez, G., & van den Bergh, O. (1992). Human evaluative conditioning: Acquisition trials, presentation schedule, evaluative style and contingency awareness. *Behavior Research and Therapy, 30,* 133–142.

Baeyens, F., Eelen, P., van den Bergh, O., & Crombez, G. (1989). Acquired affective-evaluative value. Conservative but not unchangeable. *Behaviour Research and Therapy, 27,* 279–287.

Baeyens, F., Eelen, P., & van den Bergh, O. (1990). Contingency awareness in evaluative conditioning: A case for unaware affective-evaluative learning. *Cognition and Emotion, 4,* 3–18.

Baeyens, F., Eelen, P., van den Bergh, O., & Crombez, G. (1992). The content of learning in human evaluative conditioning: Acquired valence is sensitive to US revaluation. *Learning and Motivation, 23,* 200–224.

Baeyens, F., Hermans, R., & Eelen, P. (1993). The role of CS-US contingency in human evaluative conditioning. *Behaviour Research and Therapy, 31,* 73–737.

Bakker-DePree, B. J., Defares, P. B., & Zwaan, E. J. (1970). The conditioning of evaluative meaning. *Acta Psychologica, 32,* 281–289.

Barnet, R. C., Grahame, N. J., & Miller, R. E. (1991). Comparing the magnitude of second-order conditioning and sensory preconditioning effects. *Bulletin of the Psychonomic Society, 29,* 133–135.

Barone, M. J., Miniard, P. W., & Romeo, J. B. (2000). The influence of positive mood on brand extension evaluations. *Journal of Consumer Research, 26,* 386–400.

Beggan, J. K. (1992). On the social nature of nonsocial perception: The mere ownership effect. *Journal of Personality and Social Psychology, 62,* 229–237.

Bierley, C., McSweeney, F. K., & Vannieuwkerk, R. (1985). Classical conditioning of preferences for stimuli. *Journal of Consumer Research, 12,* 316–323.

Boulding, W., Morgan, R., & Staelin, R. (1997). Pulling the plug to stop the new product drain. *Journal of Marketing Research, 34,* 164–176.

Bouton, M. (2000). A learning theory perspective on lapse, relapse, and the maintenance of behavior change. *Health Psychology, 19,* 57–63.

Bouton, M. (2002). Context, ambiguity, and unlearning: Sources of relapse after behavioral extinction. *Biological Psychiatry, 52,* 976–986.

Bower, G. H. (1981). Mood and memory. *American Psychologist, 36,* 129–148.

Brewer, W. F. (1974). There is no convincing evidence for operant or classical conditioning in adult humans. In W. B. Weimer & D. S. Palermo (Eds.), *Cognition and the symbolic process* (pp. 1–42). Oxford, UK: Erlbaum.

Brooks, D. C., Hale, B., Nelson, J. B., & Bouton, M. (1995). Reinstatement after counterconditioning. *Animal Learning and Behavior, 23,* 383–390.

Cadinu, M. R., & Rothbart, M. (1996). Self-anchoring and differentiation processes in the minimal group setting. *Journal of Personality and Social Psychology, 70,* 661–677.

Chaiken, S., Liberman, A., & Eagly, A. H. (1989). Heuristic and systematic processing within and beyond the persuasion context. In J. S. Uleman & J. A. Bargh (Eds.), *Unintended thought* (pp. 212–252). New York: Guilford.

Cialdini, R. B., & De Nicholas, M. E. (1989). Self-presentation by association. *Journal of Personality and Social Psychology, 57,* 626–631.

Clement, R. W., & Krueger, J. (2002). Social categorization moderates social projection. *Journal of Experimental Social Psychology, 38,* 219–231.

Dawson, M. E. (1973). Can classical conditioning occur without contingency learning? A review and evaluation of the evidence. *Psychophysiology, 10,* 82–86.

Dawson, M. E., & Reardon, P. (1973). Construct validity of recall and recognition postconditioning measures of awareness. *Journal of Experimental Psychology, 98*, 308–315.

Dawson, M. E., & Schell, A. (1987). Human autonomic and skeletal classical conditioning: The role of conscious cognitive factors. In G. Davey (Ed.), *Cognitive processes and Pavlovian conditioning in humans* (pp.27–55). Chichester, UK: Wiley.

De Houwer, J., Baeyens, F., & Eelen, P. (1994). Verbal evaluative conditioning with undetected US presentations. *Behaviour Research and Therapy, 32*, 629–633.

De Houwer, J., Baeyens, F., Vansteenwegen, D., & Eelen, P. (2000). Evaluative conditioning in the picture-picture paradigm with random assignment of conditioned to unconditioned stimuli. *Journal of Experimental Psychology: Animal Behavior Processes, 26*, 237–242.

De Houwer, J., Hendrickx, H., & Baeyens, F. (1997). Evaluative learning with "subliminally" presented stimuli. *Consciousness and Cognition, 6*, 87–107.

De Houwer, J., Thomas, S., & Baeyens, F. (2001). Associative learning of likes and dislikes: A review of 25 years of research on human evaluative conditioning. *Psychological Bulletin, 127*, 853–869.

De Jong, P. J., Vorage, I., & van den Hout, M. A. (2000). Counterconditioning in the treatment of spider phobia: effects on disgust, fear and valence. *Behaviour Research and Therapy, 38*, 1055–1069.

Delamater, A. R., & Lolordo, V. M. (1991). Event revaluation procedures and associative structures in Pavlovian conditioning. In L. Dachowski & C. Flaherty, *Current topics in animal learning: brain, emotion, and cognition* (pp.55–94). Hillsdale, NJ: Erlbaum.

Dijksterhuis, A. (2004). I like myself but I don't know why: Enhancing implicit self-esteem by subliminal evaluative conditioning. *Journal of Personality and Social Psychology, 86*, 345–355.

Eagly, A. H., & Chaiken, S. (1993). *The psychology of attitudes.* Fort Worth, TX: Harcourt Brace Jovanovich.

Eifert, G. H., Craill, L., Carey, E., & O'Connor, C. (1988). Affect modification through evaluative conditioning with music. *Behaviour Research and Therapy, 26*, 321–330.

Fazio, R. H. (1990). Multiple processes by which attitudes guide behavior: The MODE model as an integrative framework. In M. Zanna (Ed.), *Advances in experimental social psychology* (Vol. 23, pp. 75–109). San Diego, CA: Academic Press.

Feys, J. (1991). Briefly induced belongingness to self and preference. *European Journal of Social Psychology, 21*, 547–552.

Feys, J. (1995). Mere ownership: Affective self-bias or evaluative conditioning? *European Journal of Social Psychology, 25*, 559–575.

Field, A. P. (2000). Evaluative conditioning is Pavlovian conditioning: Issues of definition, measurement, and the theoretical importance of contingency awareness. *Consciousness & Cognition, 9*, 41–49.

Field, A. P. (2001). When all is still concealed: Are we closer to understanding the mechanisms underlying evaluative conditioning? *Consciousness and Cognition, 10*, 559–566.

Field, A. P., & Moore, A. C. (2005). Dissociating the effects of attention and contingency awareness on evaluative conditioning effects in the visual paradigm. *Cognition and Emotion, 19*, 217–243.

Fishbein, M., & Ajzen, I. (1975). *Belief, attitude, intention, and behavior.* Reading, MA: Addison-Wesley.

Fishbein, M., & Middlestadt, S. (1995). Noncognitive effects on attitude formation and change: Fact or artifact? *Journal of Consumer Psychology, 4*, 181–202.

Flaherty, K. E., & Pappas, J. M. (2000). Implicit personality theory in evaluation of brand extensions. *Psychological Reports, 86*, 807–818.

Fulcher, E. P., & Cocks, P. (1997). Dissociative storage systems in human evaluative conditioning. *Behaviour Research and Therapy, 35*, 1–10.

Fulcher, E. P., & Hammerl, M. (2001). When all is considered: Evaluative learning does not require contingency awareness. *Consciousness and Cognition, 10*, 567–573.

Gawronski, B., & Bodenhausen, G. V. (2006). Associative and propositional processes in evaluation: An integrative review of implicit and explicit attitude change. *Psychological Bulletin, 132*, 692–731.

Gawronski, B., Walther, E., & Blank, H. (2005). Cognitive consistency and the formation of interpersonal attitudes: Cognitive balance affects the encoding of social information. *Journal of Experimental Social Psychology, 41*, 618–626.

Ghuman, A. S., & Bar, M. (2006). The influence of nonremembered affective associations on preference. *Emotion, 6*, 215–223.

Goldfried, M. R., Linehan, M. M., & Smith, J. L. (1978). Reduction of test anxiety through cognitive restructuring. *Journal of Consulting and Clinical Psychology, 46*, 32–39.

Greenwald, A. G. (1968). Cognitive learning, cognitive response to persuasion, and attitude change. In A. G. Greenwald, T. C. Brock, & T. M. Edstrom (Eds.), *Psychological foundations of attitudes* (pp. 147–170). New York: Academic Press.

Greenwald, A. G., & Banaji, M. R. (1995). Implicit social cognition: Attitudes, self-esteem, and stereotypes. *Psychological Review, 102*, 4–27.

Grossman, R. L., & Till, B. D. (1998). The persistence of classically conditioned brand attitudes. *Journal of Advertising, 27*, 23–31.

Hammerl, M. (2000). I like it, but only when I'm not sure why: Evaluative conditioning and the awareness issue. *Consciousness and Cognition, 9*, 37–40.

Hammerl, M., & Grabitz, H.-J. (1996). Human evaluative conditioning without experiencing a valued event. *Learning and Motivation, 27*, 278–293.

Hammerl, M., & Grabitz, H.-J. (2000). Affective-evaluative learning in humans: A form of associative learning or only an artifact? *Learning and Motivation, 31*, 345–363.

Hebl, M. R., & Mannix, L. M. (2003). The weight of obesity in evaluating others: A mere proximity effect. *Personality and Social Psychology Bulletin, 29*, 28–38.

Heider, F. (1958). *The psychology of interpersonal relations.* New York: Wiley.

Hosoba, T., Iwanaga, M., & Seiwa, H. (2001). The effect of UCS inflation and deflation procedures on fear conditioning. *Behaviour Research and Therapy, 39*, 465–475.

Ito, T. A., Chiao, K. W., Devine, P. G., Lorig, T. S., & Cacioppo, T. (2006). The influence of facial feedback on race bias. *Psychological Science, 17*, 256–261.

Jennings, D., & Kirkpatrick, K. (2006). Interval duration effects on blocking in appetitive conditioning. *Behavioural Processes, 71*, 318–329.

Kearney, A. B. (1993). The use of covert conditioning in the treatment of obsessive compulsive disorder. In J. R. Cautela & A. J. Kearney (Eds.), *Covert conditioning casebook* (pp. 22–37). Belmont, CA: Brooks/Cole.

Koole, S. L., Dijksterhuis, A., & van Knippenberg, A. (2001). What's in a name: Implicit self-esteem and the automatic self. *Journal of Personality and Social Psychology, 80*, 669–685.

Krosnick, J. A., Betz, A. L., Jussim, L. L., & Lynn, A. R. (1992). Subliminal conditioning of attitudes. *Personality and Social Psychology Bulletin, 18*, 152–162.

Krueger, J. (2000). The projective perception of the social world: A building block of social comparison processes. In J. Suls & L. Wheeler (Eds.), *Handbook of social comparison: Theory and research* (pp. 323–351). Dordrecht, Netherlands: Kluwer.

Kruglanski, A. W., & Dechesne, M. (2006). Are associative and propositional processes qualitatively distinct? Comment on Gawronski and Bodenhausen. *Psychological Bulletin, 132*, 736–739.

Kruglanski, A. W., & Thompson, E. P. (1999). Persuasion by a single route: A view from the unimodel. *Psychological Inquiry, 10*, 83–109.

Lane, V. R. (2000). The impact of ad repetition and ad content on consumer perceptions of incongruent extensions. *Journal of Marketing, 64,* 80–91.

Lazarus, A. A. (1974). Desensitization and cognitive restructuring. *Psychotherapy: Theory, Research & Practice, 11,* 98–102.

Lazarus, R. S. (1984). On the primacy of cognition. *American Psychologist, 39,* 124–129.

Lovibond, P. F., & Shanks, D. R. (2002). The role of awareness in Pavlovian conditioning: Empirical evidence and theoretical implications. *Journal of Experimental Psychology: Animal Behavior Processes, 28,* 3–26.

Manis, M., Cornell, S. D., Moore, J. C., & Jeffrey, C. (1974). Transmission of attitude relevant information through a communication chain. *Journal of Personality and Social Psychology, 30,* 81–94.

Martin, I., & Levey, A. B. (1978). Evaluative conditioning. *Advances in Behaviour Research and Therapy, 1,* 57–101.

Martin, I., & Levey, A. B. (1987). Learning what will happen next: Conditioning, evaluation, and cognitive processes. In G. Davey (Ed.), *Cognitive processes and Pavlovian conditioning in humans* (pp. 57–81). Chichester, UK: Wiley.

Matthews, L., & Litwack, L. (1995). Cognitive restructuring. In M. Ballou (Ed.), *Psychological interventions: A practical guide to strategies* (pp. 37–53). Westport, CT: Praeger.

Niedenthal, P. M. (1990). Implicit perception of affective information. *Journal of Experimental Social Psychology, 26,* 505–527.

Nuttin, J. M. (1985). Narcissism beyond Gestalt and awareness: The name letter effect. *European Journal of Social Psychology, 15,* 353–361.

Öhman, A., Esteves, F., & Soares, J. J. F. (1995). Preparedness and preattentive associative learning: Electrodermal conditioning to masked stimuli. *Journal of Psychophysiology, 9,* 99–108.

Öhman, A., & Soares, J. J. F. (1998). Emotional conditioning to masked stimuli: Expectancies for aversive outcomes following nonrecognized fear-relevant stimuli. *Journal of Experimental Psychology: General, 127,* 69–82.

Olson, M. A., & Fazio, R. H. (2001). Implicit attitude formation through classical conditioning. *Psychological Science, 12,* 413–417.

Olson, M. A., & Fazio, R. H. (2002). Implicit acquisition and manifestation of classically conditioned attitudes. *Social Cognition, 20,* 89–104.

Olson, M. A., & Fazio, R. H. (2006). Reducing automatically activated racial prejudice through implicit evaluative conditioning. *Personality and Social Psychology Bulletin, 32,* 421–433.

Otten, S., & Wentura, D. (1999). About the impact of automaticity in the Minimal Group Paradigm: Evidence from affective priming tasks. *European Journal of Social Psychology, 29,* 1049–1071.

Otten, S., & Wentura, D. (2001). Self-anchoring and in-group favoritism: An individual profiles analysis. *Journal of Experimental Social Psychology, 37,* 525–532.

Paunovic, N. (2003). Prolonged exposure counterconditioning as a treatment for chronic posttraumatic stress disorder. *Journal of Anxiety Disorders, 17,* 479–499.

Pavlov, I. P. (1927). *Conditioned reflexes.* New York: Oxford University Press.

Pelham, B. W., Mirenberg, M. C., & Jones, J. T. (2002). Why Susie sells seashells by the seashore: Implicit egotism and major life decisions. *Journal of Personality and Social Psychology, 82,* 469–487.

Perdue, C. W., Dovidio, J. F., & Gurtman, M. B. (1990). Us and them: Social categorization and the process of intergroup bias. *Journal of Personality and Social Psychology, 59,* 475–486.

Petty, R. E., & Cacioppo, J. T. (1984). The effects of involvement on responses to argument quantity and quality: Central and peripheral routes to persuasion. *Journal of Personality and Social Psychology, 46,* 69–81.

Petty, R. E., & Cacioppo, J. T. (1986). The Elaboration Likelihood Model of persuasion. In L. Berkowitz (Ed.), *Advances in experimental social psychology* (Vol. 19, pp. 123–205). New York: Academic Press.

Petty, R. E., Cacioppo, J. T., & Goldman, R. (1981). Personal involvement as a determinant of argument-based persuasion. *Journal of Personality and Social Psychology, 41,* 847–855.

Pleyers, G., Corneille, O., Luminet, O., & Yzerbyt, V. (2007). Aware and (dis)liking: Item-based analyses reveal that valence acquisition via evaluative conditioning emerges only when there is contingency awareness. *Journal of Experimental Psychology: Learning, Memory and Cognition, 33,* 130–144.

Rachman, S. (1985). The treatment of anxiety disorders: A critique of the implications for psychopathology. In A. H. Tuma & J. D. Maser (Eds.), *Anxiety and the anxiety disorders* (pp. 453–461). Hillsdale, NJ: Erlbaum.

Rescorla, R. A., & Wagner, A. R. (1972). A theory of Pavlovian conditioning: Variations in the effectiveness of reinforcement and nonreinforcement. In A. H. Black & W. F. Prokasy (Eds.), *Classical conditioning: Vol.2. Current research and theory* (pp. 64–99). New York: Appleton.

Richardson, R., Riccio, D. C., & Smoller, D. (1987). Counterconditioning of memory in rats. *Animal Learning and Behavior, 15,* 321–326.

Rizley, R. C., & Rescorla, R. A. (1972). Associations in second-order conditioning and sensory preconditioning. *Journal of Comparative and Physiological Psychology, 81,* 1–11.

Schell, A. M., Dawson, M. E., & Marinkovic, K. (1991). Effects of potentially phobic conditioned stimuli on retention, reconditioning, and extinction of the conditioned skin conductance response.*Psychophysiology, 28,* 140–153.

Schienle, A., Schaefer, A., Walter, B., Stark, R., & Vaitl, D. (2005). Elevated disgust sensitivity in blood phobia. *Cognition and Emotion, 19,* 1229–1241.

Sherman, D. K., & Kim, H. S. (2002). Affective perseverance: The resistance of affect to cognitive invalidation. Personality and *Social Psychology Bulletin, 28,* 224–237.

Shimp, T. A., Stuart, E. W., & Engle, R. W. (1991). A program of classical conditioning experiments testing variations in the conditioned stimulus and context. *Journal of Consumer Research, 18,* 1–12.

Skowronski, J. J., Carlston, D. E., Mae, L., & Crawford, M. T. (1998). Spontaneous trait transference: Communicators take on the qualities they describe in others. *Journal of Personality and Social Psychology, 74,* 837–848.

Stapel, D. A., & Koomen, W. (2000). Distinctiveness of others, mutability of selves: Their impact on self-evaluations. *Journal of Personality and Social Psychology, 79,* 1068–1087.

Tajfel, H., Billig, M. G., Bundy, R. P., & Flament, C. (1971). Social categorization and intergroup behaviour. *European Journal of Social Psychology, 1,* 149–178.

Till, B. D., & Priluck, R. L. (2000). Stimulus generalization in classical conditioning: An initial investigation and extension. *Psychology and Marketing, 17,* 55–72.

Todrank, J., Byrnes, D., Wrzesniewski, A., & Rozin, P. (1995). Odors can change preferences for people in photographs: A cross-modal evaluative conditioning study with olfactory USs and visual CSs. *Learning & Motivation, 26,* 116–140.

Tracy, J., McFall, R. M., & Steinmetz, J. E. (2005). Effects of emotional valence and arousal manipulation on eyeblink classical conditioning and autonomic measures. *Integrative Physiological and Behavioral Science, 40,* 45–54.

Van Reekum, C., van den Berg, H., & Frijda, N. H. (1999). Cross-modal preference acquisition: Evaluative conditioning of pictures by affective olfactory and auditory cues. *Cognition and Emotion, 13*, 831–836.

Vansteenwegen, D., Francken, G., Vervliet, B., De Clercq, A., & Eelen, P. (2006). Resistance to extinction in evaluative conditioning. *Journal of Experimental Psychology: Animal Behavior Processes.*

Walther, E. (2002). Guilty by mere association: Evaluative conditioning and the spreading attitude effect. *Journal of Personality and Social Psychology, 82*, 919–934.

Walther, E., Gawronski, B., Blank, H., & Langer, T. (2007). Chaning likes and dislikes through the back door: The US-revaluation effect. Paper submitted for publication.

Walther, E., & Grigoriadis, S. (2004). Why sad people like shoes better: The influence of mood on the evaluative conditioning of consumer attitudes. *Psychology and Marketing, 21*, 755–773.

Walther, E., & Nagengast, B. (2006). Evaluative conditioning and the awareness issue: Assessing contingency awareness with the four-picture recognition test. *Journal of Experimental Psychology: Animal Behavior Processes, 32*, 454–459.

Walther, E., Nagengast, B., & Trasselli, C. (2005). Evaluative conditioning in social psychology: Facts and speculations. *Cognition and Emotion, 19*, 175–196.

Walther, E., & Trasselli, C. (2003). I like her, because I like myself: Self-evaluation as a source of interpersonal attitudes. *Experimental Psychology, 50*, 239–246.

Zajonc, B. (1980). On the primacy of affect. *American Psychologist, 39*, 117–123.

Zellner, D. A., Rozin, P., Aron, M., & Kulish, C. (1983). Conditioned enhancement of human's liking for flavor by pairing with sweetness. *Learning and Motivation, 26*, 141–160.

6

Origins of Attitudes

MICHAEL A. OLSON
RICHARD V. KENDRICK
University of Tennessee

*A*ttitudes encapsulate positive and negative feelings, beliefs, and behavioral information about all ranges of "attitude objects," from people to frozen pizza. In other words, they conveniently summarize how we feel about pretty much everything (Zanna & Rempel, 1988). Good or bad, friend or foe, before we know much about a new acquaintance, car, politician, pair of shoes, or grocery item, we tend to arrive at a decision as to whether we like or dislike them. It is the very "summary" nature of attitudes that make them so efficient, flexible, and adaptive (Eagly & Chaiken, 1993; Fazio, 2000). Because they are "precomputed" evaluations, attitudes allow us to navigate a bewilderingly complex world without having to stop and figure out from scratch, every time, whether we should get to know that new person a little better, vote for a certain politician, or buy a certain food. People could not survive without attitudes, and psychologists could not paint a full picture of human behavior without them. Given the importance of attitudes in predicting and explaining human behavior, a critical question arises: Where do they come from?

The question of the origins of attitudes is a long-standing one, not only in psychology (e.g., Allport, 1935), but in philosophy and religion as well. For example, do we naturally dislike people unlike ourselves, or are we carefully taught to hate? If our values, tastes, and opinions come from our parents, peers, and society, how do we learn them? Do we consciously choose, as it just happens to be, to have similar political attitudes as our parents, or are we "implicitly" socialized to be like them? When it comes to products and other possessions, do we deliberately consider the pros and cons of buying one car over another, or are we swayed by "superficial" features like celebrity endorsements?

These are the sorts of fascinating questions that arise in psychological research on the origins of attitudes. The question has been tackled from a variety of perspectives, with a variety of answers emerging from years of research (Eagly &

Chaiken, 1993). This diversity stems largely from the simple fact that there are multiple means by which one can come to have an attitude. I might, for example, like my Volvo because it is fun to drive and is turbo-equipped, but my wife may base her attitude on its safety features. These two bases of attitudes, the first more "emotional" and the second more "rational," comprise a major distinction researchers have made regarding the sources of our attitudes. That is, sometimes attitudes form on the basis of emotion or affect, and other times they form on the basis of beliefs or cognition. A third basis of attitudes consists of our past behavior, and as we shall see, it is indeed the case that sometimes it is our behaviors that precede our attitudes, not the other way around. The "ABCs" of attitudes (affect, cognition, and behavior), often referred to as the "tripartite" approach, serve to organize research on attitude formation, and most theories of attitude formation distinguish between these three sources (Zanna & Rempel, 1988).

However, the tripartite model provides just one means of carving up attitude formation research. As we shall elaborate later, attitudes also can be formed through "implicit" or unconscious processes, versus more "explicit" or conscious ones (Rudman, 2004). Moreover, research suggests that some attitudes can have an unlearned or inherited component (e.g., Tesser, 1993), and further research indicates that some of our attitudes might have resulted from humans' evolutionary past (Buss, 1989). The possibility that some attitudes are unlearned unleashes the "nature versus nurture" debate, but the question of whether we are born with the tendency to have positive or negative evaluations toward certain objects is one worthy of debate.

In this chapter, we describe how it is that attitudes form; that is, what processes lead to the development of attitudes. We also consider the question, not of how attitudes *can* form, but how they *do* form, via parental, peer, and social forces, in the real world. Consistent with what we might call the "grand theme" of social psychology, we will see that we are very much products of the situations in which we find ourselves.

TRIPARTITE MODEL

We can infer a person's attitude toward safe sex by determining the beliefs they have concerning safe sex, the feelings they experience toward safe sex, and whether or not they engage in practices of safe sex. Say for instance that I hold positive beliefs about how safe sex can prevent the spread of sexually transmitted diseases, as well as positive affect toward the practice of safe sex. In addition, I observe that I engage in safe sex practices. From these three pieces of information, an overall picture of my attitude toward safe sex can be derived. An attitude is typically seen as a summary of the three aspects described above (Zanna & Rempel, 1988). It is a common assumption that the affective component of an attitude is the end product, but how we feel about an object is merely one component of the attitude that combines with our cognitions and behaviors to yield an overall attitude. Also, these components need not be consistent with one another (Zanna & Rempel, 1988). The three-component or tripartite view has served as the framework from which the study of attitudes has progressed, and we shall continue this tradition by examining how these three components of attitudes help us understand how attitudes form.

We will consider attitude formation processes by examining how attitudes form from beliefs about objects, feelings toward objects, and actions directed at the objects (for a review, see Eagly & Chaiken, 1993). An attitude toward safe sex practices can develop by acquiring certain beliefs about safe sex and these cognitions can determine how one later evaluates the practice of safe sex. Also, certain emotions can become associated with safe sex, and these feelings also may determine how one evaluates safe sex. Lastly, an attitude toward safe sex may be derived from observations of past behaviors. That is, practicing (or not practicing) safe sex in the past may influence one's overall attitude concerning safe sex.

COGNITIVE ORIGINS

I may come to evaluate a particular object favorably through acquiring positive beliefs or thoughts about the object. If, for example, I read information discussing the health risks of unprotected sex, I may develop beliefs that safe sex protects against a variety of negative outcomes (e.g., AIDS, unwanted pregnancy). Attitudes develop through this thoughtful, "rational" route by creating cognitions that address whether an attitude object leads to favorable or unfavorable outcomes or possesses desirable or undesirable attributes.

Fishbein and Ajzen's (1975) expectancy-value model provides one of the best-known frameworks from which to understand the cognitive origins of attitudes (see Ajzen & Gilbert Cote, this volume). Deriving attitudes from beliefs regarding an object requires making judgments about the information associated with the object and applying this information when making an evaluation. The expectancy-value model describes the process by which we take information about an object (the "I Know" or "I Think" aspects) and use it to decide how to evaluate it. The model posits that an attitude is a function of one's beliefs and that these beliefs are a product of the expectancy and value attached to each of the perceived attributes of the attitude object. The expectancy is the perceived likelihood that the attribute will occur, and the value represents one's evaluation of the attribute. For example, in forming an attitude toward safe sex, I might think of various attributes of safe sex, determine how (un)favorable I find each attribute, and then assess the probability that each will occur. I might think that safe sex will help to prevent the transmission of an STD and that this outcome is good (value) and likely (expectancy) if safe sex is practiced. According to the model, each attribute is associated with a value and an expectancy. These are then multiplied, and the products are summed across all relevant attributes, yielding an overall attitude toward the object.

Another model of attitude formation through cognitive processes is information integration theory (Anderson, 1981). This model states that as new information is processed and interpreted, it is integrated with beliefs already held. This integration produces an attitude. Prior to integration, each piece of information undergoes a combinatorial process similar to that in the expectancy-value model.

In this process, each attribute is evaluated with a certain degree of (un)favorability and this evaluation is combined with a weight value reflecting the importance of the attribute in forming the attitude. Once we determine how we think about the various aspects of an attitude object and how important each is in determining the attitude, they can then be integrated with current attitudes and beliefs to form new attitudes. For example, I may find that practicing safe sex prevents the transmission of HIV, a favorable outcome, which is an important aspect of my attitude toward safe sex. Therefore, it will heavily influence my final attitude. Conversely, if I believe that safe sex is inconvenient—an outcome that I may find unfavorable but that I don't weigh as heavily—then it will comprise a minor portion of my complete attitude toward safe sex. In summary, according to information integration theory, attitudes can form by perceiving attributes of an object, evaluating them, determining how important these attributes are as contributions to a comprehensive evaluation of the object itself, and lastly, integrating these beliefs in memory.

Another path by which attitudes can form from cognitions about an object is described in McGuire's (1972) reception-yielding model. The model maintains a more descriptive approach to attitude formation in that it describes how perceived information regarding an object's attributes are processed and accepted. It proposes that attitudes form through a two-stage process of receiving information about the attributes of an attitude object (e.g., reading a billboard describing a political candidate's position on abortion issues), and accepting or yielding to the information in terms of what it implies about one's attitude toward the object (e.g., adjusting one's attitude toward the candidate based on the information). Although this model has been primarily applied to attitude change, it can be used to describe how recipients of information about objects perceive attributes and form attitudes based on evaluations of those attributes.

Greenwald's (1968) cognitive response model provides yet another framework to explain how attitudes form through an active thought process. Although this model too has been used primarily in the domain of persuasion, it can provide insight into how attitudes can arise from self-generated thoughts. Among the model's assumptions is that when presented with information about an attitude object, one will actively relate that information to existing knowledge of the object. This process generates thoughts or "cognitive responses" about the attitude object, and the favorability of one's thoughts determines the favorability of one's attitude toward the object. Considering the above example of safe sex practices, when I encounter information about the benefits of condom use, I will produce thoughts about the topic that relate to my existing attitudes and beliefs, and the accumulation of my favorable relative to unfavorable responses will be reflected in a more favorable attitude toward condom use.

Related to the notion that attitudes form via a cognitive process is a group of information processing theories known as dual-process models. Largely relevant for describing attitude change but certainly applicable to attitude formation in instances when no attitude previously exists, the elaboration likelihood model (ELM; Petty & Cacioppo, 1986) and the heuristic-systematic model (HSM; Chaiken & Stangor, 1987) describe how attitudes can form by way of two distinct processes. One involves cognitive processing of an object's attributes via an effortful elaboration of the qualities and characteristics of the given object (which largely resembles Greenwald's cognitive response approach), and the other relies on rather effortless, peripheral processing. Both the ELM and the HSM propose that attitudes form relative to the ability and motivation to engage in cognitive processing of the attributes and to base the evaluation of the object on the beliefs about the attitude object.

AFFECTIVE ORIGINS

Attitudes can form as a result of the emotional responses that we experience when we encounter an attitude object. For example, I may experience some emotional reaction when thinking about the benefits of safe sex practices and this affect will facilitate attitude formation by linking a feeling of positivity or negativity with the object. If I experience fear at the thought of contracting an STD and a feeling of relief at the idea of using condoms during intercourse, I will likely associate my positive feelings with safe sex practices and develop a positive attitude toward safe sex. To address the question about the mechanisms by which affective responses lead to attitude formation, we will consider three processes that lead to affectively derived attitudes: operant conditioning, classical conditioning, and mere exposure.

Operant conditioning, a process by which the frequency of a response is increased following a positive outcome and decreased following a negative outcome, can provide one mechanism for the formation of affectively based attitudes (Hull, 1951; Skinner, 1957). If interaction with the attitude object elicits a positive emotional response, then the evaluation of the attitude object will become more positive and this connection will strengthen, resulting in a positive general attitude. In a study by Hildum and Brown (1956), some students interviewed about their attitudes toward university policies were reinforced by affirmative feedback (i.e., hearing "good" vs. a mere "mm-hmmm" by the interviewer). Students who were reinforced when recalling favorable responses later demonstrated more positive attitudes toward the policies, and those reinforced when recalling negative responses demonstrated more negative attitudes toward the policies, compared to unreinforced participants. Thus, attitudes can be formed by experiencing positive or negative outcomes based on our attitudinal responses, and the more often one's responses are reinforced, the more likely that attitude will manifest itself in the future (Insko, 1965).

Another approach that addresses how attitudes form as learned dispositions is classical conditioning. Classical conditioning, while similar to operant conditioning, does not require that the person respond to an attitude object. Rather, the connection between an object and an eventual affective evaluation can develop by simply observing the pairings between a neutral object (the "conditioned stimuli" or CS) and an already positively or negatively evaluated object (Staats & Staats, 1958). Observing these covariations creates the affectively driven evaluations necessary for an attitude to form. For example, Berkowitz and Knurek (1969) created positive and negative attitudes respectively toward two CS names ("Ed" and

"George") by visually presenting these names to participants on index cards while having them repeat aloud positive and negative adjectives that were paired consistently with either name. Interestingly, these affectively generated attitudes influenced participants' subsequent rating of fictitious characters sharing the names to which they were earlier conditioned. In another study, pairings of various words with the presence (or absence) of electric shock produced evaluatively different attitudes toward those words (Zanna, Kiesler, & Pilkonis, 1970).

Research by Olson and Fazio (2001, 2002) demonstrates that attitudes can form via affective connections between an object and a response to that object without conscious awareness of the connection (Field, 2000). In these experiments, participants were recruited for a study on "attention and rapid responding," where, much like a surveillance guard, their task was to view a continuous stream of words and images on a computer screen in search of prespecified "targets." Their instructions were to ignore the filler words and images, which were purportedly interspersed to make the task more challenging, and press a key as quickly as possible whenever a target randomly appeared. The targets were Pokemon cartoon characters, and the filler items consisted of other Pokemon and a truly arbitrary collection of words (concrete, airplane) and images (an umbrella, fire hydrant, and waffles), sometimes alone and sometimes in pairs. However, on several of the trials, a prespecified Pokemon CS (which was not a target) was consistently presented with nonrepeated positive words and images (e.g., the word *awesome*, a picture of puppies) while another Pokemon CS was consistently paired with negative words and images. Posttests indicated that participants were unaware of these systematic pairings, as their attention was probably directed toward the targets. They underwent several hundred of these trials, with each CS appearing with its paired associates a total of 20 times. Afterwards, they were subjected to a measure of their preference for several of the items from the surveillance task, including the two Pokemon CSs, and were instructed to indicate their "gut" reactions to each. As predicted, participants reported more positive evaluations of the Pokemon paired with positive items than the Pokemon paired with negative items (Olson & Fazio, 2001). Later experiments indicated that this unconscious acquisition of attitudes was apparent on a subliminal priming measure, demonstrating not only that affective associations can form unconsciously, but that they can manifest unconsciously as well (Olson & Fazio, 2002; see also Walther & Langer, this volume).

Research on "mere exposure" also has shown that simply increasing the familiarity of an attitude object can create more positive attitudes toward the object (Zajonc, 1968). In a study that presented Turkish words or Chinese symbols to participants in increasing frequency, Zajonc showed that compared to others who saw the stimuli infrequently, those who observed more repetitions of the words or symbols showed a more favorable attitude toward them. Research has shown that repeated exposure to an object increases "perceptual fluency," whereby we become better at perceiving the object upon subsequent encounters, and this facilitation in perceptibility is in turn interpreted as liking for the object (Reber, Winkielman, & Schwartz, 1998). Thus, the more familiar one is with the attitude object, the more likely one is to have a positive evaluation of it. Similar to the conditioning research described above, mere exposure research outlines the ways through which attitudes can form due to affect alone, without reliance on cognitions regarding an object's attributes.

BEHAVIORAL ORIGINS

Although we can form attitudes by acquiring beliefs about the object or by experiencing some emotional state when encountering it, there are occasions when we may have encountered an object but failed to form attitudes through either of these processes. In situations when we lack either a cognitive or affective basis for an attitude, we can infer an attitude by observing our past behavior toward the object in a process of self-perception (Bem, 1972; Fazio, 1987). When the internal cues that might otherwise normally lead to an attitude are weak, we instead make attributional inferences about our behavior much like they would be done by an outside observer. Consider our earlier example. I may not have any solid beliefs about the benefits of safe sex, nor does the idea of safe sex practices elicit any emotion. However, I may recall that I have engaged in safe sex practices such as condom use, and I therefore conclude that I must have a positive attitude toward safe sex—why else would I have behaved so? This scenario exemplifies how attitudes can have a behavioral genesis whereby they (attitudes) are consistent with our self-perceived actions. For example, Bandler, Madaras, and Bem (1968) exposed participants to electric shock and manipulated whether or not they could escape the shock. The shock administered when participants could and could not escape was identical in strength, but participants rated the shocks from which they escaped to be more painful. These authors concluded that participants observed the act of ending the shock and inferred that their behavior must have been due to the shock being more intense. In another study (Strack, Martin, & Stepper, 1988), participants held pencils in their mouths while viewing cartoons and were asked to rate how funny they felt the cartoons were. Some participants held the pencil with their lips, simulating a frown, while others held it with their teeth, simulating a smile. Participants who exhibited a smile while viewing the cartoons rated them as funnier than those who frowned. Thus, in the absence of an obvious external reason for behavior, we infer an internal one, and this attribution results in a new attitude that is consistent with our actions (Bem, 1967; Linder, Cooper, & Jones, 1967).

Self-perception, and the consequent construal of internal attitudes from our overt behavior, has been shown to have the opposite effect if it is applied when one already possesses an attitude (Deci, 1971). Lepper, Greene, and Nisbett (1973) led preschoolers to engage in an enjoyable activity (drawing with Magic Markers) and promised some children a reward for participating in the activity while providing no reward for other children. When later given the chance to engage in the activity, children given the reward spent only half as much time coloring with the makers as did children who had not been given a reward. Lepper and colleagues explained that children who had played while anticipating a reward must have perceived that they did so because of the reward, whereas the others perceived that they engaged in the behavior because they liked it. Another example of how self-perception shapes attitudes is the "foot-in-the-door" phenomenon—a tendency to agree with a larger request after initially agreeing to a smaller one (Freedman & Fraser, 1966). The foot-in-the-door operates much like self-perception in that people observe that they have already behaved in a manner consistent with a request, and therefore must be willing to engage in subsequent, similar, actions.

Evidence provided above indicates that attitudes can form not only from beliefs about the objects around us and from emotions and feelings about them, but also from monitoring behavior toward an object when the former two are absent. We now turn to conceptualizations of the underlying cognitive processes involved in attitude formation, particularly those informed by recent research on "implicit" attitudes (see Devos, this volume).

IMPLICIT AND EXPLICIT ORIGINS

For years, the tripartite model has provided a kind of "theoretical umbrella" to organize and conceptualize attitudes. As evident from our review, much attitude formation research readily fits within this framework. Indeed, the majority of this research anchors itself to affect, behavior, cognition, or some combination of the three. Recent research, however, identifies other means of carving up the world of attitude formation using different distinctions. In contrast to the tripartite model that distinguishes between different kinds of attitude *content* (e.g., affect versus cognition), some current approaches distinguish between different attitude formation *processes*, independent of content. Specifically, the distinction is made between attitudes that were formed "explicitly," through a deliberate, thoughtful consideration of attitude-relevant information (e.g., Fishbein & Ajzen, 1975), and those formed "implicitly," through less effortful processes that may occur outside of conscious awareness (e.g., Olson & Fazio, 2001). Historically, attitude researchers have focused on the former, but recent years have witnessed an upsurge of interest in "implicit social cognition," the study of the automatic determinants of social behavior (Greenwald & Banaji, 1995). This research has shown that while we do sometimes stop and consider our thoughts and feelings prior to evaluating an attitude object, much of who we are and what we do, including our self-esteem, racial prejudice, and complex social behavior, is determined by processes outside of our control (e.g., Bargh & Chartrand, 1999).

Although the implicit–explicit distinction appears unrelated to the distinctions made by the tripartite model, it does seem that explicit formation processes lend themselves more to belief-based, cognitive approaches described in the expectancy value model. Implicit processes, on the other hand, tend to be more affective in nature. For example, research on mere exposure described earlier is probably implicit in most cases because people are unaware that repeated exposure to attitude objects results in more favorable evaluations of them. Likewise, evaluative conditioning is thought to result in a "gut feeling"; that is, an affective response that in many cases comes about without awareness of the systematic pairings that produced that gut feeling (Olson & Fazio, 2001). However, it also is important to recognize that affective information can lead to attitudes both implicitly and explicitly—people often are aware of the emotions that exert influence on their attitudes. Similarly, our beliefs sometimes exist beyond our awareness in ways that influence our attitudes (e.g., Betsch, Plessner, Schwieren, & Gütig, 2001). In other words, implicit and explicit processes can operate in both the "heart" and the "head."

Because of the historic emphasis on explicit formation processes, researchers have only recently begun directly addressing fundamental issues surrounding the origins of implicit attitudes. Rudman (2004) has suggested four key sources of such attitudes. The first is early life experiences—particularly those that involve indirect observations of others. Although little systematic research has addressed this possibility directly, evidence suggests that attitudes toward smoking, members of the opposite sex, and potential mates can form early in life despite little memory of the experiences that contributed to these attitudes (Rudman & Goodwin, 2004). Second, consistent with the idea that affective information lends itself more toward implicit attitude formation (Olson & Fazio, 2001), brain-imaging research suggests that automatic attitudinal responses often relate better to amygdala activation (an affective center of the brain) than the neocortical activity associated with more explicit cognition (Cunningham et al., 2004). Third, Rudman implicates "cultural biases" as potential determinants of implicit attitudes—particularly prejudicial attitudes. Evidence suggests that we tend to acquire the prejudices of our culture at an early age (Baron & Banaji, 2006; Devine, 1989), presumably through passive socialization and without our awareness or conscious consent. A noteworthy implication of this analysis is that implicitly formed attitudes can be ones with which we do not agree at an explicit level (Banaji, 2001). In the same way that groundwater can be contaminated with environmental pollutants, our minds—particularly young minds—appear to passively absorb cultural biases that may result in prejudices (and other attitudes) we may, later in life, attempt to disavow. Indeed, research on racial prejudice shows that many white individuals try to correct for their racial biases in their treatment of blacks and other minorities (Olson & Fazio, 2004), and that over time, they may progressively "purify"—to extend the analogy—their minds of racial prejudice (Devine, Plant, & Buswell, 2000).

Finally, our attitudes may form and change implicitly because of internal pressures to be consistent; that is, to hold attitudes and beliefs that agree with one another (Greenwald et al., 2002; Nosek, Greenwald, & Banaji, 2002). For example, if one has a positive automatic or implicit attitude toward the self (i.e., high "implicit self-esteem"), this would imply that one should also like other objects linked to the self (Jones, Pelham, Carvallo, & Mirenberg, 2004). Interestingly, attitudes assessed implicitly (using such reaction time techniques as the Implicit Association Test) appear to shift according to consistency principles more than attitudes assessed explicitly via traditional questionnaires (Greenwald et al., 2002).

These four potential sources of implicit attitudes—early life experiences, primarily affective experiences, cultural biases, and consistency pressure—may only scratch the surface of the various means by which attitudes form implicitly. What these sources have in common, however, is an emphasis on a lack of awareness—either of the attitude itself, or at least of the learning processes that result in the attitude. This lack of awareness has several implications. First, if it is indeed the case that many of our attitudes form implicitly, this suggests that we may not know ourselves as well as we might think. While many believe that we can call up to consciousness the totality of our attitudes and beliefs—about people, politics, products, or what-have-you— if properly prompted, it may be likely that the Ancient Greek admonishment to "know thyself" is a more formidable task than we might imagine. Second, it suggests that the explanation we provide for a given attitude may be more a post hoc justification for an attitude that already exists, and less an articulation of the attitude's underlying basis (e.g., Wilson & Schooler, 1991). Indeed, "the heart has reasons that reason does not understand" (Jacques Bénigne Bossuet), and people are quite good at producing reasons for their attitudes—even when those reasons are known not to be the source of the attitude (Nisbett & Wilson, 1977).

Relatedly, if we are unaware of some of our attitudes, then we are likely unaware of their influence. If, for example, we are unaware of our dislike for a given person (or perhaps the extent of our dislike), we may treat them more negatively than we might consciously anticipate. Similarly, we might harbor a conscious goal to treat members of different races fairly, but if we are unaware of our biases against them, we may not know to "correct" for those biases (Wegener & Petty, 1995). Prejudice might then appear in ways that we do not consciously monitor, such as nonverbal behavior (Dovidio, Kawakami, Johnson, Johnson, & Howard, 1997). Women may drift away from careers in science and engineering—not out of a conscious preference for something else, but because of socialization processes that influenced them without their awareness or consent.

Clearly, implicitly formed attitudes can be powerful influences, but this exciting area of research has only recently gained momentum (see Devos, this volume). Several conceptual and empirical ambiguities surrounding research on "implicit attitudes" are in need of clarification. First, to our knowledge, no research acknowledges the possibility that the way an attitude forms (either implicitly or explicitly) can be independent of the way it "finally" manifests. For example, a person's attitude toward a given racial group may form implicitly, but may become explicit over time as he or she reflects on it. Conversely, an explicit attitude formed deliberately through thoughtful processes may become rote with repeated use to the point that the perceiver no longer notices it. Next, researchers have tended to confound attitude measurement and attitude process by using various reaction time techniques to assess "implicit attitudes" and traditional paper/pencil questionnaire measures to assess "explicit attitudes" (Fazio & Olson, 2003). The problem with this approach is that any difference between supposed attitude types may instead reflect differences in the way each attitude was measured. Another ambiguity concerns how "automatic" the attitude is, depending on whether it is implicitly or explicitly formed. Although researchers often argue that implicit attitudes have automatic properties (i.e., they are evoked spontaneously in the present of the attitude object and can influence behavior without intention or control), many implicit attitudes probably do not start out this way. Further, explicitly formed attitudes can take on automatic properties as well. Finally, the relationship between implicit and explicit attitudes has been the subject of much debate (e.g., Dovidio, Kawakami, & Beach, 2001). Is it possible, for example, that one might have two attitudes toward the same object, one implicit and the other explicit (Wilson, Lindsey, & Schooler,

2000)? Take the domain of self-esteem. A child may, either through neglect or abuse, acquire a negative attitude toward himself implicitly, early in life. Through time, he may overcome these hardships and learn to view himself more positively through explicit processes. Does he then have two attitudes toward the self, a negative implicit attitude but a positive explicit attitude (e.g., Bosson, Swann, & Pennebaker, 2000)? Or, is there really only one "true" attitude toward a given object, the self or otherwise? This debate currently rages in the literature, with some championing the former position (e.g., Wilson et al., 2000), and others arguing the latter (e.g., Olson, Fazio, & Hermann, in press). However this debate concludes, rapidly accumulating research suggests that implicitly formed attitudes can guide us like invisible puppet strings, pulling us in one direction or another as we remain oblivious to their influence.

EVOLUTIONARY ORIGINS

Other approaches evoke evolution as the origin of some particularly important attitudes: those toward potential mates. Evolutionary theory begins with the premise that the environment rewards ("selects") organisms based on their behavior (Darwin, 1859). Organisms that engage in behaviors that the environment rewards will be more likely to survive, reproduce, and pass on genetic information to offspring. Thus, one's attitudes toward (and choice) of potential mates partially determines whether one's genes are promulgated (Trivers, 1972). Enter a critical yet simple fact: women must invest more to reproduce—months of pregnancy, birth, and the bulk of child-rearing. Men must minimally provide only a few minutes and a few sperm to reproduce. According to some theorists, these essential differences suggest that women and men will pursue different mating strategies (Buss & Schmitt, 1993). Women, owing to their greater "minimum obligatory investment," are argued to be "choosier," and interested in a mate with ambition and earning potential who can provide the resources necessary for raising offspring. Men, who are less-burdened by reproductive costs, should be less choosy, interested in greater sexual variety, and, interestingly, attuned to cues that a potential mate is "fecund," that is, able to reproduce. Data collected across a number of cultures support these predictions (Buss, 1989, 2004; Singh, 1993).

Evolutionary approaches have not been without their detractors (e.g., Eagly & Wood, 1999). Apart from an aversion social psychologists appear to have toward studying potentially "unlearned" sources of attitudes (Eagly & Chaiken, 1993; McGuire, 1969), critics point out that evolutionary approaches exaggerate differences between the sexes and ignore their overarching consensus in mate preferences. They also argue that social structural, and not necessarily evolutionary factors, contribute to sex differences in mate preferences. Specifically, women have historically had to negotiate resource acquisition through men—not because of any evolved predispositions, but simply because men tend to have greater control over important resources than do women (Eagly & Wood, 2000).

Other critics have argued that evolutionary approaches provide only limited insight to a select few attitudinal domains (cf. Tesser, 1996). But pause to consider how much our biological endowments—shaped by our evolutionary past—have contributed to human preferences for sweet versus sour foods, "high-fat" vs. "low-fat" desserts, warmth over cold, and so on. Very young infants prefer to gaze at facelike patterns over other patterns (Fantz, 1963). Evolutionary approaches have been applied to peoples' universal preferences for certain landscapes over others (Kaplan, 1992), as well as the apparently universal human tendency to be prejudiced against out-groups (Neuberg & Cottrell, 2006). In sum, while evolutionary theory is most known among attitude researchers for its controversial contribution to the domain of attitudes toward mates, it provides insights about other attitude domains as well.

GENETIC ORIGINS

Genetics research also has something to say about how our biological endowments predispose us to hold certain attitudes. Much of this research involves comparisons of identical twins (who have the same genetic makeup) who are either reared together (and hence share an environment) or reared apart (and hence experience different environmental influences). Such comparisons allow researchers to arrive at estimates of how much a given attitude or behavior is influenced by heredity and environmental factors (Bouchard, 1997). Although twin research has been criticized as an imperfect means of assessing the relative contributions of heredity and environment to beliefs, behaviors, and attitudes (Joseph, 2004), it is important to note that such research has advanced substantially our understanding of a variety of psychological disorders like alcoholism and drug addiction (Dick & Foroud, 2003).

A surprising variety of attitude domains appear to have a strong genetic component according to this research. Attitudes toward the death penalty, jazz music, censorship, divorce, certain political attitudes, and many others have relatively high hereditability indices, whereas a belief in the veracity of the bible and attitudes toward coeducation appear to be low in heritability (Martin et al., 1986; Scarr, 1981). One's belief in the importance of religion is highly heritable, but one's degree of patriotism appears not to be influenced much by genetics (Eaves, Eysenck, & Martin, 1989).

Although these findings are provocative, they beg for an explanation. The question of why some attitudes appear more heritable than others had not been addressed by searching for some elusive "jazz gene," but by attempting to link heritable attitudes to other physical and personality variables (e.g., intelligence, extroversion) that are known to have genetic components (Olson, Vernon, Harris, & Jang, 2001; Tesser, 1993). For example, given that our physiques are largely determined by genetics, it seems reasonable that a preference for certain kinds of physical activities (e.g., certain sports) would follow (Olson et al., 2001). Similarly, intelligence is somewhat genetically determined, and might reasonably be linked to certain attitudes (e.g., toward academic achievement). Genetically determined sensory structures and body chemistry might influence tastes in certain foods, music, and other hedonic activities like smoking and alcohol consumption (Tesser, 1993). Thus, whereas there is probably not a direct link between genes and attitudes, genes appear to express themselves in variety of indirect but attitude-relevant ways.

ATTITUDE SOUP: COMBINATIONS OF ATTITUDE FORMATION PROCESSES

As we have seen, attitudes can develop through a variety of processes and can be filled with a variety of content. To this point, however, the various bases of attitudes have been treated somewhat independently, as though attitudes are forged with only one kind of content via a single process. But few attitudes can be described as purely "affective," "cognitive," or "implicit." Instead, the different paths to attitude formation probably combine in a variety of ways in more naturalistic settings.

First of all, remember that the tripartite approach flexibly allows for all permutations of affect, behavior, and cognition in terms of their potential combination to a given attitude (Zanna & Rempel, 1988). A single belief, say, that Apple's Mac has a more stable operating system (OS) than Windows machines, may result in a positive attitude toward Macs based on cognition. However, the Mac's sleekly designed, aesthetically pleasing laptops tend to lend themselves toward positive affective responses. Here, both cognition and affect converge. However, if one began with a belief in the superiority of Apple's OS, one's cognitive response to Apple computers might, according to Fishbein and Middlestadt (1995), be the cause of one's affective responses. Alternatively, if one was first swayed by the Mac's aesthetic appeal, one's emotional response might color one's belief in the "facts"; that is, the stability of the OS (Petty, Schumann, Richman, & Strathman, 1993). In short, cognition and affect can contribute independently to evaluations, but they can also influence one another. Similarly, self-perceived behavior (e.g., that one tends to find oneself choosing a Mac over a PC in the computer lab) might cause the development of a belief that Macs are better or a positive affective response to Macs (Fazio, 1987).

In short, research suggests that feelings and beliefs can color our perceptions of objects, influence how they are construed, and, ultimately, evaluated and treated. Most of the time, these influences push us in consistent directions—affective responses tend to be consistent with our "factual" beliefs, and we usually make sense of "the facts" in ways that are consistent with out emotional responses. However, interesting cases arise when feelings, beliefs, and behavior disagree, such as when a smoker has a strongly positive affect response to cigarettes despite a firm belief that smoking is harmful to one's health (e.g., Chaiken & Baldwin, 1981; Stone & Fernandez, this volume).

How affect, behavior, and cognition combine to influence attitudes also can be informed by attending to the processes—implicit and explicit—by which they influence one another. For example, one's attitude toward an insurance company might be influenced implicitly, say, through mere exposure. Repeated exposure to the brand logo on various websites may result in a weak but positive affective response. When our innocent web-surfer eventually needs to look into insurance for a new car, she might be subtly drawn to this company over others, which might influence how she processes—explicitly—information about the company. The result might be a relatively strong attitude, with an implicit basis but an explicit manifestation, including both affective and cognitive components. Very little research has addressed complex questions such as these, but the possibilities are intriguing and worthy of study.

In short, affect, cognition, and behavior can combine in interesting ways, and the implicit–explicit distinction complements traditional tripartite approaches by highlighting the pervasive impact of automatic and unconscious learning mechanisms. Similarly, the contributions of evolutionary and biological approaches add to the richness of attitude formation research by augmenting approaches that emphasize learned attitudes with one's highlighting how we might be biologically "prepared" to evaluate some objects favorably or unfavorably. However, progress has been hindered by occasional declarations that one route to attitude formation supersedes another, or that attitudes don't really form from, for example, purely affective reactions. Attitudes clearly involve multiple sources—learned, innate, affective, cognitive, behavioral, implicit, and explicit, and future research will help untangle how each of these contribute to the richness of our attitudes.

"CAN" AND "DO"

Most research on attitude formation is conducted via controlled experiments within the strict confines of the laboratory. Researchers take pains to capture the attitude formation processes occurring in the natural environment and contain them in the laboratory, so this is not to say that experimental work cannot inform how attitudes form in the "real world." However, as this chapter illustrates, experimental research has led researchers to focus more on the question of how attitudes *can* form, and not necessarily on how they *do* form outside the laboratory. The "do" questions are not incompatible with the "can" questions, but instead complement them by locating points of influence in naturalistic settings where these experimentally studied formation processes presumably operate. These include one's direct experience with the attitude object, socialization processes, parents, peers, and various forms of media.

First, early research demonstrated that attitudes formed via direct experience are held more strongly than attitudes formed through observation or indirect experience (Fazio & Zanna, 1981). Attitudes based on sensory information tend to be held more confidently as well. In one study, for example, people who were allowed to taste a brand of peanut butter were more resistant to counterpersuasion than those who based their opinions on written information (Wu & Shaffer, 1987). Our own interactions with an object appear to count quite a bit in terms of our attitudes, as we get to decide for ourselves, based on our own experience, whether to like or dislike a given object.

What about attitude objects that we only hear about from others? Consistent with social psychology's emphasis on the pervasive impact people have on one another, when it comes to attitudes, no one is an island unto him- or herself. Americans tend to like American cheese, and are revolted by vegemite, an Australian staple. We hear that no one is "born racist," but that we become so after being socialized into a culture that appears to value some groups and denigrate others. By the time we reach adulthood, nearly everyone is well aware, for example, of the negative stereotypes applied to African Americans (Devine, 1989). Lest we are tempted to think that "awareness" does not amount to one's accepted attitude, research indicates that many European-Americans continue to harbor negative attitudes toward African-Americans (e.g., Olson & Fazio, 2004), and many whites confess much of their impressions of blacks are fed by media and other indirect experience (Towles-Schwen & Fazio, 2001). It is likely society's persistent negative portrayal of blacks that propagates these prejudices (e.g., crimes committed by blacks are overreported compared to those committed by whites; Dorfman & Schiraldi, 2001). Similar social influence—based on family and friends, can be found in other domains. For example, one of the best predictors of one's political attitudes are the attitudes of one's parents (e.g., Tedin, 1980), and adolescents' drug attitudes can be predicted by their peers' drug attitudes (e.g., Hawkins, Catalano, & Miller, 1992). In short, although we like to believe that we decide what to like and what to dislike through our own conscious volition, these patterns of similarity in attitudes and the experimental evidence on implicit attitude formation processes suggest otherwise. Clearly, socialization processes are a powerful influence on attitudes.

Another potentially powerful influence is advertising. Advertisers spend billions of dollars each year attempting to persuade us to buy their products, but are they successful? A full answer is well beyond the scope of this chapter, but a wide array of marketing research indicates that advertising is often effective (e.g., Lodish et al., 1995; Shimp, 2003; Wells, 1997). Interestingly, and contrary to much attitudes research suggesting that explicit, cognitive approaches are the most effective means of inducing a given attitude, much advertising appears to take a more affective, less thoughtful approach ("Battle for Your Brain," 1991). Many of the advertisements in magazines, television, and on the Internet appear devoid of facts, arguments, or any sort of cognitively based information. Imagery is used heavily, suggesting that advertisers are going for our "guts," to promote "brand awareness," and perhaps they hope to do so implicitly. Again, we may be unaware of just how much our attitudes are based on such information. In the same way that water filters cannot make the dirtiest of water pure, conscious attempts at resisting the influence of our information environments cannot remove all of the "contaminants."

CONCLUSION

We began by reviewing research on the most historically grounded and well-researched arenas of attitude formation, the tripartite approach, where affect, behavior, and cognition were treated as independent contributors to the content of our attitudes. Next we discussed the distinction between explicit and implicit formation processes, emphasizing the underappreciated role that implicit processes play in attitude formation. Evolutionary and genetic contributions were acknowledged as well, as many of our attitudes—from potential mates to jazz to political beliefs—appear to have an unlearned component. Complex combinations of different attitude components and processes were discussed, along with the power of social forces—peers, parents, culture, and advertising—on attitude formation processes.

The fervor underlying our treatment of these social forces that determine how attitudes *do* form in natural environments stems from our sense that attitude researchers, to put it bluntly, need to get out of the lab. Genocides on the order of millions, the rapid spread of AIDS in Africa, drug abuse, alcoholism, political divisions, terrorism and war, all can be linked to attitudes—toward other people, toward controlled substances, toward political and religious groups, and so on. Attitude formation research offers a fascinating window into why humans believe what they do and behave as they do, and offers literally lifesaving potential to help solve some our troubled world's most pressing problems. We hope that future researchers take attitudes as seriously as we do.

REFERENCES

Allport, G. W. (1935). Attitudes. In C. Murchison (Eds.), *Handbook of social psychology* (pp. 798–844). Worcester, MA: Clark University Press.

Anderson, N. H. (1981). Integration theory applied to cognitive responses and attitudes. In R. E. Petty, T. M. Ostrom, & T. C. Brock (Eds.), *Cognitive Responses in Persuasion* (pp. 127–133). Hillsdale, NJ: Erlbaum.

Banaji, M. R. (2001). Implicit attitudes can be measured. In H. L.Roediger, III, J. S. Nairne, I. Neath, & A. Surprenant (Eds.), *The nature of remembering: Essays in honor of Robert G. Crowder* (pp. 117–150). Washington, D.C.: American Psychological Association.

Bandler, R. J., Madaras, G. R., & Bem, D. J. (1968). Self observation as a source of pain perception. *Journal of Personality and Social Psychology, 9,* 205–209.

Bargh, J. A., & Chartrand, T. L. (1999). The unbearable automaticity of being. *American Psychologist, 54,* 462–479.

Baron, A.S., Banaji, M.R. (2006). The development of implicit attitudes: Evidence of race evaluations from ages 6, 10 & adulthood. *Psychological Science, 17,* 53–58.

Battle for your brain. (1991, August). *Consumer Reports,* 520–521.

Bem, J. D. (1967). Self-perception: An alternate interpretation of cognitive dissonance phenomena. *Psychological Review, 74,* 183–200.

Bem, D. J. (1972). Self-perception theory. In L. Berkowitz (Ed.), *Advances in experimental social psychology* (Vol. 6, pp. 1–62.). San Diego, CA: Academic Press.

Berkowitz, L., & Knurek, D. A. (1969). Label-mediated hostility generalization. *Journal of Personality and Social Psychology, 13,* 200–206.

Betsch, T., Plessner, H., Schwieren, C., & Gütig, R. (2001). I like it but I don't know why: A value-account approach to implicit attitude formation. *Personality and Social Psychology Bulletin, 27,* 242–253.

Bosson, J. K., Swann, W. B., & Pennebaker, J. W. (2000). Stalking the perfect measure of self-esteem: The blind men and the elephant revisited. *Journal of Personality and Social Psychology, 79,* 631–643.

Bouchard, T. J., Jr. (1997a). Twin studies of behavior: Old and new findings. In A. Schmitt, K. Atzwanger, K. Grammer, & K. Schäfer (Eds.), *New aspects of human ethology* (pp. 121–140). New York: Plenum.

Buss, D. M. (1989). Sex differences in human mate preferences: Evolutionary hypotheses tested in 37 cultures. *Behavioral and Brain Sciences, 12*, 1–49.

Buss, D. M. (2004). *Evolutionary psychology: The new science of the mind* (2nd ed.). Boston, MA: Allyn & Bacon.

Buss, D. M., & Schmitt, D. P. (1993). Sexual strategies theory: A contextual evolutionary analysis of human mating. *Psychological Review, 100*, 204–232.

Chaiken, S., & Baldwin, M. W. (1981). Affective-cognitive consistency and the effect of salient behavioral information on the self-perception of attitudes. *Journal of Personality and Social Psychology, 41*, 1–12.

Chaiken, S., & Stangor, C. (1987). Attitudes and attitude change. *Annual Review of Psychology, 38*, 575–630.

Cunningham, W. A., Johnson, M. K., Raye, C. L., Gatenby, J. C., Gore, J. C., & Banaji, M. R. (2004). Separable neural components in the processing of Black and White Faces. *Psychological Science, 15*, 806–813.

Darwin, C. R. (1859). *The origin of species.* London: Murray.

Deci, E. L. (1971). Effects of externally mediated rewards on intrinsic motivation. *Journal of Personality and Social Psychology, 18*, 105–115.

Devine, P. G. (1989). Stereotypes and prejudice: Their automatic and controlled components. *Journal of Personality and Social Psychology, 56*, 5–18.

Devine, P. G., Plant, E. A., & Buswell, B. N. (2000). Breaking the prejudice habit: Progress and obstacles. In S. Oskamp (Ed.), *Reducing prejudice and discrimination* (pp. 185–208). Thousand Oaks, CA: Sage.

Dick, D. M., & Foroud, T. (2003). Candidate genes for alcohol dependence: A review of genetic evidence from human studies. *Alcoholism: Clinical and Experimental Research, 7*, 868–879.

Dorfman, L., & Schiraldi, D. (2001). *Off balance: Youth, race, and crime in the news.* Washington, D.C.: Building Blocks for Youth.

Dovidio, J. F., Kawakami, K., & Beach, K. R. (2001). Implicit and explicit attitudes: Examination of the relationship between measures of intergroup bias. In R. Brown & S. Gaertner (Eds.), *Blackwell handbook of social psychology: Intergroup processes* (pp. 175–197. Malden, MA: Blackwell.

Dovidio, J. F., Kawakami, K., Johnson, C., Johnson, B., & Howard, A. (1997). On the nature of prejudice: Automatic and controlled processes. *Journal of Experimental Social Psychology, 33*, 510–540.

Eagly, A. H., & Chaiken, S. (1993). *The psychology of attitudes.* Fort Worth, TX: Harcourt Brace Jovanovich.

Eagly, A. H., & Wood, W. (1999). The origins of sex differences in human behavior. *American Psychologist, 54*, 408–423.

Eaves, L. J., Eysenck, H. J., & Martin, N. G. (1989). *Genes, culture, and personality: An empirical approach.* London: Academic Press.

Fantz, R. L. (1963). Pattern vision in newborn infants. *Science, 140*, 296–297.

Fazio, R. H. (1987). Self-perception theory: A current perspective. In M. P. Zanna, J. M. Olson, & C. P. Herman (Eds.), *Social influence:The Ontario symposium* (Vol. 5, pp. 129–150). Hillsdale, NJ: Erlbaum.

Fazio, R. H. (2000). Accessible attitudes as tools for object appraisal: Their costs and benefits. In G. Maio & J. Olson (Eds.), *Why we evaluate: Functions of attitudes* (pp. 1–36). Hillsdale, NJ: Erlbaum.

Fazio, R. H., & Olson, M. A. (2003). Implicit measures in social cognition research: Their meaning and use. *Annual Review of Psychology, 54*, 297–327.

Fazio, R. H., & Zanna, M. P. (1981). Direct experience and attitude-behavior consistency. In L. Berkowitz (Ed.), *Advances in experimental social psychology* (Vol. 14, pp. 161–202). New York: Academic Press.

Field, A.P. (2000). I like it but I'm not sure why: Can evaluative conditioning occur without conscious awareness? *Consciousness and Cognition, 9,* 13–36.

Fishbein, M., & Ajzen, I. (1975). *Belief, attitude, intention, and behavior: An introduction to theory and research.* Reading, MA: Addison-Wesley.

Fishbein, M., & Middlestadt, S. (1995). Noncognitive effects on attitude formation and change: Fact or artifact? *Journal of Consumer Psychology, 4,* 181–202.

Freedman, J., & Fraser, S. (1966). Compliance without pressure: The foot-in-the-door techniques. *Journal of Personality and Social Psychology, 4,* 195–202.

Greenwald, A. G., (1968). Cognitive learning, cognitive response to persuasion, and attitude change. In A. G. Greenwald, T. C. Brock, & T. M. Ostrom (Eds.), *Psychological foundations of attitudes* (pp. 147–170). New York: Academic Press.

Greenwald, A. G. (1981). Cognitive response analysis: An appraisal, in R. E. Petty, T. M. Ostrom, & T. C. Brock (Eds.), *Cognitive responses in persuasion* (pp. 127–133). Hillsdale, NJ: Erlbaum.

Greenwald, A. G., & Banaji, M. R. (1995). Implicit social cognition: Attitudes, self-esteem, and stereotypes. *Psychological Review, 102,* 4–27.

Greenwald, A. G., Banaji, M. R., Rudman, L.A., Farnham, S. D., & Nosek, B. A., (2002). A unified theory of implicit attitudes, stereotypes, self-esteem, and self-concept. *Psychological Review, 109,* 3–25.

Hawkins, J. D., Catalano, R. F., & Miller, J. Y. (1992). Risk and protective factors for alcohol and other drug problems in adolescence and early adulthood: Implications for substance abuse prevention. *Psychological Bulletin, 112,* 64–105.

Hildum, D. C., & Brown, R. W. (1956). Verbal reinforcement and interviewer bias. *Journal of Abnormal and Social Psychology, 53,* 108–111.

Hull, C. H. (1951). *Essentials of behavior.* New Haven, CT: Yale University Press.

Insko, C. A. (1965). Verbal reinforcement of attitude. *Journal of Personality and Social Psychology, 2,* 621–623.

Jones, J. T., Pelham, B. W., Carvallo, M., & Mirenberg, M. C. (2004). How do I love thee? Let me count the Js: Implicit egoism and interpersonal attraction. *Journal of Personality and Social Psychology, 87,* 665–683.

Joseph, J. (2004). *The gene illusion: Genetic research in psychiatry and psychology under the microscope.* New York: Algora.

Kaplan, S. 1992. Environmental preference in a knowledge-seeking, knowledge-using organism. In J. H. Barkow, L. Cosmides, & J. Tooby, (Eds.), *The adapted mind* (pp. 581–598). Oxford, UK: Oxford University Press.

Lepper, M. R., Greene, D., & Nisbett, R. E. (1973). Undermining children's intrinsic interest with extrinsic reward: A test of the "overjustification" hypothesis. *Journal of Personality and Social Psychology, 28,* 129–137.

Linder, D. E., Cooper, J., & Jones, E. E. (1967). Decision freedom as a determinant of the role of incentive magnitude in attitude change. *Journal of Personality and Social Psychology, 6,* 245–254.

Lodish, L. M., Abraham, M., Kalmenson, S., Lievelsberger, J., Lubetkin, B., Richardson, B., & Stevens, M. E. (1995). How TV advertising works: A meta-analysis of 389 real-world split-cable TV advertising experiments. *Journal of Marketing Research, 32,* 125–139.

Martin, N. G., Eaves, L. J., Heath, A. R., Jardine, R., Feingold, L. M., & Eysenck, H. J. (1986). Transmission of social attitudes. *Proceedings of the National Academy of Science, 83,* 4364–4368.

McGuire, W. J. (1969). The nature of attitudes and attitude change. In G. Lindzey & E. Aronson (Eds.), *Handbook of social psychology* (2nd ed., Vol. 3, pp. 136–314). Reading, MA: Addison-Wesley.

McGuire, W. J. (1972). Social psychology. In P. C. Dodwell (Ed.), *New horizons in psychology*. Harmondsworth, UK: Penguin.

Neuberg. S. L., & Cottrell, C. A. (2006). Evolutionary bases of prejudices. In M. Schaller, J. A. Simpson, & D. T. Kenrick (Eds.), *Evolution and social psychology* (pp. 163–187). New York: Psychology Press.

Nisbett, R. E., & Wilson, T. D. (1977). Telling more than we can know: Verbal reports on mental processes. *Psychological Review, 84*, 231–259.

Nosek, B. A., Banaji, M. R., & Greenwald, A. G. (2002b). Harvesting implicit group attitudes and beliefs from a demonstration website. *Group Dynamics, 6*, 101–115.

Olson, M. A., & Fazio, R. H. (2001). Implicit attitude formation through classical conditioning. *Psychological Science, 12*, 413–417.

Olson, M. A., & Fazio, R. H. (2002). Implicit acquisition and manifestation of classically conditioned attitudes. *Social Cognition, 20*, 89–104.

Olson, M. A., & Fazio, R. H. (2004). Trait inferences as a function of automatically activated racial attitudes and motivation to control prejudiced reactions. *Basic and Applied Social Psychology, 26*, 1–12.

Olson, M. A., Fazio, R. H., & Hermann, A. D. (in press). Reporting tendencies underlie discrepancies between implicit and explicit measures of self-esteem. *Psychological Science.*

Olson, J. M., Vernon, P. A., Harris, J. A., & Jang, K. L. (2001). The heritability of attitudes: A study of twins. *Journal of Personality and Social Psychology, 80*, 845–860.

Petty, R. E., & Cacioppo, J. A. (1986). The Elaboration Likelihood Model of Persuasion. In L. Berkowitz (Ed.), *Advances in experimental social psychology* (Vol. 19, pp. 123–205). San Diego, CA: Academic Press.

Petty, R. E., Schumann, D. W., Richman, S. A., & Strathman, A. J. (1993). Positive mood and persuasion: Different roles for affect under high- and low-elaboration conditions. *Journal of Personality and Social Psychology, 64*, 5–20.

Reber, R., Winkielman, P., & Schwartz, N. (1998). Effects of perceptual fluency on affective judgments. *Psychological Science, 9*, 45–48.

Rudman, L. A. (2004). Sources of implicit attitude. *Current Directions in Psychological Science, 13*, 80–83.

Rudman, L. A., & Goodwin, S. A. (2004). Gender differences in automatic ingroup bias: Why do women like women more than men like men? *Journal of Personality and Social Psychology, 87*, 494–509.

Scarr, S. (1981). The transmission of authoritarian attitudes in families: Genetic resemblance in social-political attitudes? In S. Scarr (Ed.), *Race, social class, and individual differences* (pp. 399–427). Hillsdale, NJ: Erlbaum.

Shimp, T. A. (2003). *Advertising, promotion, and supplemental aspects of integrated marketing communication* (6th ed.). Mason, OH: Thompson.

Singh, D. (1993). Adaptive significance of female physical attractiveness: Role of waist-to-hip ratio. *Journal of Personality and Social Psychology, 65*, 293–307.

Skinner, B. F. (1957). *Verbal behavior.* New York: Appleton-Century-Crofts.

Staats, A.W. & Staats, C.K. (1958). Attitudes established by classical conditioning. *Journal of Abnormal and Social Psychology, 11*, 187–192.

Strack, F., Martin, L. L., & Stepper, S. (1988). Inhibiting and facilitating conditions of the human smile: A nonobtrusive test of the facial feedback hypothesis. *Journal of Personality and Social Psychology, 54*, 768–777.

Tedin, K. L. (1980). Assessing peer and parent influence on adolescent political attitudes. *American Journal of Political Science, 24*, 136–154.

Tesser, A. (1993). The importance of heritability in psychological research: The case of attitudes. *Psychological Review, 100*, 129–142.

Tesser, A. (1996). The psychology of evaluation. In E. T. Higgins & A. W. Kruglanski (Eds.), *Social psychology: Handbook of basic principles* (pp. 400–432). New York: Guilford.

Towles-Schwen, T., & Fazio, R. H. (2001). On the origins of racial attitudes: Correlates of childhood experiences. *Personality and Social Psychology Bulletin, 27*, 162–175.

Trivers, R. L. (1972). Parental investment and sexual selection. In B. Campbell (Ed.), *Sexual selection and the descent of man* (pp. 136–179). Chicago: Aldine-Atherton.

Wegener, D. T., & Petty, R. E. (1995). Flexible correction processes in social judgment: The role of naive theories in corrections for perceived bias. *Journal of Personality and Social Psychology, 68*, 36–51.

Wells, W. D. (Ed.). (1997). *Measuring advertising effectiveness.* Mahwah, NJ: Erlbaum.

Wilson, T. D., Lindsey, S., & Schooler, T. Y. (2000). A model of dual attitudes. *Psychological Review, 107*, 101–126.

Wilson, T. D. & Schooler, J. W. (1991). Thinking too much: Introspection can reduce the quality of preferences and decisions. *Journal of Personality and Social Psychology 60*, 181–192.

Wu, C., & Shaffer, D. R. (1987). Susceptibility to persuasive appeals as a function of source credibility and prior experience with the attitude object. *Journal of Personality and Social Psychology, 52*, 677–688.

Zajonc, R. B. (1968). Attitudinal effects of mere exposure. *Journal of Personality and Social Psychology, 9*, 1–27.

Zajonc, R.B. (1980). Feeling and thinking: Preferences need no inferences. *American Psychologist, 35*, 151–175.

Zanna, M. P., Kiesler, C. A., & Pilkonis, P. A. (1970). Positive and negative attitudinal affect established by classical conditioning. *Journal of Personality and Social Psychology, 14*, 321–328.

Zanna, M. P., & Rempel, J. K. (1988). Attitudes: A new look at an old concept. In D. Bar-Tal & A. Kruglanski (Eds.), *The social psychology of knowledge* (pp. 315–334). Cambridge: Cambridge University Press.

7

The Role of Affect in Attitudes and Attitude Change

JOSEPH P. FORGAS

University of New South Wales

*T*he unique ability of human beings to distil and symbolically represent their social experiences, and thus form predispositions toward people and events is a key accomplishment of our species (Mead, 1934). Attitude is the key construct within social psychology that captures the complex ways in which such predispositions, once formed, come to influence social thinking and behavior (Eagly & Chaiken, 1993). Not surprisingly, the concept of attitude has long been considered one of the "most distinctive and indispensable" concepts in social psychology (Allport, 1954, p. 43), and its importance to understanding human social behavior remains undiminished to this day, as contributions to this volume attest.

The term *attitude* was first introduced into empirical social research by Thomas and Znaniecki (1928), who used this concept to analyze the changing patterns of cultural adaptation manifest by Polish emigrants to the United States. Contemporary theories see attitudes as an individual rather than a cultural construct, and suggest that attitudes comprise distinct cognitive, affective, and conative (behavioral) components (Eagly & Chaiken, 1993; see Watt, Maio, Haddock, & Johnson, this volume). Surprisingly, despite recent burgeoning interest in affective phenomena (Forgas, 2006), relatively little work has been done on the dynamic role that affective states and moods play in the way attitudes function. This chapter seeks to provide an integrative review of recent work on the role of affect in the organization and functioning of attitudes, and the role of affect in social thinking and behavior. First, a brief overview of early research in this area will be presented, followed by a summary of contemporary cognitive theories linking affect and attitudes. We then review evidence for affective influences on attitudes in a number of substantive areas, such as attitudes toward others, self-related attitudes, and intergroup attitudes, before turning to affective influences in persuasion and attitude change.

BACKGROUND

Writers, artists, and laypersons have long been fascinated by the role of feelings in attitudes and behavior. Such classic philosophers as Plato, Aristotle, Epicurus, Descartes, Pascal, Kant, and others have offered extensive analyses of how feelings come to infuse thinking, attitudes, and predispositions. Many theorists saw affect as a dangerous, invasive force that subverts rational thinking, an idea that gained its most influential expression in Freud's psychodynamic theories. However, recent advances in neuroscience, psychophysiology, and social cognition suggest that rather than viewing affect as a dangerous and disruptive influence, feelings are often a useful and even essential input to adaptive responses to social situations (Adolphs & Damasio, 2001; Damasio, 1994; Ito & Cacioppo, 2001). The last two decades saw something of an "affective revolution" in psychological research, and much of what is known about the influence of affect on attitudes has been discovered since the 1980s. In a broader sense, then, this review touches on the age-old quest to understand the relationship between the rational and the emotional aspects of human nature (Hilgard, 1980).

Why has affect been neglected for so long in psychology? It seems that the behaviorist and subsequent cognitivist paradigms that dominated empirical psychology for the past century saw little value in focusing on affective processes. Radical behaviorism explicitly excluded the study of such mental phenomena as affect and attitudes from the subject matter of psychology. The cognitive revolution in the 1960s produced little improvement, as most information processing theories also assumed that the proper purpose of cognitive research was to study cold, affectless ideation. Affect was largely seen as a source of noise and disruption. The idea that affect is an inseparable, integral, and often crucial part of how attitudes about the social world are formed and represented was not seriously entertained until the early 1980s (Bower, 1981; Zajonc, 1980).

The Primacy of Affect

Affect is a key component of attitudes, yet there has been disproportionate preoccupation with the cognitive and conative components in the past (Eagly & Chaiken, 1993). It was Zajonc (1980) who first argued that affect often constitutes the primary and determining response to social stimuli, and he recently concluded that affect indeed functions as the dominant force in social attitudes (Zajonc, 2000). Studies supporting this position show that people may acquire a powerful affective response toward a target even when they have no awareness of having encountered it before (Zajonc, 2000). Rather than seeing affect as just one, and a relatively neglected component of attitudes, Zajonc (1980) proposed that affective reactions are the major and primary driving force behind most social and interpersonal attitudes.

Affect and the Organization of Attitudes

The argument for affective primacy is also supported by studies showing that affect plays a crucial role in how people cognitively represent their attitudes about social objects. The ability to categorize and symbolically represent social experiences lies at the heart of orderly and predictable social behavior (Mead, 1934). Affective reactions seem to play a defining role in how attitudes to common, recurring social experiences are organized (Forgas, 1979, 1982; Pervin, 1976). Such affective reactions as feelings of anxiety, confidence, intimacy, pleasure, or discomfort seem to be critical in defining the implicit structure of people's cognitive representations about social encounters. Niedenthal and Halberstadt (2000) showed that "stimuli can cohere as a category even when they have nothing in common other than the emotional responses they elicit" (p. 381), suggesting that affect is indeed a primary dimension along which social attitudes are organized and represented (Zajonc, 1980, 2000). These results are not entirely unexpected. Over 30 years ago, Pervin (1976) noted that "what is striking is the extent to which situations are described in terms of affects (e.g., threatening, warm, interesting, dull, tense, calm, rejecting) and organized in terms of similarity of affects aroused by them" (p. 471).

Early Evidence for Affective Influences on Attitude Valence

In addition to playing a role in attitude structure, affect also has a more dynamic influence on the valence of attitudes. Several early studies found that feeling good seems to make our attitudes more positive, and feeling bad "infuses" our attitudes with negativity. In terms of Freud's *psychodynamic theories*, affect has a dynamic, invasive quality and can take over attitudes and judgments unless psychological resources are deployed to control these impulses. In an interesting early study, Feshbach and Singer (1957) tested the psychoanalytic prediction that attempts to suppress affect should increase the "pressure" for affect to infuse unrelated attitudes and judgments. They induced fear in their subjects through electric shocks and then instructed some of them to suppress their fear. Fearful subjects were more likely to see "another person as fearful and anxious" (p. 286), and this effect was intensified when subjects were trying to suppress their fear, consistent with the psychodynamic idea that "suppression of fear facilitates the tendency to project fear onto another social object" (Feshbach & Singer, 1957, p. 286).

Alternative *conditioning and associationist* theories suggest a different mechanism linking affect and attitudes. Although radical behaviorism denied the value of studying internal constructs, including affect and attitudes, associationist theories nevertheless had an important influence. Watson's little Albert studies showed that attitudes toward a previously neutral target (e.g., furry rabbit) can be conditioned by associating it with fear-arousing stimuli (e.g., loud noise). According to this view, all attitudes are acquired through such a pattern of complex and cumulative associations. As an early illustration of this principle, Razran (1940) found that people who were made to feel bad or good (by being exposed to highly aversive smells or receiving a free lunch) spontaneously reported significantly more negative or positive attitudes toward persuasive messages presented to them.

The conditioning approach was also used by Byrne and Clore (1970) and Clore and Byrne (1974) to explain the influence of incidental affect on interpersonal attitudes. According to this explanation, aversive environments (as unconditioned stimuli) produce negative affect (the unconditioned response) that can become associated with a new target (a person) and influence attitudes (a conditioned response) due to simple temporal and spatial contiguity. Several studies demonstrated just such a conditioning effect on interpersonal attitudes (Gouaux, 1971; Gouaux & Summers, 1973; Griffitt, 1970; see Olson & Kendirck; Walther & Langer, this volume).

COGNITIVE APPROACHES LINKING AFFECT AND ATTITUDES

Recent information processing theories offer a more subtle account of the links between affect and attitudes. Two kinds of cognitive theories have been proposed to explain affect congruency effects: *memory-based* accounts (e.g., the affect priming model; see Bower & Forgas, 2001), and *inferential* models (e.g., the affect-as-information model; see Clore, Gasper, & Garvin, 2001; Clore & Storbeck, 2006). In addition, affective states influence how social information is processed.

Affective Influences on Attitudes: The Memory Account

Several social cognitive theories suggest that affect may influence the memory structures people access when forming attitudes and responding to social situations. This principle was elaborated in the associative network model proposed by Bower (1981), who suggested that affective states should selectively prime associated thoughts and representations that are more likely to be used in constructive cognitive tasks, including attitude formation. There has been strong evidence for such mood-congruent effects in attitudes, memories, and judgments (Bower, 1981; Clark & Isen, 1982; Fiedler & Stroehm, 1986; Forgas & Bower, 1987). Affect priming, however, is most likely to occur when the affective state is strong, salient, and self-relevant, and the task involves the constructive generation of a response (Eich & Macauley, 2000; Forgas, 1995a, 2002; Sedikides, 1995).

Fiedler (1991), for example, distinguished between constructive and reconstructive cognitive processes, and argued that affect congruence in attitudes and judgments should be strongest when a task requires open, constructive processing. Tasks that simply call for the reproduction of a preexisting response and require no constructive thinking should show no affect congruence (Forgas, 1995a). Recent integrative theories, including the Affect Infusion Model (AIM; Forgas, 1995a, 2002), identify four information processing styles in terms of their (1) openness and (2) degree of constructiveness.

Affective Influences on Attitudes: The Misattribution Explanation

Alternative theories suggest that rather than computing an attitude or a judgment on the basis of recalled features of a target, individuals "may...ask themselves: 'How do I feel about it?' [and] in doing so, they may mistake feelings due to a preexisting state as a reaction to the target" (Schwarz, 1990, p. 529). This "how-do-I-feel-about-it" heuristic suggests that affective influences on attitudes are due to an inferential error, as people misattribute their affect to an unrelated attitude target.

This theory is similar to earlier conditioning models reported by Clore and Byrne (1974), suggesting an incidental—and mistaken—association between affect and an attitude object.

Recent evidence shows that the misattribution principle is only a partial explanation of affective influences on attitudes and judgments, as people only seem to rely on their affective state as a heuristic cue in rare circumstances when they lack the motivation or resources to compute a more thorough response. For example, the key experiment by Schwarz and Clore (1983) involved telephoning respondents and asking their attitudes about a number of issues. As they presumably had little personal involvement, motivation, time, or cognitive resources to engage in extensive processing to produce a response, respondents may well have relied on their prevailing mood as a shortcut to infer a response. In another study we asked almost 1,000 people who were feeling good or bad after seeing happy or sad films to complete an attitude survey on the street after leaving the movie theater (Forgas & Moylan, 1987). As they presumably had little time and capacity to engage in elaborate processing, again respondents may well have relied on their mood as a heuristic cue to infer their reaction.

Calling people's attention to the source of their affect seems to reduce or even eliminate affect congruence (Clore et al., 2001; Schwarz & Clore, 1983, 1988). This does not provide selective support for the misattribution theory, however, as is often claimed. Logically, the fact that an effect can be eliminated by emphasizing the correct source of the affect offers no evidence for how the effect occurs in the first place, when this manipulation is absent. Indeed, affect congruence in attitudes due to affect-priming mechanisms can be reversed by asking subjects to focus on their internal states (Berkowitz, 2000). In a further criticism of the affect-as-information model, Martin (2000) showed that the informational value of affective states for attitudes is not given. Rather, it is configural and depends on the particular situational context. Thus, a positive mood may inform us that a positive response is appropriate (if the setting happens to be a cabaret), but the same mood may send exactly the opposite informational signal in a different setting (e.g., a funeral). The model also has little to say about how other cues such as stimulus information and memories are combined to produce a response. In a sense, the affect as information model is really a theory of mistaken or aborted responses. Most real attitudes involve some degree of elaborate processing that involves the affect-priming rather than the affect-as-information mechanisms.

Affective Influences on Processing Strategies

So far we have looked at the informational role of affect, how it may influence the *content* and valence of attitudes. Affect may also influence the *process* of cognition, that is, *how* people think (Clark & Isen, 1982; Fiedler & Forgas, 1988; Forgas, 2000). People experiencing positive affect appear to employ less effortful and more superficial processing strategies, reach decisions more quickly, use less information, avoid demanding, systematic thinking, and are more confident about their decisions. In contrast, negative affect seems to trigger a more effortful, systematic, analytic, and vigilant processing style (Clark & Isen, 1982; Mackie & Worth, 1989;

Schwarz, 1990). Yet, more recent studies also show that positive affect can produce distinct processing advantages. Happy people also are likely to adopt more creative, open, and inclusive thinking styles, use broader categories, show greater mental flexibility, and can perform more effectively on secondary tasks (Bless, 2000; Fiedler, 2000; Hertel & Fiedler, 1994).

The processing consequences of affect were variously explained as due to affect-imposed processing limitations (Ellis & Ashbrook, 1988), or motivational factors (Clark & Isen, 1982), as people experiencing positive mood may try to maintain this pleasant state by refraining from such effortful activity as elaborate information processing. In contrast, negative affect motivates people to engage in vigilant, effortful processing as an adaptive response to improve an aversive state. In a slightly different "cognitive tuning" account, Schwarz (1990) argued that positive and negative affect have a signaling or tuning function in that they automatically inform the person of whether a relaxed, effort minimizing (in positive affect) or a vigilant, effortful (negative affect) processing style is appropriate. These accounts are consistent with evolutionary ideas about the adaptive functions of affect (Forgas, 2006; Frijda, 1986).

More recently, Bless (2000; Bless & Fiedler, 2006) and Fiedler (2000; Fiedler & Bless, 2001) have suggested a rather different explanation, arguing that positive and negative affect trigger equally effortful, but qualitatively different processing styles. Specifically, positive affect generally promotes a more *assimilative*, schema-based, top-down processing style, where preexisting ideas, attitudes, and representations dominate information processing. In contrast, negative affect produces a more *accommodative*, bottom-up, and externally focused processing strategy where attention to situational information drives thinking (Bless, 2000; Fiedler, 2000; Higgins, 2001).

Integrative Theories: The Affect Infusion Model (AIM).

Affect may thus influence both the *content*, and the *process* of how people think. However, these effects are subject to important boundary conditions, and recent integrative theories such as the Affect Infusion Model (AIM; Forgas, 2002) seek to specify the circumstances that facilitate or inhibit affect infusion. For example, affect priming is most reliably observed when cognitive tasks call for highly constructive processing that necessitates the use of memory-based information. Similarly, the inferential model is only likely to be used when people lack the motivation, ability, or resources to deal with a task more exhaustively.

The AIM predicts that affective influences on cognition depend on the processing styles recruited in different situations that can differ in terms of two features: the degree of effort, and the degree of openness of the information search strategy. By combining processing quantity (effort), and quality (openness, constructiveness) the model identifies four distinct processing styles: *direct access processing* (low effort, closed, not constructive), *motivated processing* (high effort, closed, not constructive), *heuristic processing* (low effort, open, constructive), and *substantive processing* (high effort, open, constructive). Affect infusion is most likely when constructive processing is used, such as substantive or heuristic processing. In contrast, affect should not infuse thinking when motivated or direct access processing is used. The AIM also specifies a range of contextual variables related to the *task*, the *person,* and the *situation* that influence processing choices and thus affective influences.

THE EVIDENCE FOR AFFECTIVE INFLUENCES ON ATTITUDES

As the previous review suggests, affect plays a significant and interactive role in how we represent the social world and organize and express our attitudes toward various social objects. This section will review a range of empirical studies illustrating the multiple roles of affect in attitudes, including (1) affect and attitudes toward others; (2) affective influences on attitudes about the self; (3) affect and intergroup attitudes; and (4) the role of affect in attitude change and persuasion; and the applied implications of this work.

Affect and Attitudes toward Others.

Homo sapiens is an extremely gregarious species, and our ability to represent and form attitudes about others is one of the most demanding and ubiquitous social cognitive tasks we undertake in everyday life. Several early experiments based on psychoanalytic or conditioning theories by Clore and Byrne (1974), Feshbach and Singer (1957), and Griffitt (1970) showed an affect-congruent bias in interpersonal attitudes and judgments. Even the basic process of forming an attitude based on observed behaviors can be affectively biased, theoretically, as the greater availability of affectively primed information influences the way inherently ambiguous and complex social behaviors are interpreted (Forgas & Bower, 1987). This prediction was confirmed in a study asking happy or sad participants to view a videotape based on their own social interactions with a partner from the previous day (Forgas, Bower, & Krantz, 1984), and make a series of rapid, on-line judgments evaluating the observed behaviors of themselves as well as their partners. Happy people saw significantly more positive, skilled, and fewer negative, unskilled behaviors both in themselves and in their partners than did sad subjects, and formed correspondingly more affect-congruent attitudes and judgments. Thus, affect priming can bias the way inherently ambiguous social behaviors are interpreted, and the formation of subsequent interpersonal attitudes. Even such a clear-cut behavior as a smile may be seen as friendly in a good mood but could be interpreted as awkward or condescending in a bad mood due to the greater availability in memory of affect-congruent associations. Later experiments have shown that such affect infusion into attitudes occurs even when people deal with such familiar and well-known others as their intimate partners (Forgas, 1994, 1995a).

Subsequent experiments collected reaction time and memory data to confirm that affect priming is indeed largely responsible for these effects. When happy or sad people were asked to form attitudes about others described in terms of a number of positive and negative qualities on a computer screen (Forgas & Bower,

1987), happy judges formed more positive attitudes than sad judges. Reaction latencies showed that people spent longer reading and thinking about affect-congruent information, but were faster in producing an affect-congruent judgment. These processing differences are consistent with affect-priming theories, as it should take longer to encode new affect-congruent information into a richer activated knowledge base. In contrast, producing affect-congruent attitudes should be faster because the response is already primed by the affective state.

Extended Processing Can Increase Affective Influences on Attitudes   Numerous studies support the counterintuitive prediction of the AIM that affect has a greater influence on attitudes when people need to think more extensively to deal with a more complex target, due to the greater likelihood that affectively primed associations will infuse the result (Forgas, 1993, 1994, 1995b, 2002). When attitudes are formed about a more complex and ambiguous person, more constructive processing is needed, increasing the likelihood that affectively primed information will be used. In a series of experiments (Forgas, 1993, 1995b), happy or sad participants were asked to form an attitude about couples who either were highly typical and well-matched or were atypical and mismatched in terms of race or physical attractiveness. Happy participants formed more positive attitudes than did sad participants, and these mood effects were far greater when the couples were unusual and mismatched, and thus required more extensive processing.

Similar results were obtained using verbal descriptions of more or less typical, unusual people as targets (Forgas, 1992). There was a significant mood-congruent bias in attitudes that was greater when the target was a complex, atypical person that took longer to process, facilitating affect infusion. Such affect infusion effects can also bias realistic everyday attitudes about intimately known others (Forgas, 1994). Attitudes toward partners in long-term intimate relationships showed significant affect congruence, and these effects were greater when the issues judged were complex and serious and thus required more elaborate, constructive processing. These experiments provide strong evidence for the process sensitivity of affect infusion into social attitudes, and show that even attitudes about highly familiar people can be prone to affect infusion when a more elaborate processing strategy is used.

Behavioral Consequences   One of the perennial questions in attitude research concerns the links between attitudes and behavior. Although it is frequently claimed that attitudes can predict behavior, in practice these links can be quite tenuous (Eagly & Chaiken, 1993). In this section, we will discuss some experiments that speak to a related question: If affect can influence attitudes, will it also influence subsequent social behaviors? Positive affect should thus prime positive information and produce more confident, friendly, and cooperative "approach" attitudes and behaviors, whereas negative affect should prime negative memories and produce avoidant, defensive, or unfriendly attitudes and behaviors. One field study found that affect had an affect-congruent influence on attitudes toward, and responses to a person who unexpectedly approached participants with an impromptu request (Forgas, 1998b). Students in a library received an unobtrusive mood induction, and soon afterwards were approached by another student (a confederate) who requested, either politely or impolitely, several sheets of paper needed to complete an essay. There was a clear mood-congruent pattern in attitudes and behavioral responses to the requester. Negative mood resulted in a more critical, negative attitude to the request and the requester and less compliance than did positive mood. These results suggest that affect infusion can have a significant effect on determining attitudes and behavioral responses to people encountered in realistic everyday situations. Other experiments found mood effects on strategic interpersonal behaviors such as requesting help or information (Forgas, 1999a, 1999b).

Affective states should play a particularly important role in elaborately planned interpersonal encounters such as attitudes toward future bargaining partners, and the planning and performance of complex negotiating encounters (Forgas, 1998a). We found that positive mood produced more positive and optimistic attitudes about the interaction partners and the task, led to more ambitious negotiating goals, and the formulation of more optimistic, cooperative and integrative negotiating strategies. These findings suggest that fluctuations in affective state can influence the attitudes people develop to novel social situations, the goals they set for themselves, and the way they ultimately behave in strategic interpersonal encounters. These effects occur because uncertain and unpredictable social encounters, such as a negotiating task, require open, constructive processing and affect can selectively prime the thoughts and associations used in formulating attitudes, plans, and behaviors.

Affect and Attitudes about the Self

The self represents a particularly complex, elaborate, and ambiguous attitude object, and affective states may have a particularly strong influence on self-related attitudes (Sedikides, 1995). There is good evidence for a basic affect-congruent pattern: Positive affect improves, and negative affect impairs the valence of self-attitudes (Abele & Hermer, 1993; Nasby, 1994, 1996). Similarly, when students expressed their attitudes about their success or failure on a recent exam, those in a negative mood blamed themselves more when failing, and took less credit for their successes, whereas those in a positive mood claimed credit for success but refused to accept responsibility for their failures (Forgas, Bower, & Moylan, 1990). However, these effects very much depend on the nature of the task. Nasby (1994) found that happy persons remembered more positive, and sad persons remembered more negative attributes about themselves, but only when prior ratings required an affirmative format. This result suggests that rejecting a trait as not applicable to the self may be a short and direct process less sensitive to affective influences. In contrast, affirming that a trait applies to the self calls for more elaborate thinking, enhancing the likelihood that affect will impact on the outcome.

Affective influences on attitudes about the self also depend on the extent to which the topic being considered is central or peripheral. Familiar, central aspects of the self may be less prone to affective influences (Sedikides, 1995). Central self-attitudes are what people believe is their "true" self, and are affirmed more strongly than peripheral ones (Markus, 1977; Sedikides, 1995; Sedikides & Strube, 1997; Swann, 1990). This "differential sensitivity" hypothesis was tested in an elegant series of experiments by Sedikides (1995) who found that affect had no influence on attitudes related to central traits, but had a significant mood-congruent influence on attitudes related to peripheral traits.

Self-esteem also may mediate mood effects on self-attitudes (Baumeister, 1993, 1998; Rusting, 1998, 2001). Low self-esteem persons generally have less certain and stable self-conceptions (Campbell et al., 1996), and affect may thus have a greater influence on the self-attitudes for low self-esteem individuals. This prediction was confirmed by Brown and Mankowski (1993) who found significantly greater mood effects on the self-attitudes of low self-esteem than high self-esteem individuals. Research by Smith and Petty (1995) also showed that self-esteem mediated mood effects on self-related attitudes. Mood had a significant influence on the valence of reported attitudes from their school years for low self-esteem persons, but not for the high self-esteem group. It seems that high self-esteem persons have more certain and stable self-attitudes and can respond to self-related questions by directly accessing this stable knowledge base, a process that does not allow the incidental infusion of affect into attitudes. Low self-esteem in turn may call for more open and elaborate processing and current mood may thus influence the outcome (Sedikides, 1995). Affect intensity may also influence the nature of affective influences (Larsen & Diener, 1987). Mood congruency effects may be stronger among participants who score high on affect intensity (Haddock, Zanna, & Esses, 1994), and among people who score higher on measures assessing openness to feelings as a personality trait (Ciarrochi & Forgas, 2000).

Motivated Reversal of Affect Congruence

Affect does not always just cause affect-congruence; sometimes the opposite, affect-incongruent outcome may occur. Cervone, Kopp, Schaumann, and Scott (1994) report that attitudes toward people's own *performance* on a task showed a clear affect-congruent bias. However, the opposite occurred when people were asked to express attitudes toward the minimum *standard* of performance necessary to be satisfied with themselves. Sad participants now expressed higher personal standards in an affect-incongruent pattern. It seems that negative affect may have triggered a motivated process to nominate higher expected standards, as a defensive strategy to justify their expected failure, in a process somewhat similar to self-handicapping attributions (see also Alter & Forgas, 2007, on mood effects on self-handicapping).

In another illustrative study by Sedikides (1994), sad mood participants expressed more negative, and happy participants initially expressed more positive attitudes toward themselves. However, with the passage of time, negative self-attitudes were spontaneously reversed, suggesting a motivated, spontaneous mood repair strategy. This kind of motivated correction of affective biases over time—suggesting an automatic mood management motive—was also confirmed in a series of experiments by Forgas, Ciarrochi, and Moylan (2000), showing that negative mood effects on self-attitudes were spontaneously reversed over time. These effects were closely linked to self-esteem; people who scored high on self-esteem eliminated the negativity of their self-attitudes very rapidly, whereas low self-esteem individuals persevered with negative self-attitudes much longer.

Positive Affect as a Resource   Affect has a further interesting influence on the way people process self-related attitudes. Feeling good can serve as a resource, allowing people to overcome defensiveness and deal with expressions of potentially threatening attitudes (Trope, Ferguson, & Raghunathan, 2001). Dealing with negative attitudes about the self creates a powerful motivational conflict, involving a trade-off between the immediate emotional cost and long-term information gain (Trope, 1986). It seems that affect influences the relative weight people assign to the emotional costs versus the informational benefits of receiving negative attitudes (Trope & Neter, 1994). Positive mood makes it easier to deal with threatening but diagnostic information, functioning as an emotional buffer and enabling people to absorb the affective costs of dealing with negative attitudes (Aspinwall, 1998; Reed & Aspinwall, 1998; Trope & Pomerantz, 1998). However, this effect is not universal. It is important for the negative attitudes to be seen as useful and diagnostic before people will willingly undergo the emotional cost of dealing with them (Trope & Gervey, 1998).

These effects may have important applied consequences for attitude change as well. Raghunathan and Trope (1999) evaluated the mood-as-a-resource hypothesis in the processing of health-related persuasive messages. They found that people in a positive mood not only selectively sought, but also processed in greater detail and remembered better negatively valenced arguments about health risks. In summary, affect seems to have a strong mood-congruent influence on self-related attitudes, but only when there are no motivational forces to override affect congruence, and some degree of constructive processing is employed. Affect also seems to play an important role in the structure and organization of the self-concept (Niedenthal & Halberstadt, 2000). For example, DeSteno and Salovey (1997) found that neutral mood participants structured their self-attitudes around descriptive features such as achievement and affiliation. However, the experience of positive or negative affect produced a distinct change, and self-attitudes were now structured in terms of their positive or negative valence. Thus, affect may function as a key organizing principle of self-related attitudes, whenever intense affective states are experienced.

Some Applied Consequences   The role of affect in health-related attitudes, judgments, and behaviors is an applied area that has received intense attention (Salovey, Detweiler, Steward, & Bedell, 2001). Positive or negative affective states may promote healthy or unhealthy attitudes and behaviors, and ultimately also may influence physical well-being. Several studies found a correlation between good moods and subjective health outcomes. Happy moods seem to reduce the incidence of reported physical symptoms and promote positive, optimistic attitudes and beliefs about health-related issues (Salovey & Birnbaum, 1989). It is hardly surprising that ill-health is typically associated with more negative moods. The more interesting question is whether there is a reverse effect: Can induced mood have a causal influence on reported health symptoms and attitudes? The answer is likely to be "yes." Individuals who experience negative moods, in comparison to those who experience positive moods, have more negative attitudes, report more and more severe physical symptoms, and these finding appears to be quite robust (Abele & Hermer, 1993; Croyle & Uretsky, 1987). Salovey and Birnbaum (1989) found that sick students who were suffering from cold or flu reported nearly twice as many aches and pains in negative mood than did those made to feel happy—even though there were no differences between the two groups before the mood induction.

Mood effects on health-related attitudes is thus an important predictor of actual health behaviors, including engaging in safe sex, smoking cessation, and a healthy diet (Salovey, Rothman, & Rodin, 1998). Happy persons typically have more positive attitudes toward carrying out such health-promoting behaviors (Salovey & Birnbaum, 1989), and tend to form more optimistic attitudes about the likelihood of future positive and negative events (Forgas & Moylan, 1987; Mayer, Gaschke, Braverman, & Evans, 1992; Mayer & Volanth, 1985). Although the effects of affect on health-related attitudes appear robust, the mechanisms responsible for these effects are not yet fully understood. One possibility is that affective states may directly influence the immune system and susceptibility to disease, and such effects tend to be stronger when participants are instructed to express rather than repress their mood (Labott & Martin, 1990). Individual difference variables such as optimism, affect intensity, anxiety, hope, and affect regulation skills appear to mediate many of these effects (Salovey et al., 2001). Optimism and hope can have a direct effect on health-related attitudes, immune system functioning, and produce more adaptive ideas and attitudes about how to take care of ourselves when sick (Snyder, 1994). However, these effects are subject to complex mediating influences involving such variables as immune system responses, personality characteristics, and social relationships (Salovey et al., 2001).

Affect and Intergroup Attitudes

Feelings and emotion have long been assumed to play a key role in intergroup attitudes. Early theories based on the frustration–aggression hypothesis and psychoanalytic ideas of projection and displacement suggested that aversive affective states may directly produce more negative attitudes toward out-groups. Much early research on affect and inter–group attitudes was descriptive, and analyzed the affective content of inter–group attitudes (for reviews, see Cooper, 1959; Haddock, Zanna, & Esses, 1993; Stangor, Sullivan, & Ford, 1991). Theoretical explanations suggested that conditioning plays a major role in the process that leads to negative affect coming to be associated with out-groups (Gaertner & Dovidio, 1986; Katz, 1976), consistent with other evidence showing that incidental affect can be readily associated with attitude objects as a result of conditioning processes (Clore & Byrne, 1974; Griffitt, 1970; Zanna, Kiesler, & Pilkonis, 1970). Chronic cultural conditioning—repeatedly encountering and associating certain groups with positive or negative affective states—can explain the ease with which culturally devalued groups can so readily elicit such negative emotions as anger, disgust, and resentment.

More recently, the cognitive processes that link affect and inter-group attitudes began to be explored. For example, Fiske and Pavelchak (1986) proposed that "affective tags" linked to group representations may trigger emotional responses. Memory-based and inferential theories can also explain how affect impacts intergroup attitudes. It appears that affective biases on intergroup responses are stronger when people are unaware of their feelings, lack motivation, or the cognitive resources to control their biases, and have relatively little information to go on (Bodenhausen & Moreno, 2000). A systematic framework for understanding these effects was proposed by Bodenhausen (1993), who argued that the link between affect and intergroup attitudes depends on whether affective states are long-term or short-term, and whether they are either directly elicited by an out-group or are caused by incidental factors.

Simply meeting members of out-groups in affectively nonaversive circumstances can improve attitudes to out-group members, according to the so-called contact hypothesis (Allport, 1954; Amir, 1969; Brewer & Miller, 1996; Stephan & Stephan, 1996). Contact episodes that generate positive feelings, such as successful cooperation, are likely to be even more effective (Jones, 1997). Positive affect may also promote more inclusive cognitive categorizations of social groups, potentially reducing intergroup discrimination (Dovidio, Gaertner, Isen, Rust, & Guerra, 1998; Isen, Niedenthal, & Cantor, 1992), as it recruits a more assimilative, top-down and schema-driven processing of social information (Bless, 2000; Bless & Fiedler, 2006; Fiedler, 2000). These effects will depend on what kinds of categories are most relevant in a situation. In a series of experiments, we found that when group membership is of low relevance, positive mood may well facilitate the use of in-group vs. out-group categories, and may produce greater intergroup discrimination (Forgas & Fiedler, 1996).

Contact with out-groups also may produce feelings of anxiety, uncertainty, and insecurity (Stephan & Stephan, 1985), experiences that reduce information processing capacity and amplify reliance on negative attitudes and stereotypes (Wilder & Shapiro, 1989). In experiments we found that trait anxiety significantly moderates the effects of negative mood on intergroup attitudes (Ciarrochi & Forgas, 1999). Low trait anxious whites in the United States reacted more negatively to a threatening black out-group when experiencing negative affect. Surprisingly, high trait anxious individuals showed the opposite pattern: They went out of their way to control their negative tendencies when feeling bad, and reported more positive attitudes. It appears that high trait anxiety combined with aversive affect triggered a more controlled, motivated processing strategy that reduced undesirable negative intergroup attitudes. However, not all negative affective states have the same effects: Sadness, anger and anxiety can have quite different consequences for inter-group attitudes. Sadness seems to reduce, but anger and anxiety increase reliance on stereotyped attitudes (Bodenhausen, Sheppard, & Kramer, 1994; Keltner, Ellsworth, & Edwards, 1993; Raghunathan & Pham, 1999).

Stereotyping is heavily involved in intergroup attitudes, although a full discussion of this large area of research is clearly beyond the scope of this review. Affect may influence stereotyping at each of the four stages of the stereotyping process (Gilbert & Hixon, 1991): assigning the target to a category (category identification);

accessing the features of the category (stereotype activation); interpreting the target in terms of the activated features (stereotype application); and correcting for inappropriate stereotyping (stereotype correction). As positive affect often promotes a top-down information processing strategy (Bless & Fiedler, 2006), it also may facilitate reliance on stereotypes, especially when the judgment is of low personal relevance (Forgas & Fiedler, 1996, Exp. 1). Once activated, stereotyped knowledge will influence attitudes (Bodenhausen, Macrae, & Milne, 1998). On the other hand, positive affect also may reduce negative inter-group attitudes when it promotes the use of more inclusive, superordinate categories (Dovidio, Gaertner, Isen, & Lowrance, 1995). Past work also suggests that both negative affect (Ellis & Ashbrook, 1988), and positive affect (Mackie & Worth, 1989) can reduce processing resources and so increase reliance on stereotypes. Stereotypes may also be supplemented by other information in the formation of intergroup attitudes (Bodenhausen, Macrae, & Sherman, 1999; Chaiken & Maheswaran, 1994; Duncan, 1976).

In short, affect may influence intergroup judgments both by influencing the information processing strategies used, and the way information is selected and used. As positive moods facilitate top-down, schematic processing, happy persons may produce less accurate social judgments (Forgas, 1998c; Sinclair & Mark, 1995) and are more likely to rely on stereotype information (Abele & Petzold, 1994; Bodenhausen et al., 1994; Bless, Schwarz, & Wieland, 1996). However, negative affective states other than sadness, including anger or anxiety also may increase reliance on stereotyping (e.g., Bodenhausen, Sheppard, & Kramer, 1994). Affect also has direct informational effects, simply facilitating the use of mood-congruent knowledge in intergroup attitudes. For example, in a series of studies, Esses and Zanna (1995) found that negative moods increased the tendency to form negative judgments about ethnic minorities.

As it is the case with all attitudes, stereotypes also may be influenced by people's motivated tendency to correct what they perceive as undesirable or socially unacceptable outcomes (Bodenhausen et al., 1998), including attempts to correct for affective biases (Strack, 1992). As negative affect facilitates a more cautious, defensive interpersonal style (Forgas, 1999a, 1999b), sad persons seem more likely to engage in stereotype correction (Devine & Monteith, 1993; Lambert, Khan, Lickel, & Fricke, 1997). Negative affect sometimes functions as a warning signal, triggering the motivated reassessment of intergroup attitudes (Monteith, 1993). This alerting effect of negative mood is particularly strong for individuals who are habitually anxious and score high on trait anxiety (Ciarrochi & Forgas, 1999).

AFFECT AND ATTITUDE CHANGE

Affect and Attitude Change through Persuasion

Writers on rhetoric and persuasion have long assumed that the ability to induce an emotional response in an audience is an important prerequisite for effective communication and changing attitudes. Early research on the effectiveness of

fear-arousing messages suggested that increasing fear produced increased attitude change (Boster & Mongeau, 1984). However, this effect is undermined when
fear triggers a defensive, self-protective reaction or a level of anxiety and arousal
that is distracting (Ditto & Lopez, 1992; Janis & Feshbach, 1953; Witte & Allen,
2000). In fact, fear seems most effective when the message suggests ways of avoiding negative consequences (Petty, DeSteno, & Rucker, 2001). More recent studies
have confirmed that affect does play a general role in attitude change, whether
due to persuasive communication, or to cognitive dissonance processes (Petty et
al., 2001).

All things being equal, consistent with affect congruity mechanisms, positive affect promotes a more positive response to persuasive messages, a finding
first demonstrated more than 60 years ago (Razran, 1946) and since confirmed
in a variety of studies (McGuire, 1985; Petty, Gleicher, & Baker, 1991). However,
this effect is also subject to important qualifications (Bless, Bohner, Schwarz, &
Strack, 1990; Mackie & Worth, 1989; Wegener, Petty, & Smith, 1995). Dual-process cognitive theories of the persuasion process (Eagly & Chaiken, 1993; Petty
& Cacioppo, 1986) distinguish between *systematic, central-route* and *heuristic,
peripheral route* processing. The effectiveness of persuasive messages depends on
how the message is processed (Petty et al., 2001; Petty et al., 1991). When people
pay little attention to the message and rely on simplistic, heuristic cues instead
(peripheral route processing), affect itself may function as a heuristic cue promoting a mood-congruent response to the message.

This process is very similar to the basic affect–attitude conditioning mechanism discussed earlier (e.g., Clore & Byrne, 1974; Griffitt, 1970; Razran, 1940).
Such a direct affect–attitude link can also be explained in terms of the "how do I
feel about it?" heuristic suggested by Schwarz and Clore (1983). For example, Sinclair, Mark, and Clore (1994) showed that college students were significantly more
likely to agree with persuasive messages advocating comprehensive exams when
they were interviewed on a pleasant, sunny day rather than an unpleasant, rainy
day. Direct effects of mood on attitude change are most likely when people engage
in peripheral route processing, and are neither able nor willing to engage in more
detailed analysis of the message.

The process-sensitivity of mood effects on persuasion is further illustrated in
studies by Petty, Schumann, Richman, and Strathman (1993) who asked participants to view mood-arousing films that featured a persuasive message for a pen.
Involvement was manipulated by allowing some subjects to choose a pen after viewing the ads. Positive mood generally improved responses to the ads, consistent with
heuristic processing when involvement was low. In the high involvement condition,
however, the effect was linked to a different mechanism, indicating more affect-
congruent thoughts being primed by the mood induction. Thus, affect-priming can
influence persuasion and attitude change when people adopt a systematic, central-
route strategy when processing a persuasive message. Individuals who score high
on need for cognition (Cacioppo & Petty, 1982) are habitually inclined to think
systematically, and may be especially open to such affect infusion effects.

Message valence also plays a role in linking affect and attitude change. Wegener,
Petty, and Klein (1994) found that when persuasive arguments emphasized positive

outcomes, happy mood produced more favorable responses. When the arguments pointed to the negative consequences of failing to follow the recommended course, it was negative mood that produced greater attitude change. It seems that good mood primed positive thoughts that facilitated persuasion when the message also emphasized positive outcomes, but negative affect also promoted attitude change when the message focused on negative consequences. These effects were strongest for people high in need for cognition, confirming that it was elaborate processing that produced this mood-congruent effect.

As we have seen earlier, positive and negative affect also recruit fundamentally different information processing strategies (Bless & Fiedler, 2006). Positive mood promotes the top-down heuristic processing of persuasive messages when people respond to both low- and high-quality messages the same way. Sad mood promotes more accommodative, externally focused processing that should increase the effectiveness of high-quality vs. low-quality messages (Bless et al., 1990). However, additional motivational goals may interfere with the processing consequences of affect. For example, people prefer to think and behave in ways that prolong positive affect and reduce negative affect (Clark & Isen, 1982). In an ingenious study, Wegener et al. (1995) manipulated such motivational effects by telling happy or neutral mood people that the persuasive message they were about to read would either make them happy or sad. When happy individuals believed that the message would make them sad, they did not process the message extensively and were equally influenced by high and low quality messages. However, when they thought the message would keep them happy, they engaged in more elaborate, systematic processing and showed differential persuasion in response to strong and weak arguments. These results show that the processing consequences of affect may be readily modified by motivational influences. The Flexible Correction Model (FCM) proposed by Petty and Wegener (1993; Wegener & Petty, 1997), as well as the AIM (Forgas, 2002) seeks to explain the circumstances when such motivated corrections are likely to occur. In conclusion then, affect can influence attitude change in response to persuasive messages both by selectively priming message-consistent information (Wegener et al., 1994) and by promoting an accommodative information processing style (Bless & Fiedler, 2006). These effects are highly context sensitive, however, and subject to the superimposition of motivated processing strategies (Forgas, 2002).

Affect and the Production of Persuasive Messages

Affect may also influence the effectiveness of the persuasive messages people produce to bring about attitude change (Bohner & Schwarz, 1993). Despite much research on affective influences on responding to persuasion (Petty et al., 2001), there has been little work on how such messages are produced. It may be expected that accommodative processing promoted by negative affect should produce more concrete and factual thinking and result in the production of superior persuasive messages. This prediction is consistent with much early theorizing about rhetorical effectiveness going back to Aristotle (Cooper, 1932), as well as psychological research suggesting that "expository information that is concrete...tends to be interesting and well recalled" (Sadowski, 2001, p.263).

In several recent experiments (Forgas, 2007), Australian participants received a mood induction, and then were asked to produce persuasive arguments for or against an increase in student fees, and Aboriginal land rights. Those in a negative mood produced significantly higher quality arguments on both issues. This mood effect was largely due to the greater specificity and concreteness of arguments produced in a negative mood. A further experiment replicated this finding on two completely different attitude issues, consistent with the theoretical prediction that negative mood should promote a more careful, systematic, bottom-up processing style that is more attuned to the requirements of a particular situation (Bless & Fiedler, 2006; Forgas, 2002). However, the ultimate significance of these findings depends on whether the arguments produced by happy and sad participants indeed differ in their actual persuasive power.

To test this, the arguments produced by happy or sad participants were presented to a naïve audience of 256 undergraduate students. Results showed that arguments written by negative mood participants in two experiments were significantly more successful in producing a real change in attitudes than were arguments produced by happy participants. In a final experiment in this series, persuasive attempts by happy and sad people were directed at a "partner" to volunteer for a boring experiment using a series of verbal exchanges on a computer (Forgas, 2007). Negative mood again had a significant beneficial effect on argument quality. However, the offer of a significant reward reduced mood effects, confirming a key prediction of the AIM (Forgas, 1995a, 2002), that mood effects on information processing—and subsequent social influence strategies—are strongest in the absence of motivated processing. This set of experiments confirms that attempts at attitude change using persuasive arguments are also influenced by affect. Arguments produced in a negative mood that promotes accommodative processing are not only of higher quality but are also more effective in producing genuine attitude change, largely because they contain more concrete and specific details and more factual information (Cooper, 1932). Such messages are more interesting and more memorable (Sadowski, 2001). However, when motivation is already high, mood effects tend to diminish, as predicted by the Affect Infusion Model (Forgas, 2002).

These results are consistent with other studies suggesting that negative affect typically promotes a more concrete, accommodative, externally focused information processing style that also can reduce the incidence of judgmental errors and improve eye-witness memory (Forgas, 1998c; Forgas, Vargas, & Laham, 2005). These findings may have interesting applied implications; for example, in industrial and organizational settings where encounters involving persuasive communication are very common (Forgas & George, 2001). Managing successful relationships and resolving personal conflicts also involve a great deal of persuasive communication, often in situations that are affectively charged. It is an intriguing possibility that mild negative affect may actually promote more concrete, accommodative, and ultimately, more successful attitude change strategies in real-life situations.

Affect and Dissonance-Induced Attitude Change

In addition to persuasive communication, the second major avenue for changing attitudes is based on consistency principles. As Festinger (1957) proposed many years ago, the experience of dissonance between attitudes and behaviors can be a highly potent cause of attitude change (Cooper & Fazio, 1984; Harmon-Jones, 2001; Zanna & Cooper, 1974; see Stone & Fernandez, this volume). As dissonance involves feelings of negative arousal, affect is directly implicated in this attitude change mechanism. Cognitive dissonance produces negative affect because discrepancies among cognitions challenge the clarity and certainty of our understanding of the world, and our ability to engage in effective action (Harmon-Jones, 1999, 2001; Harmon-Jones, Brehm, Greenberg, Simon, & Nelson, 1996). This analysis is consistent with Darwin's (1872/1965) evolutionary ideas about the functions of affect (see also Forgas, 2006), and functionalist theories of emotion in particular (Frijda, 1986; Izard, 1977) that predict that emotions have adaptive functions and trigger responses that have survival value.

Interestingly, some conceptualizations of dissonance theory suggest that cognitive discrepancy is neither necessary nor sufficient to produce the experience of dissonance. It is only when negative consequences are "real" and there is a degree of personal involvement that motivated attitude change should be triggered (Cooper & Fazio, 1984). However, experiments by Harmon-Jones et al. (1996) found that dissonance and subsequent attitude change also occurs when the actor's inconsistent action had no real (negative) consequences. It seems then that cognitive dissonance alone can cause negative affect even when there is no real personal involvement. This is consistent with other evidence from research on emotional appraisal, where imagined consequences appear just as effective in producing a reaction as are real consequences (Scherer, 1999).

Self-esteem seems an important factor in affective responses to cognitive discrepancy, as high self-esteem people are better able to handle negative affective states (Forgas et al., 2000; Harmon-Jones, 2001). Affective reactions also depend on the nature of the dissonance experience. Whereas belief disconfirmation is likely to produce anxiety, postdecisional dissonance is more likely to induce regret. This idea is consistent with self-discrepancy theory, which specifically predicts that qualitatively different kinds of self-discrepancies evoke qualitatively distinct affective reactions (Higgins, 1989, 2001). Several experiments suggest a direct relationship between discrepancy-produced negative affect and subsequent attitude change (Zanna & Cooper, 1974). Others, however, failed to find such a link (Elliot & Devine, 1994; Higgins, Rhodewalt, & Zanna, 1979). Measures of arousal also failed to show a direct and consistent link between electro-dermal activity and attitude change (Elkin & Leippe, 1986; Harmon-Jones et al., 1996; Losch & Cacioppo, 1990).

Harmon-Jones (2001) suggested that such inconclusive findings may be due to the attitudes measured being very resistant to change. Further, as affect intensity increases, controlled processing may take over and discrepancy reduction may not occur. Other studies also support the idea that once attention is directed at an affective state, its influence on cognition and behavior is often reduced (Berkowitz,

Jaffee, Jo, & Troccoli, 2000). The availability of alternative attributions for aversive affect may also reduce subsequent attitude change (Losch & Cacioppo, 1990). Other experiments suggest that positive affect decreases, and negative affect increases dissonance reduction and attitude change even if the source of affect is unrelated (Kidd & Berkowitz, 1976; Rhodewalt & Comer, 1979). Once consonance is restored, affective state also tends to improve (Burris, Harmon-Jones, & Tarpley, 1997; Elliot & Devine, 1994). In conclusion, affective states seem to play an important role in attitude change, influencing both the way people respond to persuasive messages, and the way they resolve attitude-behavior discrepancies. However, much work remains to be done in discovering the precise cognitive mechanisms responsible for these effects.

SUMMARY AND CONCLUSIONS

The evidence reviewed in this chapter shows that mild everyday affective states can have a highly significant influence on the way people form, maintain, and change their attitudes, and how attitudes and social information are cognitively represented and categorized (Forgas, 1979; Niedenthal & Halberstadt, 2000). Further, the experiments discussed here show that different information processing strategies play a key role in linking affect and attitudes. The multiprocess AIM (Forgas, 2002) in particular offers a simple and parsimonious explanation of when, how, and why affect infusion into attitudes is or is not likely to occur. A number of studies support the counterintuitive prediction based on the AIM that more extensive, substantive processing enhances mood congruity effects (Forgas, 1994; 1995b; Nasby, 1994, 1996; Sedikides, 1995). Affect infusion influences not only attitudes but subsequent social behaviors as well (Forgas, 1998a, 1998b; 1999a, 1999b). In contrast, affect infusion is absent whenever a social cognitive task could be performed using a simple, well-rehearsed direct access strategy, or a highly motivated strategy that offers little opportunity for primed mood-congruent information to infuse information processing (Fiedler, 1991; Forgas, 1995a). Affect infusion occurs not only in the laboratory, but also in many real-life situations, as evident in attitudes formed in intimate relationships (Forgas, 1994). Obviously, considerably more research is needed before we can fully understand affect's multiple influences on attitudes and interpersonal behavior. I hope this review will stimulate further interest in this fascinating and rapidly developing area of inquiry.

ACKNOWLEDGMENTS

This work was supported by a Professorial Fellowship from the Australian Research Council, and the Research Prize by the Alexander von Humboldt Foundation to Joseph P. Forgas. Please address all correspondence in connection with this paper to Joseph P. Forgas, at the School of Psychology, University of New South Wales, Sydney 2052, Australia; e-mail jp.forgas@unsw.edu.au. For further information on this research project, see also website at http://www.psy.unsw.edu.au/Users/JForgas/jforgas/.

REFERENCES

Abele, A., & Hermer, P. (1993). Mood influences on health-related judgments: Appraisal of own health versus appraisal of unhealthy behaviours. *European Journal of Social Psychology, 23,* 613–625.

Abele, A., & Petzold, P. (1994). How does mood operate in an impression formation task? An information integration approach. *European Journal of Social Psychology, 24,* 173–188.

Adolphs, R., & Damasio, A. (2001). The interaction of affect and cognition: A neurobiological perspective. In J. P. Forgas, (Ed.), *The handbook of affect and social cognition.* (pp. 27–49). Mahwah, NJ: Erlbaum.

Allport, G. W. (1954). *The nature of prejudice.* Reading, MA.: Addison-Wesley.

Alter, A. L., & Forgas, J. P. (2007). On being happy but fearing failure: The effects of mood on self-handicapping strategies. *Journal of Experimental Social Psychology, 43,* 947–954.

Amir, Y. (1969). Contact hypothesis in ethnic relations. *Psychological Bulletin, 71,* 319–342.

Aspinwall, L. G. (1998). Rethinking the role of positive affect in self-regulation. *Motivation and Emotion, 22,* 1–32.

Baumeister, R. F. (1993). *Self-esteem: The puzzle of low self-regard.* New York: Plenum.

Baumeister, R. F. (1998). The self. In D. T. Gilbert, S. T. Fiske, & G. Lindzey (Eds.), *The handbook of social psychology* (pp. 680–740). New York: Oxford University Press.

Berkowitz, L. (2000). *Causes and consequences of feelings.* New York: Psychology Press.

Berkowitz, L. Jaffee, S. Jo, E. & Troccoli, B. T. (2000). On the correction of feeling-induced judgmental biases. In J. P. Forgas (Ed.), *Feeling and thinking: The role of affect in social cognition* (pp. 131–152). New York: Cambridge University Press.

Bless, H. (2000). The interplay of affect and cognition: The mediating role of general knowledge structures. In J. P. Forgas (Ed.), *Feeling and thinking: The role of affect in social cognition.* (pp. 201–222). New York: Cambridge University Press.

Bless, H., Bohner, G., Schwarz, N., & Strack, F. (1990). Mood and persuasion: A cognitive response analysis. *Personality and Social Psychology Bulletin, 16,* 331–345.

Bless, H., & Fiedler, K. (2006). Mood and the regulation of information processing and behavior. In J. P. Forgas (Ed.), *Affect in social cognition and behavior* (pp. 65–84). New York: Psychology Press.

Bless, H., Schwarz, N., & Wieland, R. (1996c). Mood and the impact of category membership and individuating information. *European Journal of Social Psychology, 26,* 935–959.

Bodenhausen, G. V. (1993). Emotions, arousal, and stereotypic judgments: A heuristic model of affect and stereotyping. In D. M. Mackie & D. L. Hamilton (Eds.), *Affect, cognition, and stereotyping* (pp. 13–37). San Diego, CA: Academic Press.

Bodenhausen, G. V., & Macrae, C. N. (1998). Stereotype activation and inhibition. In R. S. Wyer, Jr. (Ed.), *Stereotype activation and inhibition: Advances in social cognition* (Vol. 11, pp. 1–52). Mahwah, NJ: Erlbaum.

Bodenhausen, G. V., Kramer, G. P., & Süsser, K. (1994). Happiness and stereotypic thinking in social judgment. *Journal of Personality and Social Psychology, 66,* 621–632.

Bodenhausen, G. V., Macrae, C. N., & Milne, A. B. (1998). Disregarding social stereotypes: Implications for memory, judgment, and behavior. In J. M. Golding & C. M.

MacLeod (Eds.), *Intentional forgetting: Interdisciplinary approaches* (pp. 349–368). Mahwah, NJ: Erlbaum.

Bodenhausen, G. V., Macrae, C. N., & Sherman, J. W. (1999). On the dialectics of discrimination: Dual processes in social stereotyping. In S. Chaiken & Y. Trope (Eds.), *Dual-process theories in social psychology* (pp. 271–290). New York: Guilford.

Bodenhausen, G. V., & Moreno, K. N. (2000). How do I feel about them? The role of affective reactions in intergroup perception. In H. Bless & J. P. Forgas (Eds.), *The role of subjective states in social cognition and behavior* (pp. 283–303). Philadelphia: Psychology Press.

Bodenhausen, G. V., Sheppard, L. A., & Kramer, G. P. (1994). Negative affect and social judgment: The differential impact of anger and sadness. *European Journal of Social Psychology, 24,* 45–62.

Bohner, G., & Schwarz, N. (1993). Mood states influence the production of persuasive arguments. *Communication Research, 20,* 696–722.

Boster, F. J., & Mongeau, P. (1984). Fear-arousing persuasive messages. In R. N. Bostrom (Ed.), *Communication yearbook* (Vol. 8, pp. 330–375). Beverly Hills, CA: Sage.

Bower, G. H. (1981). Mood and memory. *American Psychologist, 36,* 129–148.

Bower, G. H., & Forgas, J. P. (2001). Mood and social memory. In J. P. Forgas (Ed.), *The Handbook of affect and social cognition* (pp. 95–120). Mahwah, NJ: Erlbaum.

Brewer, M. B., & Miller, N. (1996). *Intergroup relations.* Pacific Grove, CA: Brooks/Cole.

Brown, J. D., & Mankowski, T. A. (1993). Self-esteem, mood, and self-evaluation: Changes in the mood and the way you see you. *Journal of Personality and Social Psychology, 64,* 421–430.

Burris, C. T., Harmon-Jones, E., & Tarpley, W. R. (1997). "By faith alone": Religious agitation and cognitive dissonance. *Basic and Applied Social Psychology, 19,* 17–31.

Byrne, D., & Clore, G. L. (1970). A reinforcement model of evaluation responses. *Personality: An International Journal, 1,* 103–128.

Cacioppo, J. T., & Petty, R. E. (1982). The need for cognition. *Journal of Personality and Social Psychology, 42,* 116–131.

Campbell, J. D., Trapnell, P. D., Heine, S. J., Katz, I. M., Lavallee, L. F., & Lehman, D. R. (1996). Self-concept clarity: Measurement, personality correlates, and cultural boundaries. *Journal of Personality and Social Psychology, 70,* 141–156.

Cervone, D., Kopp, D. A., Schaumann, L., & Scott, W. D. (1994). Mood, self-efficacy, and performance standards: Lower moods induce higher standards for performance. *Journal of Personality and Social Psychology, 67,* 499–512.

Chaiken, S., & Maheswaran, D. (1994). Heuristic processing can bias systematic processing: Effects of source credibility, argument ambiguity, and task importance on attitude judgment. *Journal of Personality and Social Psychology, 66,* 460–473.

Ciarrochi, J. V., & Forgas, J. P. (1999). On being tense yet tolerant: The paradoxical effects of trait anxiety and aversive mood on intergroup judgments. *Group Dynamics: Theory, Research and Practice, 3,* 227–238.

Ciarrochi, J. V., & Forgas, J. P. (2000). The pleasure of possessions: affective influences and personality in the evaluation of consumer items. *European Journal of Social Psychology, 30,* 631-649.

Clark, M. S., & Isen, A. M. (1982). Toward understanding the relationship between feeling states and social behavior. In A. H. Hastorf & A. M. Isen (Eds.), *Cognitive social psychology* (pp. 73–108). New York: Elsevier-North Holland.

Clore, G. L., & Byrne, D. (1974). The reinforcement affect model of attraction. In T. L. Huston (Ed.), *Foundations of interpersonal attraction* (pp. 143–170). New York: Academic Press.

Clore, G. L. Gasper, K., & Garvin, E. (2001). Affect as information. In J. P. Forgas (Ed.), *The handbook of affect and social cognition* (pp. 121–144). Mahwah, NJ: Erlbaum.

Clore, G. L., & Storbeck, J. (2006). Affect as information for social judgment, behavior, and memory. In J. P. Forgas (Ed.), *Affect in social cognition and behavior* (pp. 154–178). New York: Psychology Press.

Cooper, J. B. (1959). Emotion in prejudice. *Science, 130,* 314–318.

Cooper, J. B., & Fazio, R. H. (1984). A new look at dissonance theory. In L. Berkowitz (Ed.), *Advances in experimental social psychology* (Vol. 17, pp. 229–266). San Diego, CA: Academic Press.

Cooper, L. (1932). *The rhetoric of Aristotle.* New York: Appleton-Century.

Croyle, R. T., & Uretsky, M. D. (1987). Effects of mood on self-appraisal of health status. *Health Psychology, 6,* 239–253.

Damasio, A. R. (1994). *Descartes' error.* New York: Grosset/Putnam.

Darwin, C. (1965). *The expression of emotions in man and animals.* Chicago: University of Chicago Press. (Original work published in 1872)

DeSteno, D. A., & Salovey, P. (1997). The effects of mood on the structure of the self-concept. *Cognition and Emotion, 11,* 351–372.

Devine, P. G., & Monteith, M. J. (1993). The role of discrepancy-associated affect in prejudice reduction. In D. M. Mackie & D. L. Hamilton (Eds.), *Affect, cognition, and stereotyping: Interactive processes in group perception* (pp. 317–344). San Diego, CA: Academic Press.

Ditto, P. H., & Lopez, D. F., (1992). Motivated skepticism: Use of differential decision criteria for preferred and nonpreferred conclusions. *Journal of Personality & Social Psychology, 63,* 568–584.

Dovidio, J. F., Gaertner, S. L., Isen, A. M., & Lowrance, R. (1995). Group representations and intergroup bias: Positive affect, similarity, and group size. *Personality and Social Psychology Bulletin, 18,* 856–865.

Dovidio, J. F., Gaertner, S. L., Isen, A. M., Rust, M., & Guerra, P. (1998). Positive affect, cognition, and the reduction of intergroup bias. In C. Sedikides, J. Schopler, & C. A. Insko (Eds.), *Intergroup cognition and intergroup behavior* (pp. 337–366). Mahwah, NJ: Erlbaum.

Duncan, B. L. (1976). Differential social perception and attribution of intergroup violence: Testing the lower limits of stereotyping of Blacks. *Journal of Personality and Social Psychology, 34,* 590–598.

Eagly, A. H., & Chaiken, S. (1993). *The psychology of attitudes.* New York: Harcourt Brace Jovanovich.

Eich, E., & Macauley, D. (2000). Fundamental factors in mood-dependent memory. In: J. P. Forgas (Ed.), *Feeling and thinking: The role of affect in social cognition* (pp. 109–130). New York: Cambridge University Press.

Elkin, R. A., & Leippe, M. R. (1986). Physiological arousal, dissonance, and attitude change: Evidence for a dissonance-arousal link and a "don't remind me" effect. *Journal of Personality and Social Psychology, 51,* 55–65.

Elliot, A. J., & Devine, P. G. (1994). On the motivation nature of cognitive dissonance: Dissonance as psychological discomfort. *Journal of Personality and Social Psychology, 67,* 382–394.

Ellis, H. C., & Ashbrook, T. W. (1988). Resource allocation model of the effects of depressed mood state on memory. In K. Fiedler & J. P. Forgas (Eds.), *Affect, cognition and social behaviour* (pp. 25–43). Toronto: Hogrefe.

Esses, V. M., & Zanna, M. P. (1995). Mood and the expression of ethnic stereotypes. *Journal of Personality and Social Psychology, 69,* 1052–1068.

Feshbach, S., & Singer, R. D. (1957). The effects of fear arousal and suppression of fear upon social perception. *Journal of Abnormal and Social Psychology, 55,* 283–288.

Festinger, L. (1957). *A theory of cognitive dissonance.* Palo Alto, CA: Stanford University Press.

Fiedler, K. (1990). Mood-dependent selectivity in social cognition. In W. Stroebe & M. Hewstone (Eds.), *European review of social psychology* (Vol. 1, pp. 1–32). New York: Wiley.

Fiedler, K. (1991). On the task, the measures and the mood in research on affect and social cognition. In J. P. Forgas (Ed.), *Emotion and social judgments* (pp. 83–104). Oxford: Pergamon.

Fiedler, K. (2000). Toward an integrative account of affect and cognition phenomena using the BIAS computer algorithm. In J. P. Forgas (Ed.), *Feeling and thinking: The role of affect in social cognition.* New York: Cambridge University Press.

Fiedler, K. (2001). Affective influences on social information processing. In J. P. Forgas (Ed.), *The handbook of affect and social cognition* (pp. 163–185). Mahwah, NJ: Erlbaum.

Fiedler, K., & Bless, H. (2001). The formation of beliefs in the interface of affective and cognitive processes. In N. Frijda, A. Manstead, & S. Bem (Eds.), The influence of emotions on beliefs. New York: Cambridge University Press.

Fiedler, K., & Forgas, J. P. (1988) (Eds.). *Affect, cognition, and social behavior: New evidence and integrative attempts* (pp. 44–62). Toronto: Hogrefe.

Fiedler, K., & Stroehm, W. (1986). What kind of mood influences what kind of memory: The role of arousal and information structure. *Memory and Cognition, 14,* 181–188.

Fiske, S. T., & Pavelchak, M. A. (1986). Category-based versus piecemeal-based affective responses: Developments in schema-triggered affect. In R. M. Sorrentino & E. T. Higgins (Eds.), *Handbook of motivation and cognition* (Vol. 1, pp. 167–203). New York: Guilford.

Forgas, J. P. (1979). *Social episodes: The study of interaction routines.* London: Academic Press.

Forgas, J. P. (1982) Episode cognition: Internal representations of interaction routines. In L. Berkowitz (Ed.), *Advances in experimental social psychology* (pp. 59–104), New York: Academic Press.

Forgas, J. P. (1992). On bad mood and peculiar people: Affect and person typicality in impression formation. *Journal of Personality and Social Psychology, 62,* 863–875.

Forgas, J. P. (1993). On making sense of odd couples: Mood effects on the perception of mismatched relationships. *Personality and Social Psychology Bulletin, 19,* 59–71.

Forgas, J. P. (1994). Sad and guilty? Affective influences on the explanation of conflict episodes. *Journal of Personality and Social Psychology, 66,* 56–68.

Forgas, J. P. (1995a). Mood and judgment: The affect infusion model (AIM). *Psychological Bulletin, 117*(1), 39–66.

Forgas, J. P. (1995b). Strange couples: Mood effects on judgments and memory about prototypical and atypical targets. *Personality and Social Psychology Bulletin, 21,* 747–765.

Forgas, J. P. (1998a). On feeling good and getting your way: Mood effects on negotiation strategies and outcomes. *Journal of Personality and Social Psychology, 74,* 565–577.

Forgas, J. P. (1998b). Asking nicely? Mood effects on responding to more or less polite requests. *Personality and Social Psychology Bulletin, 24,* 173–185.

Forgas, J. P. (1998c). Happy and mistaken? Mood effects on the fundamental attribution error. *Journal of Personality and Social Psychology, 75,* 318–331.

Forgas, J. P. (1999a). On feeling good and being rude: Affective influences on language use and request formulations. *Journal of Personality and Social Psychology, 76,* 928–939.

Forgas, J. P. (1999b). Feeling and speaking: Mood effects on verbal communication strategies. *Personality and Social Psychology Bulletin, 25,* 850–863.

Forgas, J. P. (Ed.). (2000). *Feeling and thinking: the role of affect in social cognition.* New York: Cambridge University Press.

Forgas, J. P. (2002). Feeling and doing: Affective influences on interpersonal behavior. *Psychological Inquiry, 13*, 1–28.

Forgas, J. P. (Ed.). (2006). *Affect in social cognition and behavior*. New York: Psychology Press.

Forgas, J. P. (2007). When sad is better than happy: Negative affect can improve the quality and effectiveness of persuasive messages and social influence strategies. *Journal of Experimental Social Psychology, 43*, 513–528.

Forgas, J. P., & Bower, G. H. (1987). Mood effects on person perception judgements. *Journal of Personality and Social Psychology, 53*, 53–60.

Forgas, J. P., Bower, G. H., & Krantz, S. (1984). The influence of mood on perceptions of social interactions. *Journal of Experimental Social Psychology, 20*, 497–513.

Forgas, J. P., Bower, G. H., & Moylan, S. J. (1990). Praise or blame? Affective influences on attributions for achievement. *Journal of Personality and Social Psychology, 59*, 809–818.

Forgas, J. P., Ciarrochi, J. V. & Moylan, S. J. (2000). Subjective experience and mood regulation: the role of information processing strategies. In: H. Bless & J. P. Forgas (Eds.). *The message within: The role of subjective experience in social cognition* (pp. 179–202). Philadelphia: Psychology Press.

Forgas, J. P., & Fiedler, K. (1996). Us and them: Mood effects on intergroup discrimination. *Journal of Personality and Social Psychology, 70*, 36–52.

Forgas, J. P., & George, J. M. (2001). Affective influences on judgments and behavior in organizations: An information processing perspective. *Organizational Behavior and Human decision Processes, 86,* 3–34.

Forgas, J. P., & Moylan, S. J. (1987). After the movies: the effects of transient mood states on social judgments. *Personality and Social Psychology Bulletin, 13*, 478–489.

Forgas, J. P., Vargas, P., & Laham, S. (2005). Mood effects on eyewitness memory: Affective influences on susceptibility to misinformation. *Journal of Experimental Social Psychology, 41*, 574–588.

Frijda, N. (1986). *The emotions*. Cambridge, UK: Cambridge University Press.

Gaertner, S. L., & Dovidio, J. F. (1986). The aversive form of racism. In J. F. Dovidio & S. L. Gaertner (Eds.), *Prejudice, discrimination, and racism* (pp. 9–125). San Diego, CA: Academic Press.

Gilbert, D. T., & Hixon, J. G. (1991). The trouble of thinking: Activation and application of stereotypic beliefs. *Journal of Personality and Social Psychology, 60*, 509–517.

Gouaux, C. (1971). Induced affective states and interpersonal attraction. *Journal of Personality and Social Psychology, 20*, 37–43.

Gouaux, C., & Summers, K. (1973). Interpersonal attraction as a function of affective states and affective change. *Journal of Research in Personality, 7*, 254–260.

Griffitt, W. (1970). Environmental effects on interpersonal behavior: Ambient effective temperature and attraction. *Journal of Personality and Social Psychology, 15*, 240–244.

Haddock, G., Zanna, M. P., & Esses, V. M. (1993). Assessing the structure of prejudicial attitudes: The case of attitudes toward homosexuals. *Journal of Personality and Social Psychology, 65*, 1105–1118.

Haddock, G., Zanna, M. P., & Esses, V. M. (1994). Mood and the expression of intergroup attitudes: The moderating role of affect intensity. *European Journal of Social Psychology, 24*, 189–205.

Harmon-Jones, E. (1999). Toward an understanding of the motivation underlying dissonance effects: Is the production of aversive consequences necessary? In E. Harmon-Jones & J. Mills, *Cognitive dissonance: Progress on a pivotal theory in social psychology* (pp. 71–99). Washington, D.C.: American Psychological Association.

Harmon-Jones, E. (2001). The role of affect in cognitive dissonance processes. In: J. P. Forgas (Ed.), *The handbook of affect and social cognition* (pp. 237–255). Mahwah, NJ: Erlbaum.

Harmon-Jones, E., Brehm, J. W., Greenberg, J., Simon, L., & Nelson, D. E. (1996). Evidence that the production of aversive consequences is not necessary to create cognitive dissonance. *Journal of Personality and Social Psychology, 70,* 5–16.

Heider, F. (1958). *The psychology of interpersonal relations.* New York: Wiley.

Hertel, G., & Fiedler, K. (1994). Affective and cognitive influences in a social dilemma game. *European Journal of Social Psychology, 24,* 131–145.

Higgins, E. T. (1989). Self-discrepancy theory: What patterns of self-beliefs cause people to suffer? In L. Berkowitz (Ed.), *Advances in experimental social psychology, 22,* 93–136.

Higgins, E. T. (2001). Promotion and prevention experiences: relating emotions to non-emotional motivational states. In J. P. Forgas (Ed.), *The handbook of affect and social cognition* (pp. 186–211). Mahwah, NJ: Erlbaum.

Higgins, E. T., Rhodewalt, F., & Zanna, M. P. (1979). Dissonance motivation: Its nature, persistence, and reinstatement. *Journal of Experimental Social Psychology, 15,* 16–34.

Hilgard, E. R. (1980). The trilogy of mind: Cognition, affection, and conation. *Journal of the History of the Behavioral Sciences, 16,* 107–117.

Isen, A. M., Niedenthal, P., & Cantor, N. (1992). An influence of positive affect on social categorization. *Motivation and Emotion, 16,* 65–78.

Ito, T. & Cacioppo, J. (2001). Affect and attitudes: A social neuroscience approach. In: J. P. Forgas (Ed.), *The handbook of affect and social cognition* (pp. 50–74). Mahwah, NJ: Erlbaum.

Izard, C. E. (1977). *Human emotions.* New York: Plenum.

Janis, I. L., & Feshbach, S. (1953). Effects of fear-arousing communications. *Journal of Abnormal and Social Psychology, 48,* 78–92.

Jones, J. M. (1997). *Prejudice and racism* (2nd ed.). New York: McGraw-Hill.

Katz, P. A. (1976). The acquisition of racial attitudes in children. In P. A. Katz (Ed.), *Toward sthe elimination of racism* (pp 176–198). Elmsford, NY: Pergamon.

Keltner, D., Ellsworth, P. C., & Edwards, K. (1993). Beyond simple pessimism: Effects of sadness and anger on social judgment. *Journal of Personality and Social Psychology, 64,* 740–752.

Kidd, R. F., & Berkowitz, L. (1976). Effect of dissonance arousal on helpfulness. *Journal of Personality and Social Psychology, 33,* 613–622.

Labott, S. M., & Martin, R. B. (1990). Emotional coping, age, and physical disorder. *Behavioral Medicine, 16,* 53–61.

Lambert, A. J., Khan, S. R., Lickel, B. A., & Fricke, K. (1997). Mood and the correction of positive versus negative stereotypes. *Journal of Personality and Social Psychology, 72,* 1002–1016.

Larsen, R. J., & Diener, E. (1987). Affect intensity as an individual difference characteristic: A review. *Journal of Research in Personality, 21,* 1–39.

Losch, M. E., & Cacioppo, J. T. (1990). Cognitive dissonance may enhance sympathetic tonus, but attitudes are changed to reduce negative affect rather than arousal. *Journal of Experimental Social Psychology, 26,* 289–304.

Mackie, D. M., & Worth, L. T. (1989). Processing deficits and the mediation of positive affect in persuasion. *Journal of Personality and Social Psychology, 57,* 27–40.

Markus, H. (1977). Self-schemata and processing information about the self. *Journal of Personality and Social Psychology, 35,* 63–78.

Martin, L. L. (2000). Moods don't convey information: Moods in context do. In J. P. Forgas (Ed.), *Feeling and thinking: The role of affect in social cognition* (pp. 153–177). New York: Cambridge University Press.

Martin, L. L., & Clore, G. (Eds.). (2001). *Theories of cognition and affect.* Mahwah, NJ: Erlbaum.

Mayer, J. D., Gaschke, Y. N., Braverman, D. L., & Evans, T. W. (1992). Mood-congruent judgment is a general effect. *Journal of Personality and Social Psychology, 63,* 119–132.

Mayer, J. D., & Volanth, A. J. (1985). Cognitive involvement in the emotional response system. *Motivation and Emotion, 9,* 261–275.

McGuire, W. J. (1985). Attitudes and attitude change. In G. Lindzey & E. Aronson (Eds.), *The handbook or social psychology* (3rd ed., Vol. 2, pp. 233–346). New York: Random House.

Mead, G. H. (1934). *Mind, self and society.* Chicago: University of Chicago Press.

Monteith, M. J. (1993). Self-regulation of prejudiced responses: Implications for progress in prejudice-reduction efforts. *Journal of Personality and Social Psychology, 65,* 469–485.

Nasby, W. (1994). Moderators of mood-congruent encoding: Self-/Other-reference and affirmative/nonaffirmative judgement. *Cognition and Emotion, 8,* 259–278.

Nasby, W. (1996). Moderators of mood-congruent encoding and judgment: Evidence that elated and depressed moods implicate distinct processes. *Cognition and Emotion, 10,* 361–377.

Niedenthal, P., & Halberstadt, J. (2000). Grounding categories in emotional response. In J. P. Forgas (Ed.), *Feeling and thinking: the role of affect in social cognition* (pp. 357–386). New York: Cambridge University Press.

Pervin, L. A. (1976). A free-response description approach to the analysis of person-situation interaction. *Journal of Personality and Social Psychology, 34,* 465–474.

Petty, R. E., & Cacioppo, J. T. (1986). The elaboration likelihood model of persuasion. In L. Berkowitz (Ed.), *Advances in experimental social psychology* (Vol. 19, pp. 123–205). New York: Academic Press.

Petty, R. E., DeSteno, D., & Rucker, D. (2001). The role of affect in attitude change. In J. P. Forgas (Ed.), *The handbook of affect and social cognition* (pp. 212–266). Mahwah, NJ: Erlbaum.

Petty, R. E., Gleicher, F., & Baker, S. M. (1991). Multiple roles for affect in persuasion. In J. P. Forgas (Ed.), *Emotion and social judgments* (pp. 181–200). Oxford: Pergamon Press.

Petty, R. E., Schumann, D. W., Richman, S. A., & Strathman, A. J. (1993). Positive mood and persuasion: Different roles for affect under high- and low-elaboration conditions. *Journal of Personality and Social Psychology, 64,* 5–20.

Petty, R. E., & Wegener, D. T. (1993). Flexible correction processes in social judgment: correcting for context-induced contrast. *Journal of Experimental Social Psychology, 29,* 137–165.

Petty, R. E., Wegener, D. T., & Fabrigar, L. R. (1997). Attitudes and attitude change. *Annual Review of Psychology, 48,* 609–647.

Ragunathan, R., & Pham, M. T. (1999). All negative moods are not equal: Motivational influences of anxiety and sadness on decision making. *Organizational Behavior and Human Decision Processes, 79,* 56–77.

Ragunathan, & Trope, Y. (1999). Mood-as-a-resource in processing persuasive messages. Unpublished manuscript.

Razran, G. H. S. (1940). Conditioned response changes in rating and appraising sociopolitical slogans. *Psychological Bulletin, 37,* 481.

Reed, M. B., & Aspinwall, L. G. (1998). Self-affirmation reduces biased processing of health-risk information. *Motivation and Emotion, 22,* 99–132.

Rhodewalt, F., & Comer, R. (1979). Induced-compliance attitude change: Once more with feeling. *Journal of Experimental Social Psychology, 15,* 35–47.

Rusting, C. L. (2001). Personality as a mediator of affective influences on social cognition. In: J. P. Forgas (Ed.), *The handbook of affect and social cognition.* (pp. 371–391). Mahwah, N J: Erlbaum.

Rusting, C. L. (1998). Personality, mood, and cognitive processing of emotional information: Three conceptual frameworks. *Psychological Bulletin, 124*(2), 165–196.

Sadowski, M. (2001). Resolving the effects of concreteness on interest, comprehension and learning. *Educational Psychology Review, 13,* 263–281.

Salovey, P., & Birnbaum, D. (1989). Influence of mood on health-relevant cognitions. *Journal of Personality and Social Psychology, 57,* 539–551.

Salovey, P., Detweiler, J. B. Steward, W. T., & Bedell, B.T. (2001). Affect and health-relevant cognition. In J. Forgas (Ed.), *Handbook of affect and social cognition* (pp. 344–370). Mahwah, NJ: Erlbaum.

Salovey, P., Rothman, A. J., & Rodin, J. (1998). Health behavior. In D. T. Gilbert, S. T. Fiske, & G. Lindzey (Eds.), *The handbook of social psychology* (4th ed., Vol. 2, pp. 633–683). New York: McGraw-Hill.

Scherer, K. R. (1984). On the nature and function of emotion: A component process approach. In K.R. Scherer & P. Ekman (Eds.), *Approaches to emotion* (pp. 293–318). Hillsdale, NJ: Erlbaum.

Scherer, K. R. (1999). Appraisal theory. In T. Dalgleish & M. Power (Eds.), *Handbook of cognition and emotion* (pp. 637–664). Chichester, UK: Wiley.

Schwarz, N. (1990). Feelings as information: Informational and motivational functions of affective states. In E. T. Higgins & R. Sorrentino (Eds.), *Handbook of motivation and cognition: Foundations of social behaviour* (Vol. 2, pp. 527–561). New York: Guilford.

Schwarz, N., & Clore, G. L. (1983). Mood, misattribution and judgments of well being: Informative and directive functions of affective states. *Journal of Personality and Social Psychology, 45,* 513–523.

Schwarz, N., & Clore, G. L. (1988). How do I feel about it? The informative function of affective states. In K. Fiedler & J. P. Forgas (Eds.), *Affect, cognition, and social behavior* (pp. 44–62). Toronto: Hogrefe.

Sedikides, C. (1994). Incongruent effects of sad mood on self-conception valence: It's a matter of time. *European Journal of Social Psychology, 24,* 161–172.

Sedikides, C. (1995). Central and peripheral self-conceptions are differentially influenced by mood: Tests of the differential sensitivity hypothesis. *Journal of Personality and Social Psychology, 69*(4), 759–777.

Sedikides, C., & Strube, M. J. (1997). Self-evaluation: To thine own self be good, to thine own self be sure, to thine own self be true, and to thine own self be better. In M. P. Zanna (Ed.), *Advances in experimental social psychology* (Vol. 29, pp. 209–270). New York: Academic Press.

Sinclair, R. C., & Mark, M. M. (1995). The effects of mood state on judgmental accuracy: Processing strategy as a mechanism. *Cognition and Emotion, 9,* 417–438.

Sinclair, R. C., Mark, M. M., & Clore, G. L. (1994). Mood related persuasion depends on (mis)attributions. *Social Cognition, 12,* 309–326.

Smith, S. M., & Petty, R. E. (1995). Personality moderators of mood congruency effects on cognition: The role of self-esteem and negative mood regulation. *Journal of Personality and Social Psychology, 68,* 1092–1107.

Snyder, C. R. (1994). *The psychology of hope: You can get there from here.* New York: The Free Press.

Stangor, C., Sullivan, L. A., & Ford, T. E. (1991). Affective and cognitive determinants of prejudice. *Social Cognition, 9,* 359–380.

Stephan, W. G., & Stephan, C. W. (1996). *Intergroup relations.* Boulder, CO: Westview Press.

Strack, F. (1992). The different routes to social judgments: Experiential versus informational strategies. In L. L. Martin & A. Tesser (Eds.), *The construction of social judgments* (pp. 249–275). Hillsdale, NJ: Erlbaum.

Swann, W. B., Jr. (1990). To be adored or to be known? The interplay of self-enhancement and self-verification. In E. T. Higgins & R. M. Sorrentino (Eds.), *Handbook of motivation and cognition: Foundations of social behavior* (Vol. 2, pp. 408–448). New York: Guilford Press.

Thomas, W. I., & Znaniecki, F. (1928). *The Polish peasant in Europe and America.* Boston: Badger.

Trope, Y. (1986). Self-enhancement and self-assessment in achievement behavior. In R. M. Sorrentino & E. T. Higgins (Eds.), *The handbook of motivation and cognition: Foundations of social behavior* (Vol. 2, pp. 350–378). New York: Guilford.

Trope, Y., Ferguson, M., & Raghunanthan, R. (2001). Mood as a resource in processing self-relevent information. In J. P. Forgas (Ed.), *The handbook of affect and social cognition* (pp. 256–274). Mahwah, NJ: Erlbaum.

Trope, Y., & Gervey, B. (1998). Resolving conflicts among self-evaluative motives. Paper presented at the Annual Convention of Workshop of Achievement and Task Motivation. Thessaloniki, Greece.

Trope, Y., & Neter, E. (1994). Reconciling competing motives in self-evaluation: The role of self-control in feedback seeking. *Journal of Personality and Social Psychology, 66,* 646–657.

Trope, Y., & Pomerantz, E. M. (1998). Resolving conflicts among self-evaluative motives: Positive experiences as a resource for overcoming defensiveness. *Motivation and Emotion, 22,* 53–72.

Wegener, D. T., & Petty, R. E. (1997). The flexible correction model: The role of naïve theories of bias in bias correction. In M. P. Zanna (Ed.), *Advances in experimental social psychology* (Vol. 29, pp. 141–208). New York: Academic Press.

Wegener, D. T., Petty, R. E., & Klein, D. J. (1994) Effects of mood on high elaboration attitude change: The mediating role of likelihood judgments. *European Journal of Social Psychology, 24,* 25–43.

Wegener, D. T., Petty, R. E., & Smith, S. M. (1995). Positive mood can increase or decrease message scrutiny: The hedonic contingency view of mood and message processing. *Journal of Personality and Social Psychology, 69,* 5–15.

Wilder, D. A., & Shapiro, P. N. (1989). Role of competition-induced anxiety in limiting the beneficial impact of positive behavior by an outgroup member. *Journal of Personality and Social Psychology, 56,* 60–69.

Witte, K., & Allen, M. (2000). A meta-analysis of fear appeals: Implications for effective public health campaigns. *Health Education and Behavior, 27,* 591–615.

Zajonc, R. B. (1980). Feeling and thinking: Preferences need no inferences. *American Psychologist, 35,* 151–175.

Zajonc, R.B. (2000). Feeling and thinking: Closing the debate over the independence of affect. In J. P. Forgas (Ed.), *Feeling and thinking: The role of affect in social cognition* (pp. 31–58). New York: Cambridge University Press.

Zanna, M. P., & Cooper, J. (1974). Dissonance and the pill: An attribution approach to studying the arousal properties of dissonance. *Journal of Personality and Social Psychology, 29,* 703–709.

Zanna, M. P., Kiesler, C. A., & Pilkonis, P. A. (1970). Positive and negative attitudinal affect established by classical conditioning. *Journal of Personality and Social Psychology, 14,* 321–328.

IV

Attitudes
Change and Resistance

8

Information Processing Approaches to Persuasion
Integrating Assumptions from the Dual- and Single-Processing Perspectives

GERD BOHNER
Universität Bielefeld
HANS-PETER ERB
Helmut Schmidt University, Hamburg
FRANK SIEBLER
University of Tromsø

*I*n a study by Gorn (1982), undergraduates were exposed to attractive or unattractive music (the musical *Grease* or traditional Indian music) while they watched a commercial for a pen that was either blue or beige. Later they were asked to evaluate the music and received a pen of their color choice. The results showed that when *Grease* was played, the majority of participants chose the advertised color, no matter if it was blue or beige; when the disliked Indian music was played, however, the majority chose the nonadvertised color. Thus, when recipients were merely exposed to commercials, a simple association between a product and another stimulus affected their product preferences. In a second study, however, where recipients expected to make a decision, the factual information contained in the commercial proved to be more influential than the type of background music played.

In many respects, Gorn's (1982) studies are exemplary of persuasion research conducted over the last three decades. His results suggest, in a general sense, that the effects various pieces of information exert on persuasion outcomes depend on recipient states and are mediated by what the recipient makes of the information. This may imply several questions: What makes people responsive to the music in one experimental condition, but to the factual information in the other? Is there a theoretically meaningful difference between a type of information represented by the music and another type of information represented by the facts stated in the commercial? Do the respective effects of the music and the factual information represent different types of persuasion processes?

In this chapter, we present a selective review of information processing approaches to persuasion that have addressed such questions. In particular, we first contrast the dual-process approaches with the unimodel of persuasion. Then we apply the unimodel perspective to hypotheses—originally generated within the dual-processing approach—about the interplay of processing different pieces of persuasive evidence and its implications for persuasion as a sequential process. Finally, we consider the connectionist modeling of information processing in persuasion as a theoretical complement to symbolic theories.

PERSUASION AS INFORMATION PROCESSING: CONCEPTUAL ISSUES

We begin by defining some key terms. Persuasion research deals with the formation or change of attitudes through information processing, usually in response to a message about the attitude object. An attitude may be defined as a summary evaluation of an object of thought (e.g., Bohner & Wänke, 2002). One aspect that has recently been hotly debated is whether evaluations have to remain stable over an extended period and have to be stored in long-term memory to qualify as an attitude. Some researchers define attitudes as enduring concepts that are stored in memory and can be retrieved accordingly (e.g., Albarracín, Wang, Li, & Noguchi, this volume; Allport, 1935; Petty, Priester, & Wegener, 1994). This perspective has been termed the *file-drawer model* because it characterizes attitudes as mental files that individuals consult when evaluating an object (Wilson, Lisle, & Kraft, 1990; for recent theories subscribing to this view, see Cohen & Reed, 2006; Petty, 2006). In contrast, other researchers view attitudes as temporary constructions that an individual generates at the time an evaluative judgment is needed (e.g., Tourangeau & Rasinski, 1988; for reviews see Schwarz & Bohner, 2001; Wilson & Hodges, 1992). According to this "attitudes-as-constructions perspective," people do not need to retrieve a previously stored evaluation—instead, they generate an evaluative judgment based on the information that is accessible in a given situation.

In our view, the attitudes-as-constructions model is more comprehensive and parsimonious because it explains both temporal stability and change without assigning a special theoretical status to evaluations retrieved from memory as compared to other pieces of information concerning the attitude object (for discussion, see Schwarz, 2006; Schwarz & Bohner, 2001). This is not to say that stored evaluations do not exist; in fact, the persuasion theories we review often refer to such stored evaluations, which is fully compatible with our view. We simply do not assign any special status to stored evaluations as opposed to evaluations generated on-line. Accordingly, we conceive of persuasion research as studying a particular subset of the conditions that give rise to the construction of an attitude judgment. From this perspective, persuasion encompasses both attitude change and attitude formation, which we do not conceive as conceptually distinct (Schwarz & Bohner, 2001). In line with this comprehensive treatment of attitudinal judgments as temporary constructions, persuasion researchers often study responses to messages about novel or fictitious attitude objects, which recipients have never evaluated before (e.g., Chaiken & Maheswaran, 1994; Erb, Bohner, Schmälzle, & Rank, 1998).

HOW MUCH THOUGHT?

Theories of persuasion may be ordered according to the amount of effort they assign to the process of generating an attitude judgment (Petty & Cacioppo, 1981). Examples for processes influencing attitudes that seem to require little cognitive effort are: evaluative conditioning (Walther & Langer, this volume); mere exposure (Zajonc, 1968); and heuristic processing (Chaiken, 1987). The assumption of more effortful processing was at the core of the message-learning approach (Hovland, Janis, & Kelley, 1953), and later, the cognitive response approach to persuasion (Petty, Ostrom, & Brock, 1981). Whereas the message-learning approach emphasized the reception and memorizing of message content as a central element of persuasion, the cognitive response approach stresses the role of active thought processes that message recipients engage in, such as silent approval or counterarguing. More recently, the cognitive response approach was expanded by considering metacognitions and self-validating thoughts in addition to direct responses to persuasive evidence (Briñol, Petty, & Tormala, 2004; see Tormala, this volume). In comparison, the valence of recipients' cognitive responses, including their metacognitions, has proved to be a more consistent predictor of persuasion outcomes than recipients' recall of message content (see Eagly & Chaiken, 1993, chapter 6). Empirical data thus continue favoring the cognitive-response approach.

DUAL-PROCESSING MODELS

Over the last 25 years, most persuasion research has been based on two theories that incorporate assumptions of the cognitive response approach about active, effortful processing, but also contain hypotheses about less effortful processing. These two theories are the elaboration likelihood model (ELM; Petty & Cacioppo, 1986a, 1986b; Petty & Wegener, 1999) and the heuristic-systematic model (HSM; Chaiken Liberman, & Eagly, 1989; Chen & Chaiken, 1999). Each model distinguishes two prototypical modes of persuasion that are located near the endpoints of a continuum of processing effort.

The Elaboration Likelihood Model

In the ELM, these modes are called the central route, in which persuasion is mediated by effortful elaboration of message arguments and other central merits of the issue, and the peripheral route, in which persuasion results from the rather superficial, less effortful processing of peripheral cues (e.g., source attractiveness) and includes a variety of low-effort mechanisms such as mere exposure and the use of heuristics.

Basic Motivation According to the ELM, people are generally motivated to hold "correct" attitudes. Petty and Cacioppo (1986a) use this term in a very general sense and equate correctness with adaptive utility. People are thought to judge the adaptiveness of their attitudes based on a variety of standards, including social comparisons.

Continuum of Processing Effort Because people have limited resources in their striving for valid attitudes, they cannot elaborate the details of every persuasive message they receive; therefore, peripheral-route processes often prevail. Generally, elaboration likelihood varies along a continuum and depends on the motivation and ability to process a given message.

Antagonism of Routes The higher the elaboration likelihood, the greater should be the impact of central-route processing, which is mediated through the favorability of recipients' cognitive responses, and the lower should be the impact of peripheral cues on the formation of attitude judgments. The ELM's two routes are thus conceived as antagonistic in their impact on persuasion outcomes. In spite of this trade-off between processing modes, the ELM allows for central and peripheral processes to occur simultaneously (Petty & Wegener, 1998a); it does not specify, however, the exact nature of such simultaneous occurrences.

Multiple Roles for Persuasion Variables According to the ELM, variables are assigned three roles in the persuasion process: They may serve as arguments, as peripheral cues, or as factors affecting the amount or direction of elaboration. Furthermore, variables may play "multiple roles" depending on the overall elaboration likelihood (see Petty & Cacioppo, 1986a, chapter 8). For example, the attractiveness of a model who promotes a beauty product may (1) serve as a peripheral cue if elaboration likelihood is low, affecting attitudes to the product through a peripheral mechanism such as evaluative conditioning; (2) serve as a message argument if elaboration likelihood is high, increasing persuasion through issue-relevant cognitive responses ("If I use this product, I will look as good as her"); or (3) enhance the motivation or ability for central-route processing if the elaboration likelihood is in the middle range of the elaboration continuum to begin with (see Petty & Wegener, 1998a). This multiple-role assumption notwithstanding, most empirical tests of the ELM have featured source attributes (e.g., expertise, attractiveness) to operationalize peripheral cues, variations in message content to operationalize argument strength, and variations of the processing context (e.g., personal relevance; distraction) to influence processing motivation or ability (see, e.g., Kruglanski & Thompson, 1999).

Varying Argument Quality as a Methodological Tool An important methodological innovation that Petty and his colleagues have introduced is the systematic variation of argument quality. This enables researchers to study how variables influence the amount of message processing based on the result patterns these variables produce in interaction with argument quality (Petty & Cacioppo, 1986a, 1986b). This principle may be illustrated by research on distraction. Early studies had shown that distraction, not surprisingly, sometimes reduces the persuasive effect of a message; sometimes, however, quite to the contrary, recipients who were distracted while listening to a message were more persuaded than non-distracted recipients (Petty & Brock, 1981). The latter finding may seem surprising if one assumes that message learning is the main mediator of persuasion (cf. Hovland et al., 1953); if this were true, then any factor that interferes with message learning should reduce persuasion. According to the ELM, however, distraction is thought to reduce recipients' ability for central-route processing, thus disrupting the dominant cognitive responses that the message would normally elicit, whatever their valence. Because the dominant cognitive responses to a weakly argued message should be unfavorable, disrupting these responses through distraction should ultimately lead to more positive attitudes. This is exactly what Petty, Wells, and Brock (1976, Exp. 1) found in a study where distraction and argument quality were crossed in a factorial design. While their participants were listening to a message arguing for a tuition increase with either strong or weak arguments, they were asked simultaneously to monitor the position of an "X" flashing on a screen at varying time intervals, thus creating four levels of distraction intensity. The results showed that at higher (vs. lower) levels of distraction, participants who listened to the weak message reported more agreement, and participants who listened to the strong message reported less agreement. The favorability of participants' cognitive responses showed a similar pattern.

Similar interactions with argument quality have been observed for many variables that affect either the motivation or the ability to carefully process a message, including issue involvement (e.g., Petty, Cacioppo, & Goldman, 1981), the matching or mismatching of a message to recipients' chronic concerns (Petty & Wegener, 1998 b), recipients' mood (e.g., Bless, Bohner, Schwarz, & Strack, 1990; Bohner & Weinerth, 2001), or need for cognition (e.g., Bless, Wänke, Bohner, Fellhauer, & Schwarz, 1994; Cacioppo, Petty, & Morris, 1983; for an overview, see Petty & Wegener, 1998a). The research paradigm has recently been developed further by Erb and his colleagues (1998), who manipulated argument strength as a within-participants variable and assessed attitudes toward separate message aspects that had been supported by strong or weak arguments, respectively (see also Erb, Bohner, Rank, & Einwiller, 2002; Erb, Büscher, Bohner, & Rank, 2005).

Biased Elaboration Variations in motivation and capacity may not only affect the amount of thinking that recipients engage in (objective elaboration), but may also facilitate specifically positive or negative cognitive responses (biased elaboration). This results in an asymmetrical interaction of the variable in question with argument quality. For example, well-developed schemata and prior knowledge may enhance recipients' ability to elaborate arguments that are consistent with their prior attitude. To test this idea, Cacioppo, Petty, and Sidera (1982) used proattitudinal messages on abortion that featured either religious or legalistic arguments. These were presented to participants who possessed either a legalistic or a religious self-schema. In line with the ELM's biased elaboration postulate, participants generated more favorable cognitive responses and agreed more with the message if the arguments corresponded to their self-schema. As a mirror image to these results, other studies have shown that prior knowledge about an issue facilitates the refutation of counterattitudinal arguments (Wood, 1982). A motivational factor that may cause recipients specifically to counterargue a message is forewarning of persuasive intent (Petty & Cacioppo, 1977).

Consequences of Elaboration   A final ELM hypothesis addresses the consequences of the different routes to persuasion. Petty and Cacioppo (1986a) emphasize three characteristics of an attitude that are enhanced by central (vs. peripheral) route processing: Attitudes formed via the central route are more persistent, more resistant to counterpersuasion, and more predictive of behavior (Ajzen & Cote, this volume). These aspects may be interrelated and have been conceptualized as indicators of attitude strength (Bassili, this volume; Petty, Haugtvedt, & Smith, 1995). Petty and his colleagues (1995) discuss three mechanisms that may mediate the proposed effects. First, issue-relevant thinking may increase the consistency of attitude-relevant knowledge structures. Second, attitude-relevant information will be accessed repeatedly, thus rendering it more accessible. This enhances the likelihood that similar information will come to mind again in situations when the individual expresses her attitude or behaves in relation to the attitude object. Third, the individual may perceive that he invested considerable mental effort, thereby becoming more confident in the resulting attitude (for a review of relevant research, see Petty et al., 1995).

Concluding Remarks on the ELM   The ELM provides a comprehensive framework of persuasion that accommodates the effects of a wide range of variables and their interactions. The methodological innovation of varying argument quality to determine the type of effect that other variables exert in the persuasion process has advanced theory and research. Two aspects of the ELM that have been criticized are limitations of its predictive power and degree of precision (e.g., Eagly & Chaiken, 1993): First, it is often impossible to predict which of the multiple roles featured in the ELM a variable will play because the level of elaboration likelihood cannot be determined a priori. Second, although the ELM allows for the possibility that its central and peripheral processes co-occur, it does not specify exactly how and under what conditions this is going to happen. Each of these issues has been explicated more thoroughly in the heuristic–systematic model.

The Heuristic–Systematic Model

Like the ELM, the heuristic–systematic model (HSM) of persuasion comprises two processing modes: a relatively effortless heuristic mode and a more effortful systematic mode (Bohner, Moskowitz, & Chaiken, 1995; Chaiken, Liberman, & Eagly, 1989; Chen & Chaiken, 1999). Recipients are thought to achieve a balance between minimizing effort and reaching sufficient confidence in their attitude judgments. Both heuristic and systematic processing may serve any of three general motives: accuracy, defense, and impression motivation. Furthermore, the two processing modes may co-occur in either an additive or an interactive manner under specified conditions.

HSM and ELM share several core assumptions. Both postulate that processing effort varies along a continuum and is affected by a message recipient's motivation and cognitive capacity. The HSM's systematic mode is defined, much like central route processing, "as a comprehensive, analytic orientation in which perceivers access and scrutinize all informational input for its relevance and importance to their judgment task, and integrate all useful information in forming their judgments" (Chaiken et al., 1989, p. 212). The HSM differs from the ELM in the definition of its low-effort mode, its specificity regarding the interplay of processing modes, and its more detailed motivational underpinnings.

Heuristic Processing   The HSM's low-effort mode is defined both more narrowly and more specifically than the ELM's peripheral route. Heuristic processing entails the application of heuristics; that is, simple rules of inference linking elements of the persuasion setting (heuristic cues) with evaluative inferences (whereas the ELM's peripheral route comprises a wider range of low-effort mechanisms). Although heuristic processing entails little effort, its occurrence does require the presence of a heuristic cue (e.g., an expert source) and the cognitive accessibility of an applicable and relevant heuristic (e.g., "experts' statements are usually valid"). Also, individuals take into account the subjective reliability of a heuristic when making an attitude judgment (Darke et al., 1998).

Interplay of Processing Modes: The Co-Occurence Hypotheses   Systematic processing generally requires greater effort than does heuristic processing. At low levels of motivation or capacity, heuristic processing is thus thought to predominate. At higher levels of motivation and capacity, systematic processing comes into play. However, the HSM does not propose a trade-off between its processing modes. Instead, heuristic processing continues to exert an influence at high levels of processing effort, such that both processing modes jointly affect persuasion. This can happen either independently or in an interactive fashion, and the conditions of such interplay of processing modes have been described in four co-occurrence hypotheses (Bohner et al., 1995).

According to the *additivity hypothesis*, heuristic and systematic processing may exert independent main effects on attitude judgments if the outcomes of each process do not contradict each other (e.g., if a likable communicator presents convincing arguments). This hypothesis is well supported (e.g., Bohner, Frank, & Erb, 1998; Chaiken & Maheswaran, 1994; Maheswaran & Chaiken, 1991). Often, however, systematic processing yields more, and subjectively more relevant, information, such that any additional effects of heuristic processing may be impossible to detect (Chaiken et al., 1989, p. 220). This *attenuation hypothesis* also received ample support (e.g., Chaiken & Maheswaran, 1994; Maheswaran & Chaiken, 1991).

The HSM's *bias hypothesis* refers to an interaction between the two processing modes: If a persuasive message is ambiguous or has mixed content (e.g., containing both strong and weak arguments), initial heuristic inferences may guide the interpretation of the message and thus lead to cognitive responses and attitudes that are assimilated to the valence of a heuristic cue. This hypothesis was supported in a study by Chaiken and Maheswaran (1994), who varied the content ambiguity and source credibility of a consumer message about an answering machine. Participants read product information that was either clearly favorable, clearly unfavorable, or ambiguous with respect to the product's performance. This information was said to come either from a prestigious independent journal specializing in product testing (high credibility), or from sales staff at a discount retail market (low credibility). Participants reported their attitudes toward the product and listed their cognitive responses. The results showed that for participants who were highly motivated and able to process, cognitive responses and attitudes were assimilated to the credibility cue if the message was ambiguous, as predicted by the bias hypothesis. For unambiguously favorable or unfavorable messages, however, only an effect of argument strength was found, which is consistent with the attenuation hypothesis. Biasing effects of other cues were demonstrated for high versus low source consensus (Bohner, Dykema-Engblade, Tindale, & Meisenhelder, 2008; Erb et al., 1998) and for source expertise (Bohner, Ruder, & Erb, 2002).

The mirror image of assimilative bias is described in the HSM's *contrast hypothesis*: If initial, heuristic-based expectancies about a message are violated, then systematic evaluation of the arguments may lead to contrasting interpretations (Bohner et al., 1995). Specifically, the disconfirmation of positive expectancies induces a negative processing bias, whereas the disconfirmation of negative expectancies generates a positive processing bias. In line with this assumption, Bohner et al. (2002) showed that information about high or low source expertise may evoke clear expectations that the message will be strong or weak, respectively. If message content blatantly contradicted these expectations, a contrasting processing bias was observed. For example, a message ascribed to a famous expert that contained weak arguments led to more negative cognitive responses and attitudes than did the same message ascribed to a nonexpert (see also Bohner et al., 2008).

Conceptualizing the Motivation for Processing
In contrast to the ELM, the HSM defines specific external criteria determining the extent of processing motivation. According to the model's sufficiency principle, people try to attain sufficient confidence in their attitudes. They do so by considering two aspects: (1) the

sufficiency threshold (ST), defined as the level of confidence the individual would like to have, and (2) the actual confidence (AC) the individual has attained at a given moment. Whenever AC is below ST, the individual will be motivated to process (additional) information. Larger ST-AC gaps are likely to require systematic processing, whereas smaller gaps may be bridged by heuristic processing (Eagly & Chaiken, 1993, pp. 330–333). For example, if an attitude judgment has low personal relevance, both ST and AC are likely to be low and little processing effort would be expected. If personal relevance is then temporarily heightened, the ST should rise and the individual should engage in processing to close the ST-AC gap. Likewise, if both ST and AC are high, a person should expend little processing effort. Processing effort is again predicted to increase if the AC is then temporarily lowered, for instance by an unexpected discrepancy between source and content information (Maheswaran & Chaiken, 1991).

The mediating role of the ST-AC gap was first demonstrated by Bohner, Rank, Reinhard, Einwiller, and Erb (1998). These authors manipulated the ST by inducing high or low task importance and then assessed how much information participants were willing to review for upcoming social judgments. In support of the sufficiency principle, participants selected more information if task importance was high, and this effect was mediated by the size of the self-reported ST-AC gap. Importantly, this research also showed that a large ST-AC gap was a necessary, but not a sufficient, condition of increased processing effort. A further necessary condition was high task-related self-efficacy: Participants needed to perceive that they had the ability to close the ST-AC gap by increased processing.

Multiple Motives   Finally, the HSM presents a more comprehensive view of motivational states than does the ELM. It portrays the social perceiver as a "motivated tactician" (Fiske & Taylor, 1991) whose information processing may be guided by three broad motives: accuracy, defense, and impression motivation. Accordingly, people may strive to hold attitudes that are a valid reflection of reality, but they may also seek to defend important self-defining beliefs and values, or try to adopt attitudes that help them in making a good impression and "getting along" with others. This classification of processing motives was inspired by early conceptions of attitude function (e.g., Katz, 1960; Watt, Maio, Haddock, & Johnson, this volume). The impact of these qualitative differences in motivation is thought to be orthogonal to the quantitative predictions inherent in the sufficiency principle. An individual may thus be more or less confident with respect to any of the processing goals implied by the multiple-motive view.

Accuracy-motivated processing is conceptualized as relatively open-minded, whereas both defense-motivated and impression-motivated processing are depicted as selective and biased. For example, individuals who are motivated to defend a core value may selectively ignore any information that might threaten this value, may selectively use heuristics that bolster their preferred conclusion, or may selectively counterargue any opposing information they encounter. Which of these strategies will be used should partly depend on their current levels of ST and AC (Bohner & Wänke, 2002, chapter 9; Chaiken, Giner-Sorolla, & Chen, 1996).

Concluding Remarks on Dual-Processing Accounts

Dual-processing models have had an enormous impact on the field of persuasion. The ELM provides a highly comprehensive framework, includes effortful processing as well as a diversity of low-effort processes, and allows for distinctions between these processes and the various "roles" a persuasion variable may play on an empirical basis. The HSM provides a more limited conceptualization of low-effort processing, but at the same time comprises more specific motivational assumptions as well as rich and detailed predictions regarding the interplay of its processing modes. Both models were generally supported in empirical tests and helped to stimulate and guide research efforts in the area of persuasion and beyond. Recently, however, the dual-processing models have been challenged by an alternative one-process theory, which we discuss in the following sections.

THE UNIMODEL APPROACH: CONTINUOUS PARAMETERS OF EVALUATIVE JUDGMENT

How many different ways are there of being persuaded? Exactly two, according to views of the elaboration likelihood model and the heuristic-systematic model discussed above. One way is thorough and based on the effortful consideration of issue information. It represents the effortful route to persuasion afforded only under plentiful processing resources. The other way is relatively superficial, less effortful, and based on information other than issue-related content. This is the low-effort route that recipients escape to when motivation or processing resources are limited.

Empirical support for the dual-mode notions consists of demonstrations that cues interact with motivation and capacity factors in exactly the opposite way to message arguments. For example, in the Petty et al. (1981) study discussed above, issue-relevance (determining the recipients' motivational involvement in the topic) produced the opposite persuasive effects in conjunction with source expertise than in conjunction with argument quality: Whereas argument quality was the more important determinant of persuasion under high (vs. low) personal relevance, source expertise was the more important determinant under low (vs. high) relevance. These interactive results and a considerable number of similar findings (for reviews, see Eagly & Chaiken, 1993; Petty & Cacioppo, 1986a, 1986b) are consistent with the dual-mode notion that the processing of cues and the processing of message arguments are affected in contrary ways by the same, persuasion-relevant, factors (such as personal relevance of the issue).

A closer look at Petty et al.'s (1981) procedures, however, reveals that information about source expertise was presented to participants prior to the message arguments, and was considerably shorter and less complex than message argument information. It is thus possible that the reason why cue information in Petty et al.'s (1981) research had greater persuasive impact under low (vs. high) motivation is that it was less complex and appeared earlier in the processing sequence. To this end, Pierro, Mannetti, Erb, Spiegel, and Kruglanski (2005) conducted a systematic review of 19 major dual-process publications that reported the manipulation of both cue and message argument information. Independent raters who had read the method sections of these articles found that in every single instance the cue information was easier to process than the message information, and for a vast majority of these papers the cue was judged as shorter than the message information and appeared earlier than the message arguments in the processing sequence (but see Bohner, Crow, Erb, & Schwarz, 1992). Thus, it may be that the confounding of informational length, complexity, and ordinal position on the one hand with the type of information, namely cues versus message arguments, on the other hand, produced the seemingly overwhelming support for dual-process models.

Information Complexity, Length, and Ordinal Position

Kruglanski and Thompson (1999) provided a series of studies in which they tested the notion that controlling for processing difficulty (influenced by informational length, complexity, etc.) may eliminate the differences in the persuasive effects of cues and arguments. One experiment (Study 1) showed, for example, that long and complex cue information about the source's expertise exerted greater impact on recipients with high (vs. low) issue-involvement—just as long and complex message arguments had done in prior persuasion research. In another experiment, Kruglanski and Thompson (1999, Study 4) manipulated the level of issue involvement as well as the quality and ordinal position of message arguments favoring mandatory senior comprehensive exams. Brief arguments that were either strong or weak were presented early, and lengthy arguments that also were either strong or weak were presented later. The main dependent variable was participants' post-message attitude toward comprehensive exams. It was found that strong (vs. weak) initial brief arguments elicited greater agreement in the low involvement conditions, whereas no such effect was obtained under high involvement. In contrast, strong (vs. weak) subsequent and lengthy arguments elicited greater agreement in the high involvement condition, whereas no such effect was obtained under low involvement. These and related results (Kruglanski & Thompson, 1999; see also Pierro et al., 2005) show that message arguments and peripheral/heuristic cues do not necessarily interact in opposite ways with processing motivation and cognitive capacity. They suggest, instead, that qualitatively disparate types of information do not need to be processed according to qualitatively distinct modes. Rather, cues and arguments appear to function as equivalent pieces of evidence once their length, complexity, and ordinal position are controlled.

The Concept of Evidence

Kruglanski and Thompson (1999) replaced the distinction between cues and message arguments by the concept of *evidence*, which recipients of a persuasive communication use to form their final judgment. Within their *unimodel* of persuasion the term *evidence* refers to information relevant to a conclusion about the attitude object under consideration. Relevance, in this sense, implies a prior assumption of a linkage between a given piece of evidence and an appropriate conclusion, such that the affirmation of specific information (i.e., observation of the evidence) warrants the conclusion. Such prior linkage is mentally represented in the recipient's mind and constitutes a belief to which she or he subscribes. The notion of evidence is the integrative aspect of the unimodel to combine the two modes of persuasion into one. Specifically, the distinction between cues and arguments is now assumed to represent a difference in the contents of evidence rather than a qualitative difference in the persuasion process. Consider, for illustration, a persuasive communication by a renowned expert on the prohibition of Freon in household appliances. A recipient who believes that everything thinning the Ozone layer should be prohibited (prior assumption) may be persuaded by an argument stating that Freon destroys the Ozone layer (evidence) and come up with the conclusion that Freon should be prohibited. In terms of dual-mode models, such a case would represent central route or systematic processing.

In contrast, a recipient unfamiliar with this topic who neither knows that the thinning of the Ozone layer poses hazards nor believes that "anything posing a hazard should be prohibited" may still subscribe to the assumption that "if an opinion is offered by an expert, then it is valid." This assumption may lead to the (same) conclusion that Freon should be prohibited because this was suggested by a noted expert. Dual-process models have considered such reliance on source attributes (here expertise) as examples of persuasion accomplished by the heuristic or peripheral mode. Yet, from the unimodel perspective, the two examples share a fundamental similarity in that both are mediated by the use of relevant evidence to reach a conclusion. In other words, both cues and arguments are assumed to be functionally equivalent in the persuasion process. This analysis suggests that the relevance of a given piece of evidence is "in the mind of the beholder." Different recipients may find the same evidence more or less convincing, depending on the degree to which they subscribe to prior beliefs lending the given evidence its judgmental impact. In other words, there should be no universal differences in persuasiveness of different types of information: For some recipients a given cue may be more persuasive than a given message argument, whereas for others the argument may be more persuasive than the cue (Kruglanski et al., 2005). Moreover, the unimodel analysis offers a theoretical interpretation of the (up to this point intuitive and empirically derived) notion of "argument strength" in terms of the degree the recipient subscribes to a given prior belief: the stronger the subjective belief that a given argument warrants a judgment-relevant conclusion about the attitude object, the stronger the argument's persuasiveness.

Persuasive evidence can be presented in an unlimited number of forms and variations. At times it may be readily conceivable with the according prior beliefs highly accessible in the recipient's mind. In other circumstances, the evidence may have to be extracted from within a set of irrelevant details in which it is embedded. It is here where motivation and cognitive capacity considerations come into play: If the information is lengthy, complex or unclear, drawing conclusions requires considerable amounts of processing motivation and capacity.

Conversely, if processing effort is low, only relatively straightforward evidence will exert persuasive impact. In more general terms, appreciating the relevance of the information given to a specific conclusion depends on the relation of task demands (determined, e.g., by the information's length, complexity, etc.) to the recipient's processing resources. Appreciation of the information's relevance, and hence the difference in persuasion based on more versus less relevant information, would be greater if the processing resources were sufficient (vs. restricted) given high demands of the information processing task that the persuasive setting requires.

The Concept of Relevance

With regards to the mental effort that recipients invest in processing cue information and message arguments, the unimodel holds that cues versus arguments need not systematically differ. This is what initial unimodel research was about (Kruglanski & Thompson, 1999; see also Pierro et al., 2005). Differences in complexity of cues versus arguments in typical persuasion research may explain why message arguments usually did not have much persuasive impact under low capacity and motivation conditions. It was less clear, however, why cues usually did not exert much persuasive impact under high capacity conditions. To this end, Pierro, Mannetti, Kruglanski, and Sleeth-Keppler (2004) have shown that in a large proportion of studies in the persuasion literature cues are perceived as less relevant than message arguments to the attitudes measured. This led Pierro et al. (2004) to formulate a *relevance override* hypothesis whereby the impact of information depends on its relevance to the attitude issue.

Specifically, when the early information is less relevant to the attitude issue than the late information (defining an irrelevant–relevant sequence), the early information will exert impact under low capacity and motivation conditions but not under high capacity and motivation conditions where its effect will be overridden by the more relevant information that would be carefully processed under these ample resource conditions. This explains why in most persuasion studies the cues did not exert a persuasive effect under high motivation and capacity conditions. This analysis also implies that when early information is more relevant than later information, it will exert a persuasive effect irrespective of resource (capacity and motivation) conditions. Under low resource conditions it will be persuasive because it is the only information the recipient will process, and under high resource condition its implications override those of the subsequent and less relevant information (Pierro et al., 2004).

Activation of Prior Beliefs

Thus far in the persuasion literature, the notion of "rule activation" was reserved for the processing of heuristic information assumed to proceed in a "top-down" fashion (Chen & Chaiken, 1999; Eagly & Chaiken, 1993) and was viewed as irrelevant to the processing of message information assumed to proceed in a "bottom-up" fashion. For instance, in a study by Chaiken, Axsom, Liberman, and Wilson (1992, cited in Eagly & Chaiken, 1993), chronic users of a "length implies strength" heuristic (i.e., individuals for whom this rule enjoyed a high degree of chronic accessibility) were identified. In addition, the temporary accessibility of this heuristic was varied via unobtrusive priming. The results showed that both chronic and temporary accessibility affected participants' use of the "length-strength" rule, as demonstrated by higher agreement with the message when the message (which actually contained six arguments) was said to contain 10 (vs. 2) arguments.

According to the unimodel, rule activation should play the same role in the processing of message contents as it does in the processing of cues. In the case of heuristics, the heuristic cue that the message is "long," represents evidence for which the prior belief "length equals strength" can afford the conclusion that the lengthy message is convincing and should command agreement. The same process was predicted by Erb, Fishbach, and Kruglanski (2007) to take place when recipients deal with message information. In two experiments, these authors presented participants with an ad on a new ice cream brand. The message contained information that an extra amount of whipping cream was added to milk. Depending on experimental condition, for one half of the recipients the belief "cream = fat" and for the other half the belief "cream = taste" was made highly accessible via an "unrelated" priming procedure prior to message exposure. Additionally, it was assessed how much a belief combining cream with fat was chronically accessible (presumably to those persons highly conscious of their body weight due to dieting etc.). Results showed that high accessibility (temporary or chronic) of a "cream = fat" belief resulted in unfavorable attitudes, whereas recipients who did not associate cream with fat reported favorable attitudes toward the ice cream. These findings support the notion that the persuasiveness of message arguments (just like the persuasiveness of heuristic cues, as demonstrated by Chaiken et al., 1992) is affected by the activation of prior beliefs that lend relevance to the message contents.

Biased Processing

Early information can bias the processing of subsequent information provided the individual has sufficient motivation to process the latter after processing the former. Both the ELM and the HSM hold that central or systematic processing can occasionally be biased by heuristic or peripheral cues or other factors exogenous to the message (e.g., Chaiken & Maheswaran, 1994; Petty, Schuman, Richman & Strathman, 1993). Significantly, within the dual-process models, the biasing hypothesis is *asymmetrical*: Heuristic or peripheral cues are presumed to be capable of biasing subsequent processing of message information, but not vice versa (e.g., Chaiken, Duckworth & Darke, 1999; Petty, Wheeler, & Bizer, 1999). The main reason for the asymmetry is a methodological one: Because in prior persuasion studies cues typically appeared before the message, it did not make sense to ask whether their processing might be biased by the (central or systematic) processing of later arguments. However, the unimodel removes this constraint on processing sequence. It thus affords the question of whether any information type might bias the processing of any information type presented later in the persuasion sequence, supposing that the recipient invests sufficient effort to process the later appearing information.

Simply put, the early information could make accessible certain conclusions serving as input for inferences in whose light the subsequent information might be interpreted. Erb, Pierro, Mannetti, Spiegel, and Kruglanski (2007) conducted two experiments to test this idea. In the first, recipients were given information consisting entirely of message arguments. The quality of an initial argument was manipulated to be of either high or low quality. Five subsequent arguments were held constant and were of moderate quality. Processing motivation (high vs. low) was also manipulated. It was found that the early strong (weak) argument generally produced favorable (unfavorable) final attitudes. Under low motivation, recipients used the initial argument as a shortcut to the final judgments, mimicking a "cue effect" in terms of dual-process models. Under high motivation, the initial argument's quality biased the processing of the subsequent arguments, and biased processing in turn mediated the effect of the initial argument on attitudes. In their second study, Erb et al. found that an initial argument was capable of biasing the processing of subsequent communicator related (cue) information when the argument preceded but not when it followed the communicator description. Such biased processing of communicator related information mediated the effect of the initial argument on the final attitude judgments.

These results point to *processing sequence* as a previously unconsidered precondition of biased processing effects to occur (but see Erb et al., 1998). These studies also demonstrate that the processing sequence matters more than the information type in determining persuasion outcomes. Consistent with the unimodel's notion of functional equivalence of cues and arguments, arguments appear capable of serving as biasing factors (just like cues in preceding dual-process studies), and cue information may serve as the information to be biased (just like arguments in preceding dual-process studies).

To summarize, the research we have reviewed supports the basic unimodel notion that judgmental parameters such as difficulty of processing (operationalized, e.g., by the amount of information given, or the accessibility of appropriate prior beliefs), perceived relevance of the evidence (operationalized by argument quality, low or high expertise of the communicator, etc.), magnitude of processing effort (operationalized by issue involvement, etc.), or processing sequence (i.e., early or late appearing information) determine persuasion. Controlling for specific values of these parameters, the distinctions between contents or types of information (in particular, the message argument versus cue distinction) do not appear to have any persuasive effects as such. Thus, the unimodel offers an alternative to the prevalent dual-mode approaches. Still, it shares some fundamental commonalities with dual-process models, and in many aspects it grew out of insights developed by dual-process theorists. In this sense, it is perhaps better thought of as an evolution rather than a revolutionary break (Erb et al., 2003).

The unimodel has considerable generative potential for empirical research. In the studies described here, researchers manipulated the length, complexity, and ordinal position of both cues and message argument information, manipulated (and measured) the accessibility of prior beliefs and perceived relevance (of cues and arguments), and demonstrated the effects of a number of previously unconsidered factors in persuasion. Future research could also look at other dependent variables beyond attitudes per se. For example, persistence, resistance to counterpersuasion, or predictiveness for behavior may obtain as a result of the processing of any relevant evidence, rather than the elaborate processing of message arguments to which such properties of attitudes have been attributed by dual-process theorists (see above). Moreover, the unimodel offers new applied insights for successful communication. It suggests, for example, that rapid persuasion may be accomplished via simplistic message arguments (as well as via message-unrelated cues). Perhaps more importantly, it implies that when recipients are unfamiliar with the topic and hence are unable to appreciate issue related arguments, it may be possible to produce profound attitude change via relevant cue-based (vs. message-based) evidence. Or, it may be possible to enhance the accessibility of appropriate prior beliefs within the persuasive message to enable the recipient to draw the conclusion intended by the communicator. In this sense, the unimodel offers a flexible view of persuasion in which the same persuasive outcome may be attained via different means, depending on the particular characteristics of the recipients (e.g., their processing resources, their accessible beliefs, the subjectively perceived complexity of the evidence, etc.).

PERSUASION AS A SEQUENTIAL PROCESS

A considerable number of studies testing the unimodel have demonstrated that the sequence in which recipients process persuasion-relevant information can have profound effects on judgmental outcomes. Related assumptions can be found in the dual-process models as well. The ELM's multiple-roles assumption holds that sometimes a variable presented early in the persuasion sequence may affect the objective or biased processing of subsequent message arguments. However, the exact conditions giving rise to each of these effects are not specified in the ELM. Within the HSM framework, however, researchers have presented more elaborate hypotheses of how information processed early in the persuasion sequence can impact the processing of later information (e.g., the additivity, attenuation, bias, and contrast hypotheses).

Some conditions that determine which of the effects specified in the HSM's co-occurrence hypotheses is to be expected have already been identified, although the hypotheses have rarely been systematically pitted against each other (but see Bohner et al., 2002). Moreover, the HSM assumptions have been restricted to the case where the early processing of heuristic cues affects the subsequent processing of message arguments. This constraint has been removed by more recent research conducted in the realm of the unimodel. As shown, the sequence in which recipients process information plays an important role for the biased-processing phenomenon (Erb et al., 2007) and for the "relevance override" that later information may exert on earlier information (Pierro et al., 2004). Moreover, Kruglanski &

Thompson (1999) demonstrated that late information will have no impact if recipients terminate processing at a rather early stage (see also Pierro et al., 2005). This occurred irrespective of the type of evidence (cues or arguments) processed early or late. Given these findings, it makes sense to consider more closely the potential effects of different processing sequences on attitude formation. In other words, it is useful to examine how assumptions about the interplay of pieces of evidence similar to the HSM's attenuation, additivity, bias, and contrast hypotheses could be fruitfully integrated and expanded within the broader unimodel perspective. This endeavor may prove particularly useful in applied settings, because often the processing sequence is under complete control of the communicator, who can decide which evidence to present first and which to present later.

Relatedness of Early and Late Information

A rather simple, but nonetheless important first assumption regarding sequence effects refers to the question about conditions under which the processing of early evidence will have any impact at all on the processing of subsequent information. It seems obvious that any such impact would depend on whether the early information is somehow related to subsequent information. If there is no relation between pieces of information, then independent additive effects of these pieces of information would be the rule, and the sequence in which information is presented should have little impact on persuasion outcomes. If, however, there is a relation between pieces of evidence, then sequence effects are likely to occur, and the joint effects of different pieces of information would be interactive, in a similar way as specified in the HSM's bias and contrast hypotheses.

How exactly can we define relatedness of pieces of evidence? In unimodel terms, relatedness is present if the processing of early information activates inferences that serve as input to judging the evidential quality of subsequent information.

Relatedness in the Case of Two-Sided Messages   Pechmann (1992) proposed that two-sided messages may be particularly persuasive if their negative and positive aspects are "correlated" (vs. "uncorrelated") in the recipient's mind. For example, the information that a particular ice cream has many calories (a negative aspect) combined with the information that the ice cream is particularly tasty (a positive aspect) may lead to more positive evaluations of the ice cream. This is because recipients hold the belief that "ice cream that has many calories is tasty"; learning about the high calorie aspect should thus enhance the conclusion that the ice cream must indeed be tasty. Such an enhancing effect would not be observed, however, if the message contained an uncorrelated negative aspect (e.g., few container sizes).

Following up on Pechmann's (1992) reasoning, Bohner, Einwiller, Erb, and Siebler (2003) showed that the enhancing effect of correlated aspects on product attitudes requires a certain amount of processing effort and therefore, it was most clearly obtained if participants had ample (vs. little) time to study an ad.

The ad featured an Italian restaurant, and its two-sided versions contained either correlated or uncorrelated aspects. In the correlated version, the positive aspect of freshly prepared dishes was followed by the negative aspect of limited choice, whereas in the uncorrelated condition, the same positive aspect was followed by the negative aspect of lack of customer parking. Results showed that under conditions of ample processing time, participants' attitudes toward the restaurant were more positive in the correlated (vs. uncorrelated) version, and that this effect was mediated via more favorable evaluations of the positive product aspect.

Sequence effects have not been studied within this paradigm; up to now, the negative aspects were always presented after the positive aspects. We would predict, however, that the reported effects should be less strong if this sequential order were reversed. This is because by encountering the positive aspect first, a positive interpretation of the (otherwise) negative aspect is preactivated. Thus, recipients who first read that a restaurant offers freshly prepared dishes will be more likely to interpret the subsequent information about limited choice in light of a connection between limited choice and high quality, whereas recipients who first read about limited choice should be less likely to do so. It should be noted that the use of negative product aspects or, more generally, counterarguments in a two-sided message paradigm, provides a particularly strong methodological tool for assessing such "transfer" effects between pieces of persuasive information, because the otherwise negative effect of the counterarguments is turned into a positive effect by the sequence of presentation.

Relatedness and Assimilation versus Contrast Effects   Apart from this rather intriguing example of relatedness, there are other ways in which early information may be related to subsequent information. For instance, early information may elicit a favorable (or unfavorable) "first impression" about the validity or "convincingness" of the persuasive message as a whole. An example for this phenomenon was provided by a study that we reviewed earlier (Bohner et al., 2002). In that study recipients drew initial inferences about argument quality on the basis of perceived source expertise. These initial inferences led either to biased interpretations of message arguments and attitudes in line with perceived source expertise (if the arguments were ambiguous), or to contrasting interpretations and attitudes opposite to the initial inferences (if argument quality clearly contradicted these inferences). Again, we propose that effects like those observed by Bohner et al. (2002) would not be obtained if the source information were presented after the message arguments. Similarly, if the early information does not activate any inferences that are applicable to the interpretation of subsequent information, neither biased processing nor contrast effects would occur (Bohner et al., 2008). These studies and others (e.g., Erb et al., 2007) suggest that early inferences may strongly affect subsequent processing if pieces of information in the persuasion sequence are related to each other. Future theorizing and research should delineate more clearly the concept of relatedness, as well as the conditions that give rise to biased assimilation versus contrast effects once relatedness is present.

CONNECTIONIST MODELING OF INFORMATION PROCESSING IN PERSUASION: A THEORETICAL COMPLEMENT TO SYMBOLIC THEORIES

The Connectionist Approach

The previously discussed models of persuasion describe a range of cognitive processes and mental operations whereby an individual's attitude toward an object may be retrieved from long-term memory, or may be constructed on the spot, whenever an evaluative judgment is needed. As we have seen, some researchers use relatively abstract distinctions of "routes to persuasion" (ELM) or "modes of processing" (HSM); others refer to quite specific cognitive operations such as drawing syllogistic conclusions from evidence (Unimodel). Very low levels of cognition—for instance, how people identify and access required knowledge in memory—are, however, beyond the scope of these models. The connectionist approach, by contrast, views the mind as an adaptive mechanism that is equipped with simple cognitive operations such as, for instance, the mutual excitation or inhibition of ideas and concepts. More complex cognition (such as effortful processing in persuasive communication) is modeled as the result of applying simple operations repeatedly. Different from other approaches, connectionist accounts often model both the acquisition and the application of knowledge (for overviews, see Smith, 1996; Smith & DeCoster, 2000), thus providing a rather comprehensive account of empirical phenomena. Recent applications cover a broad range of domains of interest to social psychologists, for instance person perception and stereotyping (Smith & DeCoster, 1998); causal reasoning (Van Overwalle & Van Rooy, 2001); and attitude formation and change (Van Overwalle & Jordens, 2002; Van Overwalle & Siebler, 2005).

Perhaps the most striking feature of connectionist models is the theoretical parsimony that they often afford. To illustrate this, we present a simulation of Chaiken and Maheswaran's (1994) laboratory study on the HSM's bias hypothesis, which we discussed earlier. As we shall see, the connectionist model replicates the effect pattern of biased processing without having to assume an interaction between two kinds of information, as was the case in both the HSM and the unimodel.

Biased Processing in a Connectionist Network

To recapitulate, Chaiken and Maheswaran had participants read a consumer message about an answering machine. Two levels of source credibility were manipulated as a heuristic cue: The information was said to come from either a prestigious independent journal specializing in product testing (high credibility), or from sales staff at a retail market (low credibility). Argument strength was varied at three levels: The product description was either clearly favorable or clearly unfavorable with respect to the product's performance, or it comprised an ambiguous mixture of both favorable and unfavorable arguments. Finally, to induce low versus high levels of processing effort, apparent task importance was varied at two levels (low vs. high). Participants reported attitudes toward the answering machine and listed their cognitive responses. In line with predictions, Chaiken and Maheswaran found that participants in the low-importance condition reported attitudes toward the product that essentially reflected the valence of the heuristic cue (i.e., source credibility). In the high-importance condition, by contrast, attitudes reflected the favorability of the product description, provided that the description was unambiguously favorable or unfavorable. However, if the description was ambiguous, then high-importance participants' judgments were assimilated to the credibility cue. Finally, for the high- (but not low-) importance conditions, the valence of participants' cognitive responses mirrored their attitude judgments. This pattern of results is in line with the HSM's bias hypothesis.

Several connectionist simulations of Chaiken and Maheswaran's study are available in the literature (see Siebler, 2002; Van Overwalle & Siebler, 2005). To illustrate the approach, we describe a simulation by Siebler (2002) that adopts a parallel constraint satisfaction network (Read, Vanman, & Miller, 1997; Thagard, 1989; see also Kunda & Thagard, 1996). Different from more recent connectionist architectures, parallel constraint satisfaction networks do not acquire concepts and their relations in an automatic learning process; instead, these networks are compiled by the researcher (for a critique, see Van Overwalle & Siebler, 2005). For consistency with the notational convention from the original research, we label some of the network elements "cues" and others "arguments"; in unimodel terminology, these may be conceived as representing pieces of evidence requiring less versus more processing effort, respectively (see Bohner & Siebler, 1999).

As shown in Figure 8.1, the network comprised seven units or concepts, as well as six connections or associations between concepts. The network's topmost layer consisted of units representing the four kinds of information used in Chaiken and Maheswaran's study: One unit each represented a negative cue (low credibility), a positive cue (high credibility), a weak argument (unambiguously unfavorable), and a strong argument (unambiguously favorable). A special evidence unit (labeled "Observed" in Figure 8.1) served as a device of entering activation into the network. To simulate a given experimental condition, appropriate top-layer units were connected simultaneously to the special evidence unit. For instance, to simulate a condition where participants are presented with unambiguously favorable arguments stemming from a highly credible source, the evidence unit was connected (1) to the unit labeled "positive cue," and (2) to the unit labeled "strong argument" (see Figure 8.1). In ambiguous-message conditions, the evidence unit was connected to one cue unit as well as to both of the argument units. Activation was then allowed to spread, along the connections, through the network. This spreading of activation simulated the flow of thought leading from the observation of information in the environment to an attitude judgment. The network's connections were bidirectional, which means that activation could flow in either direction between any two associated concepts. Also, activation was multiplied with the weight of the connection along which it spread (as indicated by a plus or minus sign in Figure 8.1). Thus, if for instance the "negative cue" unit acquired a positive level of activation in a simulation run, it would then pass on negative activation to the "attitude judgment" unit. Finally, to model the usually smaller number of cues than

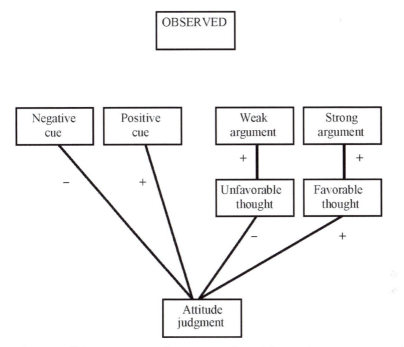

Figure 8.1   Parallel-constraint-satisfaction network used for simulating persuasion phenomena. Boxes represent concepts, lines represent associations between concepts, plus-signs (minus-signs) depict mutual excitation (inhibition) of concepts. Figure adapted from Siebler (2002).

arguments in actual persuasion studies, the connection between cue units and the attitude unit was given a (positive or negative) weight of a lesser magnitude, as compared to other connections. To simulate a given experimental condition, all units were set to neutral (zero) activation levels. Then, cue and argument(s) were connected to the evidence unit as appropriate for the condition. After some time of activation spreading, the network settled on a stable state where the units' activation levels did not change any more. At this point, the activation level of the attitude judgment unit was recorded as the network's "attitude" after high-effort processing. In addition, the attitude judgment unit's activation level from a predetermined, early stage of processing was recorded as the network's "attitude" after low-effort processing.

As shown in Figure 8.1, the attitude judgment unit could receive positive or negative activation via two paths. First, it could receive activation from cue units, and second, it could receive activation from argument units. Importantly, argument units did not feed activation directly into the attitude judgment unit. Instead, an extra layer was added to this path, reflecting the assumption that persuasion by arguments involves more thought, as compared to persuasion by cues. This difference in the length of paths from cues versus arguments to the attitude depicts the network's core mechanism. We may expect activation spreading from cue units to arrive at the attitude judgment unit relatively soon, that is, in early stages of processing. Activation spreading from argument units, in contrast, has to travel through an additional layer of cognitive responses and should thus arrive at the attitude judgment unit only at a later stage of processing. However, because of being backed by a greater number of units overall, activation arriving via the argument path should ultimately affect attitude judgments more strongly than activation arriving via the cue path. In other words, the network should reproduce a basic finding in persuasion research whereby easily processed information (e.g., heuristic cues) affects attitudes at low levels of processing effort, whereas more difficult-to-process information (e.g., argument content) affects attitudes at high levels of processing effort.

The HSM's bias hypothesis predicts an exception to that pattern: if arguments are ambiguous, then even high-effort processing should result in attitudes reflecting cue valence, due to initial heuristic inferences guiding the interpretation of the ambiguous message. A similar mechanism is assumed by the unimodel, although here, it is the unambiguous evidence presented early in a sequence that guides the interpretation of ambiguous evidence presented subsequently.

How does the network handle the case of ambiguous information? Interestingly, no special circuitry is required, and no interaction between cue and argument paths needs to be built in. Instead, we may expect biased processing to emerge automatically, for the following reasons. With both a favorable and an unfavorable argument activated, activation should spread first to both the positive and the negative cognitive-response unit, and further to the attitude judgment unit. However, if both positive and negative cognitive responses are activated, their effects on the attitude should cancel, resulting in an overall null effect of ambiguous arguments on the attitude judgment. Thus, at each level of processing effort, attitudes after ambiguous messages should be determined by cue valence alone.

Table 8.1 shows the simulation results. As expected, the sign of simulated attitudes from an early stage of processing reflected the positive or negative valence of the heuristic cue, but it did not reflect the favorability of the message. At a late stage of processing, in contrast, the sign of simulated attitudes was exclusively determined by message favorability, provided that the message was unambiguously favorable or unfavorable. If the message was ambiguous, however, then simulated attitudes reflected cue valence even at a late stage of processing. Thus, in each of twelve simulated conditions, the network model produced simulated attitudes that

TABLE 8.1   Simulated Attitudes as a Function of Cue Valence and Argument Quality, at Two Stages of Processing

| | Processing stage | | | | | |
| | early | | | late | | |
Context cue	weak	ambiguous	strong	weak	ambiguous	strong
negative	-.22	-.14	-.06	-.59	-.45	.45
positive	.06	.14	.22	-.45	.45	.59

Note. Scores represent the activation level of the network's attitude judgment unit; more positive scores indicate a more positive attitude (theoretical range –1 to +1). Table adapted from Siebler (2002).

were qualitatively in line with the HSM's bias hypothesis. Taking also the magnitude of simulated attitudes into account, the pattern of simulated means was found to correlate almost perfectly (r = .98) with the pattern of means produced by human participants in Chaiken and Maheswaran (1994).

Next, an index of thought favorability was computed from the activation levels of the cognitive-response units. This index also correlated highly with the human data (r = .97). Finally, as is typically found in studies with human participants, the association between simulated thought favorability and simulated attitudes was greater at high levels of processing effort (r = .97), as compared to low levels of processing effort (r = .73). In sum, over and above predicting appropriate patterns of means for attitudes as well as for thought valence, the network also properly reflected differences in the association of these variables at two levels of processing effort. Interestingly, although the network's two cognitive-response units were activated by their respective argument-units to exactly the same degree in ambiguous-message conditions, the cognitive-response unit that was evaluatively congruent with the active cue reached a greater magnitude of activation. This effect indicates a greater likelihood of cue-congruent than cue-incongruent thought; it was more pronounced at the late (versus the early) processing stage. Different from HSM and unimodel assumptions, that bias followed (vs. preceded) changes in the attitude-unit's activation level, as it was seen most clearly in additional cue-only conditions that we simulated. This implies that the cognitive responses assessed in actual persuasion studies may occasionally be the consequence of a newly formed attitude, rather than its antecedent.

We showed that the results of a core study in persuasive communication could readily be simulated in a basic connectionist network, with simulation results showing an excellent fit with the human data reported by Chaiken and Maheswaran (1994). With respect to the cognitive processes involved in persuasion, the simulation thus revealed parallel constraint satisfaction as a promising mechanism in explaining empirical phenomena that have previously been discussed in terms of heuristic versus systematic processing modes, or in terms of syllogistic reasoning.

More importantly, however, the connectionist simulation provides a novel and parsimonious theoretical mechanism that may lead to the result pattern typical of biased processing. Whereas both the HSMs and the unimodel's explanations refer to an interaction whereby unambiguous information guides the interpretation of ambiguous information, the connectionist model did not resort to the ambiguous information. Instead, in the ambiguous message conditions, an attitude judgment was automatically derived from the unambiguous cue information alone.

Of course we cannot conclude on the basis of this simulation that persuasion in actual people would never involve the disambiguation of ambiguous information. In fact, we do believe that people often use various bits and pieces of information in an interactive fashion, as was detailed earlier. However, that the network model fared so well in replicating the results of a core study of persuasion research alerts us of the possibility that more of our theories and models may hold undetected opportunities for greater parsimony, opportunities that may present themselves more clearly once we try and reframe these theories in a connectionist model. Concerning the effects of order and sequence in persuasion, the simulation results suggest that, in addition to manipulating the sequence of input information (as was suggested in a previous section), an assessment of the order in which relevant judgments become available to the perceiver may provide valuable insights into persuasion.

REFERENCES

Allport, G. W. (1935). Attitudes. In C. Murchison (Ed.), *Handbook of social psychology* (pp. 798–844). Worcester, MA: Clark University Press.

Bless, H., Bohner, G., Schwarz, N., & Strack, F. (1990). Mood and persuasion: A cognitive response analysis. *Personality and Social Psychology Bulletin, 16,* 331–345.

Bless, H., Wänke, M., Bohner, G., Fellhauer, R., & Schwarz, N. (1994). Need for cognition: Eine Skala zur Erfassung von Engagement und Freude bei Denkaufgaben [Need for Cognition: A scale measuring engagement in and enjoyment of thinking tasks]. *Zeitschrift für Sozialpsychologie, 25,* 147–154.

Bohner, G., Crow, K., Erb, H.-P., & Schwarz, N. (1992). Affect and persuasion: Mood effects on the processing of persuasive message content and context cues and on subsequent behaviour. *European Journal of Social Psychology, 22,* 511–530.

Bohner, G., Dykema-Engblade, A., Tindale, R. S., & Meisenhelder, H. (2008). Framing of majority and minority source information in persuasion: When and how "consensus implies correctness." *Social Psychology, 39,* in press.

Bohner, G., Einwiller, S., Erb, H.-P., & Siebler, F. (2003). When small means comfortable: Relations between product attributes in two-sided advertising. *Journal of Consumer Psychology, 13,* 454–463.

Bohner, G., Frank, E., & Erb, H.-P. (1998). Heuristic processing of distinctiveness information in minority and majority influence. *European Journal of Social Psychology, 28,* 855–860.

Bohner, G., Moskowitz, G., & Chaiken, S. (1995). The interplay of heuristic and systematic processing of social information. *European Review of Social Psychology, 6,* 33–68.

Bohner, G., Rank, S., Reinhard, M.-A., Einwiller, S., & Erb, H.-P. (1998). Motivational determinants of systematic processing: Expectancy moderates effects of desired confidence on processing effort. *European Journal of Social Psychology, 28,* 185–206.

Bohner, G., Ruder, M., & Erb, H.-P. (2002). When expertise backfires: Contrast and assimilation effects in persuasion. *British Journal of Social Psychology, 41,* 495–519.

Bohner, G., & Siebler, F. (1999). Paradigms, processes, parsimony, and predictive power: Arguments for a generic dual-process model. *Psychological Inquiry, 10,* 113–118.

Bohner, G., & Wänke, M. (2002). *Attitudes and attitude change.* Hove, UK: Psychology Press.

Bohner, G., & Weinerth, T. (2001). Negative affect can increase or decrease message scrutiny: The affect interpretation hypothesis. *Personality and Social Psychology Bulletin, 27,* 1417–1428.

Briñol, P., Petty, R. E., & Tormala, Z. L. (2004). Self-validation of cognitive responses to advertisements. *Journal of Consumer Research, 30,* 559–573.

Cacioppo, J. T., Petty, R. E., & Morris, K. J. (1983). Effects of need for cognition on message evaluation, recall, and persuasion. *Journal of Personality and Social Psychology, 45,* 805–818.

Cacioppo, J. T., Petty, R. E., & Sidera, J. (1982). The effects of a salient self-schema on the evaluation of proattitudinal editorials: Top-down versus bottom-up message processing. *Journal of Experimental Social Psychology, 18,* 324–338.

Chaiken, S. (1987). The heuristic model of persuasion. In M. P. Zanna, J. M. Olson, & C. P. Herman (Eds.), *Social influence: The Ontario Symposium* (Vol. 5, pp. 3–39). Hillsdale, NJ: Erlbaum.

Chaiken, S., Axsom, D., Liberman, A., & Wilson, D. (1992). Heuristic processing of persuasive messages: Chronic and temporary sources of rule accessibility. Unpublished manuscript, New York University.

Chaiken, S., Duckworth, K. L., & Darke, P. (1999). When parsimony fails.... *Psychological Inquiry, 10*, 118–123.

Chaiken, S., Giner-Sorolla, R., & Chen, S. (1996). Beyond accuracy: Defense and impression motives in heuristic and systematic processing. In P. M. Gollwitzer & J. A. Bargh (Eds.), *The psychology of action: Linking cognition and motivation to behavior* (pp. 553–578). New York: Guilford.

Chaiken, S., Liberman, A., & Eagly, A. H. (1989). Heuristic and systematic information processing within and beyond the persuasion context. In J. S. Uleman & J. A. Bargh (Eds.), *Unintended thought* (pp. 212–252). New York: Guilford.

Chaiken, S., & Maheswaran, D. (1994). Heuristic processing can bias systematic processing: Effects of source credibility, argument ambiguity, and task importance on attitude judgment. *Journal of Personality and Social Psychology, 66*, 460–473.

Chen, S., & Chaiken, S. (1999). The heuristic-systematic model in its broader context. In S. Chaiken & Y. Trope (Eds.), *Dual-process theories in social psychology* (pp. 73–96). New York: Guilford.

Cohen, J., & Reed, A. II. (2006). A multiple pathway anchoring and adjustment (*MPAA*) *model of attitude generation and recruitment. Journal of Consumer Research, 33*, 1–15.

Darke, P. R., Chaiken, S., Bohner, G., Einwiller, S., Erb, H.-P., & Hazlewood, J. D. (1998). Accuracy motivation, consensus information, and the law of large numbers: Effects on attitude judgment in the absence of argumentation. *Personality and Social Psychology Bulletin, 24*, 1205–1215.

Eagly, A. H., & Chaiken, S. (1993). *The psychology of attitudes*. Fort Worth, TX: Harcourt Brace Jovanovich.

Erb, H.-P., & Bohner, G. (2001). Mere consensus effects in minority and majority influence. In C. K. W. De Dreu & N. K. De Vries (Eds.), *Group consensus and minority influence: Implications for innovation* (pp. 40–59). Oxford, UK: Blackwell.

Erb, H.-P., & Bohner, G. (in press). Consensus as the key: Toward parsimony in explaining minority and majority influence. In R. Martin & M. Hewstone (Eds.), *Minority influence and innovation: Antecedents, processes, and consequences*. Hove, UK: Psychology Press.

Erb, H.-P., Bohner, G., Schmälzle, K., & Rank, S. (1998). Beyond conflict and discrepancy: Cognitive bias in minority and majority influence. *Personality and Social Psychology Bulletin, 24*, 620–633.

Erb, H.-P., Büscher, M., Bohner, G., & Rank, S. (2005). Starke und schwache Argumente als Teile derselben Botschaft: Die "Mixed-Message-Methode" zur Erfassung des kognitiven Aufwands bei der Verarbeitung persuasiver Kommunikation [Strong and weak arguments as parts of the same message: The mixed-message method for assessing processing effort in persuasion]. *Zeitschrift für Sozialpsychologie, 36*, 61–75.

Erb, H.-P., Fishbach, A., & Kruglanski, A. W. (2007). Rule accessibility and judgment across a variety of judgmental domains: Evidence for a unimodel of human judgment. Unpublished manuscript. Helmut-Schmidt-University, Hamburg.

Erb, H.-P., Kruglanski, A. W., Chun, W. Y., Pierro, A., Mannetti, L., & Spiegel, S. (2003). Searching for commonalities in human judgment: The Parametric unimodel and its dual-model alternatives. *European Review of Social Psychology, 14*, 1–47.

Erb, H.-P., Pierro, A., Mannetti, L., Spiegel, S., & Kruglanski, A. W. (2007). Biased processing of persuasive information: On the functional equivalence of cues and message arguments. *European Journal of Social Psychology, 37*, 1057–1075.

Fiske, S. T., & Taylor, S. E. (1991). *Social cognition* (2nd ed.). New York: McGraw-Hill.

Gorn, G. J. (1982). The effects of music in advertising on choice behavior: A classical conditioning approach. *Journal of Marketing Research, 46*, 94–101.

Hovland, C. I., Janis, I. L., & Kelley, H. H. (1953). *Communication and persuasion*. New Haven, CT: Yale University Press.

Katz, D. (1960). The functional approach to the study of attitudes. *Public Opinion Quarterly, 24*, 163–204.

Kruglanski, A. W., Raviv, A., Bar-Tal, D., Raviv, A., Sharvit, K., Ellis, S., Bar, R., Pierro, A., & Mannetti, L. (2005). Says who? Epistemic authority effects in social judgment. *Advances in Experimental Social Psychology, 37*, 345–392.

Kruglanski, A. W., & Thompson, E. P. (1999). Persuasion by a single route: A view from the unimodel. *Psychological Inquiry, 10*, 83–109.

Kunda, Z., & Thagard, P. (1996). Forming impressions from stereotypes, traits, and behaviors: A parallel-constraint-satisfaction theory. *Psychological Review, 103*, 284–308.

Maheswaran, D., & Chaiken, S. (1991). Promoting systematic processing in low motivation settings: The effect of incongruent information on processing and judgment. *Journal of Personality and Social Psychology, 61*, 13–25.

Pechmann, C. (1992). Predicting when two-sided ads will be more effective than one-sided ads: The role of correlational and correspondent inferences. *Journal of Marketing Research, 29*, 441–453.

Petty, R. E. (2006). A metacognitive model of attitudes. *Journal of Consumer Research, 33*, 22–24.

Petty, R. E., & Brock, T. C. (1981). Thought disruption and persuasion: Assessing the validity of attitude change experiments. In R. E. Petty, T. M. Ostrom & T. C. Brock (Eds.), *Cognitive Responses in Persuasion* (pp. 55–79). Hillsdale, NJ: Erlbaum.

Petty, R. E., & Cacioppo, J. T. (1977). Forewarning, cognitive responding, and resistance to persuasion. *Journal of Personality and Social Psychology, 35*, 645–655.

Petty, R. E., & Cacioppo, J. T. (1981). *Attitudes and persuasion: Classic and contemporary approaches*. Dubuque, Iowa: Brown.

Petty, R. E., & Cacioppo, J. T. (1986a). *Communication and persuasion: Central and peripheral routes to attitude change*. New York: Springer.

Petty, R. E., & Cacioppo, J. T. (1986b). The elaboration likelihood model of persuasion. *Advances in Experimental Social Psychology, 19*, 124–203.

Petty, R. E., Cacioppo, J. T., & Goldman, R. (1981). Personal involvement as a determinant of argument-based persuasion. *Journal of Personality and Social Psychology, 41*, 847–855.

Petty, R. E., Haugtvedt, C. P., & Smith, S. M. (1995). Elaboration as a determinant of attitude strength: Creating attitudes that are persistent, resistant, and predictive of behavior. In R. E. Petty & J. A. Krosnick (Eds.), *Attitude strength: Antecedents and consequences* (pp. 93–130). Mahwah, NJ: Erlbaum.

Petty, R. E., Ostrom, T. M., & Brock, T. C. (Eds.). (1981). *Cognitive responses in persuasion*. Hillsdale, NJ: Erlbaum.

Petty, R. E., Priester, J. R., & Wegener, D. T. (1994). Cognitive processes in attitude change. In R. S. Wyer, Jr., & T. K. Srull (Eds.), *Handbook of social cognition: Vol. 2. Applications* (2nd ed., pp. 69–142). Hillsdale, NJ: Erlbaum.

Petty, R. E., Schumann, D. W., Richman, S. A., & Strathman, A. J. (1993). Positive mood and persuasion: Different roles for affect under high- and low-elaboration conditions. *Journal of Personality and Social Psychology, 64*, 5–20.

Petty, R. E., & Wegener, D. T. (1998a). Attitude change: Multiple roles for persuasion variables. In D. Gilbert, S. T. Fiske, & G. Lindzey (Eds.), *Handbook of social psychology* (4th ed., pp. 323–390). New York: McGraw-Hill.

Petty, R. E., & Wegener, D. T. (1998b). Matching versus mismatching attitude functions: Implications for scrutiny of persuasive messages. *Personality and Social Psychology Bulletin, 24,* 227–240.

Petty, R. E., & Wegener, D. T. (1999). The elaboration likelihood model: Current status and controversies. In S. Chaiken & Y. Trope (Eds.), *Dual process theories in social psychology* (pp. 41–72). New York: Guilford.

Petty, R. E., Wells, G. L., & Brock, T. C. (1976). Distraction can enhance or reduce yielding to propaganda: Thought disruption versus effort justification. *Journal of Personality and Social Psychology, 34,* 874–884.

Petty, R. E., Wheeler, S. C., & Bizer, G. Y. (1999). Is there one persuasion process or more? Lumping versus splitting in attitude change theories. *Psychological Inquiry, 10,* 156–163.

Pierro, A., Mannetti, L., Erb, H.-P., Spiegel, S. & Kruglanski, A. W. (2005). Informational length and order of presentation as determinants of persuasion. *Journal of Experimental Social Psychology, 41,* 458–469.

Pierro, A., Mannetti, L., Kruglanski, A. W., & Sleeth-Keppler, D. (2004). Relevance override: On the reduced impact of "cues" under high-motivation conditions of persuasion studies. *Journal of Personality and Social Psychology, 86,* 251–264.

Read, S. J., Vanman, E. J., & Miller, L. C. (1997). Connectionism, parallel constraint satisfaction processes, and gestalt principles: (Re)Introducing cognitive dynamics to social psychology. *Personality and Social Psychology Review, 1,* 26–53.

Schwarz, N. (2006). Attitude research: Between Ockham's razor and the fundamental attribution error. *Journal of Consumer Research, 33,* 19–21.

Schwarz, N., & Bohner, G. (2001). The construction of attitudes. In A. Tesser & N. Schwarz (Eds.), *Blackwell handbook of social psychology: Vol. 1. Intraindividual processes* (pp. 436–457). Oxford, UK: Blackwell.

Siebler, F. (2002). *Connectionist modelling of social judgement processes.* Doctoral dissertation, University of Kent, Canterbury, UK.

Smith, E. R. (1996). What do connectionism and social psychology offer each other? *Journal of Personality and Social Psychology, 70,* 893–912.

Smith, E. R., & DeCoster, J. (1998). Knowledge acquisition, accessibility, and use in person perception and stereotyping: Simulation with a recurrent connectionist network. *Journal of Personality and Social Psychology, 74,* 21–35.

Smith, E. R., & DeCoster, J. (2000). Dual-process models in social and cognitive psychology: Conceptual integration and links to underlying memory systems. *Personality and Social Psychology Review, 4,* 108–131.

Thagard, P. (1989). Explanatory coherence. *Behavioral and Brain Sciences, 12,* 435–502.

Tourangeau, R., & Rasinski, K. A. (1988). Cognitive processes underlying context effects in attitude measurement. *Psychological Bulletin, 103,* 299–314.

Van Overwalle, F., & Jordens, K. (2002). An adaptive connectionist model of cognitive dissonance. *Personality and Social Psychology Review, 6,* 204–231.

Van Overwalle, F., & Siebler, F. (2005). A connectionist model of attitude formation and change. *Personality and Social Psychology Review, 9,* 231–274.

Van Overwalle, F., & Van Rooy, D. (2001). How one cause discounts or augments another: A connectionist account of causal competition. *Personality and Social Psychology Bulletin, 27,* 1613–1626.

Wilson, T. D., & Hodges, S. D. (1992). Attitudes as temporary constructions. In L. L. Martin & A. Tesser (Eds.), *The construction of social judgments* (pp. 37–65). Hillsdale, NJ: Erlbaum.

Wilson, T. D., Lisle, D. J., & Kraft, D. (1990). Effects of self-reflection on attitudes and consumer decisions. *Advances in Consumer Research, 17*, 79–85.

Wood, W. (1982). Retrieval of attitude-relevant information from memory: Effects on susceptibility to persuasion and on intrinsic motivation. *Journal of Personality and Social Psychology, 42*, 798–810.

Zajonc, R. B. (1968). Attitudinal effects of mere exposure. *Journal of Personality and Social Psychology Monograph Supplement, 9*(No. 2, Pt. 2), 1–27.

9

Attitude Functions in Persuasion
Matching, Involvement, Self-Affirmation, and Hierarchy

SUSAN E. WATT
University of New England

GREGORY R. MAIO, GEOFFREY HADDOCK
Cardiff University

BLAIR T. JOHNSON
University of Connecticut

*I*n years gone by, people made it common practice to arrange marriages on the basis of financial security. Some still try to ply finances as a means to marital bliss: We have a friend who once received an offer of marriage from a boyfriend who said that he had money and they would want for nothing. Yet, because he did not say he loved her, and she had no need for money, she refused his offer. Love was the only reason she would marry. This story illustrates the importance of attitude functions in persuasion. A reason was offered for why the marriage should take place, but it did not match the recipient's most important motivations, causing her to reject the proposal. As it is in relationships, so it may be in life more generally. To be effective at winning someone's agreement or support, it may be imperative to consider the motives that are important to the person.

Real-life practitioners of persuasion, including salespeople, marketers, and advertisers, often show implicit recognition of the role of motives. They discern a person's reasons for an attitude and cannily target their persuasion toward them. A good example of this process is evident in political campaigns, which are routinely won or lost on just such attempts, and where battles to win people's agreement are thus quite heated. For example, many people had taken enormous housing loans just before the 2004 Australian election. A major component of the Liberal Party of Australia's campaign was to suggest that interest rates on home loans would increase if the opposition party won the election. The Liberal Party had correctly discerned a strong concern in the electorate (to maintain housing loan interest rates) and shaped their messages to address this concern. Tailoring messages in this way is precisely what attitude functions researchers predict will make people amenable to attitude change. Indeed, the Liberal Party did win the election.

Offering a valuable theoretical perspective on these issues, the functional approach to attitudes attempts to classify and study the psychological needs that attitudes fulfill. Through classification of functions, similar sets of specific concerns are grouped into distinct categories. For example, the desire to maintain low mortgage interest rates expresses more basic needs for economic security; interest rates per se may not be the primary "motive" of interest.

This chapter focuses on the idea that these motives or attitude functions play a vital role in attitude *change*. This idea has important practical and theoretical implications. From an applied perspective, many important social interventions rely on campaigns that aim to change attitudes. Vast amounts of public money are spent on health promotion campaigns that aim to persuade people to eat a balanced diet, exercise regularly, and quit smoking. Antiracism campaigns attempt to reduce prejudice, and community protection campaigns often try to convince people not to drop litter or engage in other environmentally destructive behaviors. However, the success of these campaigns is not guaranteed. For instance, several studies of antiracism advertising in the United Kingdom found a backlash effect among individuals whose attitudes were ambivalent (i.e., both favorable and unfavorable) toward ethnic minorities and a failure of the advertisements to address the relevant functions of message recipients' attitudes may have led to this problem (Maio, Haddock, Watt, & Hewstone, in press; also see Bassili, this volume).

The functions of attitudes also may help us understand the effects of a variety of variables on persuasion. As we will show, attitude functions enable predictions about the effects of different types of message content, message sources (e.g., celebrities), and contextual factors (e.g., relationships with peers), all of which are important variables in models of persuasion. Thus, *assumptions* about attitude function are central to these models, even when the models do not explicate them.

This chapter begins by summarizing the early history of theory and research on the topic of attitude functions, which introduced some influential taxonomies of them. We then describe the role of attitude functions in understanding persuasion. Finally, the chapter examines methodological and conceptual issues in this area of research.

OF WHAT USE ARE OPINIONS?

The functional approach to attitudes originated in work conducted by two independent groups of researchers in the 1950s. Smith, Bruner, and White (1956, p. 1) started with the question "Of what use to a man are his opinions?" Based on their 10 in-depth case studies of attitudes toward Russia and communism, these scholars inductively proposed three basic functions of attitudes, including *object appraisal*, *social adjustment*, and *externalization*.

Object appraisal is "sizing up" an object for how it can advance one's own motives, goals, values, and interests. For example, attitudes toward a brand of breakfast cereal would be useful for quickly "sizing up" which ones should be approached or avoided in the supermarket aisles. One of the authors finds it easy to stay away from the Shreddies and go straight for the Fruit Loops. There is no need to think about the specific attributes of each object (e.g., low in fat and contains whole wheat vs. high in sugar and tastes great!). The attitude toward each brand captures everything needed for an immediate, effortless decision.

Social adjustment reflects the role that attitudes can play in maintaining relationships with other people. For example, agreeing with relevant others can increase social acceptance. If all our friends support a particular political party, we will feel out of place and may face social rejection if we happen to express support for a competing party. This function may affect the clothes we wear, the beverages we drink, the music that we choose to hear—anything that is observable or might be observable to others in some way.

Externalization concerns how attitudes can be affected by unresolved inner problems. For example, unresolved issues of sexual identity could be projected as hostility to gay men, lesbians, and victims of AIDS. Consequently, the individual's self-esteem is protected by being hostile to this ego-threatening group. Presumably, people are not as easily made aware of how an attitude serves this function as they are cognizant of its other functions, because when one becomes aware that his or her opinion is serving such a purpose, it quickly loses its ability to protect the self. This aspect of the function makes it difficult to study, because it requires a method to detect its nonconscious functioning.

Some researchers have suggested that object appraisal is the most primary function of attitudes (Fazio, 2000; Maio & Olson, 2000b; Sherman & Fazio, 1983). This view is consistent with Smith et al.'s (1956) conception of this function. They described it as "the creative solution to the problems posed by the existence of disparate internal demands and external or environmental demands" (p. 41). Object appraisal is the ultimate outcome of all the various influences on an attitude. This function simplifies interaction with the environment, making attitude-relevant judgments faster and easier to perform, offering obvious advantages to the attitude holder.

Similar to Smith et al. (1956), Katz and colleagues (Katz, 1960; Katz, McClintock, & Sarnoff, 1957; Sarnoff & Katz, 1954) emphasized the idea that attitude formation and attitude change must be understood in terms of the needs they serve. In contrast to the inductive approach used by Smith et al. (1956), these researchers sought to identify possible functions of attitudes deductively through theoretical analysis and to consider closely the implications of each attitude function for attitude change. They examined a range of theories dominant in psychology at that time, including Gestalt theory, learning theory, and psychoanalytic theory. Based on this analysis, Katz and his colleagues described attitudes as serving four different functions, including the (1) *instrumental, adjustive or utilitarian* function; (2) *knowledge* function; (3) *ego-defensive* function; and (4) *value-expressive* function.

The instrumental, adjustive, or utilitarian function concerns how attitudes help to maximize rewards in the external world (including the social world) and minimize penalties. Consider a person you strongly like. Because of your strong positive attitude to this person, you would probably like to stop and say hello in the street, because the interaction would be enjoyable. You may also *not* like to stop and say hello to someone you strongly dislike, because this interaction would be unpleasant and aggravating. Your attitude has helped to yield pleasant outcomes and avoid bad ones.

The knowledge function concerns a need to structure and understand those aspects of the world that impinge directly on our own lives. To illustrate this function, Katz (1960) drew on Herzog's (1944) study, which revealed that housewives liked listening to daytime radio serials because they provided information and advice. In more recent theoretical frameworks, this function resonates with the idea of need for structure (Neuberg & Newsom, 1993), which concerns the extent to which individuals prefer to structure their environment, and the need for cognitive closure (Webster & Kruglanski, 1994), which taps intolerance for ambiguity.

The knowledge function is similar to Smith et al.'s (1956) object appraisal function, because both functions emphasize the organization and utility of evaluations as a source of information. Yet there also are fundamental differences. The knowledge function concerns achieving understanding of the world, whereas the object appraisal function focuses on how an object can advance one's own interests. In this respect, object appraisal has more in common with Katz's utilitarian function. It may therefore be prudent to consider the object appraisal function as incorporating elements of both the utilitarian function and the knowledge function.

The ego-defensive function is similar to Smith et al.'s (1956) externalization function. The ego-defensive function describes a motivation to form attitudes that protect people from acknowledging basic truths about themselves or from the harsh realities of the external world. For example, we may not wish to acknowledge that we are harming the future of our own children through our negligent impact on the planet's ecology, and hence hold a hostile attitude toward environmentalists who insist on making this issue salient. In theory, this hostility protects us from confronting the threat posed by our own attitudes and behaviors.

Katz's (1960) value-expressive function is most distinct from those described by Smith et al. (1956). It describes a motivation to express attitudes that are appropriate to personal values and the self-concept. For example, we may hold positive attitudes to ethnic minorities in our community because we endorse equality for all community members. Alternatively, we may dislike a group because we feel that it possesses different values from our own (Struch & Schwartz, 1989). In either case, values are central to the attitude.

Despite the theoretical advances in the 1950s, research on attitude functions floundered in the 1960s and 1970s. Scholars criticized Smith et al.'s (1956) theory because it was an inductive analysis and had no a priori supportive data (Insko, 1967; Kiesler, Collins, & Miller, 1969). Katz and colleagues conducted some intriguing empirical tests of their theory and of the ego-defensive function in particular (discussed later in this chapter), but these tests yielded inconsistent results and used paradigms that confounded the dependent and independent variables (Kiesler et al., 1969; Shavitt, 1990). Ultimately, difficulty in identifying attitude functions a priori turned out to be a serious stumbling block in attitude functions research (Insko, 1967; Kiesler et al., 1969). Perhaps because of these issues, interest in the field waned until the 1980s, when significant methodological advances appeared.

A New Wave of Research on Attitude Function

Herek (1987) attempted a reformulation and reoperationalizion of a functional approach to attitudes. His content analysis of 110 essays on attitudes toward lesbians and gay men produced a scheme that better linked the functional approaches of Smith et al. (1956) and Katz (1960). Herek's scheme identified three primary attitude functions: *experiential-schematic, defensive,* and *self-expressive.* The experiential-schematic function captures experience with the group and knowledge of it, similar to Smith et al.'s object appraisal function; the defensive function involves the projection of unacceptable motives onto others, comparable to Smith et al.'s externalization and Katz's ego-defensive function; and the self-expressive function exists in attitudes that serve as a vehicle for expressing identity and values. Herek subsequently separated this last function into *social-expressive* and *value-expressive* portions. Herek (1987) also developed the Attitude Functions Inventory (AFI) to assess these functions. This self-report measure can be tailored to measure the functions of attitudes toward any particular object. This approach assumes that there will be individual differences in the functions of people's attitudes to the same object. Still, it does not assume that personality alone drives these differences, because functions are free to vary across situations and objects.

Shavitt's (1989, 1990) perspective was that particular objects may be better suited to some attitude functions than to others. Using content analyses of participants' descriptions of reasons for their attitudes, Shavitt identified *utilitarian, social identity,* and *self-esteem maintenance* functions, which are similar to the utilitarian, social-adjustment, and ego-defensive functions described above. Her coding scheme revealed that some objects primarily attracted particular functions. Attitudes toward utilitarian objects, such as air conditioners and coffee, were reliably utilitarian. In contrast, attitudes toward symbols of identity and values, such as the American flag and a wedding ring, reliably reflected the social identity function.

Other advances have been made in the assessment of functions at the level of the attitude object. In particular, measures of specific attitude properties can help to assess functions of particular attitudes. This potential is well illustrated within Fazio's (2000) research examining the effects of attitude accessibility on the role of the object appraisal function. In this research, attitudes that are easy to retrieve from memory (i.e., accessible) have led to quicker decisions and lower physiological reactivity when making judgments about novel objects (abstract paintings). Fazio (2000) reasoned that accessible attitudes facilitate object appraisal, which makes it easier to approach or avoid objects that are subject to positive or negative attitudes.

Together, these developments provided a useful basis for examining the role of attitude functions in predicting relevant behaviors and attitude change. For example, functions may predict relevant behaviors above and beyond the prediction afforded by simply knowing the attitude itself. To illustrate, people who love the taste of good coffee should buy a brand of coffee that they believe will taste great. That is, the strong utilitarian function of their attitude should predict their buying behavior. In contrast, people who are concerned about social justice for coffee growers should buy Fair-trade coffee, possibly disregarding whether the coffee is precisely to their taste. Here, the strong value-expressive function of their attitude would be expected to predict buying behavior. Notwithstanding these interesting implications for understanding behavior, the means for validating measures of attitude function have most often focused on tests of specific theoretical implications for persuasion. These ramifications are the focus of the remainder of this chapter.

IMPLICATIONS FOR PERSUASION

Research on attitude functions was revived when investigators began to discover a priori means to measure attitude function more directly or to manipulate the functional base of an attitude. Using these means, researchers could begin to test various effects of attitude functions. Below, we describe tests that focused on two key hypotheses: the function matching hypothesis and the message processing hypothesis.

The Function Matching Hypothesis

The functional approach provides an important basic insight into persuasion. It suggests that *attitude change occurs to meet a functional need*. Katz and his colleagues emphasized this notion from the start. They assumed that people must perceive that their attitude is no longer serving its function before any change could take place. For example, a utilitarian attitude will change if it is not fulfilling its utilitarian objectives. If you support the Liberal Party of Australia because you believe that they will protect your financial security, a member of the other political parties could try to convince you to dislike the Liberal Party by pointing out that the party has let home mortgage interest rates rise, while noting the positive impacts of their own policies on financial security. In theory, this approach would be more effective than presenting arguments that raise concerns that are irrelevant to the person's attitude. For example, if the person is *not* concerned about whether the party supports the value of peace, then it makes no sense to point out its policies regarding the military.

This *functional matching hypothesis*, as it has become known, has received extensive support across studies using a variety of approaches. The classic Yale model of persuasion (Hovland, Janis, & Kelley, 1953) proposed that to adopt a new attitude, an individual must anticipate receiving some reinforcement or incentive for attitude change. Because reinforcement may alleviate a psychologi-

cal need, this emphasis is consistent with the focus of theories of attitude function. Differing from the functional approach, the Yale model regarded incentives
as the presentation of a positive reinforcement (a reward) or a negative reinforcement (removal of something unpleasant). One example of negative reinforcement
is persuasion through fear. On being exposed to a frightening message, such as
a graphic picture of a road accident, or of oral cancer on a cigarette packet, fear
is aroused. Janis and Feshbach (1953) proposed that the reduction of fear would
take place through "silent rehearsal" of the message recommendation, leading to
changes in one's attitude. Many studies conducted by the Yale group provided
evidence consistent with the notion that message acceptance is a function of
reinforcements that are elicited by message source, message content, and the
message recipient (e.g., Hovland & Weiss, 1951; Janis, 1954; Janis & Feshbach,
1953). Nonetheless, these studies did not use a specific taxonomy of attitude
functions.

Katz and his colleagues (1957) conducted the earliest test of the functional
matching hypothesis. These researchers realized that individual differences may
predict a tendency to possess attitudes serving particular functions. They reasoned that strongly authoritarian and self-defensive personalities were more likely
to form ego-defensive attitudes and, if so, people with defensive personalities
should be more amenable to attitude change following an intervention that targets defensiveness. In an ambitious experiment, these researchers tried to reduce
prejudice through insight into how repression and projection may cause prejudice.
Ego-defense was measured on the F scale, and participants then read about the
role of repression and projection in prejudice. After presentation of the insight
message, participants with moderate defensiveness scores on the F scale showed
decreased prejudice to "Negroes" in comparison with those with low defensiveness. In contrast, the intervention did not decrease prejudice in those with high
defensiveness on the F scale. The results, then, offered only partial support for
the matching hypothesis. However, the study was flawed because the F scale also
measures prejudice, creating a confound between the independent and dependent
variables. Many studies have since examined the functional matching hypothesis
using more robust procedures, as we will illustrate shortly.

The Message Processing Hypothesis

A more controversial suggestion has been the notion that different attitude functions induce different types of message processing. Models of social influence have
taken different stances on this issue. For example, Deutsch and Gerard (1955)
provided a classic analysis of social influence that included categories found in
theories of attitude function. They described two fundamental motives for attitude
change to explain the results of experiments on conformity to majority opinion
within social groups. One motive involved a desire to conform to the expectations of other people (*normative social influence*), and the other motive involved a
desire to accept information obtained from others as evidence about reality (*informational social influence*). Normative social influence has similarities with the
social-adjustment function, whereas informational social influence is similar to the

utilitarian and knowledge functions. These types of influence were presumed to elicit different processing styles, with normative influence eliciting a simple public agreement and informational influence eliciting a validity-seeking, private, and genuine level of agreement, but there is little support for this contention (Prislin & Wood, 2005).

Kelman (1958, 1961) redrew this distinction between normative and informational influence, describing three motivational processes in attitude change: *compliance, identification*, and *internalization*. Compliance involves acceptance of an influence because of the belief that agreement will gain rewards and approval or avoid punishments and disapproval, identification involves agreement to establish or maintain a satisfying self-defining relationship to another person or a group, and internalization occurs when the content of the message is intrinsically rewarding and can be easily integrated into the individual's existing value system. Compliance and identification are similar to the social-adjustment function, because the attitudes are held to maintain relationships with others, and internalization is similar to the knowledge and ego-defensive functions because it takes into account coherence and links with the self. Again, these types of influence reflect different processing styles (e.g., Mills & Harvey, 1972). Compliance should elicit superficial processing to conform to social demands, internalization should elicit thoughtful processing that shapes public and private agreement, and identification invokes a mix of both processes.

The connection between motives and styles of processing is more evident in contemporary models of persuasion. The elaboration likelihood model (ELM: Petty & Cacioppo, 1986; Petty & Wegener, 1999) and the heuristic-systematic model (HSM: Chaiken, Liberman, & Eagly, 1989; Chen & Chaiken, 1999) each propose that the processing of persuasive messages is influenced by a need for accuracy, which is the key aspect of the knowledge function. In the ELM, attitude change occurs either through quick short-cuts (the peripheral route) or through more elaborate, cognitive processing (the central route), depending on whether people are highly motivated to form an accurate attitude *and* are able to do so. This model acknowledges that other motives can bias people's internal responses to the content of a message, but does not attempt to produce a taxonomy of these motives.

In contrast, the HSM adds two motives to the need for accuracy: *Impression management* and *defense*. Impression management involves a focus on interpersonal consequences associated with expressing a judgment (corresponds with the social-adjustment function), whereas defense is the desire to hold attitudes and beliefs that are congruent with existing self-definitional attitudes and beliefs (corresponds with the value-expression and ego-defense functions). Whereas accuracy motivation directs people to process persuasive messages carefully and respond to both the strengths and weaknesses in the arguments, impression-management motivation leads people to adopt whichever attitude best fits the social environment (Chaiken, Giner-Sorolla, & Chen, 1996), and self-defense motivation causes people to protect their self-defining attitudes and beliefs (Chen & Chaiken, 1999). In this manner, both of the latter motives arouse resistance and both prompt biased information processing that potentially gives more weight to content that favors one's *desired* attitude (to impress others or defend the self) than to content that opposes it (Lundgren & Prislin, 1998).

EVIDENCE REGARDING THE FUNCTIONAL MATCHING EFFECT

Individual Difference Approaches

DeBono and Snyder (DeBono, 1987; Snyder & DeBono, 1985) posited a connection between attitude function and individual differences in self-monitoring (Snyder, 1974, 1987). High self-monitors are people who continually monitor their relation with the environment around them, adjusting their behavior to fit the social circumstances. These people tend to agree with such items as "In different situations and with different people, I often act like very different persons." In contrast, low self-monitors are less pragmatic in focus: Instead of maintaining awareness of their relations to the social environment, they focus on principles endorsed by the self. As a result, low self-monitors base their behaviors on relevant inner sources such as values, feelings, and dispositions. They tend to agree with such items as "My behavior is usually an expression of my true inner feelings, attitudes, and beliefs." With regard to attitude functions, DeBono and Snyder concluded that high self-monitors should be more likely to exhibit social-adjustive attitudes, whereas low self-monitors should exhibit utilitarian or value-expressive attitudes.

If this link between self-monitoring and attitude function is correct, high self-monitors should be more amenable to persuasive messages (e.g., advertisements) that target social image (soft-sell), whereas low self-monitors should be more amenable to messages that target the truth (hard-sell). For example, Snyder and DeBono (1985) exposed participants to an advertisement for Canadian Club whiskey that featured a bottle of whiskey resting on a set of house designs. An image-based slogan stated "You're not just moving in, you're moving up," whereas a quality-based slogan stated "When it comes to great taste, everyone draws the same conclusion." Using messages about this and other topics, the researchers found evidence supporting the functional matching hypothesis: High self-monitors showed more preference for brands that were presented using advertisements that targeted image, whereas low self-monitors showed more preference for brands that were presented in advertisements that targeted quality. In addition, high self-monitors indicated that they would pay more money for products that were promoted by the image advertisement.

Similar effects have been found when matching high and low self-monitors with consensus or values-based arguments (DeBono, 1987). As predicted, high self-monitors are more responsive to consensus opinion, whereas low self-monitors are more responsive to value appeals. Moreover, high and low self-monitors differ predictably in their reactions to the source of a message: High self-monitors are more persuaded by attractive sources than by expert sources, whereas low self-monitors are more persuaded by expert sources than by attractive sources (DeBono & Harnish, 1988).

Using this individual difference variable, the evidence for functional matching is rather robust. This use of the self-monitoring construct was also an important methodological and theoretical advance, because the construct can successfully identify the social-adjustive and value-expressive functions a priori, while showing that there are individual differences in the motivations underlying attitudes. Thus, the same attitude could be held by different individuals for different reasons.

Other significant functional matching effects have been found in matching symbolic and values-based appeals to people who tended to value symbolic or instrumental possessions. Prentice (1987) suggested that orientations to possessions reflect the manner in which people organize their experience and derive the psychological functions of their attitudes. She tested this view by classifying the functions served by participants' most cherished possessions. Heirlooms, diaries, photos, and souvenirs are examples of symbolic possessions, because they represent important aspects of the self-concept and personal values. In contrast, stereos, TVs, boots, and bicycles might be regarded as more instrumental in nature, because of their practical utility. After indicating their cherished possessions, participants were exposed to persuasive messages on six different, unfamiliar issues, including the use of warning labels on alcohol containers, the inclusion of handicapped people in mainstream education, and whether there should be a referendum on the positioning of a naval base in a nearby location (Prentice, 1987). Each proposal explained the issue, while expressing symbolic or instrumental arguments. An example of a symbolic argument was that the referendum on the naval base would be an expression of democracy, whereas an example of an instrumental argument was that the base would bring jobs to the area. The results were mixed: Participants who most preferred their symbolic objects exhibited greater agreement with message recommendations following the symbolic arguments than following the instrumental arguments, whereas participants who most preferred the instrumental objects did not differ in their evaluations of the proposals.

Other research has examined differences in attitude function toward different attitude objects across people, rather than use objects to classify individual differences in attitude function across objects. This object-based approach is intriguing because functional matching might be employed by tailoring the persuasive message to the presumed principal function of a specific object. For example, Shavitt (1990) conducted an experiment that promoted utilitarian objects (e.g., coffee) and social identity objects (e.g., perfumes) with utilitarian or social identity advertisements. For example, the utilitarian advertisement for a brand of coffee (a utilitarian object) featured the claim, "The delicious hearty flavor and aroma of Sterling Blend coffee comes from a blend of the freshest coffee beans," whereas the social identity advertisement claimed, "The coffee you drink says something about the type of person you are. It can reveal your rare, discriminating taste." Analyses of postadvertisement attitudes revealed that for utilitarian products, participants were more persuaded by utilitarian advertisements than by social identity advertisements. In contrast, for social identity products, participants were more persuaded by social identity advertisements than by utilitarian advertisements. Similarly, Shavitt, Lowrey, and Han (1992) found that high self-monitors explained their attitudes toward social identity products using more social terms and fewer utilitarian terms than low self-monitors. However, no differences were obtained for utilitarian or multiple-function objects.

Yet another approach examines individual differences in functions of attitudes toward specific attitude objects, ranging from victims of AIDS to automobiles. A large program of research by Clary and colleagues (1998) examined differences in the functions of attitudes toward charitable volunteering activities. In this research, the investigators conceived of six potential functions of volunteering: Value-expression (e.g., promoting a worthy cause), understanding (e.g., learning through experience), career promotion (e.g., obtaining a reference), social rewards (e.g., being with people you care about), protective (e.g., escaping from personal troubles), and self-enhancement (e.g., feeling more valued and important). The researchers then developed the Volunteering Functions Inventory (VFI) to assess the extent to which these functions were important in respondents' attitudes toward volunteering. Using the VFI, the researchers found that function scores predicted receptiveness to videotaped advertisements that gave different reasons for volunteering. Specifically, participants were more persuaded by advertisements that cited reasons congruent with the dominant functions in the message recipients' attitudes than by advertisements that cited different reasons.

Rather than use individual difference constructs as a method to infer attitude functions, other research has sought to manipulate the function of an individual's attitude. For example, Murray, Haddock, and Zanna (1996) manipulated the likelihood that their Canadian participants would form a value-expressive or social-adjustive attitude toward institutionalizing the mentally ill. The first phase of the manipulation involved the completion of an "attitude functions questionnaire." The questions were loaded in a manner that encouraged responding in favor of either value-expressive or social-adjustive responses. The next phase involved giving participants (fictitious) feedback about their dominant attitude function. This feedback made their dominant function seem much more desirable and preferable to the other function. In the last phase of the manipulation, participants indicated their attitudes toward several issues and the extent to which several values affected their attitudes, or they rated their attitudes and the extent to which they had considered different reference groups in forming their attitudes. Next, in an ostensibly separate study, participants received a message advocating increased institutionalization of the mentally ill. The message linked the issue to the value of being a responsible and loving person or to the "finding" that the majority of Canadian students favored institutionalization. Murray et al.'s results indicated that participants who had received the induction of social-adjustive attitudes were in greater agreement with the social-adjustive message than the value-expressive message. This pattern was reversed for participants who received the value-expressive attitude induction. The functional matching hypothesis therefore received experimental support.

An important consideration is whether attitude functions are manipulated by priming or by threat. Priming merely makes the idea of the motive salient. For example, Maio and Olson (1995a) manipulated attitude function by presenting posters that made salient one of two reasons for donating to cancer research. In one condition, participants received a poster describing the manner in which their donations would help others, thereby promoting value-expressive benevolence values (Schwartz, 1992). In another condition, participants received a poster describing how their donations would benefit themselves, by increasing the likelihood that a cure would be discovered before they might get cancer. Validating this manipulation, subsequent correlations between participants' values of helpfulness and intentions to donate to the charity were significant after the value-expressive prime, but not after the utilitarian prime. Moreover, the relation between values and intentions occurred over and above the effects of other relevant variables, such as subjective norms regarding the behavior and perceptions of control over the performance of the behavior.

Notwithstanding such results, it may be more useful to manipulate threat to the function than to increase the salience of the function through priming. In theory, functional motives have the unique ability to maintain homeostasis. In other words, a threat to a function should trigger spontaneous or deliberate attempts to fulfill the motive more strongly. Consequently, attitude functions should respond to threats to the general motivation that they serve, over and above simple priming of the attitude function (Marsh & Julka, 2000). For instance, the need for knowledge should be activated in an ambiguous situation, or the need for value-expression should be activated if people are made to feel that they are falling short of their own values. In several experiments designed to address this issue, function matching effects were more marked as a function of priming than of manipulated threat (Marsh & Julka, 2000). More experiments are needed to examine this issue to resolve several ambiguities involved in motivational manipulations (e.g., emotional fatigue, defensiveness).

It is important to keep in mind that attitude functions predict what people *dislike*, in addition to predicting what they like. People dislike things that are harmful to their personal outcomes (utilitarian threats), threaten their values (value-expression threats), and that are unpopular among people whom they like (social-adjustment threats; see Johnson, Smith-McLallen, Killeya, & Levin, 2004). Failures to address these functions in persuasive messages may inadvertently create backlash effects. Maio et al. (in press) found *increased* derogation of ethnic outgroups following exposure to posters that were modeled after real advertisements against racism. The posters contained *brief* value-expressive and utilitarian captions (e.g., "multicultural = equality + respect", "multicultural = prosperity + progress") as arguments, and this approach may simply have made salient the functions (e.g., a utilitarian concern that too many asylum seekers might arrive) without effectively addressing them.

In sum, the reviewed research supports the matching hypothesis across a range of attitude objects and techniques. We now turn our attention to the question of *why* such functional matching effects occur. These explanations for functional matching are interesting partly because they also may help to predict when matching might produce negative effects.

Why Does Functional Matching Work?

A simple explanation for the functional matching effect is that attitude functions act as heuristics. That is, if an argument matches the attitude function, no elaboration of arguments supporting the new position is necessary. The functional match may act as a simple cue to accept the message (Petty & Wegener, 1998), and the attitude is simply altered in the direction of the argument. Yet, DeBono (1987) concluded that a simple-cue explanation is unlikely because information relating to individuals' plans, goals, and needs motivates individuals to focus attention on all relevant information in the stimulus environment (Harkness, DeBono, & Borgida, 1985).

Initial research on this topic supported the hypothesis that function matching elicits increased attention. This research found that although participants did not exhibit more thoughts about functionally matched arguments, they did have better recall for these arguments (DeBono, 1987). This result is consistent with the expectation that participants allocated more mental resources to examining and storing functionally relevant arguments. Additional research showed that participants who were exposed to messages from a source (attractive or expert) that matched the function of their attitude (social-adjustive or value-expressive) were more sensitive to the cogency of arguments (DeBono & Harnish, 1988), further suggesting greater scrutiny for function matches. At the same time, it appears that functionally-matched messages are perceived to be of higher *quality* than nonmatched messages, and perceived quality mediates the relationship between functional relevance and persuasion effects, including effects on behavior (Lavine & Snyder, 1996). Lavine and Snyder suggested that one explanation for this role of perceived quality of argument is that functionally matched arguments are consistent with an existing self-schema, and this biases the extent to which arguments are perceived as valid .

The ELM provides a useful perspective on this issue (Petty & Cacioppo, 1986; Petty & Wegener, 1999). It indicates that people should be more sensitive to the cogency of message arguments when the likelihood of message elaboration is high, as in situations where messages are relevant to the self (Petty & Wegener, 1998; see Wegener & Carlston, 2005, for a review). Following from Lavine and Snyder's (1996) evidence, function matching may cause increased self-relevance of a message. If so, the resulting message elaboration should make perceivers more likely to respond to strengths *and* weaknesses in the message. This elaboration is important because strong arguments can withstand such scrutiny, but weak arguments cannot. One way of avoiding scrutiny of weak messages when elaboration likelihood is high, then, would be to *mis*match the message. This weak message will receive less scrutiny and counterarguing than if it were functionally matched.

Petty and Wegener (1998) conducted two experiments to test this reasoning. High and low self-monitors were presented with weak or strong arguments that either matched or mismatched their attitude function (appeals to image or quality). Results revealed effects of argument strength when the message matched the function of the attitude, such that the weak message was much less persuasive than the strong message. The mismatched messages did not elicit this effect of argument strength. Overall, the weak function-matched message was the least persuasive message, consistent with Petty and Wegener's (1998) reasoning from the ELM.

These results have many interesting implications. In pragmatic terms, before working out a persuasion strategy, one should determine whether the argument is strong or weak. If it is strong, functional matching will be most effective, but if it is weak, mismatching may produce more persuasion. The results also suggest that functional matching may prompt message elaboration, but mismatching may prompt superficial processing. If this view is correct, then simple cues (e.g., source attractiveness) may be more effective when the content of messages appears mismatched to recipients' function. To our knowledge, this possibility remains to be tested.

EVIDENCE REGARDING DIFFERENT
TYPES OF MESSAGE PROCESSING

The hypothesis that different motives exert distinct effects on persuasion has been controversial. The multiple motive approach is consistent with broader theory and research suggesting that social behavior and judgment in general tend to serve multiple motives (Chaiken, Duckworth, & Darke, 1999; Katz, 1960; Maio & Olson, 2000a; Smith et al., 1956). It is also supported by Johnson and Eagly's (1989) meta-analysis of past studies that related involvement to persuasion. These researchers identified three ways of being involved with an issue: *outcome-relevant involvement*, *value-relevant involvement*, and *impression-relevant involvement*, which are logically parallel to the utilitarian, value-expressive, and social-adjustive functions, respectively. In Johnson and Eagly's scheme, involvement results from the association between an attitude and some aspect of the self-concept. In value-relevant involvement, the attitude issue is relevant to one's enduring values; in outcome-relevant involvement, the attitude issue is relevant to desired outcomes; and, in impression-relevant involvement, the issue relates to the image that one presents to others. For example, the topic of increased testing in schools may seem very relevant to personal values of creativity, freedom, and achievement (high value-relevant involvement), issues of cost (high outcome-relevant involvement), or the views of one's family and friends (high impression-relevant involvement).

Johnson and Eagly (1989) found different patterns of persuasion across different types of involvement. When outcome-relevant involvement was high, participants were more persuaded by strong arguments and less persuaded by weak arguments. When impression-relevant involvement was high, argument quality played no role in persuasion; these participants exhibited a small amount of resistance relative to their low-involvement counterparts. Value-relevant involvement was associated with less attitude change, a tendency that lessened somewhat with stronger arguments.

Johnson and Eagly (1989) documented several confounds when comparing the results of studies of the three different types of involvement. In particular, studies in the value-relevant tradition were more likely to use controversial issues for which high-involvement participants may well have held more knowledge and more polarized attitudes than their low-involvement counterparts. Also, the studies in this tradition were more likely to be based on measured rather than manipulated involvement than those in either the outcome- or impression-involvement traditions of research. Nonetheless, because no value-relevant study contained all of these flaws, and because experimental demonstrations of expected patterns were present across the literature, Johnson and Eagly concluded that the literature supported the validity of their typology (cf. Johnson & Eagly, 1990; Petty & Cacioppo, 1990).

To further clarify this typology, it is useful to consider some of the experimental demonstrations of distinct processing styles. Ostrom and Brock (1969) introduced perhaps the first and most influential methodology, the value-bonding task, for addressing the question of whether particular motives exert distinct effects on persuasion. Ostrom and Brock gave participants information to make them initially oppose Greenland's admittance into the Pan-Am Bank—a novel issue for participants. The participants then rated the importance of many social values in a list and drew connections between the issue of Greenland's acceptance and the values that they had rated as important or unimportant in the list. Next, a new pro-Greenland essay was presented, and their subsequent attitudes toward Greenland's admittance into the bank were assessed. The persuasive message elicited less agreement when participants had connected the issue to values that were important to them than when they had connected the issue to values that were unimportant to them.

This result is consistent with the view that the expression of (important) values within an attitude can lead to defensive processing of subsequent messages. Yet, this experiment did not compare the processing induced by values with the processing induced by other types of motives, such as the utilitarian motive to protect personal material outcomes. Several experiments have since addressed this issue. First, Maio and Olson (1995b) used the value-bonding task to make participants more likely to form value-expressive or utilitarian attitudes toward educational issues. In one condition, participants considered how various academic tasks (e.g., writing additional essays) promoted or threatened important social values (e.g., freedom and individualism). In the other condition, participants considered how the tasks promoted or threatened their personal outcomes. Then, in an ostensibly separate experiment, participants were told about a new potential requirement to complete comprehensive examinations at the end of their degree and were given strong or weak arguments in favor of these exams. Participants then indicated their attitudes toward the exams. Participants who considered the values or personal outcomes to be at least mildly personally important (i.e., who showed habitual bonding to values) were not affected by the strength of the arguments in favor of the exams. In contrast, after habitual bonding to important outcomes, the participants were more favorable to the exams after reading the cogent arguments than after reading the weak ones. In other words, they were sensitive to argument strength. On balance, then, it appears that the important confounds Johnson and Eagly (1989) identified do not fully account for the differences between value-relevant and outcome-relevant involvement.

We expect that awareness of these multiple motives is important to the extent that it has implications for how persuasive messages are received and used. For example, the accuracy motive may elicit the most differentiation between strong and weak information in persuasive messages. In addition, even if the other motives are associated with different confounds in practice (e.g., higher attitude strength), the motives nonetheless predict different styles of processing (Chaiken, Giner-Sorolla, & Chen, 1996). Thus, the alternate motives provide a useful (though perhaps not foolproof) heuristic for deducing message impact.

Self-Affirmation

The finding that value-relevant involvement can cause defensive message processing leads us to postulate that value-expressive attitudes may be particularly resistant to persuasion. However, as mentioned, impression-relevant involvement (and hence ego-defensive and social adjustment attitudes) also is likely to arouse resistance and prompt biased information processing. This pattern poses quite a conundrum, because many of the most important real-world issues invoke passionate feelings about values and deep concerns about others' positive regard. If we are entrenched on these issues, it may be very difficult to negotiate changes that can reduce conflict.

One recently developed intervention offers some hope for circumventing such resistance. Specifically, self-affirmation theory proposes that defensive processing of a message is reduced if the message recipient's global sense of self-worth is bolstered prior to receiving the message. Bolstering can be achieved by focusing on other valued aspects of the self, which are not threatened by the message (Aronson, Cohen & Nail, 1999; Sherman & Cohen, 2002; Steele, 1988). Commonly used techniques involve reflecting on one's central values by completing a values survey or receiving positive feedback on a personally important task. Self-affirmation allows people to feel a sense of self-integrity, which enables them to process the threat in a more open, less defensive manner. As a result, self-affirmed individuals are likely to be more responsive to counterattitudinal messages, less biased in processing of these messages, and more likely to change their attitude (Cohen, Aronson, & Steele, 2000). Self-affirmation can therefore serve to "inoculate" against defensive responses to persuasion (Jacks & O'Brien, 2004).

The hypothesized boost to self-integrity is multifaceted. According to Steele (1988), it involves seeking to maintain "a phenomenal experience of the self—self-conceptions and images—as adaptively and morally adequate, that is, as competent, good, coherent, unitary, stable, capable of free choice, capable of controlling important outcomes, and so on" (p. 262). This "phenomenal experience" should affect the motivations that are served by attitude functions. For example, if following self-affirmation the self is perceived as competent and good, there will be little need for ego-defensive attitudes. To the extent that the self has been affirmed, there is less need to defend it through one's attitudes. Similarly, if self-affirmation makes the self seem morally adequate, there will be little need to defend it through value-expressive attitudes. In addition, if the self is seen as highly adaptive and having control over important outcomes, there will be less need to defend one's utilitarian attitudes. It should also be the case that any positive effect of self-affirmation on feelings of acceptance from others should reduce the need to boost social acceptance through holding social adjustment attitudes.

From this perspective, then, self-affirmation may be an effective way to reduce resistance when attitudes serve a variety of functions. Consistent with this view, self-affirmation has been found to reduce defensive processing across differing topic domains that should logically link to different attitude functions. For example, Cohen et al. (2000) conducted research on responses to arguments regarding capital punishment and abortion—topics that should arouse mostly value-expressive attitudes. Their results showed that self-affirmed participants were more persuaded by arguments that opposed their original views on capital punishment and were more critical of arguments that supported their own attitude toward abortion.

Jacks and O'Brien (2004, Study 1) examined introductory psychology students' responses to arguments that favored increased scholarships for African Americans to attend college. This topic was likely to arouse both the value-expressive and ego-defensive attitude functions among the participants. The results showed that self-affirmed participants were more persuaded than non-self-affirmed participants. Also, in the domain of ego-defense, Cohen et al. (2005, cited in Sherman & Cohen, in press) found that self-affirmation increased trust across partisan lines when entering into negotiation. In addition, self-affirmation has also been found to reduce the stress produced by giving a speech and performing mental arithmetic in front of a hostile audience (Creswell et al., 2005).

Self-affirmation also affects receptiveness to messages that target utilitarian attitudes. Correll, Spencer, and Zanna (2004) found that self-affirmed students were more open to debate on the topic of increased tuition fees for students. This topic would have strongly implicated the utilitarian function for introductory psychology students. Similarly, Sherman, Nelson, and Steele (2000) found that self-affirmed women who were coffee drinkers were more open than non-self-affirmed women to a scientific report linking caffeine consumption with breast cancer—a threat that should implicate the utilitarian attitude function. In a similar paradigm, self-affirmation has been found to have enduring effects on risk perception and on behavioral intentions, although not on longer-term behaviors (Harris & Napper, 2005).

In sum, self-affirmation is effective in reducing defensive responses across a variety of attitude topics, reflecting diverse attitude functions (Correll, Spencer, & Zanna, 2004). An interesting issue for future research is whether this pattern argues against the distinctions among different types of involvement, because the same basic process (i.e., self-affirmation) can operate across them.

A Final Thought: An Argument for a Hierarchical Perspective on Attitude Function

Although researchers have used various definitions and categorizations of attitude functions, a fairly stable set of attitude functions has been identified. Researchers have consistently identified the following functions of attitudes: utilitarian concerns (rewards and punishments associated with an attitude object), value-expression, social relations, identity, knowledge, and self-esteem concerns. Although this convergence between researchers is encouraging, the position of these functions within each taxonomy, and the viability of other functions remain open to debate.

The number of functions identified will depend on the specificity of each function. Scientists in most disciplines struggle with the issue of how to delineate the inclusiveness of categories in any taxonomy. For example, early psychologists identifying "drives" in animal behavior initially identified a hunger drive responsible for feeding, a thirst drive, a sex drive, etc. The problem was that as they attempted to describe every possible behavior, more and more "drives" were described, resulting ultimately in a reductio ad absurdum that included drives for thumb-sucking, nail-biting, and other minutiae of behavior (McFarland, 1987).

At the inclusive end of the functions spectrum, attitude functions could be broadly divided into instrumental and symbolic functions—a similar distinction to that made by Kinder and Sears (1981) between self-interest politics and symbolic politics (Abelson & Prentice, 1989). This level of analysis has been found useful in examining the functions of intergroup attitudes (Watt, Maio, Rees, & Hewstone, 2007). At the more specific end of the spectrum, functions could vary immensely. For example, Herek (1987) discussed a possible anticipatory-evaluative function, which involves fulfilling *anticipated* benefits of an object, rather than the past benefits. Herek also distinguished between the utility of evaluations based on specific members of a category (an experiential-specific function), such as a particular member of an ethnic group (e.g., my friend Rasheed), and evaluations based on a whole category (an experiential-schematic function), such as Asians.

Attempts to address the issue of categorization may be both theory and data driven. From a theoretical perspective, one way to take into account the generality and specificity of different attitude functions might be to think in hierarchical terms. Significant advances might be made by considering whether some functions nest within one another. For example, we discussed a possible primacy of the object appraisal function, which might be seen as an overarching function of attitudes, within which all others are nested. From a data-driven point of view, functions could be identified by discovering categories that delineate meaningful differences in information processing and persuasion (suggested by Petty & Wegener, 1998). This type of approach is exemplified by research on different types of involvement in persuasion.

The debate over the distinctions among types of involvement makes it clear that the empirical method of delineating motives is not as straightforward as it may seem. The main problem is that evidence must be linked to conceptual distinctions, and this linkage has been hampered by ambiguity in descriptions of attitude functions (Greenwald, 1989). For instance, a serious difficulty occurs when distinguishing between the value-expressive and utilitarian functions (Maio & Olson, 2000b). Some values are obviously utilitarian in nature. This utilitarian nature is evident in many of the social values that emphasize self-enhancement motivations (e.g., hedonism, security). Thus, the value-expressive and utilitarian functions of attitudes are theoretically related. This relation is evident in the finding that ratings of self-enhancement oriented social values predict attitudes that serve a utilitarian function (Maio & Olson, 2000b).

This theoretical and empirical connection supports the argument for a more flexible, hierarchical view that includes utilitarian concerns as a specific sub-type of social value. Maio and Olson (2000b) suggested the new category of *goal-*

expressive attitudes to denote this type of hierarchy. They defined goal-expressive attitudes as those that *express important and relevant goals that are derived from values*. On occasion, the values could be self-transcending, reflecting concern for the welfare of other people (Schwartz, 1992). In other instances, the values could be utilitarian and self-promoting in nature. In yet other instances, the attitudes could promote other categories of goals (e.g., pursuit of freedom). More important, Maio and Olson provided evidence that attitudes can serve different goals within these broad categories. For example, attitudes toward a study skills program can reflect the utilitarian value of enjoying life or the utilitarian value of achievement, with *conflicting* implications for the attitude. Such divergence at specific, within-category levels again speaks for the importance of a hierarchical perspective on attitude functions.

CONCLUSIONS

Functional theories of attitudes provide a framework for understanding the important motivations that can underlie attitudes. These theories have many practical and theoretical implications for persuasion. The research reviewed shows that persuasive messages that take attitude functions into account tend to be more effective, provided that the messages contain strong arguments. In addition, the research suggests that value-expressive, ego-defensive, and social-adjustive attitudes may be more likely than utilitarian attitudes to arouse defensive message processing, and self-affirmation can reduce such resistance. All of these findings are important and provocative, but not definitive in their support for theories of attitude function.

Future theory and research may determine that a more complex, hierarchical model better describes the role of psychological needs in persuasion. If we are permitted to consider this issue in light of our opening description of an offer of marriage, it becomes clear that the problem may not always be whether people should marry for love *or* money. People may be more open to marriage proposals that serve a higher-order need—such as a desire for self-enhancement—proposals that offer, perhaps, both love *and* money.

AUTHOR NOTE

We are grateful to Judy Tan for her helpful comments on an earlier draft of this chapter.

REFERENCES

Abelson, R. P., & Prentice, D. A. (1989). Beliefs as possessions: A functional perspective. In A. R. Pratkanis, S. J. Breckler, & A. G. Greenwald (Eds.), *Attitude structure and function* (pp. 361–381). Hillsdale, NJ: Erlbaum.

Aronson, J., Cohen, G. L., & Nail, P. R. (1999). Self-affirmation theory: An update and appraisal. In E. Harmon-Jones & J. Mills (Eds.), *Cognitive dissonance: Progress on a pivotal theory in social psychology* (pp. 127–148). Washington, D.C.: American Psychological Association.

Chaiken, S., Duckworth, K. L., & Darke, P. (1999). When parsimony fails. *Psychological Inquiry, 10*, 118–123.

Chaiken, S., Giner-Sorolla, R., & Chen, S. (1996). Beyond accuracy: Defense and impression motives in heuristic and systematic information processing. In P. Gollwitzer & J. A. Bargh (Eds.), *The psychology of action: Linking cognition and motivation to behavior* (pp. 553–578). New York: Guilford.

Chaiken, S., Liberman, A., & Eagly, A. H. (1989). Heuristic and systematic processing within and beyond the persuasion context. In J. Uleman & J. A. Bargh (Eds.), *Unintended thought* (pp. 212–252). New York: Guilford.

Chen, S., & Chaiken, S. (1999). The heuristic-systematic model in its broader context. In S. Chaiken & Y. Trope (Eds.), *Dual process theories in social psychology* (pp. 73–96). New York: Guilford.

Clary, E. G., Snyder, M., Ridge, R. D., Copeland, J., Stukas, A. A., Haugen, J. et al. (1998). Understanding and assessing the motivations of volunteers: A functional approach. *Journal of Personality and Social Psychology, 74*, 1516–1530.

Cohen, G. L., Aronson, J., & Steele, C. (2000). When beliefs yield to evidence: Reducing biased evaluation by affirming the self. *Personality and Social Psychology Bulletin, 26*, 1151–1164.

Correll, J., Spencer, S. J., & Zanna, M. P. (2004). An affirmed self and an open mind: Self-affirmation and sensitivity to argument strength. *Journal of Experimental Social Psychology, 40*, 350–356.

Creswell, J. D., Welch, W. T., Taylor, S. E., Sherman, D. K., Gruenewald, T. L., & Mann, T. (2005). Affirmation of personal values buffers neuroendocrine and psychological stress responses. *Psychological Science, 16*, 846–851.

DeBono, K. (1987). Investigating the social-adjustive and value-expressive functions of attitudes: Implications for persuasion processes. *Journal of Personality and Social Psychology, 52*, 279–287.

DeBono, K., & Harnish, R. (1988). Source expertise, source attractiveness, and the processing of persuasive information: A functional approach. *Journal of Personality and Social Psychology, 55*, 541–546.

Deutsch, M., & Gerard, H. (1955). A study of normative and informational social influences upon individual judgment. *Journal of Abnormal Social Psychology, 51*, 629–636.

Fazio, R. H. (2000). Accessible attitudes as tools for object appraisal: Their costs and benefits. In G. R. Maio & J. M. Olson (Eds.), *Why we evaluate: Functions of attitudes* (pp. 1–36). Mahwah, NJ: Erlbaum.

Greenwald, A. G. (1989). Why are attitudes important? In A. R. Pratkanis, S. J. Breckler, & A. G. Greenwald (Eds.), *Attitude structure and function* (pp. 1–10). Hillsdale, NJ: Erlbaum.

Harkness, A. R., DeBono, K. G., & Borgida, E. (1985). Personal involvement and strategies for making contingency judgments: A stake in the dating game makes a difference. *Journal of Personality and Social Psychology, 49*, 22–32.

Harris, P. R., & Napper, L. (2005). Self-affirmation and the biased processing of threatening health-risk information. *Personality and Social Psychology Bulletin, 31*, 1250–1263.

Herek, G. (1987). Can functions be measured? A new perspective on the functional approach to attitudes. *Social Psychology Quarterly, 50*, 285–303.

Herzog, H. (1944). What do we really know about daytime listeners? In P. F. Lazarsfeld & F. N. Stanton (Eds.), *Radio research 1942–43* (pp. 3–33). New York: Duell, Sloan, & Pearce.

Hovland, C. I., Janis, I. L., & Kelley, H. H. (1953). *Communication and persuasion.* New Haven, CT: Yale University Press.

Hovland, C. I., & Weiss, W. (1951). The influence of source credibility on communication effectiveness. *Public Opinion Quarterly, 15,* 635–650.

Insko, C. A. (1967). *Theories of attitude change.* New York: Appleton-Century-Crofts.

Jacks, J. Z., & O'Brien, M. E. (2004). Decreasing resistance by affirming the self. In E. S. Knowles & J. A. Linn (Eds.), *Resistance and persuasion* (pp. 235–257). Mahwah, NJ: Erlbaum.

Janis, I. L. (1954). Personality correlates of susceptibility to persuasion. *Journal of Personality, 22,* 504–518.

Janis, I. L. & Feshbach, S. (1953). Effects of fear-arousing communications. *Journal of Abnormal and Social Psychology, 48,* 78–92.

Johnson, B. T., & Eagly, A. H. (1989). Effects of involvement on persuasion: A meta-analysis. *Psychological Bulletin, 106,* 290–314.

Johnson, B. T., & Eagly, A. H. (1990). Involvement and persuasion: Types, traditions, and the evidence. *Psychological Bulletin, 107,* 375–384.

Johnson, B. T., Smith-McLallen, A., Killeya, L. A., & Levin, K. D. (2004). Truth or consequences: Overcoming resistance to persuasion with positive thinking. In E. S. Knowles & J. A. Lin (Eds.), *Resistance and persuasion* (pp. 215–233). Mahwah, NJ: Erlbaum.

Katz, D. (1960). The functional approach to the study of attitudes. *Public Opinion Quarterly, 24,* 163–204.

Katz, D., McClintock, C., & Sarnoff, I. (1957). The measurement of ego defense as related to attitude change. *Journal of Personality, 25,* 465–474.

Kelman, H. C. (1958). Compliance, identification, and internalization: Three processes of attitude change. *The Journal of Conflict Resolution: Studies on Attitudes and Communication, 2,* 51–60.

Kelman, H. C. (1961). Processes of opinion change. *Public Opinion Quarterly, 25,* 57–78.

Kiesler, C., Collins, B., & Miller, N. (1969). *Attitude change: A critical analysis of theoretical approaches.* New York: Wiley.

Kinder, D. R., & Sears, D. O. (1981). Prejudice and politics: Symbolic racism versus racial threats to the good life. *Journal of Personality and Social Psychology, 40,* 414–431.

Lavine, H., & Snyder, M. (1996). Cognitive processing and the functional matching effect in persuasion: The mediating role of subjective perceptions of message quality. *Journal of Experimental Social Psychology, 32,* 580–604.

Lundgren, S., & Prislin, R. (1998). Motivated cognitive processing and attitude change. *Personality and Social Psychology Bulletin, 24,* 715–726.

Maio, G. R., Haddock, G., Watt, S. E., & Hewstone, M. (in press). Implicit measures and applied contexts: An illustrative examination of anti-racism advertising. In R. E. Petty, R. H. Fazio, & P. Briñol (Eds.), *Attitudes: Insights from the new wave of implicit measures.* New York: Erlbaum.

Maio, G. R., & Olson, J. M. (1995a). Relations between values, attitudes, and behavioral intentions: The moderating role of attitude functions. *Journal of Experimental Social Psychology, 31,* 266–285.

Maio, G. R., & Olson, J. M. (1995b). Involvement and persuasion: Evidence for different types of involvement. *Canadian Journal of Behavioral Science, 27,* 64–78.

Maio, G. R., & Olson, J. M. (2000a). What is a "value-expressive" attitude? In G. R. Maio & J. M. Olson (Eds.), *Why we evaluate: Functions of attitudes* (pp. 249–270). Mahwah, NJ: Erlbaum.

Maio, G. R., & Olson, J. M. (2000b). Emergent themes and potential approaches to attitude function: The Function-Structure Model of Attitudes. In G. R. Maio & J. M.

Olson (Eds.), *Why we evaluate: Functions of attitudes* (pp. 417–442). Mahwah, NJ: Erlbaum.

Marsh, K. L., & Julka, D. L. (2000). A motivational approach to experimental tests of attitude functions theory. In G. R. Maio & J. M. Olson (Eds.), *Why we evaluate: Functions of attitudes* (pp. 271–294). Mahwah, NJ: Erlbaum.

McFarland, D. J. (1987). Instinct. In R. L. Gregory (Ed.), *The Oxford companion to the mind.* (pp. 374–375). Oxford: Oxford University Press.

Mills, J., & Harvey, J. (1972). Opinion change as a function of when information about the communicator is received and whether he is attractive or expert. *Journal of Personality and Social Psychology, 21,* 52–55.

Murray, S. L., Haddock, G., & Zanna, M. P. (1996). On creating value-expressive attitudes: An experimental approach. In C. Seligman, J. M. Olson, & M. P. Zanna (Eds.), *The psychology of values: The Ontario Symposium* (Vol. 5, pp. 107–133). Mahwah, NJ: Erlbaum.

Neuberg, S., & Newsom, J. T. (1993). Personal need for structure: Individual differences in the desire for simple structure. *Journal of Personality and Social Psychology, 65,* 113–131.

Ostrom, T. M., & Brock, T. C. (1969). Cognitive bonding to central values and resistance to a communication advocating change in policy orientation. *Journal of Experimental Research in Personality, 4,* 42–50.

Petty, R. E., & Cacioppo, J. T. (1986). *Communication and persuasion: Central and peripheral routes to attitude change.* New York: Springer-Verlag.

Petty, R. E., & Cacioppo, J. T. (1990). Involvement and persuasion: Tradition versus integration. *Psychological Bulletin, 107,* 367–374.

Petty, R. E., & Wegener, D. T. (1998). Matching versus mismatching attitude functions: Implications for scrutiny of persuasive messages. *Personality and Social Psychology Bulletin, 24,* 227–240.

Petty, R. E., & Wegener, D. T. (1999). The elaboration likelihood model: Current status and controversies. In S. Chaiken & Y. Trope (Eds.), *Dual process theories in social psychology* (pp. 41–72). New York: Guilford.

Prentice, D. A. (1987). Psychological correspondence of possessions, attitudes, and values. *Journal of Personality and Social Psychology, 53,* 993–1003.

Prislin, R., & Wood, W. (2005). Social influence in attitudes and attitude change. In D. Albarracin, B. T. Johnson, & M. P. Zanna (Eds.), *The handbook of attitudes* (pp. 671–705). Mahwah, NJ: Erlbaum.

Sarnoff, I., & Katz, D. (1954). The motivational bases of attitude change. *Journal of Abnormal and Social Psychology, 49,* 115–124.

Schwartz, S. H. (1992). Universals in the content and structure of values: Theoretical advances and empirical tests in 20 countries. In M. P. Zanna (Ed.), *Advances in experimental social psychology* (Vol. 25, pp. 1–65). San Diego, CA: Academic Press.

Shavitt, S. (1989). Operationalizing functional theories of attitude. In A. R. Pratkanis, S. J. Breckler, & A. G. Greenwald (Eds.), *Attitude structure and function* (pp. 311–337). Hillsdale, NJ: Erlbaum.

Shavitt, S. (1990). The role of attitude objects in attitude functions. *Journal of Experimental Social Psychology, 26,* 124–148.

Shavitt, S., Lowrey. T., & Han. S. P. (1992). Attitude functions in advertising: The interactive role of products and self-monitoring. *Journal of Consumer Psychology, 1,* 337–364.

Sherman, D. K., & Cohen, G. L. (2002). Accepting threatening information: Self-affirmation and the reduction of defensive biases. *Current Directions in Psychological Science, 11,* 119-123.

Sherman, D. K., & Cohen, G. L. (2006). The psychology of self-defense: Self-Affirmation Theory. In M. P. Zanna (Ed.), *Advances in experimental social psychology* (Vol. 26, pp. 183–242). New York: Academic Press.

Sherman, S. J., & Fazio, R. H. (1983). Parallels between attitudes and traits as predictors of behavior. *Journal of Personality, 51,* 308–345.

Sherman, D. K., Nelson, L. D., & Steele, C. M. (2000). Do messages about health risks threaten the self? Increasing the acceptance of threatening health messages via self-affirmation. *Personality and Social Psychology Bulletin, 26,* 1046–1058.

Smith, M. B., Bruner, J., & White, R. (1956). *Opinions and personality.* New York: Wiley.

Snyder, M. (1974). The self-monitoring of expressive behavior. *Journal of Personality and Social Psychology, 30,* 526–537.

Snyder, M. (1987). *Public appearances/private realities: The psychology of self-monitoring.* New York: Freeman.

Snyder, M., & DeBono, K. G. (1985). Appeals to image and claims about quality: Understanding the psychology of advertising. *Journal of Personality and Social Psychology, 49,* 586–597.

Steele, C. M. (1988). The psychology of self-affirmation: Sustaining the integrity of the self. In L. Berkowitz (Ed.), *Advances in experimental social psychology* (Vol. 21, pp. 261–302). New York: Academic Press.

Struch, N., & Schwartz, S. H. (1989). Intergroup aggression: Its predictors and distinctness from in-group bias. *Journal of Personality and Social Psychology, 56,* 364–373.

Tykocinski, O., Higgins, E. T., & Chaiken, S. (1994). Message framing, self-discrepancies, and yielding to persuasive messages: The motivational significance of psychological situations. *Personality and Social Psychology Bulletin, 20,* 107–115.

Watt, S. E., Maio, G. R., Rees, K. J., & Hewstone, M. (2007). Functions of attitudes towards ethnic groups: Effects of level of abstraction. *Journal of Experimental Social Psychology, 43,* 441–449.

Webster, D. M., & Kruglanski, A. W. (1994). Individual differences in need for cognitive closure. *Journal of Personality and Social Psychology, 67,* 1049–1062.

Wegener, D. T., & Carlston, D. E. (2005). Cognitive processes in attitude formation and change. In D. Albarracín, B. T. Johnson, & M. P. Zanna (Eds.), *The handbook of attitudes* (pp. 493–542). Mahwah, NJ: Erlbaum.

10

A New Framework for Resistance to Persuasion
The Resistance Appraisals Hypothesis

ZAKARY L. TORMALA

Stanford University

*P*eople often are resistant to attitude change. College students enjoy drinking despite attempts by parents and university officials to curb their habits, Democrats find little merit in Republicans' views (and vice versa), Pepsi drinkers continue to prefer Pepsi even after receiving countless advertisements promoting Coke, and depressed individuals often are unconvinced by their therapists' efforts to change their views of themselves. Perhaps due to the pervasiveness of resistance in everyday life, some attitudes researchers over the years have moved from the traditional focus on eliciting successful attitude change to the explicit study of resistance to such change. A vast majority of the research conducted in this area has focused on the study of *resistance to persuasion*—that is, the act or process of defending one's attitude against persuasive attack (for reviews, see Knowles & Linn, 2004). This chapter will review some of the established findings from this resistance research and then describe a new metacognitive framework for understanding resistance.

Classic conceptualizations of resistance largely focused on the *motivation* to resist persuasion. One motivation that has received considerable attention is the motivation to maintain consistency. Cognitive dissonance theory (Festinger, 1957), for instance, suggests that people aim to resist attitude change when such change will produce incongruent, or conflicting, cognitions. The argument is that if one changes one's attitude toward something, he or she will be faced with an aversive state of tension resulting from simultaneously holding one attitude (the new one) and a series of other cognitions (e.g., old thoughts, old beliefs, knowledge of past behavior) that conflict with that attitude. The theory suggests that to avoid this aversive state of dissonance, people strive to resist persuasion. Balance theory (Heider, 1958) also emphasizes people's desire to avoid cognitive inconsistency as a motivation for resistance. According to balance theory, people resist attitude change when such change risks creating imbalanced attitude systems—that is, when change risks placing people at odds (or in agreement) with liked (disliked) others. This motivation to avoid imbalance can foster resistance to persuasion.

Approaching resistance motivation from a different perspective, other researchers have argued that people are motivated to resist persuasion to maintain independent views of themselves. Brehm's (1966) reactance theory postulates that people resist persuasion when they perceive that a persuasive message threatens or encroaches upon their personal freedom. In one demonstration, Brehm and Sensenig (1966) gave participants instructions to choose one of two alternatives in an experimental task, and then gave some participants a persuasive message telling them which alternative to select. Participants who received the message were less likely to choose the recommended alternative than were participants who did not receive the message. According to reactance theory, participants' motivation to maintain freedom or independence created resistance to the recommended course of action.

In addition to examining motivation, research also has explored the *process* of resistance—that is, the strategies people use to resist persuasion. Resistance strategies are numerous and include counterarguing persuasive messages (Brock, 1967; Killeya & Johnson, 1998; Petty & Cacioppo, 1977), bolstering initial attitudes (Lewan & Stotland, 1961; Lydon, Zanna, & Ross, 1988), derogating message sources (Tannenbaum, Macauley, & Norris, 1966), engaging in biased processing of (Lord, Ross, & Lepper, 1979) or selective exposure to attitude congruent versus incongruent information (Brannon, Tagler, & Eagly, 2007; Frey, 1986), or simply sticking with initial attitudes in a cue-based fashion (Wegener, Petty, Smoak, & Fabrigar, 2004). These mechanisms may vary in the level of cognitive effort they require, but they are all functional in helping people defend their attitudes against persuasive attacks (Eagly & Chaiken, 1995; Wegener et al., 2004).

Some research has combined the study of motivation and process to better understand the nature of resistance. For example, research on forewarning has revealed that when people are warned of an impending persuasive attack, a variety of motives can be induced which differentially affect the manner in which people respond to the attack (see Wood & Quinn, 2003 for a meta-analytic review). For instance, when people receive warnings on important or highly involving issues (especially if those warnings indicate the communicator's position), defensive motivations can lead people to engage in elaborative and biased processing in support of their attitudes or against the opposing position (e.g., anticipatory counterarguing; Petty & Cacioppo, 1977). When people receive warnings that indicate a communicator's persuasive *intent*, even without revealing the communicator's position, reactance motivations can result, leading people to resist with minimal effort simply to preserve their sense of personal freedom (Hass & Grady, 1975). Interestingly, some research has revealed that when people do not care deeply about a topic or issue, persuasive warnings can sometimes spark impression management motives that lead people to change their attitudes to be more moderate or to agree with the communicator's presumed position (Wood & Quinn, 2003). Thus, forewarnings have a complex array of effects on people's resistance (or acceptance) motivations and processes.

In addition to studying motivational and process-oriented factors in resistance, researchers have examined resistance as a *quality*, or characteristic, of some attitudes. An extensive body of research suggests that some attitudes simply are more resistant to persuasion than others. Consider the role of attitude strength, which refers to an attitude's durability and impactfulness (Krosnick & Petty, 1995). In general, strong attitudes are more durable (i.e., resistant to persuasion and persistent over time) and impactful (i.e., influential over thought and behavior) than weak attitudes. Numerous dimensions of attitude strength have been studied in the resistance domain (see Bassili, this volume). For instance, attitudes tend to be more resistant when they are highly accessible, supported by extensive knowledge, held with certainty, structurally consistent, based on cognitive elaboration, and low in ambivalence (Petty & Krosnick, 1995). Importantly, these relations have been found even in experimental studies that have manipulated attitude strength. For example, Petrocelli, Tormala, and Rucker (2007) manipulated both repeated expression and perceived social support for one's attitude to examine the effects of these variables on different aspects of attitude certainty. They found that these manipulations affected different features of certainty, and these features determined an attitude's resistance to a counterattitudinal persuasive message. The more certain people were of their attitudes, the more resistant their attitudes were to persuasion.

In addition to attitudinal properties that predict resistance, there also are certain personality characteristics associated with resistance to persuasion. Historical examples come from research on dogmatism (Rokeach, 1954) and authoritarianism (Altemeyer, 1981). More recently, researchers have investigated individual differences in meta-perceptions and their implications for resistance. For example, Briñol, Rucker, Tormala, and Petty (2004) developed an individual difference measure of people's beliefs about the degree to which they could be persuaded. This measure proved directly predictive of people's resistance or yielding to a persuasive message, particularly when people were unmotivated to think about the merits of the issue under consideration. Further exploring individual differences, Albarracín and Mitchell (2004) focused on defensive confidence or the extent to which people think they can successfully defend their attitudes against attack. They found that the more confident people were about their resistance abilities, the more willing they were to expose themselves to counterattitudinal information and, thus, the more they *changed* in response to that information. Ironically, then, people high in defensive confidence were most vulnerable to counterattitudinal information.

A NEW DIRECTION IN RESISTANCE RESEARCH

As evident from the reviewed literature, resistance to persuasion has received considerable theoretical and empirical scrutiny. Across studies, much has been learned about resistance as a motivation, as a process, and as a quality or property of a given attitude or person (see Petty, Tormala, & Rucker 2004; Tormala & Petty, 2004a). In other words, we have learned a lot about how, when, and why people tend to resist. Interestingly, though, little is known about the implications, or consequences, of resistance to persuasion. Once a person has resisted a persuasive attack, what happens to the person's attitude? In past resistance work, researchers have been mostly silent on this issue. This silence likely reflects a tacit assumption that resistance leaves the person's attitude unchanged. In contrast to the view that resistance leaves attitudes unchanged, my colleagues and I recently have proposed that resistance can have important implications for people's initial attitudes and the future lives of those attitudes. In particular, we have developed a new framework for understanding resistance, suggesting that when people resist persuasive attacks, they can become either more or less certain of their attitudes than they were to begin with.

What is attitude certainty, and why do we care about it? Attitude certainty is a dimension of attitude strength that refers to the subjective sense of conviction one has about one's attitude (Abelson, 1988; Gross, Holtz, & Miller, 1995), or the extent to which one thinks one's attitude is correct or clear in one's mind (Petrocelli et al., 2007). Past research has revealed attitude certainty to be an important dimension of people's attitudes, which has implications for an attitude's tendency to predict behavior (Bizer, Tormala, Rucker, & Petty, 2006; Fazio & Zanna, 1978), resist persuasion (Babad, Ariav, Rosen, & Salomon, 1987; Bassili, 1996; Kelley & Lamb, 1957; Petrocelli et al., 2007; Wu & Shaffer, 1987), and simply persist even when it is not being directly challenged (Bassili, 1996). The more certain one is of one's attitude, the more predictive that attitude is of behavior, the more resistant that attitude is to attack, and the more persistent or enduring that attitude is over time (see Tormala & Rucker, 2007). Although attitude certainty tends to be correlated with other dimensions of attitude strength such as attitude accessibility, importance, vested interest, and extremity (e.g., Prislin, 1996), it is also differentiable from those dimensions (Fabrigar, MacDonald, & Wegener, 2005; Franc, 1999; Krosnick, Boninger, Chuang, Berent, & Carnot, 1993; Visser, Bizer, & Krosnick, 2006). For example, a college student might hold a very negative attitude toward a tuition increase at her university—say a −3 on a scale ranging from −4 to +4—but that negative attitude could be held with high certainty (when the student knows she will always hate the idea and never change) or low certainty (when the student realizes she hasn't heard what benefits will come from the increased cash flow on campus).

THE RESISTANCE APPRAISALS HYPOTHESIS

To understand the potential impact of resistance on attitude certainty, my colleagues and I have developed a metacognitive framework for resistance to persuasion (Petty et al., 2004; Tormala & Petty, 2004a). Metacognition refers to cognition about cognition; that is, people's thoughts about their own thoughts and thought processes (Jost, Kruglanski, & Nelson, 1998; Petty, Briñol, Tormala, & Wegener, 2007; Yzerbyt, Lories, & Dardenne, 1998). Applying a metacognitive perspective to resistance to persuasion, we have postulated that when people resist persuasive attacks, they can perceive this resistance, reflect upon it, and form specifiable attribution-like inferences about their own attitudes that have implications for attitude certainty. Just as individuals can observe other people's behavior to form inferences about those people, we posit that people can observe the "behavior" of their own attitudes (e.g., resisting persuasion) to form inferences about those attitudes.

How do people's perceptions of their own resistance affect attitude certainty? Following the logic of attribution theory (Kelley, 1972), the *resistance appraisals hypothesis* suggests that resistance can leave people feeling either more or less certain of their attitudes depending on their perceptions of their resistance and the situation in which it occurs. Situational factors that foster positive appraisals of one's resistance performance should boost attitude certainty, whereas situational factors that foster negative appraisals of one's resistance performance should undermine certainty (see Figure 10.1). In other words, people should become more certain of their initial attitudes when they are impressed by their resistance and less certain of their initial attitudes when they are unimpressed by their resistance. The resistance appraisals hypothesis further suggests that these effects can occur in the absence of any differences in people's actual resistance. That is, people can resist the same message in the same way and to the same degree, but become more or less certain of their attitudes when their subjective assessment of their resistance performance leads them to a positive or a negative appraisal, respectively. Of course, when people are unsure of their resistance performance, or they form a neutral or middling appraisal of their performance, there should not be substantial certainty change in either direction. For the sake of simplicity, this chapter focuses on the more interesting cases of positive and negative appraisals.

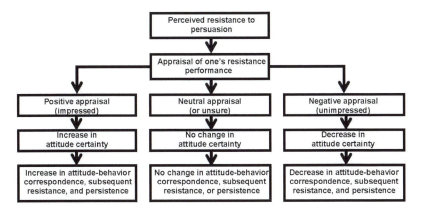

Figure 10.1   The resistance appraisals hypothesis.

Positive Resistance Appraisals

The resistance appraisals hypothesis suggests that when people resist persuasive messages, they will become more certain of their initial attitudes when they form positive appraisals of their resistance performance; that is, when they think they have done a good job resisting. Positive appraisals could stem from many sources: an individual might perceive that he or she has easily defended an attitude against a persuasive attack, that he or she has generated particularly cogent counterarguments against a persuasive attack, or that he or she has resisted an exceptionally strong attack or an attack from an expert. My colleagues and I have examined these possibilities in a series of experiments. Our basic hypothesis has been that when people perceive that they have done a good job resisting a counterattitudinal persuasive message, they infer that their attitude is correct (otherwise it would have changed), and this inference manifests as increased attitude certainty.

In an initial experiment designed to test this possibility, Tormala and Petty (2002, Experiment 1) led undergraduate participants to believe their university was considering implementation of a new policy requiring all students to pass a series of comprehensive examinations in their major areas prior to graduation. Participants were led to believe that if they failed the exams, they would be required to complete remedial coursework before a degree could be conferred. Following this basic introduction, participants received a persuasive message in favor of comprehensive exams and were induced to resist the message by generating counterarguments against it. After reading the message and listing their counterarguments, participants reported their attitudes toward comprehensive exams and indicated the certainty with which they held these attitudes. As predicted, participants became more certain of their initial attitudes after resisting the message.

This experiment provides initial evidence for the notion that people can become more certain of their attitudes when they resist persuasion. Based on this finding alone, however, ambiguity remains as to the importance of the metacognitive perspective. It could be that when people generate counterarguments to support their attitudes, they activate more attitude-relevant knowledge, which could boost certainty through changes in attitude structure or representation rather than metacognitive mechanisms (Chaiken, Pomerantz, & Giner-Sorolla, 1995; Wood, Rhodes, & Biek, 1995). However, several pieces of evidence support the metacognitive interpretation. For example, Tormala and Petty (2002) manipulated participants' perceptions of whether they had resisted or succumbed to a persuasive message and found that attitude certainty only increases when participants perceive that they have, in fact, resisted. When participants believe that they have shown some evidence of change in response to the message, even when they actually have not, they are no more certain of their attitudes than they were to begin with. Furthermore, the increase in attitude certainty is particularly likely to occur when people positively appraise their resistance performance as would be the case when people believe they have resisted a strong message or an expert source.

Resisting Strong Messages In several experiments, we manipulated participants' perception of the strength of the persuasive message they received (Tormala & Petty, 2002, 2004b). In actuality, all participants received (and resisted) the same message, but they were led to believe it was either strong or weak. Across studies, when participants perceived that they had resisted a strong attack, they became more certain of their attitudes. When participants perceived that they had resisted a weak attack (which would have created a more neutral resistance appraisal; see Figure 10.1), attitude certainty was unchanged. Moreover, this effect was mediated by participants' subjective assessments of their resistance performance. To the extent that participants believed that they resisted a strong (vs. weak) message, they rated their resistance more favorably and increased their attitude certainty accordingly (Tormala & Petty, 2002, Experiment 2). It is important to reiterate that the resisted messages did not differ in strength; all that differed was participants' perceptions of them. Furthermore, there were no differences in participants' actual resistance. All participants generated counterarguments of equal number and quality, but they perceived these counterarguments differently depending on their perceptions of the strength of the message they resisted.

Resisting Expert Sources In follow-up work, we examined source credibility as a moderator of the attitude certainty effect by manipulating the perceived expertise of the source of a counterattitudinal attack (Tormala & Petty, 2004c). In one study, participants were induced to counterargue a message that they believed came from either an expert source or an inexpert source. Although all participants counterargued the same message, only those who believed that they resisted an expert position became more certain of their attitudes (Tormala & Petty, 2004c, Experiment 1).

Summary and Implications Consistent with the resistance appraisals hypothesis, the perceived message strength (Tormala & Petty, 2002, 2004b) and source credibility (Tormala & Petty, 2004c) studies converge in suggesting that when people form positive appraisals of their resistance performance they become more certain of their initial attitudes. In essence, when people resist strong attacks or attacks from experts, they appear to view their resistance as more successful, or more diagnostic of the validity of their attitudes. In contrast, when people resist weak attacks or attacks from nonexperts, they appear to view their resistance as less successful, or less diagnostic of the validity of their attitudes. Indeed, if one resists a strong argument or an expert, one can assume that one also would have resisted a weak argument or a nonexpert. If one resists a weak argument or a nonexpert, however, one cannot assume that one also would have resisted a strong argument or expert, because it remains a possibility that stronger arguments or messages from experts would be more persuasive. In accord with the attributional logic outlined earlier, both perceived message strength and source credibility operate as augmenting or discounting situational factors (Kelley, 1972). Perceiving that one has resisted a strong message or an expert augments the impact of resistance on certainty, whereas perceiving that one has resisted a weak message or a nonexpert creates a discounting factor that attenuates or even eliminates this effect.

It should be noted that the increase in attitude certainty we have observed in these studies has proven consequential for other evaluative outcomes. In line with previous attitude certainty findings, we have found that when people become more certain of their attitudes after resisting persuasion, their attitudes become more predictive of behavioral intentions and more resistant to subsequent persuasive attacks delivered later in the experimental session (Tormala & Petty, 2002, 2004c). Thus, when it seems that a persuasive message simply has been unsuccessful because the message recipient resists it, that message actually might have been counterproductive. Specifically, to the extent that message recipients think the message (or source) they have resisted is strong (or expert), resisted messages can backfire by making the recipients more certain than ever about their attitudes, more likely to base their behavior on those attitudes, and more likely to defend those attitudes against later, even stronger, attacks. People's positive appraisals of their own resistance, then, can strengthen their attitudes.

Negative Resistance Appraisals

In contrast to the idea that people can become more certain of their initial attitudes after resisting persuasion, the resistance appraisals hypothesis also suggests that people will become *less* certain of their attitudes when they form negative appraisals of their resistance performance; that is, when they appraise their resistance as poor. Like positive appraisals, negative appraisals can stem from many sources. For example, people might form negative appraisals of their resistance if they perceive that they have struggled to resist, if they have doubts about the quality of their counterarguments, or if they have concerns about the manner in which they resisted. The resistance appraisals hypothesis holds that when people have such doubts about their resistance, they might suspect that their attitude is invalid, or at least less valid than previously thought, which undermines attitude certainty. My colleagues and I recently have been studying the conditions under which this doubt emerges.

Struggling to Resist   One possibility is that people form negative resistance appraisals when they perceive that they have struggled to resist a persuasive attack. In a test of this possibility, Tormala, Clarkson, and Petty (2006, Experiment 1) presented participants with a counterattitudinal persuasive message, which they instructed participants to counterargue. To vary resistance appraisals, Tormala et al. manipulated the circumstances surrounding the counterargument listing task. Specifically, all participants (except those in a control condition) were instructed to list four counterarguments against the message; however, whereas some participants were given ample time to articulate their counterarguments, others' counterargument time was curtailed. After completing the counterargument task, all participants reported their attitudes and attitude certainty. As predicted, attitudes did not differ across conditions, suggesting that participants were able to generate counterarguments as they read the message. Attitude certainty differed, however, in accordance with time constraints that affected participants' ability to articulate and express their arguments. Among participants who had ample time to complete the counterargument task, attitude certainty was maintained at a relatively high level. In contrast, attitude certainty decreased significantly among participants whose counterargument time was curtailed.

Generating Specious Counterarguments
A follow-up experiment (Tormala et al. 2006, Experiment 2) examined the effects of participants' perceptions of the *quality* of their counterarguments. Specifically, participants counterargued a persuasive attack on their attitudes and then received false feedback about the quality, or strength, of their counterarguments. Whereas some participants were led to believe their counterarguments were strong and convincing, others were led to believe they had generated counterarguments that were weak and unconvincing. The attitude data suggested that participants were equally resistant to persuasion across conditions; however, the false feedback manipulation influenced attitude certainty. As expected, participants who believed they had generated weak counterarguments became significantly less certain of their attitudes. Participants who believed they had generated strong counterarguments maintained a higher level of certainty.

Interestingly, and in accordance with the same attributional logic applied to positive resistance appraisals, these decreases in attitude certainty appear to be moderated by situational factors such as source credibility. This was first documented in a study that induced participants to counterargue a persuasive message from an expert versus inexpert source and then gave participants false feedback regarding the strength of their counterarguments. Attitude certainty increased when participants were led to believe that they had generated strong counterarguments against an expert (but not an inexpert) source, which replicates our past findings (Tormala & Petty, 2002, 2004c). When participants were led to believe they had generated weak counterarguments, however, the nature of this effect changed. In this condition, attitude certainty was particularly likely to *decrease* when participants perceived that they had generated weak counterarguments against a *non*expert. When participants perceived that they had generated weak counterarguments against an expert, they did not lose attitude certainty. These results are summarized in Figure 10.2.

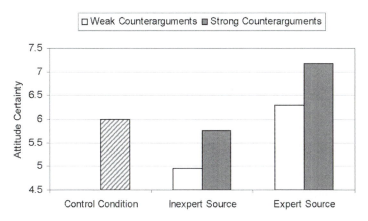

Figure 10.2 Attitude certainty as a function of the perceived strength of one's counterarguments against a persuasive attack and the expertise of the source of the attack (adapted from Tormala, Clarkson, & Petty, 2006, Experiment 3).

Following the same logic used to describe positive resistance appraisals, then, when people form negative appraisals of their resistance, variables like source credibility can provide augmenting or discounting situational factors for reduced attitude certainty (Kelley, 1972). In this case, low source credibility augments the reduction of certainty following negative resistance appraisals, whereas high source credibility operates as a discounting factor that reduces or eliminates this effect. Just as high source credibility (and perceived strong messages) can make strong resistance seem more diagnostic with respect to an attitude's validity, low source credibility (and, presumably, perceived weak messages) can make weak resistance seem more diagnostic with respect to an attitudes *in*validity.

Resisting by Illegitimate Means

In other research, my colleagues and I have been examining additional factors that can lead to negative resistance appraisals, including the possibility that people might form such appraisals when they perceive that they have resisted by illegitimate means; that is, using a strategy that is not based on consideration of the merits of a given message or position. To this point, all of the research reviewed has focused on counterarguing as the means of resistance. Our emphasis in this regard has been guided by the fact that counterarguing is a common and well-understood resistance strategy. However, while it is commonly used and studied, counterarguing might also be somewhat unique in that, in theory, it focuses on generating thoughts or information specifically targeted at the core merits of a persuasive appeal or counterattitudinal position. Thus, it is likely perceived to be a legitimate way to resist. After all, if one can successfully counterargue another's position, one's own position presumably has more merit.

Other strategies, particularly those that avoid or circumvent message content such as ignoring a message or derogating its source, might be perceived as less legitimate because they leave open the possibility that one might not have been able to generate effective counterarguments had one tried to do so. In fact, in a survey of people's self-reported resistance strategies, Jacks and Cameron (2003) found that people rated some strategies (e.g., source derogation) less favorably than others (e.g., counterarguing). To the extent that some resistance strategies are perceived as illegitimate, reliance on those strategies might foster negative resistance appraisals and, thus, reduced attitude certainty.

Tormala, DeSensi, and Petty (2007) explored these possibilities by examining resistance in the minority influence domain. In minority influence research, it has been shown that sources representing a majority opinion often induce immediate persuasion, whereas sources representing a minority opinion often induce immediate resistance (see Wood, Lundgren, Ouellette, Busceme, & Blackstone, 1994, for a review). Interestingly, though, initial resistance to minority sources has also been known to mask a hidden or delayed impact. That is, sometimes people resist minority sources in the immediate situation, but show evidence of persuasion when their attitudes are measured at a later point in time (Crano & Chen, 1998; Moscovici, 1980). Given the association between attitude certainty and attitudinal persistence, it stands to reason that certainty might play a role in some minority influence effects. Specifically, when people resist persuasive messages simply by virtue of those messages being associated with minority sources, they might perceive that they have resisted by illegitimate means. After all, in these situations people resist persuasion for reasons that have nothing to do with the merits of a given attitudinal position. To the extent that people perceive that they have done this, and they perceive that this is an illegitimate thing to do, we would expect them to lose attitude certainty and be more susceptible to delayed attitude change.

In an initial test of this hypothesis, Tormala et al. (2007, Study 1) presented undergraduate participants with a persuasive message that was attributed to a group of students representing a numerical minority (14%) or majority (86%) of the student body. As expected, participants were persuaded by the message attributed to a majority source, but resistant to the same message when it was attributed to a minority source. Importantly, though, when participants resisted the minority source, they also showed a significant decrease in attitude certainty. A follow-up experiment (Tormala et al., 2007, Study 2) extended this finding by showing that it was moderated by participants' perceptions of resisting persuasion due to the source's minority status. More specifically, Tormala et al. manipulated participants' perceptions of (1) whether they had resisted persuasion due to the minority source information, and (2) whether this was an illegitimate or legitimate thing to do. Consistent with the resistance appraisals hypothesis, attitude certainty was lowest when participants perceived that they had resisted due to the minority status of the source and believed that this was an illegitimate thing to do. Participants reported higher levels of attitude certainty when they perceived that they had not relied on the minority source information to resist, or when they perceived that they had but they believed this was a legitimate basis for resistance.

Summary and Implications   In summary, recent studies examining situations in which people struggle to communicate their reasons for resisting, subjectively assess their reasons for resisting as specious, or perceive that their reasons for resisting are illegitimate, converge on the point that people can become less certain of their original attitudes when they form negative appraisals of their own resistance. This reduction of attitude certainty, in turn, should have other important implications. In particular, if attitude certainty is undermined when people form negative appraisals of their resistance, people's attitudes should become less predictive of behavior, less persistent over time, and more vulnerable to later attack. Consistent with this notion, we have found that when people become less certain of their attitudes following initial resistance, their attitudes become less predictive of behavioral intentions (Tormala et al., 2006) and more vulnerable (i.e., less resistant) to subsequent persuasive attacks (Tormala et al., 2006; Tormala et al., 2007). In short, our studies suggest that even when it seems that a persuasive message has been unsuccessful in changing a target attitude, that message might have had a subtle yet powerful effect. In particular, depending on the circumstances surrounding resistance, the seemingly unsuccessful message might actually have weakened the target attitude, reducing its predictive utility and durability.

The Moderating Role of Elaboration

Based on the current discussion of the resistance appraisals hypothesis, it is reasonable to wonder when people engage in resistance appraisals and when they do not. That is, what determines whether people reflect upon and form inferences about their own resistance? My colleagues and I have posited that some of the same factors that determine whether people think extensively or not in general (Petty & Wegener, 1998) also determine whether people appraise their resistance performance. In particular, we have suggested that assessing one's resistance and forming an inference about attitude certainty is more likely under high rather than low levels of cognitive elaboration. The logic behind this assumption is that perceiving one's own resistance, reflecting upon it, and forming a judgment about one's attitude is a higher order, metacognitive form of thought that requires considerable motivation and ability. Indeed, to think about one's thoughts and thought processes, one must not only have thoughts, but also have thoughts about those thoughts, which means more total thoughts! Furthermore, the same variables that motivate people to care or be concerned about an object or issue (e.g., personal relevance; Petty & Cacioppo, 1979) also likely motivate people to care or be concerned about their level of attitude certainty with respect to that object or issue (Petty, Briñol, & Tormala, 2002). Thus, we would expect that metacognitive processes involved in resistance appraisals are more likely to operate at the high end rather than the low end of the elaboration continuum.

Initial research results are consistent with this expectation. Tormala and Petty (2004b), for example, examined the role of both self-reported situational elaboration and individual differences in need for cognition (Cacioppo & Petty, 1982) in moderating people's positive resistance appraisals. When elaboration was high (high self-reported elaboration, high need for cognition), participants were more certain of their attitudes after resisting a perceived strong rather than weak message. When elaboration was low (low self-reported elaboration, low need for cognition), this effect disappeared. Under low elaboration, then, people did not appear to appraise their own resistance performance, or at least they did not attend to situational factors in doing so. In related research, Tormala and Petty (2004c) examined the effect of source credibility on attitude certainty following resistance to persuasion, and tested whether this effect would be more likely under high or low cognitive load. Matching Tormala and Petty's (2004b) findings, source credibility affected attitude certainty under low cognitive load (high elaboration), but not under high cognitive load (low elaboration). Across studies, then, positive resistance appraisals appear more likely to increase attitude certainty at high rather than low levels of information processing.

On the negative appraisal side, our findings also have been consistent with the high elaboration argument. Indeed, studies exploring negative resistance appraisals have placed participants in high elaboration situations. All participants have been undergraduates led to believe their university was considering implementation of a counterattitudinal policy in the near future. This policy was personally relevant for all participants and personal relevance is a well-documented determinant of cognitive processing (e.g., Petty & Cacioppo, 1979). Thus, our findings have been consistent with the notion that negative resistance appraisals undermine attitude certainty under high elaboration conditions. We have had no low elaboration comparison groups in these studies, however, so future work is needed to understand the potential impact of negative resistance appraisals on attitude certainty when people are not motivated or able to think carefully.

RESISTANCE APPRAISALS IN CLASSIC RESISTANCE PHENOMENA

As discussed, the resistance appraisals hypothesis offers a new way to think about resistance to persuasion. This hypothesis suggests that when resistance has occurred, one's attitude might not be left unchanged. On the contrary, it might change with respect to attitude certainty, which has implications for the future life of the attitude. This perspective already has uncovered a number of new phenomena in resistance situations. Also intriguing is that the resistance appraisals hypothesis hints at new interpretations of some classic effects in resistance work that have been attributed to other processes. Although many prior findings could ultimately prove amenable to resistance appraisal explanations (e.g., minority influence effects, as reviewed), I will focus on two areas of research here: inoculation theory and the sleeper effect.

Inoculation Theory

In his groundbreaking work on inoculation theory, McGuire (1964) drew a biological analogy and argued that just as people's bodies could be inoculated against disease through exposure to initial mild doses of the disease, people's beliefs could be inoculated against attack by exposing those beliefs to initial mild attacks that were easily refuted. In one demonstration, McGuire and Papageorgis (1961) presented participants with strong persuasive attacks on various cultural truisms—beliefs that are widely shared and rarely, if ever, disputed. Immediately before these attacks, some participants were exposed to initial mild attacks that could be resisted quite easily. McGuire and Papageorgis found that participants were more resistant to the strong attack if they had been exposed to the mild attack than if they had not been exposed to the mild attack in the first place. According to McGuire (1964), the initial attack helped people realize their beliefs were assailable, which motivated them to develop protective counterarguments and provided them with practice using those counterarguments.

At first blush, inoculation effects might seem similar to some of the positive appraisal findings described in this chapter. For example, Tormala and Petty (2002) found that when people successfully resisted an initial message perceived as strong, they became more resistant to a second persuasive message delivered later in the experiment. Although the McGuire (1964) and Tormala and Petty (2002) effects appear similar, the perspectives actually are quite different. First, according to inoculation theory, the initial attack should be weak to foster subsequent resistance. In contrast, the resistance appraisals hypothesis postulates that as long as initial resistance does occur, the stronger the initial attack is perceived to be, the *more* resistant people will become to later influence. This is because attitude certainty is thought to be responsible for subsequent resistance. Moreover, because it considers the role of attitude certainty, the resistance appraisals hypothesis makes much broader predictions than does inoculation theory. The resistance appraisals hypothesis suggests that by elevating attitude certainty, initial resistance can foster subsequent resistance, subsequent persistence, and subsequent attitude-behavior correspondence (Tormala & Petty, 2002, 2004c). Inoculation theory never considered any consequences of initial resistance beyond subsequent resistance. Thus, despite their superficial similarity, inoculation effects and positive resistance appraisal effects differ in their predictions, scope, and theoretical underpinnings.

Nevertheless, the resistance appraisals hypothesis may point to a new interpretation of inoculation effects. It could be that when people resisted the initial attack in McGuire's research, this resistance prompted a positive resistance appraisal. If true, this appraisal would be expected to boost attitude certainty and, in turn, increase subsequent resistance. In fact, recent evidence from communications research suggests that attitude certainty can play a role in inoculation effects. Pfau and colleagues (e.g., Pfau et al., 2004) have conducted numerous studies to understand the nature of inoculation and have found that multiple mechanisms operate in inoculation situations. First, as originally proposed by McGuire (1964), Pfau et al. (2004) found that inoculation treatments increase the perceived threat against an attitude or belief, which motivates people to generate counterarguments to increase subsequent resistance. Interestingly, though, Pfau et al. concluded that attitude strength also plays a role. Most germane to this chapter, Pfau et al. uncovered a role for attitude certainty. In short, it appears that inoculation-based threat initially reduces attitude certainty, which motivates people to generate counterarguments to defend their attitudes. This cognitive work ultimately boosts attitude certainty and then contributes directly to resistance. Although Pfau and colleagues have not described these effects as stemming from metacognitive reasoning or resistance appraisals, the overall pattern of effects is similar to what might be predicted by the resistance appraisals hypothesis.

The Sleeper Effect

Another classic resistance finding is the sleeper effect, which refers to situations in which an initially unsuccessful persuasive message becomes more successful as time passes (Kumkale & Albarracín, 2004; Kelman & Hovland, 1953). In the typical sleeper paradigm, participants receive a strong persuasive message, which is then discredited using a discounting cue such as a low credibility source (Pratkanis, Greenwald, Leippe, & Baumgardner, 1988). Participants resist the message when the discounting cue is presented, but later, after some time has passed, the original message gains in its effectiveness and participants show evidence of delayed persuasion. Different explanations have been offered for this effect, but the most common is that the message and discounting cue become disassociated over time, which allows the message to have some impact following initial resistance (Cook, Gruder, Hennigan, & Flay, 1979).

The resistance appraisals hypothesis makes a very similar prediction regarding delayed persuasion when an initial message (particularly a strong message) is resisted solely because it is associated with a low credibility source. As noted, Tormala et al. (2007) have obtained evidence for the notion that people who perceive their means of resistance as illegitimate can negatively appraise their resistance performance and, thus, lose attitude certainty. Reduced attitude certainty, in turn, opens attitudes up to future change. To the extent that people continue thinking about the message after resisting it, delayed change should be in the direction of the original message. In essence, this mechanism would parallel the process described earlier in reference to minority influence effects.

In the sleeper effect paradigm, we would assume that people generally think it is illegitimate to resist a message solely on the basis of its source, especially when the message itself seems strong, which has been shown to make sleeper effects more likely (Priester, Wegener, Petty, & Fabrigar, 1999). According to the resistance appraisals hypothesis, when people perceive that they have resisted a message only because of its source and they believe this is an illegitimate thing to do, they should lose attitude certainty and become more likely to display the kind of delayed persuasion that is the sleeper effect. Although this metacognitive account strays from traditional perspectives on sleeper effects, it provides a testable prediction that could alter our understanding of this classic phenomenon. As a caveat, it should be noted that sleeper effects have been observed using discounting cues other than low source credibility—for instance, sometimes the message simply has been declared false (e.g., Pratkanis et al., 1988). It is unlikely that people would believe it illegitimate to resist persuasion in this circumstance. Thus, there may be some sleeper effects that are amenable to resistance appraisals accounts and some that are not. Exploring these issues should expand our understanding of both the resistance appraisals hypothesis and the sleeper effect.

RESISTANCE APPRAISALS IN ATTITUDE PERSISTENCE

This chapter has focused on resistance to attitude change in persuasion situations—that is, situations in which people receive and resist targeted persuasive appeals designed to change their attitudes. It could be that these situations are uniquely attuned to resistance appraisals because, by their very nature, they lead people to assess the evidence for and the validity of their own attitudinal position. It is reasonable to ask whether resistance appraisals also would operate in situations in which people's attitudes simply endure over time, without being directly challenged. This kind of resistance, typically termed *persistence*, is assessed by measuring a person's attitude at two points in time separated by a pre-specified period. If the attitude at Time 1 closely corresponds to the attitude at Time 2, that attitude is said to be persistent. Resistance and persistence have been treated somewhat separately in the attitudes literature, but they have much in common as both refer to situations in which an attitude could change but does not.

Although it may be true that resistance per se is more likely than persistence to prompt people to reflect upon and assess their own lack of attitude change, the resistance appraisals hypothesis would suggest that as long as people *are* thinking about their lack of change, resistance appraisals also should apply to persistence. Consider two hypothetical individuals, Ron and David. On the issue of gun control, Ron and David both hold a relatively positive attitude (say a +2 on a scale ranging from −4 to +4). Whereas Ron has held this attitude for several years, David has held this attitude for only a month. The resistance appraisals hypothesis would predict that if Ron and David perceive that they have held their attitudes for a relatively long and short time, respectively, they might feel differentially certain of those attitudes. Furthermore, this differential certainty could be *caused* by differences in their persistence appraisals. To the extent that Ron perceives that he has held his attitude for a long time, he should be more impressed with his attitude's persistence or stability. In contrast, to the extent that David perceives that he has held his attitude for a short time, he should be less impressed with his attitude's persistence or stability. The effects of David's negative appraisal could be compounded if he perceives that he has wavered or flip-flopped over time.

Some indirect evidence for this possibility comes from a correlational study showing that people's perceptions of their own attitude persistence significantly predict attitude certainty (Petrocelli & Tormala, 2006). The more persistent participants report their attitudes to be, the more certain they feel about those attitudes. Furthermore, in an experimental study, Petrocelli et al. (2007; Study 2) made a similar argument in explaining the effect of repeated attitude expression on attitude certainty. Replicating past research (e.g., Holland, Verplanken, & van Knippenberg, 2003), Petrocelli et al. found that participants were more certain of their attitudes after expressing them on several scales versus just one scale. This effect was only partially mediated by attitude accessibility. That is, repeated expression affected attitude certainty, but this effect was not fully explained by accessibility. What else could have contributed to the certainty effect? Petrocelli et al. argued that when people repeatedly express the same attitude toward an object or issue, they develop a subjective sense that they can reliably express their attitude and that it is not changing from one moment to the next. These perceptions lead people to believe that they truly know their attitude, which manifests as increased attitude certainty. Although this explanation for their findings was speculative, the argument parallels the notion of *persistence* appraisals. Factors that facilitate the perception of having held and reported one's attitude consistently over time might foster positive appraisals of one's attitude stability, thus augmenting attitude certainty.

APPLYING RESISTANCE APPRAISALS TO OTHER DOMAINS

Early research on the resistance appraisals hypothesis has expanded our understanding of what it really means to resist attitude change. Whereas researchers traditionally have been focused on understanding the antecedents of resistance (e.g., the motivation to resist, the mechanisms through which people resist, and the types of attitudes or people most likely to resist), the resistance appraisals research has revealed that it also is important to study the consequences of resistance. The tacit assumption in past resistance work has been that when a persuasive message is unsuccessful in changing the valence or extremity of a target attitude, it has failed, thus ending the story. The research reviewed in this chapter challenges this assumption, suggesting instead that when a persuasive message seems to have been unsuccessful, it nevertheless might have had a significant impact on the target attitude. Depending on people's perceptions of their resistance and the situation in which it occurs, seemingly unsuccessful persuasive messages can either undermine or build target attitude certainty.

This perspective has important implications for research in a number of other domains. For example, the notion of positive and negative resistance appraisals could be applied to health interventions and social marketing campaigns to increase and decrease the prevalence of positive and negative health behaviors, respectively. Imagine a college student who engages in excessive alcohol consumption and is resistant to antidrinking messages. In situations in which initial resistance is anticipated, influence practitioners could structure the persuasive environment to foster negative resistance appraisals among message recipients. For example, message recipients could be given very little time to counterargue or could be directly challenged to counterargue and then provided with negative feedback about the quality of their counterarguments. Employing these strategies might reduce attitude certainty among resistant individuals, thereby producing a kind of hidden persuasion that could weaken the maladaptive attitude's influence over behavior and increase that attitude's vulnerability to change.

The resistance appraisals hypothesis also might be useful in situations in which people already have positive attitudes toward healthy behaviors (e.g., condom use). A well-documented problem in health behavior research is that people often have favorable attitudes toward healthy behaviors, but fail to act in accord with those attitudes for a variety of reasons (Salovey, Rothman, & Rodin, 1998). Based on the resistance appraisals hypothesis, one intriguing and somewhat counterintuitive suggestion for strengthening attitude–behavior correspondence would be to challenge the person's positive attitude—the very attitude one hopes to strengthen! If the challenge is perceived to be cogent or coming from a high credibility source, and the person perceives that he or she has resisted it, the person should form a positive resistance appraisal and attitude–behavior correspondence should increase.

The resistance appraisals hypothesis also has potential implications for the way people perceive and reflect upon their self-concepts. In short, when people perceive that they have or have not changed over time, this perception could have implications for their level of self-certainty (for a detailed discussion of self-certainty, see Wright, 2001). Perhaps when people perceive that they have not changed their behavior or beliefs despite numerous strong attacks on those behaviors and beliefs (e.g., peer pressure), they become more certain of who they are and what they stand for. In contrast, when people perceive that they have almost changed many times, or they recall that they have found it very hard not to change or that they had poor reasons for not changing, they might be less certain of who they are and what they stand for. This notion could be applied to clinical practice. Cognitive-behavior therapy, for example has been influential in the treatment of depression (Beck & Greenberg, 1994; Ellis, 1962). The fundamental objective of this approach is to help depressed patients question the validity of their dysfunctional or maladaptive beliefs about themselves by assessing the evidence for them. The resistance appraisals hypothesis might be relevant to this technique in that it highlights new ways of both undermining certainty about in some beliefs and bolstering certainty about others.

SUMMARY AND CONCLUSIONS

Researchers have long recognized the importance of studying resistance to attitude change. As reviewed at the outset of this chapter, resistance research over the years largely has focused on understanding when, why, and how people resist. In the persuasion domain, this emphasis is a natural consequence of people's interest in identifying ways to overcome resistance as a means of increasing persuasion (Knowles & Linn, 2004). This chapter presents a metacognitive framework for resistance suggesting that in addition to understanding when, why, and how people resist persuasion, it also is important to understand the implications of this resistance for people's attitudes. That is, once people have resisted persuasion by conventional standards, what happens to their attitudes? As predicted by the resistance appraisals hypothesis, when people resist, they can perceive their resistance, assess their resistance performance, and make specifiable attribution-like inferences about their attitudes that have implications for attitude certainty. Depending on people's metacognitive assessments, attitude certainty can increase or decrease following initial resistance and this effect can alter the future lives of people's attitudes. This perspective makes interesting predictions that extend beyond the domain of traditional resistance research. Although some of these predictions await empirical scrutiny, exploring new domains from the current perspective may offer a new and innovative approach to other important areas of research and practice.

REFERENCES

Abelson, R. P. (1988). Conviction. *American Psychologist, 43,* 267–275.

Albarracín, D., & Mitchell, A. L. (2004). The role of defensive confidence in preference for proattitudinal information: How believing that one is strong can sometimes be a defensive weakness. *Personality and Social Psychology Bulletin, 30,* 1565–1584.

Altemeyer, B. (1981). *Right-wing authoritarianism.* Winnipeg, Canada: University of Manitoba Press.

Babad, E. Y., Ariav, A., Rosen, I., & Salomon, G. (1987). Perseverance of bias as a function of debriefing conditions and subjects' confidence. *Social Behavior, 2,* 185–193.

Bassili, J. N. (1996). Meta-judgmental versus operative indexes of psychological attributes: The case of measures of attitude strength. *Journal of Personality and Social Psychology, 71,* 637–653.

Beck, A. T., & Greenberg, R. L. (1994). Brief cognitive therapies. In A. E. Bergin & S. L. Garfield (Eds.), *Handbook of psychotherapy and behavior change* (pp. 230–249). New York: Wiley.

Bizer, G. Y., Tormala, Z. L., Rucker, D. D., & Petty, R. E. (2006). Memory-based versus on-line processing: Implications for attitude strength. *Journal of Experimental Social Psychology, 42,* 646–653.

Brannon, L. A., Tagler, M. J., & Eagly, A. H. (2007). The moderating role of attitude strength in selective exposure to information. *Journal of Experimental Social Psychology, 43,* 611–617.

Brehm, J. W. (1966). *A theory of psychological reactance.* San Diego, CA: Academic Press.

Brehm, J. W., & Sensenig, J. (1966). Social influence as a function of attempted and implied usurpation of choice. *Journal of Personality and Social Psychology, 4,* 703–707.

Briñol, P., Rucker, D. D., Tormala, Z. L., & Petty, R .E. (2004). Individual differences in resistance to persuasion: The role of beliefs and meta-beliefs. In E. S. Knowles & J. A. Linn (Eds.), *Resistance and persuasion* (pp. 83–104). Mahwah, NJ: Erlbaum.

Brock, T. C. (1967). Communication discrepancy and intent to persuade as determinants of counterargument production. *Journal of Experimental Social Psychology, 3,* 296–309.

Cacioppo, J. T., & Petty, R. E. (1982). The need for cognition. *Journal of Personality and Social Psychology, 42,* 116–131.

Chaiken, S., Pomerantz, E. M., & Giner-Sorolla, R. (1995). Structural consistency and attitude strength. In R. E. Petty & J. A. Krosnick (Eds.). *Attitude strength: Antecedents and consequences* (pp. 387–412). Mahwah, NJ: Erlbaum.

Cook, T. D., Gruder, C. L., Hennigan, K. M., & Flay, B. R. (1979). History of the sleeper effect: Some logical pitfalls in accepting the null hypothesis. *Psychological Bulletin, 86,* 662–679.

Crano, W. D., & Chen, X. (1998). The leniency contract and persistence of majority and minority influence. *Journal of Personality and Social Psychology, 74,* 1437–1450.

Eagly, A. H.., & Chaiken, S. (1995). Attitude strength, attitude structure, and resistance to change. In R. E. Petty & J. A. Krosnick (Eds.). *Attitude strength: Antecedents and consequences* (pp. 413–432). Mahwah, NJ: Erlbaum.

Ellis, A. (1962). *Reason and emotion in psychotherapy.* New York: Lyle Stuart.

Fabrigar, L. R., MacDonald, T. K., & Wegener, D. T. (2005). The structure of attitudes. In D. Albarracín, B. T. Johnson, & M. P. Zanna (Eds.), *The handbook of attitudes* (pp. 79–124). Mahwah, NJ: Erlbaum.

Fazio, R. H., & Zanna, M. P. (1978). Attitudinal qualities relating to the strength of the attitude-behavior relationship. *Journal of Experimental Social Psychology, 14,* 398–408.

Festinger, L. (1957). *A theory of cognitive dissonance.* Evanston, IL: Row, Peterson.

Franc, R. (1999). Attitude strength and the attitude-behavior domain: Magnitude and independence of moderating effects of different strength indices. *Journal of Social Behavior and Personality, 14,* 177–195.

Frey, D. (1986). Recent research on selective exposure to information. *Advances in Experimental Social Psychology, 19,* 41–80.

Gross, S., Holtz, R., & Miller, N. (1995). Attitude certainty. In R. E. Petty & J. A. Krosnick (Eds.), *Attitude strength: Antecedents and consequences* (pp. 215–245). Mahwah, NJ: Erlbaum.

Hass, R. G., & Grady, K. (1975). Temporal delay, type of forewarning, and resistance to influence. *Journal of Experimental Social Psychology, 11,* 459–469.

Heider, F. (1958). *The psychology of interpersonal relations.* New York: Wiley.

Holland, R. W., Verplanken, B., & van Knippenberg, A. (2003). From repetition to conviction: Attitude accessibility as a determinant of attitude certainty. *Journal of Experimental Social Psychology, 39,* 594–601.

Jacks, J. Z. & Cameron, K. A. (2003). Strategies for resisting persuasion. *Basic and Applied Social Psychology, 25,* 145–161.

Jost, J. T., Kruglanski, A. W., & Nelson, T. O. (1998). Social metacognition: An expansionist review. *Personality and Social Psychology Review, 2,* 137–154.

Kelley, H. H. (1972). Causal schemata and the attribution process. In E. E. Jones, D. E. Kanouse, H. H. Kelley, R. E. Nisbett, S. Valins, & B. Weiner (Eds.), *Attribution: Perceiving the causes of behavior* (pp. 151–174). Morristown, NJ: General Learning Press.

Kelley, H. H., & Lamb, T. W. (1957). Certainty of judgment and resistance to social influence. *Journal of Abnormal and Social Psychology, 55,* 137–139.

Kelman, H. C., & Hovland, C. I. (1953). "Reinstatement" of the communicator in delayed measurement of opinion change. *Journal of Abnormal and Social Psychology, 48,* 327–335.

Killeya, L. A., & Johnson, B. T. (1998). Experimental induction of biased systematic processing: The direct-thought technique. *Personality and Social Psychology Bulletin, 24,* 17–33.

Knowles, E. S., & Linn, J. A. (Eds.). (2004). *Resistance and persuasion.* Mahwah, NJ: Erlbaum.

Krosnick, J. A., Boninger, D. S., Chuang, Y. C., Berent, M. K., & Carnot, C. G. (1993). Attitude strength: One construct or many related constructs? *Journal of Personality and Social Psychology, 65,* 1132–1151.

Krosnick, J. A., & Petty, R. E. (1995). Attitude strength: An overview. In R. E. Petty & J. A. Krosnick (Eds.), *Attitude strength: Antecedents and consequences* (pp. 1–24). Mahwah, NJ: Erlbaum.

Kumkale, G. T., & Albarracín, D. (2004). The sleeper effect in persuasion: A meta-analytic review. *Psychological Bulletin, 130,* 143–172.

Lewan, P. C., & Stotland, E. (1961). The effects of prior information on susceptibility to an emotional appeal. *Journal of Abnormal and Social Psychology, 62,* 450–453.

Lord, C. G., Ross, L., & Lepper, M. R. (1979). Biased assimilation and attitude polarization: The effects of prior theories on subsequently considered evidence. *Journal of Personality & Social Psychology, 37,* 2098–2109.

Lydon, J., Zanna, M. P., & Ross, M. (1988). Bolstering attitudes by autobiographical recall: Attitude persistence and selective memory. *Personality and Social Psychology Bulletin, 14,* 78–86.

McGuire, W. J. (1964). Inducing resistance to persuasion: Some contemporary approaches. In L. Berkowitz (Ed.), *Advances in experimental social psychology* (Vol. 1, pp. 191–229). New York: Academic Press.

McGuire, W. J., & Papageorgis, D. (1961). The relative efficacy of various types of prior belief-defense in producing immunity against persuasion. *Journal of Abnormal & Social Psychology, 62,* 327–337.

Moscovici, S. (1980). Toward a theory of conversion behavior. In L. Berkowitz (Ed.), *Advances in experimental social psychology* (Vol. 13, pp. 209–239). New York: Academic Press.

Petrocelli, J. V., & Tormala, Z. L. (2006). *The relationship between attitude certainty and perceived persistence, perceived resistance, and the perceived correspondence between attitudes and behavior.* Unpublished manuscript, Indiana University, Bloomington, IN.

Petrocelli, J. V., Tormala, Z. L., & Rucker, D. D. (2007). Unpacking attitude certainty: Attitude clarity and attitude correctness. *Journal of Personality and Social Psychology*, 92, 30–41.

Petty, R. E., Briñol, P., & Tormala, Z. L. (2002). Thought confidence as a determinant of persuasion: The self-validation hypothesis. *Journal of Personality and Social Psychology*, 82, 722–741.

Petty, R. E., Briñol, P., Tormala, Z. L., & Wegener, D. (2007). The role of metacognition in social judgment. To appear in E. T. Higgins & A. Kruglanski (Eds.), *Social psychology: A handbook of basic principles* (2nd ed., pp. 254–284). New York: Guilford.

Petty, R. E., & Cacioppo, J. T. (1977). Forewarning, cognitive responding, and resistance to persuasion. *Journal of Personality and Social Psychology*, 35, 645–655.

Petty, R. E., & Cacioppo, J. T. (1979). Issue-involvement can increase or decrease persuasion by enhancing message-relevant cognitive responses. *Journal of Personality and Social Psychology*, 37, 1915–1926.

Petty, R. E., & Krosnick, J. A. (Eds.). (1995). *Attitude strength: Antecedents and consequences.* Mahwah, NJ: Erlbaum.

Petty, R. E., Tormala, Z. L., & Rucker, D. D. (2004). Resisting persuasion by counterarguing: An attitude strength perspective. In J. T. Jost, M. R. Banaji, & D. A. Prentice (Eds.), *Perspectivism in social psychology: The yin and yang of scientific progress* (pp. 37–51). Washington, D.C.: American Psychological Association.

Petty, R. E., & Wegner, D. T. (1998). Attitude change: Multiple roles for persuasion variables. In D. T. Gilbert, S. T. Fiske, & G. Lindzey (Eds.), *The handbook of social psychology* (Vol, 1, 323–390 New York: McGraw-Hill.

Pfau, M., Compton, J., Parker, K. A., Wittenberg, E. M., An, C., Ferguson, M., Horton, H., & Malyshev, Y. (2004). The traditional explanation for resistance versus attitude accessibility: Do they trigger distinct or overlapping processes of resistance? *Human Communication Research, 30,* 329–360.

Pratkanis, A. R., Greenwald, A. G., Leippe, M. R., & Baumgardner, M. H. (1988). In search of reliable persuasion effects: III. The sleeper effect is dead. Long live the sleeper effect. *Journal of Personality and Social Psychology, 54,* 203–218.

Priester, J. M., Wegener, D., Petty, R. E., & Fabrigar, L. (1999). Examining the psychological procesess underlying the sleeper effect: The Elaboration Likelihood Model explanation. *Media Psychology, 1,* 27–48.

Prislin, R. (1996). Attitude stability and attitude strength: One is enough to make it stable. *European Journal of Social Psychology, 26,* 447–477.

Rokeach, M. (1954). The nature and meaning of dogmatism. *Psychological Review, 61,* 194–204.

Salovey, P., Rothman, A. J., & Rodin, J. (1998). Health behavior. In D. T. Gilbert, S. T. Fiske, & G. Lindzey (Eds.), *The handbook of social psychology* (Vol. 2, pp. 633–683). New York: McGraw-Hill.

Tormala, Z. L., Clarkson, J. J., & Petty, R. E. (2006). Resisting persuasion by the skin of one's teeth: The hidden success of resisted persuasive messages. *Journal of Personality and Social Psychology.*

Tormala, Z. L., DeSensi, V. L., & Petty, R. E. (2007). Resisting persuasion by illegitimate means: A metacognitive perspective on minority influence. *Personality and Social Psychology Bulletin, 33,* 354–367.

Tormala, Z. L., & Petty, R. E. (2002). What doesn't kill me makes me stronger: The effects of resisting persuasion on attitude certainty. *Journal of Personality and Social Psychology, 83,* 1298–1313.

Tormala, Z. L., & Petty, R. E. (2004a). Resistance to persuasion and attitude certainty: A meta-cognitive analysis. In E. S. Knowles & J. A. Linn (Eds.), *Resistance and persuasion* (pp. 65–82). Mahwah, NJ: Erlbaum.

Tormala, Z. L., & Petty, R. E. (2004b). Resistance to persuasion and attitude certainty: The moderating role of elaboration. *Personality and Social Psychology Bulletin, 30,* 1446–1457.

Tormala, Z. L., & Petty, R. E. (2004c). Source credibility and attitude certainty: A metacognitive analysis of resistance to persuasion. *Journal of Consumer Psychology, 14,* 427–442.

Tormala, Z. L., & Rucker, D. D. (2007). Attitude certainty: A review of past findings and emerging perspectives. *Social and Personality Psychology Compass, 1,* 469–492.

Tannenbaum, P. H., Macauley, J. R., & Norris, E. L. (1966). Principle of congruity and reduction of persuasion. *Journal of Personality and Social Psychology, 3,* 233–238.

Visser, P. S., Bizer, G. Y., & Krosnick, J. A. (2006). Exploring the latent structure of strength-related attitude attributes. In M. Zanna (Ed.), *Advances in Experimental Social Psychology, 37,* 1–68.

Wegener, D. T., Petty, R. E., Smoak, N. D., & Fabrigar, L. R. (2004). Multiple routes to resisting attitude change. In E. S. Knowles, & J. A. Linn (Eds.), *Resistance and persuasion* (pp. 13–38). Mahwah, NJ: Erlbaum.

Wood, W., & Quinn, J. M. (2003). Forewarned and forearmed? Two meta-analytic syntheses of forewarnings of influence appeals. *Psychological Bulletin, 129,* 119–138.

Wood, W., Lundgren, S., Ouellette, J. A., Busceme, S. & Blackstone, T. (1994). Minority influence: A meta-analytic review of social influence processes. *Psychological Bulletin, 115,* 323–345.

Wood, W., Rhodes, N., & Biek, M. (1995). Working knowledge and attitude strength: The effects of amount and accuracy of information. In R. E. Petty & J. A. Krosnick (Eds.). *Attitude strength: Antecedents and consequences* (pp. 283–324). Mahwah, NJ: Erlbaum.

Wright, R. (2001). Self-certainty and self-esteem. In T. J. Owens, S. Stryker, & N. Goodman (Eds.), *Extending self-esteem theory and research: Sociological and psychological currents* (pp. 101–134). New York: Cambridge University Press.

Wu, C., & Shaffer, D. R. (1987). Susceptibility to persuasive appeals as a function of source credibility and prior experience with the attitude object. *Journal of Personality and Social Psychology, 52,* 677–688.

Yzerbyt, V. Y., Lories, G., & Dardenne, B. (1998). *Metacognition: Cognitive and social dimensions.* Thousand Oaks, CA: Sage.

V

Attitudes
Beyond Evaluation

11

Attitude Strength

JOHN N. BASSILI
University of Toronto, Scarborough

*F*ew events are as unsettling to a scientific field as the refutation of one of its most fundamental constructs. Yet, this is what happened in the field of attitudes when, following a review of studies on the relation between attitudes and behavior that found little relation between the two (Wicker, 1969), Alan Wicker declared that "it may be desirable to abandon the attitude concept" (Wicker, 1971, p. 29). How could the "attitude concept" which, less than four decades earlier had been pronounced "the most distinctive and indispensable concept in...social psychology" by no less an authority than Gordon Allport (1935, p. 798) come into such disrepute? The answer, as we will see, has a lot to do with attitude strength, because when it comes to the effect of an attitude on thought, feelings, and behavior, it is important to take into account whether the attitude is held with overwhelming conviction, whether it is a passing fancy, or in the extreme, whether it is a mere fabrication aimed at giving the appearance of knowledgeability about an issue where little actually exists.

With the benefit of hindsight, Wicker's pessimistic assessment should never have shaken social psychology's confidence in the importance of the attitude concept. History, after all, gives innumerable examples of principled as well as misguided actions taken at great personal cost by people driven by overpowering conviction. How else is one to understand, for example, the 1989 Tiananmen Square protests in Beijing or the terrorist attacks on the World Trade Center towers in New York on September 11, 2001? To this one can add the substantial historical success of election forecasting polls. As an illustration of this success, consider that the average deviation from outcomes of election predictions for winning candidates in Gallup polls going back five decades is less than 2%. In the context of such irrefutable demonstrations of the impact of attitudes on behavior, the only reasonable response to disappointing reviews such as Wicker's is to ask: why doesn't the evidence fit what common observation makes obvious?

As it turns out, several lines of inquiry took up the challenge of explaining the occasional gap between attitudes and behavior. Some of these efforts focused on the conceptualization of measures of attitudes and behavior (Fishbein & Ajzen, 1975), others on principles of aggregation that increased the representativeness of behavior indicators (Fishbein & Ajzen, 1974, 1975), and others yet on properties of the attitude itself, in particular properties having to do with its strength (Fazio & Zanna, 1981). This last approach defines one of the important developments in our understanding of when attitudes predict behavior as well as our understanding of attitude strength.

DEFINITION AND STRUCTURE OF ATTITUDE STRENGTH

When it comes to describing the properties of strong attitudes, social scientists have not been at a loss for labels. In a review of the literature published in 1985, Raden identified 11 attributes that have variously been applied to the concept of attitude strength: accessibility, affective-cognitive consistency, certainty, crystallization, direct experience, generalized attitude strength, importance, intensity, latitude of rejection, stability, and vested interest. The list does not end there. Earlier, Scott (1959) discussed attitude strength concepts that included precision, specificity, differentiation, unity and hierarchic integration. Since then, Abelson (1988) has suggested that conviction is an important attribute of strong attitudes, and the pollster Daniel Yankelovich has developed a "mushiness" index to capture attitude "volatility" (Yankelovich, Skelly, & White, 1981).

When it comes to defining attitude strength, this diversity of labels is not very useful. For one thing, the attributes described by the labels do not all fall at the same level of analysis. Some properties, like direct experience (Regan & Fazio, 1977) and vested interest (Crano, 1995), are best conceptualized as antecedents of attitude strength, whereas other properties, such as crystallization, volatility, and stability, are consequences of attitude strength (Abelson, 1988; Fazio, 1995; Miller & Peterson, 2004). Krosnick and Petty (1995) offered a more useful way to conceptualize attitude strength: They suggested that strong attitudes are attitudes that are durable in the sense of being stable and resistant to attack, and that have an impact by influencing thought and guiding behavior.

By defining strong attitudes in terms of the properties of durability and impact, Krosnick and Petty have avoided the confusion created by the multiplicity of labels previously used to refer to attitude strength. It is important to realize, however, that these two properties do not give a full account of what makes an attitude strong. For example, one can say that a police baton is strong because it is durable and does not break easily (not to mention that when it is used to knock people on the head, it influences thought and guides behavior), but these properties tell us little about the molecular properties, or the construction of the baton, that give it strength. This is why progress in our understanding of attitude strength requires a close examination of theories about the structure of attitudes and the processes responsible for their expression.

Understanding Attitude Strength Labels

Several of the strength constructs discussed above have received considerable attention from attitude researchers. Since we cannot review every one of these constructs, four properties of strength—extremity, importance, accessibility, and ambivalence—that continue to be the object of thriving research programs, will be discussed. Research on these four properties of strength illustrates nicely the kind of evidence that has been garnered on the antecedents of strong attitudes as well as on their durability and impact. Other reviews of attitude strength properties are offered by Krosnick and Abelson (1992), Miller and Peterson (2004), Raden (1985), and Scott (1968).

Extremity

It has long been common for theorists to recognize that attitudes vary in direction (whether the attitude is positive or negative) as well as in the extent to which they are endorsed (Krech & Krutchfield, 1948; Scott 1959). Thinking in terms of an attitude scale, extremity refers to the extent to which a person's attitude deviates from the midpoint in either the positive or negative direction.

Extreme attitudes have several consequences. For example, they have been found to be more resistant to counterattitudinal persuasive messages (Bassili, 1996a; Osgood & Tannenbaum, 1955), but to be more susceptible to the influence of proattitudinal ones (Lord, Ross & Lepper, 1979). Extreme attitudes also tend to be consistent with behavior (Fazio & Zanna, 1978) and are associated with assumptions that others share one's attitudes, a phenomenon known as the false consensus effect (Allison & Messick, 1988; Crano, 1983).

Several antecedents to attitude extremity have also been identified. Arguments and beliefs that are associated with the self tend to trigger ego-defensive cognitions that promote attitude extremity (De Dreu & van Knippenberg, 2005). In line with expectations about the effect of conformity pressures on opinions, social corroboration of one's attitude has been found to lead to increases in attitude extremity while contradiction leads to a decrease in extremity (Baron et al., 1996). Abelson (1995) further identifies a comprehensive set of processes that contribute to the polarization of attitudes. Among them are insults, which tend to lead people to dig their attitudinal heels in, possibly as a way of signaling that they will not tolerate further insult (Abelson & Miller, 1967). Thinking about an issue (Tesser, Martin, & Mendolia, 1995) or expressing an opinion about it repeatedly (Judd & Brauer, 1995) also tends to increase attitude extremity, probably because new cognitions are generated and old ones reinterpreted, in an attitude consistent direction during these activities.

Importance

People differ in the extent to which they consider various issues important. For some, for example, global warming is so consequential that it requires immediate changes in the way we conduct our lives; for others, it is a distant and debatable threat. It is not uncommon for public opinion pollsters to assess the importance of national issues by asking such questions as "What do you think is the most important problem facing the country today?" (CBS News Poll, May 16–17, 2006). Attitude researchers, however, have tended to focus on personal rather than national importance judgments by first asking respondents for their opinion on an issue and then following up with such questions as: "How important is this issue to you personally?" Krosnick, who with colleagues has conducted a comprehensive program of research on attitude importance, has defined the construct as "the degree to which a person is passionately concerned about and personally invested in an issue" (Krosnick, 1990, p. 60).

Important attitudes are consequential in a number of ways. They are more resistant to persuasion (Gorn, 1975; Rhine & Severance, 1970) and more stable over time (Krosnick, 1988a; Schuman & Presser, 1981). Important attitudes also impact a host of cognitive processes such as attention to attitude consistent information, and the elaboration and organization of attitude-relevant information in memory (Holbrook, Berent, Krosnick, Visser, & Boninger, 2005). Important attitudes are consequential in interpersonal affairs, influencing the perception of others' attitudes (Holtz & Miller, 1985; Krosnick, 1988b) as well as the extent to which disagreement results in dislike for others (Byrne, London, & Griffitt, 1968).

Given the multifaceted consequences of important attitudes, it is natural to inquire about their origins. Boninger, Krosnick, and Berent (1995) suggest that three factors contribute to the personal importance of an attitude: Self-interest, where a person feels that the attitude is instrumental to obtaining personally desired outcomes; social identification, where important others and groups share the attitude; and value relevance, where the individual feels that the object of the attitude is relevant to important personal values. Their studies support the role of these three antecedents to attitude importance. Research by Visser and Mirabile (2004) further reveals that attitude importance is bolstered when the individual is embedded in homogeneous social networks of people with similar views (see also Prislin, Limbert, & Bauer, 2000).

Accessibility

When asked how they feel about an issue in a public opinion survey, people sometimes answer before the interviewer has finished asking the question while at other times they hem and haw for several seconds before venturing an opinion (Bassili & Fletcher, 1991). Quick responding is an indication that the attitude comes to mind easily whereas slow responding suggests that quite a bit of thought needs to be given to the production of the response. Because of the close association between the concept of attitude accessibility and the time it takes to express an attitude, response latency has been the most common measure of accessibility (Fazio, 1995). Although measures of reaction time have played an important role in the study of psychological processes (Bassili, 2001), it is instructive to ask why response latency would serve as a measure of attitude strength? According to Fazio (1995) this is because accessible attitudes are more likely to be activated from memory upon encountering the attitude object and are, therefore, more likely to guide behavior toward it.

Fazio's research on attitude accessibility was an important contributor to solving the riddle highlighted by Wicker (1969) about inconsistencies in attitude–behavior relationships. In a carefully conducted program of research, Fazio and his colleagues have demonstrated that accessible attitudes are more consistent with behavior and more stable over time than less accessible attitudes (Fazio, Chen, McDonel, & Sherman, 1982; Fazio, Powell, & Williams, 1989; Fazio & Williams, 1986; Hodges & Wilson, 1994). In line with these findings, Bassili (1993, 1995) found in a set of election studies that for every second longer it took a respondent to express a voting intention, the probability of that intention manifesting itself in a matching cast ballot dropped by about 8%. Accessible attitudes also have been found to be more resistant to persuasion (Bassili, 1996a; Bassili & Fletcher, 1991), to accentuate biased processing of pro- and counterattitudinal information (Fazio & Williams, 1986), and to reduce the effort required to make decisions about the attitude object while increasing the quality of the decisions (Fazio, Blascovitch, & Driscoll, 1992).

Many factors are known to influence the accessibility of attitudes. Rehearsing an attitude by expressing it repeatedly increases its accessibility (Fazio et al., 1982). Social and political events that capture attention can also increase accessibility. For example, attitudes toward candidates as well as voting intentions become increasingly accessible over the course of an election campaign (Bassili & Bors, 1997; Huckfeldt, Sprague, & Levine, 2000). By contrast, social context can slow attitude expression, those holding the minority opinion being generally slower at expressing it than those holding the majority opinion (Bassili, 2003; Huckfeldt et al., 2000).

Ambivalence

Classic attitude scales conceive of attitudes as falling on a bipolar unidimensional continuum ranging from very positive to very negative. Common intuition, however, makes us all too aware that we are often of two minds about an issue, a fact that led Scott (1968) and Kaplan (1972) to point out that people can hold both a positive and a negative attitude toward the same object. For example, one can have a positive and a negative attitude toward affirmative action programs, approving of their goal to improve conditions for historically disadvantaged groups but disapproving of selection and promotion based on factors other than a candidate's qualifications and merit. Because ambivalence comprises two unipolar attitudes, it is usually calculated on the basis of responses to two questions that assess separately the positive and negative components of the attitude (Thompson, Zanna, & Griffin, 1995).

Ambivalent attitudes show many signs of weakness. For example, people with ambivalent attitudes are more likely than those low in ambivalence to adopt the prevailing consensus on an issue (Hodson, Maio, & Esses, 2001). People with ambivalent attitudes exhibit less attitude-intention and attitude-behavior consistency than people low in ambivalence (Armitage & Conner, 2000; Greene, 2005) and are more likely to yield to persuasive arguments (Armitage & Conner, 2000; Bassili, 1996a; Bell & Esses, 2002). Ambivalent attitudes also results in more extensive information processing aimed at integrating an attitude (van Harreveld, van der Plight, de Vries, Wenneker & Verhue, 2004) and can lead to psychological discomfort stemming from the ambivalence (Nordgren, van Harrelveld, & van der Pligt, 2004). Ambivalence also impacts interpersonal relations. For example, spouses with ambivalent attitudes toward their partner are less forgiving of their transgressions (Kachadourian, Finchman, & Davila, 2005).

The most important antecedent of attitude ambivalence consists of conflict among the various considerations that one brings to bear in the evaluation of an issue (Zaller, 1992). The mere presence of conflict in an individual's belief system, however, does not guarantee that this individual will feel ambivalent about an issue. Bassili (1996b, 1998) has suggested that for ambivalent feelings to result in heated intrapsychic conflict, the positive and negative evaluations of an attitude object must be simultaneously accessible; that is, they must come to mind quickly and concurrently. This idea received support in studies by Newby-Clark, McGregor, and Zanna (2002) that showed people report feeling most ambivalent when their conflicting evaluations about an attitude object are simultaneously accessible.

Other circumstances have been shown to contribute to ambivalence. Yakushko (2005) for example, reports that cultural changes in the Ukraine have contributed to ambivalent sexism (Glick & Fiske, 2001). Moreover, as most of us painfully know, eating can be associated with substantial feelings of ambivalence. Restrained eaters, in particular, have been shown to have ambivalent food attitudes (Urland & Tiffany, 2005).

Dimensionality of Attitude Strength

The review of findings on attitude extremity, importance, accessibility and ambivalence seems to paint a very similar picture of the effects of each of these properties. In each case, the property appears to be associated with many, if not all, the properties that Krosnick and Petty used to define strong attitudes, namely stability, resistance to attack, and influence on thought and behavior. Could it be that the bewildering set of labels used by past researchers to refer to properties of attitude strength are unnecessary variations on the same singular theme of strength? If so, attitude strength could most efficiently be considered a single latent construct. Alternatively, it could be that the various properties of strength define a few distinctive categories such as commitment to an issue, consistency in belief, and knowledgeability. At the extreme, it could even be that every nuance of every label used to describe properties of attitude strength is meaningful in capturing distinctive properties of the construct.

Factor Analytic Studies

A number of studies have sought to explore the dimensionality of the strength construct, and this is where the image of attitude strength as a simple single construct begins to crumble. The problem, as we will see, is not just that attitude strength has usually been found to be multidimensional, but also that it has been very difficult to identify these dimensions, the solution uncovered by each study being different from the solution suggested by other studies.

In an effort to resolve the type of problems that had triggered Wicker's (1969) rejection of the attitude construct, Abelson (1988) analyzed the results of surveys containing a large number of questions tapping conviction on several sociopolitical issues like nuclear power, abortion and welfare. The conviction items contained questions such as "Can you imagine yourself ever changing your mind?" and "Compared to most people, how much do you know about the issue?" (p. 269). Factor analysis of the these items revealed three distinct clusters relevant to *emotional commitment*, *ego preoccupation*, and *cognitive elaboration*, components that Abelson speculated were fused in the total conviction of the fanatic. A year later, Verplanken (1989) reported the structure of nine measures relevant to reading, thinking, talking, and expressing oneself about an issue, and found them to load on a single rather than three factors. The picture of the strength construct emerging from factor analytic studies was already promising to be cloudy.

The 1990s produced a spate of factor analytic studies that aimed to clarify the situation. Pomerantz, Chaiken, and Tordesillas (1995) investigated measures of attitude strength tapping certainty, importance, centrality, representativeness of values, knowledgeability, and extremity as they related to issues such as capital punishment and legalized abortion. Two factors were identified, one that the authors called *embeddedness* had to do with the extent to which the attitude object was central and important to the individual. The other, which they called *commitment*, reflected the individual's expectation that their opinion would not change, how certain they were about it, and its extremity.

In a study focusing on the impact of attitude strength on attitude stability, Prislin (1996) measured 13 strength indicators for attitudes ranging from affirmative action to pizza. Three dimensions were identified, the first consisting of *generalized attitude strength,* the second of *internal consistency* (the extent to which evaluations matched affect and cognition about the issue), and the third of *extremity* (both of affect and evaluation). Interestingly, Prislin (1996) found that the stability of an attitude over time was determined by different dimensions for different issues, and that a single dimension of strength was sufficient to promote stability. In another study that also identified three factors, 12 indicators of attitude strength were investigated in a naturalistic study of attitudes toward European monetary union in Greece (Kokkonaki, 1998). The first factor consisted of indicators such as frequency of thinking and personal involvement and was labeled *embeddedness*. The second factor consisted of indicators such as certainty, and subjective knowledge and was labeled *conviction*, while the third factor, which consisted of evaluative-affective and evaluative-cognitive consistency, was labeled *internal consistency.*

What should we make of the factor structures identified by the preceding studies? On the one hand, it is clear that there is a fair bit of variability in the number and nature of attitude strength dimensions identified. On the other hand, some factors seem to emerge with regularity across studies. For example, *commitment* in the form of certainty or conviction appears to be a fixture of the factor analytic results. The *centrality* of the issue to the person, in the form of reported importance, ego preoccupation or embeddedness, is also commonly found (Holland, Verplanken & van Knippenberg, 2003). Surprisingly, given the influential role of cognition in the realm of attitudes, cognitive indicators such as knowledgeability and accessibility are much less represented. What could be going on here?

There are several possible reasons for the inconsistency in the factor solutions yielded by various studies, and for the apparent ubiquity of some strength indicators, and scarcity of others. The first, and simplest reason, is that different studies have examined different measures of strength. Factor analysis is a data reduction procedure that analyzes interrelations among a large number of variables to identify common underlying factors. The underlying factors that emerge from the procedure are, therefore, completely dependent on the initial set of variables. If one goes back to Abelson's (1988) 18 measures of various facets of conviction and compares them to the narrower focus of Verplanken's (1989) nine measures of strength, it is hardly surprising that Abelson ended up with three factors whereas Verplanken ended up with a single one. The same logic applies to the elusive cognitive measures of attitude strength. Accessibility, in particular, has been one of the most studied and consequential properties of attitude strength, both in social psychology and in other domains such as political science (Miller & Peterson, 2004). Yet, one would hardly notice this belle if one only attended factor analytic balls. This is undoubtedly because many of the relevant studies did not measure accessibility, either by response latency or other means. In short, the factor structure that emerges from factor analyses is entirely constrained by the initial selection of variables being factor analyzed, and studies have not relied on a standard set of measures.

The second possible reason for the variability in factor solutions yielded by past studies is also statistical in nature. Krosnick, Boninger, Chuang, Berent, and Carnot (1993) pointed out that scores on attitude strength measures can be distorted by random and systematic measurement error in different ways across studies. One problem in particular involves shared measurement error that is caused by the use of similar scales to index various properties of strength. Take, for example, a hypothetical study where respondents are asked to rate on 10-point scales how knowledgeable they feel about an issue and how often they think about it, and then to indicate on 100-point "thermometer" scales how strongly they feel about the issue and how important it is to them. The correlation between the first two questions and that between the last two may well be inflated by shared method variance, and this would increase the likelihood that a factor analysis would reveal that the first two measures reflect a cognitive factor while the last two reflect an embeddedness factor. To overcome these problems, Krosnick et al. (1993) used a multitrait–multimethod confirmatory factor analysis that allowed them to estimate correlations between dimensions of attitude strength in a way that controls for measurement error and method variance. Unlike exploratory factor analysis, which finds a solution for reducing a number of variables to a smaller set of underlying factors, confirmatory factor analysis aims to test the fit between the data and particular models formulated by the researchers. One model of particular interest to Krosnick et al. was whether various indicators of attitude strength reflect a single underlying construct. Their three studies using confirmatory factor analysis demonstrated that this is *not* the case. Their results further demonstrated that while some indicators of strength are related to each other, most of them are not, and the dimensional structure they form is not clear. By controlling for measurement error and method variance, Krosnick et al.'s sophisticated methodology thus makes a powerful statement for the dimensional complexity of strength indicators.

The third reason for the dimensional complexity of strength indicators stems from the fact that researchers have mixed measures of attitude strength that differ in the way they tap into the mechanisms responsible for the representation and expression of attitudes (Bassili, 1996a). This analysis is based on an important distinction to which we now turn.

META-ATTITUDINAL VS. OPERATIVE
MEASURES OF ATTITUDE STRENGTH

The framework proposed by Bassili (1996a) distinguishes between two categories of measures of attitude strength: "meta-attitudinal" and "operative" measures. The framework is based on the realization that in survey research, it has been common to assess the strength of an attitude by asking the respondent to report directly on it. As we have seen, for example, attitude importance is usually measured by asking respondents how important an issue is to them personally. This type of measure, which is based on a self-report of the property of an attitude, is "meta-attitudinal" because it involves an impression (or attitude) regarding the attitude (see Tormala, this volume). Bassili (1996a) reasoned that this process of reflection can be unreliable because it assumes that people have direct access to properties of their attitudes when in fact these impressions are indirect and open to contextual influences.

Operative measures of attitude strength are measures that are directly linked to the cognitive processes that are responsible for attitude responses. The extremity of an attitude and response latency in expressing it are examples of operative measures of attitude strength because these measures are linked to processes responsible for attitude expression. An important postulate in the case of operative measures of strength is that responses to questions about attitudes require that the respondent process information in the context of a knowledge base relevant to the attitude query. The richness of the knowledge base and the efficiency with which it is used are important indicators of the strength of an attitude, and these indicators have the advantage of emerging from the actual processes underlying the attitude rather than on impressions of these processes Bassili (1996a; Wood, Rhodes, & Biek, 1995).

In a study of attitudes toward such policies as affirmative action and freedom of speech, Bassili measured meta-attitudinal and operative indicators of strength to assess how well they predicted the pliability and stability attitudes. The meta-attitudinal measures consisted of reported certainty, importance, strength, knowledgeability, attention, and frequency of thought about the attitude object. The operative measures consisted of the extremity of the attitude, ambivalence measured as conflict between the positive and negative evaluation toward the attitude object, and response latency. Exploratory factor analysis yielded two factors, one comprising the meta-attitudinal measures and the other the operative ones. With this initial corroboration of the distinction between meta-attitudinal and operative measures, Bassili (1996a) averaged the measures from each factor to create a meta-attitudinal and an operative index of attitude strength. The operative index proved much better than the meta-attitudinal one at predicting the pliability and the stability of attitudes.

Subsequent studies have supported the usefulness of the distinction between meta-attitudinal and operative measures of strength. In a particularly interesting exploration of attitude strength over the life cycle, Visser and Krosnick (1998) found that people are particularly susceptible to attitude change at the beginning and end of the life cycle, the middle years being characterized by fairly stable attitudes. This finding reflects the operative feature of attitudes, in that it involves a direct measure of stability. In one of their studies, Visser and Krosnick (1998) asked if people are meta-attitudinally aware of when in their life cycle their attitudes are most stable. They did so by comparing the responses of people of various ages to a question asking how likely their opinion on six political issues was to change. Perceived likelihood of change decreased steadily over the life cycle, reflecting accuracy in young people's recognition that they were highly susceptible to attitude change, but inaccuracy in older adult's assumptions about the stability of their attitudes. Interestingly, highly educated people thought of themselves as particularly open to attitude change when in fact they were very resistant to change. The disconnect between actual and perceived attitude stability led the authors to the conclusion that their data reinforce the distinction between meta-attitudinal and operative indexes of attitude strength.

Origins and Consequences Studies

The distinction between meta-attitudinal and operative indexes of strength highlight the fact that operative properties like response latency as well as meta-attitudinal impressions must come from somewhere. To avoid the indeterminacy of the factor analytic approach described above, recent studies have explored the structure of attitude strength by focusing on the origins and consequences of various strength indicators. A good example of the approach is provided by Visser, Krosnick, and Simmons (2003), who reasoned that if two strength attributes appear to be affected in the same way by other variables, and if these attributes have the same consequences on thought and behavior, then there is little to be gained by treating the attributes as distinct. If, on the other hand, two strength attributes are affected differently by other variables and have different consequences on thought and behavior, then the attributes likely represent different strength constructs.

In their studies, Visser et al. (2003) focused on the importance and certainty of attitudes on various social and political issues. A number of information processing and action outcomes associated with these attributes were explored. Attitude importance and certainty were both independently associated with the likelihood that respondents attempted to convince others to adopt their attitude. Attitude importance and certainty, however, also had many distinctive consequences. Importance was associated with the tendency to seek information that would be useful for subsequent attitudinal judgments, and was associated with turning out to vote in an election to express the attitude. These associations were not found in the case of certainty. By contrast, certainty was associated with the tendency to find more than one candidate acceptable, an association not found in the case of importance. These results suggest that attitude importance and certainty influence thought and behavior differently and therefore are best treated as distinct constructs.

Another set of studies using the origins/consequences logic for delineating the dimensionality of strength constructs focused specifically on origins of attitude importance and attitude accessibility (Bizer & Krosnick, 2001; Roese & Olson, 1994). Bizer and Krosnick (2001) reasoned that if importance and accessibility represent distinct constructs, then these two attributes should each have somewhat distinct causes. One of the most common experimental ways of increasing attitude accessibility involves getting participants to repeatedly express an attitude. Bizer and Krosnick (2001) used a repeated expression manipulation and indeed found that it increased the speed with which attitudes were subsequently expressed. The question of interest to them was whether the reported importance of the attitude also increased. Their findings showed that not only does attitude importance not increase with repeated expression, but in fact it tends to decrease slightly. This, therefore, is an example of a cause of an attitude property (accessibility) that does not affect another property (importance), which suggests that the two properties do not stem from the same underlying construct.

The preceding result does not preclude the possibility that although independent, attitude accessibility and importance may influence each other. Note in particular that attitude importance is based on a self-report, and is therefore meta-attitudinal, whereas accessibility is integral to the process of attitude expression, and is therefore operative (Bassili, 1996a). Could it be that people infer the importance they attach to an attitude by observing how quickly the attitude comes to mind when they think about it? Roese and Olson (1994) presented evidence that suggests that impressions about the importance of an attitude are derived from the speed with which the attitude comes to mind. Bizer and Krosnick (2001) challenged Roese and Olson's (1994) conclusion and provided evidence for the opposite relationship between the two constructs, namely that it is the importance that a person attaches to an attitude that causes it to become accessible. Be that as it may, these studies not only demonstrate the usefulness of looking for communalities and divergences in the causes and consequences of different strength indicators, but also the complex interdependences that can exist between them.

Using a similar approach, Holland, Verplanken, and van Knippenberg (2003) focused on the relationship between attitude accessibility and reported certainty. Certainty and accessibility have often been found to be correlated with each other (e.g., Bassili, 1993, 1996a; Pomerantz et al., 1995). Holland et al. (2003) reasoned that one possibility for the correlation is that people infer how certain they are about an attitude from the ease with which the attitude comes to mind. Attitude accessibility was manipulated through repeated expression of the attitude, a manipulation that enhanced both attitude accessibility and certainty. Further analysis demonstrated that reported certainty about the attitude was inferred from the ease with which the attitude came to mind. Interestingly, repeated expression did not influence judgments of attitude importance, a result that is consistent with Bizer and Krosnick's (2001) position on the relationship between these two attributes of strength.

Repeated expression is not the only way to influence the subjective experience of the ease with which an attitude comes to mind. Haddock, Rothman, Reber, and Schwarz (1999) asked some participants to provide three arguments relating to doctor-assisted suicide, while other participants were asked to provide seven arguments. Thinking of seven reasons in favor or against an issue is more difficult than thinking of only three. Accordingly, the subjective experience that accompanied the accessibility of information relevant to the issue would have suggested to participants who had to provide seven arguments that their attitude on the issue was not strong. The results were generally consistent with this logic, suggesting once again that meta-attitudinal properties of strength can derive from operative attitudinal processes.

ATTITUDE STRENGTH AND RESPONSE EFFECTS

As the preceding discussion suggests, attitude strength is not a simple construct. Most properties of strength seem to contribute to the stability, resistance to persuasion, and the influence of an attitude on thought and guiding behavior. Beyond this, however, things become murky. Factor analytic studies of strength measures have not revealed a clear structure, and while origins and consequences studies provide an elegant approach to exploring relations between strength measures, these studies contribute mostly to a picture of dissociation between measures rather than one of shared properties. Even in cases exploring the effect of meta-attitudinal and operative properties of strength on each other, studies have yielded varying results that suggest that these relations may be different in different contexts. To this complex picture, we must add one of the most puzzling, and also interesting, findings of all, namely the frequent failure of attitude strength to moderate response effects.

Response Effects

Response effects refer to conditions under which a response given to an attitude query is influenced by factors that are irrelevant to the attitude object. For example, support for free speech can be as much as 21% higher when respondents are asked "Do you think the United States should forbid public speeches against democracy?" than when they are asked "Do you think the United States should allow public speeches against democracy?" (Rugg, 1941). These two questions differ in tone rather than in meaning, and yet respondents treat them very differently. Other effects involve contextual variations, such as in the nature of questions preceding a particular query. For example, more respondents are in favor of a woman's right to an abortion when the question appears first than when it is preceded by a question asking about abortions "when there is a strong chance of serious defect in the baby" (Krosnick & Schuman, 1988). Context, therefore, can influence responses, and when this happens response effects are known as context effects (see Schwarz, this volume; Sudman, Bradburn, & Schwarz, 1996). Some response effects stem from the tendency of respondents to "acquiesce" or agree rather than disagree with what is stated in the question, whereas other response effects stem from a tendency to pick a middle alternative when it is offered. Schuman and Presser (1981) investigated the effect of question wording, form and context and found them to have a pervasive influence on survey responses.

Response effects are puzzling when viewed from the perspective of traditional definitions conceptualizing attitudes as summary evaluations of attitude objects (e.g., Eagly & Chaiken, 1993; Fazio, 1995). Summary evaluations, being based on prior experience with the attitude object, should be relatively stable and should reflect genuine predispositions towards it. The fact that subtle properties of questions, such as their tone or the context in which they appear, can have a substantial effect on responses, is therefore, perplexing, and raises questions about the fundamental nature of attitudes.

Attitude Strength and Response Effects

The concept of attitude strength may provide a solution to the puzzle of response effects. After all, if strong attitudes are stable and resistant to attack, then surely they should withstand variations in question tone, form, and context. In fact, survey researchers have traditionally assumed that only weak attitudes are susceptible to response effects (Converse, 1974; Payne, 1951). This logic was sensible and reassuring, until it was put to an empirical test by Krosnick and Schuman (1988). These authors analyzed 27 experiments conducted in the context of national surveys that manipulated questions variations known to produce response effects. One important aspect of these surveys is that they also asked respondents questions pertaining to three strength-related properties pertinent to the attitudes being measured: importance, intensity (strength of feelings about the issue), and certainty.

The results of Krosnick and Schuman's (1988) analyses were clear, and given the traditional assumption that only weak attitudes are susceptible to response effects, they also were surprising. Importance, intensity, and certainty did not reliably moderate the impact of variations in the order, tone, or form of question wording on responses. That is, response effects were just as pronounced for attitudes that were reported to be important, intense, and held with certainty than for those that were not. Similar findings were reported by Bishop (1990).

Counterintuitive findings invariably generate attempts to clear what appear to be empirical aberrations. Lavine, Huff, Wagner, and Sweeney (1998) reasoned that failures to find differences in the magnitude of response effects for strong and weak attitudes may be due to a methodological failure. Specifically, Krosnick and Schuman (1988) as well as Bishop (1990) assessed attitude strength with single measures of each of the strength properties. As we saw earlier, single measures often lack reliability. In their research, Lavine et al. (1998) focused on order effects caused by context items that preceded a target attitude item about a number of issues such as welfare reform and defense spending. The context items were designed to promote either conservative or liberal views on the issues. Six dimensions of strength were assessed: Importance, certainty, intensity, frequency of thought, extremity, and ambivalence. When single measures of importance and certainty were used, the results were consistent with past findings where attitude strength did not moderate response effects. When the six measures were averaged, however, context effects tended to be larger for weak attitudes than for strong attitudes.

By aggregating several strength-related measures, Lavine et al. (1998) created what they believed to be a measure of attitude strength that benefited from a broad "bandwidth." This, they felt, may be important in demonstrating that weak attitudes are more susceptible to response effects than strong attitudes. Another interesting finding was that in one of their studies, Lavine et al. (1998) used a measure of attitudinal embeddedness (the extent to which respondents felt that an attitude implied support or opposition to other issues), that single-handedly moderated the size of context effects. Thus, it could be that the nature of the strength property, as well as the methodological step of aggregation, are important in demonstrating moderation by attitude strength. The story, however, does not end here.

As we saw earlier, indicators of attitude strength can be categorized into meta-attitudinal and operative measures (Bassili, 1996a). Krosnick and Schuman's (1988) and Bishop's (1990) relied exclusively on meta-attitudinal self-reports of attitude strength. Lavine et al.'s (1998) studies contained a measure of attitude extremity as well as the measure of embeddedness, which were operative in nature. It could be, therefore, that Lavine et al.'s success in finding evidence for response effect moderation by attitude strength was due to their use of operative measures. To test this possibility, Bassili and Krosnick (2000) added three operative measures of attitude strength—response latency, extremity, and ambivalence—to an arsenal of traditional meta-attitudinal measures (reported certainty, intensity, importance, knowledgeability, and likelihood of change). The study focused on the same response effects that had been explored by Krosnick and Schuman (1988); namely, effects due to question order, the inclusion of a middle alternative, acquiescence, and tone of wording.

Bassili and Krosnick's (2000) study yielded a number of results relevant to the issues raised by prior studies. The breadth or "bandwidth" of aggregate indexes of attitude strength did not emerge as important. In no case did the meta-attitudinal or operative index of strength yield stronger effects than individual measures. This, therefore, was a failure to replicate Lavine et al.'s (1998) findings regarding aggregation, and was instead consistent with the notion that measures of strength do not reflect a single homogeneous construct. Single measures of strength did occasionally moderate a response effect (e.g., extremity moderated the magnitude of the question order effect, whereas intensity and importance moderated the tone of wording effect). However, these moderating effects were rare and inconsistent. For example, respondents with extreme views on an issue were less susceptible to order effects than respondents with moderate views, whereas respondents for whom the attitude was intense or important were *more* susceptible to tone of wording effects than respondents for whom the attitude was not intense or important! Overall, the picture that emerged from Bassili and Krosnick's (2000) study is one that suggests that different response effects occur as a result of different cognitive processes, and that different measures of attitude strength tap into these cognitive processes differently.

THEORETICAL PERSPECTIVES ON ATTITUDE STRENGTH

As the reader will have gathered from the preceding discussion, research on attitude strength has focused more on practical issues relating to the stability of attitudes and their influence on thought and behavior, than on theoretical issues relating to the underpinnings of strength. Many findings have conformed to the expectation that strong attitudes are more durable and resistant to attack than weak attitudes, and that they have more impact on thought and behavior. Other findings have been perplexing. The dimensionality of attitude strength in particular has proven complex and measures of strength have defied classification. Perhaps most perplexing is the finding that strong attitudes typically are no more impervious to response effects than weak attitudes. In closing this chapter, it is fruitful to look at the theoretical assumptions that underlie various approaches to the study of attitude strength.

Awareness and Consistency

Democratic societies are based on the assumption that citizens are competent to make choices among political options. Attitudes play an important role in this process because they are the primary mediators between information about issues in public life and the exercise of choices relevant to governance. Unfortunately, the *omnicompetent citizen*, a label coined derisively by Lippmann (1925), has proven elusive in survey research, leading theorists like Converse (1964) to suggest that in many cases, the opinions people express are reflections of "nonattitudes." This pessimistic assessment has served as the backdrop for efforts to distinguish between conditions under which attitudes have meaningful consequences from conditions where they are vacuous.

One view of strong attitudes posits that people are aware of the issues that are centrally important to them, and that issue importance has a number of antecedents and consequences that set such attitudes apart from unimportant attitudes. As we saw earlier, Krosnick and his colleagues have conducted an extensive research program on attitude importance and have garnered ample evidence for the potent role of this construct in attitudinal functioning. What is particularly interesting from a theoretical point of view is that attitude importance has many antecedents and consequences that are themselves properties of attitude strength. For example, attitude importance is influenced by self-interest, a strength property (Boninger, Krosnick, & Berent, 1995) while in turn influencing attitude accessibility (Bizer & Krosnick, 2001), as well as attention to and processing of information relevant to the attitude object (Visser, Krosnick, & Simmons, 2003), also strength properties. If attitude importance is indeed at the center of a rich web of inter-connections among strength constructs, a puzzling question arises: Why has the common-factor hypothesis of attitude strength received so little support?

The answer, I believe, is that relations among strength constructs are generally weak (see Krosnick et al., 1993) and that the view of an aware holder of attitudes who can report insightfully on what is truly important to him or her in the atti-tudinal domain is overly optimistic. Research in social cognition has repeatedly demonstrated that people are poor assessors of the factors that influence their judgments and decisions (Gilovich, 1991; Nisbett & Wilson, 1977). It is unlikely, therefore, that various measures of attitude strength will bind together consis-tently, especially when these measures are meta-attitudinal in nature.

Automatic Activation and Attitude Guidance

One of the most coherent and elegantly simple accounts of the underpinnings of attitude strength is offered by Fazio and colleagues (Fazio, 1995; Fazio, Chen et al., 1982; Fazio, Sanbonmatsu, Powell, & Kardes, 1986). According to Fazio, an attitude is represented in memory as an association between an object and a sum-mary evaluation of that object. The strength of the object–evaluation association determines the accessibility of the attitude, and therefore the likelihood that the summary evaluation will come to mind in the presence of the attitude object. Once activated in the context of the attitude object, the summary evaluation is there to guide thought and behavior toward it, a notion that has proven instrumental in solving the attitude-behavior riddle presented by Wicker (1969).

Fazio's views regarding attitude accessibility have far-reaching implications. By conceiving of attitudes as falling on a continuum defined by the strength of the object-evaluation association, Fazio provided a cognitive account of the nonatti-tudes identified by Converse (1964). Specifically, a nonattitude is an attitude that is so weak that a summary evaluation is not associated with the attitude object or, at the extreme, that the attitude object itself is not represented in memory. This last notion, incidentally, where people express opinions on issues they know nothing about is not altogether fanciful, survey researchers having documented many cases where people take a stand on entirely fictitious issues (e.g., Bishop, Tuchfarber, & Oldendick, 1986). Another feature of Fazio's theory of attitude accessibility is of crucial importance. By attributing accessibility to the strength of an association in memory, Fazio highlighted the fact that attitudinal processes often are automatic. That is, when the object–evaluation association is very strong, mere exposure to the attitude object will result in the activation of the evaluation, thus explain-ing the uncontrollable glow of approval, or the overwhelming revulsion, that one sometimes feels in reaction to a loved or despised entity.

Fazio's focus on accessibility raises the same question that we considered in relation to attitude importance as a core element of attitude strength. If accessibil-ity is such a hub in attitudinal functioning, why doesn't it provide the glue to bind all properties of strength in a single factor? The answer, I believe, is that attitudi-nal processes are a lot more fluid than the notion of object–evaluation association suggests.

Fluidity in Potentiated Recruitment

The theoretical perspectives on attitudes and attitude strength that we have discussed so far all assume that attitudes are mental constructs that are represented in memory as distinct entities that can be retrieved ready-made. Given this view, it is not surprising that cases where the attitude is slow to come to mind or where it appears inconsistent across time or domains, are often thought to involve nonattitudes. As we have seen, however, strong and weak attitudes alike are highly susceptible to contextual information, a finding that has led several theorists to suggest that rather than being represented in a ready-made fashion in memory, attitudes involve constructive processes that occur at the time they are needed (Bassili & Brown, 2005; Schwarz & Bohner, 2001; Zaller, 1992). To illustrate this view and how it accommodates attitude strength results, we now turn to the potentiated recruitment model of Bassili and Brown (2005).

The potentiated recruitment model shown in Figure 11.1 posits that attitude expression is the result of activity in large networks of microconcepts represented in an attitudinal cognitorium. These elements are associated with each other to varying degrees, and have a certain level of activation. They represent evaluatively laden bits of information from which attitudes can be constructed. Potentiation is crucial to the process of attitude construction because it determines the particular configuration of microconceptual elements that define an attitude at a certain point in time. There are four primary sources of potentiation. One source consists of recent experiences that prime particular microconcepts. Another is current information contained in eliciting conditions stemming from the encounter with the attitude object or queries about it. The third source of potentiation consists of spreading activation between associated concepts and the fourth stems from cognitive activity in working memory. One advantage of the potentiated recruitment framework is that it addresses both explicit and implicit attitude expression by positing that the output of emergent attitudes can either be go through explicit memory, where reflective processes take place, or can be more direct under conditions of unconscious or speeded responding.

How does the potentiated recruitment framework account for attitude strength? Because the framework posits that attitudes are constructed at the time they are recruited, it conceives of attitude strength as an emergent property of the potentiation recruitment process. Attitudes that are constructed quickly and effortlessly on the basis of a broad network of microconceptual elements are likely to influence thought and behavior at the same time as they give rise to meta-attitudinal impressions of strength. To the extent that such attitudes are based on highly interconnected microconceptual elements, they will be stable over time and will resist change. Properties of the attitudinal cognitorium are only one source of influence. External factors also influence attitude construction. Thus, the stronger the cues contained in the eliciting context, the prior context, and in the contents of working memory, the stronger the attitude will be at the moment of its construction.

The potentiated recruitment framework can help explain some of the puzzling results we have reviewed. Take, for example, a response effect such as support

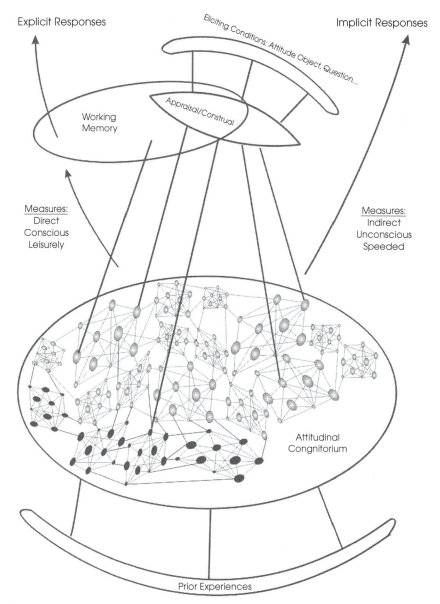

Figure 11.1   The potentiated recruitment framework (Bassili & Brown, 2005).

for free speech in response to the "forbid-allow" question variation. Why is the effect of the tone of the question equally strong for strong and weak attitudes? The answer may well be that the potentiating effect of a concept such as forbidding is likely to be at least as strong for people with strong views about free speech as it is for people with weak views. And what of strength measures' resistance to classification along a single factor? The fluid nature of attitudinal processes presented by the framework suggests that even the construal of attitude strength measures is susceptible to contextual influences. The importance of an issue, for example, is likely to vary depending on whether prior questions inquired about global warming or putting the cap on the toothpaste. To the extent that the construal of strength questions, just like the potentiation of attitudes, is highly context dependent, it is not surprising that the factor structure of strength constructs is variable.

CONCLUDING REMARKS

Krosnick and Petty's (1995) definition of attitude strength in terms of stability, resistance to attack, and influence on thought and behavior provides a good benchmark for evaluating the antecedents and consequences of various strength constructs. By this measure, most measures of attitude strength fulfill their mandate, having consequences that meet the strength benchmark in at least some circumstances, and having antecedents that are intuitively relevant to the creation of strong attitudes. The more intriguing story about attitude strength relates to variability rather than impact, variability in terms of factor structure across studies and in terms of role in moderating response effects. This variability underscores the importance of theory in accounting for attitude strength properties. The role of theory is particularly important at a time when researchers are as interested in implicit attitudes as they are in explicit ones (see Schwarz, this volume). With all the attention that has been given to the strength of explicit attitudes, very little is known about the corresponding strength of implicit ones. Thus, the challenge for future research will be not only to elucidate some of the puzzles discussed here, but also to provide an account of attitude strength in both explicit and implicit domains.

REFERENCES

Abelson, R. P. (1988). Conviction. *American Psychologist, 4,* 267–275.

Abelson, R. P. (1995). Attitude extremity. In R. E. Petty & J. A. Krosnick (Eds.), *Attitude strength: Antecedents and consequences* (pp. 25–41). Mahwah, NJ: Erlbaum.

Abelson, R. P., & Miller, J. C. (1967). Negative persuasion via personal insult. *Journal of Experimental Social Psychology, 3,* 321–333.

Allison, S. T., & Messick, D. M. (1988). The feature-positive effect, attitude strength, and degree of perceived consensus. *Personality and Social Psychology Bulletin, 14,* 231–241.

Allport, G. W. (1935). Attitudes. In C. Murchison (Ed.), *A handbook of social psychology* (pp. 798–844). Worcester, MA: Clark University Press.

Armitage, C. J., & Conner, M. (2000). Attitudinal ambivalence: A test of three key hypotheses. *Personality and Social Psychology Bulletin, 26,* 1421–1432.

Baron, R. S., Hoppe, S. I., Kao, C. F., Brunsman, B., Linneweh, B., & Rogers, D. (1996). Social corroboration and opinion extremity. *Journal of Experimental Social Psychology, 32,* 537–560.

Bassili, J. N. (1993). Response latency versus certainty as indices of the strength of voting intentions in a CATI Survey. *Public Opinion Quarterly, 57,* 54–61.

Bassili, J. N. (1995). Response latency and the accessibility of voting intentions: What contributes to accessibility and how it affects vote choice. *Personality and Social Psychology Bulletin, 21*, 686–695.

Bassili, J. N. (1996a). Meta-judgmental versus operative indexes of psychological attributes: The case of measures of attitude strength. *Journal of Personality and Social Psychology, 71*, 637–653.

Bassili, J. N. (1996b). The "how" and "why" of response latency measurement in telephone surveys. In N. Schwarz & S. Sudman (Eds.), *Answering questions: Methodology for determining cognitive and communication processes in survey research* (pp. 319–346). San Francisco: Jossey-Bass.

Bassili, J. N. (1998, July). Simultaneous accessibility: A prerequisite to heated intrapsychic conflict. In J. N. Bassili (Chair), *Response time measurement in survey research*. Symposium conducted at the meeting of the International Society of Political Psychology, Montreal, Canada.

Bassili, J. N. (2001). Cognitive indices of social information processing. In A. Tesser & N. Schwarz (Eds.), *Blackwell handbook of social psychology: Vol. 1. Intraindividual processes*. Oxford, UK: Blackwell.

Bassili, J. N. (2003). The minority slowness effect: Subtle inhibitions in the expressions of views not shared by others. *Journal of Personality and Social Psychology, 84*, 261–276.

Bassili, J. N., & Bors, D. (1997). Using response latency to increase lead time in election forecasting. *Canadian Journal of Behavioural Sciences, 29*, 231–238.

Bassili, J. N., & Brown, R. D. (2005). Implicit and explicit processes attitudes: Research, challenges and theory. In D. Albarracin, B. T. Johnson, & M. P. Zanna (Eds.), *The handbook of attitudes* (pp. 543–574). Mahwah, NJ: Erlbaum.

Bassili, J. N., & Fletcher, J. F. (1991). Response-time measurement in survey research: A method for CATI and a new look at non-attitudes. *Public Opinion Quarterly, 55*, 331–346.

Bassili, J. N., & Krosnick, J. A. (2000). Do strength-related attitude properties determine susceptibility to response effects? New evidence from response latency, attitude extremity and aggregate indices. *Political Psychology, 21*, 107–132.

Bell, D. W., & Esses, V. M. (2002). Ambivalence and response amplification: A motivational perspective. *Personality and Social Psychology Bulletin, 28*, 1143–1152.

Bishop, G. F. (1990). Issue involvement and response effects in public opinion surveys. *Public Opinion Quarterly, 55*, 331–346.

Bishop, G. F., Tuchfarber, A. J., & Oldendick, R. W. (1986). Opinions on fictitious issues: The pressure to answer survey questions. *Public Opinion Quarterly, 50*, 240–250.

Bizer, G. Y., & Krosnick, J. A. (2001). Exploring the structure of strength-related attitude features: The relation between attitude importance and attitude accessibility. *Journal of Personality and Social Psychology, 81*, 566–586.

Boninger, D. S., Krosnick, J. A., & Berent, M. K. (1995). Origins of attitude: Self-interest, social identification, and value relevance. *Journal of Personality and Social Psychology, 68*, 61–80.

Byrne, D., London, O., & Griffitt, W. (1968). The effect of topic importance and attitude similarity-dissimilarity on attraction in an intrastranger design. *Psychonomic Science, 11*, 303–304.

CBS News Poll. (2006). Retrieved July 14, 2006 from http://www.cbsnews.com/htdocs/CBSNews_polls/mayb-all.pdf.

Converse, P. E. (1964). The nature of belief systems in mass publics. In D. P. Apter (Ed.), *Ideology and discontent* (pp. 201–261). New York: Free Press.

Converse, P. E. (1974). Comment: The status of nonattitudes. *American Political Science Review, 68*, 650–660.

Crano, W. D. (1983). Assumed consensus of attitudes: The effect of vested interest. *Personality and Social Psychology Bulletin, 9*, 597–608.

Crano, W. D. (1995). Attitude strength and vested interest. In R. E. Petty & J. A. Krosnick (Eds.), *Attitude strength: Antecedents and consequences* (pp. 131–157). Mahwah, NJ: Erlbaum.

De Dreu, C. K. W., & van Knippenberg, D. (2005). The possessive self as a barrier to conflict resolution: Effects of mere ownership, process accountability, and self-concept clarity on competitive cognitions and behavior. *Journal of Personality and Social Psychology, 89*, 345–357.

Eagly, A. H., & Chaiken, S. (1993). *The psychology of attitudes.* Fort Worth, TX: Harcourt Brace Jovanovich.

Fazio, R. H. (1995). Attitudes as object-evaluation associations: Determinants, consequences, and correlates of attitude accessibility. In R. E. Petty & J. A. Krosnick (Eds.), *Attitude strength: Antecedents and consequences* (pp. 247–282). Mahwah, NJ: Erlbaum.

Fazio, R. H., Blascovich, J., & Driscoll, D. M. (1992). On the functional value of attitudes: The influence of accessible attitudes upon the ease and quality of decision making. *Personality and Social Psychology Bulletin, 18*, 388–401.

Fazio, R. H., Chen, J., McDonel, E. C., & Sherman, S. J. (1982). Attitude accessibility, attitude-behavior consistency, and the strength of the object-evaluation association. *Journal of Experimental Social Psychology, 18*, 339–357.

Fazio, R. H., Powell, M. C., & Williams, C. J. (1989). The role of attitude accessibility in the attitude-to-behavior process. *Journal of Consumer Research, 16*, 280–288.

Fazio, R. H., Sanbonmatsu, D. M., Powell, D. M., & Kardes, F. R. (1986). On the automatic activation of attitudes. *Journal of Personality and Social Psychology, 50*, 229–238.

Fazio, R. H., & Williams, C. J. (1986). Attitude accessibility as a moderator of the attitude-perception and attitude-behavior relations: An investigation of the 1984 presidential election. *Journal of Personality and Social Psychology, 51*, 505–514.

Fazio, R. H., & Zanna, M. P. (1978). Attitudinal qualities relating to the strength of the attitude-behavior relationship. *Journal of Experimental Social Psychology, 14*, 398–408.

Fazio, R. H., & Zanna, M. P. (1981). Direct experience and attitude-behavior consistency. In L. Berkowitz (Ed.), *Advances in experimental social psychology* (Vol. 14, pp. 161–202). San Diego, CA: Academic Press.

Fishbein, M., & Ajzen, I. (1974). Attitudes toward objects as predictors of single and multiple behavioral criteria. *Psychological Review, 81*, 59–74.

Fishbein, M., & Ajzen, I. (1975). *Belief, attitude, intention, and behavior: An introduction to theory and research.* Reading, MA: Addison-Wesley.

Gallup Poll Accuracy Record. (2006). Retrieved from http://poll.gallup.com/content/default.aspx?ci=18583 on July 5, 2006.

Gilovich, T. (1991). *How we know what isn't so: The fallibility of human reason in every day life.* New York: The Free Press.

Glick, P., & Fiske, S. T. (2001). Ambivalent sexism. In M. Zanna (Ed.), *Advances in experimental social psychology* (Vol. 33, pp. 115–188). San Diego, CA: Academic Press.

Gorn, G. J. (1975). The effects of personal involvement, communication discrepancy, and source prestige on reactions to communications on separatism. *Canadian Journal of Behavioural Science, 7*, 369–386.

Greene, S. (2005). The structure of partisan attitudes: Reexamining partisan dimensionality and ambivalence. *Political Psychology, 26*, 809–822.

Haddock, G., Rothman, A. J., Reber, R., & Schwarz, N. (1999). Forming judgments of attitude certainty, intensity, and importance: The role of subjective experience. *Personality and Social Psychology Bulletin, 25*, 771–782.

Hodges, S. D., & Wilson, T. D. (1994). Effects of analyzing reasons on attitude change: The moderating role of attitude accessibility. *Social Cognition, 11*, 353–366.

Hodson, G., Maio, G. R., & Esses, V. M. (2001). The role of attitudinal ambivalence in susceptibility to consensus information. *Basic and Applied Social Psychology, 23*, 197–205.

Holbrook, A. L., Berent, M. K., Krosnick, J. A., Visser, P. S., & Boninger, D. S. (2005). Attitude importance and the accumulation of attitude-relevant knowledge in memory. *Journal of Personality and Social Psychology, 88*, 749–769.

Holland, R. W., Verplanken, B., & van Knippenberg, A. (2003). From repetition to conviction: Attitude accessibility as a determinant of attitude certainty. *Journal of Experimental Social Psychology, 39*, 594–601.

Holtz, R., & Miller, N. (1985). Assumed similarity and opinion certainty. *Journal of Personality and Social Psychology, 48*, 890–898.

Huckfeldt, R., Sprague, J., & Levine, J. (2000). The dynamics of collective deliberation in the 1996 election: Campaign effects on accessibility, certainty, and accuracy. *American Political Science Review, 94*, 641–651.

Judd, C. M., & Brauer, M. (1995). Repetitive and evaluative extremity. In R. E. Petty & J. A. Krosnick (Eds.), *Attitude strength: Antecedents and consequences* (pp. 43–71). Mahwah, NJ: Erlbaum.

Kachadourian, L. K., Finchman, F., & Davila, J. (2005). Attitudinal ambivalence, rumination, and forgiveness of partner transgressions in marriage. *Personality and Social Psychology Bulletin, 31*, 334–342.

Kaplan, K. J. (1972). On the ambivalence-indifference problem in attitude theory and measurement: A suggested modification of the semantic differential technique. *Psychological Bulletin, 77*, 361–372.

Kokkinaki, F. (1998). Attitudes towards European monetary union in Greece: Antecedents, strength and consequences. *Journal of Economic Psychology, 19*, 775–796.

Krech, D., & Crutchfield (1948). *Theory and problems of social psychology.* New York: McGraw-Hill.

Krosnick, J. A. (1988a). Attitude importance and attitude change. *Journal of Experimental Social Psychology, 24*, 240–255.

Krosnick, J. A. (1988b). The role of attitude importance in social evaluation: A study of policy preferences, presidential candidate evaluations, and voting behavior. *Journal of Personality and Social Psychology, 55*, 196–210.

Krosnick, J. A. (1990). Government policy and citizen passion: A study of issue publics in contemporary America. *Political Behavior, 12*, 59–92.

Krosnick, J. A., & Abelson, R. P. (1992). The case for measuring attitude strength in surveys. In J. Tanur (Ed.), *Questions about Questions* (pp. 177–203). New York: Russell Sage.

Krosnick, J. A., Boninger, D. S., Chuang, Y. C., Berent, M. K., & Carnot, C. G. (1993). Attitude strength: One construct or many related constructs? *Journal of Personality and Social Psychology, 65*, 1132–1151.

Krosnick, J. A., & Petty, R. E. (1995). Attitude strength: An overview. In R. E. Petty & J. A. Krosnick (Eds.), *Attitude strength: Antecedents and consequences* (pp. 1–24). Mahwah, NJ: Erlbaum.

Krosnick, J. A., & Schuman, H. (1988). Attitude intensity, importance, and certainty and susceptibility to response effects. *Journal of Personality and Social Psychology, 54*, 940–952.

Lavine, H., Huff, J. W., Wagner, S. H., & Sweeney, D. (1998). The moderating influence of attitude strength on the susceptibility to context effects in attitude surveys. *Journal of Personality and Social Psychology, 75*, 359–373.

Lippmann, W. (1925). *The phantom public.* New York: Harcourt, Brace.

Lord, C. G., Ross, L., & Lepper, M. R. (1979). Biased assimilation and attitude polarization: The effects of prior theories on subsequently considered evidence. *Journal of
Personality and Social Psychology, 37,* 2098–2109.

Miller, J. M., & Peterson, D. A. M. (2004). Theoretical and empirical implications of attitude strength. *The Journal of Politics, 66,* 847–867.

Newby-Clark, I. R., McGregor, I., & Zanna, M. P. (2002). Thinking and caring about cognitive inconsistency: When and for whom does attitudinal ambivalence feel uncomfortable? *Journal of Personality and Social Psychology, 82,* 157–166.

Nisbett, R. E., & Wilson, T. D. (1977). Telling more than we can know: Verbal reports on
mental processes. *Psychological Review, 84,* 231–259.

Nordgren, L., van Harrelveld, F., & van der Pligt, J. (2004). Ambivalence, discomfort, and
motivated information processing. *Journal of Experimental Social Psychology, 42,*
252–258.

Osgood, C. E., & Tannenbaum, P. H. (1955). The principle of congruity in the prediction of
attitude change. *Psychological Review, 62,* 42–55.

Payne, S. L. (1951). *The art of asking questions.* Princeton, NJ: Princeton University
Press.

Pomerantz, E. M., Chaiken, S., & Tordesillas, R. S. (1995). Attitude strength and resistance
processes. *Journal of Personality and Social Psychology, 69,* 408–419.

Prislin, R. (1996). Attitude stability and attitude strength: One is enough to make it stable.
European Journal of Social Psychology, 26, 447–477.

Prislin, R., Limbert, W., & Bauer, E. (2000). From majority to minority and vice versa: The
asymmetrical effects of gaining and losing majority position within a group. *Journal
of Personality and Social Psychology, 79,* 385–395.

Raden, D. (1985) Strength-related attitude dimensions. *Social Psychology Quarterly, 69,*
408–419.

Regan, D. T., & Fazio, R. (1977). On the consistency between attitudes and behavior: Look
to the method of attitude formation. *Journal of Experimental Social Psychology, 13,*
28–45.

Rhine, R. J., & Severance, L. J. (1970). Ego-involvement, discrepancy, source credibility,
and attitude change. *Journal of Personality and Social Psychology, 16,* 175–190.

Roese, N. J., & Olson, J. M. (1994). Attitude importance as a function of repeated attitude
expression. *Journal of Experimental Social Psychology, 30,* 39–51.

Rugg, D. (1941). Experiments in wording of questions: II. *Public Opinion Research, 5,*
91–91.

Schuman, H., & Presser, S. (1981). *Questions and answers in attitude survey: Experiments
on question form, wording, and context.* San Diego, CA: Academic Press.

Schwarz, N., & Bohner, G. (2001). The construction of attitudes. In A. Tesser & N. Schwarz
(Eds.), *Blackwell handbook of social psychology: Intraindividual processes* (pp.
436–457). Malden, MA: Blackwell.

Scott, W. A. (1959). Cognitive consistency, response reinforcement, and attitude change.
Sociometry, 22, 219–229.

Scott, W. A. (1968). Attitude measurement. In G. Lindsey & E. Aronson (Eds.), *The handbook of social psychology* (Vol. 2, pp. 204–273). Reading, MA: Addison-Wesley.

Sudman, S., Bradburn, N. M., & Schwarz, N. (1996). *Thinking about answers: The application of cognitive processes to survey methodology.* San Francisco, CA: Jossey-Bass.

Tesser, A., Martin, L., & Mendolia, M. (1995). The impact of thought on attitude extremity
and attitude-behavior consistency. In R. E. Petty & J. A. Krosnick (Eds.), *Attitude
strength: Antecedents and consequences* (pp. 73–92). Mahwah, NJ: Erlbaum.

Thompson, M., Zanna, M., & Griffin, D. (1995). Let's not be indifferent about (attitudinal)
ambivalence. In R. E. Petty & J. A. Krosnick (Eds.), *Attitude strength: Antecedents
and consequences* (pp. 361–386). Mahwah, NJ: Erlbaum.

Urland, G. R., & Tiffany, A. (2005). Have your cake and hate it, too: Ambivalent food attitudes are associated with dietary restraint. *Basic and Applied Social Psychology, 27,* 353–360.

van Harreveld, F., van der Plight, J., de Vries, N. K., Wenneker, C., & Verhue, D. (2004). Attitudinal ambivalence and information integration in attitudinal judgment. *British Journal of Social Psychology, 43,* 431–447.

Verplanken, B. (1989). Involvement and need for cognition as moderators of belief-attitudes-intention consistency. *British Journal of Social Psychology, 28,* 115–122.

Visser, P. S., & Krosnick, J. A. (1998). Development of attitude strength over the life cycle: Surge and decline. *Journal of Personality and Social Psychology, 75,* 1389–1410.

Visser, P. S., Krosnick, J. A., & Simmons, J. P. (2003). Distinguishing the cognitive and behavioral consequences of attitude importance and certainty: A new approach to testing the common-factor hypothesis. *Journal of Experimental Social Psychology, 39,* 118–141.

Visser, P. S., & Mirabile, R. R. (2004). Attitudes in the social context: The impact of social network composition on individual-level attitude strength. *Journal of Personality and Social Psychology, 87,* 779–795.

Wicker, A. W. (1969). Attitudes versus actions: The relationship of verbal and overt behavioral responses to attitude objects. *Journal of Social Issues, 25,* 41–78.

Wicker, A. W. (1971). An examination of the "other variables" explanations of attitude-behavior inconsistency. *Journal of Personality and Social Psychology, 19,* 18–30.

Wood, W. Rhodes, N., & Biek, M. (1995). Working knowledge and attitude strength: The effects of amount and accuracy of information. In R. E. Petty & J. A. Krosnick (Eds.), *Attitude strength: Antecedents and consequences* (pp. 283–324). Mahwah, NJ: Erlbaum.

Yakushko, O. (2005). Ambivalent sexism and relationship patterns among women and men in Ukraine. *Sex Roles, 52,* 589–596.

Yankelovich, D., Skelly, F., & White, A. (1981). *The Mushiness Index: A refinement in public policy polling techniques.* New York: Yankelovich, Clancey, Shulman.

Zaller, J. R. (1992). *The nature and origins of mass opinions.* New York: Cambridge University Press.

12

Attitudinal Ambivalence

MARK CONNER
University of Leeds

CHRISTOPHER J. ARMITAGE
University of Sheffield

INTRODUCTION AND OVERVIEW

Me, ambivalent? Well, yes and no.—Anonymous

*I*n the most comprehensive single-volume review of attitudes, Eagly and Chaiken (1993) define attitude as "a psychological tendency that is expressed by evaluating a particular entity with some degree of favor or disfavor" (p. 1). Within Eagly and Chaiken's (1993) definition rests decades of research that has conceptualized attitudes as generally positive *or* negative evaluations of objects. Implicit in this definition is the idea that there is no possibility of evaluating an attitude object as both positive and negative, yet as the anonymous quote at the beginning of this chapter implies, not all attitudes are so clear-cut. Moreover, we would argue that focusing solely on positive or negative attitudes oversimplifies the concept of attitudes because even the most ardent cream cake-lover or party-hearty student will recognize negative aspects to their behavior just as the most fervent patriot might have some reservations about aspects of foreign policy (Citrin & Luks, 2005). Thus, cream cakes can be satisfying and depressing, drinking alcohol can be viewed as sociable and inappropriate, and one can love one's country while hating how it treats other countries. As we shall see later in the chapter, it is equally plausible to be sexist and yet regard women as warm, sweet, and sensitive. The concept of attitudinal ambivalence neatly encapsulates those situations in which attitudes are not polarized and where positive and negative attitudes are expressed simultaneously toward an object.

Attitudinal ambivalence is a psychological state in which "a person holds mixed feelings (positive and negative) towards some psychological object" (Gardner, 1987, p. 241); the idea was introduced into social psychology by Scott (1969). Although Kaplan (1972) and Katz and Hass (1988) among others have made significant and important contributions, mainstream research into attitudinal ambivalence was reinvigorated by Thompson, Zanna, and Griffin's (1995) chapter in Petty and Krosnick's (1995) attitude strength book. There has been an exponential growth in interest in this topic since (for reviews see Armitage & Conner, 2004, 2005; Conner & Sparks, 2002; Jonas, Brömer, & Diehl, 2000). The aim of the present chapter is to provide an update on work into attitudinal ambivalence in four broad domains. First, we examine further the conceptual and operational definitions of attitudinal ambivalence, with a particular focus on how the construct has been defined and to consider in some depth the recent distinction that has arisen between potential and felt ambivalence. Second, we explore some of the proposed antecedents of ambivalence, which we divide into top-down processes (e.g., value conflict, need for cognition), and bottom-up processes (e.g., presentation of evaluatively inconsistent information). Third, we consider the consequences of holding ambivalent attitudes for attitude stability, attitude pliability, information processing, and attitude–intention–behavior relationships (Krosnick & Petty, 1995). Finally, we consider future directions for research on attitudinal ambivalence.

CONCEPTUAL AND OPERATIONAL DEFINITIONS OF ATTITUDINAL AMBIVALENCE

Conceptual Definitions of Ambivalence

Traditionally, attitudes have been conceptualized as unidimensional bipolar constructs, meaning that individuals may only be positively disposed, negatively disposed, or neutral about a particular attitude object (such as a behavior). However, a bidimensional model of attitudes, which underlies the concept of ambivalence, challenges the unidimensional view of attitudes by arguing that individuals can simultaneously hold both positive and negative attitudes that are not perfectly (negatively) correlated with one another. In other words, it is possible for individuals to evaluate simultaneously an attitude object as positive *and* negative; that is, to be *attitudinally ambivalent*. A number of definitions for this state of ambivalence have been offered (Table 12.1; see Conner & Sparks, 2002 for further examples). For example, Thompson et al. (1995) define ambivalence as the inclination to give an attitude object "equivalently strong positive and negative evaluations" (p. 367). Most such definitions in the psychological literature make reference to the simultaneous existence of positive and negative evaluations of an attitude object. This is important because it distinguishes attitudinal ambivalence from attitude variability and attitude uncertainty, which capture temporal instability in attitudes rather than the simultaneous conflict in evaluations implied by ambivalence.

TABLE 12.1   Interpretations and Definitions of Ambivalence

the existence of simultaneous or rapidly interchangeable positive and negative feelings toward the same object or activity, with the added proviso that both the positive and negative feelings be strong. (Meehl, 1964, quoted in Emmons, 1996)

a psychological state in which a person holds mixed feelings (positive and negative) towards some psychological object. (Gardner, 1987, p. 241)

"the extent of beliefs" evaluative dissimilarity (or inconsistency). (Eagly & Chaiken, 1993, p. 123)

a conflict aroused by competing evaluative predispositions. (Breckler, 1994, p. 359)

the extent to which one's reactions to an attitude object are evaluatively mixed in that both positive (favorable) and negative (unfavorable) elements are included. (Wegener, Downing, Krosnick, & Petty, 1995, p. 460)

[an inclination] to give it [an attitude object] equivalently strong positive or negative evaluations. (Thompson et al., 1995, p. 367)

an approach-avoidance conflict—wanting but at the same time not wanting the same goal object. (Emmons, 1996, p. 326)

the simultaneous existence of positive and negative evaluations of an attitude object. (Conner & Sparks, 2002, p. 39)

Operational Definitions of Ambivalence

There is a current lack of consensus as to the best means to measure ambivalence (Breckler, 1994; Conner & Sparks, 2002; Priester & Petty, 1996; Thompson et al., 1995). Most commonly, one of two broad approaches have been adopted (Armitage & Conner, 2004). In the first, measures of *felt ambivalence* have been taken by asking people to make meta-judgments about their own levels of ambivalence. For example, Priester and Petty (1996) asked participants to rate their subjective ("felt") ambivalence on 11-point scales anchored with *feel no conflict at all* (= 0) and *feel maximum conflict* (= 10). Such measures appear to reflect particularly the felt or experienced discomfort that arises from having evaluatively inconsistent views of the same attitude object. In the second approach, measures of *potential ambivalence* employ separate measures of the positive and negative thoughts, feelings or beliefs that an attitude object produces (usually using a split semantic differential measure of attitude; Figure 12.1; Kaplan, 1972). These positive and negative reactions are then combined to yield a continuous measure of ambivalence (e.g., Thompson et al., 1995).

Each approach possesses strengths and weaknesses. For example, measures of felt ambivalence may be important in tapping the extent to which ambivalence is experienced as unpleasant. Similar to the idea of cognitive dissonance (Festinger, 1957), high levels of felt ambivalence may motivate individuals to attempt to resolve it. However, in general, such measures appear to be more open to extraneous influences that can undermine their validity (Bassili, 1996). For example, Newby-Clark, McGregor, and Zanna (2002) have shown that the relationship between felt and potential ambivalence is dependent upon the extent to which the opposing poles are salient. Thus, people's felt ambivalence may be affected by extraneous influences, and—with the exception of studies that deliberately manipulate salience—it is not clear whether the information on which to form judgments of felt ambivalence are ordinarily available to consciousness.

Measures of potential ambivalence possess some similarity to Bassili's (1996) operative indices of attitude strength. Operative indices of attitude strength (see Bassili, this volume) are derived from the attitude judgment process or its outcomes (e.g., response latency). Such measures are preferred to the extent that they do not require the respondent to combine the positive and negative evaluations in a biased manner. Nevertheless the term *potential ambivalence* would appear appropriate because the individual with high levels of potential ambivalence may not "experience" high levels of ambivalence unless both positive and negative evaluations upon which the potential ambivalence is based are similarly highly accessible (Conner & Sparks, 2002; Newby-Clark et al., 2002). An additional issue with measures of potential ambivalence concerns the best way to compute such a measure from the separate positive and negative evaluations on which it is based (Breckler, 1994; Jonas et al., 2000; Priester & Petty, 1996; Thompson et al., 1995). Kaplan (1972) suggested that in a measure of ambivalence, scores should increase as the positive and negative judgments become more polarized (both larger in value) and similar in absolute value. A variety of measures of ambivalence have been proposed to capture these conditions (see Jonas et al., 2000). Perhaps the most widely employed such equation is that devised by Griffin and presented in Thompson et al. (1995): ambivalence is calculated as half the intensity of the positive (P) and negative (N) judgments, minus the absolute difference (similarity) between the two. That is, ambivalence is denoted by the equation:

$$\text{Ambivalence} = (P+N)/2 - |P-N|,$$

where P and N are measured on unipolar scales (in absolute values) in two separate questions. So, for example, an individual who rates an attitude object on split semantic differential scales (see Figure 12.1) as both moderately positive (3) and moderately negative (3) would be assigned an ambivalence score of $(3 + 3)/2 - |3 - 3| = 3$, whereas an individual who rates the same attitude object as extremely positive (4) and not at all negative (1) would be assigned an ambivalence score of $(4 + 1)/2 - |4 - 1| = -0.5$. Interestingly, both Riketta (2000) and Priester and Petty (1996) have reported that this Griffin index is more closely correlated with felt ambivalence than any other index ($r = .62$ and $.44$, respectively), which suggests that the Griffin measure of potential ambivalence is closer to felt ambivalence than any other measure.

It also is worth noting that there is an increasing body of literature distinguishing felt from potential ambivalence in terms of antecedents and consequences. For example, Priester and Petty (2001) show intraindividual attitude conflict to be an antecedent of felt but not potential ambivalence. It would appear that whereas measures of potential ambivalence show similarities to measures of attitude strength (with higher potential ambivalence equating to weaker attitudes), measures of felt ambivalence show more complex patterns.

A (i): Semantic Differential Scale

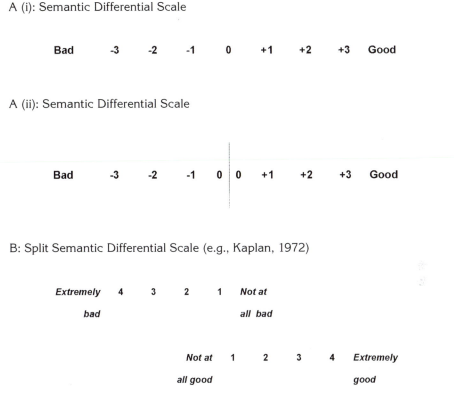

A (ii): Semantic Differential Scale

B: Split Semantic Differential Scale (e.g., Kaplan, 1972)

Figure 12.1   Evolution of the split semantic differential scale.

ANTECEDENTS OF AMBIVALENCE

Having defined attitudinal ambivalence, the question arises as to how ambivalence develops. In our view, the antecedents of ambivalence can be broadly divided into top-down and bottom-up categories. The top-down category is concerned with such chronic psychological tendencies as value conflict or individual differences that are associated with holding ambivalent attitudes. The bottom-up category consists of features in the environment, usually the attitude object itself, that can generate attitudinally ambivalent responses.

Top-Down Processes

Value conflict is often cited as a chronic antecedent of ambivalence, and has received particular attention from the field of political science (e.g., Craig & Martinez, 2005a, 2005b). Values represent core general beliefs about such desirable ends as justice, courage, and humanity, around which specific attitudes can be structured.

However, because these values are construed in the broadest possible terms, it is plausible that they will overlap and generate conflict—attitudinal ambivalence—within the more specific attitudes attached to those values. Schwartz (1992) uses the examples of self-enhancement and self-transcendence on the one hand and openness to change and conservation on the other to illustrate this point. According to Schwartz, people may perceive conflict between the need to achieve and the need to be benevolent, as well as conflict between needing stimulation and needing stability. Given that values are conceptualized in the broadest possible terms, many people may experience chronic value conflict. Consequently, several authors have hypothesized a causal link between value conflict and attitudinal ambivalence (e.g., Katz & Hass, 1988). Yet, evidence to date is still lacking, largely because creating value conflict does not seem amenable to experimental test and because the breadth with which values are conceptualized rarely induces true conflict. For example, attitudes toward giving money to charity might be unipolar even if an individual does have the need to achieve and need to be benevolent because giving money to charity can be both a sign of achievement and benevolence (cf. Armitage & Conner, 2005). The evidence that does exist is not promising—in one recent correlational study, there was only a very small zero-order relationship between value conflict and ambivalence (Craig, Martinez, & Kane, 2005). Thus, although the idea of value conflict has much intuitive appeal, it seems unlikely that it will provide a full account of how attitudinal ambivalence arises (Armitage & Conner, 2005).

Another potential chronic influence on ambivalence is personality style. In support of this idea, Thompson and Zanna (1995) showed that individual levels of ambivalence on five different attitude objects converged, thereby implying individual differences in ambivalence. Moreover, Thompson and Zanna found that people high in need for cognition, who seek out, engage in, and gain satisfaction from cognitive tasks, were less likely to be ambivalent than people low in need for cognition. Also, people high in personal fear of invalidity, who are overconcerned with making costly mistakes, were more likely to be ambivalent than people low in personal fear of invalidity. However, the effect sizes associated with these correlations were only medium-to-large in the case of need for cognition and small-to-medium in the case of personal fear of invalidity, suggesting that at best, personality style can provide only a partial account of the effects of ambivalence. It is also worth noting that Thompson and Zanna's findings have yet to be replicated in other attitude objects. However, research into alternative measures of personality has also yielded relationships to ambivalence implying strong personality correlates of ambivalence may yet be found (e.g., Sparks, Conner, James, Shepherd, & Povey, 2006). That said, it is notable that personal involvement moderated the effects reported in Thompson and Zanna's (1995) study such that greater involvement with the attitude object augmented the relationships between need for cognition and ambivalence and between personal fear of invalidity and ambivalence. This moderating role of personal involvement implies that situation specific/bottom-up processes are likely to be crucial to understanding attitudinal ambivalence, and may even exert stronger effects than top-down processes.

In summary, there is as yet little evidence to suggest that attitudinal ambivalence is dispositional or chronic, and so it may be useful to examine how attitudinal ambivalence originates from environmental stimuli.

Bottom-Up Processes

In contrast to the mixed support for the top-down approach, there is increasing evidence that attitudinal ambivalence drives people's reactions to conflicting stimuli. The obvious place to start considering these bottom-up processes is with the attitude object itself. For example, people carrying condoms have been shown to be perceived as being promiscuous (negative valuation) and self-confident (positive valuation). Drawing on this idea, Dahl, Darke, Gorn, and Weinberg (2005) used the Mason Haire shopping list technique to examine the effects on person perception of having condoms versus not having condoms on the list. The technique involves asking participants to make judgments of an individual on the basis of his or her shopping list. As predicted, people whose shopping list included condoms were rated as both more positive and more negative relative to people whose list did not include condoms. Thus, condoms represent an attitude object that is likely to arouse ambivalence.

Dahl et al.'s (2005) study implies that some attitude objects are likely to arouse greater ambivalence than others, but what kinds of attitude objects are likely to arouse attitudinal ambivalence? Research that addresses this question directly is scarce and inconclusive. For example, Conner, Povey, Sparks, James, and Shepherd (1998) examined 12 health-risk and health-protective behaviors relevant to students and found large differences in the extent to which these different behaviors produced feelings of ambivalence. However, there was no discernible pattern to the data: Whereas drinking alcohol and eating a low-fat diet produced the highest degrees of ambivalence, taking the drug ecstasy and regularly eating breakfast produced the lowest levels of ambivalence.

A clear picture as to which attitude objects naturally elicit both positive and negative reactions has not yet emerged. However, some laboratory studies have successfully induced attitudinal ambivalence. One commonly used means to induce ambivalence in the laboratory has been through overjustification. People's intrinsic motivation is undermined when they are given excessive extrinsic rewards for an intrinsically rewarding task. This overjustification effect occurs because people attribute their performance on the task to extrinsic, rather than intrinsic factors (Deci, 1971). The effect, however, does not emerge in all situations. According to Crano and Sivacek's (1984) incentive-aroused ambivalence hypothesis, overjustification induces ambivalence because an unexpected reward simultaneously provokes positive and negative responses: Rewards are intrinsically positive, yet unexpected or unjustified rewards are perceived with some degree of negativity. Thus, rather than overjustification always leading to decrements in intrinsic motivation, the ambivalent reaction makes people prone to change, and this may or may not undermine intrinsic motivation. Consistent with this hypothesis, Crano, Gorenflo, and Shackelford (1988) showed that attitudes were more readily shifted when overjustification was induced. Although the fact that direct measures of ambivalence were not taken in the Crano et al. studies is a possible limitation, the incentive-aroused ambivalence hypothesis provides a compelling account of how ambivalence could be induced.

Another way in which ambivalence has been manipulated in the laboratory has been to present people with evaluatively consistent or evaluatively inconsistent information. For example, Jonas, Diehl, and Brömer (1997) presented participants with conflicting evaluative information about several cleaning products and successfully manipulated ambivalence. A key moderator of these effects seems to be salience of the evaluatively inconsistent information. The more salient the discrepancy, the more ambivalence is felt (see Newby-Clark et al., 2002). It is plausible, then, that Conner et al.'s (1998) failure to find clear patterns of ambivalence across multiple health behaviors might be ascribed to between-participant differences in the salience of the positive and negative conflict of each individual behavior. Future studies might therefore consider salience of the positive and negative poles as a key moderator of the effects of attitudinal ambivalence.

Beyond the laboratory, societal norms and social groups also provide potentially conflicting information. For example, Glick and Fiske's (1996, 2001) research on attitudes toward women revealed *ambivalent sexism*, in which both hostile and benevolent sexist attitudes were held simultaneously. The rationale behind ambivalent sexism is that across cultures, patriarchy is widespread (Eagly & Wood, 1999). According to the traditional view of sexism, this would imply that attitudes toward women are universally hostile. In fact, this is not the case. Glick, Fiske, and colleagues argue that it is possible to engage in benevolent sexism that subjectively feels benevolent, yet reinforces prejudice by, for example, restricting the kinds of professions women can engage in because women "need to be cherished" (Glick & Fiske, 2001). Ambivalent sexism is pervasive across cultures (Glick et al., 2000). Note, however, the benevolent sexism and hostile sexism scales are positively correlated, $r = .40$ to $.50$ in U.S. samples (Glick et al., 2000), indicating that ambivalent sexism does not necessarily arise within individuals, but that there are groups of individuals within society whose attitudes toward women are either benevolent *or* hostile. Ambivalent sexism may therefore occur on a societal level, rather than the individual level (cf. Glick & Fiske, 2001).

Societal and social norms, on the other hand, can have profound effects on ambivalence within the individual. For example, Mucchi-Faina, Costarelli, and Romoli (2002) argue that even relatively simple intergroup encounters can induce ambivalence because ambivalence arises as a means to manage reactions toward social groups. A general tendency for people to prefer in-group to out-group can conflict with other motivations, such as the norm of "fairness," creating ambivalence toward both in-group and out-group. To resolve the conflict, both in-group favoritism and out-group derogation may be minimized. Consistent with this analysis, Mucchi-Faina et al. (2002) found little difference in ambivalence toward the in-group versus the out-group. However, there was greater cognition-based ambivalence than affect-based ambivalence for both in-group and out-group, suggesting that emotional reactions are less likely to conform to societal norms. Thus, consideration of affect-based and cognition-based attitudes is warranted in future studies of ambivalence.

In a similar vein, Jost and Burgess (2000) make a distinction between group justification tendencies (i.e., evaluating in-group favorably) and system justification tendencies (i.e., endorsing superiority of higher status outgroups but also the "fairness" norm; cf. Mucchi-Faina et al., 2002). As predicted, people randomly allocated to the low status groups who accepted the "system" (i.e., that higher status outgroups are superior) felt more ambivalent about their in-group than did people randomly allocated to a higher status group. In other words, the system justification tendency shifted people's positive attitudes to their in-group, thereby creating ambivalence. In a second study, Jost and Burgess (2000) replicated the effects in naturally occurring status differences between men and women, and showed that the system-justifying belief in a just world and social dominance were positively related to women's ambivalence toward a female target, but negatively related to males' ambivalence to the same female target. Note how the findings from Jost and Burgess's (2000) second study map onto those of Glick and Fiske (2001). Thus, Jost and Burgess (2000) show that acceptance of the "system" by people in lower status groups increases ambivalence toward their in-group, but decreases ambivalence toward the in-group in high status group members. In other words, societal values (system justification tendencies) interact with group norms to produce ambivalence. From this perspective, it would be interesting to see whether social dominance orientation moderated these effects such that people in lower status groups with a stronger preference for hierarchy showed even greater ambivalence toward their in-group (e.g., Pratto, Sidanius, Stallworth, & Malle, 1994).

In sum, it seems that ambivalence can arise through exposure to several different kinds of bottom-up processes, including being presented with conflicting information, through overjustification processes, by exposure to an out-group, or by societal values. In contrast with the mixed evidence for top-down processes, this analysis implies that attitudinal ambivalence tends to arise through bottom-up processes. This view is consistent with Wilson and Hodge's (1992) attitudes-as-constructions model (see also Erber, Hodges, & Wilson, 1995; Zaller & Feldman, 1992), which advances the idea that attitudes are constructed on-the-spot as and when they are needed rather than being stored in memory (see Ajzen & Gilbert Cote, this volume).

CONSEQUENCES OF AMBIVALENCE

Ambivalence as a Dimension of Attitude Strength

A growing body of literature is concerned with the consequences of holding an ambivalent attitude. In much of this research, attitudinal ambivalence has been treated as a measure of attitude strength. Lower levels of ambivalence are associated with a stronger attitude. Although there have been several empirical studies of the interrelationship of attitude strength measures (e.g., Bassili, 1996; Eagly &

Chaiken, 1995; Jonas et al., 2000; Krosnick, Boninger, Chuang, Berent, & Carnot, 1993; Pomerantz, Chaiken, & Tordesillas, 1995; Prislin, 1996), the relationship of ambivalence to the full range of attitude strength measures remains under-researched. Ambivalence is found to be associated with lower accessibility of the attitude (Bargh, Chaiken, Govender, & Pratto, 1992; Brömer, 1998), lower attitude extremity (Maio, Bell, & Esses, 1996), and lower attitude certainty (Bassili, 1996; Jonas et al., 1997), but it is unrelated to evaluative-cognitive or evaluative-affective consistency (Maio et al., 1996). However, the relationship of ambivalence to other attitude strength dimensions such as attitude importance, knowledge, interest, involvement, and intensity remains an issue for further research. In addition, currently research has tended to examine each attitude strength correlate of attitudinal ambivalence only for single attitude objects or a small set of attitude objects; the relations across a range of attitude objects needs to be further examined.

If we consider attitudinal ambivalence as a dimension of attitude strength then we might anticipate four consequences of holding an ambivalent attitude (Converse, 1995, p. xi; Krosnick & Petty, 1995). Ambivalence affects:

1. the temporal stability of attitudes,
2. the pliability of attitudes,
3. information processing, and
4. the relationship of attitudes to behavior.

A number of authors have investigated the effects of attitudinal ambivalence in relation to each of these consequences, although the evidence in support of each effect varies considerably (see Conner & Sparks, 2002 for a review).

Ambivalence and Attitude Stability

A variety of studies have demonstrated the temporal stability of strong attitudes. Indeed a number of authors have argued that attitude stability is the factor all attitude strength measures hold in common (Ajzen, 1996; Doll & Ajzen, 1992; Erber et al., 1995). Other research with intentions (e.g., Conner, Sheeran, Norman, & Armitage, 2000; Sheeran, Orbell, & Trafimow, 1999) and personality constructs (e.g., Biesanz, West, & Graziano, 1998) has noted the importance of temporal stability as a measure of the strength of a psychological construct. On this view, attitudes high in ambivalence would represent 'weak' attitudes, with lower temporal stability compared to attitudes low in ambivalence.

Several studies have tested this prediction. For example, Bargh et al. (1992) showed that respondents who gave the same evaluation to an attitude object at two time points tended to have less ambivalent attitudes than those who did not give the same evaluation. Bassili (1996) reported contrasting results; ambivalence was unrelated to stability for attitudes toward introducing quotas or toward pornography. Armitage and Conner (2000, study 1) examined the impact of ambivalence on the stability of attitudes toward eating a low fat diet over three time points in a sample of hospital workers. Potential ambivalence was assessed using a split semantic differential measure (see Figure 12.1), whereas attitudes were assessed three times using a reliable multi-item bipolar semantic differential measure. Three comparisons were possible, with time intervals of 3, 5, or 8 months between attitude measurement. The extent to which ambivalence moderated the degree of attitude stability was investigated in two ways. First, a within-subjects correlation measure of attitude stability was computed. Across respondents, this measure of the attitudinal stability was unrelated to ambivalence. Second, the authors attempted to discount any problems attributable to error variance by computing measures of attitude stability based on between-subject correlations disattenuated for measurement error. In this analysis, correlations were computed separately for the high and low ambivalence groups. In general, the degree of attitude stability was high (*mean disattenuated r* = .71), although, as might have been expected, stability was inversely related to the time interval between measurements. In no case did the differences reach significance, although they were in the predicted direction (i.e., less stability in the high ambivalence group) for comparisons over the longer time intervals.

Using a panel survey of Florida voters from 1999, Craig et al. (2005) investigated the effects of ambivalence on the temporal stability of attitudes toward abortion. Consistent with the idea that attitudinal ambivalence is an index of attitude strength, univalent attitudes exhibited greater temporal stability than ambivalent attitudes, and these effects remained even when the contributions of other dimensions of attitude strength, including importance, certainty, intensity, and commitment, were statistically controlled. Interestingly, Craig et al. (2005) also showed that framing exerted powerful effects on attitudes toward legal abortion. Both attitudes and attitudinal ambivalence associated with legal abortion were dependent on whether the procedure was presented as being elective (i.e., the woman does not want more children) or whether the circumstances were traumatic (i.e., rape, birth defect). In effect, whether abortion is presented as occurring in elective or traumatic circumstances produces different attitudes and ambivalence, and these had relatively little overlap. Even people with stable attitudes with respect to abortion in traumatic circumstances did not necessarily have stable attitudes toward abortion in elective conditions.

Consistent with Craig et al.'s conclusion that the effects of ambivalence on attitude stability are consistent across contexts, if not within individuals, Fournier (2005) examined the role of ambivalence across a variety of political contexts and in several election years. Specifically, the effect of ambivalence on temporal stability was examined for 11 decisions, measured in nine surveys conducted in the United States, UK, and Canada. Even controlling for the effects of such variables as strength of opinion and issue importance, the findings were remarkably consistent: The voting preferences of individuals who were ambivalent were less predictable than those of individuals who held univalent attitudes. The generalizability of these results is further enhanced by the fact that the magnitude of the effects was replicated across the different decisions, surveys, and countries.

Thus, research provides somewhat mixed support for the predicted impact of ambivalence on attitude stability. Larger-scale survey research, particularly on political attitudes, appears more likely to show that ambivalence significantly attenuates the stability of attitudes. It is not clear whether this is attributable to the modest effect size, which is detectable only in large studies, or that only particular attitude objects produce sufficient variation in ambivalence to affect attitude stability.

Ambivalence and Attitude Pliability

More ambivalent attitudes are expected to be more susceptible to the influence of a persuasive communication (i.e., more pliable). For example, Eagly and Chaiken (1995) argue that, "attitudes are strong to the extent that they may be well embedded in an existing attitudinal structure" (p. 414). Thus strong attitudes are held to be more securely "anchored" in knowledge structures. Given that ambivalent attitudes are based on conflicting evaluations and inconsistent information, they should be more weakly anchored and hence more pliable than univalent attitudes. Only a few studies have investigated this prediction. Bassili (1996) tested the pliability of attitudes towards three attitude objects in the face of persuasive messages. Pliability was found to be significantly related to ambivalence for two attitude objects, but not for a third (see also Pomerantz et al., 1995). MacDonald and Zanna (1998) showed individuals high in (cross-dimensional) ambivalence about a particular social group to be more susceptible to a priming manipulation in terms of their judgment about that group. Maio, Esses, and Bell (2000) found an interaction between strength of message and ambivalence on attitudes towards residents of Hong Kong, such that only in the high ambivalence group did message strength produce differential effects on attitude change.

Armitage and Conner (2000, study 2) used a simple pre-post quasi-experimental design to investigate this effect. Attitudes and levels of ambivalence toward eating a low fat diet were assessed at baseline. Five months later, participants were randomly assigned to either an attitude change or control condition and received experimental materials designed either to change attitudes or provide information only. Both sets of intervention materials included UK Government recommendations on dietary fat intake, epidemiological data on population levels of fat intake, and a description of sources of fat in the diet. The experimental intervention also included a section designed to change individual attitudes (Armitage & Conner, 2002). Based on Fishbein and Ajzen's (1975) model of belief-attitude relations, persuasive information was created to target five beliefs about eating a low fat diet that had been shown previously to distinguish between those who did and did not intend to eat a low fat diet (Armitage & Conner, 1999). The experimental and control groups did not differ at baseline on the attitude measures. The groups were split into higher and lower levels of ambivalence to test the prediction that less ambivalent attitudes are more resistant to change. Attitudes became more positive across both intervention conditions, although the change was greater in the experimental group. Of particular interest was the three-way interaction between condition, ambivalence, and time. This only approached significance, but examination of the effects of the intervention demonstrated that it had differential effects in the two ambivalence groups. For the lower ambivalence group, there was no difference between the control and experimental conditions, whereas attitudes became significantly more positive following the experimental intervention for the higher ambivalence group. The attitude intervention had significantly more impact on more ambivalent attitudes, supporting the pliability prediction.

Another aspect of the relationship between ambivalence and attitude pliability is examined in research on individuals' reactions to persuasive influences from members of their group (i.e., consensus influence). As would be expected, individuals with ambivalent attitudes appear to be especially susceptible to consensus influence. Hodson, Maio, and Esses (2001) showed that of nine attitude properties examined, only ambivalence significantly moderated the effects of consensus information on the final attitude towards social welfare. Those higher in ambivalence were more likely to change their attitudes to be more consistent with the expressed views of their peers. Other research, however, shows that highly ambivalent individuals often carefully scrutinize relevant information (Jonas et al., 1997; Maio et al., 1996), sometimes picking out flaws in the messages, and ultimately, forming more *negative* attitudes. Maio, Haddock, Watt, and Hewstone (in press) demonstrated this type of 'backfire' effect when antiracism messages were presented to people who were highly ambivalent toward ethnic minority groups. Work on response amplification shows how ambivalence toward social targets is important because of its role in forming social perceptions (Bell & Esses, 1997, 2002; Maio, Greenland, Bernard, & Esses, 2001) and regulating social relations. For example, Bell and Esses (1997) showed that only those high in ambivalence toward native peoples differed in their responses toward such groups depending on mood. Bell and Esses (2002) demonstrated that this response amplification is motivated by ambivalence reduction.

In summary, the evidence to date generally supports the idea that ambivalent attitudes tend to be more pliable in the face of persuasive messages compared to nonambivalent attitudes. Nevertheless, confirmation of this effect across a more diverse range of attitude objects would be useful, as would examination of the extent to which both potential and felt ambivalence produce similar effects.

The Impacts of Ambivalence on Information Processing

Attitudes characterized by higher levels of ambivalence are assumed to be less likely to guide processing of information about the attitude object because of their lower accessibility. Several studies found evidence that highly ambivalent (vs. univalent) attitudes are less accessible (Bargh et al., 1992; Bassili, 1996; Broemer, 1998; see Jonas et al., 2000 for a review). Reasoning that individuals with ambivalent attitudes (vs. those with nonambivalent attitudes) would take longer to integrate information into an overall attitude judgment, van der Pligt, de Vries, Manstead, and van Harreveld (2000) showed that highly ambivalent individuals had longer response latencies across three different attitude objects (see also van Harreveld, van der Pligt, de Vries, Wenneker, & Verhue, 2004). Additional research appears to support the idea that higher levels of ambivalence lead to a more systematic processing of attitude-relevant information (Hanze, 2001). Presumably, an ambivalent attitude is weaker than a nonambivalent attitude and so is less likely to produce biased processing in favor of attitude-consistent information. In support of this idea, Maio et al. (1996) showed that higher levels of ambivalence about a minority group resulted in more systematic processing of information about that group. Similarly, Broemer (1998) showed that only individuals lower in ambivalence showed a preference for attitude-congruent information in processing messages about European Monetary Union. Nordgren, van Harreveld, and van der Pligt (2006) showed that higher levels of ambivalence produced both more negative emotions and generated more one-sided thoughts designed to resolve the ambivalence. Broemer (2002) argued that ambivalence produces a bias toward preferring negative information and so ambivalent individuals should be more persuaded by negatively framed messages. In three of five studies on health behaviors, ambivalent individuals exhibited greater attitude change when faced with negatively framed messages, whereas nonambivalent individuals were more persuaded by positively framed messages. Jonas et al. (1997) suggest that the mediating mechanism for the effects of ambivalence on information processing is confidence in one's attitude: high ambivalence produces a reduction in confidence in one's attitude, which in turn leads to more systematic processing of information.

Extending this research to the political arena, McGraw and Bartels (2005) examined attitudes toward the U.S. Congress, President, and Supreme Court. At the time of data collection (1997), prevailing attitudes toward Congress were negative, suggesting that ambivalence could be created by providing positive information. In contrast, prevailing attitudes toward the President and the Supreme Court were largely positive, meaning that negative information was more likely to create ambivalence. Thus, ambivalence toward Congress was associated with more positive general political orientations, such as a greater propensity to seek positive information, whereas ambivalence toward the Supreme Court and the President was linked to more negative political orientations (e.g., disaffection for the political system). McGraw and Bartels (2005) argue that greater levels of ambivalence toward Congress and the increased levels of positive cognitive consequences associated with congressional ambivalence led to less uncertainty, more attention to politics, and greater differentiation in evaluative judgments. The same effects, however, were not observed in relation to presidential or Supreme Court ambivalence. These findings are important because the initial valence of prevailing attitudes has rarely been taken into account in work of this kind.

In summary, a number of studies suggest impacts of ambivalence on information processing, although they are not always consistent with the view of ambivalent attitudes being weaker attitudes.

Ambivalence and the Attitude–Behavior Relationship

A key prediction for a measure of attitude strength is that strong attitudes should be more likely to guide behavior than weak attitudes (Converse, 1995, p. xi; Krosnick & Petty, 1995, p. 3). As Schwartz (1978) noted, an attitude assessed at one time is unlikely to predict behavior at a later time if the attitude does not persist over the intervening time interval. Fishbein and Ajzen (1975) make a similar observation in relation to the impact of intentions on behavior (Conner et al., 2000). Some researchers (e.g., Erber et al., 1995) have argued that the greater impact of strong attitudes on behavior is solely attributable to strong attitudes' temporal stability. However, other mechanisms also may influence strong attitudes' effects on behavior. For example, Fazio (1986, 1995) has argued that attitudes influence behavior in part by shaping our perceptions of the world (the automatic activation effect). That is, the capacity of an attitude to predict behavior is partly dependent on the attitude's ability to bias perceptions of the attitude object, and the context in which the behavior is performed. Strong attitudes are assumed to be more readily accessible and so more likely to produce these biasing effects. One therefore might expect univalent attitudes to be more capable of automatic activation and thus more predictive of behavior than ambivalent attitudes.

Using models such as the Theory of Reasoned Action (Fishbein & Ajzen, 1975), which posits that intentions mediate the relationship between attitudes and behavior, researchers have examined the moderating impact of ambivalence on attitude–intention–behavior relationships (Armitage & Conner, 2004). In early examinations of this relationship, Moore (1973, 1980) demonstrated lower consistency between attitudes and behavior for those high (vs. low) in attitudinal ambivalence. However, this moderation effect is more accurately described as influencing the relationship between past behavior and attitude because measures of attitude and behavior were taken cross-sectionally. A number of studies have replicated the moderating effects of ambivalence on attitude–intention relationships cross-sectionally for such behaviors as eating a low fat diet (Armitage & Conner, 2000), smoking cessation (Lipkus, Green, Feaganes, & Sedikides, 2001), and following a vegetarian diet (Berndsen & van der Pligt, 2004). Two studies by Conner et al. (2002) examined the effects of attitudinal ambivalence on food intake prospectively and used a validated nutrition measure to obtain details about dietary intake. Study 1 tested the attitude–behavior relationship across one month and Study 2 examined the attitude–behavior relationship across three months. Consistent with predictions, both studies showed that lower levels of attitudinal ambivalence were associated with attitudes that were more predictive of behavior, and these findings remained when the effects of past behavior were statistically controlled (Conner et al., 2002, Study 2). Ambivalence moderated the attitude–behavior change relationship.

Armitage and Conner (2000, Study 1) extended these findings by controlling for the effects of behavioral intentions. The target behavior was eating a low-fat diet. This study used structural equation modeling to control the effects of measurement error. Ambivalence was measured with a split semantic differential scale, which was used to divide the sample into higher and lower ambivalence groups. A model was then fitted to the two groups with structural paths from attitude to intentions, from attitude to behavior, and from intentions to behavior allowed to vary. As we were interested in the relationship between the latent constructs (attitude, intentions, and behavior), the model was constrained such that the factor loadings for each construct were equal in the two groups (the factor loading constraint model). This allowed for direct comparisons between the regression paths for the higher and lower ambivalence groups. As predicted, the path from attitude to intention was stronger in the lower compared to the higher ambivalence group. Also as predicted, the path from attitude to behavior was stronger in the lower compared to the higher ambivalence group. These effects were present despite any evidence that ambivalence influenced attitude stability in the same data.

Importantly, not only were the effects on behavior tested across an eight-month time period, but the analyses also controlled for the effects of behavioral intention. The latter finding is of particular interest because it suggests that sufficiently univalent attitudes can by-pass intentions. This finding would is inconsistent with such models as the theory of planned behavior, which regard behavioral intentions as complete mediators of the attitude–behavior relationship (Ajzen, 1991; Ajzen & Gilbert Cote, this volume). The implication is that attitudes can be directly predictive of behavior when they are univalent; however, when attitudes are ambivalent, behavior is determined by other variables such as behavioral intentions.

A further issue in examining the moderating effects of ambivalence on the attitude–behavior relationship is the potential confound between ambivalence and attitude extremity: Univalent attitudes tend to be more extreme than ambivalent attitudes. For example, Krosnick et al. (1993) reported a correlation of $-.90$ between ambivalence and attitude extremity (see also Thompson et al., 1995) and independent manipulations of attitude extremity have been shown to increase attitude–behavior correspondence from $r = .19$ to $r = .85$ (Kallgren & Wood, 1986). Conner, Povey, Sparks, James, and Shepherd (2003) explicitly controlled for the potential confound between ambivalence and extremity of attitudes. Moreover, rather than focusing solely on between-participants analyses, Conner et al. (2003) also examined the moderating effects of ambivalence within participants by examining attitudes toward twenty healthy eating behaviors (e.g., eating a healthy breakfast, eating food containing vitamins). The within-person analyses allowed for a more focused examination of the behavioral decision-making process than traditional between-persons analyses, which assume that what a person does is best described in relation to others. Both forms of analyses produced consistent results: ambivalence moderated the attitude–behavior relationship such that greater ambivalence was associated with attenuated attitude–behavior relations. These findings are important because within- and between-persons analyses are independent, yet similar findings emerged even in the presence of alternative sources of variation (Conner et al., 2003). In summarizing these effects, Armitage and Conner (2004) estimated that across studies, the frequency-weighted correlation showed this effect of ambivalence to be substantial, with more ambivalent attitudes being less strongly correlated with behavior assessed prospectively, $r = .40$ vs. $.53$.

In summary, there appears to be fairly consistent evidence that ambivalence moderates the attitude–behavior relationship, such that higher levels of ambivalence are related to weaker relationships. It also appears that such effects are not attributable purely to temporal stability. It also appears that this moderating effect of ambivalence is not merely due to ambivalence being confounded with attitude extremity (Conner et al., 2003). Even more convincing evidence on the latter point is provided by Priester and Petty (2001), who compared safe sex behaviors of a low and a high ambivalence group, and found that ambivalence moderated the attitude–behavior relationship in the expected direction. In their analysis of respondents who expressed the most positive (extreme) attitudes, low ambivalent respondents were significantly more likely to report performing the behavior than high ambivalence respondents, despite being identical on attitude extremity.

Relatedly, research also has explored the impact of ambivalence on the relationship between intentions and behavior. For example, Conner et al. (1998) showed that ambivalence increased the relationship between intentions and use of the drug ecstasy. In contrast, Armitage and Conner (2000) reported that ambivalence decreased the impact of intentions on consumption of a low fat diet. Interestingly Sparks, Harris, and Lockwood (2004) also reported that increasing levels of ambivalence (assessed using a belief heterogeneity measure) significantly reduced the relationship between intentions and objectively assessed use of a health club. Further research is required to elucidate the factors governing the effect of ambivalence on the intention–behavior relationship (see Armitage & Conner, 2004 for further data and discussion).

Previous research on ambivalence as a moderator of attitude–behavior relationships can also be criticized for failing to employ objective measures of behavior in examining the moderating effects of ambivalence. However, Dormandy, Hankins, and Marteau (2006) reported that potential ambivalence significantly moderated the relationship between attitudes and objectively assessed behavior (uptake of a screening test based on medical records) in a sample of women. The attitude–behavior correlation was substantially stronger in the lower ambivalence compared to the higher ambivalence women ($r = .58$ vs $.27$). Thus, it seems unlikely that previous demonstrations of the moderating effect of ambivalence are attributable to biases in self-reports of behavior. It would be useful to manipulate ambivalence experimentally and observe the impact on the attitude–behavior relationship while controlling for attitude extremity and employing objective measures of behavior. Such experimental tests are required to establish a causal link between the induction of ambivalence and the attenuation of the attitude–behavior relationship.

As evident from this review, there is strong support for the idea that univalent attitudes are stronger than ambivalent attitudes (Krosnick & Petty, 1995). However, there are some weaknesses in the data collected to date that limit generalizability of these findings. We have already noted how only a modest number of these studies employ objectively measured behavior. If "thinking is for doing" as Fiske (1992) proposes, then it is important to confirm whether the ambivalence that people experience in relation to a range of objects translates into behavior. Similarly, it would be valuable to control for a greater range of potential confounding variables, most notably other indices of attitude strength (beyond extremity of attitudes). In addition, the generality of the moderation effect across different behaviors still needs to be established and demonstrated experimentally. For example, Jonas et al. (1997) and Maio et al. (1996) suggest that under certain circumstances, ambivalence can lead to stronger attitude–behavior relationships. Finally, it should be noted that the majority of these effects are found with measures of *potential* ambivalence. The extent to which such effects are similar for *felt* ambivalence remains to be demonstrated.

Other Work on Consequences of Ambivalence

Although considering ambivalence as a facet of attitude strength provides a useful framework for discussing a considerable portion of the work on ambivalence, a number of other studies examining the consequences of ambivalence (e.g., the direct vs. moderated effect of ambivalence on attitudes, intentions and behavior) do not easily fit within such a view. Rather than treating ambivalence as a moderator of attitude–behavior relationships a series of studies has treated ambivalence as a direct predictor of behavior change. Usually, such studies use measures of felt ambivalence. Such ideas are based on theories of behavior change, which suggest that increasing feelings of ambivalence may be psychologically uncomfortable (i.e., like dissonance) and so help motivate behavior change so as to reduce ambivalence. Consistent with this view, some studies have shown ambivalence to peak in individuals trying to change, compared to those either performing or not performing the behavior (Armitage & Arden, in press; Armitage, Povey, & Arden, 2003). Similarly, Lipkus et al. (2004) showed that felt ambivalence about smoking was significantly related to a desire to quit smoking in both cross-sectional and prospective samples. Costarelli and Colloca (2004) showed similar effects for ambivalence and proenvironmental intentions. Although promising, none of the studies has demonstrated that inducing ambivalence actually promotes behavior change.

In work on political attitudes, Lavine and Steenbergen (2005) argue that American public opinion often is rooted in attitudes toward particular social groups that are strongly associated with either liberal or conservative ideals. Using data from the 2000 American National Election Study, a measure of group ambivalence was derived from feelings about liberal groups (e.g., labor unions, Democrats) and conservative groups (e.g., Christian Fundamentalists, big business). In analyses controlling for a range of variables, including the effects of ambivalence toward political parties and candidates, and ideologically inconsistent group feelings, Lavine and Steenbergen (2005) reported that ambivalence toward social groups affected voters' choices involving policies, political predispositions, and candidates. More importantly, group ambivalence also was associated with differences in variables closely related to voter behavior. For example, even after controlling for the effects of ambivalence toward the candidates, people who were high in group ambivalence made later voting decisions, had less stable attitudes toward candidates, and were more likely to vote for different parties in Presidential and Congressional elections. That is, people with opposed or "consistent" attitudes to liberal and conservative groups exhibit more predictable voter behavior, whereas people who like social groups on both the left and right of the political divide make up their minds later, have unstable attitudes toward the candidates, and rely much less on the relevant issues in making their voting choice.

FUTURE DIRECTIONS FOR RESEARCH ON AMBIVALENCE

Whilst our review has shown considerable progress in understanding the ramifications of ambivalence, particularly in relation to some of its important consequences, we believe that a number of areas are worthy of further research attention. We would highlight three such key areas for research. The first is the need to further explore the *interrelationship* of felt and potential ambivalence measures. A second, related, issue is the relationship between well used measures of ambivalence, such as those based on split semantic differential measures, to other less well used measures. The third issue is concerned with the conditions under which ambivalence arises.

Felt versus Potential Ambivalence

Newby-Clark et al. (2005) provided an interesting examination of felt and potential measures of ambivalence: The "felt" approach asks people to infer and self-report their ambivalence, whereas the "potential" approach derives a measure of ambivalence from the attitude judgment process or its outcomes. As we noted earlier, generally the two are found to be only moderately related (r = .45; Riketta, submitted). Consistent with the idea that mere conflict is not sufficient to infer ambivalence, Newby-Clark et al. (2005) argue that accessibility is an important moderator of ambivalence effects, and this might explain why felt ambivalence often is only moderately correlated with potential ambivalence. More specifically, they extend the idea that the accessibility of attitudes is an important determinant of action per se by proposing that simultaneous accessibility of the positive and negative poles associated with an attitude object may be a key moderator of the relationship between felt ambivalence and potential ambivalence. This line of research taps into cognitive dissonance theory by showing that awareness of conflicted attitudes creates aversive emotional states, which people try to reduce or eliminate through processes such as suppression, distraction, or compensatory conviction (see Stone & Fernandez, this volume). Newby-Clark et al. (2005) prefer the idea of self-distraction to resolution of the conflict because they argue that changing attitudes on such value-related topics as abortion or capital punishment is likely to involve greater cognitive resources than people are likely to be willing to allocate.

Holbrook and Krosnick (2005) have extended this work by examining the structural properties of measures of felt and potential ambivalence and their consequences in the domains of abortion and capital punishment. In general, this work shows that indices designed to tap potential and felt ambivalence represent distinct constructs and, more importantly, that the two indices have different consequences for cognition and behavior. For example, whereas felt ambivalence was related to less reported interest in learning issue-relevant information, a stronger false consensus effect, and less perceived hostile media bias, greater potential ambivalence was uniquely associated with increased reports of general activism. In contrast, felt and potential ambivalence shared two consequences in common: Both were negatively related to resistance to persuasion, and both were associated with a reduced tendency to use candidates' issue positions to evaluate them. This pattern of findings was interpreted as evidence for two distinct routes by which felt and potential ambivalence exert their effects. Discomfort and the desire to reduce discomfort were hypothesized to underpin the effects of felt ambivalence. Accordingly, Holbrook and Krosnick provide evidence to suggest that people high in felt ambivalence avoid stimuli that bring their discomfort to mind. In contrast, the perception of attitude-relevant information was posited as the means by which potential ambivalence works. Presumably, because people high in potential ambivalence are aware of a range of positively and negatively valenced information, persuasive communications are likely to be interpreted as being consistent with their own attitudes, thus making their attitudes more pliable.

Given that accumulated research suggests that potential ambivalence may exist without conscious awareness, it seems plausible that potential ambivalence causes felt ambivalence. In a test of this hypothesis, Holbrook and Krosnick (2005) found that felt ambivalence failed to fully mediate the effects of potential ambivalence on resistance to persuasion, activism, information gathering, perceived consensus, perceived media bias, contents of candidate evaluations, and false consensus. The implication is that the effects of felt and potential ambivalence are independent and may have different antecedents. From a theoretical perspective, more work is needed to identify the antecedents of potential and felt ambivalence; from an applied perspective, researchers need to be cognizant of these differences between potential and felt ambivalence when choosing measures for their studies (see Priester & Petty, 2001).

Other Measures of Ambivalence

In addition to the different aspects of intra-component ambivalence, there also are likely to be discrepancies between the components of attitude, or intercomponent ambivalence (e.g., Maio et al., 2000). Intercomponent ambivalence refers to conflict between components; for example, when a large cream cake is simultaneously evaluated as "nice" (affective, positive) but "fattening" (cognitive, negative). For example, MacDonald and Zanna (1998) found that cross-dimensionally ambivalent men tended to rate their admiration for feminists as being positive, but their affection for them negatively; these men were also more likely to be influenced by unconscious priming. In other words, discrepancies between components of attitudes made attitudes weaker. To date, however, the vast majority of research into ambivalence has treated inter- and intracomponent ambivalence as being mutually exclusive: one goal for future research is to redress this balance. This suggestion is not trivial: studies that have examined intracomponent ambivalence have not controlled for the potential effects of intercomponent ambivalence. This is important because it seems likely that intercomponent ambivalence will exert a powerful effect on intracomponent ambivalence (cf. Maio et al., 2000). This might provide a further explanation for inconsistencies between the studies of intracomponent ambivalence reviewed above.

A number of studies have employed measures of ambivalence based on the degree of heterogeneity of beliefs underlying an attitude (computed in a number of different ways). For example, we have noted Sparks et al.'s (2004) work showing that such a measure moderated the intention–behavior relationship. Armitage (2003) showed that such a measure moderated the attitude–behavior relationship and that a manipulation of belief heterogeneity reduced the attitude–intention relationship. Further research on the impact of belief heterogeneity on measures of felt and potential ambivalence are warranted.

In addition to the above measures of ambivalence that focus on cognitive conflicts or cognitive-affective conflicts, other researchers have focused on emotional ambivalence based on conflicting feelings about an attitude object. Citrin and Luks's (2005) work focused on Americans' emotional reactions toward their own country. Using the 1996 General Social Survey, they examined citizens' emotional ambivalence toward the United States. There were four key findings. First, many more people reported emotional ambivalence toward the United States than expected, given the apparently prevailing backdrop of patriotic feelings. Second, emotional ambivalence did not differ across demographic lines, with people of different political persuasions, genders, ages, income levels, and ethnicities reporting similar levels of ambivalence. Third, even Americans who reported identifying strongly with their country sometimes also reported emotional ambivalence: the national identity–ambivalence correlation was modest. Fourth, although ambivalence was negatively related to patriotism, the strength of the relationship was unexpectedly modest. Interestingly, emotional ambivalence did not affect negative attitudes toward foreigners or in-group favoritism.

Recent work by Petty and colleagues has suggested that the current conceptions of ambivalence examined here could be further extended to include implicit ambivalence (i.e., conflicts between a newly formed attitude and an old, replaced attitude; Petty, 2006; Petty, Tormala, Briñol, & Jarvis, 2006). Clearly further research could usefully examine the interrelationships of these different types and measures of ambivalence. Work on both antecedents and consequences of different measures is required. However, studies such as the majority of research reviewed here can only take us so far. What is required are good manipulations of different forms of ambivalence. Such manipulations might attempt to change different forms of ambivalence directly, and examine consequences, or use the interesting approach suggested by Newby-Clark et al. (2002) in considering manipulations that change the relationship between different measures of ambivalence.

REFERENCES

Ajzen, I. (1991). The theory of planned behavior. *Organizational Behavior and Human Decision Processes, 50,* 179–211.

Ajzen, I. (1996). The directive influence of attitudes on behavior. In P. M. Gollwitzer & J. A. Bargh (Eds.), *Psychology of action* (pp. 385–403). New York: Guilford.

Armitage, C. J. (2003). Beyond attitudinal ambivalence: Effects of belief homogeneity on attitude–intention-behaviour relations. *European Journal of Social Psychology, 33,* 551–563.

Armitage, C. J., & Arden, M. A. (2007). Felt and potential ambivalence across the stages of change. *Journal of Health Psychology, 12,* 149–158.

Armitage, C. J., & Conner, M. (1999). Distinguishing perceptions of control from self-efficacy: Predicting consumption of a low fat diet using the theory of planned behavior. *Journal of Applied Social Psychology, 29,* 72–90.

Armitage, C. J., & Conner, M. (2000). Attitudinal ambivalence: A test of three key hypotheses. *Personality and Social Psychology Bulletin, 26,* 1421–1432.

Armitage, C. J., & Conner, M. (2002). Reducing fat intake: Interventions based on the theory of planned behaviour. In D. Rutter & L. Quine (Eds.), *Changing health behaviour: Intervention and research with social cognition models* (pp. 87–104). Buckingham, UK: Open University Press.

Armitage, C. J., & Conner, M. (2004). The effects of attitudinal ambivalence on attitude-intention-behavior relations. In G. Haddock & G. R. Maio (Eds.), *Contemporary perspectives on the psychology of attitudes* (pp. 121–143). Hove, UK: Psychology Press.

Armitage, C. J., & Conner, M. (2005). Attitudinal ambivalence and political opinion: Review and avenues for further research. In S. C. Craig & M. D. Martinez (Eds.), *Ambivalence, politics, and public policy* (pp. 145–184). New York: Palgrave Macmillan.

Armitage, C. J., Povey, R., & Arden, M. A. (2003). Evidence for discontinuity patterns across the stages of change: A role for attitudinal ambivalence. *Psychology and Health, 18,* 373–386.

Bargh, J. A., Chaiken, S., Govender, R., & Pratto, F. (1992). The generality of the automatic attitude activation effect. *Journal of Personality and Social Psychology, 62,* 893–912.

Bassili, J. N. (1996). Meta-judgmental versus operative indexes of psychological attributes: The case of measures of attitude strength. *Journal of Personality and Social Psychology, 71,* 637–653.

Bell, D. W., & Esses, V. M. (1997). Ambivalence and response amplification toward native peoples. *Journal of Applied Social Psychology, 27,* 1063–1084.

Bell, D. W., & Esses, V. M. (2002). Ambivalence and response amplification: A motivational perspective. *Personality and Social Psychology Bulletin, 28,* 1143–1152.

Berndsen, M., & van der Pligt, J. (2004). Ambivalence towards meat. *Appetite, 42,* 71–78.

Biesanz, J. C., West, S. G., & Graziano, W. G. (1998). Moderators of self-other agreement: Reconsidering temporal stability in personality. *Journal of Personality and Social Psychology, 75,* 467–477.

Breckler, S. J. (1994). A comparison of numerical indices for measuring attitudinal ambivalence. *Educational and Psychological Measurement, 54,* 350–365.

Broemer, P. (1998). Ambivalent attitudes and information processing. *Swiss Journal of Psychology, 57,* 225–234.

Broemer, P. (2002). Relative effectiveness of differently framed health messages: The influence of ambivalence. *European Journal of Social Psychology, 32,* 685–703.

Citrin, J., & Luks, S. (2005). Patriotic to the core? American ambivalence about America. In S. C. Craig & M. D. Martinez (Eds.), *Ambivalence and the structure of political opinion* (pp. 127–148). New York: Palgrave Macmillan.

Conner, M., Povey, R., Sparks, P., James, R., & Shepherd, R. (1998). Understanding dietary choice and dietary change: Contributions from social psychology. In A. Murcott (Ed.), *The nation's diet: The social science of food choice* (pp. 43–56). London: Longman.

Conner, M., Povey, R., Sparks, P., James, R., & Shepherd, R. (2003). Moderating role of attitudinal ambivalence within the theory of planned behaviour. *British Journal of Social Psychology, 42,* 75–94.

Conner, M., Sheeran, P., Norman, P., & Armitage, C. J. (2000). Temporal stability as a moderator of relationships in the theory of planned behaviour. *British Journal of Social Psychology, 39,* 469–493.

Conner, M., & Sparks, P. (2002). Ambivalence and attitudes. *European Review of Social Psychology, 12,* 37–70.

Conner, M., Sparks, P., Povey, R., James, R., Shepherd, R., & Armitage, C. J. (2002). Moderator effects of attitudinal ambivalence on attitude-behaviour relationships. *European Journal of Social Psychology, 32,* 705–718.

Converse, P. E. (1995). Foreword. In R. E. Petty & J. A. Krosnick (Eds.), *Attitude strength: Antecedents and consequences* (pp. xi–xvii). Hillsdale, NJ: Erlbaum.

Costarelli, S., & Colloca, P. (2004). The effects of attitudinal ambivalence on pro-environmental behavioural intentions. *Journal of Environmental Psychology, 24,* 279–288.

Craig, S. C., & Martinez, M. D. (2005a). *Ambivalence and the structure of political opinion.* New York: Palgrave Macmillan.

Craig, S. C., & Martinez, M. D. (2005b). *Ambivalence, politics, and public policy*. New York: Palgrave Macmillan.

Craig, S. C., Martinez, M. D., & Kane, J. G. (2005). Ambivalence and response instability: A panel study. In S. C. Craig & M. D. Martinez (Eds.), *Ambivalence and the structure of political opinion* (pp. 55–71). New York: Palgrave Macmillan.

Crano, W. D., Gorenflo, D. W., & Shackelford, S. L. (1988). Over-justification, assumed consensus, and attitude change—Further investigation of the incentive-aroused ambivalence hypothesis. *Journal of Personality and Social Psychology, 55*, 12–22.

Crano, W. D., & Sivacek, J. (1984). The influence of incentive-aroused ambivalence on over-justification effects in attitude change. *Journal of Experimental Social Psychology, 20*, 137–158.

Dahl, D. W., Darke, P. R., Gorn, G. J., & Weinberg, C. B. (2005). Promiscuous or confident? Attitudinal ambivalence toward condom purchase: *Journal of Applied Social Psychology, 35*, 869–887.

Deci, E. L. (1971). Effects of externally mediated rewards on intrinsic motivation. *Journal of Personality and Social Psychology, 18*, 105–115.

Doll, J., & Ajzen, I. (1992). Accessibility and stability of predictors in the theory of planned behavior. *Journal of Personality and Social Psychology, 63*, 754–765.

Dormandy, E., Hankins, M., & Marteau, T. M. (2006). Attitudes and uptake of a screening test: The moderating role of ambivalence. *Psychology and Health, 21*, 499–511.

Eagly, A. H., & Chaiken, S. (1993). *The psychology of attitudes*. Fort Worth, TX: Harcourt Brace Jovanovich.

Eagly, A. H., & Chaiken, S. (1995). Attitude strength, attitude structure, and resistance to change. In R. E. Petty & J. A. Krosnick (Eds.), *Attitude strength: Antecedents and consequences* (pp. 413–432). Mahwah, NJ: Erlbaum.

Eagly, A. H., & Wood, W. (1999). The origins of sex differences in human behavior— Evolved dispositions versus social roles. *American Psychologist, 54*, 408–423.

Eammons, R. A. (1996). Strivings and feeling: Personal goals and subjective well-being. In P. M. Gollwitzer & J. A. Bargh (Eds.), *The psychology of action: Linking cognition and motivation to behavior* (pp. 313–337). New York: Guilford.

Erber, M. W., Hodges, S. D., & Wilson, T. D. (1995). Attitude strength, attitude stability, and the effects of analyzing reasons. In R. E. Petty & J. A. Krosnick (Eds.), *Attitude strength: Antecedents and consequences* (pp. 433–454). Mahwah, NJ: Erlbaum.

Fazio, R.H. (1986). How do attitudes guide behavior? In R. M. Sorrentino & E. T. Higgins (Eds.), *Handbook of motivation and cognition: Foundations of social behavior* (Vol. 1, pp. 204–243). New York: Guilford.

Fazio, R.H. (1995). Attitudes as object-evaluation associations: Determinants, consequences, and correlates of attitude accessibility. In R. E. Petty & J. A. Krosnick (Eds.), *Attitude strength: Antecedents and consequences* (pp. 247–282). Mahwah, NJ: Erlbaum.

Festinger, L. (1957). *A theory of cognitive dissonance*. Stanford, CA: Stanford University Press.

Fishbein, M., & Ajzen, I. (1975). *Belief, attitude, intention and behavior: An introduction to theory and research*. Reading, MA: Addison-Wesley.

Fiske, S. T. (1992). Thinking is for doing—Portraits of social cognition from daguerreotype to laserphoto. *Journal of Personality and Social Psychology, 63*, 877–889.

Fournier, (2005). Ambivalence and attitude change in vote choice: Do campaign switchers experience internal conflict? In S. C. Craig & M. D. Martinez (Eds.), *Ambivalence, politics, and public policy* (pp. 27–46). New York: Palgrave Macmillan.

Gardner, P. L. (1987). Measuring ambivalence to science. *Journal of Research in Science Teaching, 24*, 241–247.

Glick, P., & Fiske, S. T. (1996). The ambivalent sexism inventory: Differentiating hostile and benevolent sexism. *Journal of Personality and Social Psychology, 70*, 491–512.

Glick, P., & Fiske, S. T. (2001). An ambivalent alliance—Hostile and benevolent sexism as complementary justifications for gender inequality. *American Psychologist, 56*, 109–118.

Glick, P., Fiske, S. T., Mladinic, A., Saiz, J. L., Abrams, D., Masser, B., et al. (2000). Beyond prejudice as simple antipathy: Hostile and benevolent sexism across cultures. *Journal of Personality and Social Psychology, 79*, 763–775.

Hanze, M. (2001). Ambivalence, conflict, and decision making: Attitudes and feelings in Germany towards NATO's military intervention in the Kosovo war. *European Journal of Social Psychology, 31*, 693–706.

Hodson, G., Maio, G. R., & Esses, V. M. (2001). The role of attitudinal ambivalence in susceptibility to consensus information. *Basic and Applied Social Psychology, 23*, 197–205.

Holbrook, A. L., & Krosnick, J. A. (2005). Meta-psychological versus operative measures of ambivalence: Differentiating the consequences of perceived intra-psychic conflicts and real intra-psychic conflict. In S. C. Craig & M. D. Martinez (Eds.), *Ambivalence, and the structure of polical opinion* (pp. 73–103). New York: Palgrave Macmillan.

Jonas, K., Brömer, P., & Diehl, M. (2000). Attitudinal ambivalence. *European Review of Social Psychology, 11*, 35–74.

Jonas, K., Diehl, M., & Brömer, P. (1997). Effects of attitudinal ambivalence on information processing and attitude–intention consistency. *Journal of Experimental Social Psychology, 33*, 190–210.

Jost, J. T., & Burgess, D. (2000). Attitudinal ambivalence and the conflict between group and system justification motives in low status groups. *Personality and Social Psychology Bulletin, 26*, 293–305.

Kallgren, C. A., & Wood, W. (1986). Access to attitude-relevant information in memory as a determinant of attitude-behavior consistency. *Journal of Experimental Social Psychology, 22*, 328–338.

Kaplan, K. J. (1972). On the ambivalence-indifference problem in attitude theory and measurement: A suggested modification of the semantic differential technique. *Psychological Bulletin, 77*, 361–372.

Katz, I., & Hass, R. G. (1988). Racial ambivalence and American value conflict: Correlational and priming studies of dual cognitive structures. *Journal of Personality and Social Psychology, 55*, 893–905.

Krosnick, J. A., Boninger, D. S., Chuang, Y. C., Berent, M. K., & Carnot, C. G. (1993). Attitude strength: One construct or many related constructs? *Journal of Personality and Social Psychology, 65*, 1132–1151.

Krosnick, J. A., & Petty, R. E. (1995). Attitude strength: An overview. In R. E. Petty & J. A. Krosnick (Eds.), *Attitude strength: Antecedents and consequences* (pp. 1–24). Mahwah, NJ: Erlbaum.

Lavine, H., & Steenberger (2005). Group ambivalence and electoral decision-making. In S. C. Craig & M. D. Martinez (Eds.), *Ambivalence, politics, and public policy* (pp. 1–26). New York: Palgrave Macmillan.

Lipkus, I. M., Green, J. D., Feaganes, J. R., & Sedikides, C. (2001). The relationship between attitudinal ambivalence and desire to quit smoking among college smokers. *Journal of Applied Social Psychology, 31*, 113–133.

Lipkus, I. M., Pollak, K. I., McBride, C. M., Schwartz-Bloom, R., Lyna, P., & Bloom, P. N. (2004). Assessing attitudinal ambivalence towards smoking and its association with desire to quit among teen smokers. *Psychology and Health, 20*, 373–387.

MacDonald, T. K., & Zanna, M. P. (1998). Cross-dimension ambivalence toward social groups: Can ambivalence affect intentions to hire feminists? *Personality and Social Psychology Bulletin, 24,* 427–441.

Maio, G. R., Bell, D. W., & Esses, V. M. (1996). Ambivalence and persuasion: The processing of messages about immigrant groups. *Journal of Experimental Social Psychology, 32,* 513–536.

Maio, G. R., Esses, V. M., & Bell, D. W. (2000). Examining conflict between components of attitudes: Ambivalence and inconsistency are distinct constructs. *Canadian Journal of Behavioral Science, 32,* 71–83.

Maio, G. R., Greenland, K., Bernard, M., & Esses, V. M. (2001). Effects of intergroup ambivalence on information processing: The role of physiological arousal. *Group Processes and Intergroup Relations, 4,* 355–372.

Maio, G. R., Haddock, G. G., Watt, S. E., & Hewstone, M. (in press). Implicit measures and applied contexts: An illustrative examination of anti-racism advertising. In R. E. Petty, R. H. Fazio, & P. Brinol (Eds.), *Attitudes: Insights from the new wave of implicit measures* (pp. ??). New York: Palgrave Macmillan.

McGraw, K.M., & Bartels, B. (2005). Ambivalence toward American political institutions: Sources and consequences. In S. C. Craig & M. D. Martinez (Eds.), *Ambivalence, and the structure of polical opinion* (pp. 105–126). New York: Palgrave Macmillan.

Moore, M. (1973). Ambivalence in attitude measurement. *Educational and Psychological Measurement, 33,* 481–483.

Moore, M. (1980). Validation of attitude toward any practice scale through use of ambivalence as a moderator. *Educational and Psychological Measurement, 40,* 205–208.

Mucchi-Faina, A., Costarelli, S., & Romoli, C. (2002). The effects of intergroup context of evaluation on ambivalence toward the ingroup and the outgroup. *European Journal of Social Psychology, 32,* 247–259.

Newby-Clark, I. R., McGregor, I., & Zanna, M. P. (2002). Thinking and caring about cognitive inconsistency: When and for whom does attitudinal ambivalence feel uncomfortable? *Journal of Personality and Social Psychology, 82,* 157–166.

Newby-Clark, I. R., McGregor, I., & Zanna, M. P. (2005). Ambivalence and accessibility: The consequences of accessible ambivalence. In S. C. Craig & M. D. Martinez (Eds.), *Ambivalence and the structure of political opinion* (pp. 33–53). New York: Palgrave Macmillan.

Nordgren, L.F., van Harreveld, F., & van der Pligt, J. (2006). Ambivalence, discomfort, and motivated information processing. *Journal of Experimental Social Psychology, 42,* 252–258.

Petty, R. E. (2006). A metacognitive model of attitudes. *Journal of Consumer Research, 33,* 22–24.

Petty, R. E., & Krosnick, J. A. (Eds.). (1995). *Attitude strength: Antecedents and consequences* (pp. 361–386). Mahwah, NJ: Erlbaum.

Petty, R. E., Tormala, Z. L., Brinol, P., & Jarvis, W. B. G. (2006). Implicit ambivalence from attitude change: An exploration of the PAST model. *Journal of Personality and Social Psychology, 90,* 21–41.

Pomerantz, E. V., Chaiken, S., & Tordesillas, R. S. (1995). Attitude strength and resistance processes. *Journal of Personality and Social Psychology, 69,* 408–419.

Pratto, F., Sidanius, J., Stallworth, L. M., & Malle, B. F. (1994). Social dominance orientation—A personality variable predicting social and political attitudes. *Journal of Personality and Social Psychology, 67,* 741–763.

Priester, J. R., & Petty, R. E. (1996). The gradual threshold model of ambivalence: Relating the positive and negative bases of attitudes to subjective ambivalence. *Journal of Personality and Social Psychology, 71,* 431–449.

Priester, J. R., & Petty, R. E. (2001). Extending the bases of subjective attitudinal ambivalence: Interpersonal and intrapersonal antecedents of evaluative tension. *Journal of Personality and Social Psychology, 80,* 19–34.

Prislin, R. (1996). Attitude strength and attitude stability: One is enough to make it strong. *European Journal of Social Psychology, 26,* 447–477.

Riketta, M. (2000). Discriminative validation of numerical indices of attitude ambivalence. *Current Research in Social Psychology, 5,* 1–9.

Riketta, M. (submitted). Convergence of direct and indirect measures of attitudinal ambivalence. Manuscript submitted for publication.

Schwartz, S. H. (1978). Temporal instability as a moderator of the attitude–behavior relationship. *Journal of Personality and Social Psychology, 36,* 715–724.

Schwartz, S. H. (1992). Universals in the content and structure of values—Theoretical advances and empirical tests in 20 countries. *Advances in Experimental Social Psychology, 25,* 1–65.

Scott, W. A. (1969). Structure of natural cognitions. *Journal of Personality and Social Psychology, 4,* 261–278.

Sheeran, P., Orbell, S., & Trafimow, D. (1999). Does the temporal stability of behavioral intentions moderate intention-behavior and past behavior-future behavior relations? *Personality and Social Psychology Bulletin, 25,* 721–730.

Sparks, P., Conner, M., James, R., Shepherd, R., & Povey, R. (2006). *Ambivalence about health-related behaviours: Relationships to personality measures.* Unpublished raw data, University of Sussex, UK.

Sparks, P., Harris, P. R., & Lockwood, N. (2004). Predictors and predictive effects of ambivalence. *British Journal of Social Psychology, 43,* 371–383.

Sparks, P., Hedderley, D., & Shepherd, R. (1992). An investigation into the relationship between perceived control, attitude variability and the consumption of two common foods. *European Journal of Social Psychology, 22,* 55–71.

Thompson, M. M., & Zanna, M. P. (1995). The conflicted individual—personality-based and domain-specific antecedents of ambivalent social attitudes. *Journal of Personality, 63,* 259–288.

Thompson, M. M., Zanna, M. P., & Griffin, D. W. (1995). Let's not be indifferent about (attitudinal) ambivalence. In R. E. Petty & J. A. Krosnick (Eds.), *Attitude strength: Antecedents and consequences* (pp. 361–386). Mahwah, NJ: Erlbaum.

Van der Pligt, J., De Vries, N. K., Manstead, A. S. R., & Van Harreveld, F. (2000). The importance of being selective: Weighing the role of attribute importance in attitudinal judgment. *Advances in Experimental Social Psychology, 32,* 135–200.

Van Harreveld, F., van der Pligt, J., de Vries, N. K., Wenneker, C., & Verhue, D. (2004). Ambivalence and information integration in attitudinal judgment. *British Journal of Social Psychology, 43,* 431–447.

Wilson, T. D., & Hodges, S. D. (1992). Attitudes as temporary constructions. In A. Tesser & L. Martin (Eds.), *The construction of social judgment* (pp. 37–65). Hillsdale, NJ: Erlbaum.

Zaller, J., & Feldman, S. (1992). A simple theory of the survey response: Answering questions versus revealing preferences. *American Journal of Political Science, 36,* 579–616.

VI

Attitudes
Mutual Impacts of Beliefs and Behaviors

13

Attitudes and the Prediction of Behavior

ICEK AJZEN and NICOLE GILBERT COTE
University of Massachusetts—Amherst

*E*valuation is a fundamental and immediate reaction to any object of psychological significance (Jarvis & Petty, 1996; Osgood, Suci, & Tannenbaum, 1957; Zajonc, 1980). We like certain individuals or groups and dislike others; we support some policies and oppose others; we prefer some products or brands over others; and we approve of some activities and disapprove of others. The term *attitude* is used to refer to these dispositions to respond with some degree of favorableness or unfavorableness to a psychological object (Eagly & Chaiken, 1993; Fishbein & Ajzen, 1975). The evaluative disposition itself is a hypothetical construct; it cannot be directly observed. We can only infer it from observable responses to the object, such as verbal expressions of like or dislike, physiological reactions, cognitive biases reflected in response latencies, or overt actions in relation to the object. Manifest responses of this kind are, however, merely fallible indicators of the latent evaluative disposition. Verbal expressions of liking are subject to social desirability biases (Paulhus, 1991), physiological reactions may reflect arousal or other reactions instead of evaluation (Kidder & Campbell, 1970), and response latencies may be indicative not of personal attitudes but of cultural stereotypes (Devine, 1989).

Given the fallibility of verbal, physiological, and cognitive indicators, measures of attitude that rely on such measures often are validated by examining their capacity to predict overt behavior with respect to the attitude object. In fact, it is usually argued that attitudes are of little value unless they can predict overt behavior (Ajzen, 2005). However, it is important to realize that overt actions can also be misleading. As Merton (1940,) noted a long time ago,

The metaphysical assumption is tacitly introduced that in one sense or another overt behavior is "more real" than verbal behavior. This assumption is both unwarranted and scientifically meaningless.... It should not be forgotten that overt actions may deceive; that they, just as "derivations" or "speech reactions" may be deliberately designed to disguise or to conceal private attitudes. (p. 20)

In this chapter we discuss the nature of attitudes and their relation to overt behavior. We examine the cognitive foundation of evaluative dispositions, the effects of global attitudes on behavior, and the prediction of specific actions from attitudes and other behavioral dispositions.

THE COGNITIVE FOUNDATION OF ATTITUDES

There is general agreement that most social attitudes are acquired, not innate. We are not born with positive attitudes toward certain candidates for political office or negative attitudes toward astrology. The great diversity of political, religious, artistic, economic, and other attitudes within and between cultures attests to the power of social background and experience in shaping our evaluative dispositions. In the course of our daily lives we acquire many different beliefs about a variety of objects, actions, and events. Thus, we may come to believe that television programs contain a great deal of violence, that men are better suited than women to hold positions of leadership, that smoking cigarettes causes heart disease, that raising taxes inhibits economic activity, and a myriad of other things. Beliefs of this kind may be formed as a result of direct observation, they may be self-generated by way of inference processes, or they may be formed indirectly by accepting information from such outside sources as friends, television, newspapers, books, and so on. Some beliefs persist over time, others weaken or disappear, and new beliefs are formed.

Although many beliefs accurately reflect reality, they can also be biased by a variety of cognitive and motivational processes. They may be irrational, based on invalid or selective information, be self-serving, or otherwise fail to correspond to reality (Allport, 1954; Eagly & Chaiken, 1993; Fishbein & Ajzen, 1975). However, no matter how they were formed or how accurate they are, beliefs represent the information we have about the world in which we live, and they form the cognitive foundation for many of our responses to aspects of that world.

The idea that beliefs form the foundation for our attitudes is embedded in the most popular model of attitude formation and structure, the expectancy-value (EV) model (Dabholkar, 1999; Feather, 1982). One of the first and most complete statements of the model can be found in Fishbein's (1963, 1967) summation theory of attitude. According to the EV model, we form beliefs about an object by associating it with certain attributes; that is, with other objects, characteristics, or events. Thus, perhaps as a result of watching a television program, we may come to believe that the government of a certain country (the object) is corrupt, imprisons innocent people, and mismanages the economy (attributes). Because the attributes that come to be linked to the object are already valued positively or negatively, we automatically and simultaneously acquire an attitude toward the object. In this fashion, we learn to like objects we believe have largely desirable characteristics, and we form unfavorable attitudes toward objects we associate with mostly undesirable characteristics. Although people can form many different beliefs about an object, it is assumed that only a relatively small number influence their attitudes at any given moment. It is these readily *accessible* beliefs that are considered to be the prevailing determinants of a person's attitude.

Specifically, the subjective value of each attribute contributes to the attitude in direct proportion to the strength of the belief; that is, the subjective probability that the object has the attribute in question. The way in which beliefs combine to produce an attitude is shown in Equation 1. As can be seen, the strength of each belief (*b*) is multiplied by the subjective evaluation (*e*) of the belief's attribute and the resulting products are summed. A person's attitude is expected to be directly proportional (α) to this summative belief index.

$$A_B \; \alpha \; \Sigma b_i e_i \qquad\qquad [1]$$

Of course, individuals are not expected to actually perform the mental calculations described by the EV model. It is merely assumed that attitude formation can be modeled as if a person were performing the stipulated calculations.

DEFINING THE PSYCHOLOGICAL OBJECT

A distinguishing characteristic of attitudes is that they involve evaluation of a particular psychological object, be it a physical entity (e.g., the Eiffel Tower), an institution (the Catholic Church), a person (President Kennedy) or group of people (homosexuals), a policy (stem cell research), an abstract concept (democracy), or any other discriminable aspect of an individual's world. We have or can readily develop dispositions to evaluate each of these kinds of objects with some degree of favorableness or unfavorableness. However, to understand the influence of attitudes on behavior we must distinguish between two fundamentally different types of attitude objects (Ajzen, 1982; Ajzen & Fishbein, 1980, 2005). One type, illustrated by the above examples, spells out no particular action that might be taken in relation to the object of interest. Evaluative dispositions with respect to this type of object will be termed *global attitudes*. The second type of attitude object is a specific behavior or category of behaviors. Examples of objects involving specific behaviors are donating money to the Catholic Church, reading a book about President Kennedy, and employing a gay person, whereas examples of behavioral categories are exercising, dieting, and studying. Evaluative dispositions with respect to psychological objects of this kind will be termed *attitude toward a behavior*.

GLOBAL ATTITUDES AND THE PREDICTION OF BEHAVIOR

Social scientists and laypersons alike have an abiding trust in the explanatory power and predictive validity of global attitudes. It appears intuitively compelling to argue, for example, that proenvironmental attitudes are conducive to participation in recycling efforts, that degree of job satisfaction influences work productivity, that prosocial attitudes determine willingness to donate blood, or that racial prejudice is responsible for biases in hiring decisions. Yet, as reasonable as it appears, empirical research has provided very little support for the idea that performance of specific behaviors can be predicted from global attitudes. In an early review of work on the attitude–behavior relation, Ajzen and Fishbein (1977) discovered that among the 102 studies reviewed, 54 had assessed global attitudes in attempts to predict specific actions. Of these studies, 25 obtained nonsignificant results and the remainder rarely showed correlations in excess of .40. A more recent meta-analysis of this literature (Kraus, 1995) revealed similarly low correlations between global attitudes and specific behaviors.

Racial Attitudes and Discriminatory Behavior: An Illustration

Perhaps the best illustration of this state of affairs comes from the extensive literature on racial prejudice and discrimination (Fiske, 1998). Indeed, some of the earliest studies regarding the relation between attitudes and behavior were conducted in this domain. A good example is the experiment reported by Himelstein and Moore (1963). A sample of white male college students first completed a scale assessing attitudes toward African Americans and, some time later, reported for an ostensibly unrelated psychology experiment. Upon arrival, the participant found another student (a confederate), either black or white, already seated in the room. While they were waiting for the experiment to begin, a (white) confederate entered the room carrying a petition to extend the university's library hours on Saturday nights. The black or white confederate was approached first and either signed or refused to sign the petition. Following this manipulation, the naive participant was asked to sign. Conformity or lack of conformity with the response of the confederate served as the measure of behavior. The data revealed virtually no effect of global attitudes toward African Americans on conformity with the black confederate.

A study by Linn (1965), which dealt with the release of interracial photographs, provides another good example. In the first phase of the experiment white female college students completed a general attitude questionnaire. Scattered among the questions were seven items that assessed global attitudes toward blacks. About four weeks later, the students were asked to help a psychological testing company that was said to be developing a new projective personality test. Students who volunteered to participate were asked to have their picture taken with a black male and to sign releases for use of the picture under a variety of increasingly public conditions. The conditions ranged from laboratory work where the picture would be seen only by professional sociologists and psychologists to use by organizations like the NAACP in a nationwide campaign for racial integration. The results of the study revealed no significant association between global attitudes toward blacks and willingness to release the interracial photographs.

The results were no more encouraging when global attitudes toward minority groups were used to predict other kinds of behavior, including administration of electric shocks (Genthner & Taylor, 1973; Larsen, Colen, von Flue, & Zimmerman, 1974), verbal conditioning to black individuals (Smith & Dixon, 1968), evaluating and sentencing a black person (Brigham, 1971), and interacting with black students during school-related activities (Bagley & Verma, 1979). In his review of this literature, Duckitt (1992, Chapter 3) concluded that the correlation between racial attitudes and measures of discrimination is at best in the weak to moderate range. Two meta-analyses (Schütz & Six, 1996; Talaska, Fiske, & Chaiken, 2004) of the relevant literature also paint a very discouraging picture. The average correlations between measures of prejudice and discrimination in these two analyses were, respectively, .29 (based on 46 effect sizes) and .26 (based on 136 effect sizes).

Implicit Racial Attitudes   In recent years a renewed challenge to the postulated relation between prejudice and discrimination has emerged (Fiske, 1998). Many investigators have pointed out that expressed stereotypical beliefs and prejudicial attitudes have declined markedly over the past decades (e.g., Dovidio, 2001; Schuman, Steeh, Bobo, & Krysan, 1997), yet discrimination against historically disadvantaged racial and ethnic groups continues to be evident in employment, education, housing, healthcare, criminal justice, and other domains (e.g., Bushway & Piehl, 2001; Crosby, Bromley, & Saxe, 1980; Daniels, 2001; Hacker, 1995; Landrine, Klonoff, & Alcaraz, 1997; Myers & Chan, 1995). Although intriguing, it must be noted that this observation is based on evidence that is at best weak and circumstantial (see Ajzen & Fishbein, 2005). There is plenty of evidence to suggest that, like expressed prejudice, overt discrimination has also declined greatly over the years (e.g., Freeman, 1973; Iceland, 2003; Jarrell & Stanley, 2004); and on the other side of the coin, there is good evidence to show that verbally expressed prejudice has by no means disappeared (Leach, Peng, & Volckens, 2000).

Whether discrimination has or has not declined to the same degree as prejudice, the immediate reaction to the apparent inconsistency between racial prejudice and discriminatory behavior was to question the validity of the measures of discriminatory attitudes (Crosby et al., 1980; McConahay, Hardee, & Batts, 1981): Because of self-presentational concerns, people were presumably reluctant to express their true (negative) feelings. There was also an assumption, however, that the nature of racial prejudice had changed over the years to become more subtle and nuanced than the blatant racism of the past (McConahay, 1986). Also, it was argued that prejudice might now be expressed more indirectly and symbolically than in the past; for example, as opposition to preferential treatment for minorities (Sears, 1988). Other theorists proposed that racial attitudes had become ambiguous or aversive, containing explicit egalitarian elements as well as more subtle and unacknowledged negative beliefs and feelings (Gaertner & Dovidio, 1986).

This revised view of the nature of contemporary prejudice provided a ready explanation for the apparent gap between low professed prejudice and high levels of discrimination. The high levels of discrimination suggested that prejudice was still very much present but that because it had become subtle and perhaps even unconscious, standard attitude scales which measure *explicit* stereotypes and prejudice were incapable of capturing it. This view led to the prediction that *implicit* attitudes—assumed to be automatically activated—guide behavior by default unless they are overridden by controlled processes.

Contemporary models of stereotyping and prejudice differ in detail, but they agree in their overall expectations regarding the predictive validity of explicit and implicit attitude measures. It is assumed that because prejudicial attitudes and discriminatory behavior with respect to racial and ethnic minorities are frowned upon in contemporary American society, many people try to inhibit their expression. Also, in addition to self-presentation biases, culturally pervasive stereotypes, even if not consciously endorsed, may be passively acquired in the process of socialization or simply by observing certain groups and social roles that co-occur repeatedly (see Devos, this volume). These beliefs and attitudes may influence behavior without a person's knowledge. Implicit measures of attitude may circumvent these problems by providing information about beliefs and attitudes that individuals may not be willing or able to self-report. Specifically, it is expected that implicit measures of prejudicial attitudes are valuable predictors of discriminatory behaviors that are not consciously monitored or that are difficult to control (e.g., facial expressions, eye contact, blushing, and other nonverbal behaviors), as well as of behaviors that people do not view as indicative of prejudice and thus are not motivated to control. They should be less predictive of behaviors that are under conscious control. With respect to explicit attitude measures the opposite pattern is expected. These measures should be predictive of behaviors that are under volitional control and whose implications for prejudice are apparent but less predictive of spontaneously emitted reactions that are not consciously monitored (Dovidio, Brigham, Johnson, & Gaertner, 1996).

Before we consider empirical tests of this hypothesis, it should be noted that the results of past studies on the relation between prejudice and discrimination discussed above are inconsistent with the prediction that explicit attitudes will be good predictors of controlled behaviors. In most of these past studies, explicit measures of global attitudes were used to predict controlled behaviors, yet contrary to what would be expected, the correlations were found to be very weak, rarely exceeding the .30 level (Wicker, 1969).

Examination of the predictive validity of implicit attitudes became possible with the development of new measurement techniques that rely on reaction times, most notably the implicit association test (IAT; Greenwald, McGhee, & Schwartz, 1998) and evaluative priming (Dovidio, Evans, & Tyler, 1986; Fazio, Jackson, Dunton, & Williams, 1995—see Fazio & Olson, 2003; Schwarz, this volume). Thus far, only a small number of studies have directly tested the hypothesis that explicit global attitudes are better predictors of controlled than of spontaneous behaviors and that implicit global attitudes predict spontaneous reactions better than controlled actions. The results of these studies have been rather disappointing. To be sure, in some instances implicit measures of prejudice have been found superior to explicit measures for the prediction of such nonverbal behaviors as blinking and eye contact (Dovidio, Kawakami, Johnson, Johnson, & Howard, 1997), the number of times whites handed a pen to an African American as opposed to placing it on the table (Wilson, Lindsey, & Schooler, 2000), as well as the friendliness of white participants in their interactions with a black person, judged by the black person on the basis of the white person's nonverbal behavior (smiling, eye contact, spatial distance, and body language) (Fazio et al., 1995; see Fazio & Olson, 2003 for a review). A similar effect was obtained in a study dealing with behavior whose implications for prejudice were ambiguous (Sekaquaptewa, Espinoza, Thompson, Vargas, & von Hippel, 2003). The critical behavior in this study was white males' choice of stereotype-consistent or inconsistent questions in a mock job interview with a black female applicant. However, even the implicit attitude measures in these studies did not do very well, with correlations rarely exceeding the .30 level observed in earlier research with explicit measures.

There also is some evidence for the advantage of explicit over implicit measures in the prediction of controlled behaviors. Thus, it has been found that in comparison to implicit measures of prejudice, explicit measures are better predictors of judgments concerning the verdict in the Rodney King trial involving police brutality toward a black person and attractiveness ratings of facial photographs of black and white individuals (Fazio et al., 1995), as well as ratings of the guilt of African-American defendants in a simulated jury trial (Dovidio et al., 1997). Note that the criterion measures in these studies were verbal judgments, not overt behaviors. Even so, predictive accuracy was modest, with correlations ranging from .24 to .54.

Perhaps the best evidence regarding the relative predictive validity of explicit and implicit global attitude measures comes from a meta-analysis of the literature (Poehlman, Uhlmann, Greenwald, & Banaji, 2005) based on 61 studies that reported data for 86 independent samples. This meta-analysis went beyond prejudice and discrimination to include data regarding a variety of other attitudinal and behavioral domains (food choice, achievement, condom use, self-esteem, smoking, political behavior, and others). The results again demonstrated the limited predictive power of global attitudes in relation to specific behaviors. Overall, the mean correlation between explicit attitude measures and various criteria, weighted for sample size, was .35, compared to a significantly lower mean correlation of .27 for implicit attitude measures. Considering only the 32 studies in the domain of racial attitudes and behavior, the mean correlation for the prediction of discriminatory responses was significantly higher when implicit (r = .25) rather than explicit (r = .13) measures of prejudice were obtained, even though the correlations were rather low in either case.

More importantly, the meta-analysis provided only very limited support for the distinct roles of implicit and explicit attitude measures. The attitudes assessed in the different studies were rated for the likelihood that they would elicit self-presentation concerns, and the behaviors were rated for their degree of controllability. The moderating effects of these factors were examined for the total sample of studies; separate analyses for racial attitudes and behaviors were not reported. As expected, the predictive validity of explicit attitude measures tended to decline with social desirability concerns ($r = -.36$) and to increase with the rated controllability of the behavior ($r = .28$). However, contrary to expectations, there was no significant effect of these variables on the correlation between implicit measures of attitude and the performance of specific behaviors.

It has often been reported that implicit attitude measures correlate only weakly with explicit measures of the same attitude (e.g., Cunningham, Preacher, & Banaji, 2001; Karpinski & Hilton, 2001; Neumann, Hülsenbeck, & Seibt, 2004). These findings suggest that implicit and explicit methods may serve to assess two distinctly different attitudes (Wilson et al., 2000), and that prediction of behavior could perhaps be improved by considering implicit and explicit measures simultaneously. However, examination of empirical studies that have assessed the same attitude by implicit and explicit means provides no support for this proposition. Zero-order correlations reveal that, in most cases, only one attitude type correlates significantly with behavior. Sometimes explicit attitudes are significant predictors and implicit attitudes are not (e.g., Asendorpf, Banse, & Muecke, 2002; Bosson, Swann, & Pennebaker, 2000; Wiers, Van Woerden, Smulders, & De Jong, 2002), whereas in other instances, implicit attitudes are significant predictors of behavior while explicit attitudes are not (e.g., Egloff & Schmukle, 2002; Hugenberg & Bodenhausen, 2003). As might therefore be expected, in these cases multiple regression analyses show that only one of the two measures makes a significant contribution to the prediction of behavior. To be sure, a few studies have found both implicit and explicit attitudes to be significantly correlated with a behavioral criterion (e.g., Czopp, Monteith, Zimmerman, & Lynam, 2004, in the case of past condom use; Maison, Greenwald, & Bruin, 2004, Study 3; Teachman & Woody, 2003). However, even here, inclusion of both measures in a regression analysis produced only a relatively small improvement in predictive validity. For example, in Czopp et al. (2004), prediction of condom use went from a correlation of .31 when only an explicit attitude measure was used to a correlation of .35 when an implicit measure was added to the prediction equation, a statistically significant but relatively small increase of 2% in explained variance. Clearly, although our understanding of sensitive beliefs and attitudes such as stereotypes and prejudice may well benefit from the measurement of explicit as well as implicit attitudes (for reviews see Blair, 2001; Fiske, 1998), the inclusion of both types of measures does not guarantee better behavioral prediction.

To summarize briefly, global attitudes are found to be rather poor predictors of specific overt behaviors. This conclusion emerges from research on the relation between racial prejudice and discrimination as well as the prediction of behavior in many other domains. Contrary to contemporary theories, the predictive validity of global attitudes tends to be relatively low whether explicit or implicit measures of attitude are employed and irrespective of social desirability concerns or the behavior's controllability.

Linking Global Attitudes to Behavior: The MODE Model

The most detailed and sophisticated account of the processes whereby global attitudes may serve to guide behavior is provided by Fazio's (1986; 1990; Fazio

& Towles-Schwen, 1999) MODE model. In this model, attitude is defined as a learned association in memory between an object and a positive or negative evaluation of that object. The attitude's strength is equivalent to the strength of this association.[1] Building on past research (Eagly, 1998), the model assumes that attitudes influence or bias perception and judgment of information relevant to the attitude object, a bias that is congruent with the valence of the attitude. Thus, people with positive attitudes toward, say, genetically modified food may evaluate new information as indicating that eating such food is safe whereas people with negative attitudes may evaluate the same information as evidence that it is dangerous. As a result, a global measure of attitude toward genetically modified food should predict consumption of such food. However, the model assumes that only strong attitudes—being chronically accessible in memory—are likely to bias perception of the situation and thus influence behavior. In work with the MODE model, the degree of an attitude's chronic accessibility in memory (i.e., its strength) is usually operationalized by measuring the latency of responses to attitudinal questions: the faster the response, the more accessible the attitude is assumed to be (e.g., Fazio & Williams, 1986; see also Fazio, 1990b).

The MODE model thus suggests that attitude strength—in the form of its accessibility in memory—plays a pivotal role in the link between attitudes and behavior. Generally speaking, relatively accessible attitudes should predict behavior better than less accessible attitudes. Support for this expectation has been obtained in several studies that have compared the predictive validity of attitudes expressed with low as opposed to high response latencies (Berger & Mitchell, 1989; Fazio, Powell, & Williams, 1989; Fazio & Williams, 1986; Kokkinaki & Lunt, 1997). In a study by Fazio, Powell, and Williams (1989), for example, college students indicated their liking or disliking for each of 100 common products (Star-Kist tuna, Planters peanuts, etc.) and, on the basis of response speed, were divided into high, moderate, and low accessibility subgroups. As a measure of behavior, participants could choose to take home five products from a set of 10 options. The attitude–behavior correlation increased with degree of accessibility, from .50 in the low accessibility group to .62 in the high accessibility group. Similarly, Fazio and Williams (1986) predicted voting choice in the 1984 Presidential election from attitudes toward the two major candidates (Reagan and Mondale) assessed several months earlier. In addition to attitude valence, the investigators assessed the accessibility of these attitudes by asking participants to respond as quickly as possible to the attitude questions and recording response latencies. As hypothesized, prediction of voting choice was significantly better for participants with relatively accessible (low latency) attitudes toward the candidates than for participants with relatively inaccessible attitudes.

Fazio's MODE model has elucidated the processes whereby global attitudes can guide performance of specific behaviors, but it leaves several important issues unresolved. First, it has been suggested that the magnitude of the attitude–behavior relation may be moderated not by attitude accessibility but by other correlated factors of attitude strength, such as certainty, amount of knowledge, or the attitude's temporal stability (Eagly & Chaiken, 1993). Support for the superior predictive validity of stable as opposed to accessible attitudes was provided by Doll and

Ajzen (1992). As expected, compared to second-hand information, direct experience with different video games raised the accessibility of attitudes toward playing those games. However, it also increased the temporal stability of these attitudes. A mediation analysis showed that the higher predictive validity of the attitude measures following direct as opposed to indirect experience could be explained better by their greater stability than by their higher level of accessibility.

Perhaps most important, any model dealing with the influence of global attitudes on specific behaviors should be able to account for the typically low attitude–behavior relations reported in the literature. In past research, investigators have tried unsuccessfully to use measures of global attitudes to predict such behaviors as job absence and turnover, various types of interaction with African Americans, participation in civil rights activities, attendance of labor union meetings, and so forth (Wicker, 1969). According to the MODE model, the observed low attitude–behavior correlations imply that participants in these studies held relatively weak attitudes, too weak to influence their definition of the event and thus guide their behavior. Without further evidence, this conjecture cannot be completely discounted, but it seems reasonable to assume that people hold fairly strong attitudes toward their jobs, their labor unions, members of minority groups, and civil rights. Strong attitudes of this kind should be chronically accessible and thus available to guide behavior. However, in actuality, even under these ideal conditions from the MODE model perspective, the observed correlations between global attitudes and specific behaviors are found to be disappointing.

Clearly then, even though attitude strength or accessibility is an important factor that can influence the relation between global attitudes and specific behaviors, by itself it cannot account for many of the relatively low correlations reported in the literature. In the remainder of this chapter we consider a different approach to the attitudinal prediction of specific behaviors.

THE PRINCIPLE OF COMPATIBILITY

The finding that as a general rule global attitudes are poor predictors of specific behaviors should come as no surprise. For global attitudes to predict a particular behavior, the behavior in question must be a valid indicator of the latent attitudinal disposition—it must reflect the global attitude of interest. However, it is unreasonable to expect any single behavior to be representative of a broad attitudinal domain. Consider, for example, the relation between global attitudes toward African Americans and willingness to have one's picture taken with a black individual of the opposite sex for a variety of purposes (Linn, 1965). Although refusal to pose for a picture with a black person may well be an indication of prejudice, this behavior can also be influenced by a variety of other factors that have nothing to do with prejudice. In fact, any single behavior in relation to African Americans is likely to be multiply determined and hence be a poor indicator of the underlying disposition; that is, the tendency to discriminate (Fishbein & Ajzen, 1974; see also Epstein, 1983).

In their review of research dealing with the attitude–behavior relation, Ajzen and Fishbein (1977) proposed that it is useful to define a behavioral criterion in terms of four facets or elements: the *action* involved, the *target* at which the action is directed, the *context* in which it occurs, and its *time* of occurrence. In a parallel manner, it is also possible to analyze any measure of attitude in terms of these four elements (i.e., the object or target that is being evaluated), and whether the evaluative measure involves a particular action, context, and time. These considerations led to the formulation of the by now widely accepted *principle of compatibility* (Ajzen, 1988; Ajzen & Fishbein, 1980). According to the principle, we can expect a strong attitude–behavior correlation only to the extent that the measures of attitude and behavior involve exactly the same action, target, context, and time elements.

Behavioral Aggregation

A global attitude is an evaluation of a target that involves no specific action, context, or time elements. A scale that assesses attitudes toward Muslims, for example, results in a score that represents a generally favorable or unfavorable evaluation of Muslims; no particular action, context, or time is specified. Because single behaviors, such as voting for a Muslim candidate in a local election or inviting a Muslim to one's home, involve specific actions and often also specific context and time elements, they are by definition not compatible with the global attitude measure. However, even if not well reflected in any single behavior, the behavioral disposition implied by a favorable or unfavorable attitude toward Muslims should become evident if we observe a broad, representative sample of behaviors with respect to Muslims (Thurstone, 1931). A multiple-act index obtained by aggregating across a variety of behaviors involves many different actions directed at the target of interest, performed in different contexts and at different points in time. Like global attitudes, such multiple-act indices thus generalize across action, context, and time elements; the only element that remains constant is the target. Consequently, we would expect a strong correlation between global attitudes and general patterns of behavior, (i.e., multiple-act aggregates).

Empirical research has provided support for this hypothesis. When the behavioral criterion is broadly representative of the behavioral domain, rather than a single arbitrarily selected action, strong relations between global attitudes and behavior are observed. For example, in a study of religiosity (Fishbein & Ajzen, 1974) several instruments were used to assess global attitudes toward religion and participants were asked to indicate whether they did or did not perform each of a set of 100 behaviors in this domain. Whereas the global attitude measures were typically poor predictors of individual behaviors (the mean correlation was about .14), they showed strong correlations (ranging from .61 to .71) with an aggregate measure across all 100 behaviors, a measure designed to reflect the general pattern of religiosity. Comparable results were reported for abortion activism (Werner, 1978) and for protection of the environment (Weigel & Newman, 1976).

Predicting Specific Actions

We have seen that global attitudes do after all have predictive validity, at least when it comes to the prediction of overall behavioral trends rather than specific actions. This conclusion is far from trivial. As social psychologists we are frequently interested in general behavioral patterns. A good case in point is the question of prejudice and discrimination discussed earlier. The logic of aggregation implies that discrimination against members of a certain group cannot be validly assessed by observing a single action. Instead, it requires consideration of a wide range of behaviors with respect to members of the group in question and selection of a representative set for observation. Although we are not aware of relevant empirical research, we would expect that a global measure of prejudicial attitudes will correlate well with such a multiple-act measure of discrimination.

The principle of compatibility can also be applied to the prediction of single behaviors. Consider, for example, students' attendance of class meetings in a certain course. Our discussion suggests that a global attitude, such as the attitude toward the course instructor, will be a poor predictor of this behavior. However, there is no need to assess a global attitude of this kind if we want to predict a specific behavior. Instead, we can obtain of measure of attitude that corresponds much more closely to the behavior in its action, target, context, and time elements, that is, the *attitude toward the behavior*. Thus we could measure students' attitudes toward attending course meetings. Indeed, investigators have assessed attitudes toward many kinds of behaviors, including attitudes toward smoking marijuana, drinking alcohol, having an abortion, participating in psychological research, and so forth. Such measures reflect rather narrow behavioral dispositions and should predict the corresponding behavior.

There is considerable support for the principle of compatibility at different levels of generality or specificity. A narrative review of 124 data sets (Ajzen & Fishbein, 1977) showed that, as expected, correlations between attitudes and behavior are substantial when these variables are assessed at compatible levels of specificity or generality; when the measures are incompatible, the correlations are very low and usually not significant. The correlation across studies between degree of compatibility and the magnitude of the attitude–behavior relation was found to be .83. However, the most compelling support for the importance of compatibility in attitude–behavior research comes from studies that have directly compared the predictive validity of attitudes that were compatible (i.e., attitudes toward behaviors) or incompatible (i.e., global attitudes toward general targets) with a single-act criterion. In Kraus's (1995) meta-analysis of eight studies that manipulated level of compatibility, the prediction of behavior from attitude toward the behavior resulted in a mean correlation of .54, whereas the mean correlation between global attitudes and single behaviors was only .13. Thus, just as global attitudes are good predictors of multiple-act measures of behavior, attitudes toward a behavior predict the specific behavior under consideration.

The Theory of Planned Behavior The principle of compatibility as applied to the prediction of specific behaviors is a central aspect of the *theory of planned* *behavior.* First described in 1985 (Ajzen, 1985), the theory of planned behavior (TPB) is today one of the most popular social-psychological models for the prediction of behavior. It has its roots in Ajzen and Fishbein's (1980) theory of reasoned action which was developed in response to the observed lack of correspondence between general dispositions, such as racial or religious attitudes, and actual behavior. Instead of dealing with broad attitudes of this kind, the TPB focuses on the behavior itself, and it goes beyond attitudes to consider such other influences on behavior as social norms and self-efficacy beliefs.

Briefly, according to the theory of planned behavior, human action is influenced by three major factors: a favorable or unfavorable evaluation of the behavior (*attitude toward the behavior*), perceived social pressure to perform or not perform the behavior (*subjective norm*), and perceived capability to perform the behavior (self-efficacy; Bandura, 1997, or *perceived behavioral control*). In combination, attitude toward the behavior, subjective norm, and perception of behavioral control lead to the formation of a behavioral intention. As a general rule, the more favorable the attitude and subjective norm, and the greater the perceived behavioral control, the stronger should be the person's intention to perform the behavior in question. The relative importance of the three predictors as determinants of intentions can vary from behavior to behavior and from population to population. Finally, given a sufficient degree of control over the behavior, people are expected to carry out their intentions when the opportunity arises. Unfortunately, although we may be able to measure some aspects of actual control, in most instances we lack sufficient information about all the relevant factors that may facilitate or impede performance of the behavior. However, to the extent that people are realistic in their judgments, a measure of *perceived* behavioral control can serve as a proxy for actual control and contribute to the prediction of the behavior in question. A schematic representation of the theory is shown in Figure 13.1. The solid arrow pointing from actual control to the intention–behavior link indicates that volitional control is expected

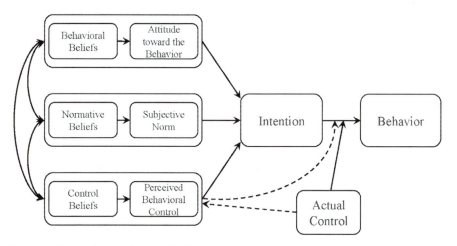

Figure 13.1   Theory of planned behavior.

to moderate the intention–behavior relation such that the effect of intention on behavior is stronger when actual control is high rather than low. That perceived behavioral control, when veridical, can serve as a proxy for actual control is shown by the dotted arrows in Figure 13.1 that connect actual control to perceived control and perceived control to the intention-behavior link.[2] (For a more detailed overview of the theory, see Ajzen, 2005.)

When applied to a particular behavior, say hiring a certain African-American applicant for a job, we would assess attitudes toward hiring the person in question, as well as perceptions of social pressure to do so (i.e., subjective norms), and perceived control over this behavior. Together, attitudes toward the behavior, subjective norms, and perceptions of control would be expected to predict intentions to hire or not to hire the applicant, and actual hiring behavior should correspond to the intention to the extent that the respondent has the authority to carry out his or her hiring decision.

The Cognitive Foundation of Behavior

The theory of planned behavior assumes that human social behavior is reasoned or planned in the sense that people take account of a behavior's likely consequences (behavioral beliefs), the normative expectations of important referents (normative beliefs), and factors that may facilitate or impede performance of the behavior (control beliefs). Although behavioral, normative, and control beliefs may sometimes be inaccurate, unfounded, or biased, attitudes, subjective norms, and perceptions of behavioral control are thought to follow spontaneously and reasonably from these beliefs, produce a corresponding behavioral intention, and ultimately result in behavior that is consistent with the overall tenor of the beliefs.

Behavioral Beliefs and Attitudes Like global attitudes, attitudes toward a behavior are assumed to be a function of beliefs, but in this case, the relevant accessible beliefs are beliefs about the behavior's likely consequences, termed behavioral beliefs. A behavioral belief is a person's subjective probability that performing a behavior of interest will lead to a certain outcome, for example, the belief that exercising (the behavior) improves physical fitness (the outcome). As described by the expectancy-value model discussed earlier, in their aggregate the behavioral beliefs are theorized to produce a positive or negative attitude toward the behavior. Specifically, the positive or negative valence of each outcome contributes to the overall attitude in direct proportion to the subjective probability that the behavior will produce the outcome in question (see Equation 1 earlier).

Normative Beliefs and Subjective Norms In an analogous fashion, accessible normative beliefs constitute the basis for perceived social pressure, or subjective norm. A normative belief is the expectation or subjective probability that a given referent individual or group (e.g., friends, family, spouse, coworkers, one's physician or supervisor) would approve or disapprove of performing the behavior under investigation. As shown in Equation 2, each accessible normative belief ($\underline{n}$) is assumed to contribute to subjective norm (*SN*) in direct proportion to the person's motivation to comply (m) with the referent individual or group, and the n x m products combine to produce the subjective norm.

$$SN \propto \Sigma n_i m_i \qquad [2]$$

Control Beliefs and Perceived Behavioral Control   Just as attitudes are assumed to be based on accessible behavioral beliefs and subjective norms on accessible normative beliefs, perceived behavioral control is assumed to be based on accessible control beliefs. These beliefs are concerned with the presence of factors that can facilitate or impede performance of the behavior. Control factors include required skills and abilities; availability or lack of time, money, and other resources; cooperation by other people; and so forth. A control belief is defined as a person's subjective probability that a given facilitating or inhibiting factor will be present. Each control belief contributes to perceived behavioral control, or a sense of self-efficacy, in direct proportion to the factor's perceived power to facilitate or impede performance of the behavior. Perceived behavioral control (*PBC*) is a function of the products of control belief (c) times perceived power (p) summed over all accessible control factors, as shown in Equation 3.

$$PBC \propto \Sigma c_i p_i \qquad [3]$$

Empirical Support for the TPB

A large number of studies have used the theory of planned behavior to examine the psychological antecedents of actions in various domains. It is beyond the scope of the present chapter to review this body of research (for summaries and meta-analyses, see Ajzen, 1991; Albarracin, Johnson, Fishbein, & Muellerleile, 2001; Armitage & Conner, 2001; Downs & Hausenblas, 2005; Godin & Kok, 1996; Hagger, Chatzisarantis, & Biddle, 2002). Generally speaking, the theory has been well supported. With regard to the prediction of behavior, many studies have substantiated the predictive validity of behavioral intentions. Reviewing different meta-analyses covering diverse behavioral domains, Sheeran (2002) reported a mean correlation of .53 between intention and behavior. Also, it has been found that the addition of perceived behavioral control can improve prediction of behavior considerably, especially when performance of the behavior is difficult (Madden, Ellen, & Ajzen, 1992). For example, in a general sample of smokers, a measure of perceived behavioral control accounted for an additional 12% of the variance in smoking behavior over and above intentions; and among postnatal women, the increase in explained behavioral variance due to perceived behavioral control was 34% (Godin, Valois, Lepage, & Desharnais, 1992).

Meta-analyses of the empirical literature have also provided evidence to show that intentions can be predicted with considerable accuracy from measures of attitudes toward the behavior, subjective norms, and perceived behavioral control (Albarracin et al., 2001; Armitage & Conner, 2001; Hagger et al., 2002; Sheeran &

Taylor, 1999). For a wide range of behaviors, attitudes are found to correlate well with intentions; across the different meta-analyses, the mean correlations ranged from .45 to .60. For the prediction of intentions from subjective norms, these correlations ranged from .34 to .42, and for the prediction of intention from perceived behavioral control, the range was .35 to .46. The multiple correlations for the prediction of intentions ranged from .63 to .71.

Finally, the meta-analysis performed by Armitage and Conner (2001) also provided evidence for the proposition that attitudes, subjective norms, and perceptions of control can be predicted from corresponding sets of beliefs. The mean correlation between the expectancy-value index of behavioral beliefs and a direct measure of attitude toward the behavior was .50, and the same mean correlation obtained between the normative belief index and subjective norm; the control belief index showed a mean correlation of .52 with perceived behavioral control.

Explaining Intentions and Behavior   A detailed examination of behavioral, normative, and control beliefs provides substantive information about a behavior's determinants. By comparing subgroups of participants who are currently performing and not performing the behavior, or those who intend to perform it in the future with those who don't, we can gain insight into the considerations that guide people's actions. Research by Conner, Sherlock, and Orbell (1998) provides an example of this form of subgroup analysis in the domain of illicit drug use. In the second of their two studies, members of a club completed a theory of planned behavior questionnaire with respect to using ecstasy in the next two months. The sample was divided into those who held positive or neutral intentions to use ecstasy in the next two months (neutral or above neutral on the intention scale) and those who held negative intentions. The two groups were then compared in terms of their behavioral, normative, and control beliefs.[3] These comparisons revealed significant differences between participants with positive and negative intentions on almost all behavioral beliefs. For example, compared with the negative intention group, participants who held positive intentions judged it more likely that using ecstasy in the next two months would give them a sense of well-being, would be exciting, and would make them sociable; and as less likely that it would bring on mood swings, lead to (undesirable) physical side effects, or lead to the use of other drugs. There were, however, no significant differences in the judged likelihood that ecstasy use would produce a feeling of lethargy or that it would lead to more frequent use of the drug.

The influence of normative beliefs on intentions was also in evidence. In general, important others (close friends, partner, parents, other club members, and other ecstasy users) were believed to disapprove of ecstasy use. However, the subgroup of participants who intended to use ecstasy in the next two months saw their close friends and partners as disapproving less than did the participants who did not intend to use the drug. The differences with respect to other club members, other ecstasy users, and parents were not statistically significant; these referents were seen as about equally disapproving of the behavior. Finally, there were also significant differences in control beliefs. For example, people who intended to use ecstasy in the next two months were less likely to believe that they would have to pay a high price for the drug, and more likely to believe that they would be offered ecstasy and be with friends who use the drug.

In short, the theory of planned behavior can provide a detailed account of the considerations that guide performance of a particular behavior. Beliefs about the behavior's likely consequences, about the normative expectations of important others, and about skills, resources, or other factors that can facilitate or impede performance of the behavior jointly influence the decision to engage or not to engage in the behavior of interest. By assessing these beliefs and comparing differences in beliefs between individuals who engage in the behavior and individuals who do not, we can gain valuable insight into the behavior's determinants.

SUMMARY AND CONCLUSIONS

In this chapter we tried to show that attitude—defined as a disposition to respond with some degree of favorableness or unfavorableness to a psychological object— is an important and very useful concept for understanding and predicting human social behavior. We have also seen, however, that a strong relation between attitudes and behavior cannot be taken for granted. Global attitudes can help us understand general patterns of behavior, but they are usually poor predictors of specific behaviors with respect to the object of the attitude. This is true whether explicit or implicit methods are used to assess global attitudes. Some insight into the effects of global attitudes on specific actions is provided by Fazio's (1990) MODE model. According to this model, only strong attitudes, readily accessible in memory, are likely to guide performance of specific behaviors. However, we have seen that even when people can be assumed to hold strong attitudes, as in the area of prejudice and discrimination, global attitudes often fail to predict specific behaviors.

It must be concluded that in many instances, global attitudes are simply too general to have much relevance for the performance of a particular behavior. Considerations associated with the specific behavior of interest have a more direct impact that can overpower whatever effect global attitudes may have. Consistent with the principle of compatibility, measures of attitude toward the behavior, measures that involve the same action, target, context, and time elements as the behavior itself, are found to predict specific actions much better than do global attitudes. Capitalizing on the principle of correspondence, the theory of planned behavior (Ajzen, 1991) has become a popular model for the prediction of specific actions. Much empirical research has confirmed the theory by showing that specific behaviors can be predicted quite well from corresponding intentions; that these intentions themselves are a function of attitudes toward the behavior, subjective norms, and perceptions of behavioral control; and that the origins of these three factors can be traced, respectively, to behavioral, normative, and control beliefs regarding the behavior of interest.

NOTES

1. Over the past two decades, the concept of attitude strength has generated considerable interest among investigators (Eagly & Chaiken, 1998; Krosnick, Boninger, Chuang, Berent, & Carnot, 1993; Petty & Krosnick, 1995; Raden, 1985). Among the indicators of attitude strength is importance of the attitudinal domain, vested interest in the topic, certainty in one's position, direct experience with the attitude object, and information and reflection about the issue (Petty & Krosnick, 1995). Although these different aspects of attitude strength tend to correlate only moderately with each other (Krosnick et al., 1993; Raden, 1985), strong attitudes—no matter how operationalized—are assumed to be relatively stable over time, to be resistant to persuasion, and to be good predictors of behavior (see Bassili, this volume).

2. Although, conceptually, perceived control is expected to *moderate* the intention–behavior relation, in practice most investigators have looked at the additive effects of intention and perceptions of control. The reason for this practice is that empirically, even when an interaction is present in the data, statistical regression analyses often reveal only main effects. To obtain a statistically significant interaction requires that intention and perceived control scores cover the full range of the measurement scale. For most behaviors, however, a majority of respondents fall on one or the other side of these continua.

3. Only differences in belief strength were reported. It is not clear whether there were significant differences in outcome evaluations, motivations to comply with referents, or the perceived power of control factors.

REFERENCES

Ajzen, I. (1982). On behaving in accordance with one's attitudes. In M. P. Zanna, E. T. Higgins, & C. P. Herman (Eds.), *Consistency in social behavior: The Ontario Symposium* (Vol. 2, pp. 3–15). Hillsdale, NJ: Erlbaum.

Ajzen, I. (1985). From intentions to actions: A theory of planned behavior. In J. Kuhl & J. Beckman (Eds.), *Action-control: From cognition to behavior* (pp. 11–39). Heidelberg, Germany: Springer.

Ajzen, I. (1988). *Attitudes, personality, and behavior*. Chicago: Dorsey Press.

Ajzen, I. (1991). The theory of planned behavior. *Organizational Behavior and Human Decision Processes, 50*, 179–211.

Ajzen, I. (2005). *Attitudes, personality, and behavior* (2nd ed.). Maidenhead, UK: Open University Press.

Ajzen, I., & Fishbein, M. (1977). Attitude–behavior relations: A theoretical analysis and review of empirical research. *Psychological Bulletin, 84*, 888–918.

Ajzen, I., & Fishbein, M. (1980). *Understanding attitudes and predicting social behavior*. Englewood-Cliffs, NJ: Prentice-Hall.

Ajzen, I., & Fishbein, M. (2005). The influence of attitudes on behavior. In D. Albarracín, B. T. Johnson, & M. P. Zanna (Eds.), *The handbook of attitudes* (pp. 173–221). Mahwah, NJ: Erlbaum.

Albarracin, D., Johnson, B. T., Fishbein, M., & Muellerleile, P. A. (2001). Theories of reasoned action and planned behavior as models of condom use: A meta-analysis. *Psychological Bulletin, 127*, 142–161.

Allport, G. W. (1954). *The nature of prejudice*. Reading, MA: Addison-Wesley.

Armitage, C. J., & Conner, M. (2001). Efficacy of the theory of planned behavior: A meta-analytic review. *British Journal of Social Psychology, 40*, 471–499.

Asendorpf, J. B., Banse, R., & Muecke, D. (2002). Double dissociation between implicit and explicit personality self-concept: The case of shy behavior. *Journal of Personality & Social Psychology, 83*, 380–393.

Bagley, C., & Verma, G. (1979). *Racial prejudice, the individual and society*. Westmean, UK: Saxon House.

Bandura, A. (1997). *Self-efficacy: The exercise of control*. New York: Freeman.

Berger, I. E., & Mitchell, A. A. (1989). The effect of advertising on attitude accessibility, attitude confidence, and the attitude–behavior relationship. *Journal of Consumer Research, 16*, 269–279.

Blair, I. V. (2001). Implicit stereotypes and prejudice. In G. B. Moskowitz (Ed.), *Cognitive social psychology: The Princeton Symposium on the Legacy and Future of Social Cognition* (pp. 359–374). Mahwah, NJ: Erlbaum.

Bosson, J. K., Swann, W. B. J., & Pennebaker, J. W. (2000). Stalking the perfect measure of implicit self-esteem: The blind men and the elephant revisited? *Journal of Personality and Social Psychology, 79*, 631–643.

Brigham, J. C. (1971). Racial stereotypes, attitudes, and evaluations of and behavioral intentions toward Negroes and whites. *Sociometry, 34*, 360–380.

Bushway, S. D., & Piehl, A. M. (2001). Judging judicial discretion: Legal factors and racial discrimination in sentencing. *Law & Society Review, 35*, 733–764.

Conner, M., Sherlock, K., & Orbell, S. (1998). Psychosocial determinants of ecstasy use in young people in the UK. *British Journal of Health Psychology, 3*, 295–317.

Crosby, F., Bromley, S., & Saxe, L. (1980). Recent unobtrusive studies of Black and White discrimination and prejudice: A literature review. *Psychological Bulletin, 87*, 546–563.

Cunningham, W. A., Preacher, K. J., & Banaji, M. R. (2001). Implicit attitude measures: Consistency, stability, and convergent validity. *Psychological Science, 121*, 163–170.

Czopp, A. M., Monteith, M. J., Zimmerman, R. S., & Lynam, D. R. (2004). Implicit attitudes as potential protection from risky sex: Predicting condom use with the IAT. *Basic and Applied Social Psychology, 26*, 227–236.

Dabholkar, P. A. (1999). Expectancy-value models. In P. E. Earl & S. Kemp (Eds.), *The Elgar companion to consumer research and economic psychology* (pp. 200–208). Cheltenham, UK: Edward Elgar.

Daniels, L. A. (2001). *State of Black America 2000*. New York: National Urban League.

Devine, P. G. (1989). Stereotypes and prejudice: Their automatic and controlled components. *Journal of Personality & Social Psychology, 56*, 5–18.

Doll, J., & Ajzen, I. (1992). Accessibility and stability of predictors in the theory of planned behavior. *Journal of Personality and Social Psychology, 63*, 754–765.

Dovidio, J. F. (2001). On the nature of contemporary prejudice: The third wave. *Journal of Social Issues, 57*, 829–849.

Dovidio, J. F., Brigham, J. C., Johnson, B. T., & Gaertner, S. L. (1996). Stereotyping, prejudice, and discrimination: Another look. In N. Macrae, C. Stangor, & M. Hewstone (Eds.), *Stereotypes and stereotyping* (pp. 276–319). New York: Guilford.

Dovidio, J. F., Evans, N., & Tyler, R. B. (1986). Racial stereotypes: The contents of their cognitive representations. *Journal of Experimental Social Psychology, 22*, 22–37.

Dovidio, J. F., Kawakami, K., Johnson, C., Johnson, B., & Howard, A. (1997). On the nature of prejudice: Automatic and controlled processes. *Journal of Experimental Social Psychology, 33*, 510–540.

Downs, D. S., & Hausenblas, H. A. (2005). The theories of reasoned action and planned behavior applied to exercise: A meta-analytic update. *Journal of Physical Activity and Health, 2*, 76-97.

Duckitt, J. H. (1992). *The social psychology of prejudice*. Westport, CT: Praeger.

Eagly, A. H. (1998). Attitudes and the processing of attitude-relevant information. In J. G. Adair & D. Belanger (Eds.), *Advances in psychological science: Vol. 1. Social, personal, and cultural aspects* (pp. 185–201). Hove, UK: Psychology Press/Erlbaum (UK).

Eagly, A. H., & Chaiken, S. (1993). *The psychology of attitudes.* Fort Worth, TX: Harcourt Brace.

Eagly, A. H., & Chaiken, S. (1998). Attitude structure and function. In D. T. Gilbert & S. T. Fiske (Eds.), *The handbook of social psychology* (4th ed., Vol. 1, pp. 269–322). Boston, MA: Mcgraw-Hill.

Egloff, B., & Schmukle, S. C. (2002). Predictive validity of an implicit association test for assessing anxiety. *Journal of Personality and Social Psychology, 83,* 1441–1455.

Epstein, S. (1983). Aggregation and beyond: Some basic issues on the prediction of behavior. *Journal of Personality, 51,* 360–392.

Fazio, R. H. (1986). How do attitudes guide behavior? In R. M. H. Sorrentino & E. Tory (Ed.), *Handbook of motivation and cognition: Foundations of social behavior* (pp. 204–243). New York: Guilford.

Fazio, R. H. (1990). Multiple processes by which attitudes guide behavior: The MODE model as an integrative framework. In M. P. Zanna (Ed.), *Advances in experimental social psychology* (Vol. 23, pp. 75–109). San Diego, CA: Academic Press.

Fazio, R. H., Jackson, J. R., Dunton, B. C., & Williams, C. J. (1995). Variability in automatic activation as an unobstrusive measure of racial attitudes: A bona fide pipeline? *Journal of Personality and Social Psychology, 69,* 1013–1027.

Fazio, R. H., & Olson, M. A. (2003). Implicit measures in social cognition research: Their meaning and uses. *Annual Review of Psychology, 54,* 297–327.

Fazio, R. H., Powell, M. C., & Williams, C. J. (1989). The role of attitude accessibility in the attitude-to-behavior process. *Journal of Consumer Research, 16,* 280–288.

Fazio, R. H., & Towles-Schwen, T. (1999). The MODE model of attitude–behavior processes. In S. Chaiken & Y. Trope (Eds.), *Dual-process theories in social psychology* (pp. 97–116). New York: Guilford.

Fazio, R. H., & Williams, C. J. (1986). Attitude accessibility as a moderator of the attitude-perception and attitude–behavior relations: An investigation of the 1984 presidential election. *Journal of Personality and Social Psychology, 51,* 505–514.

Feather, N. T. (Ed.). (1982). *Expectations and actions: Expectancy–value models in psychology.* Hillsdale, NJ: Erlbaum.

Fishbein, M., (1963). An investigation of the relationships between beliefs about an object and the attitude toward that object. *Human Relations, 16,* 233–240.

Fishbein, M. (1967). Attitude and the prediction of behavior. In M. Fishbein (Ed.), *Readings in attitude theory and measurement* (pp. 477–492). New York: Wiley.

Fishbein, M., & Ajzen, I. (1974). Attitudes towards objects as predictors of single and multiple behavioral criteria. *Psychological Review, 81,* 59–74.

Fishbein, M., & Ajzen, I. (1975). *Belief, attitude, intention, and behavior: An introduction to theory and research.* Reading, MA: Addison-Wesley.

Fiske, S. T. (1998). Stereotyping, prejudice, and discrimination. In D. T. Gilbert, S. T. Fiske, & L. Gardner (Eds.), *The handbook of social psychology* (4th ed., Vol. 2, pp. 357–411). Boston, MA: McGraw-Hill.

Freeman, R. B. (1973). Decline of labor market discrimination and economic analysis. *The American Economic Review, 63,* 280–286.

Gaertner, S. L., & Dovidio, J. F. (1986). The aversive form of racism. In J. F. Dovidio & S. L. Gaertner (Eds.), *Prejudice, discrimination, and racism* (pp. 61–89). Orlando, FL: Academic.

Genthner, R. W., & Taylor, S. P. (1973). Physical aggression as a function of racial prejudice and the race of the target. *Journal of Personality and Social Psychology, 27,* 207–210.

Godin, G., & Kok, G. (1996). The theory of planned behavior: A review of its applications to health-related behaviors. *American Journal of Health Promotion, 11,* 87–98.

Godin, G., Valois, P., Lepage, L., & Desharnais, R. (1992). Predictors of smoking behaviour: An application of Ajzen's theory of planned behaviour. *British Journal of Addiction, 87,* 1335–1343.

Greenwald, A. G., McGhee, D. E., & Schwartz, J. L. K. (1998). Measuring individual differences in implicit cognition: The implicit association test. *Journal of Personality and Social Psychology, 74,* 1464–1480.

Hacker, A. (1995). *Two nations: Black and white, separate, hostile, unequal.* New York: Ballantine Books.

Hagger, M. S., Chatzisarantis, N. L. D., & Biddle, S. J. H. (2002). A meta-analytic review of the theories of reasoned action and planned behavior in physical activity: Predictive validity and the contribution of additional variables. *Journal of Sport and Exercise Psychology, 24,* 3–32.

Himelstein, P., & Moore, J. (1963). Racial attitudes and the action of Negro and white background figures as factors in petition-signing. *Journal of Social Psychology, 61,* 267–272.

Hugenberg, K., & Bodenhausen, G. V. (2003). Facing prejudice: Implicit prejudice and the perception of facial threat. *Psychological Science, 14,* 640–643.

Iceland, J. (2003). *Poverty in America: A handbook.* Berkeley, CA: University of California Press.

Jarrell, S. B., & Stanley, T. D. (2004). Declining bias and gender wage discrimination? A meta-regression analysis. *Journal of Human Resources, 39,* 828–838.

Jarvis, W. B. G., & Petty, R. E. (1996). The need to evaluate. *Journal of Personality and Social Psychology, 70,* 172–194.

Karpinski, A., & Hilton, J. L. (2001). Attitudes and the Implicit Association Test. *Journal of Personality & Social Psychology, 81,* 774–788.

Kidder, L. H., & Campbell, D. T. (1970). The indirect testing of attitudes. In G. F. Summers (Ed.), *Attitude measurement* (pp. 333–385). Chicago: Rand McNally.

Kokkinaki, F., & Lunt, P. (1997). The relationship between involvement, attitude accessibility and attitude-behaviour consistency. *British Journal of Social Psychology, 36,* 497–509.

Kraus, S. J. (1995). Attitudes and the prediction of behavior: A meta-analysis of the empirical literature. *Personality and Social Psychology Bulletin, 21,* 58–75.

Krosnick, J. A., Boninger, D. S., Chuang, Y. C., Berent, M. K., & Carnot, C. G. (1993). Attitude strength: One construct or many related constructs? *Journal of Personality and Social Psychology, 65,* 1132–1151.

Landrine, H., Klonoff, E. A., & Alcaraz, R. (1997). Racial discrimination in minor's access to tobacco. *Journal of Black Psychology, 23,* 135–147.

Larsen, K. S., Colen, L., von Flue, D., & Zimmerman, P. (1974). Situational pressure, attitudes towards blacks, and laboratory aggression. *Social Behavior and Personality, 2,* 219–221.

Leach, C. W., Peng, T. R., & Volckens, J. (2000). Is racism dead? Comparing (expressive) means and (structural equation) models. *British Journal of Social Psychology, 39,* 449–465.

Linn, L. S. (1965). Verbal attitudes and overt behavior: A study of racial discrimination. *Social Forces, 43,* 353–364.

Madden, T. J., Ellen, P. S., & Ajzen, I. (1992). A comparison of the theory of planned behavior and the theory of reasoned action. *Personality and Social Psychology Bulletin, 18*, 3–9.

Maison, D., Greenwald, A. G., & Bruin, R. H. (2004). Predictive validity of the implicit association test in studies of brands, consumer attitudes, and behavior. *Journal of Consumer Psychology, 14*, 405–415.

McConahay, J. B. (1986). Modern racism, ambivalence, and the Modern Racism Scale. In J. F. Dovidio & S. L. Gaertner (Eds.), *Prejudice, discrimination, and racism* (pp. 91–125). San Diego, CA: Academic Press.

McConahay, J. B., Hardee, B. B., & Batts, V. (1981). Has racism declined in America? It depends on who is asking and what is asked. *Journal of Conflict Resolution, 25*, 563–579.

Merton, R. K. (1940). Fact and factitiousness in ethnic opinionnaires. *American Sociological Review, 5*, 13–28.

Myers, S. L., & Chan, T. (1995). Racial discrimination in housing markets: Accounting for credit risk. *Social Science Quarterly, 76*, 543–561.

Neumann, R., Hälsenbeck, K., & Seibt, B. (2004). Attitudes towards people with AIDS and avoidance behavior: Automatic and reflective bases of behavior. *Journal of Experimental Social Psychology, 40*, 543–550.

Osgood, C. E., Suci, G. J., & Tannenbaum, P. H. (1957). *The measurement of meaning*. Urbana: University of Illinois Press.

Paulhus, D. L. (1991). Measurement and control of response bias. In J. P. Robinson, P. R. Shaver & L. S. Wrightsman (Eds.), *Measures of personality and social psychological attitudes* (pp. 17–59). San Diego, CA: Academic Press.

Petty, R. E., & Krosnick, J. A. (Eds.). (1995). *Attitude strength: Antecedents and consequences*. Mahwah, NJ: Erlbaum.

Poehlman, T. A., Uhlmann, E., Greenwald, A. G., & Banaji, M. R. (2005). Understanding and using the implicit association test: III. Meta-analysis of predictive validity. Unpublished manuscript, Yale University.

Raden, D. (1985). Strength-related attitude dimensions. *Social Psychology Quarterly, 48*, 312–330.

Schuman, H., Steeh, C., Bobo, L., & Krysan, M. (1997). *Racial attitudes in America: Trends and interpretations* (rev. ed.). Cambridge, MA: Harvard Universitiy Press.

Schütz, H., & Six, B. (1996). How strong is the relationship between prejudice and discrimination? A meta-analytic answer. *International Journal of Intercultural Relations, 20*, 441–462.

Sears, D. O. (1988). Symbolic racism. In P. A. Katz & D. A. Taylor (Eds.), Eliminating racism: Profiles in controversy. *Perspectives in social psychology* (pp. 53–84). New York: Plenum.

Sekaquaptewa, D., Espinoza, P., Thompson, M., Vargas, P., & von Hippel, W. (2003). Stereotypic explanatory bias: Implicit stereotyping as a predictor of discrimination. *Journal of Experimental Social Psychology, 39*, 75–82.

Sheeran, P. (2002). Intention-behavior relations: A conceptual and empirical review. In W. Stroebe & M. Hewstone (Eds.), *European review of social psychology* (Vol. 12, pp. 1–36). Chichester, UK: Wiley.

Sheeran, P., & Taylor, S. (1999). Predicting intentions to use condoms: A meta-analysis and comparison of the theories of reasoned action and planned behavior. *Journal of Applied Social Psychology, 29*, 1624–1675.

Smith, E. W., & Dixon, T. R. (1968). Verbal conditioning as a function of race of the experimenter and prejudice of the subject. *Journal of Experimental Social Psychology, 4*, 285–301.

Talaska, C. A., Fiske, S. T., & Chaiken, S. (2004). *Predicting discrimination: A meta-analysis of the racial attitude–behavior literature.* Unpublished manuscript.

Teachman, B. A., & Woody, S. R. (2003). Automatic processing in spider phobia: Implicit fear associations over the course of treatment. *Journal of Abnormal Psychology, 112,* 100–109.

Thurstone, L. L. (1931). The measurement of social attitudes. *Journal of Abnormal and Social Psychology, 26,* 249–269.

Weigel, R. H., & Newman, L. S. (1976). Increasing attitude–behavior correspondence by broadening the scope of the behavioral measure. *Journal of Personality and Social Psychology, 33,* 793–802.

Werner, P. D. (1978). Personality and attitude-activism correspondence. *Journal of Personality and Social Psychology, 36,* 1375–1390.

Wicker, A. W. (1969). Attitudes versus actions: The relationship of verbal and overt behavioral responses to attitude objects. *Journal of Social Issues, 25,* 41–78.

Wiers, R. W., Van Woerden, N., Smulders, F. T. Y., & De Jong, P. J. (2002). Implicit and explicit alcohol-related cognitions in heavy and light drinkers. *Journal of Abnormal Psychology, 111,* 648–658.

Wilson, T. D., Lindsey, S., & Schooler, T. Y. (2000). A model of dual attitudes. *Psychological Review, 107,* 101–126.

Zajonc, R. T. (1980). Feeling and thinking: Preferences need no inferences. *American Psychologist, 35,* 117–123.

14

How Behavior Shapes Attitudes
Cognitive Dissonance Processes

JEFF STONE and NICHOLAS C. FERNANDEZ

University of Arizona

H ave you ever put your foot in your mouth or did something that you wish you had not done? Mistakes like these can make people feel embarrassed, somewhat ashamed, or even mortified by their actions. To feel better, people sometimes apologize or make amends for their mistake. On other occasions, however, mistakes in judgment and action cause immense psychological discomfort, especially when the actions are inconsistent with deeply cherished beliefs, values, morals, or traits that define the self-concept. When the consequences of a discrepant behavior are severe, taking responsibility may not reduce the discomfort; indeed, admitting to the mistake may make matters worse. Sometimes our only option for reducing the discomfort is to deny, trivialize, or seek justification for the immoral or incompetent act. Our need to restore a sense of integrity can, under some conditions, even lead us to distort our perceptions of what we did. The purpose of this chapter is to explore the processes of attitude and behavior change that unfold when people commit themselves to a position or a course of action, only to realize later that it was the wrong thing to do.

Few people are immune to the need to perceive consistency between attitudes and behavior. Take, for example, how some have wrestled with the ongoing war in Iraq. On March 20, 2003, U.S. and British led coalition forces invaded Iraq and declared war on the regime of Iraqi President Saddam Hussein. By the time President George W. Bush landed on the deck of the aircraft carrier Abraham Lincoln and declared that combat operations in Iraq were over, hundreds of coalition soldiers and thousands of Iraqi citizens had been killed or wounded in the fighting. Was the outcome of the invasion worth the cost of so many shattered lives? Many have argued that it was not, because the primary goal for the invasion has yet to be achieved.

One of the primary justifications for the invasion of Iraq and overthrow of Saddam Hussein was that he possessed stockpiles of weapons of mass destruction (WMD). Many leaders in the United States, including President George W. Bush, then-Secretary of Defense Donald Rumsfeld, and then-National Security Adviser Condoleezza Rice, publicly stated the belief that Hussein had WMDs and was planning to use them against Western countries. The threat of Hussein's WMDs was also stated emphatically by British Prime Minister Tony Blair on September 24, 2002, in the House of Commons:

> His weapons of mass destruction program is active, detailed, and growing.... The intelligence picture (the intelligence services)...concludes that Iraq has chemical and biological weapons, that Saddam has continued to produce them, that he has existing and active military plans for the use of chemical and biological weapons, which could be activated within 45 minutes,.... and that he is actively trying to acquire nuclear weapons capability.

Blair and other leaders argued that if Saddam Hussein had biological and chemical weapons that could be activated in less than one hour, then an invasion was necessary to prevent future terrorist attacks against Western countries. However, in the months during and following the invasion, doubts about the existence of WMD in Iraq began to emerge. Not only did Iraqi troops fail to employ any WMDs against the attacking coalition forces, but the search for the stockpile of WMDs had drawn a blank. Where was the solid evidence that Blair claimed to have seen?

Despite the early disconfirmation of his beliefs, Blair again stated his conviction in a speech to the House of Commons when he said that "There are literally thousands of sites...but it is only now that the Iraq survey group has been put together that a dedicated team of people, which includes former UN inspectors, scientists and experts, will be able to go in and do the job properly...." (He went on to state "I have no doubt that they will find the clearest possible evidence of Saddam's weapons of mass destruction."

Here, we believe, is the first indication that British Prime Minister Toni Blair was feeling the discomfort that follows from discrepant behavior. He had stated, in public, that Iraq had WMDs, but the search had failed to find any evidence of WMDs. How did he reduce his discomfort? By providing new information that dismissed the discrepancy: The reason WMDs had not been discovered was because the wrong type of people were looking for them—they were not "former UN inspectors, scientists, and experts"—who really knew what to look for. This claim allowed him to dismiss the inconsistency between his preinvasion convictions and the postinvasion reality of the missing WMD. Unfortunately, it would not last: Even after the so-called experts looked for the next seven months, no evidence of WMD was found.

How do people respond when they continue to receive information that disconfirms their firm and publicly stated beliefs? A rational person might begin to realize the mistake, accept the new information, and alter his or her beliefs to fit reality. But people are not always rational animals. As Elliot Aronson (1973) once observed, when faced with undeniable discrepancies, people become *rationaliz-*

ing animals. Rather than admitting the mistake, they often change their beliefs to justify their negative behaviors.

Six more months passed with no explanation for why the stockpiles of WMDs could not be found. Tony Blair was faced with a stark, undeniable discrepancy between his publicly stated prewar beliefs and the failure to find WMDs in Iraq. It certainly appeared to some that Blair and the other coalition leaders had misled the public to gain support for the hostile invasion of a weaker country. Pressured to admit that they had made a serious mistake in judgment, Blair told the Commons Liaison Committee in July of 2004:

> I have to accept we haven't found them (WMD) and we may never find them, we don't know what has happened to them.... They could have been removed. They could have been hidden. They could have been destroyed.

Another brilliant parry: By claiming that the WMDs were moved, hidden, or destroyed, Blair was able to maintain consistency between his statement about the existence of WMDs in Iraq, and the continued disconfirmation of his beliefs. The weapons were there all the time, but coalition forces are unable to find them because they have been moved, hidden, or destroyed. As the coalition forces continued to sweep the country but failed to turn up any evidence of usable WMDs, Blair finally apologized publicly for his mistake in a keynote Labour conference speech:

> The evidence about Saddam having actual biological and chemical weapons, as opposed to the capability to develop them, has turned out to be wrong. I acknowledge that and accept it. I simply point out, such evidence was agreed by the whole international community, not least because Saddam had used such weapons against his own people and neighboring countries.... And the problem is, I can apologize for the information that turned out to be wrong, but I can't, sincerely at least, apologize for removing Saddam.... The world is a better place with Saddam in prison.

Whereas Blair apologized for the failure to find WMDs, note that he did not apologize for the invasion of Iraq. Yes, the initial reason for the invasion was wrong, but the ends justify the means; removing Saddam from power has made the world safe. By recruiting the belief that the invasion made the world safer, Blair was able to bolster his original support for the war and reduce his discomfort over the failure to find WMDs.

Why did Tony Blair continue to bolster his beliefs about the invasion in the face of such overwhelming evidence against the existence of WMDs? Because by making irrevocable commitments to their WMD beliefs, coalition leaders were suddenly put in a position to make sense out of their seemingly irrational and incompetent behavior. They had publicly advocated going to war to depose Saddam Hussein because he had WMDs, and was therefore a danger to the coalition countries. But their version of social reality was disconfirmed when no WMDs were found. The failure to find WMDs is very problematic, because a rational analysis would suggest that perhaps it was a mistake to believe in WMDs and go to war in Iraq. That conclusion is very difficult for us to accept.

Instead of recognizing the mistake and owning up to it, many chose to bolster their beliefs in the initial position. Rather than admit that they had been wrong, some chose to strengthen their resolve. This is the power of self-justification; our need to maintain consistency between our attitudes, beliefs, and behavior can sometimes lead us to do some very strange things. When we behave in ways that contradict or challenge our own attitudes and beliefs, the discomfort we feel can motivate us to distort perceptions of our actions.

COGNITIVE DISSONANCE THEORY

In 1957, Leon Festinger described a theory called "Cognitive Dissonance" that was developed to explain the psychological processes that determine how people resolve important discrepancies between their behavior and beliefs. Festinger proposed that cognitive dissonance is a very common psychological phenomenon that many individuals experience on a daily basis. For example, cognitive dissonance is experienced when smokers, who are trying to quit, reach for yet another cigarette, or when dieters succumb to temptation and order the dessert they know they shouldn't have. It happens when consumers spend more money than they really want to spend. And it happens when serious students decide to go out partying when they know they should stay home and study for "the big test." In each of these examples, at least one of the cognitive elements (attitudes, beliefs, or behavior) is inconsistent with one or more of the other cognitive elements. The knowledge that we did not study for the exam (cognitive element 1) directly conflicts with the knowledge that we should have studied for the big test (cognitive element 2). Festinger proposed that whenever there is inconsistency between cognitions, there is cognitive dissonance.

According to Festinger (1957), the perception of cognitive dissonance induces a negative state of tension, which is similar to how people feel when they are hungry or thirsty. Like hunger or thirst, dissonance motivates people to reduce their discomfort, but in the case of dissonance, people become motivated to restore psychological consistency. The psychological processes by which people restore consistency among cognitions can lead to enduring and meaningful changes in the way we view our social world.

The Magnitude of Dissonance

Festinger proposed that when two cognitions are inconsistent, the amount of psychological discomfort that people experience depends on the importance of the cognitions. If cognitions are important, then the dissonance aroused will be much greater than when cognitions are unimportant. For example, let us say that we decide to go out to the big party and not study for the test that night. Cognitive dissonance will be induced because doing well on the test is inconsistent with failing to study the night before the exam. The magnitude of the discomfort aroused, however, will depend on how important doing well on the test is to us. If performance on the test is not important, either because it is not a class we care about, or because the exam represents only a small percentage of our grade, then the discomfort may not motivate a need to restore consistency. However, if performance on the test is important because the class is in our major or the test is worth a significant percent of our grade, then the dissonance aroused by the inconsistency would be stronger. Thus, when inconsistencies are present, the magnitude of discomfort experienced depends on the importance of the relevant cognitions.

Reducing Cognitive Dissonance

When we experience this uncomfortable state of dissonance-induced arousal, what determines how we reduce it? Festinger suggested that this could be done in a number of ways. The first and most obvious way to reduce discomfort is to change the behavioral cognition by changing the problem behavior. If the smoker decides to quit smoking then he or she would resolve the inconsistency between behavior (smoking) and knowledge of the risk of cancer that is caused by the behavior. But changing behavior is not always a viable strategy for restoring consistency. People who smoke have a difficult time quitting, and like Tony Blair, once people have committed themselves publicly to a course of action, it can be impossible to change or reverse direction. How do we deal with dissonance when we cannot change our actions or take them back? As suggested by Tony Blair's behavior following the failure to find WMD, when people are unable to undo a discrepant behavior, or make amends for it, to restore consistency they may have to change their attitudes and beliefs about what they did . This strategy for reducing the discomfort associated with dissonance can often lead to some rather puzzling and bizarre distortions of reality.

CLASSIC EXPERIMENTS ON COGNITIVE DISSONANCE

Justifying Untruths

In one of the first dissonance experiments, Festinger and Carlsmith (1959) showed evidence for the prediction that people will distort their perceptions of reality to reduce dissonance. Participants in the experiment were asked to perform a very boring task that consisted of turning a set of wooden spools on a board 1/4 turn at a time. After they completed it, the experimenter explained that the study was investigating the effect of expectations on performance. The participants were told that in their condition, no expectations were created prior to completing the spool-turning task, but in other conditions expectations were created by describing the task in advance. Participants were then asked to help out with the next session by telling the waiting participant (really a confederate of the study) that the spool-turning task was really interesting and enjoyable. Note that if participants agreed to help the experimenter, their behavior—telling the waiting confederate that the task was interesting and enjoyable—would be inconsistent with their knowledge that the task was boring. Festinger and Carlsmith predicted that the dissonance created by lying about the task could cause psychological discomfort, which could motivate participants to distort their perceptions of what they had done.

In addition, Festinger and Carlsmith manipulated the level of discomfort that participants should experience over their lie. In one condition of the study, the experimenter explained to participants that if they agreed to help, he would pay them $20 for telling the unsuspecting confederate that the task was interesting and enjoyable. However, in another condition, the experimenter said he would pay participants only $1 for telling the lie about the task. Festinger and Carlsmith reasoned that by receiving $20 for lying (big bucks in 1957), participants would experience less discomfort over the lie because the cognition "I received a lot of money" was sufficient justification for telling the lie about the task. Thus, Festinger and Carlsmith predicted that those paid $20 for lying to the confederate would not be highly motivated to distort their perceptions of their activities. In the low payment condition, the authors hypothesized that being paid $1 provided insufficient justification for misleading the other person, and as a result, the inconsistency created by telling the lie would cause the psychological discomfort associated with dissonance.

You might think that people would try to take back the lie if they could, but of course, once the confederate left the room, undoing the lie was not possible. So how could they reduce their discomfort? All participants were subsequently asked to report their experiences during the study, including how much they enjoyed the spool turning task. The results showed that participants in the $1 condition reported that the task was significantly more enjoyable than those who had told the lie for $20 or those in a control group who had not told the lie. Presumably, to reduce the inconsistency between the lie and their knowledge that the task was boring, participants in the $1 condition changed their attitude toward the task so that it was consistent with what they told the waiting confederate. This study was the first to show that the need to maintain consistency between attitudes and behavior can be powerful enough to cause people to distort their perceptions of reality.

Subsequent studies discovered that people do not need to lie to another's face to alter their attitudes for the sake of consistency. For example, Cohen (1962) showed that having (participants write an essay in which they advocated a viewpoint that was inconsistent with their own was sufficient to cause them to change their attitudes toward the topic, especially when there was insufficient justification for the behavior (i.e., participants were paid very little to write the essay). Linder, Cooper, and Jones (1967) noted that some of the attitude change effects might depend upon how much choice participants have over whether to write the essay. In a clever set of experiments, Linder et al. varied both incentive and choice to decline the request to commit a counter-attitudinal act. Both experiments showed that, consistent with a dissonance interpretation, participants changed their attitudes more under low compared to high incentive when they made the choice to write the counterattitudinal essay. In contrast, when forced to write the essay, participants attributed their inconsistent behavior to the situation, experienced less discomfort, and were less motivated to alter their attitudes to justify their behavior.

Finally, it may not be necessary to actually say something that is inconsistent with important attitudes or beliefs to feel the pinch of dissonance. Other studies suggest that when people choose to take a counterattitudinal position on an issue, the mere thought of having to write a counterattitudinal essay is sufficient to cause attitude change toward the issue, even if they never put pen to paper (Linder et al., 1967). Apparently, simply *preparing* to say something you don't believe, especially when you chose to prepare it, is sufficient to induce the discomfort and need to justify what follows from holding two inconsistent cognitions.

Justifying Difficult Decisions

Dissonance processes are not limited to the situation in which people say something they do not believe. Festinger (1957, 1964) also proposed that everyday decisions could create cognitive dissonance and the need to justify behavior. According to dissonance theory, people should be most likely to justify a decision when it involves deciding between similarly attractive alternatives. A choice between two equally attractive alternatives necessarily creates inconsistency between the positive features of the rejected alternative and the negative features of the selected alternative. For example, choosing one MP3 player over another causes dissonance when the rejected MP3 player has positive features that are not present in the chosen MP3 player, and the chosen MP3 player has negative features that are not present in the rejected MP3 player. When both options are similarly desirable, the decision is more difficult, and once one desirable item is selected over another desirable option, the inconsistency created by the decision is likely to cause discomfort.

To test this hypothesis, Brehm (1956) had participants rate their attitudes toward several consumer products including toasters, coffee makers, and blenders. Immediately following their assessments, participants were given the choice to keep one of the two appliances that they had rated. To control the level of dissonance created by the decision, Brehm also manipulated the similarity of the two appliances offered as a choice. In the "easy decision" condition, the experimenter offered participants the choice between two appliances that they had initially rated as very different from each other. Because the two alternatives were not equally desirable, selecting the more desirable product should not create much inconsistency. In the "difficult choice" condition, participants chose between two appliances that they had rated as highly desirable. The prediction was that those who made the more difficult choice between the equally desirable appliances would experience more inconsistency, and therefore more discomfort, than those who made the easier choice between two dissimilar appliances.

After choosing one product to keep, participants once again were asked to evaluate the products. How would dissonance impact their perceptions of the appliances? When people make a difficult choice, they may be overcome with regret and attempt to change their decision. Naturally, this is not always possible; many decisions are irrevocable. When people cannot change their minds but still need to reduce their discomfort, they have a tendency to justify the decision by focusing on the positive features of the chosen alternative and the negative features of the rejected alternative. Focus on the consonant elements leads to a "spreading of alternatives," whereby people change their attitudes toward the two alternatives so that the chosen alternative is viewed more favorably and the rejected alternative is viewed less favorably than before the decision. Dissonance is reduced because spreading the alternatives makes the two options subjectively less similar; with the chosen alternative now perceived as much, much better than the rejected alternative.

As hypothesized, participants in the difficult choice condition reported significantly more attitude change toward the chosen and rejected appliances compared to participants in the easy choice condition (Brehm, 1956). Subsequent research has shown that dissonance processes can cause attitude change following a wide variety of decisions, including the choice between jobs in the military (Walster, 1964), between eliminating or not eliminating student draft deferments (Crano & Messé, 1970), between horses at the race track (Knox & Inkster, 1968), between partners in close relationships (Johnson & Rusbult, 1989), collective decisions made by small groups (Zanna & Sande, 1987), and the choice between types of research in which to participate (Harmon-Jones & Harmon-Jones, 2002; Stone, 1999).

Justifying Effort

Have you ever worked very hard for something only to learn later that your efforts were not worthwhile? Such outcomes can create dissonance because working very hard is inconsistent with getting nothing in return. Reducing the discomfort and restoring consistency may be easy if you can reduce your perception of how much time and effort were expended. But when it is clear that you did everything in your power to achieve a goal that turns out to be worthless, it may be impossible to distort your perceptions of the effort. Under these conditions, to restore consistency you may have to resort to altering your perceptions of how much you gained from the waste of time and energy.

Aronson and Mills (1959) developed a study to test how people resolve the dissonance that follows from unjustified effort. Female college students in this study signed up to be part of a "sexual discussion group." To join the group, they were asked to partake in an "initiation process" to assure the experimenter that they would be comfortable talking about sex during the group meetings. After they had agreed to the screening process, they were assigned to one of two initiation conditions. In the mild initiation condition, participants were asked to read aloud sexually nonexplicit words like *petting*. Because these words were not very embarrassing, these participants did not have to work very hard to join the group. However, those assigned to the severe initiation condition were asked to read aloud sexually explicit words like *erection*. The embarrassing nature of these words caused participants in this condition to work harder to join the discussion group.

After being "initiated" the experimenter then had participants listen to a recording of the sexual discussion group ostensibly from a recent meeting. When the tape began, participants heard a technical presentation and discussion about the secondary sexual characteristics of lower vertebrates. To the participants' surprise, the group turned out to be very boring. Immediately following this, the experimenter asked participants to express their attitudes toward the group.

You might imagine that in either condition people would express a negative attitude toward the boring discussion group. But this was not the case. As predicted, participants in the severe initiation condition reported significantly more positive attitudes toward the discussion group compared to those in the mild initiation condition. Why would this be the case? Aronson and Mills (1959) suggested that participants in the severe initiation condition perceived an inconsistency between the high level of effort they expended to join the group and the realization that the group was boring and uninteresting. Working hard for nothing caused them to feel uncomfortable, but they could not deny what they endured to join the group. To reduce the dissonance, they instead changed their attitude toward the group. Why did they go through so much to join this boring group? They did so because the group was in fact interesting, and therefore, was worth the effort.

Effort justification can also account for why we come to like foods that are not very tasty. Zimbardo, Weisenberg, Firestone, and Levy (1965) showed that college students and army reservists who were encouraged to eat fried grasshoppers changed their attitudes in favor of liking grasshoppers more when the person who induced them to eat the insect was unpleasant, snobbish, and demanding compared to when the persuader was capable, well organized, and liked. Working hard to swallow a food you dislike creates dissonance, but you may not have to justify the effort if the reason for doing so was to impress an attractive date or a likeable boss. Dissonance theory predicts that you will be more motivated to like eating insects or other distasteful cuisine when implored to do so by a person you dislike.

Justifying a Failure to Act

Learning principles would suggest that to get someone to avoid a forbidden behavior, they must be threatened with a harsh punishment. Indeed, our legal system is based on this assumption: The more severe the punishment for a crime, the more motivated a person will be to avoid committing the proscribed act. Dissonance theory, in contrast, could predict that someone would be motivated to avoid a forbidden behavior if threatened with a *mild* punishment. The key to this prediction rests in how dissonance processes influence attitudes toward the forbidden behavior if in fact a person failed to act due to a mild punishment.

In one study designed to test the role of dissonance in how the threat of punishment influences attitudes, Aronson and Carlsmith (1963) allowed preschool children to play with and evaluate some toys. One of the most attractive toys was then put on a table, and the experimenter told the child that he or she was not allowed to play with the toy while he was gone. Some children were told they would receive a relatively severe punishment if they disobeyed and played with the toy: The experimenter said that he would be very angry and would take all of the toys away. Other children were told they would receive a relatively mild punishment if they disobeyed: The experimenter said that he would be "a little annoyed" if the child played with the forbidden toy. The experimenter then left the room for 10 minutes, during which time none of the children played with the forbidden toy. Then the experimenter returned to the room and had the children evaluate all of the toys again. How did the level of threatened punishment influence their attitudes toward the desirable but forbidden toy?

As predicted by dissonance theory, the children who refrained from playing with the toy following a mild threat evaluated the toy significantly more negatively than did children who had been threatened with severe consequences. To explain this difference, Aronson and Carlsmith suggested that the severe threat served as a consonant cognition that reduced dissonance between the cognitive elements "I like this toy" and "I did not play with this toy." The severe threat provided plenty of justification for not playing with the forbidden toy—who would risk having the cool toys removed? In contrast, the children in the mild punishment group did not have sufficient justification for avoiding the attractive toy; all that would happen is that the experimenter would be a little annoyed. To resolve the inconsistency between their positive attitude toward the toy and their failure to play with it, they became more negative toward the forbidden toy to justify not playing with it. As a result, they changed their attitudes to justify not playing with forbidden toy.

INVESTIGATING THE MOTIVATIONAL ENGINE THAT DRIVES COGNITIVE DISSONANCE

The research reviewed thus far makes one point clear: People will go to great lengths, and make substantial changes in their attitudes and beliefs, to restore consistency following a discrepant behavior. None of the studies covered thus far, however, show directly that people are motivated by consistency needs to change their attitudes and beliefs. This observation about what motives, desires, and goals are satisfied by changing attitudes and beliefs when dissonance is present has been a hotly debated topic for decades.

The Role of Arousal

Festinger (1957) originally proposed that inconsistencies between attitudes and behavior cause "a negative drive state" that motivates a desire to restore consistency. However, some researchers questioned whether it was the reduction of negative arousal, rather than the restoration of consistency among cognitions, that drives the changes observed in the classic studies. Showing that people feel uncomfortable and seek relief from their discomfort requires that researchers manipulate the perception of arousal directly. If varying the perception of arousal also varies the degree of attitude change following a discrepant behavior, it would suggest that the reduction of discomfort is a strong motivating force when cognitive discrepancies are present.

Zanna and Cooper (1974) reported a compelling demonstration of the arousal properties of dissonance. They used a "misattribution" technique to test whether attitude change following counter-attitudinal behavior reflects a motivation to reduce unpleasant arousal. Participants were asked to ingest a placebo pill, allegedly to investigate the effect of the drug on memory later in the session. Some participants were told that this pill would have the "side effect" of making them feel tense and aroused; others were told that the pill would make them feel relaxed;

a third group was told that the pill would have no noticeable side effects. Participants then were asked to participate in a purportedly unrelated study while they waited for the pill to be absorbed. This unrelated study involved writing a counterattitudinal essay, either under high or low choice conditions. After writing the essay, participants reported their own attitude on the issue.

The results revealed that when participants did not expect any side effects from the drug, those who wrote the essay under high choice reported more favorable attitudes toward the issue than did participants in the low choice condition. This finding replicates the standard dissonance effect showing that people will adjust their attitudes to fit their behavior when they perceive high choice or low external justification for the discrepant act. How do we know that this is driven by an unpleasant state of arousal? In the condition where high-choice participants expected the pill to create unpleasant arousal, no attitude change occurred: participants remained opposed to the topic despite having chosen to write the essay. This finding suggests that leading participants to interpret their unpleasant arousal as being caused by the pill eliminated the need to reduce dissonance by changing their attitude. In contrast, when participants expected the pill to make them feel relaxed, attitude change in the high choice condition was significantly *increased*. Apparently, participants in this condition inferred that they would be feeling even more aroused if not for the pill, and this inference heightened their motivation to reduce dissonance by changing their attitude. Zanna and Cooper (1974) concluded that dissonance is a phenomenologically aversive state of arousal, and that attitude change is driven by the need to reduce this state of discomfort (see also Higgins, Rhodewalt, & Zanna, 1979; Zanna, Higgins, & Taves, 1976).

The Role of Aversive Consequences

The question of why inconsistencies cause an aversive state of arousal was redefined in an influential review of dissonance theory presented by Cooper and Fazio (1984). In their "new look" at the data, Cooper and Fazio (1984) concluded that Festinger's original emphasis on psychological consistency was misguided; the relevant data indicated that dissonance occurs when people take personal responsibility for having committed a behavior that produced an aversive outcome. People are then motivated to change their attitudes to reduce their discomfort over the perceived consequences of the unwanted act.

Cooper and Fazio (1984) proposed that dissonance arousal begins when people engage in a behavior and then immediately evaluate the consequences of the act. Only when the behavioral consequences are perceived to fall outside of their standards and cannot be revoked do people conclude that the outcome is aversive or unwanted. People then decide if they are responsible for the consequences by evaluating whether they had choice and whether the outcome could have been anticipated or foreseen. If people perceive that they acted under their own volition, and they could have foreseen the outcome, then they accept responsibility for the behavioral outcome. The acceptance of responsibility for the aversive outcome causes dissonance arousal.

Evidence that the consequences of behavior are a necessary factor in dissonance arousal comes from studies in which dissonance-induced attitude change did not occur in the absence of any unwanted negative outcome for the behavior. In one experiment, Cooper and Worchel (1970) replicated the Festinger and Carlsmith (1959) procedure in which a naive participant was asked to tell a confederate that a very boring task was enjoyable for either $1 or $20. In addition, the study manipulated whether the lie had an aversive consequence by having the confederate express either acceptance or disbelief in the lie. The results showed that despite having lied about the task, participants came to rate the dull task as more interesting when the confederate believed their lie compared to when the lie was not believed. This and other studies led Cooper and Fazio (1984) to conclude that aversive behavioral consequences are a necessary condition for dissonance to be aroused. However, other researchers have challenged this conclusion by showing that people can be motivated by dissonance following a counter-attitudinal behavior even when their behavior had no consequences (Harmon-Jones, Brehm, Greenberg, Simon, & Nelson, 1996). Thus, not all researchers agree that dissonance simply motivates a need to reduce discomfort over an aversive consequence.

The Role of the Self

Aronson offered an altogether different perspective on dissonance processes as early as 1968. He suggested that a common thread ran through almost all dissonance studies—most involved situations that challenged people's expectancies or beliefs about themselves. To predict systematically when dissonance would occur, dissonance theory needed to take into account the firm expectations people hold for themselves and their behavior. For example, Aronson argued that the dissonance aroused in Festinger and Carlsmith's (1959) study was not due to the inconsistency between the thoughts, "I believe the tasks were boring" and "I told someone the tasks were interesting." Instead, the dissonance was aroused by the inconsistency between cognitions about the self (e.g., "I am a decent and truthful human being") and cognitions about the behavior (e.g., "I have misled a person to believe something that is not true"). Aronson concluded that "If dissonance exists it is because the individual's behavior is inconsistent with his self-concept" (1968, p. 23).

Aronson's emphasis on the self-concept shifted the motivational nature of dissonance from one of general psychological consistency to a more specific motive for self-consistency. That is, because beliefs about the self are highly important, dissonance motivates people to maintain their self-concept by changing their attitudes or beliefs. Moreover, Aronson reasoned that many of the successful dissonance experiments tacitly assumed that subjects held positive expectations for their behavior. Would misleading someone about the dullness of a task cause dissonance in people who held negative expectancies for their behavior? Aronson hypothesized that it would not; people with low self-esteem (i.e., negative expectancies) should not experience dissonance under the same conditions as people with high self-esteem (i.e., positive expectancies). Thus, the self-consistency perspective refined dissonance theory by specifying the cognitions most likely to underlie dissonance processes, and it also provided specific predictions regarding self-esteem differences in dissonance phenomena (Thibodeau & Aronson, 1992; see also Aronson, Cohen, & Nail, 1999). Several studies provided support for this view by showing that people with positive self-expectancies (Aronson & Carlsmith, 1962; Maracek & Mettee, 1972) or high self-esteem (Glass, 1964; Gibbons, Eggleston, & Benthin, 1997; Prislin & Pool, 1996) were more likely to reduce dissonance following discrepant behavior compared to people with low self-esteem.

An alternative view of how the self-concept operates in dissonance processes was advanced by research on the theory of self-affirmation (Steele, 1988). Like Aronson, Steele (1988) proposed that dissonance experiments typically induce participants to engage in actions that challenge the self-concept. One way to restore the self-concept is to eliminate the inconsistency by changing relevant attitudes or beliefs. However, dissonance reduction through attitude change is just one way people can restore the integrity of their globally positive self. According to self-affirmation theory (Steele, 1988), if the primary goal of attitude change is to restore a positive sense of the self, then any thought or action that enhances self-worth should be sufficient to reduce dissonance. The novel prediction made by self-affirmation theory was that if people can call upon other positive aspects of their self-concept, dissonance would be reduced without having to change attitudes related to the inconsistency.

Several studies show that simply reminding people of their positive self-attributes eliminates the need to change attitudes following a discrepant act. For example, Steele and Lui (1983) induced dissonance though counterattitudinal behavior and then had some participants complete a scale measuring their sociopolitical values prior to completing a measure of their attitudes toward their discrepant behavior. The data showed that dissonance-induced attitude change was eliminated when participants with strong sociopolitical values were allowed to "reaffirm" those values by completing the sociopolitical survey before their attitudes were assessed. Participants who were not value-oriented, or who did not complete the sociopolitical value measure after writing the essay, reduced dissonance by changing their attitudes. Thus, drawing on valued "self-resources" attenuates the attitude change that follows in many of the classic experimental paradigms (see McQueen & Klein, 2006, for a review).

Note that to affirm the self, people must be able to think about more positive than negative self-resources following a discrepant act. People with high self-esteem presumably have more positive attributes available for affirmation compared to people with low self-esteem. Therefore, self-affirmation should be a more effective strategy for dissonance reduction among people with high self-esteem. Steele, Spencer, and Lynch (1993) tested this prediction in an experiment in which participants with high or low self-esteem participated in the free choice paradigm (Brehm, 1956). For some of the participants, self-attributes were primed when they completed the Rosenberg self-esteem scale (1979) before making their decision; the other participants made their decision without having their self-attributes primed. The results showed that when self-attributes were primed before the dissonance-arousing choice, participants with high self-esteem showed significantly less attitude change compared to participants with low self-esteem. In a no-prime control, both self-esteem groups showed similar levels of significant post-decision justification. Interestingly, the Steele et al. (1993) pattern of self-esteem differences was exactly opposite from what is predicted by the self-consistency perspective (i.e., people with high self-esteem should show more dissonance reduction than people with low self-esteem, see Thibodeau & Aronson, 1992).

You may be wondering at this point how cognitions related to self-esteem can operate both as expectancies in dissonance arousal and as resources for dissonance reduction? Stone and Cooper (2001) proposed a new model of dissonance processes designed to explain how both processes could influence dissonance arousal and reduction. The Self-Standards Model (SSM; Stone & Cooper, 2001) maintains that people can use important attitudes, beliefs, or self-knowledge to understand the meaning of their behavior, but which criteria people use depends upon the type of information that is brought to mind or "primed" by cues in the situation.

Dissonance processes begin when, once they have acted, people evaluate their behavior against a standard of judgment, which may or may not relate to a cognitive representation of the self. For example, people can evaluate their behavior using a specific attitude or belief (Harmon-Jones et al., 1996), or using generally shared, normative considerations of what is aversive to most people (Cooper & Fazio, 1984). However, the assessment of behavior also may be based on personal, idiosyncratic standards for what is considered foolish or immoral, which tend to be linked to self-esteem. The SSM predicts that only the use of relevant personal standards in the assessment of behavior—standards that relate to idiosyncratic self-expectancies—will cause people with high self-esteem to experience more dissonance than people with low self-esteem following a discrepant behavior. Furthermore, once dissonance is aroused, the SSM predicts that the type of positive self-attributes brought to mind will determine their use as resources for dissonance reduction. For people with high self-esteem to self-affirm, they must bring to mind positive self-attributes that are unrelated to the discrepant behavior. Otherwise, research suggests that thinking about positive self-attributes that are relevant to the dissonant act will simply focus people on the discrepancy, with the resultant discomfort creating a need to justify their behavior (Aronson, Blanton, & Cooper, 1995; Blanton, Cooper, Skurnik, & Aronson, 1997). Thus, the SSM provides a framework from which to predict *when* and *how* self-esteem will moderate dissonance processes (Stone & Cooper, 2001).

Tests of the predictions made by the SSM have shown that attitude change can be a function of the predicted interaction between self-esteem and the type of standard used to assess the behavior across different classic paradigms (see Stone, 2001, 2003). For example, Stone and Cooper (2003) reported that after participants with high and low self-esteem wrote an uncompassionate essay, priming relevant positive self-attributes (e.g., compassion) caused more attitude change for participants with high self-esteem than for participants with low self-esteem. This result supports the claim that using relevant, positive self-attributes to assess the meaning of their behavior engages self-expectancies, which causes more dissonance among high compared to low self-esteem individuals. However, priming irrelevant positive self-attributes (e.g., creativity) caused more attitude change for participants with low self-esteem compared to those with high self-esteem. This supports the SSM prediction that when people focus on positive attributes that are unrelated to the cognitive discrepancy, those with high self-esteem have an easier time using them as affirmational resources compared to people with low self-esteem. As predicted by the SSM, when and how self-esteem moderated attitude change was a function of the accessibility and relevance of the positive attributes made salient after the discrepant act.

Finally, research has shown that a number of other individual differences moderate dissonance processes, including repression-sensitization (Olson & Zanna, 1982), self-monitoring (Snyder & Tanke, 1974), Machiavellianism (Epstein, 1980), preference for consistency (Cialdini, Trost, & Newsom, 1995), and attributional complexity (Stadler & Baron, 1998). When combined with research on how cognitions about the self influence dissonance processes, these findings suggest that whereas the need for consistency can be a strong force in shaping attitudes, under some conditions it may influence some people more than others. As originally observed by Festinger (1957), predicting for whom dissonance will have the greatest impact requires that the cognitions be identified that underlie the inconsistency and their importance to the people who are struggling with the discrepancy.

NEW DIRECTIONS IN DISSONANCE RESEARCH

As the theory of cognitive dissonance celebrates its 50th anniversary, researchers continue to investigate the rich and complex predictions that can be derived from the original book and the thousands of studies that have been published since 1957. In the next section, we describe some of the more recent developments in the study of how behavior can influence attitudes through cognitive dissonance processes.

Using Dissonance to Motivate Prosocial Behavior

One recent development in the study of dissonance emerged from research using hypocrisy to motivate prosocial behavior. Hypocrisy is most likely in situations in which people make a pro-attitudinal statement about the importance of performing a positive, prosocial target behavior. By itself, the proattitudinal statement is not predicted to arouse dissonance because it is neither inconsistent with people's beliefs nor capable of producing an aversive outcome. However, dissonance will occur if people are subsequently made mindful of the fact that they, themselves, do not perform the behavior they have advocated to others. Moreover, rather than changing attitudes, hypocrisy is predicted to motivate people to "practice what they preach," to initiate action toward bringing their behavior back into line with the prosocial direction of their advocacy.

The initial hypocrisy studies were designed to motivate sexually active college students to adopt the use of condoms to prevent AIDS (Aronson, Fried, & Stone, 1991; Stone, Aronson, Crain, Winslow, & Fried, 1994). Participants first made a videotaped speech in which they argued that college students should use condoms every time they have sexual intercourse. To induce hypocrisy, participants then were asked to generate a list of their previous failures to use condoms when having sexual intercourse. The results showed that when they acted hypocritically, participants reported higher intentions to use condoms in the future (Aronson et al., 1991), and when offered the opportunity, more purchased condoms, compared to participants who just advocated the use of condoms, were just made mindful of past failures to use condoms, or merely read about the dangers of AIDS (Stone et al., 1994). Other studies showed that an act of hypocrisy could motivate people to conserve more water when they shower (Dickerson, Thiboudeau, Aronson, & Miller, 1992), increase their participation in a recycling program (Fried & Aronson, 1995), and take action against policies that discriminate against minority group members (Son Hing, Li, & Zanna, 2002).

Why do people change their behavior and not their attitudes following an act of hypocrisy? According to Stone and colleagues, it is because an act of hypocrisy challenges a sense of self-integrity that people are motivated to uphold. The most direct way to restore self-integrity is to bring behavior back into line with the prosocial standards advocated in the speech. Stone, Weigand, Cooper, and Aronson (1997) tested this assumption by inducing hypocrisy about AIDS and condom use, and then simultaneously offering more than one behavioral option for dissonance reduction. Specifically, participants were offered one option that would solve the hypocritical discrepancy directly (e.g., condom purchase) and one that would allow affirmation of the self without solving the discrepancy directly (e.g., a donation to a homeless shelter). Participants then were allowed to choose which behavior they wanted to enact at the completion of the study. The results showed that when offered only the affirmation option (i.e., donation), 83% of those in the hypocrisy condition used it. However, when the affirmation option was offered alongside the option that would directly restore self-integrity (i.e., condom purchase), 78% chose the direct option, and only 13% chose the affirmation option. This study showed that when dissonance follows from an act of hypocrisy, people are primarily motivated to restore their self-integrity by changing the target behavior, even when other options for dissonance reduction, such as self-affirmation, are available and easy to complete.

There is at least one condition under which people may use attitude change rather than behavior change to resolve a hypocritical discrepancy. In a hypocrisy study on recycling, Fried (1998) manipulated the public nature of past failures to recycle. In one condition, after participants completed the mindfulness task, an experimenter read aloud their past failures to recycle. When later offered the opportunity to volunteer for a recycling program, participants who were publicly identified as failing to practice what they preached did not opt to improve their recycling behavior; instead, they changed their attitude to be more negative toward recycling behavior. In contrast, when past failures to recycle were kept private from the experimenter, participants were more likely to volunteer for a recycling program. These data suggest that when people are publicly associated with past failures to practice what they preach, they may feel embarrassed or ashamed of their past behavior, and this motivates them to justify their past transgressions through attitude change. But if allowed to privately "discover" their past failures on their own, the need to restore self-integrity motivates people to take action designed to improve their behavior in the future.

Recall that Festinger originally predicted that when behavior is inconsistent with beliefs, people often change their behavior to reduce the inconsistency. The hypocrisy research illustrates conditions under which people appear to avoid justifying their failures and instead focus on changing future behavior to restore a sense of consistency.

The Role of Culture in Dissonance

You may have wondered if dissonance and the need for consistency varies across cultures. In his original book, Festinger (1957) noted that prevailing "cultural mores and norms" can determine whether or not two cognitions are inconsistent. He observed that the same behavior might be perceived as inconsistent in one culture, but completely consistent with cultural mandates for behavior in another. He provided many examples of how culture not only determines what cognitions are inconsistent, but also how culture could influence the choice of dissonance reduction strategy.

The role of culture in determining dissonance, however, did not receive widespread attention from researchers until an influential review by Markus and Kitayama (1991). They called attention to the possibility that differences in the way the self is construed in collectivistic or interdependent cultures limit the generalizability of numerous processes, including those assumed to underlie cognitive dissonance. Citing several failures to replicate dissonance effects in collectivistic cultures like Japan, Markus and Kitayama concluded that people with an interdependent self-concept might not experience the motive for psychological consistency in the same way as people from an independent or individualistic culture. More recent research has provided support for Festinger's (1957) idea that dissonance operates under different conditions across cultures. For example, Kitayama (2002) showed that dissonance occurred among Japanese subjects only when they viewed a counterattitudinal act from the perspective of others. Similarly, Hoshino-Browne and colleagues (2005) found that Asian-Canadians with strong Asian identities showed significantly more postdecision justification when their decision would affect a close friend as opposed to the self. In contrast, European-Canadians and Asian-Canadians with a weak Asian identity were more likely to justify a difficult decision they made for themselves than a decision made for a close friend. Cross-cultural researchers are only now beginning to understand the full dynamics of how culture influences the dissonance processes that influence attitude change.

The Role of the Group in Dissonance

Researchers have begun to explore the interpersonal nature of dissonance processes (e.g., Cooper & Stone, 1999; Zanna & Sande, 1987), specifically, how a discrepant behavior enacted by another individual can influence attitude change in an observer. Sakai (1999) reported an experiment in which two individuals (one a confederate) completed a boring task modeled after Festinger and Carlsmith (1959). The experimenter then asked the confederate to tell the next participant (also a confederate) that the task was interesting. To introduce a feeling of "common fate," the confederate then turned to the naive participant and proposed that they tell the lie together. The confederate stated that he would do all the talking, but he then asked the participant if this would be okay. During the advocacy, the confederate and participant sat together facing the waiting confederate, but the naive participant did not partake in telling the waiting confederate that the task was interesting. In a control condition, the confederate agreed to tell the lie but did not address the participant as his partner, and during the advocacy, the participant stood off in a corner of the room while the confederate told the lie. The results showed that observers in the "common-fate" condition took more responsibility for their partner's behavior, and in a conceptual replication of the classic finding, also rated the boring task as more interesting than did observers in the control condition. The data suggest that agreeing to participate in a counter-attitudinal conspiracy, even if one is only tangentially involved, can cause dissonance and the motivation for attitude change.

In a different approach, research by Norton, Monin, Cooper, and Hogg (2003) investigated whether people can suffer "vicarious dissonance" when they share a social identity with someone whom they observe commit a counterattitudinal behavior. In one experiment, participants overheard an in-group or out-group member make a speech that was counterattitudinal for the observer. The data showed that participants who identified most with the in-group showed the most attitude change in the direction of the actor's intended speech, even when the speech was not actually delivered, but only when the actor was known to disagree with the statement (see Smith & Hogg, this volume). Another experiment showed that attitude change in the observers was moderated by the in-group actor's choice to make the counterattitudinal speech and the extent to which the actor's speech had foreseeable aversive consequences. However, witnessing an in-group member commit a counterattitudinal behavior did not induce "personal" psychological discomfort in the observer; rather, it induced a relatively high level of "vicarious discomfort"—the discomfort observers imagined feeling if they were in the actor's shoes. These and other studies (e.g., Matz & Wood, 2005) indicate that, as Festinger (1957) proposed, social groups can be both sources of dissonance and sources of dissonance reduction.

CODA: HOW BEHAVIOR SHAPES ATTITUDES

In a broad sense, dissonance theory describes how people make sense of the world when they find themselves acting in a surprising or irrational way. As the research illustrates, our own behavior occasionally catches us off guard, especially when we decide to do things that, despite our best intentions, turn out poorly for others and for ourselves. Dissonance can occur when we spontaneously say or do something and immediately realize the mistake. At other times, however, dissonance can occur when we plan carefully and start off in a direction that makes sense, but then after a time, new information becomes available that suggests our behavior is unwise or immoral. This may be what happened to the coalition leaders like Tony Blair. At the time they started the war, the information they had led to the conclusion that Iraq had WMDs, and an invasion was necessary to insure the safety of the coalition countries. But within a few months, it became clear that the information about the existence of WMDs was wrong and that the stated primary objective of the war would never be achieved. Blair and the other leaders who advocated for the war on the basis of the WMDs intelligence likely experienced cognitive dissonance, and to reduce their discomfort and restore consistency, they became motivated to change their attitudes and beliefs about the intelligence, the existence of WMDs, and the war itself.

What makes dissonance processes so interesting is that the changes people undertake in the service of consistency can deviate from the reality perceived by the rest of us. Consider the various strategies that Tony Blair used at different times to reduce his dissonance. In the early stages of the war, Blair reduced dissonance by suggesting that the WMDs existed, we just had the wrong people looking for them. This amounts to denying that a discrepancy exists (Abelson, 1959). Months later as the evidence against WMDs grew, Blair appeared to adopt a different strategy by suggesting that the WMDs were there, but they could not be found because they may have been moved, hidden, or destroyed. Festinger (1957) originally noted that when it is not possible to change one of the dissonant cognitions, adding new cognitive elements to bolster either dissonant element could reduce the magnitude of dissonance. It appears that Blair may have opted for this strategy by suggesting that the WMDs were there, but adding the "new possibility" that they could not be found because they had been moved, hidden or destroyed. Finally, after over a year of searching and finding no WMDs, Blair resorted to yet another dissonance reduction strategy: He apologized for being wrong about the existence of WMD, but not for removing Saddam Hussein from power. Festinger also predicted this maneuver when he suggested that people could reduce dissonance by trivializing the inconsistency. Blair acknowledged that he had made a mistake, but that this mistake was small in comparison to the more important goal of removing a disliked leader from office. Or as Festinger (1957) would have it, "Here, the total dissonance is reduced by reducing the *importance* of the existing dissonance" (p. 22, emphasis added). Indeed, research shows that people will sometimes resort to trivializing their behavior in order to reduce dissonance (Simon, Greenberg, & Brehm, 1995).

The potential problem is that by trivializing the discrepancy in this way, Blair actually created another inconsistency to ponder: If Saddam Hussein and his military did not possess WMDs, how did removing him from power make the world safer? Blair's answer to this question would likely motivate further changes in attitudes and beliefs to reduce dissonance and maintain consistency with his original perception of reality.

REFERENCES

Abelson, R. P. (1959). Modes of resolution of belief dilemmas. *Journal of Conflict Resolution, 3,* 343–352.

Aronson, E. (1968). Dissonance theory: Progress and problems. In R. Abelson, E. Aronson, W. McGuire, T. Newcomb, M. Rosenberg, & P. Tannenbaum (Eds.), *Theories of cognitive consistency: A sourcebook* (pp. 5–27). Chicago: Rand McNally.

Aronson, E. (May, 1973). The rationalizing animal. *Psychology Today*. American Psychological Association.

Aronson, J., Blanton, H., & Cooper, J. (1995). From dissonance to disidentification: Selectivity in the self-affirmation process. *Journal of Personality and Social Psychology, 68*(6), 986–996.

Aronson, E., & Carlsmith., J. M. (1962). Performance expectancy as a determinant of actual performance. *Journal of Abnormal and Social Psychology, 65*, 178–182.

Aronson, E., & Carlsmith, J. M. (1963). Effect of the severity of threat on the devaluation of forbidden behavior. *Journal of Abnormal and Social Psychology, 66*, 584–588.

Aronson, J., Cohen, G. L., & Nail, P. R. (1999). Self-affirmation theory: An update and appraisal. In E. Harmon-Jones & J. Mills (Eds.), *Cognitive dissonance: Progress on a pivotal theory in social psychology* (pp. 127–148). Washington, D.C.: American Psychological Association.

Aronson, E., Fried, C. B., & Stone, J. (1991). Overcoming denial and increasing the use of condoms through the induction of hypocrisy. *American Journal of Public Health, 81*, 1636–1638.

Aronson, E., & Mills, J. (1959). The effect of severity of initiation on liking for a group. *Journal of Abnormal and Social Psychology, 59*, 177–181.

Blanton, H., Cooper, J., Skurnik, I., & Aronson, J. (1997). When bad things happen to good feedback: Exacerbating the need for self-justification with self-affirmations. *Personality and Social Psychology Bulletin, 23*, 684–692.

Brehm, J. (1956). Postdecision changes in the desirability of alternatives. *Journal of Abnormal and Social Psychology, 52*, 384–389.

Cialdini, R. B., Trost., M. R., & Newsom, J. T. (1995). Preference for consistency: The development of a valid measure and the discovery of surprising behavioral implications. *Journal of Personality and Social Psychology, 69*, 318–328.

Cohen, A. R. (1962). An experiment on small rewards for discrepant compliance and attitude change. In J. W. Brehm & A. R. Cohen (Eds.), *Explorations in cognitive dissonance* (pp. 73–78). New York: Wiley.

Cooper, J., & Fazio, R. H. (1984). A new look at dissonance theory. In L. Berkowitz (Ed.), *Advances in Experimental Social Psychology* (Vol. 17, pp. 229–262). Hillsdale, NJ: Erlbaum.

Cooper, J., & Stone, J. (2000). Cognitive dissonance and the social group. In D. J. Terry & M. A. Hogg (Eds.), *Attitudes, behavior, and social context: The role of norms and group membership* (pp. 227–244). Mahwah, NJ: Erlbaum.

Cooper, J., & Worchel, S. (1970). Role of undesired consequences in arousing dissonance. *Journal of Personality and Social Psychology, 16*, 199–206.

Crano, W. D., & Messé, L. A. (1970). When *does* dissonance fail? The time dimension in attitude measurement. *Journal of Personality, 38*, 493–508.

Dickerson, C., Thibodeau, R., Aronson, E., & Miller, D. (1992). Using cognitive dissonance to encourage water conservation. *Journal of Applied Social Psychology, 22*, 841–854.

Epstein, G. F. (1969). Machiavelli and the devil's advocate. *Journal of Personality and Social Psychology, 11*, 38–41.

Festinger, L. (1957). *A theory of cognitive dissonance*. Evanston, IL: Row, Peterson.

Festinger, L. (1964). *Conflict, decision, and dissonance*. Stanford, CA: Stanford University Press.

Festinger, L., & Carlsmith, J. M. (1959). Cognitive consequences of forced compliance. *Journal of Abnormal and Social Psychology, 58*, 203–210.

Fried, C. B. (1998). Hypocrisy and identification with transgressions: A case of undetected dissonance. *Basic and Applied Social Psychology, 20*, 145–154.

Fried, C. B., & Aronson, E. (1995). Hypocrisy, misattribution, and dissonance reduction. *Personality and Social Psychology Bulletin, 21*(9), 925–933.

Gibbons, F. X., Eggleston, T. J., & Benthin, A. (1997). Cognitive reactions to smoking relapse: The reciprocal relation of dissonance and self-esteem. *Journal of Personality and Social Psychology, 72,* 184–195.

Glass, D. (1964). Changes in liking as a means of reducing cognitive discrepancies between self-esteem and aggression. *Journal of Personality, 32,* 531–549.

Harmon-Jones, E., Brehm, J. W., Greenberg, J., Simon, L., & Nelson, D. E. (1996). Evidence that the production of aversive consequences is not necessary to create cognitive dissonance. *Journal of Personality and Social Psychology, 70*(1), 5–16.

Harmon-Jones, E., & Harmon-Jones, C. (2002). Testing the action-based model of cognitive dissonance: The effect of action orientation on postdecisional attitudes. *Personality and Social Psychology Bulletin, 28,* 711–723.

Harmon-Jones, E., & Mills, J. (1999). *Cognitive dissonance: Progress on a pivotal theory in social psychology.* Washington, D.C.: American Psychological Association.

Higgins, E. T., Rhodewalt, F., & Zanna, M. P. (1979). Dissonance motivation: Its nature, persistence, and reinstatement. *Journal of Experimental Social Psychology, 15,* 16–34.

Hoshino-Browne, E., Zanna, A. S., Spencer, S. J., Zanna, M. P., Kitayama, S., & Lackenbauer, S. (2005). On the cultural guises of cognitive dissonance: The case of Easterners and Westerners. *Journal of Personality and Social Psychology, 89,* 294–310.

Johnson, D. J., & Rusbult, C. E. (1989). Resisting temptation: Devaluation of alternative partners as a means of maintaining commitment in close relationships. *Journal of Personality and Social Psychology, 57,* 967–980.

Kitayama, S. (2002). *Culture, self and dissonance.* Paper presented at the Society for Experimental Social Psychology, Columbus, OH.

Knox, R. E., & Inkster, J. A. (1968). Postdecision dissonance at post time. *Journal of Personality and Social Psychology, 8,* 319–323.

Linder, D. E., Cooper, J., & Jones, E. E. (1967). Decision freedom as a determinant of the role of incentive magnitude in attitude change. *Journal of Personality and Social Psychology, 6,* 245–254.

Maracek, J., & Mettee, D. (1972). Avoidance of continued success as a function of self-steem, level of esteem certainty, and responsibility for success. *Journal of Personality and Social Psychology, 22,* 98–107.

Markus, H. R., & Kitayama, S. (1991). Culture and self: Implications for cognition, emotion, and motivation. *Psychological Review, 98,* 224–253.

Matz, D. C., & Wood, W. (2005). Cognitive dissonance in groups: The consequences of disagreement. *Journal of Personality and Social Psychology, 88,* 22–37.

McQueen, A., & Klein, W. (2006). Experimental manipulations of self-affirmation: A systematic review. *Self and Identity, 5,* 289–354.

Norton, M. I., Monin, B., Cooper, J., & Hogg, M. A. (2003). Vicarious dissonance: Attitude change from the inconsistency of others. *Journal of Personality and Social Psychology, 85,* 47–62.

Olson, J. M., & Zanna, M. P. (1982). Repression-sensitization differences in responses to a decision. *Journal of Personality, 50*(1), 46–57.

Prislin, R., & Pool, G. J. (1996). Behavior, consequences, and the self: Is all well that ends well. *Personality and Social Psychology Bulletin, 22,* 933–948.

Rosenberg, M. (1979). *Conceiving the self.* Malabar, FL: Krieger.

Sakai, H. (1981). Induced compliance and opinion change. *Japanese Psychological Research, 22,* 32–41.

Simon, L., Greenberg, J., & Brehm, J. (1995). Trivialization: The forgotten mode of dissonance reduction. *Journal of Personality and Social Psychology, 68*(2), 247–260.

Snyder, M., & Tanke, E. D. (1976). Behavior and attitude: Some people are more consistent than others. *Journal of Personality, 44,* 510–517.

Son Hing, L. S., Li, W., & Zanna, M. P. (2001). Inducing hypocrisy to reduce prejudicial responses among aversive racists. *Journal of Experimental Social Psychology, 38*(1), 71–78.

Stalder, D. R., & Baron, R. S. (1998). Attributional complexity as a moderator of dissonance-produced attitude change. *Journal of Personality and Social Psychology, 75,* 449–455.

Steele, C. M. (1988). The psychology of self-affirmation: Sustaining the integrity of the self. In L. Berkowitz (Ed.), *Advances in Experimental Social Psychology* (Vol. 21, pp. 261–302). Hillsdale, NJ: Erlbaum.

Steele, C. M., & Lui, T. J. (1983). Dissonance processes as self-affirmation. *Journal of Personality and Social Psychology, 45,* 5–19.

Steele, C. M., Spencer, S. J., & Lynch, M. (1993). Dissonance and affirmational resources: Resilience against self-image threats. *Journal of Personality and Social Psychology, 64*(6), 885–896.

Stone, J. (1999). What exactly have I done? The role of self-attribute accessibility in dissonance. In E. Harmon-Jones & J. Mills (Eds.), *Cognitive dissonance: Progress on a pivotal theory in social psychology* (pp. 175–200). Washington, D.C.: American Psychological Association.

Stone, J. (2001). Behavioral discrepancies and construal processes in cognitive dissonance. In G. Moskowitz (Ed.), *Cognitive social psychology: The Princeton symposium on the legacy and future of social cognition* (pp. 41–58). Hillsdale, N.J.: Erlbaum.

Stone, J. (2003). Self-consistency for low self-esteem in dissonance processes: The role of self-standards. *Personality and Social Psychology Bulletin, 29,* 846–858.

Stone, J., Aronson, E., Crain, A. L., Winslow, M. P., & Fried, C. B. (1994). Inducing hypocrisy as a means of encouraging young adults to use condoms. *Personality and Social Psychology Bulletin, 20*(1), 116–128.

Stone, J., & Cooper, J. (2001). A self-standards model of cognitive dissonance. *Journal of Experimental Social Psychology, 37,* 228–243.

Stone, J., & Cooper, J. (2003). The effect of self-attribute relevance on how self-esteem moderates dissonance processes. *Journal of Experimental Social Psychology, 39,* 508–515.

Stone, J., Wiegand, A. W., Cooper, J., & Aronson, E. (1997). When exemplification fails: Hypocrisy and the motive for self-integrity. *Journal of Personality and Social Psychology, 72*(1), 54–65.

Thibodeau, R., & Aronson, E. (1992). Taking a closer look: Reasserting the role of the self-concept in dissonance theory. *Personality and Social Psychology Bulletin, 18*(5), 591–602.

Walster, E. (1964). The temporal sequence of post-decision dissonance. In L. Festinger (Ed.), *Conflict, decision, and dissonance* (pp. 112–128). Palo Alto, CA: Stanford University Press.

Zanna, M. P., & Cooper, J. (1974). Dissonance and the pill: An attribution approach to studying the arousal properties of dissonance. *Journal of Personality and Social Psychology, 29,* 703–709.

Zanna, M. P., Higgins, E. T., & Taves, P. A. (1976). Is dissonance phenomenologically aversive? *Journal of Experimental Social Psychology, 12,* 530–538.

Zanna, M. P., & Sande, G. N. (1987). The effect of collective actions on the attitudes of individual group members: A dissonance analysis. In M. P. Zanna, J. M. Olson, & C. P. Herman (Eds.), *Social influence: The Ontario symposium* (Vol. 5, pp. 151–163). Hillsdale, NJ: Erlbaum.

Zimbardo, P. G., Weisenberg, M., Firestone, I., & Levy, B. (1965). Communicator effectiveness in producing public conformity and private attitude change. *Journal of Personality, 33,* 233-255.

VII

Attitudes
The Social Context

15

Social Identity and Attitudes

JOANNE R. SMITH
University of Exeter, UK

MICHAEL A. HOGG
Claremont Graduate University, USA

> In short, man's socialization is revealed mainly in his attitudes formed in relation to the values or norms of his reference group or groups. (Sherif, 1936, p. 203)

> The investigation of attitudes brings us to the center of the person's social relations and to the heart of the dynamics of social processes. (Asch, 1952, p. 577)

As these quotes attest, early influential social psychologists viewed attitudes and the social contexts in which attitudes are formed, changed, and expressed as inextricably linked. Despite this, surprisingly little attention has been directed toward the interplay of attitudes with social context. The social psychological study of attitudes almost universally adopts a conceptualization of attitudes as intraindividual cognitive structures—as individual cognitive representations that are acquired and possessed by individuals and which, to a great extent, are a part of human individuality (Bohner & Wanke, 2002; Eagly & Chaiken, 1993; Fazio & Olson, 2003; Maio & Haddock, in press). What is missing or underemphasized in all this is that our attitudes are rarely idiosyncratic—more often than not they are grounded in the groups we belong to and they serve to define and proclaim who we are in terms of our relationships to others who are members of the same or different groups.

Attitudes are powerful bases for making group stereotypical or normative inferences about other attitudes and about behaviors and customs—they let us construct a norm-based persona that reduces uncertainty and regulates social interaction. Attitudes are grounded in social consensus defined by group membership. Many, if not most, of our attitudes reflect and even define groups with which we identify. We are autobiographically idiosyncratic, but our attitudes are actually attached to group memberships that we internalize to define ourselves.

In this chapter we promote a group-centric orientation to attitudes and describe what the social identity approach contributes to our understanding of attitudes and attitudinal phenomena. The main point we make is that attitudes are grounded in group memberships; thus, attitude research must consider more completely the way in which attitudes are socially formed, configured, and enacted. This is not to say that attitudes are not cognitively represented by individual people: they are. Rather, we emphasize the way that attitudes are normative and embedded in wider representational and ideological systems attached to social groups and categories. Attitudes map the contours of social groups and shared identities. Attitude phenomena are impacted significantly by social identity processes. They are socially structured and grounded in social consensus, group memberships, and social identities. Our analysis of attitudes comes from the social psychology of group processes and intergroup relations, rather than the social psychology of attitudes. More specifically, it comes from social identity theory (Hogg & Abrams, 1988; Tajfel & Turner, 1986; Turner, Hogg, Oakes, Reicher, & Wetherell, 1987) and the metatheory that frames social identity theory (Abrams & Hogg, 2004).

We present a social identity perspective on attitudes (also see Hogg & Smith, 2007) that draws on, integrates, and extends basic principles of classic and contemporary social identity theory. After a brief review of the current state of research on attitudes and the social context, we introduce social identity theory and focus on what it has to say about attitudes—how attitudes are embedded in descriptive and prescriptive group *prototypes*, how attitudes become group normative, how social categorization of self assigns group attitudes to self via *depersonalization*, and how social identity processes underpin influence in groups and the development and communication of normative attitudes. We discuss research on the impact of social identity processes on attitude change and persuasion, focusing on persuasion, dissonance, minority influence, and the third-person effect. Finally, we examine the impact of social identity processes on the relationship between people's attitudes and their behavior. In each section, we present theory and review research conducted primarily, but not exclusively, in our research group over the past 10 to 15 years to illustrate our central argument that attitude phenomena are affected significantly by social identity processes.

ATTITUDES AND THE SOCIAL CONTEXT

The historical treatment and neglect of the social context in attitudes research may reflect early individualistic definitions of attitudes, and a focus on individuals rather than groups as the unit of analysis (e.g., F. Allport, 1919; G. Allport, 1935). Attitudes are viewed primarily as cognitive representations in the mind of the individual: they are "mental and neural states of readiness to respond" (G. Allport, 1935, p. 810). This individualistic orientation has persisted in the study of attitudes, with attitude researchers focusing on the analysis of the psychological processes and structures of individuals at the expense of attention to the social environment (Eagly & Chaiken, 1993; Prislin & Wood, 2005). However, there have been increasing calls in recent years for researchers to consider and integrate social factors into investigations of attitude dynamics (Prislin & Christensen, 2005; Prislin & Wood, 2005).

Some research has acknowledged the impact of the social context on attitudes and attitude phenomena. However, such research has distinguished attitudes (as an informational determinant of action; see Deutsch & Gerard, 1955) from the social context (as a normative determinant of action). That is, the distinction between informational influence (e.g., message or argument quality) and normative influence (e.g., source) is retained. In research on attitude–behavior relations, the social context is seen as a background factor, rather than as a fundamental component of attitudes. In the attitude change literature, source characteristics, such as group membership, are often seen to operate through peripheral or heuristic routes, such that any change in attitudes attributed to these variables is less "true", stable, and enduring (e.g., Chaiken, 1987; cf. Mackie & Queller, 2000).

Thus, even when research has examined issues related to the social environment or social context, it has narrowed in on issues related to social influence, rather than broadening the scope to include the wider social environment of group memberships and social identities (see Prislin & Wood, 2005, for a review). Research has focused on the individual and interpersonal aspects of the processes by which attitudes are changed (e.g., Briñol & Petty, 2005) and has treated the social context as a set of stimuli that act upon an individual, either in the form of social pressures and expectations (norms) or in the form of social motivations (impression management). There has been little attention given to conceptualizing the structure of the social environment in terms of the social norms, social identities, and sociostructural factors that affect the formation, stability, and expression of attitudes.

Within the attitude field, advances have been made, particularly in minority influence research (e.g., Crano, 2001; Prislin, Limbert, & Bauer, 2000). However, as noted by Eagly and Chaiken (2005), progress has not been rapid and many challenges remain in situating and studying attitudes within a complex and dynamic social landscape. What is needed is a reconceptualization of attitudes as fundamentally entwined with the social environment and inherently social, rather than simply reducing the social context to the inclusion of norms (norms as the "social appendage"). After all, attitudes are socially learned, socially changed, and socially expressed. By highlighting the impact of the social environment on individual attitudes, we can gain a more complete insight into the motivational complexities that drive attitudinal phenomena.

One way to facilitate this change in emphasis is to approach the conceptualization of attitudes from the perspective of the social psychology of groups and intergroup relations rather than the social psychology of the individual and interpersonal interactions. In this way attitudes are treated as an aspect of group life, rather than an aspect of individuality. Social identity theory is a powerful group perspective in social psychology that allows just such an analysis.

SOCIAL IDENTITY THEORY AND ATTITUDES

Since its origins in the early 1970s, social identity theory has developed into a comprehensive and integrated analysis of the dynamic relationship among the self-concept, group memberships, group processes, and intergroup behavior (e.g., Tajfel, 1972). The concept of social identity is the unifying principle at the heart of the social identity approach. For Tajfel (1972), social identity represents "the individual's knowledge that he belongs to certain social groups together with some emotional and value significance to him of his group membership" (p. 292). Social identity is not merely the knowledge that one is a member of a group and of the defining attributes of group membership, it also involves an emotional and motivational attachment to the group. Recent statements and overviews of social identity theory in its contemporary form can be found in Hogg (2003, 2006). Here we describe only those aspects that are relevant to a social identity analysis of attitudes and attitude phenomena.

Prototypes and Normative Attitudes

People cognitively represent a social group (e.g., a nation, a religion, an ethnic group) as a category *prototype*—a fuzzy set of category attributes that are related to one another in a meaningful way. These prototypes simultaneously capture similarities within the group and differences between the group and other groups or people who are not in the group (Hogg, 2005). Category attributes can include how people look, dress, speak, behave, feel, and of, course, their attitudes toward objects, events, people, and so forth. Generally, these attributes are relatively organized so that they "appear" to be meaningfully related and consistent with one another. So, attitudinal components of a group prototype will generally appear consistent—an appearance of consistency that may be subsumed by a wider ideology or world view (Larrain, 1979; Thompson, 1990), or value system (Rohan, 2000) that the perceiver believes the group subscribes to.

Prototypes not only describe categories but also evaluate them and prescribe membership-related attributes. They specify how people ought to behave as category members, what attitudes they ought to hold, and so forth. Prototypes chart the contours of social groups, and tell us not only what characterizes a group, but how that group is different from other groups. In this sense prototypes are norms; that is, because a particular perception, behavior, or attitude is shared within a group, it is normative of that particular group (Sherif, 1936; Turner, 1991). Thus, prototype-based attitudes are normative—they are shared within a group. Prototypes maximize "entitativity" or the property of a category that makes it appear a cohesive and clearly structured entity that is distinct from other entities (Campbell, 1958; Hamilton & Sherman, 1996). Also, prototypes obey the *metacontrast principle*—their configuration maximizes the ratio of perceived intergroup differences to intragroup differences, and thus accentuates perceived similarities within groups and differences between groups (Tajfel, 1959).

The prototype is the position that best defines what the group has in common compared to other relevant out-groups. Moreover, because social identity is defined comparatively and dynamically, in-group prototypes are also defined comparatively and can vary with the social context. Intergroup and intragroup behavior are inextricable—what happens between groups affects what happens within groups, and vice versa. Attitudes and attitudinal phenomena are related to self-definition in group prototypical terms to the extent that they are tied to group and intergroup dynamics.

Depersonalization and Referent Informational Influence

One of the key insights of social identity theory, elaborated by self-categorization theory (Turner et al., 1987), is that the process of categorization of self and others, *depersonalizes* one's perception of self and others and depersonalizes one's own behavior. When we categorize people (in-group members, out-group members, or ourselves), we view them not as idiosyncratic individuals, but through the lens of the group prototype. We assign prototypical attributes to them, and we interpret and expect behavior, including their attitudes, to conform to our prototype of the group. In this way, social categorization generates stereotype or norm consistent expectations regarding people's attitudes and conduct. Categorization of self, self-categorization, configures and changes self-conception to match the identity described by the category, and transforms one's perceptions, attitudes, feelings, and conduct to conform to the category prototype.

Self-categorization and depersonalization account for the social cognitive process that causes people to internalize group attributes and behave in line with group norms—it explains how people internalize in-group normative attitudes as their own attitudes. When people categorize themselves as members of a group and perceive that the group is important to them, there is an assimilation of the self to the group prototype. The norms, stereotypes, attitudes, and other properties that are commonly ascribed to the social group become internalized; they become subjectively interchangeable with personal norms, stereotypes, and attitudes, influencing thought and guiding action.

The social influence process associated with identification-based conformity is *referent informational influence* (Hogg & Turner, 1987; Turner, 1982), in which conformity to the group norm evolves through three stages. First, individuals must categorize and identify as a group member. Next, a context-specific prototype is constructed from available and usually shared social comparative information (e.g., the expressed attitudes of others). This newly formed prototype serves to describe and prescribe beliefs, attitudes, feelings, and behaviors that maximize intergroup differences and minimize intragroup differences (the metacontrast principle). Finally, group members internalize the prototype through assimilation of the self to the prototype (depersonalization), and use it as a guide to their own behavior as a group member. Because the prototype is internalized as part of the individual's self-concept, it exerts influence over behavior even in the absence of surveillance by other group members. Once the norm has been identified, self-categorization produces normative behavior, including subscription to attitudes. It is through this process of referent informational influence that individuals come to learn about the group and appropriate ways of behavior.

Referent informational influence differs in a number of ways from other accounts of influence processes that distinguish normative influence to conform to the positive expectations of others from informational influence to accept information from another as evidence about reality (Deutsch & Gerard, 1955; Kelley, 1952). For example, for referent informational influence, people conform to a norm, not to the behavior of specific other individuals, and they conform because they are group members, not to validate physical reality or to avoid social disapproval. Because the norm is an internalized representation, people can conform to it in the absence of surveillance by group members. Conformity involves private acceptance of a norm that defines a group in which individuals include themselves and with which they identify (Abrams & Hogg, 1990; Turner, 1991; Turner & Oakes, 1989).

DISCOVERING THE NORMATIVENESS OF ATTITUDES

One of the key arguments of the social identity analysis of attitudes is that certain attitude effects flow from the perception or knowledge that an attitude is normative of a self-inclusive group with which one identifies. However, it is not always easy for a person to determine whether an attitude is normative—sometimes people miss what is normative, distort the norm, or get the norm entirely wrong (e.g., pluralistic ignorance; Prentice & Miller, 1996). We can learn the normativeness of attitudes and behaviors by observing or interacting with people. As we shall see, people can impart norms relatively passively by example, or through more active persuasion.

Behavioral Averaging, Group Polarization, and Normative Attitudes

Sherif's (1935, 1936) autokinetic studies are classic demonstrations of how people develop and learn group norms. Participants in small groups called out their estimates of the amount of movement of a light source—the source was not actually moving but appeared to move due to an illusion called the autokinetic effect. Sherif found that people quickly adjusted their judgments into a tight range around the average of the group's initial judgments. A norm had emerged. Furthermore, the norm persisted even when all original members of the group had left and the group had entirely new members (Jacobs & Campbell, 1961; MacNeil & Sherif, 1976). Social identity research has demonstrated that this norm formation is accelerated, and the group norm is more tightly convergent, when participants identify strongly with the group (Abrams, Wetherell, Cochrane, Hogg, & Turner, 1990).

Sherif's norm formation studies, along with most other studies of norms, assume that a group norm is the average in-group position. However, from a social identity perspective norms do not have to be the average in-group position. Prototypes, as individual representations of group norms, are formed from intra- and intergroup comparisons that obey the metacontrast principle; thus, prototypes polarize norms to differentiate between groups. As the intergroup comparative context changes, the in-group norm also changes to maintain intergroup differentiation.

This idea has been tested using variants of the group polarization paradigm (Isenberg, 1986; Moscovici & Zavalloni, 1969) in which group discussion, or mere exposure to fellow group members' attitudes, produces a final group attitude that is more extreme than the average of the initial members' attitudes in a direction away from the out-group. A number of social identity studies have found that attitudinal polarization is more extreme when members identify more strongly with the group (e.g., Abrams et al., 1990; Mackie, 1986; Mackie & Cooper, 1984; Turner, Wetherell, & Hogg, 1989) or in times of uncertainty (e.g., Sherman, Hogg, & Maitner, in press). Hogg, Turner, and Davidson (1990), for example, demonstrated that group members' attitudes shifted towards a perceived normative attitude that best defined the group in contrast to other groups even in the absence of actual group discussion and interaction.

This research on norm formation and group polarization shows that attitudes are responsive to social context. People use others' attitudes, particularly when they share a social identity with those others, to construct a group norm that specifies what attitudes are normative. People use this normative information to configure their own attitudes. Group members deduce the content of a social identity from shared membership in a social category and the wider social context of intergroup relations (Postmes, Haslam, & Swaab, 2005).

Communication and Normative Attitudes

Although mere exposure to others' attitudes allows one to construct an attitudinal norm, many group contexts involve at least some degree of discussion that often is oriented toward making a group decision or arriving at a group position. However, such group interactions also are overwhelmingly about establishing, negotiating, or confirming group attitudes, norms, and identity (Hogg & Reid, 2006). Group members infer or induce the content of a social identity (norms, attitudes, rules) from intragroup communication and the individual contributions of group members (Postmes et al., 2005). Communication serves to construct norms and identity—communication provides the means by which abstract characteristics of the group can be translated into a concrete situational norm or prototype that applies to actions within a specific context. In a study of electronic communication, Postmes, Spears, and Lea (2000) demonstrated that over time, groups converged in both the content and the stylistic form of their messages, producing attributes that were distinctive to the group and decreasing within-group heterogeneity. There also is evidence that over time, majority views and norm-consistent attitudes tend to dominate, and that group discussion strains out norm-inconsistent attitudes, narrowing the group's scope to focus on norm-consistent attitudes (Kashima, 2000). Members who espouse nonnormative attitudes often are discredited (Marques, Abrams, & Serôdio, 2001), and direct criticism of groups is tolerated more if the critic is viewed as an in-group, not an out-group, member (Hornsey, 2005; Hornsey & Imani, 2004).

ATTITUDE CHANGE

In this section, we apply the social identity perspective on attitudes to the area of attitude change and examine how social identity can, at the cognitive level, change our attitudes. We already have seen how self-categorization depersonalizes our attitudes so that they conform to the in-group prototype, and that this represents genuine attitude change not superficial behavioral compliance. This is the most fundamental and basic way in which social identities and groups affect attitudes (see Abrams et al., 1990; Haslam, Oakes, McGarty, Turner, & Onorato, 1995; Hogg et al., 1990; McGarty, Turner, Hogg, David, & Wetherell, 1992; Turner et al., 1989).

Persuasion

Early research on attitude change viewed source or communicator characteristics as a key variable in determining the effectiveness of an attitude change attempt. Sources high in attractiveness, expertise, and so forth produced more attitude change and were more persuasive than other sources (e.g., DeBono & Telesca, 1990; Hovland & Weiss, 1951). However, less attention was given to the impact of shared group membership between the source and the audience on persuasion.

Research has shown that the social identity, shared or otherwise, of the individuals in the source and audience roles can have considerable impact on both the processing and eventual effectiveness of persuasive appeals. According to the social identity approach, when social identity is salient, the validity of persuasive information is (psychologically) established by in-group norms (Turner, 1991). Thus, because in-group messages are perceived as more subjectively valid than out-group messages, people should be more influenced by in-group than out-group sources.

Research supports this contention: Persuasive messages lead to greater attitude change when they are presented by a source who shares the message recipients' group membership than when they are presented by a source who does not share this membership (Abrams et al., 1990; McGarty, Haslam, Hutchison, & Turner, 1994; Wilder, 1990). However, this effect is not due merely to heuristic processes or compliance—in-group sources can persuade through a number of different mechanisms, depending on the circumstances. The mere presence of an in-group source can act as a persuasive cue, leading to increased acceptance, especially when the group's position on the issue is clear (Mackie, Gastardo-Conaco, & Skelly, 1992) or under low elaboration conditions such as a novel attitude topic (Fleming & Petty, 2000). However, an in-group message can motivate systematic and effortful processing, especially on group-relevant or group-defining issues (Mackie, Worth, & Asuncion, 1990; van Knippenberg & Wilke, 1992) or when the message is delivered by a prototypical or representative group member (van Knippenberg, Lossie, & Wilke, 1994). Thus, the processes of attitude change are influenced by social identities and shared group memberships. The social context of groups determines what information is deemed to be persuasive and the processes by which attitudes are changed.

Dissonance

One of the best established accounts of attitude change is offered by cognitive dissonance theory (Festinger, 1957; for a recent review see Cooper, 2007; Stone & Fernandez, this volume). Specifically, when people realize that their behavior is inconsistent with their attitude, they experience dissonance that must be resolved, and because behavior is hard to deny, it is usually the attitude that must change. Although one of the first studies of dissonance focused on how members of a group turned to one another to help reduce their dissonance when a prophecy failed (Festinger, Riecken, & Schachter, 1957), most research on attitude change through dissonance is focused on individual cognition (but see Matz & Wood, 2005).

From a social identity perspective, we would expect that people who experience dissonance may be vigilant about the behavior and reactions of other people. In many contexts it would matter a great deal whether that other person shared the same group membership. McKimmie and colleagues (2003) found that participants who behaved counterattitudinally experienced less dissonance and attitude change when they knew that another participant had also behaved counterattitudinally, but only when they shared a salient common in-group membership with that person.

Group norms may play a complicated role in producing this identity-contingent effect. On the one hand, in-group normative support for one's underlying attitude may bolster the attitude, or it may actually make dissonance even more acute. On the other hand, normative support for one's attitude-inconsistent behavior may protect one from dissonance and attitude change. Invoking the notion of meta-consistency, McKimmie, Terry, and Hogg (2006) go further to suggest that what may be particularly important is whether or not the other in-group member has engaged in counterattitudinal behavior like oneself. Dissonance and attitude change is reduced if a fellow in-group member also has behaved counterattitudinally (McKimmie et al., 2003). In a similar vein, Robertson and Reicher (1997) have argued that people experience dissonance if their behavior is inconsistent and there is no normative support for their inconsistency. However, if there is support (i.e., others in the group also behave in ways that are inconsistent with attitudinal norms), dissonance is reduced.

Vicarious Dissonance

Another way that social identity processes may influence dissonance and attitude change is through vicarious dissonance. Cooper and Hogg (2002) argue that if you observe someone else experiencing dissonance because they have behaved counterattitudinally, then you as an observer will vicariously experience dissonance and change your attitudes—but only if you share a salient social identity with the other person. This idea fits well with other research showing that shared identity facilitates perspective taking (Batson, Early, & Salvarini, 1997), increases empathy (Davis, 1994), and enhances vicarious emotions (Hatfield, Cacioppo, & Rapson, 1994).

Cooper and associates have published five studies using classic dissonance paradigms (Monin, Norton, Cooper, & Hogg, 2004; Norton, Monin, Cooper, & Hogg, 2003) that provide support for their vicarious dissonance theory. In these studies, participants experienced greater dissonance and attitude change when they observed a fellow member of a salient in-group behave in a way that would cause the actor to experience dissonance. For example, participants who heard a member of a group with which they strongly identified agree to deliver a counterattitudinal speech experienced elevated discomfort. However, this discomfort was reduced by changing their own attitude in the direction of the position espoused by the speaker (Norton et al., 2004). Vicarious dissonance processes, and the processes outlined in McKimmie et al.'s (2006) meta-consistency effect, show that the experience of dissonance, which can affect attitudes, can be fundamentally influenced by group memberships and social identities.

Minority Influence

Despite the fact that group norms are generally grounded in wide majority consensus, and that groups are motivated to maintain agreement and avoid disagreement, minorities can be very effective in modifying or changing the attitudes and behaviors represented by the majority norm—indeed active minorities are an important vehicle for social change (Moscovici, 1976). Research on minority influence shows that minorities are very effective in changing majority attitudes if the minority's position is novel and the minority adopts a consistent yet flexible style of social influence and persuasion (e.g., Martin, Hewstone, & Gardikiotis, this volume; Mugny, 1982; Nemeth, 1986; Ziegler, Diehl, Zigon, & Fett, 2004).

Not all minorities are equally effective in producing attitude change. Perceptions of shared group membership between the majority and the minority are a critical determinant of the success of minority influence. That is, in-group minorities, but not out-group minorities, produce change. David and Turner (1996, 1999) conducted a series of experiments to test the relative impact of in-group and out-group majorities and minorities. In addition to demonstrating that the immediate influence of in-groups was positive (i.e., toward the source's position), and the immediate influence of out-groups was negative (i.e., away from the source's position), these studies highlighted the power of in-group minorities to produce greater attitude change over time. Crano (2001) has proposed a leniency contract model to account for the ability of in-group minorities to produce majority opinion change. Integrating insights from both social identity and information processing approaches, Crano argues that in-group minorities exert influence because of the lenient evaluation afforded members of the same social category. Provided that the minority does not pose a threat to the majority, shared group membership allows for relatively open-minded elaboration, because the majority attempts to understand the unexpected position held by this minority of fellow in-group members, which ultimately creates pressures for attitude change.

One consequence of successful minority influence is not just change in the individual attitudes of group members. Successful minority influence also changes the structure and meaning of minority and majority groups. Prislin and her colleagues have highlighted the dynamic nature of minority influence (see Prislin & Christensen, 2005, for a review). For example, majorities who find themselves in a new minority position tend to agree with the newly emerging attitudinal consensus (Prislin et al., 2000) and to interpret attitudinal differences within the group as diversity rather than deviance (Prislin, Brewer, & Wilson, 2002). In contrast, successful minorities bolster their attitudes by enhancing attitudinal importance, restricting what are considered as acceptable attitudes, and expressing less tolerance of minority views. It is clear that changes in the attitudinal landscape influence the social context of identities just as changes in the social context of identities influence the attitudinal landscape.

The Third-Person Effect

Social identity processes not only influence persuasion and attitude change processes, they also influence the extent to which individuals perceive that they, and those around them, are influenced by persuasion attempts. The third-person effect refers to the tendency for people to perceive that others are more influenced by persuasive communications than they are themselves (Davison, 1983). Moreover, people act on the basis of these distorted perceptions: attitudinal and behavioral change may result from the belief that the options of others have been altered (e.g., Gunther, 1995).

From a social identity perspective, third-person perceptions should be highly sensitive to the categorization of self and other into relevant in-groups and out-groups. Perceptions of influence are dependent on salient social identities—perceived self-other differences in persuasibility are affected by the social context and reflect in-group norms about the acceptability of acknowledging influence. Duck and associates (Duck, Hogg, & Terry, 1999, 2000; Duck, Terry, & Hogg, 1998) have demonstrated that evaluations of influence are governed by group memberships and the extent to which being influenced is normative for the relevant in-group or out-group (see also Reid & Hogg, 2005). When it is normative to resist persuasion, such as for negative media content (e.g., pornography, violence), individuals will see themselves and members of their in-group as highly resistant and see members of the out-group as less resistant (a third-person effect). In contrast, when it is normative to acknowledge persuasive influence, such as for positive media content (e.g., public health announcements), individuals will see themselves and members of their in-group as quite yielding and see other targets as less so (a reverse third-person effect or a first-person effect).

A social identity account for the third-person effect has been supported in a number of areas, including political campaigning (Duck, Terry, et al., 1998), public service advertising (Duck, Hogg, et al., 1999), and the relative influence of different media (Reid & Hogg, 2005). Third-person effects are dynamic and influenced by changing intergroup contexts—these perceptions can change suddenly and dramatically over time in response to changes in the current status and power structure (Duck, Terry, et al., 1998) or changes in the target of social comparison (Reid & Hogg, 2005). Thus, perceptions of the relative impact of persuasive communications are context-dependent and fluid and reflect salient social comparisons and social identities within the immediate social context.

ATTITUDES AND ACTION

One of the key issues in attitude research has been the relationship between attitudes as internal representations and overt behavior (what people say and do). Indeed, one of the reasons that researchers and practitioners are interested in attitudes is because it is assumed that attitudes predict action (see Aizen, this volume). If you cannot predict behavior from attitudes, or vice versa, then attempts to change people's health related, consumer or voting behavior via public education, propaganda, and advertising are pointless.

Attitude–Behavior Relations

Early attitude researchers often assumed, in line with common opinion, that attitudes translate into overt behavior, despite evidence that attitudes and behavior were largely unrelated (Kutner, Wilkins, & Yarrow, 1952; LaPiere, 1934). Although early reviews of the field suggested that attitudes typically did not predict behavior well (Wicker, 1969), it is now generally accepted that there is a relationship between attitudes and action (Kraus, 1995), and recent research has focused on elucidating under what conditions attitudes influence behavior (the "when" question; Zanna & Fazio, 1982). One of the most influential outcomes of this line of research was the acknowledgment that it is necessary to take into account other variables in addition to attitude to understand fully the nature of the attitude–behavior relationship.

Of particular relevance to social identity theory is the role of norms in attitude–behavior correspondence. The theories of reasoned action (Ajzen & Fishbein, 1980; Fishbein & Ajzen, 1974) and planned behavior (Ajzen, 1989) are notable in their inclusion of a role for social norms. These models argue that subjective norms influence attitude–behavior consistency. What is meant by this is that if one knows that significant other individuals (e.g., friends, family members) approve of engaging in a particular behavior, one's attitude is more likely to translate into behavior. However, although normative support does improve attitude–behavior correspondence, research shows the effect to be surprisingly small. A number of meta-analyses have suggested that the predictive ability of the subjective norm construct is limited (Farley, Lehmann, & Ryan, 1981; Hausenblaus, Carron, & Mack, 1997) and that subjective norm is the weakest predictor of behavior (Armitage & Conner, 2001). The weakness of the link between norms and behavior even led Ajzen (1991) to conclude that personal factors are the primary determinants of behavior.

According to Terry and Hogg (1996, 2001), one reason for this relatively weak effect may be the way that norms are conceptualized. In the theories of reasoned action and planned behavior norms are separated from attitudes—attitudes are "in here" (private, internalized cognitive constructs), whereas norms are "out there" (public, external pressures representing the cumulative expectations of others). This conceptualization of norms is different from that used by social identity theory (Turner, 1991), and by much of contemporary social psychology of groups (Brown, 2000).

Drawing on the social identity perspective, Terry and Hogg and their associates (Terry & Hogg, 1996, 2001; Terry, Hogg, & Duck, 1999; Terry, Hogg, & White, 2000) argue that attitudes are more likely to express themselves as behavior if the attitude (and associated behaviors) are normative properties of a social group with which people identify. In circumstances where membership of a particular social group becomes a salient basis of self-definition, attitudes and group norms come to govern our own behavior. Attitudes express themselves as behavior if they are group normative and if group membership is salient. Thus, it can be predicted that the relationship between attitude and behavior will be strengthened when group members perceive that the attitude is normative for the group and weakened when group members perceive that their attitude is out of step with the group.

In two tests of the theory of planned behavior, Terry and Hogg (1996) examined longitudinally students' intentions to exercise regularly and to engage in sun-protective behavior. They found that the perceived norms of a specific and behaviorally relevant reference group were related positively to students' intention to engage in health behaviors. These intentions were significantly stronger among participants who identified strongly with the reference group. Other field research has replicated this effect in studies of smoking in young people (Schofield, Pattison, Hill, & Borland, 2001), healthy eating behavior (Astrom & Rise, 2001; Louis, Davies, Terry, & Smith, 2007), recycling behavior (Terry, Hogg, & White, 1999), and environmental behavior (Fielding, Terry, Masser, & Hogg, in press).

Subsequent experimental and field studies have replicated this finding and have explored moderators and boundary conditions. These studies, which have examined a range of attitude issues (e.g., campus and political issues, career choice), have demonstrated consistently that the attitude–behavior relationship is strengthened when group members are exposed to an in-group norm supportive of their initial attitude, and weakened when exposed to a nonsupportive in-group norm, but only when group membership is salient or when individuals identify strongly with the group (Smith & Terry, 2003; Terry, Hogg, & McKimmie, 2000; Wellen, Hogg, & Terry, 1998; White, Hogg, & Terry, 2002). Furthermore, it has been shown that group members are sensitive to the relevance of an attitude to the group. Attitudes that are more central or relevant to a group are perceived to be more personally important and relevant to group members and, in turn, are more predictive of behavior (Smith, Terry, Crosier, & Duck, 2005).

In addition, Terry, Hogg, and colleagues have demonstrated that social factors, such as the salience or importance of social identity and group norms, have more impact on the attitude–behavior relationship than more cognitive factors, such as attitude accessibility or mode of decision making (Smith & Terry, 2003; Terry, Hogg, & McKimmie, 2000; Wellen et al., 1998). For example, Smith and Terry (2003) considered simultaneously attitude accessibility and mode of decision-making as the cognitive factors associated with Fazio's (1990) MODE model (motivation and opportunity as determinants of mode of behavioral decision making) and identification and in-group norms as the social factors associated with the social identity approach. Contrary to the predictions of the MODE model, two studies found that attitude accessibility had no effect on behavioral intention or behavior, and that in-group norms influenced behavioral intentions and behavior in both the spontaneous and deliberate decision-making modes. Furthermore, group norms had a stronger effect for high identifiers in the deliberative, as opposed to the spontaneous, decision-making conditions, suggesting that individuals who are strongly identified with a group are motivated to process group-relevant information carefully and effortfully (see also Mackie & Queller, 2000).

Research within the social identity approach to attitude–behavior relations has also focused on the motivations that may underlie group-mediated attitude–behavior consistency. According to uncertainty-identity theory (Hogg, 2000, 2007) feelings of self-related uncertainty motivate people to identify with self-inclusive groups and to identify more strongly with such groups. Research has shown that self-related uncertainty influences the attitude–behavior relationship. Smith, Hogg, Martin, and Terry (2007) report two studies in which feelings of self-uncertainty were manipulated and participants were exposed to attitude-congruent, attitude-incongruent, or ambiguous group norms. In both studies, more self-uncertain participants expressed greater intentions to behave in line with their attitudes when their attitude was normative for the in-group, whereas more certain participants' behavioral intentions were unrelated to the level of normative support. Thus, conformity to group norms is enhanced when individuals feel uncertain, suggesting that the desire to resolve uncertainty may underpin group-normative behavior.

In addition to an epistemic, uncertainty-related motive, group members also conform to group norms for strategic, self-presentation reasons. Drawing on recent research and theorizing on the strategic expression of social identity (Reicher, Spears, & Postmes, 1995), Smith and colleagues (Smith, Terry, & Hogg, 2006, 2007) have shown that strategic concerns, such as those associated with accountability to particular audiences, influence the expression of group-normative attitudes and behavior. In two experiments, Smith et al. manipulated level of normative support and response context (anonymity vs. accountability). In addition, the importance of the social identity to the individual was either measured (Study 1) or manipulated (Study 2). Across both studies, it was found that low identifiers, or individuals in low-salience contexts, were more inclined to follow an in-group norm when accountable to the in-group than when anonymous to the in-group, suggesting that these individuals may be more subject to self-presentational concerns, such as a desire for positive evaluations (see also Barreto & Ellemers, 2000). In contrast, high identifiers, or individuals in high-salience contexts, were more likely to follow the in-group norm in anonymous conditions. This latter effect, which is inconsistent with past research and theorizing on the communicative aspects of group behavior (e.g., Emler, 1990) was thought to reflect an intrinsic motivation on the part of high identifiers and high-salience participants to act and perceive themselves as worthy group members. That is, and in line with self-determination theory (Deci & Ryan, 2000), individuals who are intrinsically motivated to engage in particular courses of action, such as high identifiers engaging in group-normative behavior, are more likely to engage in the action in anonymous conditions because such behavior cannot be attributed to external constraints and, therefore, may be more diagnostic of loyalty to the group.

This growing body of research in the attitude–behavior context highlights the widespread and pervasive influence of group factors on the attitude–behavior relationship. Social identity and group norms influence the attitudes and actions of *all* group members under a range of decision-making conditions and in a range of social contexts.

Collective Action

According to the social identity analysis of attitudes, people are more likely to behave in line with their attitudes if the attitudes and behaviors are normative of a salient social group with which they identify strongly. The more definitional of the norm the attitudes and behavior are, and the more injunctive the norm itself is, the stronger the likelihood. This idea has important implications for collective mobilization, the study of how individual attitudes are transformed into collective action (Klandermans, 1997; Reicher, 2001; Stürmer & Simon, 2004; Tyler & Smith, 1998), and how and why people who have sympathetic attitudes towards an issue become mobilized as activists or participants. From a social identity perspective, collective action that is attitude-consistent is most likely when the attitude and action are normative of a group with which people identify and therefore feel motivated to follow. The normative attitude coordinates group members to advance group interests, translating the group-normative attitude in actions that generate benefits to the group and the individual group member. Ultimately, it is group identification that increases the probability of social action and collective protest (Stürmer & Simon, 2004).

Identification is associated directly with collective action, independently of "rational" cost-benefit analyses (Simon et al., 1998; see also Kelly & Breinlinger, 1995). Identity, and the norms associated with that identity, influence perceptions of the consequences of collective action (Louis, Taylor, & Neil, 2004). Individuals will strategically conform to, or violate, in-group and out-group norms to acquire benefits for the group and avoid costs (Louis, Taylor, & Douglas, 2005). Furthermore, for individuals who identify with a particular group, engagement in collective action may be less about the effectiveness of the action in influencing public opinion or one's opponents, and more about the effectiveness of the action in building an oppositional or political movement (Hornsey et al., 2006). The decision to engage in collective action, and collective mobilization itself, is shaped and guided by social identity, normative attitudes, and normative behavior.

SUMMARY AND CLOSING COMMENTS

The study of attitudes, how they are structured, how they are formed, how they change, and how they influence behavior, has always lain close to the heart of social psychology. Although it is clearly acknowledged that attitudes are formed, sustained, and changed through social interaction, traditional research on the social psychology of attitudes has focused on the intraindividual dimensions of attitudes and on processes of interindividual influence and persuasion that produce attitude change. The wider social context of attitudes as normative attributes of social groups and identities located in intergroup contexts has, but for some notable exceptions (Crano, 2001, in press; Prislin & Wood, 2005), been conspicuously underresearched.

In this chapter we document and explain how the social context can be integrated more completely into the study of attitudes by approaching the study of attitudes from the perspective of social identity theory. We have described how social identity theory conceptualizes attitudes, viewing them as normative attributes of social groups that define who we are and provide us with an identity in society. This social identity function of attitudes means that attitude phenomena are closely tied to collective self-conception and to the dynamics of group life and intergroup relations. By considering attitudes from a social identity perspective, we can see how three common motives for attitude phenomena—the need to understand reality, the need to achieve a positive and coherent self-concept, and the need to relate to others and convey an appropriate impression to them (Chen & Chaiken, 1999; Prislin & Wood, 2005)—can all be satisfied by the processes of self-categorization and social identification.

The processes of social categorization and prototype-based depersonalization associated with social identity translate group normative attitudes into individually held attitudes—cognitive representations in the mind of individuals. Social identity processes also influence how we construct and perceive group norms and who or what is most influential in providing norm-relevant information. Because normative attitudes delineate and define groups relative to other groups, they tend to be polarized in social identity contexts. Furthermore, this self-definitional function of attitudinal norms means that group-defining attitudes are more likely to be reflected in behavior when people identify strongly with a group—a process that can mobilize sympathizers to engage in collective action and social protest.

There is relatively robust empirical evidence for much of the social identity analysis of attitudinal phenomena. However, there are avenues for further research in a number of areas; for example, the role of dissonance processes in social identity related to attitude change (Cooper & Hogg, 2002) and the role of uncertainty in social identity mediated normative attitudinal structure (Hogg, 2007). The study of implicit attitudes, which has become popular in recent years (see Devos, this volume; Greenwald et al., 2002), is another avenue for future research—prompting the question of the extent to which social identity processes influence implicit, as well as explicit, attitude phenomena. On a more practical note, one challenge is to apply the social identity analysis of attitudes more consistently to issues of social concern such as health behaviors, environmental behaviors, and prejudice and discrimination. Some advances in this domain have been made (e.g., Fielding et al., in press; Terry & Hogg, 1996, 2001), but more research needs to be done to realize fully the social and theoretical impacts of this approach. Many exciting and interesting challenges remain in studying attitudes under conditions that take into account the complex embedding of attitudes in group and intergroup contexts that extend over time.

All in all, however, we hope we have shown how social identity theory provides an integrative group-based analysis of attitudes and attitude phenomena—an approach that explicitly ties attitudes to the wider social context of social identities, social groups, and the dynamics of intergroup relations. This perspective provides a powerful and fresh complement to the more traditional social psychological approach to attitudes that focuses on the individual and on interindividual interaction.

AUTHOR NOTES

We would like to acknowledge the valuable empirical and conceptual contributions made over the years by our colleagues and collaborators in the Centre for Research on Group Processes at the University of Queensland to the development of some of the ideas presented in this article. Their work is liberally cited in the chapter.

Correspondence concerning this chapter should be addressed to Joanne Smith, j.r.smith@exeter.ac.uk, or Michael Hogg, michael.hogg@cgu.edu.

REFERENCES

Abrams, D., & Hogg, M. A. (1990). Social identification, self-categorization and social influence. *European Review of Social Psychology, 1,* 195–228.

Abrams, D., & Hogg, M. A. (2004). Metatheory: Lessons from social identity research. *Personality and Social Psychology Review, 8,* 98–106.

Abrams, D., Wetherell, M. S., Cochrane, S., Hogg, M. A., & Turner, J. C. (1990). Knowing what to think by knowing who you are: Self-categorization and the nature of norm formation, conformity, and group polarization. *British Journal of Social Psychology, 29,* 97–119.

Ajzen, I. (1989). Attitude structure and behaviour. In A. R. Pratkanis, S. J. Breckler, & A. G. Greenwald (Eds.), *Attitude structure and function* (pp. 241–274). Hillsdale, NJ: Erlbaum.

Ajzen, I. (1991). The theory of planned behavior. *Organizational Behavior and Human Decision Processes, 50,* 179–211.

Ajzen, I., & Fishbein, M. (1980). *Understanding attitudes and predicting social behavior.* Englewood Cliffs, NJ: Prentice Hall.

Allport, F. (1919). Behavior and experiment in social psychology. *Journal of Abnormal and Social Psychology, 14,* 297–306.

Allport, G. W. (1935). Attitudes. In C. Murchison (Ed.), *Handbook of social psychology* (pp. 789–844). Worchester, MA: Clark University Press.

Armitage, C. J., & Conner, M. (2001). Efficacy of the theory of planned behavior: A meta-analytic review. *British Journal of Social Psychology, 40,* 471–499.

Asch, S. (1952). *Social psychology.* Englewood Cliffs, NJ: Prentice-Hall.

Astrom, A. N., & Rise, J. (2001). Young adults' intentions to eat healthy food: Extending the theory of planned behavior. *Psychology and Health, 16,* 223–237.

Barreto, M., & Ellemers, N. (2000). You can't always do what you want: Social identity and self-presentational determinants of choices to work for a low status group. *Personality and Social Psychology Bulletin, 26,* 891–906.

Batson, C. D., Early, S., & Salvarani, G. (1997). Perspective taking: Imagining how another feels versus imagining how you would feel. *Personality and Social Psychology Bulletin, 23,* 751–758.

Bohner, G., & Wanke, M. (2002). *Attitudes and attitude change.* New York: Psychology Press.

Briñol, P., & Petty, R. E. (2005). Individual differences in attitude change. In D. Albarracin, B. T. Johnson, & M. P. Zanna (Eds.), *The handbook of attitudes* (pp. 575–615). Hillsdale, NJ: Erlbaum.

Brown, R. J. (2000). *Group processes* (2nd ed.). Oxford, UK: Blackwell.

Campbell, D. T. (1958). Common fate, similarity, and other indices of the status of aggregates of persons as social entities. *Behavioral Science, 3,* 14–25.

Chaiken, S. (1987). The heuristic model of persuasion. In M. P. Zanna, J. M. Olson, & C. P. Herman (Eds.), *Social influence: The Ontario symposium* (Vol. 5, pp. 3–39). Hillsdale, NJ: Erlbaum.

Chen, S., & Chaiken, S. (1999). The heuristic-systematic model in its broader context. In S. Chaiken & Y. Trope (Eds.), *Dual process theories in social psychology* (pp. 73–96). New York: Guilford.

Cooper, J. (2007). *Cognitive dissonance: Fifty years of classic theory.* London: Sage.

Cooper, J., & Hogg, M. A. (2002). Dissonance arousal and the collective self: Vicarious experience of dissonance based on shared group membership. In J. P. Forgas & K. D. Williams (Eds.), *The social self: Cognitive, interpersonal, and intergroup perspectives* (pp. 327-341). New York: Psychology Press.

Crano, W. D. (2001). Social influence, social identity, and in-group leniency. In C. W. K. de Dreu & N. K. de Vries (Eds.), *Group consensus and minority influence: Implications for innovation* (pp. 122–143). Oxford: Blackwell.

Crano, W. D. (in press). Task, group status, elaboration, and leniency: Majority and minority influence in attitude formation and attitude change. In R. Martin & M. Hewstone (Eds.), *Minority influence and innovation: Antecedents, processes and consequences.* Hove, UK: Psychology Press.

David, B., & Turner, J. C. (1996). Studies in self-categorization and minority conversion: Is being a member of the out-group an advantage? *British Journal of Social Psychology, 35,* 179–199.

David, B., & Turner, J. C. (1999). Studies in self-categorization and minority conversion: The in-group minority in intragroup and intergroup contexts. *British Journal of Social Psychology, 38,* 115–134.

Davis, M. H. (1994). *Empathy: A social psychological approach.* Boulder, CO: Westview Press.

Davison, W. P. (1983). The third-person effect in communication. *Public Opinion Quarterly, 52,* 1–15.

DeBono, K. G., & Telesca, C. (1990). The influence of source physical attractiveness on advertising effectiveness: A functional perspective. *Journal of Applied Social Psychology, 20,* 1383–1395.

Deci, E. L., & Ryan, R. M. (2000). The "what" and "why" of goal pursuits: Human needs and the self-determination of behavior. *Psychological Inquiry, 11,* 227–268.

Deutsch, M., & Gerard, H. B. (1955). A study of normative and informational social influences upon individual judgment. *Journal of Abnormal and Social Psychology, 51,* 629–636.

Duck, J. M., Hogg, M. A., & Terry, D. J. (1999). Social identity and perceptions of media persuasion: Are we always less influenced than others? *Journal of Applied Social Psychology, 29,* 1879–1899.

Duck, J. M., Hogg, M. A., & Terry, D. J. (2000). The perceived impact of persuasive messages on "us" and "them." In D. J. Terry & M. A. Hogg (Eds.), *Attitudes, behavior, and social context: The role of norms and group membership* (pp. 265–291). Mahwah, NJ: Erlbaum.

Duck, J. M., Terry, D. J., & Hogg, M. A. (1998). Perceptions of a media campaign: The role of social identity and the changing intergroup context. *Personality and Social Psychology Bulletin, 24,* 3–16.

Eagly, A. H., & Chaiken, S. (1993). *The psychology of attitudes.* Belmont, CA: Thomson.

Eagly, A. H., & Chaiken, S. (2005). Attitude research in the 21st century: The current state of knowledge. In D. Albarracin, B. T. Johnson, & M. P. Zanna (Eds.), *The handbook of attitudes* (pp. 743–767). Hillsdale, NJ: Erlbaum.

Emler, N. (1990). A social psychology of reputation. *European Review of Social Psychology, 1,* 171–193.

Farley, J. U., Lehmann, D. R., & Ryan, M. J. (1981). Generalising from "imperfect" replication. *Journal of Business, 54,* 597–610.

Fazio, R. H. (1990). Multiple processes by which attitude guide behavior: The MODE model as an integrative framework. In M. P. Zanna (Ed.), *Advances in experimental social psychology* (Vol. 22, pp. 75–109). San Diego, CA: Academic Press.

Fazio, R. H., & Olson, M. A. (2003). Implicit measures in social cognition research: Their meanings and use. *Annual Review of Psychology, 54,* 297–327.

Festinger, L. (1957). *A theory of cognitive dissonance.* Stanford, CA: Stanford University Press.

Festinger, L., Riecken, H., & Schachter, S. (1956). *When prophecy fails.* Minneapolis: University of Minnesota Press.

Fielding, K. S., Terry, D. J., Masser, B., & Hogg, M. A. (in press). Integrating social identity and the theory of planned behaviour to explain decisions to engage in sustainable agricultural practices. *British Journal of Social Psychology.*

Fishbein, M., & Ajzen, I. (1974). Attitudes toward objects as predictors of single and multiple behavior criteria. *Psychological Review, 81,* 59–74.

Fleming, M. A., & Petty, R. E. (2000). Identity and persuasion: An elaboration likelihood approach. In D. J. Terry & M. A. Hogg (Eds.), *Attitudes, behavior, and social context: The role of norms and group membership* (pp. 171–199). Mahwah, NJ: Erlbaum.

Greenwald, A. G., Banaji, M. R., Rudman, L. A., Farnham, S. D., Nosek, B. A., & Mellott, D. S. (2002). A unified theory of implicit attitudes, stereotypes, self-esteem, and self-concept. *Psychological Review, 109,* 3–25.

Gunther, A. (1995). Overrating the X-rating: The third-person perception and support for censorship of pornography. *Journal of Communication, 45,* 27–38.

Hamilton, D. L., & Sherman, S. J. (1996). Perceiving persons and groups. *Psychological Review, 103,* 336–355.

Haslam, S. A., Oakes, P. J., McGarty, C., Turner, J. C., & Onorato, S. (1995). Contextual changes in the prototypicality of extreme and moderate out-group members. *European Journal of Social Psychology, 25,* 509–530.

Hatfield, E., Cacioppo, J. T., & Rapson, R. L. (1994). *Emotional contagion.* New York: Cambridge University Press.

Hausenblaus, H. A., Carron, A. V., & Mack, D. E. (1997). Application of the theories of reasoned action and planned behavior in exercise behavior: A meta-analysis. *Journal of Sport and Exercise Psychology, 19,* 36–51.

Hogg, M. A. (2000). Subjective uncertainty reduction through self-categorization: A motivational theory of social identity processes. *European Review of Social Psychology, 11*, 223–255.

Hogg, M. A. (2003). Social identity. In M. R. Leary & J. P. Tangney (Eds.), *Handbook of self and identity* (pp. 462–479). New York: Guilford.

Hogg, M. A. (2005). Uncertainty, social identity and ideology. In S. R. Thye & E. J. Lawler (Eds.), *Advances in group processes* (Vol. 22, pp. 203–230). New York: Elsevier.

Hogg, M. A. (2006). Social identity theory. In P. J. Burke (Ed.), *Contemporary social psychological theories* (pp. 111–136). Palo Alto, CA: Stanford University Press.

Hogg, M. A. (2007). Uncertainty-identity theory. In M. P. Zanna (Ed.), *Advances in experimental social psychology* (Vol. 39, pp. 69–125). San Diego, CA: Academic Press.

Hogg, M. A., & Abrams, D. (1988). *Social identifications: A social psychology of intergroup relations and group processes.* London: Routledge.

Hogg, M. A., & Reid, S. A. (2006). Social identity, self-categorization, and the communication of group norms. *Communication Theory, 16*, 7–30.

Hogg, M. A., & Smith, J. R. (2007). Attitudes in social context: A social identity perspective. *European Review of Social Psychology, 18*, 89–131.

Hogg, M. A., & Turner, J. C. (1987). Social identity and conformity: A theory of referent informational influence. In W. Doise & S. Moscovici (Eds.), *Current issues in European social psychology* (Vol. 2, pp. 139–182). Cambridge, UK: Cambridge University Press.

Hogg, M. A., Turner, J. C., & Davidson, B. (1990). Polarized norms and social frames of reference: A test of the self-categorization theory of group polarization. *Basic and Applied Social Psychology, 11*, 77–100.

Hornsey, M. J. (2005). Why being right is not enough: Predicting defensiveness in the face of group criticism. *European Review of Social Psychology, 16*, 301–334.

Hornsey, M., Blackwood, L., Fielding, K. S., Louis, W. R., Mavor, K., Morton, T., et al. (2006). Identity and motivated collective action: Goal orientations and effectiveness ratings at a political demonstration. *Journal of Applied Social Psychology, 36*, 1701–1722.

Hornsey, M. J., & Imani, A. (2004). Criticising groups from the inside and the outside: An identity perspective on the intergroup sensitivity effect. *Personality and Social Psychology Bulletin, 30*, 365–383.

Hovland, C. I., & Weiss, W. (1951). The influence of source credibility on communication effectiveness. *Public Opinion Quarterly, 15*, 635–650.

Isenberg, D. J. (1986). Group polarization: A critical review. *Journal of Personality and Social Psychology, 50*, 1141–1151.

Jacobs, R. C., & Campbell, D. T. (1961). The perpetuation of an arbitrary tradition through several generations of a laboratory microculture. *Journal of Abnormal & Social Psychology, 62*, 649–658.

Kashima, Y. (2000). Maintaining cultural stereotypes in the serial reproduction of narratives. *Personality and Social Psychology Bulletin, 26*, 594–604.

Kelley, H. H. (1952). Two functions of reference groups. In G. E. Swanson, T. M. Newcomb, & E. L. Hartley (Eds.), *Readings in social psychology* (2nd ed., pp. 410–414). New York: Holt, Rinehart & Winston.

Kelly, C., & Breinlinger, S. (1995). Attitudes, intentions, and behavior: A study of women's participation in collective action. *Journal of Applied Social Psychology, 25*, 1430–1445.

Klandermans, B. (1997). *The social psychology of protest.* Oxford, UK: Blackwell.

Kraus, S. J. (1995). Attitudes and the prediction of behavior: A meta-analysis of the empirical literature. *Personality and Social Psychology Bulletin, 21*, 58–75.

Kutner, B., Wilkins, C., & Yarrow, P. R. (1952). Verbal attitudes and overt behavior involving racial prejudice. *Journal of Abnormal and Social Psychology, 47,* 649–652.

LaPiere, R. T. (1934). Attitudes versus actions. *Social Forces, 13,* 230–237.

Larrain, J. (1979). *The concept of ideology.* London: Hutchinson.

Louis, W. R., Davies, S., Smith, J., & Terry, D. (2007). Pizza and pop and the student identity: The role of referent group norms in healthy and unhealthy eating. *Journal of Social Psychology, 147,* 57–74.

Louis, W. R., Taylor, D. M., & Douglas, R. L. (2005). Normative influence and rational conflict decisions: Group norms and cost-benefit analyses for intergroup behavior. *Group Processes and Intergroup Relations, 8,* 355–374.

Louis, W. R., Taylor, D. M., & Neil, T. (2004). Cost-benefit analyses for your group and your self: The rationality of decision-making in conflict. *International Journal of Conflict Management, 15* (2), 110–143.

Mackie, D. M. (1986). Social identification effects in group polarization. *Journal of Personality and Social Psychology, 50,* 720–728.

Mackie, D. M., & Cooper, J. (1984). Attitude polarization: The effects of group membership. *Journal of Personality and Social Psychology, 46,* 575–585.

Mackie, D. M., Gastardo-Conaco, M. C., & Skelly, J. J. (1992). Knowledge of the advocated position and the processing of in-group and out-group persuasive messages. *Personality and Social Psychology Bulletin, 18,* 145–151.

Mackie, D. M., & Queller, S. (2000). The impact of group membership on persuasion: Revisiting "Who says what to whom with what effect?". In D. J. Terry & M. A. Hogg (Eds.), *Attitudes, behavior, and social context: The role of norms and group membership* (pp. 135–156). Mahwah, NJ: Erlbaum.

Mackie, D. M., Worth, L. T., & Asuncion, A. G. (1990). Processing of persuasive in-group messages. *Journal of Personality and Social Psychology, 58,* 812–822.

MacNeil, M., & Sherif, M. (1976). Norm change over subject generations as a function of arbitrariness of prescribed norms. *Journal of Personality and Social Psychology, 34,* 762–773.

Maio, G., & Haddock, G. (in press). *The science of attitudes.* London: Sage.

Marques, J. M., Abrams, D., & Serôdio, R. (2001). Being better by being right: Subjective group dynamics and derogation of in-group deviants when generic norms are undermined. *Journal of Personality and Social Psychology, 81,* 436–447.

Matz, D. C., & Wood, W. (2005). Cognitive dissonance in groups: The consequences of disagreement. *Journal of Personality and Social Psychology, 88,* 22–37.

McGarty, C., Haslam, S. A., Hutchison, K. J., & Turner, J. C. (1994). The effects of salient group memberships on persuasion. *Small Group Research, 25,* 267–293.

McGarty, C, Turner, J. C., Hogg, M. A., David, B., & Wetherell, M. S. (1992). Group polarization as conformity to the prototypical group member. *British Journal of Social Psychology, 31,* 1–20.

McKimmie, B. M., Terry, D. J., & Hogg, M. A. (2006). *Dissonance reduction in the context of group membership: The role of meta-consistency.* Manuscript submitted for publication.

McKimmie, B. M., Terry, D. J., Hogg, M. A., Manstead, A. S. R., Spears, R., & Doosje, B. (2003). I'm a hypocrite, but so is everyone else: Group support and the reduction of cognitive dissonance. *Group Dynamics, 7,* 214–224.

Monin, B., Nortin, M. I., Cooper, J., & Hogg, M. A. (2004). Reacting to an assumed situation vs. conforming to an assumed reaction: The role of perceived speaker attitude in vicarious dissonance. *Group Processes and Intergroup Relations, 7,* 207–220.

Moscovici, S. (1976). *Social influence and social change.* London: Academic Press.

Moscovici, S., & Zavalloni, M. (1969). The group as a polarizer of attitudes. *Journal of Personality and Social Psychology, 12,* 125–135.

Mugny, G. (1982). *The power of minorities*. London: Academic Press.

Nemeth, C. (1986). Differential contributions of majority and minority influence. *Psychological Review, 93*, 23–32.

Norton, M. I., Monin, B., Cooper, J., & Hogg, M. A. (2003). Vicarious dissonance: Attitude change from the inconsistency of others. *Journal of Personality and Social Psychology, 85*, 47–62.

Postmes, T., Haslam, S. A., & Swaab, R. I. (2005). Social influence in small groups: An interactive model of social identity formation. *European Review of Social Psychology, 16*, 1–42.

Postmes, T., Spears, R., & Lea, M. (2000). The formation of group norms in computer-mediated communication. *Human Communication Research, 26*, 341–371.

Prentice, D. A., & Miller, D. T. (1996). Pluralistic ignorance and the perpetuation of social norms by unwitting actors. In M. P. Zanna (Ed.), *Advances in experimental social psychology* (Vol. 28, pp. 161–209). New York: Academic Press.

Prislin, R., Brewer, M., & Wilson, D. J. (2002). Changing majority and minority positions within a group versus an aggregate. *Personality and Social Psychology Bulletin, 28*, 504–511.

Prislin, R., & Christensen, P. N. (2005). Social change in the aftermath of successful minority influence. *European Review of Social Psychology, 16*, 43–74.

Prislin, R., Limbert, W., & Bauer, E. (2000). From majority to minority and vice versa: The asymmetrical effects of gaining and losing majority position within a group. *Journal of Personality and Social Psychology, 79*, 385–395.

Prislin, R., & Wood, W. (2005). Social influence in attitudes and attitude change. In D. Albarracin, B. T. Johnson, & M. P. Zanna (Eds.), *The handbook of attitudes* (pp. 671–706). Hillsdale, NJ: Erlbaum.

Reicher, S. D. (2001). The psychology of crowd dynamics. In M. A. Hogg & R. S. Tindale (Eds.), *Blackwell handbook of social psychology: Group processes* (pp. 182–207). Oxford, UK: Blackwell.

Reicher, S. D., Spears, R., & Postmes, T. (1995). A social identity model of deindividuation phenomena. *European Review of Social Psychology, 6*, 161–198.

Reid, S. A., & Hogg, M. A. (2005). A self-categorization explanation for the third-person effect. *Human Communication Research, 31*, 129–161.

Robertson, T., & Reicher, S. (1997). Threats to self and the multiple inconsistencies of forced compliance: Some preliminary investigations into the relationship between contradictions and claims to identity. *Social Psychological Review, 1*, 1–15.

Rohan, M. J. (2000). A rose by any name? The values construct. *Personality and Social Psychology Review, 4*, 255–277.

Schofield, P. E., Pattison, P. E., Hill, D. J., & Borland, R. (2001). The influence of group identification on the adoption of smoking norms. *Psychology and Health, 16*, 1–16.

Sherif, M. (1935). A study of some social factors in perception. *Archives of Psychology, 27*, 1–60.

Sherif, M. (1936). *The psychology of social norms*. New York: Harper.

Sherman, D. K., Hogg, M. A., & Maitner, A. (in press). Perceived polarization: Reconciling ingroup and intergroup perception under uncertainty. *Group Processes and Intergroup Relations*.

Simon, B., Loewy, M., Sturmer, S., Weber, U., Freytag, P., Habig, C., et al. (1998). Collective identification and social movement participation. *Journal of Personality and Social Psychology, 74*, 646–658.

Smith, J. R., Hogg, M. A., Martin R., & Terry, D. J. (2007). Uncertainty and the influence of group norms in the attitude-behaviour relationship. *British Journal of Social Psychology, 46*, 769–792.

Smith, J. R., & Terry, D. J. (2003). Attitude-behaviour consistency: The role of group norms, attitude accessibility, and mode of behavioural decision-making. *European Journal of Social Psychology, 33,* 591–608.

Smith, J. R., Terry, D. J., Crosier, T., & Duck, J. M. (2005). The importance of the relevance of the issue to the group in attitude-intention consistency. *Basic and Applied Social Psychology, 27,* 163–170.

Smith, J. R., Terry, D. J., & Hogg, M. A. (2006). Who will see me? The impact of type of audience on willingness to display group-mediated attitude-intention consistency. *Journal of Applied Social Psychology, 36,* 1173–1197.

Smith, J. R., Terry, D. J., & Hogg, M. A. (2007). Social identity and the attitude-behaviour relationship: Effects of anonymity and accountability. *European Journal of Social Psychology, 37,* 239–257.

Stürmer, S., & Simon, B. (2004). Collective action: Towards a dual-pathway model. *European Review of Social Psychology, 15,* 59–99.

Tajfel, H. (1959). Quantitative judgement in social perception. *British Journal of Psychology, 50,* 16–29.

Tajfel, H. (1972). La catégorisation sociale [Social categorization]. In S. Moscovici (Ed.), *Introduction à la psychologie sociale* (Vol. 1, pp. 272–302). Paris: Larousse.

Tajfel, H., & Turner, J. C. (1986). The social identity theory of intergroup behavior. In S. Worchel & W. Austin (Eds.), *Psychology of intergroup relations* (pp. 7–24). Chicago: Nelson-Hall.

Terry, D. J., & Hogg, M. A. (1996). Group norms and the attitude-behavior relationship: A role for group identification. *Personality and Social Psychology Bulletin, 22,* 776–793.

Terry, D. J., & Hogg, M. A. (2001). Attitudes, behaviour, and social context: The role of norms and group membership in social influence processes. In J. P. Forgas & K. D. Williams (Eds.), *Social influence: Direct and indirect processes* (pp. 253–270). New York: Psychology Press.

Terry, D. J., Hogg, M. A., & Duck, J. M. (1999). Group membership, social identity, and attitudes. In D. Abrams & M. A. Hogg (Eds), *Social identity and social cognition* (pp. 280–314). Oxford, UK: Blackwell.

Terry, D. J., Hogg, M. A., & McKimmie, B. M. (2000). Attitude-behaviour relations: The role of in-group norms and mode of behavioural decision-making. *British Journal of Social Psychology, 39,* 337–361.

Terry, D. J., Hogg, M. A., & White, K. M. (1999). The theory of planned behaviour: Self-identity, social identity and group norms. *British Journal of Social Psychology, 38,* 225–244.

Terry, D. J., Hogg, M. A., & White, K. M. (2000). Attitude-behavior relations: Social identity and group membership. In D. J. Terry & M. A. Hogg (Eds.), *Attitudes, behavior, and social context: The role of norms and group membership* (pp. 67–94). Mahwah, NJ: Erlbaum.

Thompson, J. B. (1990). *Ideology and modern culture: Critical social theory in the era of mass communication.* Stanford, CA: Stanford University Press.

Turner, J. C. (1982). Towards a cognitive redefinition of the social group. In H. Tajfel (Ed.), *Social identity and intergroup relations* (pp. 15–40). Cambridge, UK: Cambridge University Press.

Turner, J. C. (1991). *Social influence.* Buckingham, UK: Open University Press.

Turner, J. C., Hogg, M. A., Oakes, P. J., Reicher, S. D., & Wetherell, M. S. (1987). *Rediscovering the social group: A self-categorization theory.* Oxford, UK: Blackwell.

Turner, J. C., & Oakes, P. J. (1989). Self-categorization and social influence. In P. B. Paulus (Ed.), *The psychology of group influence* (2nd ed., pp. 233–275). Hillsdale, NJ: Erlbaum.

Turner, J. C., Wetherell, M. S., & Hogg, M. A. (1989). Referent informational influence and group polarization. *British Journal of Social Psychology, 28,* 135–147.

Tyler, T. R., & Smith, H. J. (1998). Social justice and social movements. In D. T. Gilbert, S. T. Fiske, & G. Lindzey (Eds.), *The handbook of social psychology* (4th ed., Vol. 2, pp. 595–629). Boston: McGraw-Hill.

van Knippenberg, D., Lossie, N., & Wilke, H. (1994). In-group prototypicality and persuasion: Determinants of heuristic and systematic processing. *British Journal of Social Psychology, 33,* 289–300.

van Knippenberg, D., & Wilke, H. (1992). Prototypicality of arguments and conformity to in-group norms. *European Journal of Social Psychology, 22,* 141–155.

Wellen, J. M., Hogg, M. A., & Terry, D. J. (1998). Group norms and attitude-behavior consistency: The role of group salience and mood. *Group Dynamics: Theory, Research, and Practice, 2,* 48–56.

White, K. M., Hogg, M. A., & Terry, D. J. (2002). Improving attitude–behavior correspondence through exposure to normative support from a salient in-group. *Basic and Applied Social Psychology, 24,* 91–103.

Wicker, A. W. (1969). Attitudes versus actions: The relationship of verbal and overt behavioral responses to attitude objects. *Journal of Social Issues, 25,* 41–78.

Wilder, D. A. (1990). Some determinants of the persuasive power of in-groups and out-groups: Organization of information and attribution of independence. *Journal of Personality and Social Psychology, 59,* 1202–1213.

Zanna, M. P., & Fazio, R. H. (1982). The attitude-behavior relation: Moving towards a third generation of research. In M. P. Zanna, E. T. Higgins, & C. P. Herman (Eds.), *Consistency in social behavior: The Ontario Ssymposium* (Vol. 2, pp. 283–301). Hillsdale, NJ: Erlbaum.

Ziegler, R., Diehl, M., Zigon, R., & Fett, T. (2004). Source consistency distinctiveness and consensus: The three dimensions of the Kelley ANOVA model of persuasion. *Personality and Social Psychology Bulletin, 30,* 352–364.

16

Persuasion from Majority and Minority Groups

ROBIN MARTIN
Aston University, Birmingham, UK

MILES HEWSTONE
University of Oxford, UK

PEARL Y. MARTIN
Aston University, Birmingham, UK

ANTONIS GARDIKIOTIS
Aristotle University of Thessaloniki, Thessaloniki, Greece

New opinions are always suspected, and usually opposed, without any reason but because they are not already common—John Locke (1632–1704), *Essay Concerning Human Understanding*, dedicatory epistle.

*T*here are numerous attempts to influence our opinions every day. These attempts can come from many directions—reading a newspaper, listening to the television/radio, or hearing a debate are all situations where one person or group is trying to change the attitudes and opinions of another person or group. Often people try to support (or denigrate) a particular position by claiming that many people, *the majority*, or a relatively few people, *the minority*, support that position. It is this aspect of attitude change that is the subject of this chapter and it addresses the basic research question of whether people are more influenced when they believe a position is supported by either a numerical majority or minority.

Before proceeding, we need to define what the terms *majority* and *minority* mean. There are at least three ways to define these terms. First, we might simply resort to the number of people in each group, with the majority group being numerically larger than the minority group. Second, we can define these terms with reference to normative positions (that is, opinions and beliefs that reflect "accepted" standards in society). In this sense, the majority typically holds the normative position and the minority the antinormative or deviant position. Finally, we can refer to the power relationship between the source and recipient of influence; that is, the ability of the source to exert influence over the recipient. Majorities are considered to be high in power, whereas minorities are low in power as they are often discriminated against and marginalized in society. Using these dimensions, one might define a majority as the numerically larger group that holds the normative position and has power over others. In contrast, minorities tend to be numerically small, hold antinormative positions, and lack power over others. We stress that this is a generalized definition and there are exceptions; for example, blacks in South Africa during the period of apartheid were the numerically larger group in the population but lacked power.

Research in this area has gone through four distinct phases and it is this historical development that shapes this review. The first phase (pre-1970) focused on how the majority was able to cause individuals to conform or comply with its position. The second phase of research (late 1960s to 1980) reversed this question and focused on understanding the conditions under which a minority can influence the attitudes of the majority. The main research question of the first two phases of research were the identification of the key factors that inhibit or facilitate majority or minority influence. The third phase of research (1980 to the present) combined the first two phases and examined both majority and minority influence within the same paradigm. The main research question focused on the psychological processes underlying majority and minority influence and what impact they had on attitude change. The fourth, and current, phase of research is a continuation of the third phase where the examination of majority and minority influence is undertaken through the application of theories and methodologies derived from the persuasion literature (early 1990s to the present). The emphasis in this research has been to examine the different information processing strategies employed by recipients of either a majority or a minority persuasive message and to detail the contingency factors that determine when they will be utilized.

Our review follows these four chronological phases. However, because research relevant to the first and second phases of research (examining either majority or minority influence) has been reviewed extensively before (e.g., Cialdini & Goldstein, 2004; Levine & Russo, 1987; Maass & Clark, 1984: Maass, West, & Cialdini, 1987), we only briefly review them here. Instead, we focus in this chapter upon reviewing research relevant to the third and four phases (examining both majority and minority together and developments from the cognitive response approach). In addition, we include a section that examines current and future research developments in the area. Finally, due to space limitations, we have endeavored to cite only a few examples of relevant research in each section and direct the reader to other sources that can provide more details (e.g., Dreu & De Vries; 2001; Martin & Hewstone, 2003a; in press).

PHASE 1: EARLY RESEARCH ON MAJORITY INFLUENCE AND CONFORMITY (PRE-1970)

The first studies of social influence examined the conditions under which an individual yields or conforms to a numerical majority (e.g., Asch, 1951; Crutchfield, 1955). These studies typically involved objective judgment tasks (such as judging the length of lines), and exposed participants to the erroneous responses of a numerical majority. The research question was, would naïve participants agree with a majority of people who gave the obviously wrong judgment? Research has consistently shown that they do. Bond and Smith (1996), in a meta-analytic review of 133 studies conducted in 17 countries with the classic Asch line-judgment paradigm, found robust evidence that individuals conform to the judgments of a numerical majority even when that majority gave the obviously wrong response.

Explanations of conformity are based on the functionalist perspective of small-group behavior derived from work by Festinger (1950). According to Festinger, there are pressures for uniformity within groups to reach consensus, particularly when there is an explicit group goal. These pressures create a psychological dependency of the individual on the group. Festinger argued that individuals are dependent on others for social approval and verification of opinions and beliefs. In this sense, the majority is able to satisfy both these needs: first, because people generally wish to belong to majority groups, and, second, because people accept as true, opinions that are widely shared (Jones & Gerard, 1967). Building on these ideas, Deutsch and Gerard (1955) made a distinction between two social influence processes underlying conformity: *normative social influence* ("an influence to conform with the positive expectations of others," p. 629) and *informational social influence* ("an influence to accept information obtained from another as evidence about reality," p. 629).

The distinction between normative and informational influence has shaped much of the subsequent research in this area. People conform to the majority because they believe the majority provides a valid source of evidence about reality (informational influence) or because majority membership is desirable and protects against group rejection (normative influence). There is ample evidence supporting each of these explanations (Allen, 1975, for a review), showing situations where both normative and informational factors can lead to increased or decreased conformity. For example, when the normative value of the group increases (increasing similarity or attractiveness) conformity increases (Allen, 1975; Deutsch & Gerard, 1955). However, conformity is reduced in situations where surveillance by the majority is low (e.g., when group members' responses are anonymous to the majority) (Asch, 1956; Deutsch & Gerard, 1955). In terms of informational factors, research shows that reducing the majority's credibility as a source of information (e.g., making it inconsistent by having defectors from the majority) reduces conformity (Asch,

1951). Increasing the majority's ability to act as a valid source of information about reality (e.g., increasing group size or increasing task uncertainty) can increase conformity (Crutchfield, 1955; Gerard, Wilhelmy, & Connolley, 1968).

Notwithstanding the impact Deutsch and Gerard's framework has had on the whole social influence literature, Prislin and Wood (2005) have criticized the interpretation of it, which emphasizes only whether people are (public settings) or are not (private settings) under *surveillance*. According to the normative–informational distinction, social influence based on normative influence is temporary, and evidenced in public settings, but not maintained in private settings when judgments do not have social consequences. Informational influence yields enduring change in judgments, however, and holds in both private and public settings. In contrast to this view, Prislin and Wood emphasize that normative motives can have informational consequences that hold up later in time, and in private settings.

The fact that conformity rates can be affected by manipulating normative and informational motives does not, by itself, demonstrate that there are two separate processes. The dual process route has been routinely questioned (e.g., Kelman, 1958; see also the critical evaluation by Turner, 1991). Contemporary views have suggested consideration of four major motives underlying social influence (Prislin & Wood, 2005): effective action, building and maintaining relationships, managing the self-concept, and understanding. This approach emphasizes the goals of the *target* of influence, rather than the influencing agent.

The focus of this first phase of research was on how the majority influenced the individual, and this neglected the possibility that the individual (or minority) could influence the majority. According to the dependency account of conformity, minorities lack the resources to make majority members dependent on them (such as, power, status, size) and therefore do not have the means to enforce normative or informational influence. Therefore, according to the conformity approach, social influence can only flow from those who have the power to create psychological dependency (such as a majority) to those who do not (such as a minority). Deviancy, within the functionalist approach, was seen as dysfunctional and a threat to group harmony; consequently, deviants either conform to the group or face rejection.

PHASE 2: EARLY RESEARCH ON MINORITY INFLUENCE AND INNOVATION (LATE 1960S TO 1980)

Nearly all the research until the late 1960s had focused on how the majority can make individuals conform to their position. Yet, history is replete with examples of individuals and minorities who have had a tremendous impact on the majority in society (from the "ancients," such as Galileo, Freud, and Copernicus; to the "moderns," Bob Geldof, Noam Chomsky, and Aung San Suu Kyi). It was this observation in the late 1960s by a French social psychologist, Serge Moscovici that led to a theoretical reshaping of the area. Moscovici argued that if social influence only relied on conformity to the majority, then it would be difficult to see how groups changed, new ideas developed, and innovation might occur. Moscovici argued that there had been a "conformity bias" in the literature, with nearly all research focusing on majority influence, and that this had led to the dominance of the functionalist approach toward social influence, with its reliance on dependency as its explanatory variable (Moscovici & Faucheux, 1972). The problem with the functionalist approach is that it takes a unilateral or asymmetrical perspective on social influence that views influence as flowing only *from* the majority *to* the minority.

In his ground-breaking book, *Social Change and Social Influence*, Moscovici (1976) argued against the functionalist approach as an explanation of social influence, and instead proposed what he called a "genetic" model. At the heart of his approach was the proposition that all attempts at social influence create conflict between the source and the recipient of influence. Contrary to previous research that had only focused on the majority, Moscovici argued that minorities can, and often do, create conflict because they challenge the dominant majority view and, in so doing, offer a new and different perspective. Because people wish to avoid conflict, they will typically dismiss the minority position—often attributing its deviancy to an underlying, undesirable psychological dimension (Papastamou, 1986) such as seeing the minority as "crazy," "provocative," or "unstable." In order for the minority to avoid these negative attributions it must demonstrate that it is certain and committed to its position, that it will not compromise, and that its members believe that the majority should change to its position. Moscovici argued that by adopting such a *behavioral style* the minority could make the majority reconsider its own beliefs and consider the minority's position as a viable alternative. Moscovici defined the minority's behavioral style as the "way in which the behavior is organized and presented...to provoke the acceptance or rejection of a judgment... the fact that it maintains a well defined point of view and develops it in a coherent manner" (Moscovici, Lage, & Naffrechoux, 1969, p. 366). Moscovici (1976) identified five key aspects of behavioral style (consistency, investment, autonomy, rigidity, and fairness). By standing up to the majority, the minority shows that it is certain, confident, and committed to its position and will not be easily swayed.

Some of the first studies of minority influence employed a color perception task and showed that a minority that consistently called a blue slide green, led some majority members to also call the same slide green (e.g., Moscovici et al., 1969; Nemeth, Swedlund, & Kanki, 1971). Whereas many of the initial studies employed a color perception task, Mugny (1975; for review see, 1982) extended this research by examining minority influence on a range of social attitudes that were topical within the participants' population (in Swiss society, for example, topics included pollution, acceptance of foreign workers, and military service). Mugny also complemented the notion of behavioral style by making a distinction between two negotiating styles of influence, a rigid style where the minority refuses to compromise on any issue, and a flexible style where the minority is prepared to adapt to the majority position and accept certain compromises. In a series of studies, across a range of attitudes, Mugny showed that a minority that used the flexible style was more likely than one that used the rigid style to influence the majority, especially on a direct level.

To explain why behavioral style is important to minority influence, Moscovici relied on Kelley's (1967) attribution theory to explain how attributions that are derived from the minority's behavior lead to attitude change (for alternative perspectives, see Eagly & Chaiken, 1993). By consistently adopting its position, the minority is visible within the group and attracts attention (Schachter, 1951). Response consistency leads to attributions of certainty and confidence, especially when the minority is seen to reject publicly the majority position (for recent work on behavioral style see Buschini, 1998). Such a style of behavior creates two types of conflict within members of the majority: one cognitive (from an increase in response diversity) and the other social (from threatened interpersonal relations). Because the majority is unable to discredit the minority, it resolves this conflict by questioning its own position and considering the minority's position as a valid alternative.

Evidence in favor of the genetic model can be drawn from various lines of research. For example, studies have shown that key aspects of the minority's behavioral style are important in determining influence; these include response consistency (e.g., Moscovici et al., 1969), flexibility (e.g., Mugny, 1975), and minority consensus (e.g., Nemeth, Wachtler, & Endicott, 1977). Although there is much evidence to show that key behavioral styles do increase minority influence, and that these lead to self-reported perceptions of minority confidence and competence, there is no evidence that these attributions actually mediate influence (see Maass & Clark, 1984, for a critical evaluation).

Although Moscovici's early theorizing about minority influence received some criticisms (e.g., Levine, 1980; Turner, 1991), it was clearly extremely important in placing the study of active minorities on the research agenda. Moreover, it questioned the dominant functionalist account of influence that viewed social influence as invariably flowing from those with power (majorities) to those without power (minorities), and instead showed that influence is a reciprocal, or dialectical, process. As Moscovici (1976) argued, people can be both the source *and* the recipient of influence.

PHASE 3: COMPARING MAJORITY AND MINORITY INFLUENCE (MID-1970S TO 1990)

Having examined majority and minority influence research as separate phenomena, the next logical step was to compare majority and minority influence within the *same* paradigm. This research led to the development of several theoretical approaches. Although we recognize that there are many ways to organize these theories, we have found it useful to do this around two broad explanations, each of which subsumes several theories. We term these the *conflict* and *group-identification* approaches.[1]

Conflict-Based Models

This section reviews two of the main theories that examine majority and minority influence primarily through the resolution of conflict and how this affects underlying psychological processes.

Conversion Theory   Moscovici's (1980, 1985) conversion theory is widely regarded as the dominant theoretical perspective in this area. Moscovici argues that all forms of influence, whether from a majority or minority, result in conflict and that individuals are motivated to reduce that conflict. However, Moscovici proposes that people employ different processes, with different outcomes, depending on whether the source of the conflict is a majority or a minority. In the case of majority influence, individuals engage in a *comparison process* whereby they concentrate attention on "what others say, so as to fit in with their opinions or judgments" (1980, p. 214). Because people perceive that there are benefits from identification with a majority, they conform to the majority position without examining the content of the majority's message in detail. The outcome of majority influence is public compliance with the majority position with little or no private attitude change. Although social comparison might underpin majority influence, it cannot do so for minority influence because, as Moscovici argues, people typically wish to avoid association with undesirable deviant groups. However, minorities do have an advantage vis-à-vis majorities in that they are distinctive, in the sense that they stand out from the majority. This distinctiveness encourages a *validation process* leading one to "examine one's own responses, one's own judgments, in order to confirm and validate them...to see what the minority saw, to understand what it understood' (1980, p. 215). Minority influence may not lead to public agreement, but because of concerns over being categorized as a (deviant) minority member (Mugny, 1982), the close examination of the minority's arguments may bring about attitude conversion on an indirect or private level.

Conversion theory was developed from Moscovici's (1976) earlier genetic model, but it represents such a major change that it might be considered a separate theory. In the case of majority influence more emphasis is placed in conversion theory on the normative value associated with majority group membership, and less on the majority's ability to act as a verifier of information in the genetic model. In the case of minority influence there is less emphasis on an attribution account (as in the genetic model), but more on a cognitive explanation where influence results from the degree of evaluation of the minority's message. The most notable difference concerns the concept of "behavioral style" which was pivotal in the genetic model (Moscovici, 1976) but is seldom mentioned in conversion theory (Moscovici, 1980). In conversion theory it is the minority's distinctiveness, rather than its style of behavior, that triggers a validation process that can lead to conversion.

Research testing conversion theory can be grouped into three main hypotheses:

1. *The direction-of-attention* hypothesis: majority influence causes people to focus on the relationship between themselves and the source of influence, whereas minority influence causes people to focus on the content of the minority message. In support of this hypothesis some research has shown that majorities do encourage individuals to focus attention on the relationship between themselves and members of the majority (interpersonal focus) whereas a minority leads to greater attention being focused on the content of the minority's message (message focus) (e.g., Guillon & Personnaz, 1983). Other research examines this hypothesis through the ability of people to recall the source's message. If people do focus

more on the content of the minority message, as Moscovici argues, then one might predict people will recall more arguments when attributed to a minority than a majority source. However, research evidence for this hypothesis is mixed, with as many studies showing superior message recall for a majority (e.g., Mackie, 1987) as for a minority (e.g., Moscovici, Mugny & Papastamou, 1981) source. A consistent problem in these studies is that recall measures are almost universally taken after attitude (and other dependent variable) measurements making it difficult to make a direct link between the source's message and later recall.

2. *The content-of-thinking* hypothesis: majority influence leads to a superficial examination of the majority's argument, whereas minority influence leads to a detailed evaluation of the minority's arguments. This hypothesis has been interpreted as suggesting that a minority will lead to more detailed message evaluation, involving great cognitive effort (quantity) and to a better quality of thinking (quality) than does a majority. Research examining the level of message evaluation (quantity) has employed messages which contained either weak (and nonpersuasive) arguments or strong (and persuasive) arguments in order to determine whether message scrutiny has occurred. If participants are motivated and able to process a message, they should be more persuaded by the strong than the weak message (Petty & Cacioppo, 1986). The results of studies crossing source status and message quality have been mixed, with some supporting conversion theory and some not (e.g., Baker & Petty, 1994; De Dreu & De Vries, 1993; Martin & Hewstone, 2003b; Martin, Hewstone, & Martin, 2007). In reviewing these studies, Martin and Hewstone (2003b) concluded that overall research favors conversion theory, by showing greater message scrutiny for a minority source, and that some of the discrepancies in the findings might be due to differences in the persuasion topics employed. In addition, Martin et al. (2007) have shown that many of these findings can be understood as an interaction between source status and the processing demands present at the time of message exposure and that conversion theory applies best when processing demands are neither too low nor too high (see Martin & Hewstone, 2008). This issue is considered in more detail later in the chapter.

Research examining whether minorities lead to the generation of a different pattern of arguments and counterarguments (quality) than do majorities, in an attempt to evaluate the message, has produced inconsistent results. These studies, which employed a thought-listing technique to elicit participants' elaborations of the message, have yielded results suggestive of differences in the quality of thinking following majority and minority influence but there is not a consistent pattern (e.g., Maass & Clark, 1983; Mackie, 1987; Mucchi-Faina, Maass & Volpato, 1991). It is likely that these inconsistencies are due to a variety of factors including differences in methodologies used to collect participants' thoughts and variations in how these thoughts were coded.

3. *The differential-influence* hypothesis: majority influence leads to more public/direct influence than private/indirect influence, whereas minority influence leads to the opposite. This hypothesis has received the most research attention. In a review of the literature, Maass et al. (1987) identified four dimensions of influence employed to examine this hypothesis: (a) *time*—influence measured immediately following exposure to the source versus influence measured latter in time (e.g.,

Crano & Chen, 1998; Moscovici et al., 1981); (b) *specificity*—influence specific to the message versus influence that goes beyond the message and considers a wider set of issues. This dimension is commonly referred to as "direct" and "indirect" influence, respectively (e.g., Alvaro & Crano, 1997; Mugny & Pérez, 1991); (c) *privacy*—responses made in public versus those that are made anonymously and in private (e.g., Maass & Clark, 1983; Martin, 1988) and (d) *awareness*—participants are aware of the connection between source message and influence dimension, versus not being aware of this connection (e.g., Moscovici & Personnaz, 1980). Support for conversion theory comes from a meta-analysis of 97 studies, across the types of measures noted above, by Wood, Lundgren, Ouellette, Busceme, and Blackstone (1994) who concluded that "Minority impact was most marked on measures of influence that were private from the source and indirectly related to the content of the appeal and less evident on direct private influence measures and on public measures" (p. 323).

One of the most provocative lines of research has focused on Moscovici and Personnaz's (1980) finding that a minority, but not a majority, can cause a perceptual conversion. Using the "blue-green slide paradigm," they measured both manifest and latent levels of influence (corresponding to the "awareness" dimension above). After viewing a blue slide, participants gazed at a white screen on which a color started to appear. This color is the chromatic afterimage and is the complementary color of the original stimulus (in this case blue). They found that when the minority called the blue slide green participants started to see the afterimage closer to the complementary color of green (i.e., red-purple). When the majority called the blue slide green, however, the participant's afterimage judgment was closer to the complementary color of blue (i.e., yellow). Because there is no obvious link between slide and afterimage color, the latter result is taken to represent an unconscious or latent level of influence. If true, these results are remarkable and suggest that a consistent minority changed people's perceptual code. Replications of these findings have, however, been mixed (see Martin & Hewstone, 2001, for a review). Martin (1998) conducted five replications of the original study and found that the results obtained by Moscovici and Personnaz (1980) could be explained by a number of methodological factors including variations in the number of slide presentations per experimental phase and participant suspiciousness (see also Sorrentino, King, & Leo, 1980). Despite these concerns, research still continues with this paradigm (e.g., Laurens & Moscovici, 2005).

In summary, it is widely recognized that Moscovici played a pivotal role in the development of majority and minority influence. He was the first person to systematically research the conditions under which a minority can influence a majority and in so doing emphasized that influence can flow in both directions and not simply from a majority to a minority as had earlier been assumed. Many aspects of conversion theory have received support, as indicated above, and the theory has been the backbone for many future theoretical developments in this area, as will become clear as this chapter unfolds.

Convergent–Divergent Theory   The second major model of majority and minority influence is the convergent–divergent theory proposed by Nemeth (1986,

1995). Nemeth proposes that majority and minority influence induces people to engage in different styles of thinking, which lead to different outcomes. Much of Nemeth's theorizing rests on two assumptions; first, the "false-consensus heuristic" (Ross, Greene & House, 1977), which states that people expect to share the same attitude as the majority, and to differ from the minority and, second, that the experience of stress narrows a person's focus of attention (Easterbrook, 1959). Based on these assumptions, Nemeth argues that exposure to a counterattitudinal majority breaks the consensus expectation and this leads people to narrow their focus of attention on the content of the majority's message. This is referred to as *convergent thinking*, which is characterized by a "convergence of attention, thought, and the number of alternatives considered" (Nemeth, 1986, p. 25). By contrast, exposure to a counterattitudinal minority is consistent with the consensus expectation (people expect to disagree with the minority). This does not lead to stress, and therefore people can engage in a wider range of issues, some of which may not have been proposed by the minority. Nemeth refers to this as *divergent thinking* which involves "a greater consideration of other alternatives, ones that were not proposed but would not have been considered without the influence of the minority" (Nemeth, 1986, p. 25).

Nemeth's theory differs from conversion theory in many ways. Perhaps the major difference concerns the analysis of majority influence. According to conversion theory, people comply with the majority without considering its arguments in detail. In contrast, Nemeth claims that because a counterattitudinal majority breaks the consensus expectations, people actively process the majority's message but do so in a convergent way—focusing only on the immediate issues to do with the majority's arguments. In the case of minority influence, both models state that people will actively process the minority arguments, but Nemeth goes further to suggest that this will involve a much wider range of issues than that stated in the message.

What is radical about Nemeth's perspective is that it suggests minorities can lead individuals to consider a wider range of alternatives than was contained in the minority's original arguments, and that this can result in improved judgments and performance. Therefore, minorities can lead to the detection of new and better ideas and solutions, and in so doing can increase creativity. In testing this hypothesis, researchers have typically employed objective tasks (such as the stroop test, or identifying anagrams) where it is possible to quantify performance and hence compare the results of being exposed to a numerical majority or minority. The results support Nemeth's theory. In tasks where performance benefits from divergent thinking, minority influence has been shown to lead to better performance than majority influence (e.g., Nemeth & Kwan, 1987; Nemeth & Wachtler, 1983), but on tasks where performance benefits from convergent thinking, majority influence leads to better performance than minority influence (e.g., Nemeth, Mosier & Chiles, 1992; Peterson & Nemeth, 1996). Furthermore, minority influence has been shown to lead to the generation of more creative and novel judgments than does majority influence (e.g., Mucchi-Faina et al., 1991; Nemeth & Kwan, 1985; Nemeth & Wachtler, 1983).

Another line of research has examined more directly the types of thinking following majority and minority influence. For example, research shows that minority influence leads to the use of multiple strategies in solving problems, whereas majority influence leads individuals to focus on the majority-endorsed strategy (Butera, Mugny, Legrenzi, & Pérez, 1996; Nemeth & Kwan, 1987). Finally, research shows that minority influence encourages issue-relevant thinking, whereas majority influence leads to message-relevant thinking (e.g., De Dreu & De Vries, 1993; De Dreu, De Vries, Gordijn, & Schuurman, 1999).

Nemeth's theory yields interesting insights into the processes of majority and minority influence and it offers the tantalizing prospect that minorities can lead to improved performance through stimulating creativity (see also work on devil's advocacy; e.g., Nemeth, Brown, & Rogers, 2001). However, most of the research has employed cognitive tasks to measure task performance and more research is needed to determine whether compatible findings can be observed on attitudes (for an exception, see Martin & Hewstone, 1999).

Group-Identification Based Approaches

Whereas the conflict approaches focus on intragroup processes, the group-identification approaches focus on both the intergroup *and* intragroup processes with particular reference to the role of identification processes.

Conflict-Elaboration Theory   Conflict-elaboration theory was developed by Mugny, Pérez, and their colleagues (Mugny, Butera, Sanchez-Mazas, & Pérez, 1995; Pérez & Mugny, 1996: for empirical tests of the model, see Brandstätter et al., 1991; Butera et al., 1996). The model is similar to conversion theory, in that it proposes that divergence from a source of influence causes conflict; and how this conflict is handled depends on whether it originates from a majority or minority source. However, unlike conversion theory, which focuses on conflict *resolution*, this approach considers conflict *elaboration*, a process that "refers to the way people give meaning to this divergence" (Mugny et al., 1995, p. 161). Another major difference is that conflict-elaboration theory places a great deal of importance on the role of group identification in shaping psychological processes.

The nature of the conflict elaboration and the types of influence depends on the type of task and the source introducing the divergence. Two contingency variables are associated with the type of task. The first concerns the *relevance of making an error*. If the task is objective with a clearly correct response (with all other responses being wrong), the cost to the individual of an error is high, whereas if the task is one where objectively correct responses cannot be determined, the cost of making an error is low. The second dimension concerns whether the responses are *socially anchoring*. If the response defines the individual within a particular group membership, it is socially anchoring, but if the response does not define an individual within a social category, the task is not socially anchoring. Crossing these two dimensions leads to four social situations, each of which is associated with different psychological processes involved in conflict elaboration.

Conflict-elaboration theory is a general theory of social-influence phenomena, across many social situations, with one of these quadrants being particularly relevant to the typical majority and minority influence scenario (this involves subjective tasks that are socially anchoring). The conflict associated with a source in this situation is determined by the meaning attached to it in terms of in-group or out-group membership. When the source is the in-group, as one may assume a majority would be, normative influence would be increased, and conformity to the majority position will occur with little need to consider the content of the majority message (similar to Moscovici's comparison process). When the source is an out-group such as a minority, and thereby associated with negative connotations, agreement would be threatening to self-image, and an identification conflict arises. Private and indirect influence can occur through a process of dissociation between social comparison and validation, whereby targets of influence resolve the intergroup conflict, because "Only then can subjects focus their attention on the content of the minority position" (Mugny et al., 1995, p. 166). The conflict-elaboration theory proposes hypotheses similar to those of Moscovici, suggesting that a majority source leads to minimal processing of its message whereas a minority source can lead to detailed consideration of its message especially when social comparison processes are weak.

Self-Categorization Theory

The role of group identification on social influence is central to the self-categorization theory analysis of majority and minority influence. The fundamental assertion of self-categorization theory (Turner, 1991) is that only those who are similar to self (on dimensions relevant to influence) can be agents of influence. This is because similar others provide consensual validation for one's opinions whereas dissimilar others do not. Perceiving oneself as dissimilar from others (e.g., out-group or minority) can be a basis for explaining, and dismissing, the difference in opinions. Self-categorization theory does not claim that similar others always have influence, as individuals may resist change by recategorizing themselves, the group, and the relevance of the influence topic, or by acting on the source to change their opinions.

In applying self-categorization theory to majority and minority influence, David and Turner (1996, 1999, 2001), suggested that a minority will have influence only if it is defined as the target's in-group. The categorization of the minority as different from self reduces its influence. According to self-categorization theory, indirect influence occurs when there is a shift in perspective from intragroup to intergroup. In the intergroup perspective, individuals perceive the minority in a wider context and begin to see the minority as "part of 'us' rather than 'them', basically on our side, standing for basic values that 'we' all share" (Turner, 1991, p. 171). In this case, the minority can lead to an indirect change without it being apparent on the direct level.

Unlike the other theories discussed in this chapter, self-categorization theory is a single-process theory, proposing that majority and minority influence are affected by the same process, with the outcomes of this process determined by the in-group/out-group status of the source. In support of this, David and Turner

(1996, 1999) found majority compliance and minority conversion only when the source of influence was categorized as similar to the target of influence (which is consistent with conversion theory). When the source was characterized as being dissimilar to the target of influence, there was no direct or indirect influence. However, there is little support for self-categorization theory's claim that only in-group minorities lead to indirect attitude change. In fact, there is much evidence to show that out-group minorities can have considerable indirect influence and often greater influence than the in-group minority (e.g., Martin, 1988; Mugny, Kaiser & Papastamou, 1983; Pérez & Mugny, 1987; for a review see Pérez & Mugny, 1998). Finally, research within the self-categorization theory framework has failed to show that self-categorization is the mediating process between source status and influence (for an exception, see Gordijn, Postmes, & De Vries, 2001).

The Context/Comparison Model   The final model we will consider in this section is the context/comparison model developed by Crano (Crano, 2001; Crano & Alvaro, 1998). This model identifies two processes that are important in determining whether there is direct or indirect influence: message elaboration and source derogation. If the message concerns *weak or unvested attitudes*, an in-group minority can be persuasive because it is perceived by majority members as being distinctive, and this leads to message elaboration (in a similar way as proposed by conversion theory). If the minority is part of the in-group, it is unlikely to be derogated by the majority because the attitude dimension has little implication for in-group membership. Majorities, however, are unlikely to lead to much influence because the majority is not distinctive and therefore does not trigger message elaboration. If the message concerns *vested or central attitudes*, targets of in-group minority influence are reluctant to be identified with the minority position, yet there is a reluctance to derogate other in-group members. This leads to what Crano and Alvaro (1998) term the "leniency contract," which allows the target to elaborate on the in-group minority's message without source derogation, "open-mindedly, with little defensiveness or hostility" (Crano & Alvaro, 1998, p. 180), and this can lead to indirect attitude change. In the case of out-group minorities, however, the source is derogated, resulting in little direct or indirect influence. Because the message relates to important group-relevant dimensions, there can be compliance without message elaboration leading to influence on both a public or direct level.

Research supporting the context/comparison model comes from various studies by Crano and colleagues (e.g., Alvaro & Crano, 1997; Crano & Chen, 1998; Crano & Hannula-Bral, 1994). One area that needs more attention is the causal psychological processes involved. The model proposes various mediating factors (such as source distinctiveness, majority-group acceptance, and identification), and future research could usefully identify when these operate. Moreover, the distinction between weak and central attitudes is an important one, as there has been surprisingly little research that examines the role of the topic on majority and minority influence.

PHASE 4: THE COGNITIVE-RESPONSE ERA (MID-1980S TO THE PRESENT)

One of the major developments in recent research into majority and minority influence has been the application of concepts, and methodologies to the study of social influence that are derived from the cognitive-response approach to persuasion. This is an information-processing approach that focuses on how people's cognitions are affected by persuasive arguments, and how this affects the acceptance (or rejection) of these arguments. The extent to which a message encourages people to generate thoughts that are consistent with that message determines whether they will be influenced by it. In contrast, if a message leads people to generate thoughts counter to the message (or neutral ones or none at all), then attitudes will not be affected by the message. The application of methodologies developed within the cognitive-response approach has offered new ways to examine the processes involved in majority and minority influence. The most notable development has been the application of the thought-listing methodology to examine people's cognitions. This is now widely used in the majority and minority influence literature to assess cognitive activity, which is then used as a mediating variable between source status and influence.

One of the major theoretical outcomes of this approach has been the development of the *objective-consensus approach* (Mackie, 1987; see also De Vries, De Dreu, Gordijn, & Shuurman, 1996). In direct contradiction to conversion theory, this approach proposes that people are more likely to process a majority than a minority message. Two reasons are given for this prediction; first, the majority exerts informational influence (people believe the majority view is valid and therefore likely to process the arguments); and, second the majority breaks consensus expectations (a counterattitudinal majority breaks expectations and this motivates people to analyze majority arguments to understand the discrepancy). By contrast, exposure to a counterattitudinal minority does not lead to informational influence, nor does it break the consensus heuristic and, consequently, one is less likely to process the minority's message.

Mackie (1987) reported a number of studies showing that majorities led to greater cognitive thought elaboration and indirect attitude change than did minorities. However, in the wider literature, there is relatively little evidence for the proposition that majorities promote more messages processing than minorities, and that this leads to greater private attitude acceptance. Indeed, Wood et al.'s (1994) meta-analytic review described above tends to support conversion theory: minorities lead to greater private and indirect attitude change.

Baker and Petty (1994) have built on this approach to develop the *source-position congruency model*. According to this perspective, greater message processing occurs when the situation is "imbalanced" or unexpected (i.e., counterattitudinal majority or proattitudinal minority) than when the situation is "balanced' or expected (i.e., proattitudinal majority or counterattitudinal minority). When expectancies are violated, recipients of influence attempts are surprised and this motivates them to examine the source's message in more detail in order to resolve the inconsistency. Across two studies they provided some evidence that source-position congruity moderates when people will process a majority or minority message (but see Martin & Hewstone, 2003b, for an alternative account).

A more explicit integration of the cognitive response approach with majority and minority influence has been proposed by Martin and Hewstone (Martin & Hewstone, 2003b, 2008; Martin, Hewstone, & Martin, 2003; Martin, Martin, Smith, & Hewstone, 2007; Martin et al., 2007). They draw on a parallel, first noted by Maass and Clark (1983), between Moscovici's concepts of comparison/validation and the nonsystematic/systematic processing strategies proposed in models of persuasion, such as the Elaboration Likelihood Model (ELM; Petty & Wegner, 1999), and the Heuristic/Systematic Model (HSM; Chen & Chaiken, 1999).

Essentially this approach makes two broad sets of predictions concerning (1) the types of processes underlying majority and minority influence and when they occur, and (2) the consequences for attitudes following majority and minority influence. The first set of predictions states that the effects of source status (majority vs. minority) vary along an elaboration continuum (the extent to which the situation allows or encourages elaboration of the source's message). When the elaboration demands are low (e.g., the topic is low in personal relevance), message recipients do not process the source's arguments and attitudes can be guided through simple heuristics (such as the majority is more likely to be right than the minority). When elaboration demands are high (e.g., the topic is high in personal relevance), then people will attend to, and process, both the majority and minority arguments and there should be attitude change in both situations. However, most influence situations to which people are exposed are not characterized by either very low or high processing demands but, rather, are located at an intermediate level. In this situation, Martin and Hewstone, believe conversion theory should apply; that is, systematic processing of only the minority arguments. Evidence in favor of this prediction has been found in two studies reported by Martin et al. (2007) who examined majority and minority influence at different levels of processing demands (low, intermediate, and high). Results showed that both a majority and minority can lead to systematic processing of its arguments, and to attitude change, depending on the processing demands that occur during message exposure. The second set of predictions concerns the nature of the attitudes that are formed following majority and minority influence. According to the persuasion literature, attitudes formed through systematic processing are "strong" (Krosnick, Boninger, Chuang, Berent, & Carnot, 1993) in terms of being more resistant to counterpersuasion, persistent over time, and more predictive of behavior than attitudes formed via nonsystematic processing. Evidence has been shown that minorities lead to "strong" attitudes in that attitudes following minority influence were more resistant to counterpersuasion (Martin et al., 2003), more persistent over time (Martin & Hewstone, 2008), and better predictors of behavior (Martin et al., 2007) compared to attitudes formed following majority influence.

It is clear that the impact of the cognitive-response approach will continue to grow with the potential to offer greater insights into the processes of majority and minority influence. However, we raise two potential concerns. First, this approach reinforces the importance of information-processing strategies in understanding social influence. The cognitive response approach, by virtue of its methodologies, places much emphasis on cognitive processes to the neglect of normative issues. Yet we know from experience that exposure to a minority leads to both a cognitive and an emotional reaction. There is a danger that a purely cognitive approach would overlook affective and motivational factors, which are closely associated with social cognition and, indeed, form key aspects of it (see Forgas, 2001, and this volume). Second, an exclusive focus on the information processing strategies that arise from majority and minority influence has the potential to neglect *why* these sources have influence, and the process of interaction between target and source of influence.

CURRENT AND FUTURE RESEARCH DEVELOPMENTS

In conducting this review we were encouraged by the fact that this topic continues to attract considerable research attention: not only in terms of the number of publications but also the number of active scholars in the area. In this section we review two major areas of research activity concerning structural aspects of majority and minority influence and applied applications.

The first area of recent research development concerns renewed interest in the *structural aspects* of majority and minority influence, such as the numerical size of the majority and minority (e.g., Erb, Bohner, Hewstone, Werth, & Reinhard, 2006; Gardikiotis, Martin, & Hewstone, 2005), group congruence of opinion (e.g., Phillips, 2003), and dynamic changes in group status from one source group to another (e.g., Clark, 2001; Prislin & Christensen, 2005). This research is promoting a debate over the role of consensus information for majority- and minority-group membership (e.g., Erb & Bohner, 2001; also see Bohner, Erb, Siebler, this volume). In addition, research is examining the role of individual differences (e.g., Shuper & Sorrentino, 2004), the social representation of majorities and minorities (e.g., Gardikiotis, Martin, & Hewstone, 2005; Laurens & Viaud, 2000), and the role of both cultural factors and norms (e.g., Ng & Van Dyne, 2001). While research continues to examine the *different levels of influence* as summarized above, it is increasingly focusing on the cognitive implications of influence in terms of strategies people adopt when being influenced (e.g., Laughlin, 1992), the reasons people give for changing their attitudes (e.g., Laurens & Masson, 1996), and the consequences of attitude change for the structure of attitudes (e.g., Gruenfeld, Thomas-Hunt, & Kim, 1998; Martin et al., 2007, Mucchi-Faina & Cicoletti, 2006).

The second area of research development concerns more *applied research and situational awareness* of the effects of majority and minority influence. While planned field experiments that directly test majority and minority influence are unlikely to be conducted (due to ethical reasons), contemporary research is applying the findings of basic research to real-life issues and/or in more ecologically valid situations. These include studies of the interaction between majority and minority in group situations (e.g., Prislin & Christensen, 2005; Smith, Tindale, & Anderson, 2001), examining real-life minority movements and political groups (e.g., Smith & Diven, 2002), the effects of minority opinions on group decision making (e.g., Schulz-Hardt, Brodbeck, Mojzisch, Kerschreiter & Frey, 2006;

Velden, Beersma, & De Dreu, 2007), the ability of minorities to change peoples' behavior (e.g., Falomir-Picastor, Butera, & Mugny, 2002; Martin et al., 2007), and in understanding innovation in organizations (e.g., De Dreu & Beersma, 2001; De Dreu & West, 2001).

Our prediction is that future research will continue to focus on these two broad areas, with further advances in the application of theoretical knowledge to the understanding of the role of minorities in contemporary society.

CONCLUDING REMARKS

The aim of this chapter was to review research in the area of majority and minority influence. We are particularly concerned with the crucial role of minorities in innovation, introducing new perspectives on old problems, and bringing new ideas to our attention. As the words of John Locke underline, in our opening quote, new ideas are too often opposed for no reason other than that they are novel. Space restrictions meant, however, that we have had to be selective in this review, and we chose to focus mostly on reviewing the main theoretical models and recent developments in the area.

We chose to categorize the theories according to whether they are conflict- or group-identification based. We recognize that there are other categorization systems that can be made (such as, single vs. dual process, main vs. contingency models). We chose this categorization because we believe that the concepts of "conflict" and "identification" are pivotal in understanding majority and minority influence. We stress, however, that our allocation of theories into the conflict- and group-identification based categorizes is not mutually exclusive—most of the theories have some element of both aspects. This is best seen in the conflict elaboration model which integrates both conflict and identification processes. We hope that the roles of conflict and identification, in these and other models, will become more explicitly articulated in future theoretical developments.

We wish to comment on the standard methodology now employed in examining majority and minority influence—the attitude-change paradigm (pretest, message exposure, posttest) with its emphasis on information processing. Majority and minority status are defined in purely numerical terms, and participants receive the same (usually counterattitudinal) message to allow comparisons between the different sources of influence. Generally, these studies strip the social situation to a minimum with no contact between source and recipient of influence. The integration of the majority and minority research traditions (our Phase 3 above), especially through the framework of persuasion, has brought theoretical and methodological gains. It has, however, also resulted in a loss of the distinctive aspects that were associated with each research tradition and reduced studies to the examination of informational aspects with little regard to normative issues that had been pivotal in initial theorizing in both areas. This leads us to voice the concern that contemporary research, by its design and emphasis on informational aspects, is distorting theoretical developments. Future research needs to address this issue, and use a variety of paradigms to examine both informational and normative aspects of influence. Concepts such as "dependency" and "behavioral style," which were crucial to early theoretical advances, are almost completely overlooked in contemporary work—mainly, we believe, because they do not fit the current vogue for information-processing paradigms and theories.

Following from the above, we would also welcome more research examining the causal processes involved in majority and minority influence. Extrapolating from variations of dependent variables is not, by itself, sufficient unless there is clear evidence that these were determined by theoretically relevant mediating variables. Some researchers have risen to this challenge by using regression procedures to conduct mediational analyses to test the role of various mediators in determining influence (e.g., Baker & Petty, 1994; Erb, Bohner, Schmaelzle, & Rank, 1998; Gordijn et al., 2001; Martin et al., 2007). However, more can be achieved using structural equation modeling to examine the relationship between antecedents, mediating factors, and outcomes of influence. We believe that this will provide a much better understanding of majority and minority influence as well as more exacting testing of the various theoretical models.

We end this chapter by referring back to Moscovici's (1976) seminal book, *Social Influence and Social Change*. In that book Moscovici drew a parallel between majority influence, compliance, and social control, and between minority influence, innovation, and social change. Many scholars, ourselves included, have internalized this parallel and thus equate majorities with control and minorities with change. The research reviewed in this chapter has made us question this assumption as it clearly shows that both majorities and minorities can be agents of change *and* control: our quest is to know exactly when, and how, each occurs.

NOTE

1. In this chapter we have chosen not to review the mathematical models of social influence—such as, Latané and Wolf's (1981) *social impact model*, and Tanford and Penrod's (1984), *social-impact model*—because they do not currently attract any research attention. These models analyze majority and minority influence in terms of mathematical equations based on such factors as the source's strength (as in status), immediacy (as in physical closeness), and number (how many people hold that position). The more the majority or minority has these factors the greater is their influence, although the relationship is not linear. Martin and Hewstone (2003a) outlined several problems associated with these models in explaining majority and minority influence, the most notable being that they do not consider the influence of the source beyond the public or direct level, and therefore they cannot explain the private and indirect influence often observed with minority influence.

REFERENCES

Allen, V. L. (1975). Social support for nonconformity. In L. Berkowitz (Ed.), *Advances in experimental social psychology* (Vol. 8, pp. 1–43). New York: Academic Press.

Alvaro, E. M., & Crano, W. D. (1997). Indirect minority influence: Evidence for leniency in source evaluation and counterargumentation. *Journal of Personality and Social Psychology, 72*, 949–964.

Asch, S. E. (1951). Effects of group pressure upon the modification and distortion of judgments. In H. Guetzhow (Ed.), *Groups, leadership, and men* (pp. 177–190). Pittsburgh: Carnegie Press.

Asch, S. E. (1956). Studies of independence and conformity. A minority of one against a unanimous majority. *Psychological Monographs: General and Applied*. Whole No. 416.

Baker, S. M., & Petty, R. E. (1994). Majority and minority influence: Source-position imbalance as a determinant of message scrutiny. *Journal of Personality and Social Psychology, 67*, 5–19.

Bond, R., & Smith, P. B. (1996). Culture and conformity: A meta-analysis of studies using Asch's (1952b, 1956) line judgment task. *Psychological Bulletin, 119*, 111–137.

Brandstätter, V., Ellemers, N., Gaviria, E., Giosue, F., Huguet, P., Kroon, M., Morchain, P., Pujal, M., Rubini, M., Mugny, G., & Pérez, J. A. (1991). Indirect majority and minority influence: An exploratory study. *European Journal of Social Psychology, 21*, 199–211.

Buschini, F. (1998). L'impact des messages aux styles d'expression positif ou negatif en fonction du statut minoritaire ou majoritaire de la source d'influence [The impact of messages on positive and negative styles of expression in the functioning of minority or majority status as a source of influence]. *Cahiers Internationaux de Psychologie Sociale, 39*, 9–22.

Butera, F., Mugny, G., Legrenzi, P., & Pérez, J. A. (1996). Majority and minority influence, task representation and inductive reasoning. *British Journal of Social Psychology, 35*, 123–136.

Chen, S., & Chaiken, S. (1999). The heuristic-systematic model in its broader context. In S. Chaiken & Y. Trope (Eds.), *Dual-process theories in social psychology* (pp. 73–96). New York: Guilford.

Cialdini, R. B., & Goldstein, N. J. (2004). Social influence: Compliance and conformity. *Annual Review of Psychology, 55*, 591–621.

Clark, R. D., III (2001). Effects of majority defection and multiple minority sources on minority influence. *Group Dynamics, 5*, 57–62.

Crano, W. D. (2001). Social influence, social identity, and ingroup leniency. In C. K. W. De Dreu & N. K. De Vries (Eds.), *Group consensus and innovation* (pp. 122–143). Oxford: Blackwell.

Crano, W. D., & Alvaro, E. M. (1998). The context/comparison model of social influence: Mechanisms, structure, and linkages that underlie indirect attitude change. In W. Stroebe & M. Hewstone (Eds.), *European Review of Social Psychology* (Vol. 8, pp. 175–202). Chichester, UK: Wiley.

Crano, W. D., & Chen, X. (1998). The leniency contract and persistence of majority and minority influence. *Journal of Personality and Social Psychology, 74*, 1437–1450.

Crano, W. D., & Hannula-Bral, K. A. (1994). Context/categorization model of social influence: Minority and majority influence in the formation of a novel response norm. *Journal of Experimental Social Psychology, 30*, 247–276.

Crutchfield, R. S. (1955). Conformity and character. *American Psychologist, 10*, 191–198.

David, B., & Turner, J. C. (1996). Studies in self-categorization and minority conversion: Is being a member of the outgroup an advantage? *British Journal of Social Psychology, 35*, 179–199.

David, B., & Turner, J. C. (1999). Studies in self-categorization and minority conversion: The ingroup minority in intragroup and intergroup contexts. *British Journal of Social Psychology, 38*, 115–134.

David, B., & Turner, J. C. (2001). Majority and minority influence: A single process self-categorization analysis. In C. K. W. De Dreu & N. K. De Vries (Eds.), *Group consensus and innovation* (pp. 91–121). Oxford: Blackwell.

De Dreu, C. K. W., & Beersma, B. (2001). Minority influence in organizations: Its origins and implications for learning and group performance. In C. K. W. De Dreu & N. K. De Vries (Eds.), *Group consensus and innovation* (pp. 258–283). Oxford: Blackwell.

De Dreu, C. K. W., & De Vries, N. K. (1993). Numerical support, information processing and attitude change. *European Journal of Social Psychology, 23*, 647–663.

De Dreu, C. K. W., & De Vries, N. K. (Eds.). (2001). *Group consensus and innovation.* Oxford, UK: Blackwell.

De Dreu, C. K. W, De Vries, N. K., Gordijn, E., & Schuurman, M. (1999). Convergent and divergent processing of majority and minority arguments: Effects on focal and related attitudes. *European Journal of Social Psychology, 29*, 329–348.

De Dreu, C. K. W., & West, M. A. (2001). Minority dissent and team innovation: The importance of participation in decision making. *Journal of Applied Psychology, 86*, 1191–1201.

Deutsch, M., & Gerard, H. G. (1955). A study of normative and informational social influence upon individual judgment. *Journal of Abnormal and Social Psychology, 51*, 629–636.

De Vries, N. K., De Dreu, C. K. W., Gordijn, E., & Schuurman, M. (1996). Majority and minority influence: A dual interpretation. In W. Stroebe & M. Hewstone (Eds.), *European review of social psychology* (Vol. 7, pp. 145–172). Chichester, UK: Wiley.

Easterbrook, J. A. (1959). The effect of emotion on the utilization and the organization of behavior. *Psychological Review, 66*, 183–201.

Eagly, A. H., & Chaiken, S. (1993). *The psychology of attitudes.* Fort Worth, TX: Harcourt Brace Jovanovich.

Erb, H. P., & Bohner, G. (2001). Mere consensus effects in minority and majority influence. C. K. W. De Dreu & N. K. De Vries (Eds.), *Group consensus and innovation* (pp. 40–59). Oxford: Blackwell.

Erb, H. P., Bohner, G., Hewstone, M., Werth, L., & Reinhard, M-A. (2006). Large minorities and small majorities: Interactive effects of inferred and explicit consensus on attitudes. *Basic and Applied Social Psychology, 28*, 221–231.

Erb, H. P., Bohner, G., Schmaelzle, K., & Rank, S. (1998). Beyond conflict and discrepancy: Cognitive bias in minority and majority influence. *Personality and Social Psychology Bulletin, 24*, 620–633.

Falomir-Picastor, J. M., Butera, F., & Mugny, G. (2002). Persuasive constraint and expert versus non-expert influence in intention to quit smoking. *European Journal of Social Psychology, 32*, 209–222.

Festinger, L. (1950). Informal social communication. *Psychological Review, 57*, 271–282.

Forgas, J. P. (Ed.). (2001). *The handbook of affect and social cognitions.* Mahwah, NJ: Erlbaum.

Gardikiotis, A., Martin, R., & Hewstone, M. (2005). Group consensus in social influence: Type of consensus information as a moderator of majority and minority influence. *Personality and Social Psychology Bulletin, 31*, 1163–1174.

Gerard, H. B., Wilhelmy, R. A., & Connolley, E. S. (1968). Conformity and group size. *Journal of Personality and Social Psychology, 8*, 79–82.

Gordijn, E., Postmes, T., & de Vries, N. K. (2001). Devil's advocate or advocate of oneself: Effects of numerical support on pro- and counterattitudinal self-persuasion. *Personality and Social Psychology Bulletin, 27*, 395–407.

Gruenfeld, D. H., Thomas-Hunt, M. C., & Kim, P. H. (1998). Cognitive flexibility, communication strategy, and integrative complexity in groups: Public versus private reactions to majority and minority status. *Journal of Experimental Social Psychology, 34,* 202–226.

Guillon, M., & Personnaz, B. (1983). Analyse de la dynamique des representations des conflits minoritaire et majoritaire [An analysis of the dynamics of representations of minority and majority conflicts]. *Cahiers de Psychologie Cognitive, 3,* 65–87.

Jones, E. E., & Gerard, H. B. (1967). *Foundations of social psychology.* New York: Wiley.

Kelley, H. H. (1967). Attribution theory in social psychology. In D. Levine (Ed.), *Nebraska symposium on motivation* (pp. 192–241). Lincoln: University of Nebraska Press.

Kelman, H. C. (1958). Compliance, identification, and internalization: Three processes of attitude change. *Journal of Conflict Resolution, 2,* 51–60.

Latané, B., & Wolf, S. (1981). The social impact of majorities and minorities. *Psychological Review, 88,* 438–453.

Laughlin, P. R. (1992). Influence and performance in simultaneous collective and individual induction. *Organizational Behavior and Human Decision Processes, 51,* 447–470.

Laurens, S., & Masson, E. (1996). Critique du sens commun et changement social: Le rôle des minorités [A critique of shared feeling and social change: The role of minorities]. *Cahiers Internationaux de Psychologie Sociale, 32,* 13–32.

Laurens, S., & Moscovici, S. (2005). The confederate's and others' self-conversion: A neglected phenomenon. *Journal of Social Psychology, 145,* 191–207.

Laurens, S., & Viaud, J. (2000). Influence minoritaire versus majoritaire sur la representation de la distribution des opinions d'autrui [The influence of the minority vs. the majority on the representation of the diffusion of altruistic views]. *Cahiers Internationaux de Psychologie Sociale, 46,* 26–33.

Levine, J. M. (1980). Reaction to opinion deviance in small groups. In P. B. Paulus (Ed.), *Psychology of group influence* (pp. 375–429). Hillsdale, NJ: Erlbaum.

Levine, J. M., & Russo, E. M. (1987). Majority and minority influence. In C. Hendrick (Ed.), *Group processes: Review of personality and social psychology* (Vol. 8, pp. 13–54). Newbury Park, CA: Sage.

Maass, A., & Clark, R. D., III (1983). Internalization versus compliance: Differential processes underlying minority influence and conformity. *European Journal of Social Psychology, 13,* 197–215.

Maass, A., & Clark, R. D., III (1984). Hidden impact of minorities: Fifteen years of minority influence research. *Psychological Bulletin, 95,* 428–450.

Maass, A., West, S., & Cialdini, R. B. (1987). Minority influence and conversion. In C. Hendrick (Ed.), *Group processes: Review of personality and social psychology* (Vol. 8, pp. 55–79). Newbury Park, CA.: Sage.

Mackie, D. M. (1987). Systematic and nonsystematic processing of majority and minority persuasive communications. *Journal of Personality and Social Psychology, 53,* 41–52.

Martin, R. (1988). Ingroup and outgroup minorities: differential impact upon public and private responses. *European Journal of Social Psychology, 18,* 39–52.

Martin, R. (1996). Minority influence and argument generation. *British Journal of Social Psychology, 35,* 91–103.

Martin, R. (1998). Majority and minority influence using the afterimage paradigm: A series of attempted replications. *Journal of Experimental Social Psychology, 34,* 1–26.

Martin, R., Gardikiotis, A., & Hewstone, M. (2002). Levels of consensus and majority and minority influence. *European Journal of Social Psychology, 32,* 645–665.

Martin, R., & Hewstone, M. (1999). Minority influence and optimal problem-solving. *European Journal of Social Psychology, 29,* 825–832.

Martin, R., & Hewstone, M. (2001). Afterthoughts on afterimages: A review of the literature using the afterimage paradigm in majority and minority influence. In C. De

Dreu & N. De Vries (Eds.), *Group innovation: Fundamental and applied perspectives* (pp. 15–39). Oxford: Blackwell.

Martin, R., & Hewstone, M. (2003a). Social influence processes of control and change: Conformity, obedience to authority, and innovation. In M. A. Hogg & J. Cooper (Eds.), *Sage handbook of social psychology* (pp. 347–366). London: Sage.

Martin, R., & Hewstone, M. (2003b). Majority versus minority influence: When, not whether, source status instigates heuristic or systematic processing. *European Journal of Social Psychology, 33*, 313–330.

Martin, R., & Hewstone, M. (2008). Majority versus minority influences, message processing and attitude change: The Source-Context-Elaboration Model. In M. Zanna (Ed.), *Advances in experimental social psychology* (Vol. 40, pp. 237–326). San Diego, CA: Academic Press.

Martin, R., & Hewstone, M. (Eds.) (in press). *Minority influence and innovation: Antecedents, processes and consequences.* Hove, UK: Psychology Press.

Martin, R., Hewstone, M., & Martin, P. Y. (2003). Resistance to persuasive messages as a function of majority and minority source status. *Journal of Experimental Social Psychology, 39*, 585–593.

Martin, R., Hewstone, M., & Martin, P. Y. (2007). Systematic and heuristic processing of majority- and minority-endorsed messages: The effects of varying outcome relevance and levels of orientation on attitude and message processing. *Personality and Social Psychology Bulletin, 33*, 43–56.

Martin, R., Martin, P. Y., Smith, J., & Hewstone, M. (2007). Majority and minority influence and prediction of behavioural intentions and behaviour. *Journal of Experimental Social Psychology, 43*, 763–771.

Moscovici, S. (1976). *Social influence and social change.* London: Academic Press.

Moscovici, S. (1980). Toward a theory of conversion behavior. In L. Berkowitz (Ed.), *Advances in experimental social psychology* (Vol. 13, pp. 209–239). New York: Academic Press.

Moscovici, S. (1985). Social influence and conformity. In G. Lindsey & E. Aronson (Eds.), *The handbook of social psychology* (3rd ed., Vol. 2, pp. 347–412). New York: Random House.

Moscovici, S., & Faucheux, C. (1972). Social influence, conformity bias and the study of active minorities. In L. Berkowitz (Ed.), *Advances in experimental social psychology* (Vol. 6, pp. 149–202). New York: Academic Press.

Moscovici, S., Lage, E., & Naffrechoux (1969). Influence of a consistent minority on the responses of a majority in a color perception task. *Sociometry, 32*, 365–380.

Moscovici, S., Mugny, G., & Papastamou, S. (1981). "Sleeper effect" et/ou effet minoritaire? Etude théorique et expérimentale de l'influence sociale à retardement ["Sleeper effect" and/or the minority effect? A theoretical and experimental study of delayed social influence]. *Cahiers de Psychologie Cognitive, 1*, 199–221.

Moscovici, S., & Personnaz, B. (1980). Studies in social influence: V. Minority influence and conversion behavior in a perceptual task. *Journal of Experimental Social Psychology, 16*, 270–282.

Mucchi-Faina, A., & Cicoletti, G. (2006). Divergence vs. ambivalence: Effects of personal relevance on minority influence. *European Journal of Social Psychology, 36*, 91–104.

Mucchi-Faina, A., Maass, A., & Volpato, C. (1991). Social influence: The role of originality. *European Journal of Social Psychology, 21*, 183–197.

Mugny, G. (1975). Negotiations, image of the other and the process of minority influence. *European Journal of Social Psychology, 5*, 209–228.

Mugny, G. (1982). *The power of minorities.* London: Academic Press.

Mugny, G., Butera, F., Sanchez-Mazas, M., & Pérez, J. A. (1995). Judgements in conflict: The conflict elaboration theory of social influence. In B. Boothe, R. Hirsig, A. Helminger, B. Meier, & R. Volkart (Eds.), *Perception-evaluation-interpretation* (pp. 160–168). Göttingen: Hogrefe & Huber.

Mugny, G., Kaiser, C., & Papastamou, S. (1983). Influence minoritaire, identification et relations entre groupes: Etude expérimentale autour d'une votation [Minority influence, identification and relations between groups: An experimental study around an election]. *Cahiers de Psychologie Sociale, 19*, 1–30.

Mugny, G., & Pérez, J. (1991). *The social psychology of minority influence.* Cambridge, UK: Cambridge University Press.

Nemeth, C., (1986). Differential contributions of majority and minority influence. *Psychological Review, 93*, 23–32.

Nemeth, C., (1995). Dissent as driving cognition, attitudes and judgements. *Social Cognition, 13*, 273–291.

Nemeth, C. J., Brown, K., & Rogers, J. (2001). Devil's advocate versus authentic dissent: Stimulating quantity and quality. *European Journal of Social Psychology, 31*, 707–720.

Nemeth, C. J., & Kwan, J. (1985). Originality of word associations as a function of majority and minority influence. *Social Psychology Quarterly, 48*, 277–282.

Nemeth, C. J., & Kwan, J. (1987). Minority influence, divergent thinking and detection of correct solutions. *Journal of Applied Social Psychology, 17*, 788–799.

Nemeth, C. J., Mosier, K., & Chiles, C. (1992). When convergent thought improves performance: Majority vs. minority influence. *Personality and Social Psychology Bulletin, 18*, 139–144.

Nemeth, C. J., Swedlund, M., & Kanki, B. (1974). Patterning of the minority's response and their influence on the majority. *European Journal of Social Psychology, 4*, 53–64.

Nemeth, C. J., & Wachtler, J. (1983). Creative problem solving as a result of majority vs minority influence. *European Journal of Social Psychology, 13*, 45–55.

Nemeth, C. J., Wachtler, J., & Endicott J. (1977). Increasing the size of the minority: Some gains and some losses. *European Journal of Social Psychology, 7*, 15–27.

Ng, K. Y., & Van Dyne, L. (2001). Individualism-collectivism as a boundary condition for effectiveness of minority influence in decision making. *Organizational Behavior and Human Decision Processes, 84*, 198–225.

Papastamou, S. (1986). Psychologization and processes of minority and majority influence. *European Journal of Social Psychology, 16*, 165–180.

Pérez, J. A., & Mugny, G. (1987). Paradoxical effects of categorization in minority influence: When being an outgroup is an advantage. *European Journal of Social Psychology, 17*, 157–169.

Pérez, J. A., & Mugny, G. (1996). The conflict elaboration theory of social influence. In E. H. Witte & J. H. Davis (Eds.), *Understanding group behavior: Small group processes and interpersonal relations* (Vol. 2, pp. 191–210). Mahwah, NJ: Erlbaum.

Pérez, J. A., & Mugny, G. (1998). Categorization and social influence. In S. Worchel & J.M. Francisco (Eds.), *Social identity: International perspectives* (pp. 142–153). London: Sage.

Peterson, R., & Nemeth, C. J. (1996). Focus versus flexibility: Majority and minority influence can both improve performance. *Personality and Social Psychology Bulletin, 22*, 14–23.

Petty, R. E., & Cacioppo, J. T. (1986). *Communication and persuasion: Central and peripheral routes to attitude change.* New York: Springer-Verlag.

Petty, R. E., & Wegener, D. T. (1999). The elaboration likelihood model: Current status and controversies. In S. Chaiken & Y. Trope (Eds.), *Dual-process theories in social psychology* (pp. 37–72), New York: Guilford.

Phillips, K. W. (2003). The effects of categorically based expectations on minority influence: The importance of congruence. *Personality and Social Psychology Bulletin, 29*, 3–13.

Prislin, R., & Christensen, P. N. (2005). Social change in the aftermath of successful minority influence. In W. Stroebe & M. Hewstone (Eds.), *European review of social psychology* (Vol. 16, pp. 43–73). Hove, E. Sussex: Psychology Press.

Prislin, R., & Wood, W. (2005). Social influence in attitudes and attitude change. In D. Albarracín, B. T. Johnson, & M. P. Zanna (Eds.), *The handbook of attitudes* (pp. 671–706). Mahwah, NJ: Erlbaum.

Ross, L., Greene, D., & House, P. (1977). The "false consensus effect": An egocentric bias in social perception and attribution processes. *Journal of Experimental Social Psychology, 13*, 279–301.

Schachter, S. (1951). Deviation, rejection, and communication. *Journal of Abnormal and Social Psychology, 46*, 190–207.

Schulz-Hardt, S., Brodbeck, F. C., Mojzisch, A., Kerschreiter, R., & Frey, D. (2006). Group decision making in hidden profile situations: Dissent as a facilitator for decision quality. *Journal of Personality and Social Psychology, 91*, 1080–1093.

Shuper, P. A., & Sorrentino, R. M. (2004). Minority versus majority influence and uncertainty orientation: processing persuasive messages on the basis of situational expectancies. *Journal of Social Psychology, 144*, 127–147.

Smith, C. M., & Diven, P. J. (2002). Minority influence and political interest groups. In V. C. Ottati & R. S. Tindale (Eds.), *The social psychology of politics: Social psychological applications to social issues* (pp. 175–192). New York: Kluwer Academic.

Smith, C. M, Tindale, R. S., & Anderson, E. M. (2001). The impact of shared representations on minority influence in freely interacting groups. In C. K. W. De Dreu & N. K. De Vries (Eds.), *Group consensus and innovation* (pp. 183–200). Oxford: Blackwell.

Sorrentino, R. M., King, G., & Leo, G. (1980). The influence of the minority on perception: A note on a possible alternative explanation. *Journal of Experimental Social Psychology, 16*, 293–301.

Tanford, S., & Penrod, S. (1984). Social influence model: A formal integration of research on majority and minority influence processes. *Psychological Bulletin, 95*, 189–225.

Turner, J. C. (1991). *Social influence*. Milton Keynes, UK: Open University Press.

Velden, F. S., Beersma, B., & De Dreu, C. K. W. (2007). Majority and minority influence in group negotiation: The moderating effects of social motivation and decision rules. *Journal of Applied Psychology, 92*, 259–268.

Wood, W., Lundgren, S., Ouellette, J. A., Busceme, S., & Blackstone, T. (1994). Minority influence: A meta-analytic review of social influence processes. *Psychological Bulletin, 115*, 323–345.

17

Normative Beliefs as Agents of Influence
Basic Processes and Real-World Applications

P. WESLEY SCHULTZ, JENNIFER J. TABANICO,
and TANIA RENDÓN

California State University, San Marcos

*O*ne of the fundamental tenets of social psychology is that individuals are influenced by others. From the earliest days of empirical social psychology, research has shown that the mere presence of others influences people's behavior (Triplett, 1897; see also Strube, 2005). But social influence goes far beyond the mere presence of others. From our observations and perceptions of how other people think, feel, and act, we infer what is normal and acceptable in a given context. These inferences, in turn, serve as guides for our own actions. Research on the influence of social norms has a long history, and over the years, a number of widely accepted truths have emerged. In this chapter, we examine these widely held "truths" in light of recent field experiments. We begin with definitions and distinctions between different types of norms, discuss norms as agents of influence, and examine five widely accepted ideas about the effects of normative beliefs on behavior. We conclude by summarizing three broad perspectives on the influence of normative beliefs and highlight avenues for future research. A consistent theme recurs across this chapter: social influence associated with normative beliefs is more robust, and more complex, than suggested by the widely held "truths" of social psychology.

SOCIAL NORMS AND RELATED CONCEPTS

Social norms are the common and accepted behaviors for a specific situation. They are "rules and standards that are understood by members of a group, and that guide and/or constrain human behavior without the force of laws" (Cialdini & Trost, 1998, p. 152). Social norms are what is done or what is approved. That is, social norms describe the level of a behavior within a particular group, or the level of approval for the behavior. When psychologists talk about social norms, however, they typically refer to an individual's beliefs about the behaviors and evaluations of group members. These normative beliefs reside in the mind of the individual, and can vary considerably in their degree of accuracy. For example, a college student might falsely believe that a high percentage of his or her peers get drunk on weekends, when in fact the true percentage is quite small. Similarly, a Tennessee resident might erroneously believe that a majority of smokers in their state throw their cigarette butts on the ground. Normative beliefs refer to the perception, and not the reality. Normative beliefs are social in nature—referring to what other people think and do. By comparison, individuals also hold personal norms, which are rules or standards for their own behavior (Kallgren, Reno, & Cialdini, 2000).

Much of the early work on social norms was conducted under the umbrella of *conformity,* a process in which changes in behavior are brought about by witnessing the actions of other people. Unlike other types of social influence, conformity does not result from a direct request. Instead, the influence is subtle, and involves changing one's behavior to be consistent with the behavior of others in the group. The findings from early studies on conformity suggested that individuals were strongly influenced by their perceptions of others—in fact, it could even lead them to say things that they knew were incorrect. Deutsch and Gerard (1955) offered a useful distinction for the motivational forces that lead to conformity. *Normative social influence* describes conformity to a group norm brought about by a desire to be liked by the group members. Because of its emphasis on *liking*, normative social influence operates in situations in which the person belongs to the group and cares about the evaluations of the other group members. Because of this concern, normative social influence should be particularly powerful when the person's behavior is subject to surveillance by other group members. In contrast, *informational social influence* operates outside of group membership, and the individual is not motivated by a concern about the evaluations of other group members. Informational social influence describes conformity to a group norm brought about by a desire to be correct. Both processes can influence behavior, but they operate in different contexts and have different underlying motivational bases.

A more recent distinction was offered by Cialdini and colleagues (Cialdini, Kallgren, & Reno, 1991), who separated descriptive from injunctive normative beliefs. *Descriptive norms* refer to a person's perception of what is commonly done in a situation; they characterize the perceptions about behaviors of group members. *Injunctive norms* refer to a person's beliefs about what others in the group approve (or disapprove) of doing. Injunctive norms are prescriptive. While these two beliefs often are highly correlated, there is enough discrepancy to treat them as separate. In addition, evidence suggests that they exert independent influences on behavior and that experimental manipulations can affect one, the other, or both simultaneously (Cialdini, 2003; Cialdini et al., 2005).

Before proceeding, it is important to clarify some definitional issues. Throughout this chapter, we use the term *influence* to refer to psychological change—particularly change in behavior, but also change of cognitive and affective features like attitudes or intentions. By *social influence*, we mean psychological change brought about as a result of the behavior of other people. We use the term *persuasion* to refer to psychological change that is intentionally induced. Such change typically is characterized by a change agent delivering a message with the intent of inducing change in an individual. Given the 50 years of work differentiating informational and normative social influence, we have chosen to adhere to this terminology. However, research over the past 50 years has not clearly established the motivational distinction between informational and normative social influence (Turner, 1991), and we occasionally use the term *normative social influence* more broadly to refer to behavior change brought about by an individual's perceptions of what others do or value, regardless of the motivational underpinnings.

NORMS AS LEVERS OF PERSUASION

Considerable research has shown that normative beliefs predict behavior. Across a range of domains and research traditions, beliefs about what other people do, and approve of doing, are strongly related to an individual's behaviors. Although the causal connections between normative beliefs and behavior were disputed for many years, it now seems clear that normative beliefs can exert a direct influence on behavior (Cialdini & Goldstein, 2004; Goldstein & Cialdini, in press). We should point out that the reverse has also been established—once an individual acts, his or her normative beliefs will shift as well (Monin & Norton, 2003), but for the purposes of this chapter, we begin from the established finding that normative beliefs can cause behavior.

As the debate among researchers about the causal relationship between normative beliefs and behavior came to resolution in the early 1990s, norms became increasingly invoked in studies of persuasion, and they have been seen as a "lever" of influence in applied research (Goldstein & Cialdini, in press). Since the early 1990s, social norms have been used widely in "social marketing" campaigns targeting alcohol consumption among college students, and normative education has emerged as a promising approach for reducing substance use in adolescents. It has since been applied to address many other social issues, including traffic safety, tax compliance, academic success, sexual assault prevention, and a range of environmental issues (littering, recycling, and energy conservation; National Social Norms Resource Center, 2006). Importantly, the applied projects called into question some of the basic "truths" about the influence of social norms and began to explore moderators of the influence effects. Do social norms influence some behaviors more strongly than others? For whom is it strongest? How do we best convey a normative message to maximize its persuasive impact? In the following section, we examine several "truths" about the influence of social norms on behavior, along the way summarizing results from recent studies. We focus on five widely accepted truths about social norms:

- Normative beliefs only result from social interaction.
- Normative beliefs only influence behavior when they come from a close referent group.
- Normative beliefs only influence behavior in ambiguous situations.
- Normative beliefs only influence public behaviors.
- People know when they have been influenced by normative information.

NORMATIVE BELIEFS ONLY RESULT FROM SOCIAL INTERACTION

Normative beliefs are generally viewed as resulting from social interaction (Prentice & Miller, 1993). Indeed, much of the early research on normative social influence used real people in staged settings to convey information about the norm. For example, Sherif's (1936) studies on the autokinetic effect used groups of participants (usually three) whose judgments on a task were publicized to the other participants. Similarly, Asch (1956) used confederates to convey normative information in his studies of conformity, as did Latané and Darley (1968) in their studies of pluralistic ignorance. While this tradition is still used (and widely cited as *the* approach to normative social influence), other procedures have been employed in which normative information is conveyed through nonsocial channels. That is, although seeing other people act can clearly provide information about the social norms in a given context, social interaction is not required. Individuals use a variety of cues, social and nonsocial, to draw inferences about the behavior of others. Examples abound of nonsocial sources of normative information:

- Trails through a natural area tell us where other people have walked (Winter, 2002),
- Posted signs supply information about what people in the area value (Tabanico, Butler, Shakarian, & Schultz, 2006),
- A banner posted in a college campus that "most students have 4 or fewer drinks when they party" (Johannessen & Glider, 2003),
- A billboard message that "48% of Tennesseans polled say that they have knowingly thrown trash on the street. About 1 in 5 people say they do this on a regular basis" (Keep Tennessee Beautiful, 2006),
- A pile of swept litter in a parking lot tells us that others in this area disapprove of littering (Cialdini, Reno, & Kallgren, 1990),
- Music MP3 sites provide feedback about the number of times a song has been downloaded, giving us information about its popularity (Salganik, Dodds, & Watts, 2006),

- An e-mail notification from Amazon.com that other people who have bought X, have also purchased Y.

Each of these examples conveys normative information, but none requires direct social interaction. Indeed, none of the examples above involve any contact with another person.

Despite an abundance of nonsocial sources of normative information, the bulk of the research to date has relied primarily on social interaction to convey or activate a normative belief. Two common approaches that rely heavily on social interaction are seeing other people act, and guided group discussion. However, nonsocial sources such as passive media attempts to convey normative beliefs also have been used. In the following section, we examine the impact of both social and nonsocial normative information on subsequent behavior.

Seeing Other People Act

The prototypical paradigm for studying normative social influence is through a staged situation in which participants witness other people acting in a speci-fied way. These other people are most often confederates, but the effect has also been studied using naïve groups. In a now-classic study, Milgram, Bickman, and Berkowitz (1969) staged a gawking experiment on the streets of New York City. In the first trial, a single individual stopped on a crowded city street and looked upward. The consequence—almost no one cared. Only 4% of passersby stopped, and less than half looked up. The study was conducted a second time after the area had cleared, with five confederates gawking upward. This time, 18% of pass-ersby stopped to look. In the third variation, 15 confederates gawked upward. This time, 40% of passersby stopped and nearly 90% of them looked up—an incident that stopped city traffic. These results are consistent with classic psy-chological research on modeling and observational learning which has clearly documented that seeing another individual act in a particular way can shape one's subsequent behavior (Bandura, Ross, & Ross, 1961). However, the results of the gawking study suggest a mechanism that goes beyond simple imitation of modeled behavior. That is, if it were a basic modeling effect, we would expect to see the same number of passersby imitating the modeled gawking behavior regardless of whether the behavior was modeled by one person or by a group.

Similar results showing the power of witnessing the behavior of others can be found in studies of pluralistic ignorance. For example, Latané and Darley (1968) showed that participants who witnessed *in*action by others were less likely to act themselves. In their study, participants completed questionnaires in a waiting room, either alone, or in groups of three. As they waited, smoke was piped into the room. When alone, 75% of participants left the room to report it. However, when in a group with two confederates who continued working on the questionnaire, only 10% left the room despite the fact that the room became filled with smoke. A variation of the study contained groups of three real participants (no confederates), in which the reporting rate was 38%.

Guided Discussions

A variation of the influence that results from seeing others act comes from studies on guided group discussions. Whereas most of the initial research on the influence of social norms used confederates to convey the norm, guided discussions involve a group of people coming together to discuss a specific problem or behavior. The discussion is facilitated in such a way that desirable attitudes and behaviors are encouraged by the group leader, and undesirable behaviors are downplayed. Lewin (1952) used this guided discussion approach to change food habits of U.S. families during World War II. Groups of 13 to 17 participants heard either a persuasive lecture or participated in a group discussion. The discussion focused on obstacles that prevented "housewives like themselves" from buying and preparing uncommon foods for their families (e.g., beef hearts, kidneys). Toward the end of the sessions, these groups discussed preparation techniques for the novel foods. Results showed that only 3% of the women who attended the lecture subsequently served the novel foods, whereas 32% did so after participating in the discussion.

The guided discussion technique has been used in several more-recent applied experiments. For example, Donaldson, Graham, Piccinin, and Hansen (1995) used the approach to reduce alcohol and substance use among more than 12,000 adolescents (see also Hansen & Graham, 1991). The experimental condition consisted of facilitated group discussions that corrected student misperceptions about the prevalence and acceptability of alcohol and drug use among peers. Results showed lower subsequent substance use rates among students in the normative education conditions compared to students in control or resistance skills programs. Furthermore, the effectiveness of the normative education was mediated through a reduction in descriptive and injunctive norms about substance use. Interestingly, the traditional resistance skills training programs (e.g., D.A.R.E.) resulted in an undesirable *increase* in normative beliefs. Schroeder and Prentice (1998), and Haines and Spears (1996) provide additional examples of guided discussions used to reduce alcohol use among students.

Another example of guided group discussion comes from Werner and colleagues' work to reduce the use of toxic household products (Werner & Brown, 2006; Werner, Byerly, & Sansone, 2004). Similar to Lewin's findings, group discussion was substantially more successful than a persuasive lecture about changing attitudes toward nontoxic alternatives (Werner et al., 2004), and intentions to use nontoxics (Werner & Brown, 2006). Further, the effectiveness of the group discussion (vs. lectures) was mediated by perceived group endorsement. That is, the discussions led to attitude change *because* participants believed that others endorsed the new behavior. In content analyses of the discussions, Werner and Brown (2006) found that the persuasive impact of the groups was enhanced when students asked more questions and shared their knowledge about nontoxics. However, when students commented on the reasons for using toxic products, it fostered a norm of use, resulting in a boomerang effect. Werner's presenters had initially encouraged students to describe their use of toxics as a way of increasing audience involvement and participation. They did not anticipate this negative effect.

The potential for boomerang effects as a result of group discussion was further illustrated by Mann, Nolen-Hoeksema, and Huang (1997), who sought to reduce the prevalence of eating disorders among female college students. Groups of 10 to 20 female participants engaged in a group discussion led by two students with a history of eating disorders—one anorexic and one bulimic. The two-part intervention was intended to promote awareness, provide information, and teach skills related to the problem of eating disorders. The results showed that compared with controls the intervention led to an *increase* in symptoms of eating disorders among participants in the discussion. Furthermore, the program led to an *increase* in the perceived prevalence of eating disorders among students on campus. For example, following the intervention, participants in the discussion, groups estimated that 20% of their fellow students "vomit for weight loss," compared with 14% for controls.

Normative Feedback

The techniques described above generally use social interaction to convey or acti-vate a normative belief. However, recent studies have shown that similar effects can be obtained using passive media. For example, Schultz (1999) disseminated normative information about the recycling rates among residents served by a curb-side collection program. Over a four-week period, residents received hand-written information about the percentage of households in the community that recycled that week (descriptive group norm). The results showed that after eight weeks, residents who received the normative feedback recycled significantly more fre-quently and more material than residents in control conditions, and the effect was particularly strong for residents who were initially recycling at a low rate. Interest-ingly, there also was a trend toward a *decrease* in recycling by residents who were previously recycling at high rates. This study suggests that a passive media-deliv-ered normative feedback was used as a standard against which residents compared their own behavior.

In a recent extension, we demonstrated the potential for normative messages to produce boomerang effects. That is, for residents who already engaged in the desired behavior, receiving a message that others engaged in the desired behavior less often than they did actually produced a *reduction* in the desirable actions (Schultz, Nolan, Cialdini, Goldstein, & Griskevicius, 2007). In this study, commu-nity residents received normative feedback about the level of energy consumption among other households in their community, along with a comparison to their own level of consumption. The results showed that this information caused a reduction in energy conservation among residents who were consuming more than the aver-age. However, for residents who were initially consuming *less* than the average, the feedback produced a boomerang effect—these residents actually *increased* their energy use (Figure 17.1)!

Fortunately, our findings also suggest a pathway for eliminating these boomer-ang effects. In a second experimental condition, residents received an added injunc-tive element to the normative feedback. Those who consumed less than the average received a hand-drawn smiley face ☺ on the feedback card, whereas residents who

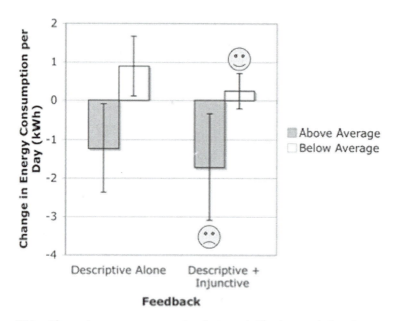

Figure 17.1   Change in energy consumption for households above or below the norm. *Source:* Modified from data and figure presented in Schultz, P. W., Nolan, J., Cialdini, R., Goldstein, N., & Griskevicius, V. (2007). The constructive, destructive, and reconstructive power of social norms. *Psychological Science, 18,* 429–434.

consumed more than the average received a sad face ☹. This added injunctive element successfully eliminated the boomerang effect. Households that consumed low levels of energy continued to do so even after receiving normative information indicating that others in their community consumed more than they did.

The normative feedback approach also has been applied to domains other than conservation. For example, Neighbors, Larimer, and Lewis (2004) used normative feedback to reduce binge drinking among college students. Using a computer interface, participants completed survey measures of their reasons for drinking, normative beliefs about the drinking behavior of others, and self-reported drinking behavior. Next, participants in the experimental condition received immediate computer-delivered feedback that included a summary of their perceived drinking norms compared with actual drinking norms, as well as a comparison of their self-reported drinking behavior with the average college student drinking behavior. Follow-up measures at three- and six-month intervals showed a significant reduction in perceptions of peer drinking and actual drinking behavior at both the three- and six-month follow-ups. The intervention was particularly effective for students who reported drinking primarily for social reasons.

Normative Messages

The studies described here provided highly personalized normative information through a variety of media. However, several studies have produced significant changes in behavior and intentions by providing more generic normative messages in both controlled laboratory environments (Blanton, Stewart, & VandenEijnden, 2001) and in the field (Perkins, Haines, & Rice, 2005; Schultz, Khazian, & Zaleski, in press). For example, Blanton et al. (2001) used printed normative information (bogus newspaper articles) to change the intentions of college students to get flu shots. In the laboratory, printed normative messages have successfully changed behavioral intentions across a variety of behaviors, from condom use (Buunk, Vanden Eijnden, & Siero, 2002) to driving (Groeger & Chapman, 1997).

Extending these laboratory findings to the field, a number of studies have used print media, such as posters, flyers, mouse pads, and billboards, to change behaviors (Perkins, Haines, & Rice, 2005). Most of this work has been conducted under an applied "social marketing" framework, particularly in university programs intended to reduce rates of binge drinking, but also to address a range of social issues. For example, Nolan (2004) successfully reduced energy consumption among California residents by placing door hangers with normative messages on residents' front doors. Interestingly, the normative messages used in this campaign were more successful at changing behavior than messages that targeted environmental protection or financial savings, despite the fact that residents did not rate the normative messages as motivational. This is an interesting point to which we will return to later.

NORMATIVE BELIEFS ONLY INFLUENCE BEHAVIOR WHEN THEY COME FROM A CLOSE REFERENT GROUP

Are we more, or perhaps less, likely to conform to the norms of our peers than the norms of strangers? On the one hand, we care more about the evaluations of our peers than of strangers, and so we should be more likely to act in ways that are consistent with them. On the other hand, if we feel accepted by our peers, we should feel a greater freedom to express our individuality. The early literature on normative social influence suggested that conforming to the norm often was motivated by a desire to be liked by our group (Deutsch & Gerard, 1955). The argument that group membership moderates the strength of conformity to a group norm has been elaborated in subsequent research within the social identity/social categorization framework (Ellemers, Spears, & Doosje, 2002; Hogg, 2003; Terry & Hogg, 1996; Turner, 1982; Van Knippenberg, 2000). From this line of inquiry, social influence results from a process of self-categorization and occurs in situations in which individuals perceive that they are similar to other group members (a process termed *referent informational influence*). It is the process of self-categorization that generates conformity, rather than the potential for social reward or punishment from in-group members. To illustrate, Abrams, Wetherell, Cochrane, Hogg, and Turner (1990) reported a series of studies examining the role of self-categorization on social influence. The first study in the series utilized the Sherif (1936) paradigm, in which participants estimated the movement of a light in an autokinetic task. When the task was performed in a group, responses became more similar over time, indicating the formation of a social norm. The greatest conformity occurred in the control condition where the participant was generally deindividualized (this was the typical condition used by Sherif, since the autokinetic effect requires a completely darkened room) and when participants perceived that they were part of a single large group. In contrast, under conditions where divergent social categorizations were made salient (i.e., you belong to group H, or to group J), conformity to the norm set by confederates was minimized.

Similar results were shown in Study 2, using the Asch (1956) line paradigm. The highest level of conformity occurred in the condition where confederates were from an in-group (other psychology students at a prestigious neighboring university) rather than an out-group (ancient history majors from the neighboring university), and when responses were made publicly (stated verbally by three confederates, and then aloud by the true participant, who always responded last). Interestingly, when responses were given privately by the participant but publicly by the confederates, there were no differences in conformity as a result of in-group/out-group categorization—both groups showed a moderate level of conformity.

Although these results showed a decrease in social influence on public behaviors resulting from normative information about an out-group, they do not provide clear evidence for increased influence resulting from greater identification with an in-group. While the latter is implied—a normative belief will exert stronger social influence when it comes from a close referent group—it has not been clearly established (Rimal et al., 2005). In the research by Abrams et al. (1990), the in-group was quite generic (students from a neighboring university with the same major). Consistent with Abrams et al., other studies have shown that a generic referent group (e.g., the general public), but not an out-group, can exert considerable social pressure. Goldstein, Cialdini, & Griskevicius (under review) examined the relative impact of different referent groups on the influence of normative information. In their studies, normative messages were provided to hotel guests on an in-room placard urging them to reuse their bath towels. The results showed that descriptive normative messages motivated more conservation behavior, but there was no evidence that a referent group that was relevant to a respondents' own in-group led to greater conformity. The descriptive norm message was successful despite the fact that it was associated with a referent group that was not particularly meaningful (other hotel guests). The authors concluded that the power of different referent groups to exert social influence "did not map onto the extent to which individuals would consider those identities personally meaningful and important to them." We reached a similar conclusion in a study of conservation behavior by guests at an upscale timeshare resort (Schultz, Khazian, & Zaleski, in press; see also Dittes & Kelley, 1956; Harper & Tuddenham 1964).

We are not suggesting that social influence does not occur as a result of normative information about a similar referent group—there seems clear evidence that it does. Rather, we are suggesting that normative information about a *generic* referent group provides sufficient motivation to induce conformity, and that increasing the degree of similarity to the referent group does little to strengthen its influence. Interestingly, there also is evidence that normative information about an out-group can also induce conformity for private behaviors.

NORMATIVE BELIEFS ONLY INFLUENCE BEHAVIOR IN AMBIGUOUS SITUATIONS

In novel or ambiguous situations, where we are uncertain of the appropriate course of action, we should be more likely to use others as a guide for our behaviors. Indeed, a third "truth" about the influence of normative beliefs is that it applies most strongly to ambiguous situations. In the classic research on the formation and influence of social norms, Sherif (1936) purposely selected an ambiguous context, commenting that the autokinetic effect was "a fluid and ambiguous situation for which individuals did not have previously established standards" (p. ix). In later work, Darley and Latané (1970) commented that the bystander effect would be less likely in situations that were familiar to the person. Contradicting this reasoning are many examples where normative social influence produced large effects in familiar situations—for example, a person's home (Schultz, 1999; Schultz et al., 2007), a frequented parking structure (Cialdini et al., 1991), or a familiar campus residence hall (Cialdini et al., 1991). While it seems clear that normative information can powerfully influence behavior in novel or ambiguous situations, it also seems clear that norms are ever-shifting and changing, and that even in familiar environments behavior is influenced by normative information. However, at this point, it remains unclear whether norms operate the same way in both types of situations. Research is needed to determine whether familiar situations are also characterized by a certain degree of social uncertainty that allows norms to influence behavior or if other processes are involved.

NORMATIVE BELIEFS ONLY INFLUENCE PUBLIC BEHAVIORS

A fourth "truth" about the influence of social norms is that it is stronger for public than for private behaviors (Deutsch & Gerard, 1955; Insko, Drenan, Solomon, Smith, & Wade, 1983). As Miller et al. (2000) summarized:

> ...social norms often produce public behavior that is inconsistent with individuals' private attitudes. Norms are properties of situations and of groups, not of individuals. They develop through processes that have only an indirect and partial connection to the characteristics and views of those who are influenced by them. Therefore, it is not surprising that the normative behavior that is exhibited in public settings is frequently counterattitudinal for some or even most of the people who are enacting it. (p. 97)

Much of the research and theorizing on this issue has been conducted using Deutsch and Gerard's (1955) distinction, where normative influence is presumed to work in public domains, and informational influence in private (French & Raven, 1959; Kelman, 1961). However, a number of studies have shown large and robust normative social influence effects for private behaviors. In a series of rigorous field experiments, Goldstein et al. (under review) and Schultz et al. (in press) showed that normative messages produced substantial changes in behavior among hotel guests urged to reuse their bath towels (a private behavior). Similarly, we found normative social influence effects for household energy conservation (Schultz et al., 2007). Despite the largely private behavior of conserving energy in the home, descriptive normative information produced changes in behavior. This behavior change not only occurred outside the controlled confines of the experimental laboratory environment, but in a familiar and largely private environment.

The presumed transient nature of normative social influence also is inconsistent with studies showing longer-term changes in behavior. The accepted wisdom here is that normative social influence only endures as long as others have surveillance over the behavior (Prislin & Wood, 2005, p. 674). To illustrate, let us consider a study by Darley and Latané (1970). In their experiment:

> A girl sat on a bench in the waiting room of Grand Central. Soon another girl sat on a bench facing her. They recognized each other and began a conversation. One girl had been shopping, and announced that she had just bought a Frisbee. The other girl asked to see it, and the first girl threw it to her. They then began to toss it back and forth. Apparently by accident, the Frisbee was thrown to a third person and the reaction of this third person (an experimental confederate), was the independent variable of the study. That person either enthusiastically joined in throwing the Frisbee or accused the two girls of being childish and dangerous, and kicked the Frisbee back across the gap.

The girls in the experiment continued to toss the Frisbee, and threw it to other bystanders sitting in the area. Results from 170 bystanders showed strikingly different results: when the confederate joined in the play, 86% responded (i.e., tossed it back). As Darley and Latané (1970) commented: "In this condition, the problem was not to start interaction, but to terminate it." However, when the confederate sanctioned the girls, only 17% of bystanders responded when thrown the Frisbee. Later, the sanctioning confederate either left the location, or stayed. When she stayed, only 11% of bystanders participated, but when she left, the number rose to 60%.

These short-term effects are consistent with the theorized public nature of normative social influence, but they are inconsistent with other studies that have shown longer-lasting effects of normative influence on behavior. Indeed, many of these effects have been shown to go far beyond the original time period of the manipulation. For example, in study of normative social influence to promote curbside recycling, Schultz (1999) reported behavioral changes resulting from a descriptive norm message that lasted eight weeks (see also Schultz et al., 2007). Similarly, a number of applied studies summarized above on guided group discussions have shown effects lasting days, months, and even years (Donaldson et al., 1995; Neighbors et al., 2004; Werner et al., 2006).

A possible reconciliation here centers on the nature of the manipulated norm. In the early research, like the Frisbee study by Darley and Latané (1970), the manipulated norm was injunctive. That is, "other people will disapprove of me if I play Frisbee in the Grand Central terminal." In contrast, the results showing longer-lasting effects have focused primarily on descriptive norm message. That is, "other students who are like me don't drink alcohol." These studies suggest that descriptive normative messages can be internalized, thereby providing a standard against which an individual can compare his/her behavior. Such internalized normative beliefs can transcend time and situation (cf. Kelman, 1961). Injunctive norms, on the other hand, are more fluid, can be more easily activated by aspects of the context, are more likely to influence public than private behavior, and have shorter-term effects.

PEOPLE KNOW WHEN THEY HAVE BEEN INFLUENCED BY NORMATIVE INFORMATION

Another insight that has emerged from the field experiments is that normative social influence generally is underestimated (Khazian, Goldstein, Schultz, & Cialdini, 2003). That is, people do not believe that they are influenced by the actual or perceived behavior of others. To illustrate, in a recent study on energy conservation, we asked California residents to rate various reasons for their "decision to conserve energy." The most highly rated reasons were environmental protection, social responsibility, and saving money. "Because other people do it" was rated as *least* important. However, when examining the relationship between various beliefs about energy conservation and self-reported behavior, we found that normative beliefs were the *strongest* predictors of energy conservation. A follow-up field experiment showed that providing residents with normative information about the conservation behavior of others in their community caused a reduction in household energy consumption (Nolan, 2004). Appeals to environmental protection, social responsibility, and saving money failed to produce significant changes in behavior. Yet, when asked how persuasive they found the distributed information, households in the normative condition rated it as less persuasive than those who received environmental, social responsibility, or financial information (even though the latter three did not produce significant changes in behavior!).

The findings of the two studies summarized above support Nisbett and Wilson's (1977) conclusion that people have difficulty identifying the influence of external factors on their judgment processes. More importantly, these studies demonstrate that normative social influence in particular often is severely underestimated. See also Nolan, Schultz, Cialdini, Griskevicius, & Goldstein, in press.

THEORETICAL APPROACHES

The research results summarized in the preceding section show large and robust influence effects for normative information. Social norms are conveyed through a variety of channels, and they can both spur and guide an individual's behaviors. We have examined some established "truths" about the influence of normative beliefs, and concluded that the effects are more robust and long-lasting than previously thought. In the next section, we turn our attention to theoretical models of normative social influence.

The Focus Theory of Normative Conduct

The focus theory of normative conduct is built on two main assertions: First, the theory makes a distinction between descriptive norms (norms of "is") and injunctive norms (norms of "ought"), and proposes that each of these norms motivates behavior differently. Second, and unique to the focus theory of normative conduct, is that the capacity of norms to guide behavior is stronger when the norm is activated. Moreover, when two inconsistent norms exist simultaneously, the norm that is activated, or made most salient, will have the greater influence on subsequent behavior (Cialdini, Reno, & Kallgren, 1990). To test these ideas, Cialdini et al. (1990) conducted a series of studies in which they varied the amount of litter present in various field settings. The settings were either relatively clean to depict a low descriptive norm for littering (not many people litter here), or noticeably littered to depict a high descriptive norm for littering (people litter here). In addition to manipulating the descriptive norm for littering in the situation, the experimenters also manipulated the salience of the norm by having a confederate either drop trash into the environment or walk past it. In a clean or a littered environment, participants were given an opportunity to litter a handbill placed on the windshield of their vehicle after witnessing the confederate. Results supported the assertion that the most salient norm takes precedence. That is, while participants littered significantly more into the littered environment than the clean environment, the *least* littering occurred when participants saw a confederate drop trash into a clean environment. By littering into a clean environment, the confederate was able to shift the focus of the participants onto the descriptive norm that "people don't litter here."

Extending these findings beyond littering, Tabanico et al. (2006) conducted a laboratory experiment to examine applicability of the focus theory to a popular community-based crime prevention effort. The laboratory experiment used a virtual community tour to assess the effect of "neighborhood watch" sign presence and content on community perceptions and fear of crime. It was hypothesized that posted neighborhood watch signs might inadvertently draw focus to the descriptive normative message that "crime happens" in the area and, as a result, lead to an increase in perceptions about crime rates and likelihood of victimization. Results revealed that the descriptive normative information about crime that is included on many types of signs caused a significant increase in perceived crime rates and likelihood of victimization, and decreased perceptions of community safety.

As these studies demonstrate, focus theory predicts that the norm that is most salient is the one that ultimately will guide behavior. However, recall that an increasing number of social marketing campaigns are disseminating normative information through mass media. Can these messages manipulate focus as gracefully and effectively as it has been done in experimental settings? According to Cialdini et al. (under review), the likely answer is "no." However, they recommend that the inclusion of a retrieval cue might bring the correct norm into consciousness at the onset of behavior. This notion was tested in a controlled laboratory environment, using a series of Public Service Announcements (PSAs), which manipulated the focus of a littering norm (descriptive vs. injunctive) along with placement of a retrieval cue. After viewing one of four PSAs, participants were placed in a situation where they had the opportunity to litter a soiled paper towel into a stairwell. The results showed that PSAs that linked an injunctive normative message directly to a prominent retrieval cue successfully reduced littering (Cialdini et al., 2005; see also Chekroun & Brauer, 2002).

Norms as Standards

A second theoretical perspective on normative social influence views norms as internalized standards (Haines, Perkins, Rice, & Barker, 2005; Linkenbach, in press; Perkins et al., 2005). This approach, sometimes referred to as the social norms model (Perkins, 2003a), has been applied to a broad range of social issues (National Social Norms Resource Center, http://www.mostofus.org). Unlike focus theory, which emphasizes the contextual salience of a normative belief, the norms-as-standard model treats norms as a construct that is generally stable across situations. That is, individuals hold normative beliefs about many behaviors, and these beliefs directly influence behavior. There is no consideration of conflicting normative beliefs, or a distinction between different types of norms (injunctive vs. descriptive).

From the norms-as-standards perspective, behavior change is likely to result from changes in normative beliefs. In creating messages that target normative beliefs, two variables are crucial. First, normative beliefs are best changed using messages from a close referent group (other students on my campus, Montana tax payers like me, etc.). Second, normative beliefs are more likely to change if the message recipient processes the message and believes it. To do this, normative messages designed according to this framework typically present normative information in the form of research findings. For example, a radio message that states "Most Montanans—3 out of 4—Wear Seatbelts" or a television ad that "MOST of us (70%) are tobacco free." The model postulates that if these messages are going to change behavior, they must be attended to, recalled, and ultimately reflected in a shift in normative beliefs (Perkins, 2003b).

Deviance Regulation Theory

An alternative theoretical perspective on normative social influence emphasizes an individual's desire to distinguish him- or herself from the group. Deviance regulation theory (DRT) suggests that people are motivated by the desire to maintain a positive self-image, both public and private, and that they maintain this self-image by choosing desirable ways of deviating from social norms and by avoiding undesirable ways of deviating (Blanton & Christie, 2003). Because individuals want to "stick out" in a good way, they seek positive prototypes that are consistent with their self-image and avoid negative prototypes. People conform or deviate from an established norm in such a way that their positive self-image is enhanced. As a result, the focus of an effective persuasive attempt depends largely on whether or not the desired behavior is the norm.

From the DRT perspective, then, a persuasive attempt that seeks conformity to the norm should associate negative attributes to deviation from the norm, rather than the positive attributes to conformity. If the desired behavior is the norm, ("most sexually active students use condoms") then persuasive attempts should focus on the negative attributes of students who choose to deviate from the norm ("students who don't use condoms are irresponsible"). Conversely, if the desired behavior is not the norm ("most students do not practice safe sex") then the persuasive attempt should focus on the positive attributes associated with those who deviate from the norm ("students who use condoms are responsible"). To test this assumption, Blanton, Stuart, and VandenEijnden (2001) used positive and negatively framed messages to evaluate the extent to which negative and positive attributions toward deviating from the norm influence an individual's behavior. In one study, college students were presented with one of two news articles that contained bogus information about the social norm for getting flu shots. One article stated that past research had found that the *majority* of students would get shots. The other article stated that past research had shown that only a *minority* of students would get flu shots. Next, students were presented with either a positively or negatively framed message about the personality correlates of those who chose immunization. The positively framed message described the desirable attributes of people that get flu shots. The negatively framed message described the undesirable attributes of people who do not get flu shots. When getting flu shots was presented as the norm, intentions to get a flu shot were higher among students presented with a negatively framed message about those who do not get flu shots. Similarly, when not getting flu shots was presented as the norm, intentions to get a flu shot were higher when positively framed messages about those who did were presented.

UNRESOLVED QUESTIONS

Despite the volume of both basic and applied psychological research on the topic of normative social influence, there are several unanswered questions and unresolved issues. First, several relevant social psychological principles have yet to be integrated into a social norms paradigm despite the fact that normative beliefs are clearly involved in the processes. Two such principles where the process of normative social influence is most apparent are the false consensus and false uniqueness effects.

The Desire to Be Different

Although not widely applied to the process of normative social influence, other social psychological concepts warrant consideration in the present discussion (Epley & Dunning, 2000; Pronin, Gilovich, & Ross, 2004). In studies on perceptions of others (i.e., descriptive normative beliefs) versus self, research consistently shows a tendency to view self as acting in more desirable ways, and less undesirable ways, than other people. For example, individuals think they are more charitable, kind, considerate, and sincere than most other people. At the same time, individuals believe that they are less gullible, persuadable, and unethical than others. This sense of false uniqueness is quite pervasive, and has been reported across a range of behavioral domains (Monin & Norton, 2003).

The source of these perceptual biases is unclear. Is the distortion due to a rosy view of self, or a misperception of other people? On the one hand, there is considerable evidence that we hold misperceptions about the behavior of others. For example, in a study of alcohol consumption, Perkins et al. (2005) found that 71% of university students in a nationwide study overestimated the number of drinks consumed by students on their campus "the last time they partied." Students erroneously believed that their peers drank more than they really did (see also Prentice & Miller, 1993). On the other hand, empirical evidence suggests that people also are bad judges of themselves (Epley & Dunning, 2000). For example, when confronted by someone making a sexist remark, women tend to believe that they would be more likely to disagree and confront the perpetrator of the comment than they really were (Swim & Hyers, 1999). Underlying this false uniqueness effect is a basic desire to be different, and this notion helps to explain several patterns in the norms literature. First, we consistently find that people do not believe that they are influenced by the thoughts and behaviors of other people, when in fact the data suggest that they are. Second, as postulated by the deviance regulation theory, people want to be different from the group in ways that are positive.

Others Do as I Do

A related, yet conceptually distinct concept from false uniqueness is the notion of false consensus. Ross, Greene, and House (1977) coined the term *false consensus effect* to describe the tendency for people to overestimate the extent to which their own attributes, choices, and judgments are common, while simultaneously viewing alternative responses as uncommon. The false consensus phenomenon has been well documented and the effect has been demonstrated across a wide range of attributes and behaviors (Monin & Norton, 2003; Ross et al., 1977; Suls & Wan, 1987). For example, adolescents who smoke estimate that a greater number of adolescents smoke than do nonsmokers (Sherman, Presson, Chassin, Corty, & Olshavsky, 1983) and that people with high fear make higher population estimates of fear than people with low fear (Suls & Wan, 1987). In a more recent study conducted during a water shortage crisis, Monin and Norton (2003) found that participants who took one or more showers during a shower ban gave higher estimates of students who also showered (72%) than those who did not take any showers (44%). These findings call into question the causal effects of normative beliefs on behavior. In fact, taken together with findings summarized throughout this paper, they suggest that causation may operate in both directions, and that there is a basic pressure not to deviate from the norm in large or undesirable ways.

Dual Cognitive Processes?

A second unresolved issue pertains to the cognitive process through which normative beliefs influence behavior (Van Knippenberg, 2000; Watt & Hogg, this volume). The results from the research to date do not fit into a single theoretical framework. On the one hand are many examples of normative social influence that suggest a deliberate processing of normative information. On the other hand, many of the findings summarized here appear to follow an automatic pathway (Aarts & Dijksterhuis, 2003).

Here we highlight two lines of research that have taken a more deliberate, central route approach to normative social influence. First are the studies on social identity as a moderator of normative social influence (Ellemers, Spears, & Doosje, 2002; Hogg, 2003; Van Knippenberg, 2000). These studies suggest that participants actively process the nature of the normative information, evaluate its relevance to self, and choose a course of action that maintains their identity (see Pronin, Gilovich, & Ross, 2004). Second are applied studies on normative education in which messages are devised to correct student misperceptions about the prevalence of drinking among peers. The effectiveness of these campaigns often is gauged by the extent to which they change students' normative beliefs—again, implying an active processing of the message, with persuasion occurring when the student believes and agrees with it (Perkins, 2002; 2003b). Consistent with this perspective, Werner et al. (2004) showed that the persuasive effect of moderated group discussions was *mediated* by a change in normative beliefs.

Evidence also suggests that some normative influence occurs outside of awareness. Cialdini (2001) described this (social proof) process as operating through a "click-whirr" mechanism that requires little cognitive elaboration. From this perspective, normative messages might influence behavior through a peripheral route, operating through nonconscious processes. Consistent with this view are studies by Bargh and colleagues (Bargh & Chartrand, 1999; Bargh, Gollwitzer, Lee-Chai, Barndollar, & Trotschel, 2001) on the automaticity of behavior. For example, Bargh et al. (2001) showed that priming participants with cooperation-related words resulted in greater cooperation in a resource dilemma task. Importantly, this increase in cooperation occurred without awareness from participants. Other suggestive evidence for this nonconscious pathway comes from our studies on energy conservation. As summarized above, survey respondents substantially underreported the extent to which they were influenced by normative information. Yet field experiments showed that normative messages *did* cause a change in behavior (Nolan et al., in press).

Research on the processes underlying normative influence is sparse, and the existing results are mixed. The pathway mediating persuasive normative message effects on behavior change is not obvious. Does a normative message need to be believable to be persuasive? Do normative beliefs need to change in order for normative messages to change behavior? These questions should inspire future research.

An Affective Pathway?

Finally, we want to suggest that affective responses to normative information may play an important role in the way in which behavior is influenced. The moderator effect of attitudes in normative social influence has remained largely unexplored. Here we highlight several instances where the effectiveness of normative influences appears to be moderated by an individual's attitude toward the behavior. In the early 1970s, the "Keep America Beautiful" organization produced and aired a public service announcement to address the problem of littering along the nation's highways. The public service announcement began with a Native American, "Iron Eyes Cody," canoeing down a river. As he makes his way through the water, it becomes apparent the water is severely polluted, full of debris and litter (a clear descriptive norm for littering). The PSA concludes with a motorist speeding down the highway, throwing trash out of his car window. As the trash splatters at Iron Eyes' feet, the camera pans in on a single teardrop rolling down his face (an anti-littering injunctive norm). This particular public service announcement had such an impact that it was rated as the 16th greatest television commercial of all time by *TV Guide* ("The Fifty Greatest," 1999). However, academics have criticized the ad, warning that it and similar messages may produce a boomerang effect by presenting a misalignment of norms and focusing on the undesirable descriptive message that littering is common (Cialdini, 2003; Goldstein & Cialdini, in press). Despite the negative attention the Keep America Beautiful PSA has received from the academic community, people with strong anti-littering attitudes, such as program planners, react differently to this type of message. In direct opposition to the focus theory of normative conduct postulate that this approach should actually produce an increase in littering, program planners throughout the country have consistently reported that the "Iron Eyes Cody" commercial changed their lives and reinforced their devotion to maintaining a clean environment. Although anecdotal, this evidence suggests that those who hold strong personal or moral beliefs about an issue may react differently to normative information than those who are less passionate about the issue.

Several researchers have highlighted the way in which the moral basis for an attitude interacts with normative information. For example, although Von Borgstede, Dahlstrand, and Biel (1999) successfully used normative messages to change behavioral intentions for water conservation, blood donation, transit use, and purchasing organic food, their manipulation was unsuccessful at affecting behavioral intentions toward organ donation. In fact, low normative information about organ donation was associated with the greatest *increase* in behavioral intention (contrary to hypotheses). Von Borgstede et al. (1999) speculated that a strong established norm for organ donation might have moderated the effect of the normative information in this case. That is, "if people believe that there is a strong need for action, and learn that few are prepared to act for the common good, then they feel a stronger responsibility to act themselves" (p. 12).

In a more direct test of the moderating role of attitudes in normative social influence, Hornsey, Majkut, Terry, and McKine (2003) examined both public and private conformity with respect to attitudes that had a clear moral dimension. In two experiments, participants were told that they were part of either the majority or the minority with respect to their opinions toward two morally charged issues: recognition of gay couples (Study 1) and government apology to Aborigines (Study 2). Results showed that private behaviors of participants whose attitudes had a weak moral basis were influenced by the group norm. In contrast, participants who had a strong moral basis for their attitude were not affected by the norm. Among all participants there was a general lack of conformity for public compared to private behaviors.

The studies summarized here suggest that having a strong attitude toward the behavior may reduce or even reverse the direction of normative social influence. That is, people with strong morally based attitudes toward the behavior might be resistant to normative information or they may even react against it, a type of boomerang effect. If a person feels strongly about a behavior (e.g., it is important for parents to give their children experiences in nature), hearing normative information about other people not practicing the behavior (e.g., only 10% of families ever go camping with their children) could instill a sense of indignation and ultimately embolden the behavioral tendency (e.g., "I'm definitely taking *my* kids camping"). As Hornsey et al. (2003) stated, "although fear of social censure is a real phenomenon, there are circumstances where people's need to be [morally] right might override their need to be accepted" (p. 320). Such results would be consistent with the deviance regulation theory, if the attitude served to frame the behavior in a positive way. This possibility has yet to be tested empirically.

Although the last 100 years of social psychological research has begun to paint a picture of the ways in which people are influenced by norms, there remain unresolved issues. While the evidence is clear that normative beliefs can have a direct causal effect on behavior, it also is clear that a number of variables can moderate both the strength and direction of this effect (Rimal et al., 2005). The discrepancy of one's own behavior from the norm, normative information about an out-group vs. in-group, and the degree of norm salience have all been shown to moderate the strength of normative social influence effects. Contrary to established wisdom, the ambiguity of the situation and the public vs. private nature of the behavior are inconsistent moderators. Indeed, recent field studies have shown strong normative influence for familiar situations and for private behaviors. Other less-studied moderators include culture (or self-construal), personal relevance (Rimal et al., 2005), personality variables like self-monitoring (Perrine & Aloise-Young, 2004), and such fundamental motives as self-protection and mate selection (Griskevicius, Goldstein, Mortensen, Cialdini, & Kenrick, 2006). Finally, although there are several broad theoretical models of normative social influence, none has fully captured the breadth of these processes. This provides a fertile ground for future research ventures into the influence of social norms.

AUTHOR'S NOTE

Address correspondences to Wesley Schultz, Department of Psychology, California State University, San Marcos, CA 92096, wschultz@csusm.edu.

Preparation of this chapter was supported by a grant from the U.S. Department of Justice to the first two authors, and a National Institutes of Health RISE Fellowship to the third author.

Our appreciation goes to the many students who have worked on the program of research outlined in this chapter: Dulcinea Contreras, Azar Khazian, Lelani Lumaban, Jessica Nolan, and Adam Zaleski.

REFERENCES

Aarts, H., & Dijksterhuis, A. (2003). The silence of the library: Environment, situational norm and social behavior. *Journal of Personality and Social Psychology, 84,* 18–28.

Abrams, D., Wetherell, M., Cochrane, S., Hogg, M. A., & Turner, J. C. (1990). Knowing what to think by knowing who you are: Self-categorization and the nature of norm formation, conformity and group polarization. *British Journal of Social Psychology, 29,* 97–119.

Asch, S. E. (1956). Studies of independence and conformity: A minority of one against a unanimous majority. *Psychological Monographs, 70*(9), 1–70.

Bandura, A. Ross, D., & Ross, S. (1961). Transmission of aggression through imitation of aggressive models. *Journal of Abnormal and Social Psychology, 63,* 575–582.

Bargh, J., & Chartrand, T. (1999). The unbearable automaticity of being. *American Psychologist, 54,* 462–479.

Bargh, J., Gollwitzer, P., Lee-Chai, A., Barndollar, K., & Trotschel, R. (2001). The automated will: Nonconscious activation and pursuit of behavioral goals. *Journal of Personality and Social Psychology, 81,* 1014–1027.

Blanton, H., & Christie, C. (2003). Deviance regulation: A theory of action and identity. *Review of General Psychology, 7,* 115–149.

Blanton, H., Stuart, A. E., & VandenEijnden, R. J. J. M. (2001). An introduction to deviance-regulation theory: The effect of behavioral norms on message framing. *Personality and Social Psychology Bulletin, 27,* 848–858.

Buunk, B. P., VandenEijnden, R. J. J. M., & Siero, F. E. (2002). The double-edged sword of providing information about the prevalence of safer sex. *Journal of Applied Social Psychology, 32,* 684–699.

Chekroun, P., & Brauer, M. (2002). The bystander effect and social control behavior: The effect of the presence of others on people's reaction to norm violations. *European Journal of Social Psychology, 32,* 853–867.

Cialdini, R. B. (2001). *Influence: Science and practice* (4th ed.). Boston: Allyn & Bacon.

Cialdini, R. B. (2003). Crafting normative messages to protect the environment. *Current Directions in Psychological Science, 12,* 105–109.

Cialdini, R. B., Barrett, D. W., Bator, R., Demaine, L., Sagarin, B. J., Rhoads, K. v. L., & Winter, P. L. (2005). Activating and aligning social norms for persuasive impact. Manuscript submitted for publication.

Cialdini, R., & Goldstein, N. (2004). Social influence: Compliance and conformity. *Annual Review of Psychology, 55,* 591–621.

Cialdini, R. B., Kallgren, C. A., & Reno, R. R. (1991). A focus theory of normative conduct: A theoretical refinement and reevaluation of the role of norms in human behavior. *Advances in Experimental Social Psychology, 21,* 201–234.

Cialdini, R. B., Reno, R. R., & Kallgren, C. A. (1990). A focus theory of normative conduct: Recycling the concept of norms to reduce littering in public places. *Journal of Personality and Social Psychology, 58,* 1015–1026.

Cialdini, R. B., & Trost, M. R. (1998). Social influence: Social norms, conformity, and compliance. In D. T. Gilbert, S. T. Fiske, & G. Lindzey (Eds.), *Handbook of social psychology* (4th ed., Vol. 2, pp. 151–193). New York: McGraw-Hill.

Darley, J. D., & Latané, B. (1970). Norms and normative behavior: Field studies on social interdependence. In J. Macaulay & L. Berkowitz (Eds.), *Altruism and helping behavior* (pp. 83–101). New York: Academic Press.

Deutsch, M., & Gerard, H. B. (1955). A study of normative and informational social influences upon individual judgment. *Journal of Abnormal & Social Psychology, 51,* 629–636.

Dittes, J. E., & Kelley, H. H. (1956). Effects of different conditions of acceptance upon conformity to group norms. *Journal of Abnormal and Social Psychology, 53,* 100–107.

Donaldson, S. I., Graham, J. W., Piccinin, A. M., & Hansen, W. B. (1995). Resistance-skills training and onset of alcohol use: Evidence for beneficial and potentially harmful effects in public schools and private Catholic schools. *Health Psychology, 14,* 291–300.

Ellemers, N., Spears, R., & Doosje, B. (2002). Self and social identity. *Annual Review of Psychology, 53,* 161–186.

Epley, N., & Dunning, D. (2000). Feeling "holier than thou": Are self-serving assessments produced by errors in self- or social prediction? *Journal of Personality and Social Psychology, 79,* 861–875.

Fifty Greatest TV Commercials of All Time, The. (1999, July), *TV Guide,* pp. 2–34

French, J. R., & Raven, B. (1959). The bases of social power. In D. Cartwright (Ed.), *Studies in social power.* Ann Arbor, MI: Institute for Social Research.

Goldstein, N. J., & Cialdini, R. B. (in press). Using social norms as a lever of social influence. In A. Pratkanis (Ed.), *The science of social influence: Advances and future progress.* Philadelphia, PA: Psychology Press.

Goldstein, N. J., Cialdini, R. B., & Griskevicius, V. (under review). A room with a viewpoint: Using normative appeals to motivate environmental conservation in a hotel setting. Unpublished manuscript. Arizona State University. Tempe, AZ.

Griskevicius, V., Goldstein, N. J., Mortensen, C. R., Cialdini, R. B., & Kenrick, D. T. (2006). Going along versus going alone: When fundamental motives facilitate strategic (non)conformity. *Journal of Personality and Social Psychology, 91,* 281–294.

Groeger, J. A., & Chapman, P. R. (1997). Normative influences on decisions to offend. *Applied Psychology: An International Review, 46,* 265–285.

Haines, M. P., & Spears, S. F. (1996). Changing perception of the norm: A strategy to decrease binge drinking among college students. *Journal of American College Health, 45*(3), 134–140.

Haines, M. P., Perkins, H. W., Rice, R., & Barker, G. (2005). *Guide to marketing social norms for health promotion in schools and communities* (pdf). DeKalb, IL: National Social Norms Resource Center.

Hansen, W. B., & Graham, J. W. (1991). Preventing alcohol, marijuana, and cigarette use among adolescents: Peer pressure resistance training vs. establishing conservative norms. *Preventive Medicine, 20,* 414–430.

Harper, F. B. W., & Tuddenham, R. D. (1964). The sociometric composition of the group as a determinant of yielding to a distorted norm. *The Journal of Psychology, 58,* 307–311.

Hogg, M. A. (2003). Social identity. In M. R. Leary & J. P. Tangney (Eds.), *Handbook of self and identity* (pp. 462–479). New York: Guilford.

Hornsey, M. J., Majkut, L., Terry, D. J., & McKimme, B. M. (2003). On being loud and proud: Non-conformity and counter-conformity to group norms. *British Journal of Social Psychology, 42,* 319–335.

Insko, C., Drenan, S., Solomon, M., Smith, R., & Wade, T. (1983). Conformity as a function of the consistency of positive self-evaluation with being liked and being right. *Journal of Experimental Social Psychology, 19*, 341–358.

Johannessen, K., & Glider, P. (2003). The University of Arizona's campus health social norms media campaign. In H. W. Perkins (Ed.), *The social norms approach to preventing school and college age substance abuse: A handbook for educators, counselors, and clinicians* (pp. 3–18). San Francisco, CA: Jossey-Bass.

Kallgren, C., Reno, R., & Cialdini, R. (2000). A focus theory of normative conduct: When norms do and not affect behavior. *Personality and Social Psychology Bulletin, 26*, 1002–1012.

Khazian, A., Goldstein, N., Schultz, P. W., & Cialdini, R. (2003, February). A survey of normative beliefs about energy conservation. Poster presented at the annual meeting of the Society for Personality and Social Psychology, Los Angeles, CA.

Keep Tennessee Beautiful. (2006). *Stop litter: Tennessee's had enough. Have you?* http://www.stoplitter.org/

Kelman, H. (1961). Process of opinion change. *Public Opinion Quarterly, 25*, 57–78.

Latané, B., & Darley, J. M. (1968).). Group inhibition of bystander intervention. *Journal of Personality and Social Psychology, 10*, 215–221.

Lewin, K. (1952). Group discussion and social change. In G. E. Swanson et al. (Eds.), *Readings in social psychology* (pp. 459–473). New York: Holt.

Linkenbach, J.W. (in press). Marketing highlight: Drinking and driving. In P. Kotler, N. Roberto, & N. Lee (Eds.), *Social marketing*. Thousand Oaks, CA: Sage.

Mann, T., Nolen-Hoeksema, S., & Huang, K. (1997). Are two interventions worse than one? Joint primary and secondary prevention of eating disorders in college females. *Health Psychology, 16*, 215–225.

Milgram, S., Bickman, L., & Berkowitz, L. (1969). Note on the drawing power of crowds of different size. *Journal of Personality and Social Psychology, 13*, 79–82.

Miller, D. T., Monin, B., & Prentice, D. (2000). Pluralistic ignorance and inconsistency between private attitudes and public behaviors. In D. Terry (Ed.), *Attitudes, behavior and social context: The role of norms and group membership* (pp. 95–114). Mahwah, NJ: Erlbaum.

Monin, B., & Norton, M. I. (2003). Perceptions of fluid consensus: Uniqueness bias, false consensus, false polarization, and pluralistic ignorance in water conservation crisis. *Personality and Social Psychology Bulletin, 29*, 559–567.

National Social Norms Resource Center. (2006). Online resource accessed September 4, 2006: http://www.socialnorms.org.

Neighbors, C., Larimer, M. E., & Lewis, M. A. (2004). Targeting misperceptions of descriptive drinking norms: Efficacy of a computer delivered personalized normative feedback intervention. *Journal of Consulting and Clinical Psychology, 72*, 434–447.

Nisbett, R. E., & Wilson, T. D. (1977). Telling more than we can know: Verbal report on mental processes. *Psychological Review, 84*, 231–259.

Nolan, J. (2004). Home energy conservation as a social dilemma: Exploring the role of social uncertainty. Unpublished master's thesis, California State University, San Marcos, CA.

Nolan, J., Schultz, P. W., Cialdini, R., Griskevicius, V., & Goldstein, N. (in press). Normative social influence is underdetected. *Personality and Social Psychology Bulletin*.

Perkins, H. W. (2002). Social norms and the prevention of alcohol misuse in collegiate contexts. *Journal of Studies on Alcohol, 14* 164–172.

Perkins, H. W. (2003a). The emergence and evolution of the social norms approach to substance abuse prevention. In H. W. Perkins (Ed.), *The social norms approach to preventing school and college age substance abuse: A handbook for educators, counselors, and clinicians* (pp. 3–18). San Francisco, CA: Jossey-Bass.

Perkins, H. W. (2003b). The promise and challenge of future work using the social norms model. In H. W. Perkins (Ed.), *The social norms approach to preventing school and college age substance abuse: A handbook for educators, counselors, and clinicians* (pp. 280–296). San Francisco, CA: Jossey-Bass.

Perkins, H. W., Haines, M. P., & Rice, R. (2005). Misperceiving the college drinking norm and related problems: A nationwide study of exposure to prevention information, perceived norms and student alcohol misuse. *Journal of Studies on Alcohol, 66*(4), 470–478.

Perrine, N. E., & Aloise-Young, P. A. (2004). The role of self-monitoring in adolescents' susceptibility to passive peer pressure. *Personality and Individual Differences, 37,* 1701–1716.

Prentice, D. A., & Miller, D. T. (1993). Pluralistic ignorance and alcohol use on campus: Some consequences of misperceiving the social norm. *Journal of Personality and Social Psychology, 64,* 243–256.

Prislin, R., & Wood, W. (2005). Social influence in attitudes and attitude change. In D. Albarracín, B. T. Johnson, & M. P. Zanna (Eds.), *The handbook of attitudes* (pp. 671–706). Mahwah, NJ: Erlbaum.

Pronin, E., Golivich, T., & Ross, L. (2004). Objectivity in the eye of the beholder: Divergent perceptions of bias in self vs. others. *Psychological Review, 111,* 781–799.

Rimal, R. N., Lapinski, M. K., Cook, R. J., & Real, K. (2005). Moving toward a theory of normative influences: How perceived benefits and similarity moderate the impact of descriptive norms on behaviors. *Journal of Health Communication, 10,* 433–450.

Ross, L., Greene, D., & House, P. (1977). The false consensus effect: An egocentric bias in social perception and attribution processes. *Journal of Experimental Social Psychology, 13,* 279–301.

Salganik, M., Dodds, P., & Watts, D. (2006). Experimental study of inequality and unpredictability in an artificial cultural market. *Science, 311,* 854–856.

Schroeder, C. M., & Prentice, D. A. (1998). Dispelling pluralistic ignorance to reduce excessive alcohol use among college students. *Journal of Applied Social Psychology, 28,* 2150–2180.

Schultz, P. W. (1999). Changing behavior with normative feedback interventions: A field experiment of curbside recycling. *Basic and Applied Social Psychology, 21,* 25–36.

Schultz, P. W., Khazian, A., & Zaleski, A. (in press). Using normative social influence to promote conservation among hotel guests. *Social Influence.*

Schultz, P. W., Nolan, J., Cialdini, R., Goldstein, N., & Griskevicius, V. (2007). The constructive, destructive, and reconstructive power of social norms. *Psychological Science, 18,* 429–434.

Sherif, M. (1936). *The psychology of social norms.* New York: Harper.

Sherman, S. J., Presson, C. C., Chassin, L., Corty, E., & Olshavsky, R. (1983). The false consensus effect in estimates of smoking prevalence: Underlying mechanisms. *Personality and Social Psychology Bulletin, 9,* 197–207.

Strube, M. (2005). What did Triplett really find? Contemporary analysis of the first experiment in social psychology. *American Journal of Psychology, 118,* 271–286.

Suls, J., & Wan, C. K. (1987). In search of the false-uniqueness phenomenon: Fear and estimates of social consensus. *Journal of Personality and Social Psychology, 52,* 211–217.

Swim, J. K. & Hyers, L. (1999). Excuse me—What did you just say?! Women's public and private responses to sexist remarks. *Journal of Experimental Social Psychology, 35,* 68–88.

Tabanico, J., Butler, H., Shakarian, T., & Schultz, P. W. (2006, May). Unintended consequences of normative messages: Looking out for Neighborhood Watch. Paper presented at the annual meeting of the Association for Psychological Science, New York.

Terry, D. J., & Hogg, M. A. (1996). Group norms and the attitude-behavior relationship: A role for group identification. *Personality and Social Psychology Bulletin, 22,* 776–793.

Triplett, N. (1897). The dynamogenic factors in pacemaking and competition. *American Journal of Psychology, 9,* 507–533. Available online at: http://psychclassics.yorku. ca/Triplett.

Turner, J. (1982). Towards a cognitive redefinition of the social group. In H. Tajfel (Ed.), *Social identity and intergroup relations.* Cambridge, UK: Cambridge University Press.

Turner, J. (1991). *Social influence.* Milton Keynes, UK: Open University Press.

Van Knippenberg, D. (2000). Group norms, prototypicality, and persuasion. In D. Terry (Ed.), *Attitudes, behavior and social context: The role of norms and group membership* (pp. 157–170). Mahwah, NJ: Erlbaum.

Von Borgstede, C., Dahlstrand, U., & Biel, A. (1999). From ought to is: Large-scale social dilemmas. *Goteborg Psychological Reports, 29,* 1–20.

Werner, C., & Brown, B. (2006, July). *Embedding environmental behaviors in their social-environmental-policy contexts.* Symposium presented at the International Congress of Applied Psychology, Athens, Greece.

Werner, C., Byerly, S., & Sansone, C. (2004). Changing intentions to use toxic household products through guided group discussion. *Special Issue: 18th IAPS Conference,* 147–156.

Winter, P. L. (2002). *What is the best wording to use on signs? The impact of normative message types on off-trail hiking.* Unpublished manuscript. U.S. Department of Agriculture, Forest Service.

Author Index

Subject Index